Lecture Notes in Artificial Intelligence 1555

Subseries of Lecture Notes in Computer Science
Edited by J. G. Carbonell and J. Siekmann

Lecture Notes in Computer Science

Edited by G. Goos, J. Hartmanis and J. van Leeuwen

Springer

Berlin
Heidelberg
New York
Barcelona
Hong Kong
London
Milan
Paris
Singapore
Tokyo

Jörg P. Müller Munindar P. Singh
Anand S. Rao (Eds.)

Intelligent Agents V

Agent Theories, Architectures, and Languages

5th International Workshop, ATAL'98
Paris, France, July 4-7, 1998
Proceedings

Springer

Series Editors

Jaime G. Carbonell, Carnegie Mellon University, Pittsburgh, PA, USA
Jörg Siekmann, University of Saarland, Saarbrücken, Germany

Volume Editors

Jörg P. Müller
John Wiley & Sons Ltd., International House
Ealing, London W5 5DB, UK
E-mail: jpm@wis-dev.wiley.co.ik

Anand S. Rao
Mitchell Madison Group
Level 49, 120 Collins St.
Melbourne, Victoria 3000, Australia
E-mail: anand_rao@mmg.net.au

Munindar P. Singh
Department of Computer Science, North Carolina State University
Raleigh, NC 27695-8206, USA
E-mail: singh@ncsu.edu

Cataloging-in-Publication data applied for

Die Deutsche Bibliothek - CIP-Einheitsaufnahme

Intelligent agents V : agent theories, architectures, and languages ;
5th international workshop ; proceedings / ATAL'98, Paris, France,
July 4 - 7, 1998. Joerg P. Mueller ... (ed.). - Berlin ; Heidelberg ;
New York ; Barcelona ; Hong Kong ; London ; Milan ; Paris ;
Singapore ; Tokyo : Springer, 1999
    (Lecture notes in computer science ; Vol. 1555 : Lecture notes in
    artificial intelligence)
    ISBN 3-540-65713-4

CR Subject Classification (1998): I.2.11, I.2, C.2.4, D.2, F.3

ISBN 3-540-65713-4 Springer-Verlag Berlin Heidelberg New York

© Springer-Verlag Berlin Heidelberg 1999
Printed in Germany

Typesetting: Camera-ready by author
SPIN 10693229   06/3142 – 5 4 3 2 1 0   Printed on acid-free paper

Preface

The leading edge of computer science research is notoriously fickle. New trends come and go with alarming and unfailing regularity. In such a rapidly changing field, the fact that research interest in a subject lasts more than a year is worthy of note. The fact that, after *five* years, interest not only remains, but actually continues to *grow* is highly unusual. As 1998 marked the fifth birthday of the International Workshop on Agent Theories, Architectures, and Languages (ATAL), it seemed appropriate for the organizers of the original workshop to comment on this remarkable growth, and reflect on how the field has developed and matured.

The first ATAL workshop was co-located with the Eleventh European Conference on Artificial Intelligence (ECAI-94), which was held in Amsterdam. The fact that we chose an AI conference to co-locate with is telling: at that time, we expected most researchers with an interest in agents to come from the AI community. The workshop, which was planned over the summer of 1993, attracted 32 submissions, and was attended by 55 people. ATAL was the largest workshop at ECAI-94, and the clear enthusiasm on behalf of the community made the decision to hold another ATAL workshop simple. The ATAL-94 proceedings were formally published in January 1995 under the title *Intelligent Agents*, and included an extensive review article, a glossary, a list of key agent systems, and — unusually for the proceedings of an academic workshop — a full subject index. The high scientific and production values embodied by the ATAL-94 proceedings appear to have been recognized by the community, and resulted in ATAL proceedings being the most successful sequence of books published in Springer-Verlag's *Lecture Notes in Artificial Intelligence* series.

ATAL-95 was held at the International Joint Conference on AI, which in 1995 was held in Montreal, Canada. The number of submissions leapt to 55, and the workshop was attended by 70 people. Since many international conferences fail to attract this many submissions and delegates, it was decided at this point to make ATAL an annual event. It was also decided to hold ATAL-96 in Europe, following the successful model of ATAL-94 by co-locating with ECAI-96, which was held in Budapest, Hungary. We received 56 submissions, and the workshop was attended by about 60 delegates. For ATAL-97, it was felt that the workshop was sufficiently mature that it merited its own event, and so the conference was located immediately before the AAAI-97 conference in Providence, Rhode Island. It was attended by about 75 delegates. ATAL-98 was co-located with the "Agents World" series of events, held in Paris in July 1998. 90 submissions were received, and 139 delegates registered for ATAL.

In the five years since ATAL-94, the landscape of the computing world has changed almost beyond recognition. Even seasoned veterans of the historically fast-moving IT environment have been surprised by the current rate of change. Perhaps the simplest way we can sum up these changes is by noting that the first ATAL was also the last not to have a World Wide Web (WWW) page. In 1999, on the eve of the new millennium, it would be unthinkable for a serious academic conference or workshop not to have a dedicated WWW site. The changes brought about by the explosion of the Internet into worldwide public and corporate awareness are well documented, and it is not appropriate for us to add to the mountain of comment (and hyperbole). However, it is important to note that the rise of the Internet had a significant impact on the development of the agent field itself. By the summer of 1994 it was becoming clear that the Internet would be a major proving ground for agent technology (perhaps even the "killer application"), although the full extent of this interest was not yet apparent.

The emergence of agents on and for the Internet gave rise to a new, associated software technology, somewhat distinct from the "mainstream" of agent research and development. In the summer of 1994, a California-based company called General Magic was creating intense interest in the idea of *mobile agents* — programs that could transmit themselves across an electronic network and recommence execution at a remote site. At the time, General Magic were distributing a widely-read white paper that described "Telescript" — a programming language intended to realize the vision of mobile agents. In the event, it was not Telescript, but another programming language that caught the imagination of the Internet community: Java. When Netscape incorporated a Java virtual machine into their Navigator browser, and hence brought the idea of applets into the mainstream, they gave Java an enormous impetus, both as a way of animating the Internet, but also as a powerful, well-designed object-oriented programming language in its own right. A number of mobile agent frameworks were rapidly developed and released as Java packages, and interest in Telescript rapidly waned. As we write this preface in late 1998, Java is the programming language of choice not just for agent systems, but also, it seems, for most other applications in computing.

Mobile agent technology was not the only other agent technology beginning to make its presence felt at the time of the first ATAL. The summer of 1994 saw the publication of a special issue of *Communications of the ACM* with the title "intelligent agents". Many of the articles in this special issue described a new type of agent system, that acted as a kind of "expert assistant" to a user working with a particular class of application. The vision of agents as intelligent assistants was perhaps articulated most clearly by Pattie Maes from MIT Media Lab, who described a number of prototype systems to realize the vision. Such user interface agents rapidly caught the imagination of a wider community, and in particular, the commercial possibilities of such technologies was self-evident. A number of agent startup companies were founded to commercialize this technology (many of which have by now either been sold or gone bust). Current interest in such agents comes, to a great extent, from the possibility of using them in electronic commerce scenarios, where they negotiate on behalf of their "owner".

The commercial interest in agents in the latter half of the 1990s has not been limited to venture capitalists and "small scale" agent systems. Perhaps one of the most encouraging long-term trends for agent technology is the idea of agents as a software engineering paradigm. The level of interest in this concept has been evidenced in several ways. For example, the number of large-scale industrial-strength agent systems being developed and deployed is an obvious indicator. However, the degree of interest is perhaps best illustrated by the attempts currently underway to develop international standards for agent communication. Although some tentative steps towards standard agent communication languages were taken by the KQML/KIF community in the USA in the early 1990s, it is the FIPA initiative, started in 1995, which currently appears to be the best candidate for a standard agent communication framework.

Turning more specifically to the ATAL workshops, a number of smaller scale trends have emerged, echoing to some extent the more visible changes in the computing world itself. One obvious indicator that agent technology is beginning to mature is that far fewer *new* agent architectures are being developed. It seems that authors are taking architectures off the shelf, rather than developing their own. In this vein, the belief-desire-intention (BDI) class of architectures has become particularly prominent. This work represents a paradigm example of the ATAL ethos — there is a well-defined theory, which relates more or less directly to specific architectures or programming languages. On the theoretical side, there has been an increasing trend towards more integrated models; that is, theories which cover a wider proportion of an agent's decision making and acting capabilities.

We noted above that five years sometimes seems like a long time for an academic workshop. Incredibly, when ATAL began, there were no conferences dedicated to agent technology. In contrast, the agent research community is now served by at least two major international scientific conferences (the *International Conference on Multi-Agent Systems* and the *International Conference on Autonomous Agents*), as well as a dedicated journal (*Autonomous Agents and Multi-Agent Systems*). That agent technology is able to comfortably support this degree of interest tells us that agents have a good chance of succeeding as a technology. We hope that ATAL will continue to play its part in this development, maintaining its current high level of scientific and production values, and serving a vibrant, rich research and development community.

To close, we would like to take this opportunity to thank those who have made ATAL the success we sincerely believe it is today. In particular, our thanks go to Jörg Müller, Munindar Singh, Anand Rao, and Milind Tambe, who have all acted as organizers for ATAL, and helped to shape it through their dedication and vision. In addition, we would like to thank those who have played various other special roles throughout the first five years, including Klaus Fischer, Michael Fisher, Mike Georgeff, Piotr Gmytrasiewicz, David Kinny, John-Jules Ch. Meyer, and Jan Treur. Also thanks to the program committee members, and finally, to Alfred Hofmann, our editor at Springer-Verlag, whose support and genuine enthusiasm for a well-produced volume has helped establish ATAL as a premier forum for publishing agent research.

November 1998

Michael Wooldridge
Nicholas R. Jennings

Workshop Organization

Organizing Committee

Jörg P. Müller   (GENERAL CHAIR)
(John Wiley & Sons, Inc., UK)

Munindar P. Singh   (AMERICAS CHAIR)
(North Carolina State University, USA)

Anand S. Rao   (ASIA / PACIFIC RIM CHAIR)
(Mitchell Madison Group, Australia)

Mike Wooldridge   (BDI SPECIAL TRACK)
Queen Mary and Westfield College, UK

John-Jules Ch. Meyer (LANGUAGES SPECIAL TRACK)
Utrecht University, NL

Nicholas R. Jennings
Queen Mary and Westfield College, UK

Program Committee

Ron Arkin	(USA)	Pete Bonasso	(USA)
Hans-Dieter Burkhard	(Germany)	Cristiano Castelfranchi	(Italy)
Keith Decker	(USA)	Frank Dignum	(NL)
Ed Durfee	(USA)	Jacques Ferber	(France)
Klaus Fischer	(Germany)	Michael Fisher	(UK)
Stan Franklin	(USA)	Fausto Giunchiglia	(Italy)
Piotr Gmytrasiewicz	(USA)	Afsaneh Haddadi	(Germany)
Henry Hexmoor	(USA)	Mark d'Inverno	(UK)
Nick Jennings	(UK)	David Kinny	(Australia)
Kurt Konolige	(USA)	Sarit Kraus	(Israel)
Yves Lespérance	(Canada)	James Lester	(USA)
John-Jules Ch. Meyer	(Netherlands)	Jeff Rosenschein	(Israel)
Onn Shehory	(USA)	Wei-Min Shen	(USA)
Carles Sierra	(Spain)	Kurt Sundermeyer	(Germany)
Katia Sycara	(USA)	Milind Tambe	(USA)
Gil Tidhar	(Australia)	Jan Treur	(Netherlands)
Mike Wooldridge	(UK)		

Additional Reviewers

John Barbour	Massimo Benerecetti	Frances Brazier	Bruno Caprile
Lawrence Cavedon	Rosaria Conte	Marco Daniele	Frank de Boer
Joeri Engelfriet	Rino Falcone	Petra Funk	C. M. Jonker
Ralf Kühnel	Jürgen Lind	Serafini Luciano	Charlie Ortiz
Rina Schwartz	Luciano Serafini	Ziying Shao	Steven Shapiro
David Tremaine	Wiebe van der Hoek	Pascal van Eck	Gero Vierke

Foreword

It is a particular pleasure for me to contribute, from the publisher's point of view, a few paragraphs as foreword and acknowledgement on the occasion of this fifth volume of the Intelligent Agents subline within the LNCS/LNAI series. One might object that the fifth anniversary of a workshop series is nothing special. In the fast moving area of agent technology, however, the continued success of a highly reputed workshop series deserves the attention usually reserved for achievements of longer duration. To my knowledge, there is no other series of workshops or conferences explicitly devoted to agents from its very beginning that has such a long and well-established tradition. We are proud to have been the publishers of ATAL, from its inception and in its entirety (vols. 890, 1037, 1193, 1365, and 1555 in LNAI), and we look forward to continuing this successful cooperative effort into the future.

When in October/November 1994, the initiators of the ATAL workshop series and editors of the first ATAL volume (LNAI 890), Michael J. Wooldridge and Nicholas R. Jennings, prepared their manuscript for publication, Mike gave me a call during which he impressed me by stating that they were ready to invest time and effort "to make this a book that is really useful to the community". This attitude seemed remarkable to me since I had rarely experienced LNCS/LNAI volume editors who volunteered to do extra work to make post-workshop proceedings more than just a collection of papers. We went on to discuss various options for increasing the value of their book; the resulting volume features a unique survey article by Mike and Nick with a comprehensive bibliography, a glossary of key terms, an annotated list of systems, and a subject index. These added-value components and the careful selection of thoroughly reviewed and revised full papers made the volume an excellent state-of-the-art survey, designed for use by scientists active in the area as a standard source of reference and by newcomers to agents research and development as an ideal starting platform. As a consequence, the volume quickly exceeded all expectations: I had expected the initial print run of 1000 copies to cover demand for the volume's entire life cycle (of about 10 years), but already in October 1995, after only 10 months on the market, LNAI 890 had sold out and it has been reprinted twice since. Such an unexpected sales success had hardly ever happened before in the history of LNCS/LNAI.

Mike and Nick were later joined in the co-editing of subsequent ATAL volumes by (chronologically) Jörg P. Müller, Milind Tambe, Anand Rao, and Munindar P. Singh. Here too, cooperation was excellent and successful, and it went beyond ATAL. In all of the volumes published so far, the editors have improved their workshop documentations by adding special features to the high-quality papers selected in increasingly competitive reviewing processes. From ATAL II onward, the Intelligent Agents volumes have appeared with the new blue-and-yellow jacket cover that distinguishes high-profile titles on hot topics from the many proceedings in the series. In a certain sense, it's a pity that LNAI 890, which is a state-of-the-art survey volume par excellence, was not released with the distinctive jacket cover, as an LNCS/LNAI de luxe. However, this first ATAL book was instrumental in the introduction of the LNCS/LNAI jacket cover concept, and there is certainly greater merit in the establishment of quality standards reflected in a new concept line than in being just one volume in such a line. While recently evaluating a new LNAI publication proposal, I became aware that also the scientific community shares this appreciation of the special nature of the publication concept introduced by ATAL: as an argument of trying to convince us to accept the project, the proposers assured us that they "would do the book in the Wooldridge-Jennings style, like LNAI 890".

Fortunately, the success of ATAL in LNAI has helped attract quite a number of other agent-related projects. Over the years we have succeeded in building a whole publication line around ATAL; with about 15 volumes released annually, LNCS/LNAI seems to be understood by the agents community as one of its premier publication forums. For me personally, agent technology is presently, perhaps along with cryptology, the most exciting subfield of computer science and artificial intelligence, with great promise for the future both as a computing paradigm and a software technology. I am very happy to see that people from distributed AI, who popularized the concept of agents and have been the driving force behind agent technology for years, are now actively seeking the cooperation of the core computer-science community — notably of researchers in traditional distributed computing, networking, programming, software engineering, information systems, multimedia, cryptology, electronic commerce, telecommunications, and human-computer interaction — in order to cope with the problems that emerge in the context of large-scale intelligent applications. This cooperation will undoubtedly advance the state of the art in theory, and both the development community and practitioners interested in everyday private and professional applications will certainly benefit from the results of these efforts.

On the occasion of the fifth anniversary of the ATAL success story, I would like to convey my congratulations to the ATAL community in general and to the aforementioned persons and friends in particular. The devoted and professional cooperation that Springer-Verlag has enjoyed is very much appreciated on our end, and I personally would like to express sincere thanks to all "ATALians" who have shared their visions, thoughts, ideas and publication plans with me and, in doing so, have taught me a bit about a fascinating new technology.

ATAL ad multos annos!

Heidelberg, January 1999   Alfred Hofmann

Contents

Section IV: Languages

Introduction

Every year, putting together the first few paragraphs to start the new *Intelligent Agents* book is one of the hardest parts of the exercise of being a book editor. Thanks to Mike Wooldridge and Nick Jennings, who kindly accepted our offer of writing an "ATAL fifth anniversary preface", this task has been greatly simplified this year. Their description of the evolution of the field and of the *Intelligent Agents* series from its origin in 1994 to the ATAL-98 workshop gives the reader a good perspective on the overall direction of this exciting area. It allows us to use the remainder of this introduction to focus exclusively on the contents of ATAL-98 (on which this book is based), rather than tracing the history of the field.

This book, the fifth in the *Intelligent Agents* series, is structured into four sections. Section I (*belief-desire-intention*) is based on the special track on BDI agents held at ATAL-98. The other three sections reflect the main topics of the series, i.e., *agent theories* (Section II), *agent architectures* (Section III), and *agent languages* (Section IV). Throughout these sections, you will find a rich collection of technical papers that were accepted for presentations for the ATAL-98 workshop.

In addition, the book contains two contributions summarizing two panel discussions that were held at ATAL-98: *The Belief-Desire-Intention Model of Agency* in Section I, and *Agent Languages and their Relationship to other Programming Paradigms*, in Section IV. We would also like to draw your attention to the *Classified Index to Volumes I to V of the Intelligent Agents Series* on pages 427ff. This index applies the classification of agent-related research and development activities used in the AGENTLINK project to all papers published in the *Intelligent Agents* series. Its objective is to enable quick access to all papers in the series, and at the same time provide a taxonomy that we hope proves helpful to the reader in structuring the field.

Finally, it should be mentioned that three of the papers contained in this book were granted special awards at ATAL-98. The papers *Goal Satisfaction in Large Scale Agent-Systems: A Transportation Example* by Sarit Kraus, Onn Shehory, and Osher Yadgar, and *Content-Based Routing as the Basis for Intra-Agent Communication* by Nikolaos Skarmeas and Keith Clark shared the ATAL-98 Best Paper Award. The paper *Control Structures of Rule-Based Agent Languages* by Koen Hindriks, Frank de Boer, Wiebe van der Hoek, and John-Jules Ch. Meyer was chosen as the Best Student Paper.

In the remainder of the introduction, we provide short summaries of the individual contributions to this book.

Section I: Belief-Desire-Intention

The belief-desire-intention (BDI) model is probably the most popular approach to describe and model intelligent agents. BDI theories have been around for more than a decade; different logics, operational models, architectures, and applications have been developed. This section reflects the prominent role of BDI theories and architectures within intelligent agents research. It contains an invited contribution by Georgeff, Pell, Pollack, Tambe, and Wooldridge, and four technical presentations.

The Future of the BDI Model: There are a number of issues regarding the practical usefulness of BDI models - the gap between sophisticated BDI logics and their links to practical systems. More recently, a number of attempts have been made at bridging this gap and on extending the BDI model to incorporate other aspects of rational agency. This contribution is the summary of a panel discussion held at ATAL-98. The authors, Mike Georgeff, Barney Pell, Martha Pollack, Milind Tambe, and Mike Wooldridge, address a number of issues related to the future development of the BDI model.

Mora et al. — *BDI models and systems:* Admittedly, there still is a considerable gap between theories and models of belief-desire-intention on the one hand, and today's implemented systems built according to the BDI paradigm, on the other hand. Research aimed at bridging this gap between theoretical and practical approaches has been receiving increasing attention in recent years (see also the Proceedings of ATAL-96 and ATAL-97). In their paper *BDI Models and Systems - Bridging the Gap, Mora et al.* tackle this issue by adopting an Extended Logic Programming (ELP) model with explicit negation. The mental state of an agent is expressed in this language. The advantage of the approach is that the approach offers both a logical specification and an operational specification of BDI agents.

Van Eijk et al. — *Information-passing and belief revision:* Agents and multiagent systems are first and foremost software (and sometimes hardware) systems. As such, they must be implemented through some means of programming, which in turn presupposes the existence of well-defined programming languages. Since agents and multiagent systems are typically defined using a rich set of concepts dealing with cognition and communications, desirable languages must include those concepts as well. Accordingly, quite a few such "agent-oriented" programming languages have been defined. However, current agent programming languages usually are weak in terms of both their concurrency aspects and their operational semantics. This paper seeks to alleviate this problem by developing a rigorous operational semantics for some varieties of information-passing among agents. The passing of information through communication has natural ramifications on how the beliefs of the communicating agents are revised. This paper builds on previous work in traditional concurrency theory and shows how it may be lifted to apply in multiagent settings.

Schild — *BDI logics and logics of concurrency:* BDI logics took their initial inspiration from the standard logics of concurrency and epistemic logics. The paper *On the relationship between BDI logics and standard logics of concurrency* goes back to the original roots of BDI logics. Comparing BDI logics to logics of concurrent programs, the author shows how the two-dimensional semantic structure used in the basic BDI theory, across worlds and time points, can be collapsed into a single dimension. This allows the author to express a very powerful result, namely that the propositional μ-calculus subsumes the standard BDI logics, BDI_{CTL} and the more expressive BDI_{CTL^*}. As a result, the substantial body of research done on standard logics of concurrency can now be transferred to BDI logics, making Schild's contribution very significant. For instance, it is possible to provide the first complete axiomatization of Rao and Georgeff's BDI theory.

Wooldridge and Parsons — Intention reconsideration: Reconsideration of intentions has always been recognized as a central part of practical reasoning and hence central to BDI logics. However, so far the topic has received only informal and experimental treatment. In their paper on *Intention reconsideration reconsidered, Wooldridge and Parsons* redress this situation by giving a formal treatment of intention reconsideration and the bigger issue of meta-level control. They provide a formal framework for discussing the soundness and completeness of meta-level control strategies with respect to real-time task environments. The framework is illustrated by a number of scenarios showing examples of practical reasoning tasks that can be achieved using the model provided in this paper. This work provides the foundation for investigating different meta-level control strategies for BDI agents in different task environments.

Hunsberger — Shared plans: When multiple agents occupy a shared environment and cooperate in that environment, the notion of collaborative planning becomes crucial. The theory of SharedPlans is an extension of the BDI model to multiple agents. This paper continues this tradition, based on the shared plans paradigm developed in the seminal work by Grosz and Kraus. By introducing an explicit representation of the choices made by a group of agents, called the SharedPlan Tree, Hunsberger simplifies the meta-predicate definitions. This leads to a simplified theory of SharedPlans without compromising its overall expressiveness. In particular, Hunsberger's formalism enables conditions to be specified under which a set of basic, desirable properties of agents and their SharedPlans may be proven (e.g., when does an agent's belief that it has a plan entail that it has such a plan).

Section II: Agent Theories

The majority of the seven papers in the *Agent Theories* section deal with macro-level issues of agency. The first three papers (Conte *et al.*, Bazzan *et al.*, Ossowski and García-Serrano) investigate foundations of cooperation and social action, such as norms, moral sentiments, and the impact of social structure). Rustogi and Singh investigate preconditions for efficient co-ordination in multiagent systems. The next two papers, by Benerecetti *et al.* and Engelfriet *et al.* address the important question of how properties of multiagent systems can be verified. Finally, Jung's contribution addresses micro-level foundations of agency, describing how layered agents can be represented as holonic structures.

Conte et al. — *Norm acceptance:* The investigation of norms and social conventions in multi-agent systems has become an important topic in agent research. Application areas that can greatly benefit from norm-aware agents are legal expert systems as well as agents involved in commerce transactions and negotiations. An important question in the context of norms in multi-agent systems is how autonomous agents can recognize and evaluate norms, and accept them as *normative beliefs*, and thus as a basis for the formation of *normative goals*. This paper proposes a formal logical model of normative beliefs and goals for autonomous agents that, by treating norms as first-class citizens, allows agents to reason about normative beliefs and normative goals and thus provides them with two types of autonomy related to the normative decision process, i.e.: Whether to accept a norm in the first place, and whether to comply to a norm once the agent has accepted it.

Bazzan et al. — Moral sentiments: The investigation of self-interested, rational agents has a long tradition in DAI and game theory. This paper proposes a complementary approach: To enrich models of rational agents by an *emotional stance*, i.e., by the capability to decide whether or not to behave rationally based on emotional grounds. Emotional processing should be balanced with rational processing in the decision-making process of autonomous agents. The authors present a series of experimental results to support their thesis. Ironically (or maybe not), the basis of their experiments is the Iterated Prisoner's Dilemma (IPD), a testbed for rational, utilitarian agents since the days of Axelrod. Their experiments confirm the well-known result that groups of "egoistic, rational fools" (i.e., agents that always defect) lose out in the IPD. In addition, the results seem to suggest that in the IPD, the more altruists (i.e., agents that always cooperate) are in a group, the better they, and the group as a whole, perform. Thus, what seems irrational from an individual point of view, turns out to be rational from a societal perspective.

Ossowski and García-Serrano — Social structure: So far, research on social aspects of agenthood has mainly focused on heterogeneous multiagent societies. This paper investigates the role of social structure in Distributed Problem Solving (DPS), where agents are often centrally designed to achieve or maintain global goals. The authors start out from a set of self-interested agents, and formalize possible relationships and dependence structures between individuals, groups, and their respective plans. The authors then extend this basic model by introducing a normative structure, allowing an agent designer to modify the "natural" dependence structures to support the emergence of a desired global functionality.

The authors describe illustrate the effect of social structure on social coordination by means of a bargaining scenario and describe a distributed algorithm to compute its outcome. Finally, the paper sketches the ProsA$_2$ agent architecture, a layered agent architecture providing a normative layer, a first attempt of a framework to implement normative theories as the ones described by Jung and Bazzan *et al.* in this volume.

Rustogi and Singh — Effective coordination: An important challenge in building agent-based systems is in ensuring that the agents coordinate properly with one another. Coordination is especially difficult when the agents act more or less autonomously and make apparently independent decisions based on their local knowledge. This paper studies the conceptual underpinnings of coordination in such decentralized settings seeking to identify the measurable concepts that most affect success in coordinating. A better understanding of such measurable concepts can lead to refined architectures for agents that must participate in decentralized multiagent systems, and to more effective methodologies for the construction of such agents. Based on empirical results from a simulated environment, this paper argues that the success of the agents in coordinating with others depends not only on their local knowledge, but also on the choices available to them, their inertia in seeking local optima, and their shared knowledge. These concepts can be measured from the agents' construction and from the structure of the multiagent system in which they function.

Benerecetti et al. — *Model-checking multiagent systems:* As agent-based and multi-agent systems become prevalent and are employed in a variety of serious applications, it is becoming increasingly important to develop techniques to validate them. Some of the best techniques are based on formal logic. Among those, the technique of *model checking* has been gaining much attention, since it was first proposed by Clarke and Emerson in the early 1980s. In contrast to theorem proving, which is a more traditional application of logic, model checking is about testing if a given specification is satisfied by a given model. The model itself is derived from a proposed implementation of the specification. The model check is successful if and only if the implementation is sound. Importantly, for a wide range of useful logics, model checking proves to be significantly less computationally complex than theorem proving. The present paper develops a model checking approach for multiagent systems by accommodating beliefs, desires, and intentions—the so-called BDI concepts commonly used in the specification of agents.

Engelfriet et al. — *Compositional verification of multiagent systems:* Everyone agrees on the importance of verifying agents and multiagent systems. A lot of progress has been made on specific techniques and approaches for verification. However, to verify complex systems as part of routine engineering practice remains an important challenge, to a large extent because of the complexity of the verification task. One of the nice properties of well-designed systems is their inherent compositional structure. The present paper develops an approach to exploiting this structure. It proposes a temporal epistemic logic that reflects the evolving knowledge of different agents. The paper gives some valuable metatheoretic results on the notion of provability in a logic as lifted to compositional models. The temporal ingredients of this logic are based on a simplified version of the "declarative past $\Rightarrow$ imperative future" doctrine of METATEM, but with an explicit notion of default persistence. The paper applies this approach to a multiagent system for cooperative information gathering.

Jung — *Emergent mental attitudes in layered agents:* Every agent theory—at least implicitly—involves some agent architecture and every agent architecture—at least implicitly—involves some agent theory. This is because the claims of any theory can be made only relative to some type of agents—this is reflected in an architecture of the agents being described. Conversely, the choice of components of any architecture is guided by some theoretical notion, whether or not fully formalized. One important class of theories is based on cognitive concepts such as beliefs, desires, and intentions. Correspondingly, BDI architectures are a general class of agent architectures. Many practical agent architectures are layered; yet they involve some informal references to BDI. This paper fills the gap between theory and practice by developing a formal model of BDI for agents built according to the layered architecture INTERRAP. Jung's model is based on the notion of *holon*, a unit of organization, and treats layered agents as holons with the layers as subholons. It then relates the beliefs, desires, and intentions of holons at different levels in the hierarchy.

Section III: Agent Architectures

The development of control architectures for intelligent agents has been a prevalent topic within the agents community throughout the 1990s. This section addresses difference aspects of agent architectures, such as their relationship to applications (Müller), architectures of the individual agent (the papers by Fisher and Piaggio), and multi-agent architectures (Rachlin *et al.*, Shehory *et al.*, as well as Stone and Veloso).

Müller— Agent architectures and applications: The objective of this paper is to provide designers of agent systems with a set of guidelines allowing them to choose the right agent architecture for a given application domain. The paper starts from an empirical analysis of a large number of architectures presented in the literature. Based on this analysis, Müller proposes a classification of the architectures according to two criteria, i.e.: the material state of agents (hardware, software) and the primary mode of agent-environment interaction (autonomous agents, multiagents, assistant agents). Combinations of the three criteria result in a taxonomy of six basic types of agent applications. The paper then offers a set of guidelines indicating which agent architectures are useful for which class of applications. The guidelines include general (e.g., *Check first whether your application really requires agents*) as well as specific hints for designers (e.g., *Do not use heavy-weight layered architectures for light-weight Internet software agents applications*).

Fisher — Abstract agent architectures: This paper proposes a unified meta model for the representation of agent architectures. Its underlying observation is that today's agent architectures, most of which are layered, are based on largely different models and frameworks, which makes it difficult to compare and to verify them. Fisher proposes to employ the logical language Concurrent METATEM to describe the computational architecture of an agent. He defines four levels of refinement for representing agents by logical descriptions, starting from a monolithic logical description for an agent up to associating individual layers within an architecture with groups of sub-agents with different internal communication and execution properties. Fisher extends the Concurrent METATEM language by the concept of a group of agents, and by allowing to control execution of and communication between agents in and across groups. Fisher's model of recursively defining agents by groups of sub-agents is similar to the approach described by Jung (in this volume).

Piaggio— HEIR: HEIR is an agent architecture for autonomous robots. What makes HEIR special compared to traditional layered architectures seen in earlier *Intelligent Agents* books is that it explicitly foregoes a hierarchical structuring of reactive and deliberative layers. Rather, a HEIR agent consists of three, non-hierarchically organized components: a reactive, a deliberative, and a diagrammatic component. The use of a diagrammatic component to maintain procedural and diagrammatic knowledge (e.g., a sequence of Figures showing how to serve a tennis ball) is a further interesting feature of the HEIR architecture. Each component in HEIR is designed as a group of *experts*, comparable to behaviors or skills in layered architectures. The primary communication mechanism employed by experts is a specific publish—subscribe protocol. The HEIR architecture has been evaluated by building a mobile robot. Related approaches defining an agent recursively by sets of sub-agents found in this book are those by Jung and by Fisher.

Rachlin et al. — A-TEAMS: A-TEAMS are a generic approach for solving complex dynamic problems (e.g., scheduling problems) through asynchronous teams of agents. Thus, A-TEAMS describes a multiagent architecture rather than an architecture for a single agent. Different types of agents take on different tasks in the A-TEAMS architecture: Constructors create new initial solutions, optimizers improve existing solutions, and destroyers dispose of poor solutions. Agents cooperate implicitly, by sharing a space of solutions (see the paper by Dury *et al.* for reactive constraint satisfaction agents that deal with conflicts in problem solving). A-TEAMS differ in this way from the team activity model presented by Stone and Veloso (in this volume). The development of A-TEAMS is supported by a class library and a team configuration language. The A-TEAMS architecture has been used in different applications, including paper mill scheduling, steel mill scheduling, and wafer start planning for semiconductor manufacturing.

Shehory, Kraus, and Yadgar — *Goal satisfaction:* An important problem in the construction of agent systems, especially large-scale ones, is in deciding how tasks are assigned to the agents. Traditional approaches either require an organizational structure of some sort or explicit communication and negotiation among the agents. This paper develops an alternative approach, which borrows its metaphor and techniques from the domain of physics. In this approach, agents are modeled simply as dynamic particles that interact with another; goals are modeled as static particles. Goal satisfaction is modeled as a collision between a dynamic particle and a static particle. An interaction among agents is modeled as a collision between two dynamic particles. The agents transition from one state to another based on the agents, goals, and obstacles that surround them. The approach is applied to a transportation problem where agents must make freight deliveries in a (simulated) city represented by a graph. In adapting physics for multiagent systems, the paper also includes the seed of an interesting methodology for constructing physics-based solutions to distributed problems.

Stone and Veloso — *Flexible team structure:* Whereas the papers by Conte *et al.*, Ossowski and García-Serrano, and Bazzan *et al.* provide theoretical accounts of concepts of concepts of social coordination in agent societies, Stone and Veloso's contribution investigates a practical model that allows agent teams that operate in *periodic team synchronization* domains to dynamically modify their structure and the way tasks are decomposed among them, in order to cope with short-term or long-term changes in the environment. As an example for a periodic team synchronization domain, the authors use the ROBOCUP robotic soccer scenario: during the game, agents need to act autonomously, relying on off-line agreements made in periods of reliable and safe communication.

The paper proposes an architecture for the individual team member, consisting of a representation of the world state, a set of behaviors, and knowledge about team agreements. The team structure relies on the concept of formations, comprising a set of roles as well as subformations (i.e., subsets of roles from the formation). The paper reports empirical results on different formation switching strategies, indicating amongst others that dynamic, flexible formation switching outperforms more rigid strategies.

Section IV: Agent Languages

With the success of agent technology come languages, tools, and methodologies to support the design, the implementation, and verification of agent-based systems. This section highlights various important areas in research on agent languages and agent-oriented programming, including their relationship to other programming paradigms (Meyer), a survey of design methodologies (Iglesias *et al.*), the AGENTIS agent development platform (Kinny), component-based agent construction (Skarmeas and Clark), semantics of agent communication languages (Chaib-draa and Vanderveken), rule-based and constraint-based approaches (Hindriks *et al.* and Dury *et al.*), as well as the introduction of agent cloning for load balancing (Shehory *et al.*)

Agent languages and other programming paradigms: Over the past years, a variety of proposals for agent-oriented languages have been proposed in the literature. However, these proposals have had hardly any influence on *mainstream* programming. Today's professional programmers' choice are Java, C++, relational and object-oriented databases, and distribution object frameworks such as CORBA, DCOM, or RMI. Before this background, a panel was held at ATAL-98 to discuss the relationship between agent-oriented programming and other programming models. This contribution summarizes the positions supported by the panelists: Jean-Pierre Briot, Keith Clark, Jacques Ferber, Carl Hewitt, and John-Jules Ch. Meyer.

Iglesias et al. — *Methodologies survey:* With the increasing use of agents in industrial and commercial applications, research on methodologies for building complex agent systems has been gaining in importance. The methodologies for agent-oriented systems are mostly extensions of traditional object-oriented or knowledge engineering methodologies. In particular, they cover areas that traditional approaches do not or not sufficiently cover, such as: speech-act based communication and its semantics, autonomy and goal orientation, reflexivity, and modeling social relationships. In *A Survey of Agent-Oriented methodologies, Iglesias et al.* provide a good description of all the methodologies derived from these two traditions. The paper also raises important open issues related to agent-oriented methodologies that deserve a more detailed analysis, such as their relationship to agent architectures.

Kinny — AGENTIS: In this paper, the author describes a methodology for specifying agents and their interaction that is partly inspired by similar work in object-oriented methodologies. Key components of the methodology are an *agent model* and an *agent interaction model*. The agent model describes standard agent types, and has its analog in the object model of object-oriented analysis and design models. The interaction model, which is the focus of this paper, provides explicit notions of services and tasks, as well as interaction protocols that provide reliable concurrent provision of these services and tasks. Unlike the approaches of KQML and FIPA that aim to provide a comprehensive set of primitives for agent communication the AGENTIS approach is based on a small set of communication acts that are used to form complex interaction protocols.

Skarmeas and Clark — Content-based routing: In the paper *Content-based Routing as the Basis for Intra-Agent Communication*, the authors introduce the notion of component-based software construction to agent-oriented systems. Their primary view of an agent is that of integrating pre-existing software modules, corresponding to individual domain or problem-solving capabilities. Skarmeas and Clark propose an agent architecture that facilitates the easy integration of pre-existing components by using an active message board for communication between the different components of an agent. The message routing mechanism is based on so-called message pattern, that can be registered with the message board, and enable *content-based* routing of messages in between agent components. In addition, content-based routing of messages adds greater flexibility and robustness to the design.

Chaib-draa and Vanderveken — Success, satisfaction, and recursion: The theory of speech acts has often provided the foundation for communication between agents. The contribution of this paper is to unify the two important notions of conditions of success of an illocutionary act and the conditions of satisfaction (or truth) of an illocutionary act. Chaib-draa and Vanderveken provide a formalism based on the situation calculus, that provides the necessary model to reason about knowledge and action, and makes an appropriate trade-off between expressiveness and tractability. The approach described in this paper has two important applications: Firstly, it supports the analysis and the interpretation of speech acts among humans as well as software agents; secondly, it also provides the foundations for an adequate semantics of agent communication languages, such as KQML.

Hindriks et al. *— Control structures for rule-based agent languages:* As implemented agent-oriented systems have matured, agent languages that abstract useful constructs of such systems have emerged. The authors separate the basic structures of such agent languages from their control structure. This is based on the observation that all interpreters for rule-based agent programming languages implement some generic functions, i.e., selection of applicable rules from a set of rules, and the ordering of the applicable rules. By doing this, the authors are able to discuss the meta-level interpreters for such agent languages. It also provides a common framework for comparing the different agent languages. The formalization of this two-level approach is done using transition systems. The authors show how their formal tools and meta programming language can be used to design interpreters for three agent programming languages described in the literature, i.e.: AGENT-0, AgentSpeak(L), and 3APL.

Dury et al. *— Reactive constraint satisfaction:* Constraint satisfaction is an important paradigm in computing today. Specifying constraints is often a natural way to capture the requirements of an application as well as the available knowledge in the given domain. This paper considers one of the many applications of constraints—specifically, in the assignment of land-use categories in a farming territory in the Vittel plateau in north-east France. The assignment must respect potential admissible uses of the land, its soil properties, and proximity to human settlements. For this interesting real-life problem, the paper develops an approach in which a number of reactive agents form groups representing the different use categories compete to acquire regions of the available territory. The approach is shown to have some nice properties, such as that it is "anytime"—meaning that its solution quality improves over time and a well-defined solution is available whenever you choose to halt the execution.

Shehory et al. — *Agent cloning:* One of the challenges faced by current multiagent system designs is that of load management or balancing. As a system or specific agents within it get overload, some actions must be taken to restore performance. Traditional approaches to this problem involve (a) task distribution and redistribution where the assigned tasks are split differently among the available agents, or (b) agent migration where an overloaded agent may be transported (somewhat like an operating system level process) to a computer that has additional available processing power. The present approach, by contrast, advocates *cloning*, whereby a copy or clone of an overloaded agent is created and used to share some of the tasks of the original agent. This approach best applies to cases where an agent and its clone can perform the given tasks more efficiently than the original agent by itself. A natural situation would be where the clone can be migrated to another host thus balancing the load on the hosts as well as improving the performance on the assigned tasks.

The Belief-Desire-Intention Model of Agency

Michael Georgeff[*]   Barney Pell[†]   Martha Pollack[‡]
Milind Tambe[#]   Michael Wooldridge[×]

[*] Australian AI Institute, Level 6, 171 La Trobe St
Melbourne, Australia 3000
georgeff@aaii.oz.au

[†] RIACS, NASA Ames Research Center
Moffett Field, CA 94035-1000, USA
pell@ptolemy.arc.nasa.gov

[‡] Department of Computer Science/Intelligent Systems Program
University of Pittsburgh, Pittsburgh, PA 15260, USA
pollack@cs.pitt.edu

[#] Computer Science Department/ISI, University of Southern California
4676 Admiralty Way, Marina del Rey, CA 90292, USA
tambe@isi.edu

[×] Department of Electronic Engineering, Queen Mary and Westfield College
University of London, London E1 4NS, United Kingdom
M.J.Wooldridge@qmw.ac.uk

1 Introduction

Within the ATAL community, the belief-desire-intention (BDI) model has come to be possibly the best known and best studied model of practical reasoning agents. There are several reasons for its success, but perhaps the most compelling are that the BDI model combines a respectable philosophical model of human practical reasoning, (originally developed by Michael Bratman [1]), a number of implementations (in the IRMA architecture [2] and the various PRS-like systems currently available [7]), several successful applications (including the now-famous fault diagnosis system for the space shuttle, as well as factory process control systems and business process management [8]), and finally, an elegant abstract logical semantics, which have been taken up and elaborated upon widely within the agent research community [14, 16].

However, it could be argued that the BDI model is now becoming somewhat dated: the principles of the architecture were established in the mid-1980s, and have remained essentially unchanged since then. With the explosion of interest in intelligent agents and multi-agent systems that has occurred since then, a great many other architectures have been developed, which, it could be argued, address some issues that the BDI model fundamentally fails to. Furthermore, the focus of agent research (and AI in general) has shifted significantly since the BDI model was originally developed. New advances in understanding (such as Russell and Subramanian's model of "bounded-optimal agents" [15]) have led to radical changes in how the agents community (and more generally, the artificial intelligence community) views its enterprise.

The purpose of this panel is therefore to establish how the BDI model stands in relation to other contemporary models of agency, and where it should go next.

2 Questions for the Panelists

The panelists (Georgeff, Pell, Pollack, and Tambe) were asked to respond to the following questions:

1. *BDI and other models of practical reasoning agents.*
   Several other models of practical reasoning agents have been successfully developed within the agent research and development community and AI in general. Examples include (of course!) the Soar model of human cognition, and models in which agents are viewed as utility-maximizers in the economic sense. The latter model has been particularly successful in understanding multi-agent interactions. So, how does BDI stand in relation to these alternate models? Can these models be reconciled, and if so how?
2. *Limitations of the BDI model.*
   One criticism of the BDI model has been that it is not well-suited to certain types of behaviour. In particular, the basic BDI model appears to be inappropriate for building systems that must learn and adapt their behaviour – and such systems are becoming increasingly important. Moreover, the basic BDI model gives no architectural consideration to explicitly multi-agent aspects of behaviour. More recent architectures, (such as InteRRaP [13] and TouringMachines [5]) do explicitly provide for such behaviours at the architectural level. So, is it necessary for an agent model in general (and the BDI model in particular) to provide for such types of behaviour (in particular, learning and social ability)? If so, how can the BDI model be extended to incorporate them? What other types of behaviour are missing at an architectural level from the BDI model?
3. *Next steps.*
   What issues should feature at the top of the BDI research agenda? How can the relationship between the theory and practice of the BDI model be better understood and elaborated? Programming paradigms such as logic programming have well-defined and well-understood computational models that underpin them (e.g., SLD resolution); BDI currently does not. So what sort of computational model might serve in this role? What are the key requirements to take the BDI model from the research lab to the desktop of the mainstream software engineer?

3 Response by Georgeff

The point I wanted to make in this panel was that the notions of complexity and change will have a major impact on the way we build computational systems, and that software agents — in particular, BDI agents — provide the essential components necessary to cope with the real world. We need to bring agents into mainstream computer science, and the only way we can do that is to clearly show how certain agent architectures can cope with problems that are intractable using conventional approaches.

Most applications of computer systems are algorithmic, working with perfect information. But in a highly competitive world, businesses need systems that are much more complex than this — systems that are embedded in a changing world, with access to

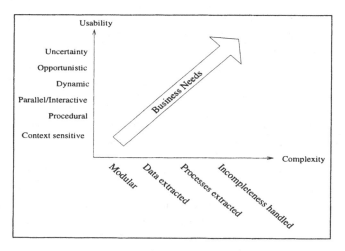

Fig. 1. Business Drivers

only partial information, and where uncertainty prevails. Moreover, the frequency with which the behaviour of these systems needs to be changed (as new information comes to light, or new competitive pressures emerge), is increasing dramatically, requiring computer architectures and languages that substantially reduce the complexity and time for specification and modification. In terms of Figure 1, business needs are driving to the top right hand corner, and it is my contention that only software agents can really deliver solutions in that quadrant.

As we all know, but seem not to have fully understood (at least in the way physicists have) the world is complex and dynamic, a place where chaos is the norm, not the exception. We also know that computational systems have practical limitations, which limit the information they can access and the computations they can perform. Conventional software systems are designed for static worlds with perfect knowledge — we are instead interested in environments that are dynamic and uncertain (or chaotic), and where the computational system only has a local view of the world (i.e., has limited access to information) and is resource bounded (i.e., has finite computational resources). These constraints have certain fundamental implications for the design of the underlying computational architecture. In what follows, I will attempt to show that Beliefs, Desires, and Intentions, and Plans are an essential part of the state of such systems.

Let us first consider so-called Beliefs. In AI terms, Beliefs represent knowledge of the world. However, in computational terms, Beliefs are just some way of representing the state of the world, be it as the value of a variable, a relational database, or symbolic expressions in predicate calculus. Beliefs are essential because the world is dynamic (past events need therefore to be remembered), and the system only has a local view of the world (events outside its sphere of perception need to be remembered). Moreover, as the system is resource bounded, it is desirable to cache important information rather than recompute it from base perceptual data. As Beliefs represent (possibly) imperfect information about the world, the underlying semantics of the Belief component should conform to belief logics, even though the computational representation need not be symbolic or logical at all.

Desires (or, more commonly though somewhat loosely, Goals) form another essential component of system state. Again, in computational terms, a Goal may simply be the value of a variable, a record structure, or a symbolic expression in some logic. The important point is that a Goal represents some desired end state. Conventional computer software is "task oriented" rather than "goal oriented"; that is, each task (or subroutine) is executed without any memory of why it is being executed. This means that the system cannot automatically recover from failures (unless this is explicitly coded by the programmer) and cannot discover and make use of opportunities as they unexpectedly present themselves.

For example, the reason we can recover from a missed train or unexpected flat tyre is that we know where we are (through our Beliefs) and we remember to where we want to get (through our Goals). The underlying semantics for Goals, irrespective of how they are represented computationally, should reflect some logic of desire.

Now that we know the system state must include components for Beliefs and Goals, is that enough? More specifically, if we have decided upon a course of action (let's call it a plan), and the world changes in some (perhaps small) way, what should we do — carry on regardless, or replan? Interestingly, classical decision theory says we should always replan, whereas conventional software, being task-oriented, carries on regardless. Which is the right approach?

Figure 2 demonstrates the results of an experiment with a simulated robot trying to move around a grid collecting points [11]. As the world (grid) is dynamic, the points change value and come and go as the robot moves and plans — thus a plan is never good for long. The y axis of the graph shows robot efficiency in collecting points, the x axis the speed of change (i.e., the rate at which the points in the grid are changing). The "cautious" graph represents the case in which the system replans at every change (i.e., as prescribed by classical decision theory), and the "bold" graph in which the system commits to its plans and only replans at "crucial" times. (The case of conventional software, which commits to its plans forever, is not shown, but yields higher efficiency than classical decision theory when the world changes slowly, but rapidly becomes worse when the world changes quickly). In short, neither classical decision theory nor conventional task-oriented approaches are appropriate — the system needs to commit to the plans and subgoals it adopts but must also be capable of reconsidering these at appropriate (crucial) moments. These committed plans or procedures are called, in the AI literature, *Intentions*, and represent the third necessary component of system state. Computationally, Intentions may simply be a set of executing threads in a process that can be appropriately interrupted upon receiving feedback from the possibly changing world.

Finally, for the same reasons the system needs to store its current Intentions (that is, because it is resource bound), it should also cache generic, parameterized Plans for use in future situations (rather than try to recreate every new plan from first principles). These plans, semantically, can be viewed as a special kind of Belief, but because of their computational importance, are sensibly separated out as another component of system state.

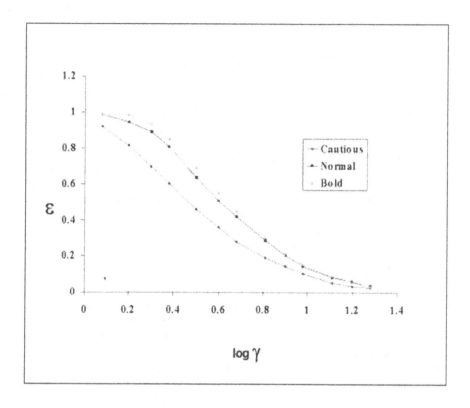

Fig. 2. Rational Commitment

In summary, the basic components of a system designed for a dynamic, uncertain world should include some representation of Beliefs, Desires, Intentions and Plans, or what has come to be called a BDI agent. I have said here nothing about the way in which these components are controlled and managed, which is of course crucial to the way in which BDI agents cope with uncertainty and change in a way that is not possible with conventional systems. There is much in the literature about this, and many different and interesting approaches.

Finally, because of the logical or physical distribution of information and processing, it is important that agent systems be distributed, giving rise to so-called multi-agent systems. Apart from the usual benefits provided by distributed systems, multi-agent systems also have the substantial benefit of containing the spread of uncertainty, with each agent locally dealing with the problems created by an uncertain and changing world.

4 Response by Pollack

I want to begin by clarifying the distinction between three things:

- Models of practical reasoning that employ the folk-psychology concepts of belief, desire, and intention, perhaps among others. Let's call these Belief-Desire-Intention (BDI) models.
- Particular BDI models that center on claims originally propounded by Bratman [1] about the role of intentions in focusing practical reasoning. Specifically, Bratman argued that rational agents will tend to focus their practical reasoning on the intentions they have already adopted, and will tend to bypass full consideration of options that conflict with those intentions. Let's call this Bratman's Claim, and let's call computational models that embody this claim IRMA models (for the "Intelligent Resource-Bounded Machine Architecture" described in [2]).
- The Procedural Reasoning System (PRS) [7, 6], a programming environment for developing complex applications that execute in dynamic environments and can best be specified using BDI concepts.

One can reject Bratman's Claim, but still subscribe to the view that BDI models are useful; the converse, of course, is not true.[1] And while it is possible to build a PRS application that respects Bratman's Claim — indeed, as mentioned in the Introduction, several successful applications have done just this — it is also possible to build PRS applications that embody alternative BDI models. It is up to the designer of a PRS application to specify how beliefs, desires, and intentions affect and are influenced by the application's reasoning processes; there is no requirement that these specifications conform to Bratman's Claim.

The questions set out in the Introduction might in principle be asked of each of the three classes of entity under consideration: BDI models, IRMA models, or PRS-based applications. However, I think it makes the most sense here to interpret them as being addressed at IRMA models, in part because these are the most specific of the three classes (it would be difficult to address all BDI models within a few pages), and in part because IRMA models have received significant attention within the AI community, both in their realization in several successful applications, and in a number of detailed formal models.

Bratman's Claim addresses at a particular, albeit central, question in practical reasoning: how can an agent avoid getting lost in the morass of options for action available to it?[2] The formation of intentions and the commitments thereby entailed are seen as a mechanism — possibly one amongst many — for constraining the set of options about which an agent must reason. Practical reasoning tasks such as means-end reasoning

---

[1] However, one could reject all BDI models, including IRMA ones, arguing that they have no explanatory value. The debate over this question has raged in the philosophical literature; see, e.g., Carrier and Machamer [3, Chap. 1-3].

[2] Bratman actually came at things the other way round. He wondered why humans formed intentions and plans, and concluded that doing so provides them with a way of focusing their practical reasoning.

and the weighing of alternatives remain important for IRMA agents. But IRMA agents' intentions help focus these reasoning tasks.

In response to the first question posed, then, it seems clear that both Soar and the utility maximization models include important ideas that can potentially be integrated in an IRMA agent. As just noted, IRMA agents still need to perform means-end reasoning (in a focused way), and Soar, with its chunking strategies, can make the means-end reasoning process more efficient. Again, IRMA agents still need to weigh alternatives (in a focused way), and to do this they may use the techniques studied in the literature on economic agents. It has been generally accepted for many years that agents cannot possibly perform optimizations over the space of all possible courses of action [17]. Bratman's Claim is aimed precisely at helping reduce that space to make the required reasoning feasible.

The second question concerns the development of techniques to enable IRMA agents to learn and to interact socially. Certainly, if Bratman's Claim is a viable one, then it must be possible to design IRMA agents who can learn and can interact with one another. However, all that is required is that Bratman's Claim be compatible with (some) theories of learning and social interaction: Bratman's Claim *itself* does not have to tell us anything about these capabilities.[3] To date, I see no evidence that there is anything in either Bratman's Claim or its interpretation in IRMA models that would make an IRMA agent inherently poorly suited to learning or social interaction.

The third question asks about an appropriate research agenda for those interested in IRMA models. What seems most crucial to me is the development of computationally sound accounts of the various practical reasoning tasks that must be performed by IRMA agents. There has been a great deal of attention paid to questions of commitment and intention revision, and this is not surprising, given that these questions are central to Bratman's Claim. But there are other reasoning tasks that all IRMA agents must perform as well. For example, they must deliberate about alternatives that are either compatible with their existing plans or have "triggered an override" [2]); recently, John Horty and I have been developing mechanisms for weighing alternatives in the context of existing plans [10]. Another example is hinted at in my earlier comments· all IRMA agents need to be able to perform means-end reasoning. But unlike standard means-end reasoning in AI (plan generation), an IRMA agent must do this reasoning taking account its existing plans. Work on plan merging, notably that of Yang [18], may be relevant here. One final example: IRMA agents must be capable of committing to partial plans. If they were required always to form complete plans, they would over-commit, and filter out too many subsequent options as incompatible. But this then entails that IRMA agents must have a way of deciding when to add detail to their existing plans— when to commit to particular expansions of their partial plans. To my knowledge, this question has not been investigated yet.

In addressing questions like these, we need to focus, at least for now, on the development of computationally sound mechanisms: algorithms and heuristics that we can employ in building IRMA agents (perhaps using PRS). Formal underpinnings can, and if at all possible, should accompany these mechanisms, but unless they underpin specific algorithms and heuristics they seem unlikely to have much impact.

---

[3] However, it might contribute to them; see, e.g., Ephrati *et al.* [4] for some preliminary work on using the intention-commitment strategy in multi-agent settings to increase cooperation.

5 Response by Tambe

I was invited on this panel as a representative of the Soar group with particular interests in multi-agent systems. Thus, in this short response, I will mainly focus on the relationship between Soar and BDI models. For the sake of simplicity, one key assumption in my response is considering PRS, dMARS, and IRMA to be the paradigmatic BDI architectures. Of course, it also should be understood that despite my twelve years of research using Soar, I alone cannot possibly capture all of the diverse set of views of Soar researchers.

I will begin here by first pointing out the commonality in Soar and BDI models. Indeed, the Soar model seems fully compatible with the BDI architectures mentioned above. To see this, let us consider a very abstract definition of the Soar model. Soar is based on operators, which are similar to reactive plans, and states (which include its highest-level goals and beliefs about its environment). Operators are qualified by preconditions which help select operators for execution based on an agent's current state. Selecting high-level operators for execution leads to subgoals and thus a hierarchical expansion of operators ensues. Selected operators are reconsidered if their termination conditions match the state. While this abstract description ignores significant aspects of the Soar architecture, such as (i) its meta-level reasoning layer, and (ii) its highly optimized rule-based implementation layer, it will sufficient for the sake of defining an abstract mapping between BDI architectures and Soar as follows:

1. *intentions* are selected operators in Soar;
2. *beliefs* are included in the current state in Soar;
3. *desires* are goals (including those generated from subgoaled operators); and
4. *commitment strategies* are strategies for defining operator termination conditions. For instance, operators may be terminated only if they are achieved, unachievable or irrelevant.

Bratman's insights about the use of commitments in plans are applicable in Soar as well. For instance, in Soar, a selected operator (commitment) constrains the new operators (options) that the agent is willing to consider. In particular, the operator constrains the problem-space that is selected in its subgoal. This problem-space in turn constrains the choice of new operators that are considered in the subgoal (unless a new situation causes the higher-level operator itself to be reconsidered). Interestingly, such insights have parallels in Soar. For instance, Newell has discussed at length the role of problem spaces in Soar.

Both Soar and BDI architectures have by now been applied to several large-scale applications. Thus, they share concerns of efficiency, real-time, and scalability to large-scale applications. Interestingly, even the application domains have also overlapped. For instance, PRS and dMARS have been applied in air-combat simulation, which is also one of the large-scale applications for Soar.

Despite such commonality, there are some key differences in Soar and BDI models. Interestingly, in these differences, the two models appear to complement each other's strengths. For instance, Soar research has typically appealed to cognitive psychology and practical applications for rationalizing design decisions. In contrast, BDI architectures have appealed to logic and philosophy. Furthermore, Soar has often taken an empirical approach to architecture design, where systems are first constructed and some of the underlying principles are understood via such constructed systems. Thus, Soar includes modules such as chunking, a form of explanation-based learning, and a truth maintenance system for maintaining state consistency, which as yet appear to be absent from BDI systems. In contrast, the approach in BDI systems appears to be to first clearly understand the logical or philosophical underpinnings and then build systems.

Based on the above discussion, it would appear that there is tremendous scope for interaction in the Soar and BDI communities, with significant opportunities for cross-fertilization of ideas. BDI theories could potentially inform and enrich the Soar model, while BDI theorists and system builders may gain some new insights from Soar's experiments with chunking and truth maintenance systems. Yet, there is an unfortunate lack of awareness exhibited in both communities about each others' research. The danger here is that both could end up reinventing each others' work in different disguises.

In my own work, I have attempted to bridge this gap, roughly based on the mapping defined above. For instance, Cohen and Levesque's research on joint intentions [12], and Grosz and Kraus's work on SHAREDPLANS [9] has significantly influenced the STEAM system for teamwork, which I have developed in Soar. However, this is just one such attempt. This panel discussion was an excellent step to attempt to bridge this gap in general.

Acknowledgements

Thanks to David Kinny, who helped to generate the questions and issues raised on the panel.

References

1. M. E. Bratman. *Intentions, Plans, and Practical Reason.* Harvard University Press: Cambridge, MA, 1987.
2. M. E. Bratman, D. J. Israel, and M. E. Pollack. Plans and resource-bounded practical reasoning. *Computational Intelligence*, 4:349–355, 1988.
3. M. Carrier and P. K. Machamer, editors. *Mindscapes: Philosophy, Science, and the Mind.* University of Pittsburgh Press, Pittsburgh, PA, 1997.
4. E. Ephrati, M. E. Pollack, and S. Ur. Deriving multi-agent coordination through filtering strategies. In *Proceedings of the Fourteenth International Joint Conference on Artificial Intelligence (IJCAI-95)*, pages 679–687, Montréal, Québec, Canada, August 1995.
5. I. A. Ferguson. Integrated control and coordinated behaviour: A case for agent models. In M. Wooldridge and N. R. Jennings, editors, *Intelligent Agents: Theories, Architectures, and Languages (LNAI Volume 890)*, pages 203–218. Springer-Verlag: Berlin, Germany, January 1995.
6. M. P. Georgeff and F. F. Ingrand. Decision-making in an embedded reasoning system. In *Proceedings of the Eleventh International Joint Conference on Artificial Intelligence (IJCAI-89)*, pages 972–978, Detroit, MI, 1989.

7. M. P. Georgeff and A. L. Lansky. Reactive reasoning and planning. In *Proceedings of the Sixth National Conference on Artificial Intelligence (AAAI-87)*, pages 677–682, Seattle, WA, 1987.

8. M. P. Georgeff and A. S. Rao. A profile of the Australian AI Institute. *IEEE Expert*, 11(6):89–92, December 1996.

9. B. Grosz and S. Kraus. Collaborative plans for group activities. In *Proceedings of the Thirteenth International Joint Conference on Artificial Intelligence (IJCAI-93)*, pages 367–373, Chambéry, France, 1993.

10. J. F. Horty and M. E Pollack. Option evaluation in context. In *Proceedings of the Seventh Conference on Theoretical Aspects of Rationality and Knowledge (TARK-98)*, 1998.

11. D. Kinny and M. Georgeff. Commitment and effectiveness of situated agents. In *Proceedings of the Twelfth International Joint Conference on Artificial Intelligence (IJCAI-91)*, pages 82–88, Sydney, Australia, 1991.

12. H. J. Levesque, P. R. Cohen, and J. H. T. Nunes. On acting together. In *Proceedings of the Eighth National Conference on Artificial Intelligence (AAAI-90)*, pages 94–99, Boston, MA, 1990.

13. J. P. Müller. *The Design of Intelligent Agents (LNAI Volume 1177)*. Springer-Verlag: Berlin, Germany, 1997.

14. A. S. Rao and M. Georgeff. Decision procedures of BDI logics. *Journal of Logic and Computation*, 8(3):293–344, 1998.

15. S. Russell and D. Subramanian. Provably bounded-optimal agents. *Journal of AI Research*, 2:575–609, 1995.

16. K. Schild. On the relationship between BDI logics and standard logics of concurrency. In J. P. Müller, M. P. Singh, and A. S. Rao, editors, *Intelligent Agents V — Proceedings of the Fifth International Workshop on Agent Theories, Architectures, and Languages (ATAL-98)*, Lecture Notes in Artificial Intelligence. Springer-Verlag, Heidelberg, 1999. In this volume.

17. H. A. Simon. A behavioral model of rational choice. *Quarterly Journal of Economics*, 69:99–118, 1995.

18. Q. Yang. *Intelligent Planning: A Decomposition and Abstraction Based Approach*. Springer-Verlag: New York, 1997.

BDI Models and Systems: Reducing the Gap

Michael C. Móra*‡, José G. Lopes†*, Rosa M. Viccari‡** and Helder Coelho *

* CPGCC/II, Universidade Federal do Rio Grande do Sul
  Bloco IV, Campus do Vale, Av. Bento Gonçalves 9500, Porto Alegre, RS, Brasil
  {michael,rosa}@inf.ufrgs.br

† CENTRIA/DI – Universidade Nova de Lisboa
  Quinta da Torre – 2825 Monte da Caparica – Portugal
  gpl@di.fct.unl.pt

‡ II – Pontifícia Universidade Católica do Rio Grande do Sul
  Prédio 30 – Av. Ipiranga 6618, Porto Alegre, RS, Brasil
  michael@inf.pucrs.br

* DI/FCUL – Universidade de Lisboa
  Bloco C5, Piso 1, Campo Grande, 1700 Lisboa, Portugal
  hcoelho@di.fc.ul.pt

Abstract. Beliefs-Desires-Intentions models (or BDI models) of agents have been around for quit a long time. The purpose of these models is to characterize agents using anthropomorphic notions, such as mental states and actions. However, despite the fact that many systems have been developed based on these models, it is a general concern that there is a gap between those powerful BDI logics and practical systems. The purpose of this paper is to present a BDI model that, besides being a formal model of agents, is also suitable to be used to implement agents. Instead of defining a new BDI logic or choosing an existing one, and extending it with an operational model, we define the notions of belief, desires and intentions using a logic formalism that is both well-defined and computational.

Keywords: BDI models; mental states modeling; agent architectures; logic programming.

1 Introduction

Beliefs-Desires-Intentions models (or BDI models) of agents have been around for quite a long time. The purpose of these models is to characterize agents using anthropomorphic notions, such as mental states and actions. Usually, these notions and their properties are formally defined using logical frameworks that allow theorists to analyze, to specify and to verify rational agents,like in [10] [26] [29] [31] [25] [17](among others).

---

* Supported by project DIXIT/JNICT.
** Supported by CNPq/Brazil.

However, despite the fact that many systems have been developed based on these models ([8,16,11,17], to mention some), it is a general concern that there is a gap between those powerful BDI logics and practical systems. We believe that the main reason for the existence of this gap is that the logical formalisms used to define the models do not have an operational model that support them. By an operational model we mean proof procedures that are correct and complete with respect to the logical semantics, as well as mechanisms to perform different types of reasoning needed to model agents [20,21].

There are, at least, two major approaches that may be used to overcome this limitation of BDI models. One is to extend existing BDI logics with appropriate operational models so that agent theories become computational. This is the approach taken by Rao, in [25], where he defines a proof procedure for the propositional version of his BDI logic[26]. Also, Bell in [4] develops a computational theory that can be applied to his formalizations of goal hierarchies[5]. Still, Schild's[27] representation of Rao and Georgeff's[26] BDI theory with standard logic of concurrency follows this approach.

The other approach is to define BDI models using a suitable logical formalism that is both powerful enough to represent mental states and that has operational procedures that allow us to use the logic as a knowledge representation formalism, when building the agent. This is the path followed by Corrêa and Coelho[11], where they define their SEM architecture using situation theory[15] as their underlying formalism and use Nakashima's operational model[23,13]. This is also the approach we follow in this paper.

The purpose of this paper is to present a BDI model that, besides being a formal model of agents, is also suitable to be used to implement agents. Instead of defining a new BDI logic or choosing an existing one, and extending it with an operational model, we define the notions of belief, desires and intentions using a logical formalism that is both well-defined and computational. The formalism we are using is *logic programming extended with explicit negation* (ELP) with the *Well-Founded Semantics eXtended for explicit negation* (WFSX). ELP with WFSX (simply ELP, from now on) extends normal logic programs with a second negation named *explicit*[1] *negation*. This extension allows us to explicitly represent negative information (like a belief that a property P does not hold, or an intention that a property Q should not hold) and increases the expressive power of the language. When we introduce negative information, we may have to deal with contradictory programs[1]. The ELP framework, besides providing the computational proof procedure for theories expressed in its language, also provides a mechanism to determine how to minimally change a logic program in order to remove contradictions. Our model benefits from these features provided by the logical formalism.

As it is usually done[10,30,17], we focus on the formal definition of mental states and on how the agent behaves, given such mental states. But, contrasting with these former approaches, our model is not only an agent specification, but it may also be executed in order to verify the actual agent behavior, as well as it may be used as reasoning mechanism by actual agents. We depart from Bratman's analysis[9], where he states

---

[1] In contrast with the usual *negation as failure* or *negation by default* of normal logic programs, which is called *implicit negation* in the ELP context.

that, along with desires and beliefs, intentions is a fundamental mental state. There-fore, initially we define these three mental states and the static relations between them, namely constraints on consistency among those mental states. Afterwards, we advance with the definition of dynamic aspects of mental states, namely how the agent chooses its intentions, and when and how it revises its intentions[2].

The paper is organized as follows: in section 2, we present the ELP formalism and the reasoning mechanisms it provides; in section 3, we present an action and time theory based on a variation of the event calculus[24] that is used to define the mental states; in section 4, we present our agent model; in section 5, we discuss some related and future work and draw some conclusions.

2 Extended Logic Programming

Unlike normal logic programs, where negative information is only stated implicitly (i.e., a proposition is false only if it cannot be proved to be true), extended logic programs have a second kind of negation that allows us to explicitly represent negative informa-tion. If, on one hand, this second negation increases the representational power of the language, it may also introduce contradictory information in programs. Therefore, it is necessary to assign some meaning to contradictory programs and to be able to deal with contradiction. The paraconsistent version of the $WFSX$ semantics, $WFSX_P$, assigns meaning to contradictory programs and is used as a tool by the revision mechanism that restores consistency to contradictory programs. This revision mechanism may be used to perform several kinds of reasoning, as we will see bellow.

An extended logic program (ELP) is a set of rules $H \leftarrow B_1, \ldots, B_n, not\ C_1, \ldots, not\ C_m$ (m,n $\geq$ 0), where $H, B_1, \ldots, B_n, C_1, \ldots, C_m$ are objective literals. An objective literal is either an atom A or its explicit negation $\neg A$. The symbol not stands for negation by default and $not\ L$ is a default literal. Literals are either objective or default literals and $\neg\neg L \equiv L$. The language also allows for integrity constraints of the form $A_1 \lor \ldots \lor A_l \Leftarrow B_1, \ldots, B_n, not\ C_1, \ldots, not\ C_m$ (m,n $\geq$ 0; l $\geq$ 1) where $A_1, \ldots, A_l, B_1, \ldots, B_n, C_1, \ldots, C_m$ are objective literals, stating that at least one of the A_i (i $\geq$ 1), should hold if its body $B_1, \ldots, B_n, not\ C_1, \ldots, not\ C_m$ (m,n $\geq$ 0) holds. Particularly, when $A = \perp$, where $\perp$ stands for *contradiction*, it means that a contradiction is raised when the constraint body holds. The set of all objective literals of a program P is the extended Herbrand base of P denoted by $\mathcal{H}(P)$.

In order to assign meaning to ELP programs, we need the notions of interpretation of ELP clause[3]. Roughly, an interpretation of an ELP program is a set of literals that verifies the coherence principle: if $\neg L \in T$ then $L \in F$. A literal L is true in an

---

[2] As we stated before, our concern is the definition of agents' behavior in terms of their mental states. Therefore, its beyond the scope of this work to treat dynamic aspects of beliefs, as belief revision. Notice, however, that opposed to models like the ones defined in [10,30,17] and others, the logical grounds on which we base our definitions are suitable to define belief revision strategies and to be used by agents as a reasoning tool for truth maintenance. See [2,19] for two different approaches on this matter.

[3] For a formal definition, see [1].

interpretation I if $L \in I$, L is false in I if $not\ L \in I$, and L is undefined, otherwise. An interpretation I is a model for program P iff, for every clause L in P, $I \models_P L$.

2.1 Program Revision and Non-Monotonic Reasoning

As we stated before, due to the use of explicit negation, programs may be contradictory. In order to restore consistency in programs that are contradictory with respect to $WFSX$, the program is submitted to a revision process that relies on the allowance to change the truth value of some set of literals. This set of literals is the set of *revisable literals*, and can be any subset of $\mathcal{H}$ for which there are no rules or there are only facts in the program. No other restriction is made on which literals should be considered revisable. They are supposed to be provided by the user, along with the program.

The revision process changes the truth value of revisable literals in a minimal way and in all alternative ways of removing contradiction. *Minimally revised programs* can be defined as those programs obtained from the original one after modifying the subsets of revisable literals.

The ability to represent negative information, along with a well-defined procedure that restores consistency in logic program, makes ELP suitable to be used to perform different forms of non-monotonic reasoning [1]. In particular, we are interested in two of these forms of non-monotonic reasoning, namely *defeasible reasoning* and *abductive reasoning*.

Defeasible Reasoning A defeasible rule is a rule of the form *Normally if A then B*. ELP allows us to express defeasible reasoning and to give meaning to a set of rules (defeasible or not) when contradiction arises from the application of the defeasible rules. To remove contradiction, we revise the truth value of revisable literals in the body of the defeasible rules.

Abductive Reasoning Abductive reasoning consists of, given a theory T and a set of observations O, to find a theory Δ such that $T \cup \Delta \models O$ and $T \cup \Delta$ is consistent. In the ELP context, an abductive framework P' is a tuple $\langle P, Abd, IC \rangle$, where P is an extended logic program, Abd is the set of abducible literals and IC is the set of integrity constraints. An observation O has an abductive explanation Δ iff $P' \cup \Delta \models_P O$ and $P \not\models_P \Delta$. We may abduce a theory Δ that explains such observations making each of these observations O a new integrity constraint $O \Leftarrow$ and revising the program with revisable set Abd (recall that a program is contradictory iff for some literal L in program P, $P \models L$ and $P \models \neg L$, or a constraint is not satisfied).

Preferred Revisions Sometimes, it may be necessary to state that we do not only want the minimal revisions provided by the formalism, but also that we prefer revisions that have a certain fact only after finding that no other revisions including other facts exist. The ELP formalism allows us to express preferences over the order of revisions using a labeled directed acyclic and/or graph defined by rules of the form[14]:

$$Level_0 \ll Level_1 \wedge Level_2 \wedge \ldots Level_n (n \geq 1)$$

$Level_i$ nodes in the graph are preference level identifiers. To each of these levels is associated a set of revisables denoted by $\mathcal{R}(Level_i)$. Rules like the one above for $Level_0$ state that we want to consider revisions for $Level_0$ only if, for some rule body, its levels have been considered and there are no revisions at any of those levels. The root of the preference graph is the node denoted by **bottom**.

3 The Event Calculus

When we reason about pro-attitudes like desires and intentions, we need to deal with properties that should hold at an instant of time and with actions that should be executed at a certain time. Therefore, in order to represent them and to reason about them, we need to have a logical formalism that deals with actions and time. In this work, we use a modified version of the Event Calculus (EC) proposed in [24]. This version of the EC allows events to have a duration and an identification, instead of being instantaneous and identified to the instant of time the event occurs. As a consequence, events may occur simultaneously. The predicate $holds\_at$ defining the properties that are true at a specific time is:

$$
\begin{aligned}
holds\_at(P, T) \leftarrow\ & happens(E, T_i, T_f), \\
& initiates(E, T_P, P), T_P < T, \\
& T_P >= T_i, persists(T_P, P, T). \\
persists(T_P, P, T) \leftarrow\ & not\ clipped(T_P, P, T). \\
clipped(T_P, P, T) \leftarrow\ & happens(C, T_{ci}, T_{cf}), \\
& terminates(C, T_C, P), \\
& T_C >= T_{ci}, not\ out(T_C, T_P, T). \\
out(T_C, T_P, T) \leftarrow\ & (T \leq T_C); (T_C < T_P).
\end{aligned}
$$

The predicate $happens(E, T_i, T_f)$ means that event E occurred between T_i and T_f; $initiates(E, T, P)$ means that event E initiates P at time T; $terminates$ (E, T, P) means that event E terminates P at time T; $persists(T_P, P, T)$ means that P persists since T_P until T (at least). We assume there is a special time variable Now that represents the present time. Note that a property P is true at a time T ($holds\_at(P, T)$), if there is a previous event that initiates P and if P persists until T. P persists until T if it can not be proved by default the existence of another event that terminates P before the time T. We need additional rules for the relation between not holding a property and holding its negation and we also need to define the relation between the two kinds of negation:

$$
\begin{aligned}
holds\_at(\neg P, T) \leftarrow\ & \neg holds\_at(P, T). \\
\neg holds\_at(P, T) \leftarrow\ & not\ holds\_at(P, T).
\end{aligned}
$$

The predicates that will be abduced need to be related by some integrity rules, namely:

$$
\perp \Leftarrow happens(E, T_{1i}, T_{1f}), happens(E, T_{2i}, T_{2f}),
$$

$$not(T_{1i} = T_{2i}, T_{1f} = T_{2f}).$$
$$\bot \Leftarrow happens(E, T_i, T_f), \ not(T_f < T_i).$$
$$\bot \Leftarrow happens(E, T_i, T_f), not(act(E, A)).$$

that state, respectively, that events cannot be associated to different time intervals, that events cannot have a negative duration and that events must have an associated action.

The EC allows us to reason about the future, by hypothetically assuming a sequence of actions represented by $happens/3$ and $act/2$ predicates and verifying which properties would hold. It also allows us to reason about the past. In order to know if a given property P holds at time T, the EC checks what properties remain valid after the execution of the actions that happened before T. We are now ready to define the agent's model.

4 The Agent Model

Now that we have the logical formalism set, we start defining the BDI model. We depart from Bratman's analysis about intentions, its role in rational reasoning and how it relates to beliefs and desires. According to Bratman[9], since agents are assumed to be resource-bounded, they cannot continuously evaluate their competing beliefs and desires in order to act rationally. After some reasoning, agents have to commit to some set of choices. It is this choice followed by a commitment that characterizes the intentions. Our model does not define a complete agent, but only the cognitive structure that is part of the agent model.

Definition 1 (Agent Cognitive Structure). An *agent cognitive structure* is a tuple $Ag = \langle \mathcal{B}, \mathcal{D}, \mathcal{I}, \mathcal{T}Ax \rangle$ where

- $\mathcal{B}$ is the set of agent's beliefs;
- $\mathcal{D}$ is the set of agent's desires;
- $\mathcal{I}$ is the set of agent's intentions;
- $\mathcal{T}Ax$ is the set of time axioms, as defined in section 3.

This cognitive structure contains both the mental states that compose the agent and the rules that govern the interaction of these mental states (and, consequently, the agent's behavior).

We should now define every component of this structure. We start by defining desires. Desires are related to the state of affairs the agent eventually wants to bring about. But desires, in the sense usually presented, does not necessarily drive the agent to act. That is, the fact of an agent having a desire does not mean it will act to satisfy it. It means, instead, that before such an agent decides what to do, it will be engaged in a reasoning process, confronting its desires (the state of affairs it wants to bring about) with its beliefs (the current circumstances and constraints the world imposes). The agent will choose those desires that are possible according to some criteria. In other words, desires constitute the set of states among which the agent chooses what to do. Notice that, since agents are not committed to their desires, they need not to be consistent, neither with other desires nor with other mental states.

Definition 2 (Desires Set). The *desires* of an agent is a set of sentences of the form

$$\mathcal{D} = \{holds\_at(des(D, Ag, P, Atr), P) \leftarrow Body\}$$

where D is the desire identification, P is a property, T is a time point, Ag is an agent identification and A is list of attributes. *Body* is any conjunction of literals. An agent desires that a property P holds at time T iff

$$(holds\_at(des(D, Ag, P, Atr), T) \leftarrow Body) \in \mathcal{D},$$

for some D, Ag, Atr.

Our definition of desires allows the agent to have a desire that a certain property holds (or does not hold) in a specific instant of time (when T is instantiated). Desire clauses may be facts, representing states the agent may want to achieve whenever possible, or rules, representing states to be achieved when a certain condition holds. The attributes associated to each desire define properties, like urgency, importance or priority[3,12,22] that are used by the agent to choose the most appropriate desire (see bellow).

Beliefs constitute the agent's information attitude. They represent the information agents have about the environment and about themselves.

Definition 3 (Beliefs Set). The *beliefs* of an agent is a consistent extended logic program $\mathcal{B}$, i.e. $\mathcal{B} \not\models_P \bot$. An agent believes agent A believes a property P holds at time T iff $\{\mathcal{B} \cup \mathcal{T}Ax\} \models_P holds\_at(bel(A, P), T)$.

We assume that the agent continuously updates its beliefs to reflect changes it detects in the environment. Describing the belief update process is beyond the scope of this paper. We just assume that, whenever a new belief is added to the beliefs set, consistency is maintained.

As we stated before, intentions are characterized by a *choice* of a state of affairs to achieve, and a *commitment* to this choice. Thus, intentions are viewed as a compromise the agent assumes with a specific possible future. This means that, differently from desires, an intention may not be contradictory with other intentions, as it would not be rational for an agent to act in order to achieve incompatible states. Also, intentions should be supported by the agent's beliefs. That is, it would not be rational for an agent to intend something it does not believe is possible. Once an intention is adopted, the agent will pursue that intention, planning actions to accomplish it, re-planning when a failure occurs, and so on. These actions, as means that are used to achieve intentions, must also be adopted as intentions by agents.

Definition 4 (Intentions Set). The *intentions* of an agent at a time T is the set

$$\mathcal{I} = \{X/X = int\_that(I, Ag, P, A) \vee X = int\_to(I, Ag, Act, A)\}$$

where I is the intention identification, P is a property, Ag is an agent, A is a list of attributes, Act is an action, and such that

1. $holds\_at(int\_that(I, Ag, P, A), T)$ or $holds\_at(int\_to(I, Ag, Act, A), T)$;
2. $\forall int\_that(I, Ag, P, A) \in \mathcal{I}.(Now \leq T)$;

3. $\forall int\_to(I, Ag, Act, A) \in \mathcal{I}.(Now \leq T)$;

4. $\forall int\_to(I, Ag, Act, A) \in \mathcal{I}.(\{\mathcal{B} \cup \mathcal{T} Ax\} \not\models_P (happens(E, T, T_F), act(E, Act)))$;

5. $\exists \Delta.(P' \cup \Delta \not\models_P \bot)$, where

   (a) P' is the abductive framework $\langle \{\mathcal{B} \cup \mathcal{T} Ax\}, \{happens/3, act/2\}, IC(\mathcal{I})\rangle$;

   (b) $IC(\mathcal{I})$ is set of constraints generated by intentions, defined as

   $$holds\_at(bel(Ag, P), T) \Leftarrow$$

   for every $int\_that(I, Ag, P, A)$ in $\mathcal{I}$ and

   $$happens(E, T, T_f) \Leftarrow$$
   $$act(E, Act) \Leftarrow$$

   for every $intends\_to(I, Act, T, A)$ in $\mathcal{I}$;

An agent intends that a property P holds at time T iff $\mathcal{B} \cup \mathcal{T} Ax \cup \mathcal{R} \models_P holds\_at($ $int\_that\ (I, Ag, P, A), T)$, and it intends to execute an action Act at time T iff $\mathcal{B} \cup \mathcal{T} Ax \cup \mathcal{R} \models_P holds\_at(int\_to\ (I, Act, P, A), T)$.

The definition of intentions enforces its rationality constraints. Conditions 2 and 3 state that an agent should not intend something at a time that has already past. Condition 4, the non-triviality condition[10] states that an agent should not intend something it believes is already satisfied or that will be satisfied with no efforts by the agent. Condition 5 states that an agent only intends something it believes is possible to be achieved, i.e., if it believes there is a course of actions that leads to the intended state of affairs. When designing an agent, we specify only the agent's beliefs and desires. It is up to the agent to choose its intentions appropriatly from its desires. Those rationality constraints must also be guaranteed during this selection process. Notice also that we are able to avoid the *side-effect problem*[9]. Bratman states that *an agent who intends to do α an believes that doing α would imply β does not have to also intend β*. In our definition, an agent does not intend the *side-effects* of its intentions, as the side-effects are not in the intentions set[4]. To fully avoid this problem, it is also important, when we define how the agent selects its intentions and how and and how and when to revise them, that we characterize commitment in a way that side-effects of adopted intentions do not prevent agents from adopting intentions, neither that side-effects make agents revise their intentions.

Example 5 (Warehouse Robot). This is a toy example to illustrate the use of the formalism. Suppose there is a robot rbt that should take all the objects placed in an input counter and store those objects in a warehouse. It also must recharge its batteries whenever they run out of charge.

---

[4] This is similar to the belief base approach, but it is simpler because we do not have to include the derivations in the base, as with belief bases.

Desires

$\perp \Leftarrow holds\_at(des(\_,rbt, bel(rbt, bat\_chged),_\}\,), T),$
$\quad holds\_at(des(\_,rbt, bel(rbt, stored(O)),_\}\,), T).$
$holds\_at(des(1, rbt, bel(rbt, bat\_chged), [0.5]), T).$
$holds\_at(des(2, rbt, bel(rbt, stored(O)), [0.3]), T) \leftarrow holds\_at(bel(rbt,$
$\qquad\qquad\qquad\qquad\qquad\qquad\qquad\qquad\qquad\qquad input(O)), T).$

Beliefs

$initiates(E, T_f, bel(rbt, bat\_chged)) \leftarrow happens(E, T_i, T_f),$
$\qquad\qquad\qquad\qquad\qquad\qquad\qquad\qquad act(E, charge).$
$terminates(E, T, bel(rbt, bat\_chged)) \leftarrow happens(E, T, T),$
$\qquad\qquad\qquad\qquad\qquad\qquad\qquad\qquad act(E, sense\_low\_bat).$
$initiates(E, T_f, bel(rbt, stored(O))) \leftarrow happens(E, T_i, T_f),$
$\qquad\qquad\qquad\qquad\qquad\qquad\qquad\qquad act(E, store(O)).$
$initiates(E, T_i, bel(rbt, input(O))) \leftarrow happens(E, T_i, T_i),$
$\qquad\qquad\qquad\qquad\qquad\qquad\qquad\qquad act(E, put\_input(O)).$
$terminates(E, T_i, bel(rbt, input(O))) \leftarrow happens(R, T_i, T_f),$
$\qquad\qquad\qquad\qquad\qquad\qquad\qquad\qquad act(E, store(O)).$
$happens(e1, t1, t2). \; act(e1, input(o1)).$

The agent definition describes only its desires and beliefs. Intentions will be adopted as the agent tries to satisfy its desires.

4.1 Originating Intentions

Once we have characterized intentions and related mental states, it is necessary to define how these mental states interact to produce the agent's behavior, namely how agents select intentions and when and how agents revise selected intentions. Agents choose their intentions from two different sources: from its desires and as a refinement from other intentions. We start by defining the creation of intentions from desires.

By definition, there are no constraints on the agent's desires. Therefore, an agent may have conflicting desires, i.e., desires that are not jointly achievable. Intentions, on the other hand, are restricted by rationality constraints (as shown before). Thus, agents must select only those desires that respect those constraints. We start by defining those desires that are eligible to be chosen and the notion of candidate desires set.

Definition 6 (Eligible Desires). Let $\mathcal{D}$ be the agent's desires. We call *eligible desires* at a time T the set

$$\mathcal{D}' = \{des(D, Ag, P, A) \,/\, [holds\_at(des(D, Ag, P, A), T) \leftarrow Body) \in \mathcal{D}] \wedge$$
$$Now \le T \wedge (\mathcal{B} \models_P Body) \wedge$$
$$\{\mathcal{B} \cup \mathcal{T}Ax\} \models_P \neg holds\_at(bel(Ag, P), T)\}$$

Eligible desires are those desires the agent believes are not satisfied. Recall that, according to rationality constraints in section 4, it is not rational for an agent to intend something it believes is already achieved or that is impossible. Notice that if a desire is conditional, then the agent should believe this condition is true.

As the initial set of desires, eligible desires may also be contradictory. Therefore, it is necessary to determine those subsets of the eligible desires that are jointly achievable. In general, there may be more than one subset of the eligible desires that are jointly achievable. Therefore, we should indicate which of these subsets are preferred to be adopted as intentions. We do this through the preference relation defined bellow.

Definition 7 (Desires Preference Relation $<_{Pref}$). Let $\mathcal{D}$ be the agent's desires, $\mathcal{D}'$ the set of eligible desires from $\mathcal{D}$, $\mathcal{P}(\mathcal{D}')$ the power set of $\mathcal{D}'$ and $R, S \in \mathcal{P}(\mathcal{D}')$. We say that $R <_{Pref} S$ (R is less preferred than S) if the biggest value for importance occurring in S and not occurring in R is bigger than the biggest value for importance occurring in R and no

t occurring in S; if there is no such biggest value in S, than R is less preferred than S if S has more elements than R.

According to this definition, the agent should prefer to satisfy first the most important desires. Additionally to preferring the most important ones, the agent adopts as much desires as it can.

Example 8. Given the set

$$D' = \{des(1, Ag, a, [0.5]), des(2, Ag, b, [0.3]),$$
$$des(3, Ag, c, [0.3]), des(4, Ag, d, [0.2])\}$$

of eligible desires:

1. for $d_1 = \{des(2, Ag, b, [0.3]), des(4, Ag, c, [0.2])\}$ and $d_2 = \{des(1, Ag, a, [0.5])\}$, we have $(d_1 <_{Pref} d_2)$. That is, d_1 is less preferred than d_2, since $A = 0.5$ for d_2 and $A' = 0.3$ for d_1;
2. for $d_3 = \{des(3, Ag, c, [0.3])\}$, we have $d_3 <_{Pref} d_1$, as $A = 0.2$ for both d_1 and d_3, but $\#d_3 < \#d_1$ ($\#d$ stands for cardinality of set d).

Notice that the preference relation is a pre-order relation. For instance, if an agent were to choose between $d_4 = \{des(2, Ag, b, [0.3])\}$ and $d_5 = \{des(3, Ag, c, [0.3])\}$, based only on the importance of desires and maximization of desires satisfied, it would not prefer either of them. And, indeed, according to the preference relation, we have that neither $(d_4 <_{Pref} d_5)$ nor $(d_5 <_{Pref} d_4)$. Based on this preference order, we define the preference graph that will be used to revise the mental states and the revision process.

Definition 9 (Desires Preference Graph). Let $\mathcal{D}$ be the agent's desires and $\mathcal{D}'$ the set of eligible desires from $\mathcal{D}$. Let *Revisable* be the set

$$Revisable = \{unsel(D)/\exists des(D, Ag, P, A) \in \mathcal{D}'\}$$

and *index* : $\mathcal{P}(Revisable) \longrightarrow \aleph^+$ a function from the power set of *Revisable* to natural numbers (zero excluded) that attributes a level number to elements of $\mathcal{P}(Rev)$. The *desires preference graph* is the graph defined by

1. $Rev(\textbf{bottom}) = \{happens(E, T_i, T_f), act(E, A)\}$;
2. $Rev(i) = R \cup \{happens(E, T_i, T_f), act(E, A)\}$, where $R \in \mathcal{P}(Revisable)$ and $i = index(R)$;

3. $i \ll$ **bottom**, where $i = index(R)$, $R \in \mathcal{P}(Revisable)$ and $\not\exists S \in \mathcal{P}$ $(Revisable)$. $(S <_{Pref} R)$;

4. $j \ll k_1, \ldots, k_n$, where $j = index(R)$, $k_i = index(S_i)$ $(1 \leq i \leq n)$, $R, S_i \in \mathcal{P}(Rev)$ $(1 \leq i \leq n)$ and R is an antecedent of S.

The desires graph definition starts by defining the set of revisable literals, i.e., the set of literals that will have their truth value changed when performing revision in order to select a subset of desires. According to the definition, to each desire D there is a revisable literal $unsel(D)$ associated to it. Next, it defines a numbering function (the $index$ function) that assigns to each set composed by elements of $Revisable$ a number. This number is used as the level numbers (see section 2 about preferred revisions) in the preference graph. At the root of the preference graph (**bottom** level) the revisable literals are $happens/3$ and $act/3$, i.e., we try to see if there is a course of actions that jointly satisfies all the eligible desires. If this is not the case, then we have to select a subset of the eligible desires. This is the role of the $unsel/1$ literals. Their initial value is false and, as we may see in definition 10, they are attached to each eligible desire as a default literal. Therefore, initially they have no influence in the evaluation of desires. If we cannot find a course of actions to satisfy all eligible desires, we have to start checking subsets of $\mathcal{D}'$. The preference graph states that we prefer to revise first the $unsel/1$ literals associated with less important desires, and second preserving as many eligible desires as we can. That is, when revising the eligible desires set, the preferred revisions are those that eliminate first the less important desires, and the least possible amount of desires, as shown in the definition bellow.

Definition 10 (Candidate Desires Set). Let $\mathcal{D}$ be the agent's desires and $\mathcal{D}'$ the set of eligible desires from $\mathcal{D}$ with a preference graph associated with it. We call *candidate desires set* any set

$$\mathcal{D}'_C = \{des(D, Ag, P, A)/(des(D, Ag, P, A) \in \mathcal{D}') \wedge$$
$$(P' \cup \Delta \not\models_P \bot)]\} \wedge$$
$$[\exists \Delta.(\mathcal{B} \cup \mathcal{T}Ax \cup \mathcal{R} \cup \Delta \models_P (holds\_at(bel(Ag, P), T), not\ unsel(D)))$$

where

1. P' is the abductive framework

$$\langle \mathcal{B} \cup \mathcal{T}Ax \cup \mathcal{R}, \{happens(E, T_i, T_f), act(E, Act), unsel(D)\}, IC \rangle;$$

2. IC is a set of constraints of the form
   - $\{holds\_at(bel(Ag, P), T) \Leftarrow not\ unsel(D)\}$ for every $des(D, Ag, P, A)$ in $\mathcal{D}'$;
   - the constraints $IC(\mathcal{I})$ generated by intentions (see definition 4).

In the revision process, we mix abductive reasoning with defeasible reasoning, where the literal $unsel(D)$ is defeasible. Its intuitive meaning is *"Desire D should not be selected as an intention"*. If the agent believes it is possible to satisfy all of its desires (if it can abduce actions that satisfy all desires and satisfy all constraints), it will find a revision that contains only $happens/3$ and $act/2$. When constraints may not be all concurrently satisfied, it means that the adoption of all desires as intentions leads to contradictions, i.e., they are not jointly satisfiable.

Notice that contradictions do not arise if the actions necessary to satisfy two different intentions have contradictory effects. Recall that, according to the EC axioms, a property P holds if there is an action that initiates it or, alternatively, if $\neg P$ implicitly does not hold, and vice-versa for $\neg P$. Therefore, actions that make contradictory properties hold in fact just cancel each other. This allows us to avoid the *side-effect problem*[9]. If we allowed for this kind of situations to raise contradictions, we would be making the agent preclude intentions that have contradictory consequences, but that are not directly contradictory with each other, and making the agent intend the logical consequences of its intentions. On the other hand, if an action necessary to satisfy an intention cancels a property that is also an intention, a constraint is violated and that course of action is rejected. In this case, the revision will try to defeat intentions, changing the truth value of $unsel(D)$ literals. According to the preference graph, it will try to defeat those constraints that represent the less important desires, trying to preserve the maximum of the most important ones.

As we mentioned before, the desires preference relation is not an order relation. Therefore, it is possible to have more than one candidate set after a revision. However, if we consider only achievability and desires attributes as decision criteria, it makes no difference for the agent to adopt any of the candidate desires set[5][5].

Definition 11 (Primary Intentions). Let $\mathcal{D}$ be the agent's desires, $\mathcal{D}'_C$ a candidate desires set from $\mathcal{D}$. The *primary intentions* of an agent is the set $\{int\_that(D, Ag, P, A) \mid des(D, Ag, P, A) \in Des'_C)\}$

Intentions as Refinements from Intentions Once the agent adopts its intentions, it will start planning to achieve those intentions. During planning, the agent will form intentions that are relative to pre-existing intentions. That is, they "refine" their existing intentions. This can be done in various ways, for instance, a plan that includes an action that is not directly executable can be elaborated by specifying particular way of carrying out that action; a plan that includes a set of actions can be elaborated by imposing a temporal order on that set[18]. Since the agent commits to the adopted intentions, these previously adopted intentions constrain the adoption of new ones. That is, during the elaboration of plans, a potential new intention is only adopted if it is not contradictory with the existing intentions and with beliefs.

Definition 12 (Relative Intentions). Let $\mathcal{I}_P$ be the set of primary intentions. A *planning process* is a procedure that, for each $i \in \mathcal{I}_P$, will generate a set of temporal ordered actions $\mathcal{I}_R$ that achieve i, such $\mathcal{B} \cup \mathcal{T}Ax \cup \mathcal{I}_P \cup \mathcal{I}_R$ is non-contradictory. The set $\mathcal{I}_R$ are the *relative intentions* of the agent.

---

[5] The revision process provided by the ELP framework defines a *sceptical revision*[1], that is the revision formed by the union of all the minimal program revision. This kind of approach prevents the agent from having to choose one of the minimal revisions. However, for intentions, this is not adequate, since we would like our agents to try to satisfy all the eligible desires it can.

The non-contradiction condition enforces again the notion of commitment, i.e., once an intention is adopted it constrains the adoption of new intentions.

Example 13 (cont. from example 5). As the robot starts working, it verifies what it is going to do (it adopts intentions). According to our definitions, it initially selects its eligible desires.

$$\mathcal{D}' = \{des(2, rbt, bel(rbt, stored(a1)), [0.3])\}$$

Since there is only one desire to be satisfied, there are no conflicts and it is adopted as a primary intention, i.e.,

$$\mathcal{I}_P = \{int\_that(1, rbt, bel(rbt, stored(a1)), [0.3])\}$$

Notice that none of the rationality constraints have been violated. Only one action is enough to satisfy its intention, namely

$$\mathcal{I}_R = \{int\_to(2, rbt, bel(rbt, store(a1)), [0.3])\}$$

4.2 Revising Intentions

In the previous section, we defined how the agent chooses its intentions. As we have seen, weighing motivations and beliefs means finding inconsistencies in competing desires, checking valid desires according to beliefs and intentions, resolving constraints imposed by intentions and desires, i.e., very expensive reasoning activities. It is now necessary to define *when* the agent should perform this process[33].

We argue that it is not enough to state that an agent should revise its intentions when it believes a certain condition holds, like to believe that an intention has been satisfied or that it is no longer possible to satisfy it, as this suggests that the agent needs to verify its beliefs constantly. Instead, we take the stance that it is necessary to define, along with those conditions, a mechanism that triggers the reasoning process without imposing a significant additional burden on the agent. Our approach is to define those conditions that make the agent start reasoning about intentions as constraints over its beliefs. Recall that we assume that an agent constantly has to maintain its beliefs consistent, whenever new facts are incorporated.

Definition 14 (Trigger from Intentions). Let $\mathcal{B}$ be the agent's beliefs set and $\mathcal{I}$ its intentions. We add to $\mathcal{B}$ the following *trigger constraints*:

- $(\perp \Leftarrow Now > T, not\ rev\_int)$, for each $(int\_that(I, Ag, P, A), int\_to(I, Ag, Act, A)) \in \mathcal{I}$;
- $(\perp \Leftarrow happens(E, T_i, T_f), act(E, Act), not\ rev\_int$, for each $int\_to(I, Ag, Act, A)) \in \mathcal{I}$.

The literal rev_int is part of the revisable set of beliefs, and its initial value is *false*. Whenever the agent revises its beliefs and one of the conditions for revising beliefs hold, a contradiction is raised. We identify such contradiction by testing if rev_int is in the selected revision for the beliefs set, i.e., if it has to have its truth value modified in order to restore consistency. The intention revision process is triggered when one of these constraints is violated.

The conditions we have defined so far are the usual ones defined by formal models of agents. As we have seen before, this characterization of intentions may lead to some fanatical behavior. Therefore, we need to adopt additional constraints that will avoid those unwanted behaviors. We take the stance that the same reasons that originated intentions may be used to break commitment associated to them[7]. If we accept that an intention originated from desires, it is reasonable to state that it is not rational to persist with an intention whose reasons are superseded by more urgent or important ones. The agent's normal behavior would be to weigh its competing desires and beliefs, selecting its intentions. The agent would commit to these intentions and they would constitute the filter of admissibility for other intentions. Also, the agent would try to satisfy those intentions, until successful accomplishment, impossibility (as usually defined), or *until some of his other desires that were not selected before would become eligible*, or *until the desires that originated them would not be eligible anymore*, re-activating the revision process that would weigh (again) competing desires and beliefs. Since the notion of commitment is preserved, the agent would not start this process every time there is a change in beliefs, but only if relevant conditions trigger the intention revision process, changing the agent's focus of attention[6]. These triggers are determined by the desires pre-conditions. We model this triggers using an approach similar to the normative constraints in [28,32].

Definition 15 (Trigger Constraints from Desires). Let $\mathcal{D}$ be the agent's desires and $\mathcal{D}'$ the set of eligible desires from $\mathcal{D}$. We define *trigger constraints from desires* as

1. For every $des(D,Ag,P,A) \leftarrow Body \in \mathcal{D}$ and not in $\mathcal{D}'$ with importance A bigger that the biggest importance in intentions, we define a trigger constraint $\bot \Leftarrow Body$, $not\ rev\_int$;

2. given the set of actions Δ abduced by the agent (see definition 10), for each $des(D, Ag, P, A) \in (\mathcal{D}' - \mathcal{D}'_C)$ with importance A bigger that the biggest importance in intentions, we define a trigger constraint $\bot \Leftarrow C_1, \ldots, C_n, not\ rev\_int$, where C_i $(1 \leq i \leq n)$ are the conditions the agent could not bring about when selecting the candidate desires set.

The first constraint trigger is formed by the pre-conditions of those desires that were not eligible and that are more important than those that were evaluated. It means that if the pre-conditions of such desires become true, these desires (that were not considered during reasoning) become eligible. Therefore, it is necessary to re-evaluate desires and beliefs to check if this new desire may be brought about. The second constraint is formed by the pre-conditions of those eligible desires that, although more important, were not relevant when the agent made his choice. Notice that there are no triggers for those desires that were eligible but that were ruled out during the choice of a revision. This is so because they had already been evaluated and they have been considered less important than the other desires. Therefore, it is of no use to trigger the whole process again (i.e., to shift the agent's attention) to re-evaluate them.

Example 16 (cont. from example 5). The robot would have as triggers in its beliefs

$$\bot \Leftarrow happens(E, T_i, T_f), act(E, store(a1)), not\ rev\_int.$$
$$\bot \Leftarrow holds\_at(bel(rbt, \neg bat\_chged), T), not\ rev_i nt.$$

Suppose that, while executing the $store(a1)$ action, an event with $sense\_low\_bat$ happens. This would raise a contradiction in the belief revision, as property $bel(rbt, bat\_chged)$ would hold and would make the robot revise its desires and intentions. Now, the eligible desires would be

$$\mathcal{D}' = \{des(1, rbt, bat\_chged, [0.5]), des(2, rbt, stored(a1), [0.3])\}$$

But these are conflicting desires, therefore we must choose an appropriate subset of desires. There desires preference graph would be

$Rev(1) = \{unsel(2)\} \cup Rev(\mathbf{bottom})$ $\qquad$ $Rev(2) = \{unsel(1)\}\cup$
$\qquad\qquad\qquad\qquad\qquad\qquad\qquad\qquad\qquad\qquad Rev(\mathbf{bottom})$
$Rev(3) = \{unsel(1), unsel(2)\} \cup Rev(\mathbf{bottom})$
$1 \ll \mathbf{bottom} \qquad 2 \ll 1 \qquad 3 \ll 2$

and would produce as candidate desire set $\mathcal{D}'_C = \{des(1, rbt, bel(rbt, bat\_chged), [0.5])\}$. The robot's intentions then would be $\mathcal{I}_P = \{int\_that(1, rbt, bat\_chged), [0.5])\}$ and $\mathcal{I}_R = \{int\_to(2, rbt, charge, [0.5])\}$.

5 Conclusion

The main contribution of this paper is to provide a formal model of agents that reduces the gap between agent specification and agent implementation. Adopting ELP as the underlying formalism has both preserved the main characteristics of formal models, namely the ability to formally define and verify agents, and has provided machinery the agent may use to reason. Besides that, our model presents other advantages, such as modelling both static and dynamic aspects of pro-active mental states[20] (see also [21] for a comparison of our work with many other formal BDI models). Our next step is to focus on the evolution of plans and communication, on how this affects the stability of intentions and integrate it to our framework.

References

1. J.J. Alferes and L.M. Pereira. *Reasoning with Logic Programming.* Springer-Verlag, Berlin, DE., 1996. Lecture Notes in Artificial Intelligence Series (LNAI 1111).

2. J.J. Alferes, L.M. Pereira, and T. Przymusinski. Belief revision in non-monotonic reasoning and logic programming. In C. Pinto-Ferreira and N.J. Mamede, editors, *Proceedings of the Seventh Portuguese Conference on Artificial Intelligence (EPIA'93)*, Berlin, Germany, 1995. APIA, Springer-Verlag. Lecture Notes on Artificial Intelligence (LNAI 990).

3. L. Beaudoin. *Goal Processing in Autonomous Agents.* PhD thesis, Birmingham University, Birmingham, UK, August 1994.

4. J. Bell. A planning theory of practical reasoning. In *Proceedings of the AAAI'95 Fall Symposium on Rational Agents Concepts*. AAAI, 1995.

5. J. Bell and Z. Huang. Dynamic goal hierarchies. In *Proceedings of the Second Workshop on Practical Reasoning and Rationality*, London, England, 1997. AISB Workshop Series.

6. L.M. Botelho and H. Coelho. Agents that rationalize their decisions. In *Proceedings of the II International Conference on Multi-Agent Systems*, Kyoto, Japan, 1996. AAAI Org.

7. M. Bratman. Planning and the stability of intentions. *Minds and Machines*, 2:1–16, 1992.

8. M. Bratman, D.J. Israel, and M.E Pollack. Plans and resource bounded practical reasoning. *Computational Intelligence*, 4:349–355, 1988.

9. M.E. Bratman. What is intention? In P.R. Cohen, J.L. Morgan, and M. Pollack, editors, *Intentions in Communication*, chapter 1. The MIT Press, Cambridge, MA, 1990.

10. P.R. Cohen and H.J. Levesque. Intention is choice with commitment. *Artificial Intelligence*, 42:213–261, 1990.

11. M. Corrêa and H. Coelho. Around the architectural approach to model conversations. In *Proceedings of the Fifth European Workshop on Modelling Autonomous Agents and Multi-Agents Worlds (MAAMAW'93)*, 1993.

12. M. Corrêa and H. Coelho. A framework for mental states and agent architectures. In *Proceedings of the MASTAS Workshop at EPIA'97*, 1997.

13. M. Corrêa and S. Mendes. A computational approach to situation theory based on logic programming to design cognitive agents. In *Advances in Artificial Intelligence: Proceedings of the 12th Brazilian Symposium on Artificial Intelligence*. Springer-Verlag, 1995. (Lecture Notes on Artificial Intelligence 991).

14. C. Damásio, W. Nejdl, and L.M. Pereira. Revise: An extended logic programming system for revising knowledge bases. In *Knowledge Representation and Reasoning*. Morgan Kaufmann inc., 1994.

15. K. Devlin. *Logic and Information*. Cambridge University Press, 1991.

16. M. Georgeff and A. Lansky. Reactive reasoning and planning. In *Proceedings of the National Conference of Artificial Intelligence (AAAI'91)*. AAAI inc., 1991.

17. A. Haddadi. *Communication and Cooperation in Agent Systems: a Pragmatic Theory*. Springer-Verlag, Berlin, DE., 1996. Lecture Notes in Artificial Intelligence Series (LNAI 1056).

18. K. Konolige and M. Pollack. A representationalist theory of intentions. In *Proceedings of the XII International Joint Conference on Artificial Intelligence (IJCAI'93)*, Chambéry, France, 1993. IJCAI inc.

19. R. Li and L.M. Pereira. Knowledge assimilation in domains of actions: A possible causes approach. *Journal of Applied Non-Classical Logic*, 1996. Special issue on Inconsistency Handling in Knowledge Systems.

20. M.C. Móra, J.G. Lopes, H. Coelho, and R. Viccari. Affecting the stability of intentions. In E. Costa, editor, *8th Portuguese Conference on Artificial Intelligence*. Springer-Verlag, 1997.

21. M.C. Móra, J.G. Lopes, H. Coelho, and R. Viccari. Modelling agents with extended logic programa. In *International Workshop on Engineering of Intelligent Systems*. ICSC co., 1998.

22. N. Moussale, R.M. Viccari, and M. Corrêa. Tutor-student interaction modelling in an agent architecture based on mental states. In D. Borges and C. Kaestner, editors, *Advances in Artificial Intelligence: Proceedings of the Thirteenth Brasilian Symposium on Artificial Intelligence*, Berlin, Germany, 1996. SBC, Springer-Verlag. Lecture Notes in Artificial Intelligence (LNAI 1159).

23. H. Nakashima, I. Ohsawa, and Y. Kinoshita. Inference with mental situation. Technical report, Umezono, Tsukuba, Ibaraki, Japan, 1981. (TR-91-7).

24. J. Quaresma and J.G. Lopes. A logic programming framework for the abduction of events in a dialogue system. In *Proceedings of the Workshop on Automated Reasoning*, London, England, 1997. AISB Workshop Series.

25. A.. Rao. Agentspeak(1): BDI agents speak out in a logical computable language. In *Proceedings of the European Workshop on Modelling Autonomous Agents and Multi-Agents Worlds 1996 (MAAMAW'96)*, Berlin, Germany, 1996. Springer-Verlag.

26. A.S. Rao and M.P. Georgeff. Modelling rational agents within a BDI-architecture. In R. Fikes and E. Sandewall, editors, *Proceedings of the Knowledge Representation and Reasoning'91 (KR&R'91)*, San Mateo, CA., 1991. Morgan Kauffman Publishers.

27. K. Schild. On the relationship between BDI logics and standard logics of concurrency. In J. P. Müller, M. P. Singh, and A S. Rao, editors, *Intelligent Agents V — Proceedings of the Fifth International Workshop on Agent Theories, Architectures, and Languages (ATAL-98)*, Lecture Notes in Artificial Intelligence. Springer-Verlag, Heidelberg, 1999. In this volume.

28. M. Schroeder, Iara de Almeida Móra, and Luís Moniz Pereira. A deliberative and reactive diagnosis agent based on logic programming. In J. P. Müller, M. J. Wooldridge, and N. R. Jennings, editors, *Intelligent Agents III — Proceedings of the Third International Workshop on Agent Theories, Architectures, and Languages (ATAL-96)*, volume 1193 of *Lecture Notes in Artificial Intelligence*, pages 293–308. Springer-Verlag, Heidelberg, 1997.

29. Y. Shoham. Agent-oriented programming. *Artificial Intelligence*, 60:51–92, 1993.

30. M. Singh. *Multiagent systems: a theoretical framework for intentions, know-how, and communications*. Springer-Verlag, Heidelberg, Germany, 1994. Lecture Notes in Artificial Intelligence (LNAI 799).

31. B. van Linder, W. van der Hoek, and J. J. Ch. Meyer. Formalizing motivational attitudes of agents: On preferences, goals, and commitments. In M. Wooldridge, J. P. Müller, and M. Tambe, editors, *Intelligent Agents II — Proceedings of the Second International Workshop on Agent Theories, Architectures, and Languages (ATAL-95)*, volume 1037 of *Lecture Notes in Artificial Intelligence*, pages 17–32. Springer-Verlag, Heidelberg, 1996.

32. G. Wagner. A logical and operational model of scalable knowledge and perception-based agents. In *Proceedings of the European Workshop on Modelling Autonomous Agents and Multi-Agents Worlds 1996 (MAAMAW'96)*, Berlin, Germany, 1996. Springer-Verlag.

33. M. J. Wooldridge and S. D. Parsons. Intention reconsideration reconsidered. In J. P. Müller, M. P. Singh, and A. S. Rao, editors, *Intelligent Agents V — Proceedings of the Fifth International Workshop on Agent Theories, Architectures, and Languages (ATAL-98)*, Lecture Notes in Artificial Intelligence. Springer-Verlag, Heidelberg, 1999. In this volume.

Information-Passing and Belief Revision in Multi-Agent Systems

Rogier M. van Eijk, Frank S. de Boer,
Wiebe van der Hoek and John-Jules Ch. Meyer

Utrecht University, Department of Computer Science
P.O. Box 80.089, 3508 TB Utrecht, The Netherlands
{rogier, frankb, wiebe, jj}@cs.uu.nl

Abstract. We define a programming language for multi-agent systems in which agents interact with a common environment and cooperate by exchanging their individual beliefs on the environment. In handling the information they acquire, the agents employ operations to expand, remove and update their individual belief bases. The overall framework, which generalises traditional concurrent programming concepts, is parameterised by an information system of constraints. Such a system is used to represent the environment as well as the beliefs of the agents. We give the syntax of the programming language and develop an operational semantics in terms of a transition system.

1 Introduction

A lot of effort has been made in the development of programming languages for multi-agent systems that cover typical agent concepts like beliefs, desires, intentions, commitments, speech acts, communication, cooperation and so on. However, we believe that most of the concurrency aspects of the existing multi-agent languages lack a clear modular structure, which is mainly due to the intricacies of the interactions between the various agent features. The significance of a modular design, which is also discussed in the contributions of Fisher [11] and Engelfriet *et al.* [9] in this volume, is reflected by the fact that most of the existing multi-agent languages are not yet fully understood from a semantical point of view.

In order to obtain a well-structured and semantically well-understood multi-agent programming language, we advocate an *incremental* approach to the design of such languages. Our starting point, like that of the contribution of Schild on BDI logics in this volume [21], lies in the traditional concepts and mechanisms introduced and studied in the research area of concurrency theory. Notably, we consider concepts like communication, synchronisation and parallelism. We generalise these concepts in order to model epistemic features of agents reflecting on their actions, observations and interactions. One of the main characteristics of this generalisation, as presented in this paper, is the shift from a traditional *value-passing* to a more general *information-passing* mechanism.

In particular, we study the implications of information-passing in a context of interacting agents that act upon and reason about a common world.

In our opinion the present framework will provide a solid basis for further extensions dealing with the motivational attitudes as desires and intentions that are for instance described in [4, 19]. Moreover, the incremental and modular development advocated in this paper, provides a framework for the study of interactions between the epistemic and motivational attitudes of agents.

In a preliminary paper [6] we examined an abstract programming language for agents interacting with and passing information about an environment, which was represented by a store of constraints. The store, which we called the *work-space*, satisfied the property that once some information was contained in it, this information would indefinitely be present. The restriction to environments satisfying this property, enabled us to concentrate on setting up the general programming framework. In the present paper, we drop the assumption of the monotonic-increasing behaviour of the environment and allow information to be removed from the workspace as well. This has a major impact on the agents in the framework, as the information available to them, obtained from observations and communication, need not be true with respect to the *current* environment.

1.1 Beliefs and Updates

We view multi-agent systems as systems composed of interacting agents that inhabit an external environment (see [25] for more details). To keep their feet in the environment, the agents are usually assigned a mental state consisting of beliefs, goals, intentions and so on. In this paper, we focus on the way agents cope with the information they acquire about their environment. We explicitly state one mentalistic notion of agency: the agents' beliefs about their environment. More specific, we assume each agent in the framework maintains a private store of information, called a *belief base*, constituting its beliefs on the environment. Whenever the agent acquires new information, it examines the effects on its current belief base and if necessary updates it in conformity with the newly acquired data.

In multi-agent systems, there are at least two sources of new information: the agents' ability of observing the environment and secondly, their ability to share information by means of communication. To understand the issues at stake, let us consider the multi-agent system in figure 1. It is composed of a building consisting of a waiting room and a service room, and several agents that are staying either in the waiting room, in the service room or outside the building. We focus on an agent A staying in the waiting room and which is able to observe the number, say x, of agents in this room. Additionally, there is an agent B that keeps track of the number of agents that are inside the building, which is the sum of the number x of agents in the waiting room and the number y of agents in the service room, without being able to observe x and y separately. We assume that the agents A and B are able to communicate with each other via some communication channel. Let us consider an initial situation in which the agent B has observed the assertion $x + y = 10$; i.e. the fact that there are 10 agents inside the building. The belief base of the agent A is empty. Next, the following subsequent events take place:

- (e1) The agent A observes that the number of waiting agents (including himself) equals 8; that is, it observes the assertion $x = 8$.
- (e2) The agent B communicates the assertion $x + y = 10$ to the agent A.
- (e3) The agent B communicates the assertion $x = 6$ to the agent A.
- (e4) One agent leaves the service room through the building's exit. (Note that this cannot be observed by the agent A.) The agent B reports this event by communicating the assertion $x + y = 9$ to A.
- (e5) One of the waiting agents leaves the waiting room. The agent A comes to know about the new situation by observing the assertion $x = 7$.

We examine some strategies the agents might employ to deal with the information coming available to them after the occurrences of events $e1 - e5$. We remark that we abstract from any notion of time and assume that the assertions observed by an agent itself are considered to be more reliable than the assertions obtained by means of communication.

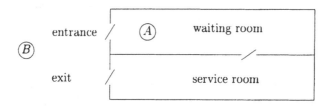

Fig. 1. A multi-agent system

The naive approach The first approach to the process of belief updating that comes to mind is one in which each agent maintains a belief base that is updated with every new fact it acquires. Hence, if the agent A uses this strategy, after events $e1$ and $e2$, its belief base contains the facts $x = 8$ and $x+y = 10$. However, after the occurrence of event $e3$, the belief $x = 8$ of the agent A is overruled by the assertion $x = 6$. We note that this is not a wise thing to do, as the agent has observed with its own eyes a fact contradicting $x = 6$.

The discriminating approach The discriminating approach tries to solve the problem sketched above; agents acting according to this strategy only accept information from communication that is consistent with their current belief base. Hence, by employing this strategy, after event $e3$, the agent A rejects the assertion $x = 6$, as it is inconsistent with its belief base; the agent holds on to its belief $x = 8$ instead. This approach is however not entirely satisfactory in the light of event $e4$. Using the strategy A rejects the information $x + y = 9$ about the new situation, as it is inconsistent with its current belief base. However, considering the situation at hand, we note that this is not a wise thing to do.

The splitting approach I To overcome the drawback of the discriminating approach, we propose a strategy (as suggested in [16]) in which the belief base is divided in two sections: the beliefs resulting from observations (*the observational beliefs*) and beliefs resulting from communication (*the communicational beliefs*). This situation is depicted in figure 2. The labels in this diagram represent the

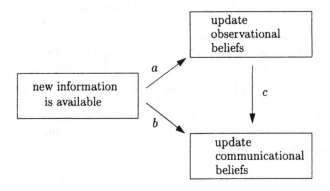

Fig. 2. A belief update scheme

circumstances under which the agent decides to update its beliefs. Obviously, by introducing a split belief base, we have to be careful that the agent's beliefs stay consistent. The procedure is as follows. Whenever the agent observes new information (denoted as condition *a* in this figure), its observational beliefs are updated with this recent information. If it obtains new information by means of communication and the communicational beliefs that would result are consistent with the observational beliefs (condition *b* in figure 2), the update of the communicational beliefs is carried out. Finally, in case after an update of the observational beliefs, the agent's communicational beliefs have become inconsistent with these beliefs (condition *c*), the agent should recover from this inconsistency. For instance, after event $e4$ in which the new information $x + y = 9$ comes available, the communicational belief $x + y = 10$ of the agent A is overwritten by this new information. Subsequently, after event $e5$, the agent's observational belief $x = 8$ is overwritten by the assertion $x = 7$, while the communicational belief $x + y = 9$ is left intact, as it is still consistent with the new observational beliefs. We remark that in the imaginary situation A possesses the communicational belief $x = 6$, this belief should be removed from the communicational beliefs after the observation of the assertion $x = 7$.

The splitting approach II We claim that the approach outlined above is still not entirely satisfactory. To see this, let us examine the event $e5$ in more detail. Without having any additional information, the agent A has no clue about the effects of its observation $x = 7$ on the total number of agents in the building, as it is for instance not able to distinguish between the case that one of the waiting agents has left the building through the entrance without being served; that is, $x + y = 8$, and the case that a waiting agent has entered the service room; i.e. $x + y = 9$. Hence, there is no explicit ground for keeping the belief $x + y = 9$. To deal with this, we propose a strategy in which after an observation that conflicts with the agent's observational beliefs, the corresponding communicational beliefs are also erased. Applying this strategy, the communicational belief $x + y = 9$ of the agent A is erased after an observation of the assertion $x = 7$. We remark that the new observation might serve as a trigger to get a decisive answer about the current relation between x and y by means of communication with agent B.

The approaches described in this section reveal some possible update strategies and belief base representations. In order to show the consequences of a particular strategy on the development of a programming language, we develop the multi-agent programming framework in the light of splitting approach II.

1.2 The Workspace and Integrity Constraints

Besides the ability to observe the workspace and the ability to communicate, the agents are also able to establish facts in the section of the workspace that constitutes their expertise. In describing these establishments, we employ the notion of an *integrity constraint* from the database literature, which expresses a property that the structure and behaviour of the data in the workspace must satisfy at all times [24]. We will distinguish between two types of integrity constraints. One type is constituted by the *persistent* constraints, which once present in the information store can never be removed from it. The other integrity constraints are given by the *hard* constraints, which need not necessarily be represented in the workspace itself, but should be obeyed by the workspace at all times. In the multi-agent situation outlined above, an example of a persistent constraint is the fact that the number of agents in the building is equal to the sum of the number of agents in the waiting and the service room. Additionally, hard constraints are for example the universal facts about integers. The programming framework we describe includes a construct to identify persistent constraints in the workspace. Additionally, we assume that the agents have access to a background theory consisting of the hard constraints the workspace obeys.

The rest of the paper is organised as follows. In the next section we describe the information system underlying the programming language. Subsequently, we define the syntax and the operational semantics of the language in section 3 and 4, respectively. We conclude in section 5 by outlining several directions for future extensions of the framework.

2 Constraint Systems

In order to stay close to well-understood concepts from the field of concurrent programming and additionally to concentrate on setting up the framework, we focus on the so-called constraint languages to represent information. We use these languages to represent the workspace and the belief bases of the agents; they are constructed by the accumulation of constraints, denoted by $\wedge$, and the hiding of constraints given by an operation $\exists$. The latter logical operation is used as a uniform mechanism to describe workspace changes as well as belief base updates.

Definition 1 A *constraint system* is a tuple:

$$\langle\, Var, \mathcal{L}, C, \vdash, \wedge, true, false, \exists\,\rangle,$$

where *Var* is a set of variables and $\mathcal{L}$ is a constraint language covering a collection C of primitive constraints and the constants *true* and *false*. Additionally, if $x \in Var$ and $\varphi, \psi \in \mathcal{L}$ then $\varphi \wedge \psi$, $\exists_x \varphi \in \mathcal{L}$, which denote the accumulation of φ and ψ and the hiding of constraints on x in φ, respectively. The operator $\vdash$ represents an information-ordering on $\mathcal{L}$.

We will refer to the variables occurring in a constraint φ by $var(\varphi)$. Additionally, we will use the meta-variables $\varphi \in \mathcal{L}$ and $\psi \in \mathcal{L}$ to denote arbitrary constraints, $\sigma \in \mathcal{L}$ to denote workspaces and $B \in \mathcal{L} \times \mathcal{L}$ to denote belief bases. An example of a constraint system for the multi-agent system outlined in the introduction is one in which $Var = \{w, x, y, z\}$ and the variable x refers to the number of agents in the waiting room, y denotes the number of agents in the service room, z is the number of agents in the building and w refers to the total number of agents in the system. Typical primitive constraints are assertions like $x + y = z$, $z \leq w$, $y \geq 0$ and so on.

If $\mathbf{x}$ denotes the vector $x_1, \ldots, x_n$ then $\exists_\mathbf{x}$ abbreviates $\exists_{x_1} \cdots \exists_{x_n}$. The *projection* of φ to the variables $\mathbf{x}$ is defined by:

$$\Pi_\mathbf{x}\varphi =_{def} \exists_\mathbf{y}\varphi,$$

where $\mathbf{y} = var(\varphi) \setminus \mathbf{x}$. For instance, $\Pi_w(w + x = y \wedge x = y)$ is defined to be $\exists_{x,y}(w + x = y \wedge x = y)$, which is logically equivalent to $w = 0$.

3   Syntax of the Programming Language

We define an agent-oriented programming language for agents interacting in a shared environment. The language builds upon concepts underpinning several well-understood concurrent programming paradigms; viz. Concurrent Constraint Programming (CCP) [20,5], Communicating Sequential Processes (CSP) [13] and Algebra of Communicating Processes (ACP) [1]. The communication Analogous to CCP, the language is parameterised by a constraint system $\langle\, Var, \mathcal{L}, C, \vdash,$ $\wedge, true, false, \exists\,\rangle$. It is intended for programming agent systems that are built from agents operating in parallel that interact with an external environment represented by a workspace $\sigma \in \mathcal{L}$. The framework is outlined in figure 3. The left-hand side of the diagram shows the interaction mechanisms between the

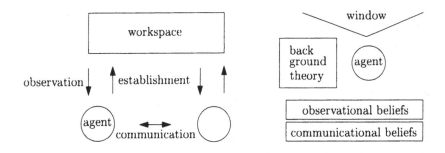

Fig. 3. The agents' interactions and information sources

agents: they observe the workspace, establish facts in it and additionally communicate with each other. The right-hand side of the figure depicts the information sources that are available to the agents. Each agent maintains a private belief base consisting of its observational and communicational beliefs, has access to a background theory consisting of the hard constraints the workspace satisfies and additionally, possesses a private window through which it observes the workspace.

Definition 2 *(Syntax of the programming language)*
Given a formula $\varphi \in \mathcal{L}$, a vector of variables $\mathbf{x}$, a communication channel c and a belief base $B \in \mathcal{L} \times \mathcal{L}$, we define atomic actions a, programming statements S and agent systems A as follows:

$$a ::= \mathsf{est}_{\mathbf{x}}(\varphi) \mid \mathsf{ver}(\varphi) \mid \mathsf{non\_ver}(\varphi) \mid \mathsf{obs}(\mathbf{x}) \mid \mathsf{send}(c, \varphi) \mid \mathsf{receive}(c, \varphi)$$
$$S ::= S_1 \mathbin{\&} S_2 \mid a; S \mid S_1 + S_2 \mid P \mid \mathsf{skip}$$
$$A ::= (\mathbf{x}, S, B) \mid A_1 \parallel A_2 \mid \mathsf{pers}_{\varphi} A \mid \delta_c(A)$$

An agent system A in the language is defined to be either a basic agent $(\mathbf{x}, S, B)$, the parallel composition $\parallel$ of two agent systems, a construct $\mathsf{pers}_{\varphi} A$ meaning that the constraint φ in the workspace is persistent during the execution of the agent system A, or an encapsulated agent system $\delta_c(A)$ in which the communication channel c is local to the agents in A.

The basic agents are denoted as $(\mathbf{x}, S, B)$, in which $\mathbf{x}$ is a vector of variables, S a program and B a belief base. The behaviour of the agents is given by the execution of primitive actions for establishing changes in the workspace, (non-) verifying constraints, observing the workspace and communicating with other agents. Each agent is controlled by means of a program S composed of familiar programming constructs; viz. & expressing parallel execution, ; denoting the prefixing operator, + standing for non-deterministic choice, P denoting a call to a procedure P and skip standing for the statement that always succeeds and has no side effects. We assume a set W of (recursive) procedure declarations of the form $P :: S$, where P denotes the name and S the body of the procedure. Additionally, the construct $a \to \mathsf{skip}$ is usually abbreviated to a.

An agent's belief base $B \in \mathcal{L} \times \mathcal{L}$ is constituted by the beliefs B^o which are obtained by observing the environment and the beliefs B^c obtained from communication; we will denote it as (B^o, B^c). Abusing notation we will sometimes write B to denote $B^o \wedge B^c$. Moreover, we will write B^s (beliefs from source s) to denote either B^o or B^c. Each agent $(\mathbf{x}, S, B)$ is additionally assigned an expertise on the environment, modeled by the variables $\mathbf{x}$.[1] These variables give rise to a window on the workspace; i.e. the part of the workspace concerning the agent's expertise variables. Additionally, we require that the agents do not establish constraints other than those on the variables $\mathbf{x}$. For instance, in the example mentioned above, the expertise of the agent A is given by the variable x (the number of agents in the waiting room), whereas that of the agent B is given by z (the number of agents in the building). As in the framework we assume the vector $\mathbf{x}$ to be static, we usually suppress it from notation and write (S, B) rather than $(\mathbf{x}, S, B)$. We define an agent's window on the workspace to be the part of the workspace concerning the agent's accessible variables; i.e. the workspace from which the constraints on the inaccessible variables are hidden.

Definition 3 A *window* on a workspace σ with respect to the variables $\mathbf{x}$, is defined as: $window(\sigma, \mathbf{x}) =_{def} \Pi_{\mathbf{x}} \sigma$.

The meaning of the programming constructs should become clear in the subsequent section where we discuss their operational semantics.

4 Operational Semantics

In the theory of belief updates [14] there is a traditional distinction between three types of operations; viz. expansions, erasures and updates. An expansion of a belief base with φ is the addition of φ regardless of the potential inconsistency of the resulting base. An erasure of φ from a belief base is an adjustment such that it no longer derives φ. An update with φ is an adjustment of the belief base such that it is consistent and derives φ. In our framework, each agent will employ each of these operations to maintain its belief base. To decide whether to expand, to erase, or to update its beliefs, we assume each agent has access to a background theory Φ constituted by the hard constraints the workspace is subjected to. The decision whether new information is consistent with the agent's current beliefs is then made in the light of this background theory Φ.

Definition 4 Given the background theory Φ, a constraint $\varphi \in \mathcal{L}$ is defined to be *consistent* if $(\Phi \wedge \varphi) \nvdash false$.

We subsequently define the three belief update operators the agents in the framework employ. Consider a belief $B^s \in \mathcal{L}$, a constraint $\varphi \in \mathcal{L}$ and a vector $\mathbf{x}$ of variables.

---

[1] In [8] we study a refinement in which an expertise is given by a signature rather than by a collection of accessible variables. In this light, we can for example model the situation that an agent is able to observe the fact that x is a block; that is, $block(x)$, whereas it is not capable of observing that it is a red block; that is, $red(x)$.

First, the expansion operation defined by

$$expand(B^s, \varphi) =_{def} B^s \wedge \varphi,$$

yields a (possibly inconsistent) belief base consisting of the conjunction of B^s and φ.

Secondly, given a constraint ψ we define the operation:

$$erase(B^s, \mathbf{x}) =_{def} \exists_{\mathbf{x}} B^s \wedge \psi,$$

where ψ denotes the persistent beliefs on the variables $\mathbf{x}$ with $B^s \vdash \psi$. This operation hides in B^s all constraints on the variables $\mathbf{x}$ but the constraints that are identified to be persistent. In this paper, we will not further consider these persistent beliefs and assume ψ to be *true*.

Finally, we define the operation:

$$update(B^s, \varphi) =_{def} \begin{cases} expand(B^s, \varphi) & \text{if } B^s \wedge \varphi \text{ is consistent} \\ expand(erase(B^s, var(\varphi)), \varphi) & \text{otherwise.} \end{cases}$$

The update of B^s is either the expansion with φ, or in case this yields an inconsistent belief, the hiding of the constraints on the variables occurring in φ, succeeded by the expansion with φ.

4.1 Transition Systems

In this section we develop an operational semantics of the language by means of a transition system (due to Plotkin cf. [17]). Such a system is used for the formal derivation of transitions. A transition takes a system from one configuration to a subsequent configuration. It is of the form $\langle A, \sigma \rangle \xrightarrow{\alpha} \langle A', \sigma' \rangle$ denoting that the agent system A in the workspace σ performs a computation step that changes the workspace to σ'. The agent system A' represents the part of A that still needs to be executed. The label α is either an internal computation step τ, a local computation step $c \,!\, \varphi$ of sending the constraint φ along the communication channel c, or a local computation step $c \,?\, \varphi$ of receiving a constraint φ along the channel c. The transition system is composed of transition rules, which are of the form:

$$\frac{\langle A_1, \sigma \rangle \xrightarrow{\alpha_1} \langle A'_1, \sigma' \rangle \ \dots \ \langle A_n, \sigma \rangle \xrightarrow{\alpha_n} \langle A'_n, \sigma' \rangle}{\langle A, \sigma \rangle \xrightarrow{\alpha} \langle A', \sigma' \rangle} \ cond$$

The rule says that the transition below the line can be derived if the transition above the line can be derived and *cond* holds. A transition rule with several transitions below the line, is used to abbreviate a collection of rules, each having one of them as its conclusion. Axioms of the transition system are those rules with no transitions above the line.

We identify a special symbol E denoting termination. Additionally, we define the statement $E \, \& \, E$ as well as the agent systems (E, B), $E \parallel E$, $\mathsf{pers}_\varphi E$ and $\delta_c(E)$ all to be equal to E.

4.2   Transition Rules

In the rules below we assume that B denotes the belief base (B^o, B^c), while B' represents the base $(B^{o'}, B^{c'})$.

Definition 5 (*Transition for establishing*)

$$\langle(\mathsf{est}_\mathbf{x}(\varphi), B), \sigma\rangle \xrightarrow{\tau} \langle(E, B), \sigma'\rangle \qquad \text{if } \sigma' \text{ is consistent}$$

where $\sigma' = \exists_\mathbf{x} \sigma \wedge \varphi$.

The action $\mathsf{est}_\mathbf{x}(\varphi)$ yields a consistent workspace in which the information on the variables $\mathbf{x}$ is exactly given by φ.

Example 1. This example and the subsequent ones refer to the multi-agent system outlined in the introduction. Consider the initial workspace comprised of the fact that the sum of the number x of agents in the waiting room and the number y of agents in the service room equals 10, and the fact that there are 8 agents in the waiting room; that is, $x + y = 10 \wedge x = 8$. An agent's exit from the service room through the building's exit (event $e4$) is modeled by $\mathsf{est}_y(y = 1)$; i.e. the establishment that the current constraints on y are given by $y = 1$. The result of this action is a new workspace $\exists_y(x + y = 10 \wedge x = 8) \wedge y = 1$, which is logically equivalent to $x = 8 \wedge y = 1$. We remark that for instance the action $\mathsf{est}_y(x + y = 9)$ would yield an equivalent workspace.

Definition 6 (*Transition for verifying*)

$$\langle(\mathsf{ver}(\varphi), B), \sigma\rangle \xrightarrow{\tau} \langle(E, B'), \sigma\rangle \qquad \text{if } window(\sigma) \vdash \varphi$$

where $B^{o'} = update(B^o, \varphi)$ and

$$B^{c'} = \begin{cases} B^c & \text{if } B^o \wedge \varphi, \ B^c \wedge B^{o'} \text{ consistent} \\ erase(B^c, var(\varphi)) & \text{otherwise} \end{cases}$$

The action $\mathsf{ver}(\varphi)$ is successful whenever the constraint φ is implied by the agent's window; the observational beliefs are subsequently updated with φ. In case φ is inconsistent with the observational beliefs or in case the communicational beliefs have become inconsistent with the new observational beliefs, the communicational beliefs on $var(\varphi)$ are erased.

Example 2. Consider the situation in which the agent A has the beliefs $B^o = (x = 8)$ and $B^c = (x + y = 9)$; i.e. it has observed that the number of agents in the waiting room equals 8 and has heard that the sum of the number of agents in the waiting room and the number of agents in the service room equals 9. Now consider the situation after event $e5$; that is, the agent is able to successfully perform the action $\mathsf{ver}(x = 7)$. As the constraint $x = 7$ is inconsistent with the agent's observational beliefs, the agent's new observational beliefs are given by $B^{o'} = update(B^o, x = 7)$, which equals $(x = 7)$. Additionally, as φ is inconsistent with B^o, the agent's communicational beliefs are updated to become $\exists_x(x + y = 10)$, which is logically equivalent to *true*.

Definition 7 *(Transition for non-verifying)*

$$\langle(\mathsf{non\_ver}(\varphi), B), \sigma\rangle \overset{\tau}{\longrightarrow} \langle(E, B'), \sigma\rangle \qquad \text{if } window(\sigma) \nvdash \varphi$$

where $B^{o\prime} = \begin{cases} erase(B^o, var(\varphi)) & \text{if } B^o \vdash \varphi \\ B^o & \text{otherwise} \end{cases}$ and

$$B^{c\prime} = \begin{cases} erase(B^c, var(\varphi)) & \text{if } B^o \vdash \varphi \\ B^c & \text{otherwise} \end{cases}$$

The action non_ver(φ) succeeds if the formula φ is not implied by the agent's window on the workspace. The observational and communicational beliefs are updated in case the formula φ is one of the observational beliefs.

Definition 8 *(A statement for testing)*

$$\mathsf{test}(\varphi) =_{def} \mathsf{ver}(\varphi) + \mathsf{non\_ver}(\varphi).$$

The statement test(φ) abbreviates the non-deterministic choice between the verification an the non-verification of φ. As in this case exactly one of the guards $window(\sigma) \nvdash \varphi$ and $window(\sigma) \vdash \varphi$ is valid, it boils down to a deterministic choice.

Example 3. Consider the agent A possessing the belief base $(x = 8. x + y = 9)$. After the occurrence of event $e5$ in which one of the waiting agents leaves the waiting room, a possible execution of test($x = 8$) would change the agent's belief base to $(true, true)$ as the information $x = 8$ is no longer valid in the workspace.

Definition 9 *(Transition for observing)*

$$\langle(\mathsf{obs}(\mathbf{y}), B), \sigma\rangle \overset{\tau}{\longrightarrow} \langle(E, B'), \sigma\rangle$$

where B' is defined like in the where-clause of definition 6 with $\varphi = \Pi_{\mathbf{y}}\sigma$.

The action obs($\mathbf{y}$) is a highly informative observation that yields all information on the variables $\mathbf{y}$ that is visible through the agent's window on the workspace.

Example 4. Consider the situation just before event $e1$, in which the workspace is given by $x + y = 10 \wedge x = 8$ and the belief base of the agent A by $(true, true)$. The agent performs obs(x) to update its belief base with the current information on the variable x, which yields the base $(x = 8, true)$.

We will next consider communication. We focus on agents that are sincere in the sense that they only communicate constraints they believe to be true; i.e. constraints from their belief base.

Definition 10 *(Transition for sending)*

$$\langle(\mathsf{send}(c, \varphi), B), \sigma\rangle \overset{c\,!\,\varphi}{\longrightarrow} \langle(E, B), \sigma\rangle \qquad \text{if } B \vdash \varphi$$

Example 5. Consider the event $e3$ in which the agent B possesses the beliefs $B^o = (x + y = 10)$ and $B^c = (x = 6)$ about the workspace $(x + y = 10 \wedge x = 8)$. Despite that it conflicts with the current workspace, the agent might communicate the constraint $x = 6$, as it is not aware of this conflict.

Definition 11 *(Transition for receiving)*

$$\langle(\mathsf{receive}(c, \psi), B), \sigma\rangle \xrightarrow{c\,?\,\varphi} \langle(E, B'), \sigma\rangle \quad \text{if } B' \vdash \psi$$

where $B^{o\prime} = B^o$ and

$$B^{c\prime} = \begin{cases} update(B^c, \varphi) & \text{if } B^o \wedge update(B^c, \varphi) \text{ consistent} \\ B^c & \text{otherwise} \end{cases}$$

In the transition, the constraint ψ serves as a direction for the communication, whereas the constraint φ is the actual information received. The action $\mathsf{receive}(c, \psi)$ is successful in case the update of the agent's communicational beliefs with the formula φ, which is received along the channel c, yields a belief base from which ψ is derivable. Because observations are preferred over communicational beliefs, the observational beliefs are left intact.

Example 6. First, consider the situation just before event $e3$ in which the agent A possesses the beliefs $B^o = (x = 8)$ and $B^c = (x + y = 10)$. In case the agent performs $\mathsf{receive}(c, true)$ and receives the constraint $x = 6$ from the agent B, there is no change of the agent's belief base as $update(B^c, x = 6)$ which equals $(x = 6)$ is inconsistent with the its observational beliefs; i.e. we have $B' = B$. Secondly, after event $e4$ in which the agent performs $\mathsf{receive}(c, true)$, the reception of the assertion $x + y = 9$, yields the belief base $(x = 8, x + y = 9)$. As a final example we mention that after event $e5$, the agent A might execute the statement $\mathsf{receive}(c, x + y = 8) + \mathsf{receive}(c, x + y = 9)$ to receive information about the current relation between x and y.

Definition 12 (Inference rules for prefixing and procedure calls) If $P :: S \in W$

$$\frac{\langle(a, B), \sigma\rangle \xrightarrow{\alpha} \langle(E, B'), \sigma'\rangle}{\langle(a; S, B), \sigma\rangle \xrightarrow{\alpha} \langle(S, B'), \sigma'\rangle} \qquad \frac{\langle(S, B), \sigma\rangle \xrightarrow{\alpha} \langle(S', B'), \sigma'\rangle}{\langle(P, B), \sigma\rangle \xrightarrow{\alpha} \langle(S', B'), \sigma'\rangle}$$

The computation step of a prefixed statement $a; S$ consists of the transition of its prefix a. The statement S denotes the part of the statement that is subsequently to be executed. Secondly, the transition of a procedure call P, is given by a transition of its body S.

Definition 13 (Inference rules for non-deterministic choice and skip)

$$\frac{\langle(S_1, B), \sigma\rangle \xrightarrow{\alpha} \langle(S_1', B'), \sigma'\rangle}{\langle(S_1 + S_2, B), \sigma\rangle \xrightarrow{\alpha} \langle(S_1', B'), \sigma'\rangle} \qquad \langle(\mathsf{skip}, B), \sigma\rangle \xrightarrow{\tau} \langle(E, B), \sigma\rangle$$
$$\langle(S_2 + S_1, B), \sigma\rangle \xrightarrow{\alpha} \langle(S_1', B'), \sigma'\rangle$$

The transition of the non-deterministic choice can be derived by the transition of one of its operands. The execution of the statement skip always succeeds and leaves the belief base and workspace intact.

Definition 14 *(Inference rules for parallel composition)*

$$\frac{\langle A_1, \sigma \rangle \xrightarrow{\alpha} \langle A_1', \sigma' \rangle}{\begin{array}{c} \langle A_1 \parallel A_2, \sigma \rangle \xrightarrow{\alpha} \langle A_1' \parallel A_2, \sigma' \rangle \\ \langle A_2 \parallel A_1, \sigma \rangle \xrightarrow{\alpha} \langle A_2 \parallel A_1', \sigma' \rangle \end{array}} \qquad \frac{\langle A_1, \sigma \rangle \xrightarrow{c\,?\,\varphi} \langle A_1', \sigma \rangle \quad \langle A_2, \sigma \rangle \xrightarrow{c\,!\,\varphi} \langle A_2', \sigma \rangle}{\begin{array}{c} \langle A_1 \parallel A_2, \sigma \rangle \xrightarrow{\tau} \langle A_1' \parallel A_2', \sigma \rangle \\ \langle A_2 \parallel A_1, \sigma \rangle \xrightarrow{\tau} \langle A_2' \parallel A_1', \sigma \rangle \end{array}}$$

A computation step of the agent system $A_1 \parallel A_2$ is given by the computation step of either A_1 or A_2, or the communication of a constraint φ along a channel c between an agent in A_1 and an agent in A_2. We stress that the labels $c\,?\,\varphi$ and $c\,!\,\varphi$ refer to local computation steps of the agent systems A_1 and A_2, while the *actual* communication takes place during the execution step of their parallel composition $A_1 \parallel A_2$ or $A_2 \parallel A_1$.

Definition 15 *(Inference rule for persistent constraints)*

$$\frac{\langle A, \sigma \rangle \xrightarrow{\alpha} \langle A', \sigma' \rangle}{\langle \mathsf{pers}_\varphi A, \sigma \rangle \xrightarrow{\alpha} \langle \mathsf{pers}_\varphi A', \sigma' \rangle} \qquad \text{if } \sigma \vdash \varphi \text{ implies } \sigma' \vdash \varphi$$

A transition of $\mathsf{pers}_\varphi A$ in a workspace σ can be derived from a transition of A, if either the resulting workspace σ' derives φ or the original workspace σ does not derive φ. This implies that once the persistent constraint φ is derivable from the workspace, it will be derivable after every transition of the agent system.

Example 7. Consider the following integrity constraint expressing that the number of agents in the building is given by the sum of the number of agents in the waiting room and the number of agents in the service room: $z = x + y$. The construct $\mathsf{pers}_{z\,=\,x+y} A$ takes care that during the execution of the agent system A the persistent constraint $z = x + y$ is not removed from the workspace.

Definition 16 *(Inference rule for local channels)*

$$\frac{\langle A, \sigma \rangle \xrightarrow{\alpha} \langle A', \sigma' \rangle}{\langle \delta_c(A), \sigma \rangle \xrightarrow{\alpha} \langle \delta_c(A'), \sigma' \rangle} \qquad \text{if } \alpha \text{ does not involve the channel } c$$

The transition of the agent system $\delta_c(A)$ can be derived from a transition of A in case this involves an internal computation step (denoted as τ) or an intention to communicate along a channel other than c. In other words, agents in the agent system A cannot communicate via the communication channel c with agents located outside A.

4.3 Semantics of the Language

The above described transition system gives rise to an operational semantics for the language. We identify the notion of a computation.

Definition 17 A *computation* is a sequence

$$\langle A_0, \sigma_0 \rangle \xrightarrow{\alpha_0} \langle A_1, \sigma_1 \rangle, \; \langle A_1, \sigma_1 \rangle \xrightarrow{\alpha_1} \langle A_2, \sigma_2 \rangle, \; \cdots$$

of derived transitions between subsequent configurations of an agent system. Such a sequence is finite if it has a final configuration from which no transition is derivable. In case this configuration is of the form $\langle E, \sigma \rangle$ we identify the corresponding computation to have successfully *terminated*; in all other cases we say that the computation has *deadlocked*. A computation is *non-terminating* if the sequence of transitions is infinite.

Before we give an operational semantics of the language we state the property that in a computation the belief bases of the basic agents stay consistent.

Theorem 1 If all belief bases B of the basic agents (S, B) in the initial agent system A_0 are consistent and if σ_0 is consistent then it holds for each configuration $\langle A_i, \sigma_i \rangle$ $(i = 0, 1, 2, \ldots)$ in the computation

$$\langle A_0, \sigma_0 \rangle \xrightarrow{\tau} \langle A_1, \sigma_1 \rangle, \; \langle A_1, \sigma_1 \rangle \xrightarrow{\tau} \langle A_2, \sigma_2 \rangle, \; \cdots$$

that for all (S, B) in A_i the belief base B is consistent.

The operational semantics of a programming language is usually given by a notion of *observables*, which denote what is to be observed of a computation. One observable for our language is the final workspace of a terminating computation. Other observables are for instance those taking account of the epistemic attitudes of agents and those dealing with non-terminating computations.

Definition 18 *(Observables of successfully terminating agent systems)*

$$\mathcal{O}(A)(\sigma) \;=\; \{\sigma_n \mid \langle A, \sigma \rangle \xrightarrow{\tau} \langle A_1, \sigma_1 \rangle, \cdots, \langle A_{n-1}, \sigma_{n-1} \rangle \xrightarrow{\tau} \langle E, \sigma_n \rangle \}$$

5   Conclusions and Future Research

The framework presented in this paper is to be considered a first step in the development of a theoretically well-founded methodology for the top-down design of multi-agent systems. In the development of such a methodology we distinguish two major stages. The first is one in which a suitable programming language is crystallised that incorporates all the prominent concepts characterising multi-agent systems. Additionally in this phase, the dynamical behaviour of the language is developed by means of an operational semantics. In the second stage, this operational characterisation is moulded into a compositional description of the multi-agent language, as such descriptions for example, would give rise to top-down design facilities as well as specification and verification techniques. The paper of Engelfriet *et al.* in this volume [9] outlines a compositional verification method that is based on temporal multi-epistemic logic.

Secondly, an interesting application of our framework lies in the analysis and comparison of the concurrency aspects dealing with communication in existing multi-agent languages like DESIRE [2], Concurrent METATEM [10], AGENT-0 [22], Agent-Speak(L) [18] and ConGolog [15]. Other possible future applications of our communication mechanism are in the formalisation of *negotiating* agents.

We will conclude by a short summary of the many possible future research directions. In [8] we study an extension of the framework covering general first-order information systems rather than constraint systems. As in agent systems like DESIRE, communication comes along with a translation facility, we intend to extend our framework with a general logical translation mechanism. In [7] we describe an initial framework to understand such mechanisms. Another issue is the incorporation of beliefs on (the beliefs of) the other agents in the system in addition to the beliefs on the environment. Other aspects are the incorporation of object-oriented aspects like inheritance and subtyping and the introduction of extra levels of belief in addition to the observational and communicational beliefs (for instance default beliefs, see [16] and [3]). Yet another issue is the introduction of the notions of real-time and agent identity. In such a setting the reliability of assertions might also be judged in the light of associated time stamps and the sender's identity. Additionally, the communication primitives in our framework explicitly specify the communication channel that constraints are to be send along. A future extension might be the incorporation of content-based routing, which constitutes a form of communication where such destination channels need not to be specified in advance (cf. [23]). Finally, we mention the other mentalistic attitudes usually assigned to agents like desires, intentions and commitments. A possible approach to an extension covering these attitudes might be along the lines of [12].

References

1. J.A. Bergstra and J.W. Klop. Process algebra for synchronous communication. *Information and Control*, 60:109–137, 1984.
2. F. Brazier, B. Dunin-Keplicz, N. Jennings, and J. Treur. Formal specification of multi-agent systems: a real-world case. In *Proceedings of International Conference on Multi-Agent Systems (ICMAS'95)*, pages 25–32. MIT Press, 1995.
3. G. Brewka. Preferred subtheories: An extended logical framework for default reasoning. In *Proceedings International Joint Conference on Artificial Intelligence*, pages 1043–1048. Morgan Kaufmann, 1989.
4. P. Cohen and H.J. Levesque. Intention is choice with commitment. *Artificial Intelligence*, 42:213-261, 1990.
5. F.S. de Boer, J.N. Kok, C. Palamidessi, and J.J.M.M. Rutten. Non-monotonic concurrent constraint programming. In *Proceedings of the International Logic Programming Symposium*, pages 315–333, Vancouver Canada, 1993.
6. R. M. van Eijk, F.S. de Boer, W. van der Hoek, and J.-J.Ch. Meyer. A language for modular information-passing agents. Technical report UU-CS-1997-16, Universiteit Utrecht, Department of Computer Science, 1997.
7. R. M. van Eijk, F.S. de Boer, W. van der Hoek, and J.-J.Ch. Meyer. Constructing translations between individual vocabularies in multi-agent systems. In F. Giunchiglia, editor, *Proceedings of Eigth International Conference on Artificial Intelligence: Methodology, Systems and Applications (AIMSA'98)*, volume 1480

of *Lecture Notes on Computer Science*, pages 240–253, Sozopol, Bulgaria, 1998. Springer-Verlag.

8. R.M. van Eijk, F.S. de Boer, W. van der Hoek, and J.-J.Ch. Meyer. Systems of communicating agents. In *Proceedings of the 13th Biennial European Conference on Artificial Intelligence (ECAI-98)*, pages 293–297, Brighton, UK, 1998. John Wiley & Sons, Ltd.

9. J. Engelfriet, C. M. Jonker, and J. Treur. Compositional verification of multi-agent systems in temporal multi-epistemic logic. In J. P. Müller, M. P. Singh, and A. S. Rao, editors, *Intelligent Agents V — Proceedings of the Fifth International Workshop on Agent Theories, Architectures, and Languages (ATAL-98)*, Lecture Notes in Artificial Intelligence. Springer-Verlag, Heidelberg, 1999. In this volume.

10. M. Fisher. A survey of concurrent METATEM– the language and its applications. In *Proceedings of First International Conference on Temporal Logic (ICTL'94)*, volume 827 of *LNCS*, pages 480–505. Springer-Verlag, 1994.

11. M. Fisher. Representing abstract agent architectures. In J. P. Müller, M. P. Singh, and A. S. Rao, editors, *Intelligent Agents V — Proceedings of the Fifth International Workshop on Agent Theories, Architectures, and Languages (ATAL-98)*, Lecture Notes in Artificial Intelligence. Springer-Verlag, Heidelberg, 1999. In this volume.

12. K.V. Hindriks, F.S. de Boer, W. van der Hoek, and J.-J.Ch. Meyer. A formal semantics for an abstract agent programming language. In M.P. Singh, A. Rao, and M.J. Wooldridge, editors, *Proceedings of Fourth International Workshop on Agent Theories, Architectures and Languages (ATAL'97)*, volume 1365 of *LNAI*, pages 215–229. Springer-Verlag, 1998.

13. C.A.R. Hoare. Communicating sequential processes. *Communications of the ACM*, 21(8):666–677, 1978.

14. H. Katsuno and A.O. Mendelzon. On the difference between updating a knowledge base and revising it. In J. Allen, R. Fikes, and E. Sandewall, editors, *Proceedings of International Conference on Principles of Knowledge Representation and Reasoning (KR'91)*, pages 387–394, Massachusetts, 1991. Morgan Kaufmann.

15. Y. Lespérance, H.J. Levesque, F. Lin, D. Marcu, R. Reiter, and R.B. Scherl. Foundations of a logical approach to agent programming. In *Proceedings of IJCAI'95 International Workshop on Agent Theores, Architectures and Languages (ATAL'95)*, volume 1037 of *LNAI*, pages 331–346. Springer-Verlag, 1996.

16. B. van Linder, W. van der Hoek, and J.-J.Ch. Meyer. Seeing is believing - and so are hearing and jumping. In *Topics in Artificial Intelligence (Proc. AIIA'95)*, volume 992 of *LNCS*, pages 402–423. Springer-Verlag, 1995.

17. G. Plotkin. A structured approach to operational semantics. Technical Report DAIMI FN-19, Computer Science Department, Aarhus University, 1981.

18. Anand S. Rao. Agentspeak(L): BDI agents speak out in a logical computable language. In W. van der Velde and J.W. Perram, editors, *Agents Breaking Away*, volume 1038 of *LNAI*, pages 42–55. Springer-Verlag, 1996.

19. A.S. Rao and M.P. Georgeff. Modeling rational agents within a BDI-architecture. In J. Allen, R. Fikes, and E. Sandewall, editors, *Proceedings of International Conference on Principles of Knowledge Representation and Reasoning (KR'91)*, pages 473–484, Cambridge, Massachusettes, 1991.

20. V.A. Saraswat and M. Rinard. Concurrent constraint programming. In *Proceedings of Seventeenth ACM Symposium on Principles of Programming Languages*, pages 232–245, 1990.

21. K. Schild. On the relationship between BDI logics and standard logics of concurrency. In J. P. Müller, M. P. Singh, and A. S. Rao, editors, *Intelligent Agents V — Proceedings of the Fifth International Workshop on Agent Theories, Architectures, and Languages (ATAL-98)*, Lecture Notes in Artificial Intelligence. Springer-Verlag, Heidelberg, 1999. In this volume.

22. Y. Shoham. Agent-oriented programming. *Artificial Intelligence*, 60:51–92, 1993.

23. N. Skarmeas and K. L. Clark. Content based routing as the basis for intra-agent communication. In J. P. Müller, M. P. Singh, and A. S. Rao, editors, *Intelligent Agents V — Proceedings of the Fifth International Workshop on Agent Theories, Architectures, and Languages (ATAL-98)*, Lecture Notes in Artificial Intelligence. Springer-Verlag, Heidelberg, 1999. In this volume.

24. J.D. Ullman and J. Widom. *A First Course in Database Systems*. Prentice Hall, New Jersey, 1997.

25. M. Wooldridge and N. Jennings. Intelligent agents: theory and practice. *The Knowledge Engineering Review*, 10(2):115–152, 1995.

On the Relationship Between BDI Logics and Standard Logics of Concurrency

Klaus Schild

Daimler-Benz AG, Research and Technology 3
Alt-Moabit 96A, D-10559 Berlin, Germany
schild@dbag.bln.daimlerbenz.com

Abstract. The behavior of an agent is mainly governed by the specific way it handles the rational balance between information and deliberation. Most popular among the formalisms capturing this very balance is Rao and Georgeff's BDI theory. This formalism has been proposed as a language for specifying agents in an abstract manner or, alternatively, for verifying various properties of agents implemented in some other programming language. In mainstream Computer Science, there are formalisms designed for a similar purpose as the BDI theory, though not specifically aiming at agents, but at concurrency in general. These formalisms are known as logics of concurrent programs. In this paper, these two frameworks are for the first time compared with each other. The result shows that the basic BDI theory, BDI_{CTL^*}, can be captured within a standard logic of concurrency. The logic relevant here is Kozen's propositional μ-calculus. The μ-calculus turns out to be even *strictly* stronger in expressive power than BDI_{CTL^*}, while enjoying a computational complexity which is not higher than that of BDI_{CTL^*}'s small fragment CTL. This correspondence brings us in a position to give the first complete axiomatization of Rao and Georgeff's full theory.

1 Introduction

It is widely accepted that the behavior of any agent is mainly governed by the specific way it handles the rational balance between its beliefs, desires, and intentions [1]. *Beliefs* describe the informational state of an agent, *desires* its motivational state, and *intentions* its deliberative state. These three notions turned out to be a proper abstraction tool for characterizing the behavior of an agent—just like an object and a method is the right abstraction for object-oriented programming [19, p28]. Most popular among the formalisms capturing exactly this balance is Rao and Georgeff's BDI theory [13]. In this framework, beliefs, desires, and intentions are introduced as independent modalities Bel, Des, and Intend. The specific inter-relationships between the basic modalities are then given by special axioms. These axioms are known as different kinds of realisms. Axioms of this kind describe the fundamental static relationships between the basic modalities; see Chapter 7 of [15] for a thorough overview. However, the possible ways as to how these relationships may change over time are not covered. These dynamic aspects are captured by specific *commitment strategies*. The most important commitment strategy is about how long an agent maintains its goals. In Rao and Georgeff's theory, the pursuit of a goal can be captured by $Intend(a, A\Diamond\alpha)$. This expression means that agent a intends to eventually achieve α, no matter how the future will evolve. The fact that a proposition will eventually come true is expressed by $\Diamond$, while A is to be read as "for all possible courses of future events." The question here is how long an agent should maintain $\mathsf{Intend}(a, \mathsf{A}\Diamond\alpha)$. It seems to be reasonable for an agent to give up this intention as soon as the agent believes α has already been attained. This is exactly what $\mathsf{Bel}(a, \alpha)$ denotes. Another reason might be that the agent believes the intention not to be attainable any more. This condition can be expressed with the help of the E-operator, which reads "for at least one possible course of future events." The relevant truncation condition thus translates into $\neg\mathsf{Bel}(a, \mathsf{E}\Diamond\alpha)$. The until operator U then allows us to formulate a proper axiom of change:

$$\mathsf{A}\Big(\mathsf{Intend}(a, \mathsf{A}\Diamond\alpha) \ \mathsf{U} \ \big(\mathsf{Bel}(a, \alpha) \vee \neg\mathsf{Bel}(a, \mathsf{E}\Diamond\alpha)\big)\Big).$$

These are the essential ingredients of Rao and Georgeff's theory. It has been argued that this theory can be used to specify agents in an abstract manner or, alternatively, to verify agents implemented in some other programming language. The first alternative requires proper tools that ensure the consistency of the overall specification. One such tool is an axiomatization; a more powerful tool is a decision procedure. A complete axiomatization and a decision procedure is known only for a small fragment of Rao and Georgeff's theory [15]. This fragment is not able to express such a simple temporal formulae as $\mathsf{A}\Diamond(\alpha \wedge \mathsf{X}\alpha)$, where X reads "at the next time instant." This leaves Rao and Georgeff's theory somewhat incomplete. The situation is not better when the BDI theory is to be used to verify agents implemented in some other programming language. Here, a proper model checker is required. Such a model checker also exists for only a small fragment of the BDI theory [14].

In mainstream Computer Science, there are formalisms designed for a similar purpose as the BDI theory, though not specifically aiming at agents, but at concurrency in general. These formalisms are known as logics of concurrent programs. This immediately raises the question of how these frameworks are related to each other, which is the issue considered in this paper. We shall compare the BDI theory with a standard logic of programs, known as the propositional μ-calculus. In this formalism a modal formula like $\mathsf{Bel}(a, \alpha)$ can be rephrased as $[bel\text{-}a]\alpha$, which reads "for every termination of the program $bel\text{-}a$, the postcondition α holds." This reading, especially the interpretation of a's beliefs as a primitive program, may appear unorthodox; however, it is perfectly equivalent to the original one. The distinguishing characteristic of the μ-calculus is its ability to express recursion. This turned out to be a rather powerful approach. Recursion is uniformly captured by special fixed point operators. The recursive definition of $\mathsf{A}\Diamond\alpha$, for instance, is $\mu X.(\alpha \vee [next]X)$. If the program $next$ is interpreted as a successor relation, then this inductive definition denotes the least set X such that for every $s \in X$, either α holds at s or all successors of s are also contained in X. Even an involved formula such as $\mathsf{A}(\alpha \ \mathsf{U} \ \beta)$ can be defined recursively. The relevant inductive definition is $\mu X.\big(\beta \vee (\alpha \wedge [next]X)\big)$. This paper shows that in this way actually *every* formula of Rao and Georgeff's theory can be expressed. This observation is of interest on its own as it clarifies the relationship between the two frameworks. A more concrete outcome is that it solves the longstanding problem of a complete axiomatization of the full BDI theory. This is because for the propositional μ-calculus a complete axiomatization is already known.

The paper is organized as follows. First we give a brief introduction into basic modal logic, the very basis of Rao and Georgeff's whole theory. The BDI theory itself is then introduced in a step by step manner, beginning with the computation tree logic CTL*. The foundations of logics of concurrent programs are then given in order to show how the BDI theory can be captured within this framework. The paper closes with a brief discussion of some theoretical as well as practical consequences of this observation.

2 Basic Modal Logic

Modal logic allows us to apply special modal operators to conventional formulae. $\mathbf{K}_i\alpha$ is such a modal formula. It can be read as "i knows (or believes in) α." Meaning is given to such modal operators by relativizing the truth of formulae. A formula may or may not be true, depending on the specific possible world in which we are. $\mathbf{K}_i\alpha$ is then true in a particular possible world w iff α is true in all possible worlds that are imaginable from w's point of view. What is actually imaginable is represented by a simple binary relation among possible worlds, referred to as *accessibility relation*. The ultimate meaning of a modal operator depends on the specific restrictions imposed on this very relation. The condition of reflexivity, for instance, distinguishes knowing from believing. The normal modal logic $\mathbf{K}_{(m)}$ is not committed to any such interpretation and, thus, considers *every* accessibility relation admissible. The relevant mathematical definitions are as follows.

Definition 1. Let $\mathbf{Mod} = \{\mathbf{K}_1, ..., \mathbf{K}_m\}$ be a set of modal operators. The admissible formulae of the *propositional modal logic* $\mathbf{K}_{(m)}$ are defined by the following three formation rules.

F1 Each atomic proposition is a formula.
F2 If α and β are formulae, then so are $\alpha \wedge \beta$ and $\neg\alpha$.
F3 If α is a formula and $\mathbf{K}_i \in \mathbf{Mod}$, then $\mathbf{K}_i\alpha$ is a formula as well.

We shall make use of the standard conventions for $\vee$, $\rightarrow$, $\leftrightarrow$, *true*, and *false*.

Definition 2. A *Kripke structure* is a tuple $M = \langle S, \mathcal{R}, L \rangle$. The first component, S, is a nonempty set, the elements of which are called the *possible worlds* in M. The second component, $\mathcal{R}$, is a binary relation over S, referred to as an *accessibility relation*. The remaining third component, L, is a function mapping every $s \in S$ to a set of atomic propositions. $L(s)$ yields all those atomic propositions that are true in s.

This defines a Kripke structure with a single accessibility relation. For multiple modalities, the definition can be extended in a canonical manner: If for each i ($1 \le i \le m$), $\langle S, \mathcal{R}_i, L \rangle$ forms a Kripke structure, then so does $\langle S, \mathcal{R}_1, ..., \mathcal{R}_m, L \rangle$.

The semantic relation $\models$ properly interprets formulae of $\mathbf{K}_{(m)}$. In particular, each formula is interpreted relative to a particular Kripke structure M and a state s in that structure. $M, s \models \alpha$ is to be read as "α holds in state s of M." The reference to M may be omitted whenever it is understood. The exact definition of $\models$ is as follows.

F1 $s \models p$ iff $p \in L(s)$.
   $s \models \alpha \wedge \beta$ iff $s \models \alpha$ and $s \models \beta$.

F2 $s \models \neg\alpha$ iff $s \models \alpha$ does not hold.
F3 $s \models K_i \alpha$ iff for every $s' \in S$ such that $s\mathcal{R}_i s'$, $s' \models \alpha$.

Definition 3. Let C be a class of Kripke structures. A formula α is said to be *satisfiable over C* iff there is at least one Kripke structure M and at least one state s in M such that $M, s \models \alpha$. Moreover, α is *valid over C*, in symbols $\models_C \alpha$, iff $\neg\alpha$ is not satisfiable over C. Finally, we say that α and α' are *equivalent* over C iff $\models_C \alpha \leftrightarrow \alpha'$. The reference to C may be omitted whenever it denotes the class of *all* Kripke structures.

This should be enough to make the paper self-contained. For a more thorough introduction into propositional modal logic the reader is referred to [8].

3 Rao & Georgeff's BDI Theory

Rao and Georgeff's theory is built upon two main building blocks. One building block is a special temporal logic, called CTL*, particularly suited for branching time. The second component is a collection of traditional modalities capturing the beliefs, desires, and intentions of each single agent. We begin with the temporal logic.

Definition 4. The admissible formulae of the *computation tree logic* CTL are categorized into two classes, *state formulae* and *path formulae*.

S1 Each atomic proposition is a state formula.
S2 If α and β are state formulae, then so are $\alpha \wedge \beta$ and $\neg\alpha$.
S3 If α is a path formula, then Eα and Aα are state formulae.
P If α and β are state formulae, then Xα and α U β are path formulae.

The definition of the *full computation tree logic* CTL* extends that of CTL by replacing P with the following three formation rules.

P1 Each state formula is also a path formula.
P2 If α and β are path formulae, then so are $\alpha \wedge \beta$ and $\neg\alpha$.
P3 If α and β are path formulae, then so are Xα and α U β.

State formulae of CTL* are interpreted relative to a particular Kripke structure $M = \langle S, \mathcal{R}, L \rangle$ and an element s of S. Here, the elements of S are to be thought of as *states* (or *points in time*) rather than possible worlds. Consequently, $\mathcal{R}$ is a *successor relation* rather than an accessibility relation among possible worlds. Another specialty of CTL and CTL* is that some formulae are not interpreted relative to a particular state. These are the path formulae. What is relevant here are full paths. A *full path* in M is an infinite sequence $\chi = s_0, s_1, s_2, \ldots$ of states in M such that for every $i \geq 0$, $s_i \mathcal{R} s_{i+1}$. We say that such a full path *starts at s* iff $s_0 = s$.

The definition of $\models$ for CTL* is given below. The definition makes use of the following convention. If $\chi = s_0, s_1, s_2, \ldots$ is a full path in M, then χ^i ($i \geq 0$) denotes exactly the same infinite sequence as χ, except that the first i components are omitted. For example, χ^1 denotes the suffix path $s_1, s_2, \ldots$

S1 $s \models p$ iff $p \in L(s)$.

S2 $s \models \alpha \land \beta$ iff $s \models \alpha$ and $s \models \beta$.

$\quad s \models \neg\alpha$ iff $s \models \alpha$ does not hold.

S3 $s \models \mathsf{E}\alpha$ iff there is at least one full path χ in M starting at s such that $\chi \models \alpha$.

$\quad s \models \mathsf{A}\alpha$ iff for every full path χ in M starting at s, $\chi \models \alpha$.

P1 If α is a state formula and χ starts at s, then $\chi \models \alpha$ iff $s \models \alpha$.

P2 $\chi \models \alpha \land \beta$ iff $\chi \models \alpha$ and $\chi \models \beta$.

$\quad \chi \models \neg\alpha$ iff $\chi \models \alpha$ does not hold.

P3 $\chi \models \mathsf{X}\alpha$ iff $\chi^1 \models \alpha$.

$\quad \chi \models \alpha \mathsf{U} \beta$ iff there is at least one $i \geq 0$ such that $\chi^i \models \beta$ and for all j ($0 \leq j < i$), $\chi^j \models \alpha$.

Note that the definitions for A and E make sense only if there is actually at least one full path starting at s. For a state with no such full path, $\mathsf{A}\alpha$ would always be true, while $\mathsf{E}\alpha$ would be false, no matter which particular formula α denotes. This is why the following condition is usually imposed on $\mathcal{R}$. For every $s \in S$, there is at least one $s' \in S$ such that $s\mathcal{R}s'$. This property is called *seriality*. It guarantees that for every state there is always at least one full path in M starting at that state.

An $\mathcal{R}$-serial Kripke structure is also called a branching-time structure. This class does not only cover tree-like structures. It is well-known, however, that any $\mathcal{R}$-serial Kripke structure can be unwound into an equivalent infinite tree, see e.g. [4, p1012]. Equivalence means here that the truth value of no CTL*-formula is affected.

The unary temporal operator $\Diamond$ can be defined as a special case of the binary U-operator, while $\Box$ is the dual of $\Diamond$.

$$\Diamond\alpha \stackrel{\text{def}}{=} \textit{true } \mathsf{U} \alpha,$$

$$\Box\alpha \stackrel{\text{def}}{=} \neg\Diamond\neg\alpha.$$

This is the temporal logic that Rao and Georgeff employ in their theory. Now for the full BDI theory.

Definition 5. Let **Agent** $= \{1, ..., m\}$ be a set of agent identifiers. $\mathrm{BDI_{CTL^*}}$ extends the definition of CTL* just by one additional formation rule:

S4 If α is a state formula and $i \in$ **Agent**, then $\mathsf{Bel}(i, \alpha)$, $\mathsf{Des}(i, \alpha)$, and $\mathsf{Intend}(i, \alpha)$ are formulae as well.

$\mathrm{BDI_{CTL^*}}$ thus combines CTL* with a collection of conventional modal operators. This means that the underlying semantics involves two dimensions rather than just one: a dimension of possible worlds, along which **Bel**, **Des**, and **Intend**, are interpreted, and a dimension of time, along which the temporal formulae are evaluated. Therefore, the truth of a formula not only depends on the current state, but also on the particular possible world in which we are. This is what we call a specific situation. A *situation* is an ordered pair consisting of a possible world and a state.

According to Rao and Georgeff, each state has its own accessibility relations. Take a belief accessible relation $\mathcal{B}$. Each state $s \in S$ has a specific accessibility relation $\mathcal{B}^s \subseteq W \times W$. This does make sense because the beliefs of an agent are expected to evolve over time. But then we end up with a ternary relation $\mathcal{B} \subseteq W \times S \times W$.

Vice versa, each possible world $w \in W$ has its own successor relation $\mathcal{R}^w$. This does make sense, too. The successor relation captures the different courses the environment may evolve. The different trajectories that an agent believes may come true are indeed subject to the specific possible world from which the agent observes the environment. This is why $\mathcal{R}$ is a ternary relation of the type $\mathcal{R} \subseteq S \times W \times S$.

Rao and Georgeff take these two different types of ternary relations as a starting point for a proper semantics of $\mathrm{BDI_{CTL^*}}$. We slightly diverge from their original definition in [15]. Instead of considering $\mathcal{B}$ and $\mathcal{R}$ as ternary relations, we treat them as binary relations among *situations*. In particular, $\mathcal{B}(w, s, w')$ is encoded as $\mathcal{B}(\langle w, s \rangle, \langle w', s \rangle)$ and $\mathcal{R}(s, w, s')$ as $\mathcal{R}(\langle w, s \rangle, \langle w, s' \rangle)$. Thus $\mathcal{B}$ always leaves the relevant states unchanged, while $\mathcal{R}$ leaves the possible worlds unchanged. What we gain by this alternative formulation is that $\mathrm{BDI_{CTL^*}}$ can be given a semantics in terms of a conventional (though special) Kripke structure, obeying the conditions just described. It is thus not necessary to diverge from conventional Kripke semantics, as Rao and Georgeff do. The exact definition of the special Kripke structures relevant here is as follows.

Definition 6. A Kripke structure $M = \langle \Delta, \mathcal{R}, \mathcal{B}, \mathcal{D}, \mathcal{I}, L \rangle$ forms a *situation structure* if each of the following three conditions is met.

1. Δ is a set of situations.
2. $w' = w$ whenever $\langle w, s \rangle \mathcal{R} \langle w', s' \rangle$.
3. $s' = s$ whenever $\langle w, s \rangle \mathcal{B} \langle w', s' \rangle$ and similarly for $\mathcal{D}$ and $\mathcal{I}$.

The canonical extension to the multiple-agent case is left to the reader. Now, the definition of the semantic relations $M, s \models \alpha$ and $M, \chi \models \alpha$ is exactly the same as the one for CTL*, except that here M is a situation structure rather than a simple Kripke structure. The definition, of course, has to be extended to cope with the additional modal operators.

S4 $s \models \mathrm{Bel}(i, \alpha)$ iff for every $s' \in S$ such that $s\mathcal{B}_i s'$, $s' \models \alpha$.
  $s \models \mathrm{Des}(i, \alpha)$ iff for every $s' \in S$ such that $s\mathcal{D}_i s'$, $s' \models \alpha$.
  $s \models \mathrm{Intend}(i, \alpha)$ iff for every $s' \in S$ such that $s\mathcal{I}_i s'$, $s' \models \alpha$.

A formula α of $\mathrm{BDI_{CTL^*}}$ is then said to be satisfiable over $\mathcal{C}$ iff there is at least one $\mathcal{R}$-serial situation structure $M \in \mathcal{C}$ and at least one situation s (or full path χ) in M such that $M, s \models \alpha$ (or $M, \chi \models \alpha$). The notion of validness and equivalence are the same as for $\mathbf{K}_{(m)}$.

4 Logics of Concurrency

Kripke-style semantics turned out to be widely applicable. It not only is a proper semantic framework for mental attitudes, but can equally well capture time. And there is even more to it. Pratt [12] first argued that possible worlds could also be viewed as *program states*. In doing so we can interpret accessibility relations as nondeterministic programs. This is in accord with the common view of programs as state transitions. This is why propositional modal logic as it stands constitutes a basic framework for reasoning about programs. In fact, the modal formula $K_a\alpha$ can be read as "postcondition α holds after any successful termination of the program a." For such a reading the notation $[a]\alpha$ is usually preferred in favor of $K_a\alpha$. If $\langle a\rangle\alpha$ abbreviates $\neg[a]\neg\alpha$, the termination of the program a can be captured by $\langle a\rangle true$. The termination of two programs running concurrently is then expressed by $\langle a\rangle true \wedge \langle b\rangle true$.

Whenever this alternative interpretation is put into effect, modal logics are referred to as *dynamic logics*. The term *dynamic* reflects the fact that the underlying intuition is about states and their transitions. The dynamic interpretation of $K_{(m)}$ is known as *Hennessy-Milner Logic*. What makes this logic somewhat impractical is that it includes only primitive programs. It does not include such fundamental programming facilities as executing two programs consecutively, nor does it cover while-loops or if-then-else guards. Fischer and Ladner [7] proposed not to confine dynamic formulae to primitive programs only. They suggest the following fundamental repository for constructing programs.

$a; b$ meaning "run a and b consecutively in order;"

a^* meaning "repeat a a nondeterministically chosen number of times ≥ 0;"

$a \cup b$ meaning "nondeterministically execute either a or b;"

$\alpha?$ meaning "test α and continue if the result is true."

This repository actually forms a good basis for programs with while-loops and if-then-else guards. These standard program schemes can be implemented with Fischer and Ladner's repository as follows.

$$\textbf{if } \alpha \textbf{ then } a \textbf{ else } b \overset{\text{def}}{=} (\alpha?; a) \cup (\neg\alpha?; b),$$

$$\textbf{while } \alpha \textbf{ do } a \overset{\text{def}}{=} (\alpha?; a)^*; \neg\alpha.$$

Fischer and Ladner [7] coined the relevant extension of Hennessy-Milner Logic *propositional dynamic logic* (or *PDL* for short). PDL achieved considerable attention, in particular because of its expressive power. However, it was also observed that some fundamental properties of programs are not covered. One such property is the perpetual repetition of a program. It was Streett who first observed that this basic property is not expressible in PDL; see [10, p540]. He thus proposed to introduce an additional formula, Δa, specifically devoted to the perpetual repetition of a program. It turned out that the simultaneous perpetual repetition of two programs cannot be expressed within this extension either.

Kozen [11] proposed an elegant solution to these limitations in expressive power. He argued that Hennessy-Milner Logic just lacks a fundamental means of recursion not only to cover the full expressive power of PDL, but also to avoid its limitations. Recursion can be expressed by two special fixed-point operators, he further argued. One is the least fixed-point operator $\mu X.\alpha$, which reads "the least X such that α." If α involves at least one occurrence of the variable X, then $\mu X.\alpha$ is recursive. An example is $\mu X.(p \vee \langle a\rangle X)$. This formula denotes the least set of states S_X containing all states in which either p is true or from which at least one execution of a leads to a state in S_X. This is an inductive definition of the PDL-formula $\langle a^*\rangle p$. If the variable X occurs only positively in $\mu X.\alpha$, the relevant induction is guaranteed to have always a unique solution. The greatest fixed-point operator $\nu X.\alpha$ works similarly. The formula $\nu X.(p \vee \langle a \rangle X)$ is interpreted in the same way as its counterpart above, except that here the greatest set S_X is considered. The distinguishing characteristic between a least and a greatest fixed-point operator is that the former requires a recursion to terminate, while the latter does not. Least fixed-points are thus used for eventualities, while greatest-fixed points express invariances. The relevant mathematical definitions are as follows.

Definition 7. Let **Var** be a distinguished set of atomic propositions. These atomic propositions are referred to as *variables*. The *propositional μ-calculus* extends $\mathbf{K}_{(m)}$ by the following additional formation rule.

F4 If α is a formula and X is a variable, then $\mu X.\alpha$ and $\nu X.\alpha$ are formulae as well. For $\mu X.\alpha$ and $\nu X.\alpha$ being admissible formulae, we additionally require that in α X occurs only in the scope of an even number of negation signs.

Formulae of the propositional μ-calculus are interpreted exactly in the same way as in $\mathbf{K}_{(m)}$, with a single additional interpretation rule that is shown below. This interpretation rule uses the following convention. If α is a formula and M a Kripke structure, then let $[\![\alpha]\!]_M$ denote the set of all those states in M in which α holds.

F4 $M, s \models \mu X.\alpha$ iff s is a member of the least fixed point of a certain function $f :$ $2^S \to 2^S$. This function maps every $S' \subseteq S$ to $[\![\alpha]\!]_{M'}$, where M' is identical with M, except that $L(X)$ is S'. Similar, $s \models \nu X.\alpha$ iff s is a member of the greatest fixed point of f.

Nowadays, the propositional μ-calculus has become something like a standard logic of programs. At least partly, this popularity is due to the fact that Kozen [11] himself showed that the propositional μ-calculus does not only cover the whole expressive power of PDL, but that it is even strictly stronger in expressive power. This result still holds if PDL is augmented by the repeat construct Δa. Another positive result is that the propositional μ-calculus enjoys essentially the same computational complexity as PDL. Just like PDL, it is complete for deterministic exponential time [16, 5]. Walukiewicz [18] was able to solve also the longstanding problem of finding a complete axiomatization for the full propositional μ-calculus.

5 BDI Theory Phrased in μ-Calculus' Terms

So far we introduced two different formalisms, one for describing the behavior of BDI agents, the other one devoted to concurrency in general. The question arises how these two formalisms are related to each other.

A first quite obvious observation is that the standard logic of concurrency that we just introduced strictly subsumes all temporal operators of Rao and Georgeff's BDI theory. We refer here to the well-known fact that the propositional μ-calculus strictly subsumes CTL* [4, p1066]. For CTL, we can employ the following equivalences over

$\mathcal{R}$-serial Kripke structures.

$$\models \quad \mathsf{EX}\alpha \leftrightarrow \langle next\rangle\alpha,$$
$$\models \quad \mathsf{AX}\alpha \leftrightarrow [next]\alpha,$$
$$\models \mathsf{E}(\alpha \mathrel{U} \beta) \leftrightarrow \mu X.\big(\beta \vee (\alpha \wedge \langle next\rangle X)\big),$$
$$\models \mathsf{A}(\alpha \mathrel{U} \beta) \leftrightarrow \mu X.\big(\beta \vee (\alpha \wedge [next]X)\big).$$

Here, *next* is a distinguished primitive program representing the successor relation $\mathcal{R}$. For CTL* we additionally have:

$$\models \quad \mathsf{E}\neg\mathsf{X}\alpha \leftrightarrow \langle next\rangle\neg\alpha,$$
$$\models \quad \mathsf{A}\neg\mathsf{X}\alpha \leftrightarrow [next]\neg\alpha,$$
$$\models \mathsf{E}\neg(\alpha \mathrel{U} \beta) \leftrightarrow \nu X.\big(\alpha \vee (\neg\beta \wedge \langle next\rangle X)\big),$$
$$\models \mathsf{A}\neg(\alpha \mathrel{U} \beta) \leftrightarrow \nu X.\big(\alpha \vee (\neg\beta \wedge [next]X)\big).$$

Note that the last two equivalences include as special cases the relevant translations for $\mathsf{E}\square\gamma$ and $\mathsf{A}\square\gamma$. To see this, just assign α with *true*. Note also that these eight equivalences do not cover *all* CTL*-formulae. One formula that is not covered is $\mathsf{E}\big((\alpha \mathrel{U} \beta) \wedge \neg(\alpha' \mathrel{U} \beta')\big)$. This is not to say that for this formula there is no equivalent μ-calculus formulae at all. As a matter of fact, for every formula of CTL* there is an equivalent formula of the propositional μ-calculus, though the translation is not always succinct [3, Theorem 3.2].

This result shows that the propositional μ-calculus covers the expressive power of $\mathrm{BDI}_{\mathrm{CTL}^*}$'s temporal operators. It is also possible to encode the belief, desire, and intention modalities of $\mathrm{BDI}_{\mathrm{CTL}^*}$, though this is not as easy as it might appear at first glance. Consider the following quite obvious translations, where the *bel-i*'s, *des-i*'s, and *intend-i*'s are pairwise distinct primitive programs.

$$\models \quad \mathsf{Bel}(i, \alpha) \leftrightarrow [bel\text{-}i]\alpha,$$
$$\models \quad \mathsf{Des}(i, \alpha) \leftrightarrow [des\text{-}i]\alpha,$$
$$\models \mathsf{Intend}(i, \alpha) \leftrightarrow [intend\text{-}i]\alpha.$$

This kind of translation works fine as long as we consider the belief, desire, and intention modalities of $\mathrm{BDI}_{\mathrm{CTL}^*}$ in isolation, while ignoring the temporal operators—just as we already know that the temporal logic of $\mathrm{BDI}_{\mathrm{CTL}^*}$ is covered by the μ-calculus if we consider only that part of $\mathrm{BDI}_{\mathrm{CTL}^*}$. The problem here is that it is not clear whether the constituent translations also work when considering $\mathrm{BDI}_{\mathrm{CTL}^*}$ as a whole, that is, with $\mathrm{BDI}_{\mathrm{CTL}^*}$'s distinguished two-dimensional situation semantics taken into account. In what follows we shall show how the two dimensions of $\mathrm{BDI}_{\mathrm{CTL}^*}$ can be collapsed into a single dimension without effecting the truth of any formula. In particular, we shall see how a two-dimensional situation structure can be encoded as a conventional one-dimensional Kripke structure that meets a special structural condition. This condition forbids certain loops in the relevant structure. In particular, there must not be any loop of a length greater than 1 running first through a sequence of edges labeled with $\mathcal{R}$ or its inverse and, then, through a sequence of edges labeled with $\mathcal{B}_i, \mathcal{D}_i, \mathcal{I}_i$, including their inverses. This condition is called *situation compatibility*. This structural condition stems from the definition of a situation structure. In every situation structure, $\mathcal{R}$ must leave the first dimension unchanged, while the $\mathcal{B}_i$, $\mathcal{D}_i$, and $\mathcal{I}_i$ must leave the second dimension unchanged. If there was a loop of the kind above, all nodes would be identical, resulting in a loop of length 1.

Definition 8. A Kripke structure $M = \langle S, \mathcal{R}, \mathcal{B}_1, \mathcal{D}_1, \mathcal{I}_1, ..., \mathcal{B}_m, \mathcal{D}_m, \mathcal{I}_m, L \rangle$ is *situation compatible* iff, when seen as an undirected graph, it contains no path through the nodes $s_1, ..., s_n, s_1$ such that $s_1, ..., s_n$ are pair-wise distinct, $n \geq 2$, and the corresponding sequence of edges is labeled with $\mathcal{R}^+(\mathcal{B}_1 \cup ... \cup \mathcal{I}_m)^+$.

For a tree-like Kripke structure this condition is easy to meet. The only precondition is that for each i $(1 \leq i \leq m)$, $\mathcal{R} \cap \mathcal{B}_i = \emptyset$ and similarly for $\mathcal{D}_i$ and $\mathcal{I}_i$. We call this property $\mathcal{R}$-*uniqueness*.

Proposition 9. *Let α be an arbitrary formula of* BDI$_{\text{CTL}}$. *Then the following two statements are equivalent.*

(a) α *is satisfiable over situation structures.*
(b) α *is satisfiable over situation-compatible Kripke structures.*

Proof. We first prove that (a) implies (b). It suffices to show that every situation structure is also a situation-compatible Kripke structure. Take an arbitrary situation structure $M = \langle \Delta, \mathcal{R}, \mathcal{B}_1, \mathcal{D}_1, \mathcal{I}_1, ..., \mathcal{B}_m, \mathcal{D}_m, \mathcal{I}_m, L \rangle$. This situation structure is a Kripke structure, as is every situation structure. It remains to show that M is situation compatible. If M was not situation compatible, when viewed as an undirected graph, it would contain at least one path through nodes $\langle w_1, s_1 \rangle, ..., \langle w_n, s_n \rangle, \langle w_1, s_1 \rangle$ such that $n \geq 2$, $\langle w_1, s_1 \rangle, ..., \langle w_n, s_n \rangle$ are pair-wise distinct situations, and the corresponding sequence of edges is labeled with $\mathcal{R}^+(\mathcal{B}_1 \cup ... \cup \mathcal{I}_m)^+$. But then, according to Definition 6, $w_1, ..., w_k$ would be identical, for some k $(1 \leq k \leq n)$, and so would be $s_k, ..., s_n, s_1$. This would just mean that $\langle w_k, s_k \rangle$ equals $\langle w_1, s_1 \rangle$, contradicting the assumption that $\langle w_1, s_1 \rangle ... \langle w_n, s_n \rangle$ are pair-wise distinct. This proves that every situation structure is actually a situation-compatible Kripke structure.

Now, for the reverse direction, (b) implies (a). Take an arbitrary situation-compatible Kripke structure $M = \langle S, \mathcal{R}, \mathcal{B}_1, \mathcal{D}_1, \mathcal{I}_1, ..., \mathcal{B}_m, \mathcal{D}_m, \mathcal{I}_m, L \rangle$. Here, we view M as a directed graph $\langle S, \mathcal{R} \cup \mathcal{B}_1 ... \cup \mathcal{I}_m \rangle$. Consider the following rewriting rules, transforming M into an isomorphic situation structure.

$$s \leadsto \langle w_{new}, s \rangle \qquad \text{if } s \in S \text{ is a starting state;}$$
$$\langle w, s \rangle \xrightarrow{\mathcal{R}} s' \leadsto \langle w, s \rangle \xrightarrow{\mathcal{R}} \langle w, s' \rangle \text{ if } s' \in S;$$
$$s \xrightarrow{\mathcal{R}} \langle w, s' \rangle \leadsto \langle w, s \rangle \xrightarrow{\mathcal{R}} \langle w, s' \rangle \text{ if } s \in S;$$
$$\langle w, s \rangle \xrightarrow{\mathcal{X}_i} s' \leadsto \langle w, s \rangle \xrightarrow{\mathcal{X}_i} \langle s', s \rangle \text{ if } s' \in S \text{ and } \mathcal{X}_i \neq \mathcal{R};$$
$$s \xrightarrow{\mathcal{X}_i} \langle w, s' \rangle \leadsto \langle s, s' \rangle \xrightarrow{\mathcal{X}_i} \langle w, s' \rangle \text{ if } s \in S \text{ and } \mathcal{X}_i \neq \mathcal{R}.$$

The first rewriting rule means that a node s is replaced by $\langle w_{new}, s \rangle$ whenever $s \in S$ is a distinguished starting state. If M is a connected graph, then exactly one state of S must be such a distinguished starting state; otherwise, each maximal connected subgraph must contain exactly one starting state. In each case, we require w_{new} to be a fresh element not contained in S. The second rewriting rule means that a node s' be substituted by $\langle w, s' \rangle$ whenever there is an edge leading from $\langle w, s \rangle$ to this node such that $\mathcal{R}$ is among the edge's labels.

All the rewriting rules are applied to M until no rule is applicable any longer. Let us call this transformed graph M'. If M is situation compatible, then M' is a situation structure isomorphic to M. Now, consider $M, s \models \alpha$. Choose s as a starting state. It is not too hard to verify that $M, s \models \alpha$ iff $M', \langle w_{new}, s \rangle \models \alpha$. □

This shows that a two-dimensional situation structure can be encoded in a conventional one-dimensional Kripke structure and vice versa, if only the latter does not contain certain loops of a length greater than 1. With the well-known technique of unwinding, it can be shown that we can get rid of this structural condition, too. This is because we can unwind every Kripke structure into an equivalent $\mathcal{R}$-unique tree, which is always situation compatible.

Theorem 10. *Let α be an arbitrary formula of $\mathrm{BDI}_{\mathrm{CTL}^*}$. Then the following two statements are equivalent.*

(a) *α is satisfiable over situation structures.*
(b) *α is satisfiable over Kripke structures.*

At this stage we have circumvented the main stumbling block preventing us from extending Emerson *et al.*'s [3] result on CTL^* to $\mathrm{BDI}_{\mathrm{CTL}^*}$.

Theorem 11. *The propositional μ-calculus with an additional $\mathcal{R}$-seriality constraint is strictly stronger in expressive power than $\mathrm{BDI}_{\mathrm{CTL}^*}$.*

Note that the additional seriality constraint on the μ-calculus' side stems from the fact that CTL^* always imposes this constraint, while the μ-calculus does not do so. There is a standard method for encoding seriality directly within the μ-calculus. If $\mathcal{P}$ is the union of all primitive programs, then $[\mathcal{P}^*]\langle next \rangle true$ is a correct encoding of seriality.

6 Some Consequences of the Correspondence

From Theorem 11 we have learned that we can rephrase every formula of $\mathrm{BDI}_{\mathrm{CTL}^*}$ as an equivalent formula of the propositional μ-calculus with an additional $\mathcal{R}$-seriality constraint. This observation immediately yields a complete axiomatization of full $\mathrm{BDI}_{\mathrm{CTL}^*}$. We just have to translate $\mathrm{BDI}_{\mathrm{CTL}^*}$-formulae into the propositional μ-calculus. We can then resort to complete axiomatization from [18] and add to it an axiom for $\mathcal{R}$-seriality. The axiom for $\mathcal{R}$-seriality is as follows.

$$\langle next \rangle true.$$

When translated properly, all other axioms of the BDI theory can be taken from the original theory.

Theorem 12. *There is a complete axiomatization for $\mathrm{BDI}_{\mathrm{CTL}^*}$ and, thus, also for Rao and Georgeff's full BDI theory.*

This positive result might give us the hope that the upper computational complexity bound for μ-calculus also carries to the full BDI theory. This would give us a complete computational account of Rao and Georgeff's theory. However, the situation here is somewhat more involved. One problem is that the translation into the μ-calculus is succinct only for BDI$_{\text{CTL}}$. What we know for sure is that at least for this subset the upper computational complexity bound of the μ-calculus does apply.

Theorem 13. *Deciding satisfiability of* BDI$_{\text{CTL}}$*-formulae is complete for deterministic exponential time.*

A further complication is the axioms for, say, different kinds of realisms. These axioms are an integral part of the overall theory. Like most axioms, these axioms are actually *axiom schemes* and, thus, second order in nature. Take weak realism. *Weak realism* means that a proposition α may be among an agent's desires only if $\neg\alpha$ is not among the agent's beliefs [15]. This translates into the following axiom.

$$\text{Des}(a, \alpha) \rightarrow \neg\text{Bel}(a, \neg\alpha).$$

As it stands a decision algorithm for deciding satisfiability or validness is not able to handle axioms of this kind. In the μ-calculus, however, it is possible to encode some special axioms as a conventional formula. The axiom of weak realism is an example of such an axiom. To see how this works we have to consider weak realism more thoroughly. In semantic terms weak realism simply means that $\mathcal{B}_i \cap \mathcal{D}_i \neq \emptyset$ [15]. The first observation is that we can partition $\mathcal{B}_i$ into $\mathcal{B}_i \setminus \mathcal{D}_i$ and $\mathcal{B}_i \cap \mathcal{D}_i$ and, similarly, $\mathcal{D}_i$ into $\mathcal{D}_i \setminus \mathcal{B}_i$ and $\mathcal{B}_i \cap \mathcal{D}_i$. Each of these three disjoint sets is represented by a distinguished primitive program. Call these programs $b\bar{d}$-i, bd-i, and $\bar{d}b$-i, where bd-i is to capture the common intersection $\mathcal{B}_i \cap \mathcal{D}_i$. Consequently, the complex program $b\bar{d}$-$i \cup bd$-i represents $\mathcal{B}_i$ and, similarly, $\bar{d}b$-$i \cup bd$-i captures $\mathcal{D}_i$. In this case, $\mathcal{B}_i$ and $\mathcal{D}_i$ are presented by two *complex* programs rather than by two primitive ones. It remains to guarantee that $\mathcal{B}_i \cap \mathcal{D}_i$ is not empty. This is exactly what $[\mathcal{P}^*]\langle bd$-$i\rangle true$ does if $\mathcal{P}$ is the union of all primitive programs. The overall encoding is even succinct.

The procedure for *(pure) realism* is similar. Pure realism has been put forward by Cohen and Levesque [2]. In semantic terms it means that $\mathcal{D}_i \subseteq \mathcal{B}_i$. This subset relation is equivalent to $\mathcal{B}_i = \mathcal{B}_i \cup \mathcal{D}_i$. This suggests representing $\mathcal{B}_i$ by the complex program b-$i \cup d$-i, while the primitive program d-i captures $\mathcal{D}_i$. The programs b-$i \cup d$-i and d-i then enjoy Cohen and Levesque's pure realism constraint. We conclude:

Theorem 14. *Under the pure realism constraint, deciding satisfiability of* BDI$_{\text{CTL}}$*-formulae is complete for deterministic exponential time, and so is deciding satisfiability of* BDI$_{\text{CTL}}$*-formulae under the weak realism constraint.*

It is not clear whether strong realism can also be encoded along the lines above. This is because strong realism is a complex structural condition rather than a simple set-theoretical one [15].

7 Conclusion

A distinguishing characteristic of BDI$_{\text{CTL}}$* is its two-dimensional semantics. This non-standard semantics is due to the combination of modalities Bel, Des, and Intend with the temporal operators of CTL*. Bel, Des, and Intend are interpreted over a dimension of possible worlds, while the temporal operators refer to a dimension of time. The first important observation of this paper is that such a two-dimensional semantics can be encoded as a conventional one-dimensional Kripke structure obeying a certain structural condition. If a conventional Kripke structure obeys this condition, then it encodes a specific two-dimensional structure. Vice versa, every two-dimensional structure has an equivalent one-dimensional Kripke structure that meets this structural condition. Another important observation is that, without loss of generality, we can assume that *every* conventional Kripke structure does obey this structural condition. If a Kripke structure did not have this property, it could be unwound into an equivalent structure that actually meets the relevant structural condition. In this way, we can ultimately get rid of the two-dimensional situation semantics of BDI_{CTL^*}. This is not what one might expect in view of the various negative results on two-dimensional modal logics [9].

¿From the literature it is known that the propositional μ-calculus strictly subsumes the full computation tree logic CTL*. When considering a conventional one-dimensional Kripke semantics for BDI_{CTL^*}, it becomes quite obvious that this result can be extended to BDI_{CTL^*}. Now, confining ourselves to a conventional one-dimensional semantics for BDI_{CTL^*} is exactly what we are allowed to do. We end up with the conclusion that the propositional μ-calculus strictly subsumes BDI_{CTL^*}. Despite its expressive power, the μ-calculus enjoys essentially the same computational complexity as BDI_{CTL^*}'s small fragment CTL. Both the propositional μ-calculus and CTL are known to be complete for deterministic exponential time.

An immediate consequence of this subsumption is a complete axiomatization for Rao and Georgeff's full BDI theory. We have learned that every BDI_{CTL^*}-formula can be translated into an equivalent formula of the μ-calculus. But then we can employ Walukievicz's complete axiomatization of the propositional μ-calculus also for BDI_{CTL^*}. If convenient we can add proper axioms for Bel, Des, and Intend, including axioms for the different types of realisms and commitment strategies. Of course, these axioms have to be translated as well. By this procedure we can obtain the first complete axiomatization of Rao and Georgeff's full BDI theory. Up until now, a complete axiomatization is only known for the much weaker BDI_{CTL} [15].

Unfortunately, the upper computational complexity bound for μ-calculus does not so easily apply to BDI_{CTL^*}. One problem is that the translation into the μ-calculus is succinct only for BDI_{CTL}. At least for this subset of BDI_{CTL^*} the upper computational complexity bound does apply. A further complication are the axioms for, say, different kinds of realisms. Like most axioms, these axioms are actually *axiom schemes* and, thus, second order in nature. The decision algorithms for the propositional μ-calculus are not able to handle such second-order formulae. Some special axioms can be encoded anyway. This is in particular true for pure realism and weak realism. In these cases, the upper computational complexity bound for the propositional μ-calculus also applies to BDI_{CTL}. Among the different types of realism, only strong realism resist a direct encoding and, thus, makes it necessary to modify the decision algorithms themselves.

A more practical consequence might arise from the various model-checker tools available for the μ-calculus. If agents are implemented by finite state automata, we can check whether these implementations meet certain properties. This is what model checking means. Even with the properties phrased in the powerful μ-calculus, such tests are efficient [6]. There are also several practical model-checker tools available [17]. With the correspondence worked out in this paper, these tools become also relevant for the BDI theory.

Acknowledgements

I would like to thank my colleagues Stefan Bussmann and Afsaneh Haddadi as well as the anonymous referees for their invaluable comments on a draft version of this paper.

References

1. M. E. Bratman. *Intentions, Plans, and Practical Reason.* Harvard University Press: Cambridge, MA, 1987.
2. P. R. Cohen and H. J. Levesque. Intention is choice with commitment. *Artificial Intelligence*, 42:213–261, 1990.
3. E. A. Emerson, C. S. Jutla, and A. P. Sistla. On model-checking for fragments of mu-calculus. In C. Courcoubetis, editor, *Computer Aided Verification: Proc. of the 5th International Conference CAV'93*, pages 395–396. Springer-Verlag, Berlin, Heidelberg, 1993.
4. E. A. Emerson. Temporal and modal logic. In Jan van Leeuwen, editor, *Handbook of Theoretical Computer Science*, volume B, pages 995–1072. Elsevier, Amsterdam, The Netherlands, 1990.
5. E. A. Emerson and Ch. S. Jutla. The complexity of tree automata and logics of programs (extended abstract). In *Proceedings of the 29th Annual Symposium on Foundations of Computer Science*, pages 328–337, 1988.
6. E. A. Emerson and Ch.-L. Lei. Efficient model checking in fragments of the propositional mu-calculus (extended abstract). In *Proceedings of the 1st Annual IEEE Symposium on Logic in Computer Science*, pages 267–278, Boston, MA, 1986.
7. M. J. Fischer and R. E. Ladner. Propositional dynamic logic of regular programs. *Journal of Computer and System Science*, 18:194–211, 1979.
8. J. Y. Halpern and Y. Moses. A guide to completeness and complexity for modal logics of knowledge and belief. *Artificial Intelligence*, 54:319–379, 1992.
9. D. Harel. Recurring dominoes: Making the highly undecidable highly understandable. In *Topics in the Theory of Computation: Selected Papers of the International Conference on Foundations of Computation Theory*, pages 51–71. North-Holland, 1983.
10. D. Harel. Dynamic logic. In D. Gabbay and F. Guenther, editors, *Handbook of Philosophical Logic*, volume 2, pages 497–604. Reidel, Dordrecht, The Netherlands, 1984.
11. D. Kozen. Results on the propositional μ-calculus. *Theoretical Computer Science*, 27:333–354, 1983.
12. V. R. Pratt. Semantical considerations on Floyd-Hoare logic. In *Proceedings 17th IEEE Symposium on Foundations of Computer Science*, pages 109–121, 1976.
13. A. S. Rao and M. P. Georgeff. Modeling rational agents within a BDI-architecture. In R. Fikes and E. Sandewall, editors, *Proceedings of the 2nd International Conference on Principles of Knowledge Representation and Reasoning*, pages 473–484, 1991.
14. A. S. Rao and M. P. Georgeff. A model-theoretic approach to the verification of situated reasoning systems. In *Proceedings of the 13th International Joint Conference on Artificial Intelligence*, pages 318–324, Chambery, France, 1993.

15. A. S. Rao and M. P. Georgeff. Formal models and decision procedures for multi-agent systems. Technical Note 61, Australian AI Institute, Level 6, 171 La Trobe Street, Melbourne, Australia, 1995.

16. S. Safra. On the complexity of ω-automata. In *Proceedings of the 29th Annual Symposium on Foundations of Computer Science*, pages 319–327, 1988.

17. P. Stevens. The edinburgh concurrency workbench. http://www.dcs.ed.ac.uk/home/cwb, 1997.

18. I. Walukiewicz. On completeness of the μ-calculus. In *Proceedings of the 8th Annual IEEE Symposium on Logic in Computer Science*, pages 136–146, Montreal, Canada, 1993.

19. M. Wooldridge. Agent-based software engineering. *IEE Proceedings Software Engineering*, 114(1):26–37, 1997.

Intention Reconsideration Reconsidered

Michael Wooldridge and Simon Parsons

Department of Electronic Engineering
Queen Mary and Westfield College
University of London
London E1 4NS, United Kingdom
{M.J.Wooldridge, S.D.Parsons}@elec.qmw.ac.uk

Abstract. In this paper, we consider the issue of designing agents that successfully balance the amount of time spent in reconsidering their intentions against
the amount of time spent acting to achieve them. Following a brief review of
the various ways in which this problem has previously been analysed, we motivate and introduce a simple formal model of agents, which is closely related
to the well-known belief-desire-intention model. In this model, an agent is explicitly equipped with mechanisms for deliberation and action selection, as well
as a meta-level control function, which allows the agent to choose between deliberation and action. Using the formal model, we define what it means for an
agent to be optimal with respect to a task environment, and explore how various
properties of an agent's task environment can impose certain requirements on its
deliberation and meta-level control components. We then show how the model
can capture a number of interesting practical reasoning scenarios, and illustrate
how our notion of meta-level control can easily be extended to encompass higher-
order meta-level reasoning. We conclude with a discussion and pointers to future
work.

1 Introduction

Much of the research activity from the intelligent agent community in the mid-to-late
1980s was focussed around the problem of designing agents that could achieve an effective balance between *deliberation* (the process of deciding *what to do*) and *means-ends
reasoning* (the process of deciding *how to do it*) [2]. One particularly successful approach that emerged at this time was the *belief-desire-intention* (BDI) paradigm [5, 2,
10, 13]. The development of the BDI paradigm was to a great extent driven by Bratman's
theory of (human) practical reasoning [1], in which *intentions* play a central role. Put
crudely, since an agent cannot deliberate indefinitely about what courses of action to
pursue, the idea is it should eventually *commit* to achieving certain states of affairs, and
then devote resources to achieving them. These chosen states of affairs are intentions,
and once adopted, they play a central role in future practical reasoning [1, 3].

A major issue in the design of agents that are based upon models of intention is that
of when to *reconsider* intentions. An agent cannot simply maintain an intention, once
adopted, without ever stopping to reconsider it. From time-to-time, it will be necessary
to check, (for example), whether the intention has been achieved, or whether it is believed to be no longer achievable [3]. In such situations, it is necessary for an agent to

deliberate over its intentions, and, if necessary, to *change focus* by dropping existing intentions and adopting new ones. Kinny and Georgeff undertook an experimental study of different intention reconsideration strategies [6]. They found that *dynamic* environments — environments in which the rate of world change was high — tend to favour *cautious* intention reconsideration strategies, i.e., strategies which frequently stop to reconsider intentions. Intuitively, this is because although such agents incur the costs of deliberation, they do not waste effort attempting to achieve intentions that are no longer viable, and are able to exploit new opportunities as they arise. In contrast, *static* environments — in which the rate of world change is low — tend to favour *bold* intention reconsideration strategies, which only infrequently pause to reconsider intentions.

Our aim in this paper is to consider the question of when to deliberate (i.e., to reconsider intentions) *versus* when to act from a formal point of view, in contrast to the experimental standpoint of Kinny and Georgeff [6]. We develop a simple formal model of practical reasoning agents, and investigate the behaviour of this model in different types of task environment. In this agent model, (which is very closely related to the BDI model [5, 2, 10]) an agent's internal state is characterised by a set of beliefs (information that the agent has about its environment) and a set of intentions (commitments the agent has made about what states of the world to try and achieve). In addition, an agent has a deliberation function, which allows it to reconsider and if necessary modify its intentions, and an action function, which allow it to act towards its current intentions. These functions are mediated by a *meta-level control* function. The purpose of the meta-level control function is simply to choose between deliberation and action. The meta-level control function thus acts somewhat like the interpreter in the PRS [5], but more closely resembles the meta-plans that are used to manage an agent's intention structures in the PRS.

The remainder of this paper is structured as follows. In section 2 we present our formal model of agents, and we define what it means for an agent to be optimal with respect to a particular *task environment*. In section 3, we investigate what it means for a task environment to be *real time*, and discuss the relationships that must hold between an agent's meta-level control and deliberation components in order for an agent to act optimally in such task environments. In particular, we define notions of soundness and completeness for meta-level control and deliberation strategies, and show that an optimal meta-level control function must be sound and complete with respect to a deliberation function in an important class of real-time task environments. In section 4, we show how our formal framework can capture a number of typical practical reasoning scenarios (taken from [2]). In section 5, we generalise our model of meta-level control to capture *higher-order* meta-level reasoning strategies (intuitively, strategies to determine what sort of meta-level reasoning function to use), and we integrate these with our agent model. Finally, in section 6, we present some conclusions and issues for future work.

2 Agents and Environments

In this section, we formalise a simple model of practical reasoning agents and the environments they occupy, and define what we mean by a *run* or *history* of an agent in an environment. An overview of our agent model is given in Figure 1.

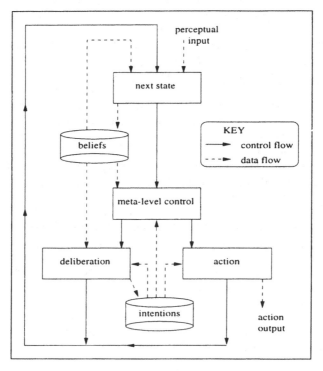

Fig. 1. Meta-level control, deliberation, and action in an architecture for practical reasoning agents.

Before discussing this model in detail, it is important to make several points clear. First, the architecture is emphatically *not* intended to be a proposal for a new implementable agent architecture in the sense of the PRS, INTERRAP, and so on [15]. Rather, it is intended to be an *abstraction* of the key functional components of the BDI architecture, which we find to be useful for analysis purposes. Second, note that although the architecture is closely related to the BDI model of agency, it also has some key differences. Perhaps most importantly, the reader will note that *desires* are missing. Desires in a BDI agent are essentially "options" or "possibilities" available to the agent. The agent chooses and commits to a subset of its desires, which then become intentions. Desires are thus used by an agent during the process of intention formation, and in particular, they are not a key component of the intention reconsideration process, which is our primary object of study in this paper. Hence they are subsumed within the deliberation component of our architecture. If one were to actually *implement* the deliberation component of our architecture, then it might well be useful to employ desires — but at our analysis level, they do not play any useful role.

Returning to Figure 1, our agents have two main data structures: a *belief set* and an *intention set*. An agent's beliefs represent information that the agent has about its environment. In implemented agent systems (such as PRS [5]), beliefs are often represented symbolically, as PROLOG-like facts, but they may simply be variables of a PASCAL-like programming language. However they are represented, beliefs correspond to an agent's *information state*. Let B be the set of all beliefs. For the most part, the contents of B will not be of concern to us here. However, it is often useful to suppose that B contains formulae of some logic, so that, for example, it is possible to determine whether two beliefs are mutually consistent or not. An agent's actions at any given moment are guided by its *intention set*, which represents its *focus*: the "direction" of its activities. Intentions may be thought of as states of affairs that an agent has committed to bringing about. Formally, let I be the set of all intentions. Again, we are not concerned here with the contents of I. As with beliefs, however, it is often useful to assume that intentions are expressed in some sort of logical language. An agent's *local state* will then be a pair (b, i), where $b \subseteq B$ is a set of beliefs, and $i \subseteq I$ is a set of intentions. The local state of an agent is its internal state: a snapshot of its information and focus at any given instant. Let $L = \wp(B) \times \wp(I)$ be the set of all internal states. We use l (with annotations: $l', l_1, \ldots$) to stand for members of L. If $l = (b, i)$, then we denote the belief component of l by b_l, and the intention component of l by i_l.

Agents do not operate isolation: they are situated in *environments*; we can think of an agent's environment as being everything external to the agent. (This external component may, of course, include other agents; we leave the exploration of this possibility to future work.) We assume that the environment external to the agent may be in any of a set $E = \{e, e', \ldots\}$ of states.

Together, an agent and its environment make up a *system*. The *global* state of a system at any time is thus a pair containing the state of the agent and the state of the environment. Formally, let $G = E \times L$ be the set of all such global states. We use g (with annotations: $g, g', \ldots$) to stand for members of G.

2.1   Choice, Deliberation, and Action

As Figure 1 illustrates, our agents have four main components, which together generate their behaviour: a *next-state function*, a *meta-level control function*, a *deliberation function*, and an *action function*. The *next state* function can be thought of as a *belief revision function*. On the basis of the agent's current state and the state of the environment, it determines a new set of beliefs for the agent, which will include any new information that the agent has perceived. An agent's next-state function thus realises whatever *perception* the agent is capable of. Formally, a next-state function is a mapping $\mathcal{N} : E \times \wp(B) \to \wp(B)$.

The next component in our agent architecture is meta-level control. The idea here is that at any given instant, an agent has two choices available to it. It can either *deliberate* (that is, it can expend computational resources deciding whether to change its focus), or else it can *act* (that is, it can expend resources attempting to actually achieve its current intentions). Note that we assume the only way an agent can *change* its focus (i.e., modify its intentions) is through explicit deliberation. To represent the choices (deliberation versus action) available to an agent, we will assume a set $C = \{d, a\}$, where d denotes deliberation, and a denotes action. The purpose of an agent's *meta-level control function* it to choose between deliberation and action. If it chooses to deliberate, then the agent subsequently deliberates; if its chooses to act, then the agent subsequently acts. Formally, we can represent such strategies as functions $\mathcal{M} : L \rightarrow C$, which on the basis of the agent's internal state, decides whether to deliberate (d) or act (a).

The *deliberation* process of an agent is represented by a function that, on the basis of an agent's internal state (i.e., its beliefs and intentions), determines a new set of intentions. Formally, we can represent this deliberative process via a function $\mathcal{D} : L \rightarrow \wp(I)$.

If an agent decides to act, rather than deliberate, then it is acting to achieve its intentions. To do so, it must decide *which* action to perform. The action selection component of an agent is essentially a function that, on the basis of the agent's current state, returns an action, which represents that which the agent has chosen to perform. Let $Ac = \{\alpha, \alpha', \ldots\}$ be the set of actions. Formally, an action selection function is a mapping $\mathcal{A} : L \rightarrow Ac$.

Finally, we define an agent to be a 5-tuple $(\mathcal{M}, \mathcal{D}, \mathcal{A}, \mathcal{N}, l_0)$, where $\mathcal{M}$ is a meta-level control function, $\mathcal{D}$ is a deliberation function, $\mathcal{A}$ is an action selection function, $\mathcal{N}$ is a next-state function, and $l_0 \in L$ is an *initial state*.

Before proceeding any further, we state some assumptions upon which later results depend. First, note that although we choose to abstractly model the components of an agent as functions, they will be ultimately be implemented by programs of some kind. If f is a program, then we write $cost_f$ for the *time cost* of f. The idea is that if f has time cost $O(g(n))$ and f' has time cost $O(h(n))$, where $O(g(n)) > O(h(n))$, then $cost_f > cost_{f'}$. We assume that the cost of deliberation is approximately equal to the cost of acting (i.e., $cost_{\mathcal{D}} \simeq cost_{\mathcal{A}}$). Second, we assume the cost of meta-level control is very much smaller than the cost of deliberation (i.e., $cost_{\mathcal{M}} \ll cost_{\mathcal{D}}$).

2.2 Runs

Recall that an agent is situated in an environment, and that such an environment may be in any of a set E of states. In order to represent the effect that an agent's actions have on an environment, we introduce a *state transformer* function, τ (cf. [4, p154]). The idea is that τ takes as input an environment state $e \in E$ and an action $\alpha \in Ac$, and returns the environment state that would result from performing α in e. Thus $\tau : E \times Ac \rightarrow E$. We are implicitly assuming that environments are *deterministic*: there is no uncertainty about the result of performing an action in some state [11, p46]. In addition, we assume that the only way an environment state can change is through the performance of an action on the part of an agent (i.e., the environment is *static* [11, p46]). Dropping these assumptions is not particularly problematic and does not alter any of our results, although it does make the formalism somewhat more convoluted. We leave the reader to make the required modifications. Formally, we define an environment *Env* to be a triple (E, τ, e_o), where E is a set of environment states as above, τ is a state transformer function, and $e_0 \in E$ is the initial state of *Env*.

A *run* of an agent/environment system can be thought of as an infinite sequence:

$$r : g_0 \xrightarrow{c_0} g_1 \xrightarrow{c_1} g_2 \xrightarrow{c_2} g_3 \xrightarrow{c_3} \cdots \xrightarrow{c_{u-1}} g_u \xrightarrow{c_u} \cdots$$

In such a run, g_0 is the initial state of the system (comprised of the initial state of the environment and the initial state of the agent) and $c_0 \in C$ is the *choice* dictated by the agent's meta-level control function on the basis of it's initial state. The state $g_1 = (e_1, l_1)$ is that which results after the agent has made its choice c_0. If the agent chose to *act* (that is, if $c_0 = a$), then $e_1 = \tau(e_0, \mathcal{A}(l_0))$ and $l_1 = (\mathcal{N}(e_0, b_{l_0}), i_{l_0})$, that is, the environment state e_1 is that which results from the agent performing its chosen action in the initial state, and the internal state l_1 is that which results from the agent updating its beliefs via its belief revision function and not changing its intentions (since it did not deliberate).

If, however, the agent chose to *deliberate* at time 0 (i.e., if $c_0 = d$) then $e_1 = e_0$ (i.e., the environment remains unchanged, since the agent did not act), and $l_1 = (\mathcal{N}(e_0, b_{l_0}), \mathcal{D}(l_0))$ (i.e., the agent's beliefs are updated as in the previous case, and the agent's intentions are updated through its deliberation function $\mathcal{D}$.

Formally, an infinite sequence $(g_0, g_1, g_2, \ldots)$ over G represents a run of an agent $Ag = (\mathcal{M}, \mathcal{D}, \mathcal{A}, \mathcal{N}, l_0)$ in an environment $Env = (E, \tau, e_0)$ iff $g_0 = (e_0, l_0)$ and $\forall u \in I\!N$, we have

$$g_{u+1} = \begin{cases} (e_u, (\mathcal{N}(e_u, b_{l_u}), \mathcal{D}(l_u))) & \text{if } \mathcal{M}(l_u) = d \\ (\tau(e_u, \mathcal{A}(i_{l_u})), (\mathcal{N}(e_u, b_{l_u}), i_{l_u})) & \text{if } \mathcal{M}(l_u) = a. \end{cases}$$

We will denote by $r(Ag, Env)$ the run of agent Ag in environment Env, and let Run be the set of all possible runs.

2.3 Optimal Behaviour

In order to express the *value*, or *utility* of a run, we introduce a function $V : Run \to I\!R$, which assigns real numbers indicating "payoffs" to runs. Thus V essentially captures a standard decision-theoretic notion of utility. We will assume that there is some upper bound to the utility that V assigns to a run, so there will always be one or more "optimal" runs. The function V represents a *performance measure* against which an agent will be measured.

A *task environment* is defined to be a pair (Env, V), where Env is an environment, and $V : Run \to I\!R$ is a utility function. We say an agent Ag is *optimal* with respect to a task environment (Env, V) if there is no agent Ag' such that $V(r(Ag', Env)) > V(r(Ag, Env))$. Again, this is in essence the by-now standard notion of an optimal agent (cf. [12, p583]).

Viewed at its most abstract, an agent is simply an action selection or decision-making function, which maps perceptual inputs to actions [11, p34]. The architectural components of an agent — its meta-level control function, deliberation, action, and next-state function — are there *in the service* of this decision making. An obvious question is therefore whether or not we can define what it means for such a component to be optimal. Let us consider the case of the meta-level control. Suppose that in some situation, the meta-level control function chose to deliberate rather than act, and as a consequence, the agent lost some utility. (Imagine that the agent was about to be hit by a speeding car, and instead of choosing to jump, chose to deliberate about which way to jump.) Then clearly, the meta-level control function was sub-optimal in this case — it would have done better by choosing differently. This leads us to the following definition: a meta-level control function $\mathcal{M}$ is *sub-optimal* if there is some other meta-level control function $\mathcal{M}'$ such that if the agent used $\mathcal{M}'$ instead of $\mathcal{M}$, it would obtain a higher utility. Formally, if $(\mathcal{M}, \mathcal{D}, \mathcal{A}, \mathcal{N}, l_0)$ is an agent, then $\mathcal{M}$ if optimal (with respect to (Env, V), $\mathcal{D}$, $\mathcal{A}$, and $\mathcal{N}$) if there is no $\mathcal{M}'$ such that $V(r(\mathcal{M}', \mathcal{D}, \mathcal{A}, \mathcal{N}, l_0), Env) > V(r(\mathcal{M}, \mathcal{D}, \mathcal{A}, \mathcal{N}, l_0), Env)$. In a similar way, we can define optimality for $\mathcal{D}$, $\mathcal{A}$, and $\mathcal{N}$ — the details are left to the reader. Notice that optimality of a component is defined not only with respect to a task environment, but also with respect to the other components of an agent. The following theorem captures the relationship between optimality for an agent and the optimality of its components.

Theorem 1 *If an agent is optimal with respect to some task environment, then the components of that agent are mutually optimal.*

Proof. Suppose $Ag = (\mathcal{M}, \mathcal{D}, \mathcal{A}, \mathcal{N}, l_0)$ is globally optimal with respect to (Env, V), but that one component is sub-optimal. Assume this component is $\mathcal{M}$ (the cases for $\mathcal{D}$, $\mathcal{A}$, or $\mathcal{N}$ are identical). Then $V(r(\mathcal{M}', \mathcal{D}, \mathcal{A}, \mathcal{N}, l_0), Env) > V(r(\mathcal{M}, \mathcal{D}, \mathcal{A}, \mathcal{N}, l_0), Env)$ for some $\mathcal{M}'$ such that $\mathcal{M}' \neq \mathcal{M}$. But in this case, Ag is not optimal with respect to (Env, V), which is a contradiction.

Notice that the implication in this theorem cannot be strengthened to a biconditional: the fact that the components of an agent are mutually optimal does imply that the agent is itself optimal. We can think of agents that have mutually optimal components but that are globally sub-optimal as having achieved a kind of local maxima: an optimality of sorts, but not the best that could be achieved.

To make the concept of a valuation function and task environment concrete, we consider the Tileworld scenario, introduced by Pollack and Ringuette [9], and used by Kinny and Georgeff in their investigation into agent commitment strategies [6]. In this scenario, the environment is a two-dimensional "grid world". The agent is situated in this grid world, and can move around it in single steps. The grid world is also occupied by a number of randomly distributed blocks, and holes into which an agent can shove blocks. An agent does this by moving around the world, pushing blocks ahead of it. The "optimal" agent is the one that, on average, maximises the number of blocks shoved into holes. The valuation function V_{TW} for the Tileworld can simply be defined as $V_{TW}(r) = blocks(r)/unsuccessful(r)$ where $blocks(r)$ denotes the number of blocks that were successfully shoved into holes during r and $unsuccessful(r)$ denotes the number of time steps on r during which a block was not shoved into a hole. Note that the valuation function V_{TW} ranges from 0 (the agent failed to shove any block into a hole), to 1 (a block was shoved into a hole at every time step).

An agent entering such a Tileworld could, in principle, compute an optimal plan for shoving blocks into holes, (although as a variant of the travelling salesman problem, the computation of such a plan would be NP-complete). However, decision making in the Tileworld is complicated by the fact that blocks themselves appear and disappear at random. The agent has no way of knowing in advance where holes will appear or disappear, and if it is to operate effectively, it must monitor such environmental changes, and, where appropriate, modify its course of action. We will return to the Tileworld and comment further on this issue in the following section.

For the remainder of this paper, we will be particularly concerned with the relationship between just two of the components of an agent: its meta-level control function and deliberation component. We shall therefore assume from here on that an agent's next-state function and action function are fixed and optimal.

3   Real-Time Task Environments

It should be clear that the performance of an agent is very much dependent on the nature of the task environment in which it is situated. An agent that performs badly in one task environment may do well in one that has different properties [11, p46]. An understanding of the relationship between agents and the task environments they occupy is therefore likely to be of great benefit when we come to build agents that will operate in real environments.

Arguably the most important everyday class of task environments are those that come under the banner of *real-time*. Put at its most abstract, a real-time task environment is simply one in which time plays a part in the evaluation of an agent's performance [12, p585]. It is possible to identify several different sorts of real-time task environments, for example:

- those in which the agent must bring about some state of affairs as quickly as possible — the sooner it achieves this state of affairs, the higher its payoff;
- one in which an agent is required to repeat some task, with the optimal agent being the one that repeats the task as often as possible.

Real-time task environments are problematic because, in general, if an agent is to operate successfully in such an environment, then it must successfully trade-off the amount of time it spends deliberating against the amount of time it spends acting. For if an agent deliberates indefinitely, then it will typically never achieve anything (cf. the notion of reactivity in [15])[1].

Formally defining what it means for a task environment to be real-time is not simple, since, as the examples above indicate, the concept of real-time actually encompasses a number of related properties. Rather than attempt to present such a general definition, we define a class of task environments in which *wasted effort is penalised*. We argue that this concept captures many aspects of real-time task environments.

How might an agent waste effort? There are essentially two possibilities. First, an agent is wasting effort if it is expending resources attempting to achieve the "wrong" intentions. Consider the Tileworld, discussed in the preceding section. Suppose an agent has observed some block, and has formed an intention to shove that block into a particular hole. Now if the agent is attempting to achieve this intention even when that hole

---

[1] It is easy to construct providential task environments, in which an optimal agent is one that always chooses to deliberate or always chooses to act. However, we argue that such task environments do not correspond to many interesting real-world situations.

has vanished, then it is in some sense wasting effort. It would do better to reconsider its intentions. A similar waste of effort occurs if an agent fails to exploit a serendipitous situation (for example when a hole appears to the side of an agent, making it possible to obtain additional utility).

A second type of wasted effort occurs if an agent has "correct" intentions, but is not acting on them — in such a situation, an agent is engaging in unnecessary deliberation. For example, suppose an agent in the Tileworld has an intention of shoving some particular block into a hole, and stops to deliberate. After deliberation, the agent's intentions are unchanged, and it continues to push the same block to the same hole. In this case, all other things being equal, the utility accorded to the agent would be less than it would have obtained by not deliberating at all (since the value *unsuccessful*(r) has increased). The agent would thus have done better by simply acting instead.

In order to formally define what we mean for an agent to waste effort, we must first define what it means for an agent to have *optimal intentions*. Intuitively, an agent has optimal intentions if there is no good reason for changing them — if, given the information available to the agent, an optimal deliberation function would not choose to change them. Formally, if $(\mathcal{M}, \mathcal{D}, \mathcal{A}, \mathcal{N}, l_0)$ is an agent that is currently in state (b, i), and that is situated in task environment (Env, V), then its intention set i is optimal for $\mathcal{M}, \mathcal{A}, \mathcal{N}, l_0$ iff $\mathcal{D}((b, i)) = i$. Note that the notion of an optimal intention set is inherently *relative* to a specific agent. An intention set that is optimal for one agent may well not be optimal for another. An agent $Ag = (\mathcal{M}, \mathcal{D}, \mathcal{A}, \mathcal{N}, l_0)$ in task environment (Env, V) is then said to waste effort iff $r(Ag, Env) = (g_0, \ldots)$ and for some $u \in \mathbb{N}$ we have either i_{l_u} is optimal for $\mathcal{M}, \mathcal{A}, \mathcal{N}, l_0$ and $c_u = d$ or else i_{l_u} is not optimal for $\mathcal{M}, \mathcal{A}, \mathcal{N}, l_0$ and $c_u = a$. Finally, a task environment is said to penalise wasted effort iff any optimal agent for this task environment does not waste effort.

Let us now turn to the relationship between meta-level control and deliberation for task environments that penalise wasted effort. The possible interactions between meta-level control and deliberation in such task environments are summarised in Table 1 (adapted and extended from [2, p353]). Consider situation (1). In this situation, the agent does not have optimal intentions, and hence would do well to deliberate. However, it does not choose to deliberate and hence the meta-level reasoning function that chose to act was sub-optimal. In situation (2), the agent again has sub-optimal intentions, but this time chooses to deliberate, rather than act. Unfortunately, the agent's deliberation function $\mathcal{D}$ does not change focus, and is thus sub-optimal. Situation (3) is essentially the same as situation (2), but this time, the deliberation function *does* change focus. While it is clear that the meta-level reasoning function is optimal in this situation, it is not certain that the deliberation function is optimal, since we do not know what the old intentions were replaced with. However, it would certainly be sub-optimal *not* to change intentions.

In situation (4), the agent has optimal intentions, and does not choose to deliberate. Since the intentions are optimal, the meta-level control function is obviously correct not to deliberate in this situation, and is hence optimal. In situation (5), the agent has optimal intentions, but this time chooses to deliberate; the deliberation function, however, does not change focus. Hence while the meta-level control function is clearly sub-optimal, the deliberation function is optimal. Situation (6) is as situation (5), except

Situation number	Optimal intentions?	Chose to deliberate?	Changed focus?	$\mathcal{M}$ optimal?	$\mathcal{D}$ optimal?
1	No	No	—	No	—
2	No	Yes	No	Yes	No
3	No	Yes	Yes	Yes	Maybe
4	Yes	No	—	Yes	—
5	Yes	Yes	No	No	Yes
6	Yes	Yes	Yes	No	No

Table 1. Practical Reasoning Situations (cf. [2])

that this time, the deliberation function changes focus. In this case, both the meta-level control and deliberation components must be sub-optimal, since the agent wasted time deliberating, and then modified its intentions despite the fact that there is no reason to do so.

From the discussion above, we can extract the following simple principle: for task environments that penalise wasted effort, a meta-level control function should choose to deliberate *only* when its corresponding deliberation function would change focus. We will say a meta-level control function $\mathcal{M}$ is *sound* with respect to an optimal deliberation function $\mathcal{D}$ iff whenever $\mathcal{M}$ chooses to deliberate, $\mathcal{D}$ chooses to change focus (i.e., if $M(l) = d$ implies $\mathcal{D}(l) \neq i_l$). Similarly, we say $\mathcal{M}$ is *complete* with respect to $\mathcal{D}$ iff whenever $\mathcal{D}$ *would* change focus, $\mathcal{M}$ chooses to deliberate (i.e., if $\mathcal{D}(l) \neq i_l$ implies $M(l) = d$). We can easily establish the following result, which relates sound and complete meta-level control strategies to task environments that penalise wasted effort.

Theorem 2 *For task environments that penalise wasted effort, an optimal agent has a meta-level control function that is sound and complete with respect to its deliberation function.*

Proof. Assume an arbitrary agent $(\mathcal{M}, \mathcal{D}, \mathcal{A}, \mathcal{N}, l_0)$ is optimal with respect to some task environment that penalises wasted effort. We need to show that $\mathcal{M}$ is sound and complete with respect to $\mathcal{D}$. For soundness, start by assuming that $\mathcal{M}$ is not sound with respect to $\mathcal{D}$. Then for some $l \in L$, we have $\mathcal{M}(l) = d$ (the meta-level control function says deliberate) but that $\mathcal{D}(l) = i_l$ (the deliberation function does not choose to change focus). But by definition, this is a waste of effort, hence $(\mathcal{M}, \mathcal{D}, \mathcal{A}, \mathcal{N}, l_0)$ cannot be optimal, which is a contradiction, so $\mathcal{M}$ is sound. For completeness, start by assuming that $\mathcal{M}$ is not complete with respect to $\mathcal{D}$. Hence for some $l \in L$, we have $\mathcal{D}(l) \neq i_l$ but that $\mathcal{M}(l) = a$. But this is a waste of effort, hence $(\mathcal{M}, \mathcal{D}, \mathcal{A}, \mathcal{N}, l_0)$ cannot be optimal, which is a contradiction, so $\mathcal{M}$ is complete.

An optimal meta-level control function for task environments that penalise wasted effort thus has a kind of oracle for its corresponding deliberation function. One might therefore wonder what is the point of having both meta-level control *and* deliberation components, as an optimal meta-level control function need only run the deliberation function as a subroutine to see if it would change focus, and choose to deliberate just in case the deliberation function *does* change focus. Formally, such a meta-level control function would be defined as follows:

$$\mathcal{M}(l) = \begin{cases} a & \text{if } \mathcal{D}(l) = i_l \\ d & \text{otherwise.} \end{cases}$$

This would indeed be a successful strategy if the cost of the meta-level control function was approximately equal to the cost of deliberation (i.e., if $cost_\mathcal{M} \simeq cost_\mathcal{D}$). However, as we pointed out earlier, we require that the cost of meta-level control be *significantly less* than that of deliberation ($cost_\mathcal{M} \ll cost_\mathcal{D}$). Under this assumption, running the deliberation component in order to decide whether to deliberate is not an option.

4 An Example

In the previous section, we discussed the notion of a real-time task environment, and investigated the relationship between meta-level control and deliberation in such task environments. In this section, we show how four illustrative practical reasoning scenarios (introduced in [2]) can be represented within our framework. (More accurately, Bratman and colleagues give six scenarios, since there are two variants each of scenarios one and four. However, these variants are meaningless in our framework.)

4.1 Scenario One

All four scenarios are based on the following basic story: Rosie is an agent that has been assigned the task of repairing a malfunctioning VDU. As a result of some task analysis, she has decided that this might best be done by replacing the CRT (which she believes is burnt out), and so she has adopted the intentions of going to the VDU armed with a replacement CRT, and then using this new tube to fix the VDU. In the first scenario, Rosie arrives at the VDU to find that the CRT is not burnt out: the contrast has just been turned way down. She therefore has the option of fixing the VDU by adjusting the contrast. This information is sufficient for her meta-level control function to decide that it is worth deliberating, and in so doing, Rosie finds that adjusting the contrast is cheaper than replacing the CRT. She thus adopts the new intention of adjusting the contrast. She then acts, adjusting the contrast and completes her initial task.

In this, and all other scenarios, we represent Rosie's world as a set of propositions. The propositions of interest to us are summarised in Table 2. While the intended interpretation for most of these is self-evident, some require additional explanation: s is intended to capture the presence of the additional CRT in scenarios three and four; b_1 is intended to capture the fact that Rosie knows that if it is possible to fix the VDU by just adjusting the contrast then this is a better option than using the CRT she carries with her; b_2 is intended to capture the fact that rewiring the faulty CRT is the best option, and b_3 is intended to capture the fact that an additional CRT in scenarios three and four is superior to the CRT she carries with her.

In addition, we will also represent Rosie's possible intentions as propositions: see Table 2. Again, most of these are self-explanatory, but i_v is needed to capture Rosie's initial progress from wherever she picks up the first CRT to wherever the broken VDU is.

Beliefs	
w	VDU working
c	CRT burnt out
d	Contrast turned down
b_1	Adjust contrast is better
r	CRT can be fixed by re-wiring
b_2	Re-wiring is better
s	Spare VDU
b_3	Spare VDU is better

Intentions	
i_o	Fix VDU using original CRT
i_c	Fix VDU by adjusting contrast
i_r	Fix VDU by re-wiring
i_a	Fix VDU by using alternative CRT
i_v	Go to VDU

Table 2. Rosie's Possible Beliefs and Intentions

For simplicity we will assume that each of these intentions can be achieved by a single action (though each of these could equally well be a series of actions). Thus the action to achieve intention i_r is α_r, the action to achieve intention i_v is α_v, and so on.

We can now formalise Rosie's reasoning. Initially the state of the world is $e_0 = \{\neg w, \neg c, d\}$ (the VDU is not working, the CRT is not burnt out, and the contrast is turned down). Rosie's initial internal state l_0 is thus: $(\{\neg w, c, \neg d, b_1\}, \{i_v, i_o\})$. She thus begins scenario one with false beliefs, since she wrongly believes that the CRT is burned out. Note that Rosie's beliefs also include the preference information b_1. She initially has two intentions: to fix the VDU using the original CRT, and to go to the VDU.

The first part of Rosie's operation is to decide whether to deliberate or act. She chooses to act, and executes the action α_v that achieves her intention i_v, and thus arrives at the VDU. At this point she deliberates, and removes the now-achieved intention of moving to the VDU from her intention set, so that the previously adopted intention of fixing the VDU using the CRT she brought with her becomes the main focus. At this point she can identify the real state of the world, and her next-state function $\mathcal{N}$ updates her beliefs to reflect this. Her internal state becomes: $l_1 = (\{\neg w, \neg c, d, b_1\}, \{i_o\})$. The state of the external world is unchanged: $e_1 = e_0$.

Rosie again applies her meta-level control function:

$$\mathcal{M}(l) = \begin{cases} d \text{ if } \{\neg c, d, b_1\} \subseteq b_l \text{ or } \{\neg c, r, b_2\} \subseteq b_l \text{ or } \{c, s, b_3\} \subseteq b_l \\ a \text{ otherwise.} \end{cases}$$

Thus there are three situations in which she will choose to deliberate, all of which can be glossed as "there is now some reason to suspect that there is a better alternative to repair the VDU". Clearly this is just an illustrative fragment of the complete meta-level control function which is appropriate to this example. Since Rosie now believes $\neg c$, she chooses to deliberate. That is, $\mathcal{M}(l_1) = d$ since the CRT is known to not be burnt out, the contrast is known to be turned down, and it is known that adjusting the contrast gives a better means of fixing the VDU than replacing the CRT. To find the result of deliberation, we need to define $\mathcal{D}$. We have:

$$\mathcal{D}(l) = \begin{cases} \{i_c\} & \text{if } \{\neg c, d, b_1\} \subseteq b_l \\ \{i_r\} & \text{if } \{\neg c, r, b_2\} \subseteq b_l \\ \{i_a\} & \text{if } \{c, s, b_3\} \subseteq b_l \\ l_i & \text{otherwise.} \end{cases}$$

The deliberation function $\mathcal{D}$ thus decides to adjust the contrast: $\mathcal{D}(l_1) = \{i_c\}$. Note that $\mathcal{D}$ should really check that the agent has a means of adopting the intention before it decides to adopt it — if Rosie is unable to adjust the contrast (because she has the wrong kind of gripper for instance) then however good a solution this might be, there is no point in changing focus to try and achieve it. For our purposes, we can ignore this subtlety, however.

After deliberation, Rosie's internal state becomes: $l_2 = (\{\neg w, \neg c, d, b_1\}, \{i_c\})$, while the external world remains unchanged: $e_2 = e_1 = e_0$. This time $\mathcal{M}$ chooses to act, and since $\mathcal{A}(l_2) = \alpha_c$, the contrast is adjusted, which repairs the VDU. This change in the world causes Rosie to revise her beliefs about the state of the VDU and the contrast control. The final state of the environment is thus $e_3 = \{w, \neg c, \neg d\}$, while Rosie's internal state is $l_3 = (\{w, \neg c, \neg d, b_1\}, \emptyset)$.

The complete run for scenario one is thus:

$$r_1 : g_0 \xrightarrow{a_v} g_1 \xrightarrow{d} g_2 \xrightarrow{a_c} g_3$$

4.2 Scenario Two

In this scenario, Rosie arrives at the VDU to find that the CRT is not burnt out and can be fixed by re-wiring. However, this fix will only be short term, and the CRT will soon burn out anyway. This information is sufficient for Rosie's meta-level control function to decide it is not worth deliberating to see if she is able to fix the VDU by rewiring, and so she acts, replacing the CRT in line with her unchanged intention. The start this scenario is described by:

$$e_0 = \{\neg w, \neg c, r\}$$
$$l_0 = (\{\neg w, c, \neg r, \neg b_2\}, \{i_v\})$$

So, although the CRT is not burnt out and the VDU can be fixed by re-wiring (facts that Rosie initially does not know), Rosie *does* know that re-wiring is a worse option than replacing the CRT. After moving to the VDU, popping the intention stack, and revising beliefs, just as in the previous scenario, the environment state remains unchanged but Rosie's internal state is $l_1 = (\{\neg w, \neg c, r, \neg b_2\}, \{i_o\})$.

Rosie then applies her meta-level control function, and despite the fact that there is reason for her to suspect that deliberation might lead to an alternative means of repairing the VDU (a situation which is actually true), $\mathcal{M}$ returns a because Rosie also knows that fixing the CRT by re-wiring is a worse option than the one she has already. Thus she can reject the idea of changing her focus without going as far as establishing whether or not she can build a new plan in order to fix the VDU. Having decided to act, Rosie performs $A(i_o) = \alpha_o$ and the situation becomes:

$$e_2 = \{w, \neg c, r\}$$
$$l_2 = (\{w, c, r, \neg b_2\}, \emptyset)$$

The complete run for Scenario Two is thus:

$$r_2 : g_0 \xrightarrow{a_v} g_1 \xrightarrow{a_o} g_2$$

4.3 Scenario Three

In Scenario Three, Rosie arrives at the VDU to find a spare (and therefore free) CRT sitting by the terminal, but notes that the spare is inferior to the tube she brought with her. Her meta-level control mechanism therefore realises that there is no advantage to seeing if the new tube can be used, and so chooses to act. Rosie then replaces the CRT in line with her original intention. Scenario Three thus begins with the following state of affairs:

$$e_0 = \{\neg w, c, s\}$$
$$l_0 = (\{\neg w, c, \neg s, \neg b_3\}, \{i_v\})$$

As before, Rosie proceeds to the VDU and this time finds the spare tube. After belief revision, the environment state remains unchanged but Rosie's internal state becomes $l_1 = (\{\neg w, c, s, \neg b_3\}, i_0)$. This time $\mathcal{M}$ tells her to act, because the newly visible CRT is worse than the one she is carrying with her. She acts, $A(l_1) = \alpha_o$ by replacing the CRT and the situation becomes:

$$e_2 = \{\neg w, \neg c, s\}$$
$$l_2 = (\{\neg w, \neg c, s, \neg b_3\}, \emptyset)$$

The complete run for Scenario Three is thus:

$$r_3 : g_0 \xrightarrow{a_v} g_1 \xrightarrow{a_o} g_2$$

4.4 Scenario Four

In Scenario Four, Rosie arrives at the VDU to again find a spare CRT sitting by the terminal, and this time notes that the spare is superior to the tube she brought with her. Her meta-level control mechanism therefore realises that there is considerable advantage to seeing if the new tube can be used since the saving in the cost of the tube is greater than the cost of deliberation. So she chooses to deliberate. Deliberation results in the adoption of the intention to use the new tube, and Rosie then replaces the CRT in line with this new intention. This scenario is almost the same as the third, except that this time the "new" CRT is superior to the one that Rosie brings with her. Thus the initial situation is:

$$e_0 = \{\neg w, c, s\}$$
$$l_0 = (\{\neg w, c, \neg s, b_3\}, \{i_v\})$$

After moving to the VDU and revising beliefs, the environment is unchanged ($e_1 = e_0$) but Rosie's internal state is $l_1 = (\{\neg w, c, s, b_3\}, \{i_0\})$. This time $\mathcal{M}(l_1) = d$ and $\mathcal{D}(l_1) = \{i_a\}$. After this, the environment state again remains unchanged but Rosie's internal state is $l_2 = (\{\neg w, c, s, b_3\}, \{i_a\})$, and Rosie proceeds to act $\mathcal{A}(l_2) = \alpha_a$ giving the following global state:

$$e_3 = \{\neg w, \neg c, s\}$$
$$l_3 = (\{\neg w, \neg c, s, b_3\}, \emptyset)$$

The complete run for Scenario Four is thus:

$$r_1 : g_0 \xrightarrow{a_v} g_1 \xrightarrow{d} g_2 \xrightarrow{a_a} g_3$$

There are several points to note about this example. The first is that both $\mathcal{M}$ and $\mathcal{D}$ are optimal for the cases given. There is no set of actions which could be chosen to give a better result. The second is that it is easy to alter the example so that Rosie is not optimal. Consider what would happen in Scenario Four if she had no means of using the additional CRT (which would mean that there was no intention i_a, or, worse no action α_a for achieving i_a). $\mathcal{M}$ would choose to deliberate since the CRT is superior, but either this deliberation would not change the intentions (if there was no i_a), or when Rosie came to act on the changed intention, she would be unable to achieve that intention and would have to revert to i_o. The final point to note is that it is this consideration of intentions and actions which justifies our assumption that the time cost of $\mathcal{M}$ is less than that of $\mathcal{D}$. Deliberation will typically involve an expensive activity such as building and evaluating the quality of plans to achieve some set of alternative intentions. Although that activity might be as simple as looking to see if there is some alternative intention which can be adopted, as here, it is still an overhead.

5 Generalised Meta-Level Reasoning

In this section, we will sketch out how an agent might use *higher-order* meta-level control strategies in its architecture, and what role such strategies might play. What do we mean by a higher-order meta-level control function? Let us refer to the meta-level control strategies as described above as *first-order* meta-level strategies. Such strategies merely choose whether to deliberate or to act. A *second-order* meta-level control function can be thought of as *selecting* which first-order meta-level control function to use. For example, a second-order meta-level control function might examine the agent's beliefs to see how dynamic the agent's environment is. If it determines that the environment is highly dynamic (i.e., the rate of world change is high [6]), then it might select a cautious first-order meta-level control function — one which frequently causes the agent to deliberate. If, in contrast, the environment is relatively static (the rate of world change is low), then it might select a *bold* meta-level control function (one that favours action over deliberation).

It is easy to imagine an agent with a "tower" of such meta-level control strategies, with nth-order function selecting which function to use at level $n - 1$. The idea is very similar to the use of meta-language hierarchies in meta-logic [8, 14].

We can incorporate such higher-order meta-level reasoning into our formal model with ease. First, let $MLC_1 = L \to C$ be the set of all *first-order* meta-level control strategies. These are the meta-level control strategies that we discussed above. Then define $MLC_u = L \to MLC_{u-1}$, for all $u \in I\!N$ such that $u > 1$. Thus MLC_2 is the set of all second-order meta-level control strategies, MLC_3 is the set of all third-order meta-level control strategies, and so on. An agent becomes a 5-tuple, $(\mathcal{M}_n, \mathcal{D}, \mathcal{A}, \mathcal{N}, l_0)$, where $\mathcal{M}_n$ is an nth order meta-level control function and the agent's other components are as before. Given this, we can redefine what it means for a run to represent a history of an agent in an environment. Formally, an infinite sequence $(g_0, g_1, g_2, \ldots)$ over G represents a run of an agent $Ag = (\mathcal{M}_n, \mathcal{D}, \mathcal{A}, \mathcal{N}, l_0)$ in an environment $Env = (E, \tau, e_0)$ iff $g_0 = (e_0, l_0)$ and $\forall u \in I\!N$, we have

$$
g_{u+1} = \begin{cases} (e_u, (\mathcal{N}(e_u, b_{l_u}), \mathcal{D}(l_u))) & \text{if } \mathcal{M}_n(l_u) \overbrace{(l_u) \cdots (l_u)}^{n-1 \text{ times}} = d \\ (\tau(e_u, \mathcal{A}(i_{l_u})), (\mathcal{N}(e_u, b_{l_u}), i_{l_u})) & \text{if } \mathcal{M}_n(l_u) \underbrace{(l_u) \cdots (l_u)}_{n-1 \text{ times}} = a. \end{cases}
$$

Notice that agents which make use of higher-order meta-level control are strictly speaking no more powerful than "ordinary" agents, as defined earlier. For every higher-order agent there is an "ordinary" agent that behaves in exactly the same way. The point is that from the point of view of an agent designer, it may make sense to divide the functionality of the agent up into different levels of meta-reasoning.

6 Conclusions

In this paper, we have investigated the relationship between the deliberation, action, and meta-level control components of a practical reasoning architecture. While this relationship has previously been investigated from an experimental perspective (particularly by Kinny [6]), we have in contrast attempted a formal analysis. We have demonstrated how it is possible to construct a simple but, we argue, realistic model of practical reasoning agents of the type investigated by Kinny and Georgeff, and we have established some basic properties of such agents when placed in different types of task environment. We have focussed in particular on real-time task environments, since these are, we believe, the most common class of real-world task environment that one encounters. Our work, which attempts an (admittedly preliminary) formal analysis of the relationship between agent and environment, is similar in spirit to that of [7].

This work was originally instigated in an attempt to relate the work of Russell and Subramanian on bounded-optimal agents (i.e., agents that perform as well as any agent can do under certain architectural constraints [12]) to the increasingly large literature on BDI agents [5, 2, 10, 13]. While this initial investigation led us into some areas we had not initially anticipated visiting, we believe that investigating the implications of bounded-optimal agents for BDI model will be an interesting research issue, and one that we hope to investigate in future work. Another issue that we hope to consider is the moving from individual agents to multi-agent systems.

Acknowledgments. This paper has benefited enormously from comments by Rogier van Eijk, Koen Hindriks, Jörg Müller, Tim Norman, Barney Pell, and Martha Pollack.

References

1. M. E. Bratman. *Intentions, Plans, and Practical Reason.* Harvard University Press: Cambridge, MA, 1987.
2. M. E. Bratman, D. J. Israel, and M. E. Pollack. Plans and resource-bounded practical reasoning. *Computational Intelligence,* 4:349–355, 1988.
3. P. R. Cohen and H. J. Levesque. Intention is choice with commitment. *Artificial Intelligence,* 42:213–261, 1990.
4. R. Fagin, J. Y. Halpern, Y. Moses, and M. Y. Vardi. *Reasoning About Knowledge.* The MIT Press: Cambridge, MA, 1995.
5. M. P. Georgeff and A. L. Lansky. Reactive reasoning and planning. In *Proceedings of the Sixth National Conference on Artificial Intelligence (AAAI-87),* pages 677–682, Seattle, WA, 1987.
6. D. Kinny and M. Georgeff. Commitment and effectiveness of situated agents. In *Proceedings of the Twelfth International Joint Conference on Artificial Intelligence (IJCAI-91),* pages 82–88, Sydney, Australia, 1991.
7. J. P. Müller. The right agent (architecture) to do the right thing. In J. P. Müller, M. P. Singh, and A. S. Rao, editors, *Intelligent Agents V — Proceedings of the Fifth International Workshop on Agent Theories, Architectures, and Languages (ATAL-98),* Lecture Notes in Artificial Intelligence. Springer-Verlag, Heidelberg, 1999. In this volume.
8. D. Perlis. Meta in logic. In P. Maes and D. Nardi, editors, *Meta-Level Architectures and Reflection,* pages 37–49. Elsevier Science Publishers B.V.: Amsterdam, The Netherlands, 1988.
9. M. E. Pollack and M. Ringuette. Introducing the Tileworld: Experimentally evaluating agent architectures. In *Proceedings of the Eighth National Conference on Artificial Intelligence (AAAI-90),* pages 183–189, Boston, MA, 1990.
10. A. S. Rao and M. Georgeff. Decision procedures of BDI logics. *Journal of Logic and Computation,* 8(3):293–344, 1998.
11. S. Russell and P. Norvig. *Artificial Intelligence: A Modern Approach.* Prentice-Hall, 1995.
12. S. Russell and D. Subramanian. Provably bounded-optimal agents. *Journal of AI Research,* 2:575–609, 1995.
13. K. Schild. On the relationship between BDI logics and standard logics of concurrency. In J. P. Müller, M. P. Singh, and A. S. Rao, editors, *Intelligent Agents V — Proceedings of the Fifth International Workshop on Agent Theories, Architectures, and Languages (ATAL-98),* Lecture Notes in Artificial Intelligence. Springer-Verlag, Heidelberg, 1999. In this volume.
14. R. Turner. *Truth and Modality for Knowledge Representation.* Pitman Publishing: London, 1990.
15. M. Wooldridge and N. R. Jennings. Intelligent agents: Theory and practice. *The Knowledge Engineering Review,* 10(2):115–152, 1995.

Making SharedPlans More Concise and Easier to Reason About*

Luke Hunsberger
luke@eecs.harvard.edu

Harvard University
Cambridge, MA USA

Abstract. SharedPlans is a general theory of collaborative planning that accommodates multi-level action decomposition hierarchies and explicates the process of expanding partial plans into full plans [5, 6]. This paper presents a reformulation of SharedPlans that simplifies the Shared-Plans definitions without sacrificing their expressiveness, and enables the specification of conditions under which a set of important theorems about agents and their SharedPlans may be proven to hold. A representative set of such theorems is presented.

1 Introduction

"Collaboration must be designed into systems from the start; it cannot be patched on." [4]

"Simply fitting individual agents with precomputed coordination plans will not do, for their inflexibility can cause severe failures in teamwork."[12]

When a group of agents get together to work on some complex group action, whether it be a group of helicopter agents embarking on a scouting mission [12] or a group of people making dinner [5], collaboration does not just happen. It requires the existence or formation of mutual beliefs about the capabilities and commitments of the agents involved, the adoption by individual agents of various intentions (not only *intentions-to* do various actions, but also *intentions-that* certain propositions hold), and a variety of group decision-making and planning processes. Grosz and Kraus's SharedPlans [5, 6] is a general theory of collaborative planning that requires no notion of irreducible joint intentions, accommodates multi-level action decomposition hierarchies, models the collaborative support provided by group members to those agents or subgroups responsible for doing constituent actions, specifies what it means for a group of agents to have a *partial* plan, and explicates the process of elaborating a partial plan into a full plan. Recent implementations of SharedPlans include a collaborative interface agent for an air travel application [10] and a collaborative multi-agent

---

* The author thanks Barbara J. Grosz for her invaluable guidance during the preparation of this paper. This research has been supported by National Science Foundation grants IRI 95-25915, IRI-9618848 and CDA-94-01024.

system for electronic commerce [7]. In addition, to test, evaluate and improve the theory, the author is currently developing an agent architecture that follows the SharedPlans specifications.

In SharedPlans, the plans of individual agents and groups of agents are modelled by *meta-predicates* that is, abbreviations for complex logical expressions involving predicates and the following modal operators.

Operator	Instantiation	Interpretation
Bel	$Bel(G, \phi)$	Agent G believes proposition ϕ.
Int.To	$Int.To(G, A)$	Agent G intends to do action A.
Int.Th	$Int.Th(G, \phi)$	Agent G intends that proposition ϕ hold.
MB	$MB(GR, \phi)$	Group GR mutually believe proposition ϕ.

In the original formulation, henceforth called V_1 (for *Version 1*), the meta-predicate definitions use existential quantification to refer to various agents, subgroups and actions involved in a plan, thereby making it difficult to reason about such things as the conditions under which a group's mutual belief that they have a SharedPlan entails that they do in fact have such a plan.[2] This paper presents a reformulation of SharedPlans, henceforth called V_2, that simplifies and reorganizes the meta-predicate definitions without sacrificing their expressiveness, and enables the specification of knowledge conditions under which a set of important theorems about agents and their SharedPlans may be proven.[3] This paper thus represents a step in the direction of making SharedPlans more practical to implement and reason about, not only for the agents themselves, but also for theorists studying the agents.

V_1 is reviewed in Section 2; V_2 is presented in Section 3; sample theorems and their proofs are given in Section 4; related work is discussed in Section 5; and concluding remarks are given in Section 6.

2   The Original Formulation of SharedPlans: V_1

2.1   Actions and Recipes in V_1

In V_1, actions are either *basic* or *complex*. A basic action is a single-agent action that is treated as atomic and, under certain conditions, is assumed to be executable at will. A complex action may be a single-agent or multi-agent action and is treated as decomposable. A *recipe* for a complex action, A, is a set of actions, $\{A_1, \ldots, A_n\}$, and constraints, $\{\rho_1, \ldots, \rho_m\}$, such that the doing of those actions under those constraints constitutes the doing of A. A *partial* recipe is a set of actions and constraints that can be expanded into a complete recipe. Multi-agent complex actions are assumed to be ultimately decomposable into single-agent

---

[2] A typical difficulty stems from the fact that $Bel(G, (\exists x)P(x))$ does not, in general, entail $(\exists x)Bel(G, P(x))$.

[3] To simplify the presentation, the case of "contracting out" actions to other agents is ignored, as are parameters not central to the discussion, such as constraints, time, and intentional context.

actions (basic or complex); single-agent complex actions are assumed to be ultimately decomposable into basic actions. Recursive decomposition gives rise to an *action decomposition hierarchy*. An action decomposition hierarchy is called complete if (1) the decomposition of each action in the hierarchy corresponds to a complete recipe, and (2) all leaf actions are basic actions.

2.2 Intention-To and Individual Plans in V_1

The modal operator $Int.To$ models the intention of an agent G to do a single-agent action A. If A is basic, then G intending to do A requires that G believe it is able to execute A and that G be committed to doing so:

$$Basic(A) \wedge Int.To(G, A) \Rightarrow Bel(G, Exec(G, A)) \wedge Commit(G, A).$$

If A is complex, then G intending to do A requires either that G have a *Full Individual Plan* (modelled by the FIP meta-predicate) for doing A or that G have a *Partial Individual Plan* (PIP) for doing A accompanied by an *associate* plan for elaborating its partial plan into a full plan:[4]

$$Complex(A) \wedge Int.To(G, A) \Rightarrow FIP \otimes (PIP \wedge FIP^{Elab}).[5]$$

An agent G has a Full Individual Plan for doing A if: (1) G has a complete recipe for doing A, (2) G intends to do each action in that recipe, and (3) G has a subordinate FIP to do each complex action in that recipe. The requirements for a Partial Individual Plan are much weaker. G's recipe for doing A may be partial or even empty as long as G has an associate plan for extending the partial recipe into a complete recipe. In addition, G need not yet have formed intentions to do the actions comprising its partial recipe; G need only believe that it is *able* to do those actions. The ability of an agent to do a single-agent action is modelled by the *Can-Bring-About* (CBA) meta-predicate which, like $Int.To$, is defined in two parts to handle both basic and complex actions.

In the context of an individual plan, an action in the decomposition hierarchy is called *resolved* if the agent intends to do that action. Furthermore, a complex action resolved by a FIP is called *fully resolved*. Using this terminology, a full plan is characterized by a complete action decomposition hierarchy, each action of which has been resolved, the complex actions fully resolved. On the other hand, a partial plan is characterized by a possibly incomplete action decomposition hierarchy, some or all actions of which may be unresolved.

2.3 SharedPlans in V_1

V_1 provides analogous definitions for the plans of groups of *two* or more agents. A group of agents GR have a SharedPlan (SP) to do some multi-agent action, A, either by having a Full SharedPlan (FSP) to do A or by having a Partial SharedPlan (PSP) to do A accompanied by an associate plan to elaborate the partial plan into a full plan: $SP \Rightarrow FSP \otimes (PSP \wedge FSP^{Elab})$.

---

[4] Such associate plans are required to be FIPs to avoid problems of infinite recursion.

[5] The arguments of FIP and PIP have been omitted to simplify the presentation.

Unlike *Int.To*, the *SP* meta-predicate is not a modal operator. A SharedPlan is reducible to the individual plans, beliefs and intentions of the various group members; it does not correspond to any sort of irreducible joint intention.

In the context of a SharedPlan, a single-agent action A_i in the decomposition hierarchy is called resolved if: (1) an agent G_i has been selected to do A_i, (2) G_i intends to do A_i, and (3) the other members of the group have a set of supportive mutual beliefs and intentions-that G_i succeed.[6] Similarly, a multi-agent action A_j is called resolved if: (1) a subgroup GR_j has been selected to do A_j, (2) GR_j has a SharedPlan to do A_j, and (3) the other members of the group have a set of supportive mutual beliefs and intentions-that GR_j succeed. As with Individual Plans, a complex action resolved by a full plan (whether a *FIP* or a *FSP*) is called fully resolved. Thus, a Full SharedPlan is characterized by a complete action decomposition hierarchy, each action of which has been fully resolved, while a Partial SharedPlan is characterized by a possibly incomplete action decomposition hierarchy, some or all actions of which may be unresolved. (Incidentally, if a complex action in a partial plan is itself resolved by a mere partial plan, the recipe associated with that action may be only partial or even empty.) To elaborate a partial plan into a full plan, for each complex action in the decomposition hierarchy, the agent or group selected to work on that action must select (perhaps incrementally) a recipe for doing that action and, for each action in that recipe, must select an agent or subgroup that is able to do it. The ability of a group to do a multi-agent action is modelled by the *Can-Bring-About-Group* (*CBAG*) meta-predicate.

The following chart illustrates the coverage of the V_1 meta-predicates and the *Int.To* modal operator.

V_1	Basic Actions	*Int.To*	---	---	*CBA*
	Single-Agent Complex Actions		*FIP*	*PIP*	
	Multi-Agent Actions (≥ 2 agents)	*SP*	*FSP*	*PSP*	*CBAG*

3 The Reformulation of SharedPlans: V_2

3.1 Actions and Plans in V_2

In V_2, for complex actions, the distinction between single-agent and multi-agent actions is deemphasized. Instead, single-agent groups are allowed and an Individual Plan is simply a SharedPlan of a single-agent group. In addition, the V_2 definitions of *SP*, *FSP*, *PSP* and *CBAG* are made more concise than their V_1 counterparts through the selective use of a new meta-predicate, *Basic-Can-Bring-About* (*B.CBA*), and a new modal operator, *Basic-Intention-To* (*B.Int.To*), defined by those portions of the V_1 definitions of *CBA* and *Int.To* that deal with basic actions. The following chart illustrates the coverage of the V_2 meta-predicates and the *B.Int.To* modal operator.

| V_2 | Basic Actions | *B.Int.To* | --- | --- | *B.CBA* |
| | Complex Actions (≥ 1 agents) | *SP* | *FSP* | *PSP* | *CBAG* |

---

[6] The properties of *intentions-that* are discussed in detail by Grosz & Kraus [6].

3.2 Plan Trees in V_2

In the process of constructing a SharedPlan, various agents and subgroups may make numerous planning decisions (e.g., selecting recipes and assigning agents to actions) in a distributed fashion and at every level of the evolving action decomposition hierarchy. In V_1, even decisions that have already been made, such as those concerning the elements of a full plan, are modelled implicitly using existential quantification. In V_2, SharedPlan Trees (SPTs) are used to explicitly represent the choices already made by a group working on some SharedPlan. Each node of an SPT corresponds to an action in the incrementally-selected and possibly incomplete action decomposition hierarchy and is explicitly classified according to whether that action is basic or complex, and resolved or unresolved (*vis à vis* the plan). Thus, there are four types of nodes, as summarized below:

Node Type	Node Representation	Action Characteristics	
β	$\langle I_\beta, G_\beta, A_\beta \rangle$	basic	resolved
κ	$\langle I_\kappa, GR_\kappa, A_\kappa \rangle$	complex	resolved
ϵ	$\langle I_\epsilon, A_\epsilon \rangle$	basic	unresolved
μ	$\langle I_\mu, A_\mu \rangle$	complex	unresolved

where $I_\beta, I_\kappa, I_\epsilon$ and I_μ are unique identifiers; $A_\beta, A_\kappa, A_\epsilon$ and A_μ are actions; G_β is an agent (nominally the agent selected to do the action, A_β); and GR_κ is a group of agents (nominally the subgroup selected to do the action, A_κ). All identifiers, agent names and action names are assumed to be rigid designators.

In a SharedPlan Tree, only κ nodes may have child nodes but these child nodes may be of any of the four types. The set of β child nodes of a given node are termed its βset. Similarly, the sets of κ, ϵ and μ child nodes of a given node are termed its κset, its ϵset, and its μset, respectively.

Because all actions involved in a full plan are, by definition, resolved, a Full Plan Tree (FPT) has only β and κ nodes. Partial plans, however, may have unresolved actions and hence a Partial Plan Tree (PFT) may have nodes of any of the four types. In addition, partial plans typically have a variety of associate plans corresponding to complex planning actions, such as selecting a recipe (*SelRec*), elaborating a partial plan into a full plan (*Elab*), or selecting an agent or subgroup to do some action (*SelAgt* or *SelSgr*). Thus, each node in a Partial Plan Tree may have one or more additional plan trees associated with it as summarized below.

Node Type	Type of Associate Plan	Functional Notation for Corresponding Plan Tree	Abbreviation for Plan Tree
κ	Elaborate	$ElabPT(\langle I_\kappa, GR_\kappa, A_\kappa \rangle)$	PT_κ^{Elab}
	Select Recipe	$SelRecPT(\langle I_\kappa, GR_\kappa, A_\kappa \rangle)$	PT_κ^{SelRec}
ϵ	Select Agent	$SelAgtPT(\langle I_\epsilon, A_\epsilon \rangle)$	PT_ϵ^{SelAgt}
μ	Select Subgroup	$SelSgrPT(\langle I_\mu, A_\mu \rangle)$	PT_μ^{SelSgr}

Definition. Given some κ node, $N = \langle I, GR, A \rangle$, the **SharedPlan Tree** (or subtree) rooted at N is a 7-tuple:

$$\langle N, \beta set, \kappa set, \epsilon set, \mu set, ElabPT, SelRecPT \rangle,$$

where βset, κset, ϵset and μset are sets of β, κ, ϵ and μ nodes, respectively, such that for each $\langle I_\kappa, GR_\kappa, A_\kappa \rangle$ in κset, the object given by $PlanTree(\langle I_\kappa, GR_\kappa, A_\kappa \rangle)$, abbreviated as PT_κ, is itself a SharedPlan Tree. In a **Full Plan Tree**, $ElabPT$ and $SelRecPT$ are NIL, ϵset and μset are empty, and each PT_κ is itself a Full Plan Tree. In a **Partial Plan Tree**, $ElabPT$ is a Full Plan Tree (and hence not NIL) and $SelRecPT$ is either NIL or a Full Plan Tree.

3.3 V_2 Definitions

V_2 definitions of $B.CBA$, $B.Int.To$, $CBAG$, SP, FSP and PSP are given in Figs. 1 and 2. The definitions of $B.CBA$ and $B.Int.To$ are simply those portions of the V_1 definitions of CBA and $Int.To$ that deal with basic actions. The V_2 definitions of $CBAG$, SP, FSP and PSP are generalizations of their V_1 counterparts in that they allow for single-agent groups. Thus, in V_2 there is no need for a separate set of meta-predicates to handle single-agent plans. The V_2 definitions of $CBAG$, FSP, PSP and SP also differ from their V_1 counterparts in that each takes an explicit plan tree,

$$PT_\alpha = \langle \langle I_\alpha, GR_\alpha, A_\alpha \rangle, \beta set_\alpha, \kappa set_\alpha, \epsilon set_\alpha, \mu set_\alpha, PT_\alpha^{Elab}, PT_\alpha^{SelRec} \rangle,$$

as its only argument. For brevity, the symbol PT_α is used instead of the 7-tuple; but it should be kept in mind that the 7-tuple is the actual argument. For example, $FSP(PT_\alpha)$ represents that the group GR_α has a Full SharedPlan to do the action A_α using the plan tree PT_α.[7]

The V_2 definitions of FSP and PSP are given in terms of subsidiary meta-predicates to distinguish the top-level and recursive portions of the definitions. Making this distinction reflects a fundamental tenet of SharedPlans, namely, that while the entire group needs to be directly involved in the topmost level of a plan, only the agents selected to do a given subaction need to be directly involved in the corresponding subplan. Making this distinction also enables precise specification of the knowledge conditions and mutual beliefs needed for the theorems presented in Section 4.

$FSP.Top$ and $PSP.Top$ model the top-level (or non-recursive portion) of a SharedPlan. As such, their specifications are restricted to the top level of the plan tree (i.e., the root node and its immediate children). For example, they specify various intentions and mutual beliefs pertaining to the immediate children of the root node; but they do not specify, directly or indirectly, anything pertaining to nodes further down in the tree. $FSP.Rec$ and $PSP.Rec$, on the other hand, encapsulate the recursive portions of the FSP and PSP definitions. As such,

---

[7] In cases where it is desirable to explicitly indicate the group and possibly the action involved, they are included as parameters of the plan tree symbol, as in the fragments, $FSP(PT_\kappa(GR_\kappa))$ and $(\exists PT)FSP(PT(GR_\kappa, A_\kappa))$, from the FSP definition.

(Basic) Can-Bring-About

$B.CBA(G, A) \equiv$

   $Basic(A)$
   $\wedge$
   $Exec(G, A)$

(Basic) Intention-To

$B.Int.To(G, A) \equiv$

   $Bel(G, B.CBA(G, A))$
   $\wedge$
   $Commit(G, A)$

SharedPlan

$SP(PT_\alpha) \equiv$

   $FSP(PT_\alpha) \otimes PSP(PT_\alpha)$

Can-Bring-About (Group)

$CBAG(PT_\alpha) \equiv$

   $PT_\alpha^{Elab} = PT_\alpha^{SelRec} = \text{NIL}$
   $\wedge$
   $\epsilon set_\alpha = \mu set_\alpha = \emptyset$
   $\wedge$
   $Top(PT_\alpha) \in Recipes(A_\alpha)$
   $\wedge$
   $(\forall \langle I_\beta, G_\beta, A_\beta \rangle \in \beta set_\alpha)$
    $G_\beta \in GR_\alpha$
    $\wedge$
    $B.CBA(G_\beta, A_\beta)$
   $\wedge$
   $(\forall \langle I_\kappa, GR_\kappa, A_\kappa \rangle \in \kappa set_\alpha)$
    $GR_\kappa \subseteq GR_\alpha$
    $\wedge$
    $CBAG(PT_\kappa(GR_\kappa))$

Full SharedPlan

$FSP(PT_\alpha) \equiv FSP.Top(PT_\alpha) \wedge FSP.Rec(PT_\alpha),$
where

  Full SharedPlan: Top-Level Portion

  $FSP.Top(PT_\alpha) \equiv F_1 \wedge F_2 \wedge F_3 \wedge F_4 \wedge F_5 \wedge F_6 \wedge F_\beta \wedge F_\kappa$
  where
    $F_1 \equiv (PT_\alpha^{Elab} = \text{NIL})$
    $F_2 \equiv (PT_\alpha^{SelRec} = \text{NIL})$
    $F_3 \equiv (\epsilon set_\alpha = \emptyset)$
    $F_4 \equiv (\mu set_\alpha = \emptyset)$
    $F_5 \equiv MB_\alpha((\forall G \in GR_\alpha)Int.Th(G, Do(GR_\alpha, A_\alpha)))$
    $F_6 \equiv MB_\alpha(Top(PT_\alpha) \in Recipes(A_\alpha))$
    $F_\beta \equiv (\forall \langle I_\beta, G_\beta, A_\beta \rangle \in \beta set_\alpha)F_{\beta_0} \wedge F_{\beta_1} \wedge F_{\beta_2} \wedge F_{\beta_3}$
    $F_\kappa \equiv (\forall \langle I_\kappa, GR_\kappa, A_\kappa \rangle \in \kappa set_\alpha)F_{\kappa_0} \wedge F_{\kappa_2} \wedge F_{\kappa_3}$
    where
      $F_{\beta_0} \equiv G_\beta \in GR_\alpha$
      $F_{\beta_1} \equiv B.Int.To(G_\beta, A_\beta)$
      $F_{\beta_2} \equiv MB_\alpha(B.Int.To(G_\beta, A_\beta) \wedge B.CBA(G_\beta, A_\beta))$
      $F_{\beta_3} \equiv MB_\alpha((\forall G \in GR_\alpha, G \neq G_\beta)Int.Th(G, B.CBA(G_\beta, A_\beta)))$
      and
      $F_{\kappa_0} \equiv GR_\kappa \subseteq GR_\alpha$
      $F_{\kappa_2} \equiv MB_\alpha((\exists PT)FSP(PT(GR_\kappa, A_\kappa)) \wedge CBAG(PT(GR_\kappa, A_\kappa)))$
      $F_{\kappa_3} \equiv MB_\alpha((\forall G \in GR_\alpha, G \notin GR_\kappa)$
          $Int.Th(G, (\exists PT)CBAG(PT(GR_\kappa, A_\kappa))))$

  Full SharedPlan: Recursive Portion
  $FSP.Rec(PT_\alpha) \equiv (\forall \langle I_\kappa, GR_\kappa, A_\kappa \rangle \in \kappa set_\alpha)FSP(PT_\kappa(GR_\kappa))$

Fig. 1. V_2 definitions of $B.CBA, B.Int.To, CBAG, SP$ and FSP

Partial SharedPlan

$PSP(PT_\alpha) \equiv PSP.Top(PT_\alpha) \land PSP.Rec(PT_\alpha),$

where

Partial SharedPlan: Top-Level Portion

$PSP.Top(PT_\alpha) \equiv P_1 \land P_2 \land P_3 \land P_4 \land P_5 \land P_\beta \land P_\kappa \land P_\epsilon \land P_\mu$

where

$\quad P_1 \equiv (PT_\alpha^{Elab} \neq \text{NIL})$

$\quad P_2 \equiv FSP(GR_\alpha, Elab(GR_\alpha, A_\alpha, Top(PT_\alpha)), PT_\alpha^{Elab})$

$\quad P_3 \equiv (PT_\alpha^{SelRec} = \text{NIL}) \Rightarrow MB_\alpha(Top(PT_\alpha) \in Recipes(A_\alpha))$

$$P_4 \equiv (PT_\alpha^{SelRec} \neq \text{NIL}) \Rightarrow \begin{cases} MB_\alpha((\exists PT)((Top(PT_\alpha) \subset Top(PT)) \\ \qquad\qquad \land CBAG(PT(GR_\alpha, A_\alpha)))) \\ \land \\ FSP(GR_\alpha, SelRec(GR_\alpha, A_\alpha, Top(PT_\alpha)), \\ \qquad\qquad PT_\alpha^{SelRec}) \end{cases}$$

$\quad P_5 \equiv MB_\alpha((\forall G \in GR_\alpha)Int.Th(G, Do(GR_\alpha, A_\alpha)))$

$\quad P_\beta \equiv (\forall \langle I_\beta, G_\beta, A_\beta \rangle \in \beta set_\alpha)F_{\beta_0} \land F_{\beta_1} \land P_{\beta_{2.1}} \land P_{\beta_{2.2}} \land F_{\beta_3}$

$\quad P_\kappa \equiv (\forall \langle I_\kappa, GR_\kappa, A_\kappa \rangle \in \kappa set_\alpha)F_{\kappa_0} \land P_{\kappa_{2.1}} \land P_{\kappa_{2.2}} \land F_{\kappa_3}$

$\quad P_\epsilon \equiv (\forall \langle I_\epsilon, A_\epsilon \rangle \in \epsilon set_\alpha)P_{\epsilon_1} \land P_{\epsilon_2}$

$\quad P_\mu \equiv (\forall \langle I_\mu, A_\mu \rangle \in \mu set_\alpha)P_{\mu_1} \land P_{\mu_2}$

where

$\quad F_{\beta_0}, F_{\beta_1}, F_{\beta_3}, F_{\kappa_0}$ and F_{κ_3} are as in the FSP definition

and

$\quad P_{\beta_{2.1}} \equiv MB_\alpha(B.Int.To(G_\beta, A_\beta))$

$\quad P_{\beta_{2.2}} \equiv (\forall G \in GR_\alpha)Int.Th(G, MB_\alpha(B.CBA(G_\beta, A_\beta)))$

$\quad P_{\kappa_{2.1}} \equiv MB_\alpha((\exists PT)SP(PT(GR_\kappa, A_\kappa)))$

$\quad P_{\kappa_{2.2}} \equiv (\forall G \in GR_\alpha)Int.Th(G, MB_\alpha((\exists PT)CBAG(PT(GR_\kappa, A_\kappa))))$

$\quad P_{\epsilon_1} \equiv MB_\alpha((\exists G \in GR_\alpha)B.CBA(G, A_\epsilon))$

$\quad P_{\epsilon_2} \equiv FSP(GR_\alpha, SelAgt(GR_\alpha, A_\epsilon), PT_\epsilon^{SelAgt})$

$\quad P_{\mu_1} \equiv MB_\alpha((\exists GR \subseteq GR_\alpha, PT)CBAG(PT(GR, A_\mu)))$

$\quad P_{\mu_2} \equiv FSP(GR_\alpha, SelSgr(GR_\alpha, A_\mu), PT_\mu^{SelSgr})$

Partial SharedPlan: Recursive Portion

$PSP.Rec(PT_\alpha) \equiv (\forall \langle I_\kappa, GR_\kappa, A_\kappa \rangle \in \kappa set_\alpha)SP(PT_\kappa(GR_\kappa))$

Fig. 2. V_2 definition of PSP

their specifications refer to the plan subtrees rooted at the κ children of the root node. For example, $FSP.Rec$ requires that the subgroup selected to do the action corresponding to a κ child of the root node have a Full SharedPlan using the plan subtree rooted at that node.

In the V_2 definitions, clauses of the form $MB(GR_\alpha, \phi)$ appear so frequently that they are abbreviated as $MB_\alpha(\phi)$. In addition, the $CBAG$, FSP and PSP definitions refer to $Top(PT_\alpha)$ which denotes the set of actions in the top-level decomposition of PT_α. For example, $Top(PT_\alpha) \in Recipes(A_\alpha)$ represents that the top-level decomposition of A_α in the plan tree PT_α is a (complete) recipe for doing A_α. Finally, the V_1 requirement that a PSP be accompanied by an Elab FSP has been folded into the V_2 definition of PSP in clause P_2.

4   Theorems about Agents and Their SharedPlans

Under what knowledge conditions does an agent's belief that it has, say, a Full Individual Plan (*FIP*) entail that it does in fact have such a plan? In other words, what conditions would ensure that $Bel(G, FIP(G, \alpha, R_\alpha))$ entails $FIP(G, \alpha, R_\alpha)$, for some agent G, some action α, and some recipe R_α? The existential quantification in the V_1 meta-predicate definitions makes questions such as these difficult to answer. For example, in the above case, knowledge conditions might be sought such that the following holds:

$$Bel(G, (\exists R_\delta) FIP(G, \delta, R_\delta)) \models (\exists R_\delta) Bel(G, FIP(G, \delta, R_\delta)),$$

where δ is an action in the recipe R_α. But existential quantifiers may not, in general, be extracted from the scope of modal belief operators.

In V_2, the use of explicit plan trees as arguments in the various meta-predicate definitions eliminates such problems and allows a number of important theorems about agents and their SharedPlans to be formulated and proven. The theorems specify sets of knowledge conditions and sets of mutual beliefs such that under those knowledge conditions the agents have a SharedPlan if (or only if) they hold the specified mutual beliefs. For each action, A, in the decomposition hierarchy, the knowledge conditions stipulate that only those agents selected to work on A need know the top-level contents of the plan subtree associated with A. Similarly, only those agents selected to work on A need participate in the mutual beliefs about whether or not they satisfy the top-level requirements of a SharedPlan. For the theorems pertaining to full plans, the sets of knowledge conditions and mutual beliefs are completely specified and detailed proofs are given. For the theorems pertaining to partial plans and SharedPlans in general, space limitations preclude such a full treatment. Thus, these theorems are simply stated along with brief sketches of the issues involved in their proofs.

Before presenting the theorems, some background assumptions about the belief and mutual belief modal operators are given that lead to preliminary results used throughout the rest of this section. In addition, some assumptions about actions, commitments and intentions-that are made. In all that follows, all free variables are implicitly universally quantified and plan trees are assumed to have finite depth.

4.1   Background Assumptions and Preliminary Results

Bel, the modal belief operator, is assumed to satisfy the standard $KD45$ and necessitation axioms [3]. MB, the modal operator for mutual belief, is assumed to cover arbitrary nestings of *Bel*. Consequently, the following preliminary results are valid for arbitrary propositions ϕ and ψ.

(P1) $Bel(G, \phi \wedge \psi) \Leftrightarrow Bel(G, \phi) \wedge Bel(G, \psi)$
(P2) $Bel(G, Bel(G, \phi)) \Leftrightarrow Bel(G, \phi)$
(P3) $MB(GR, \phi \wedge \psi) \Leftrightarrow MB(GR, \phi) \wedge MB(GR, \psi)$
(P4) $MB(GR, MB(GR, \phi)) \Leftrightarrow MB(GR, \phi)$

Next, it is assumed that the universe of nodes is fixed. As a result, when the variable of quantification ranges over nodes, both the Barcan formula (B2) and its converse (B1), given below, are valid [3].

(B1) $Bel(G, (\forall x)P(x)) \Rightarrow (\forall x)Bel(G, P(x))$
(B2) $(\forall x)Bel(G, P(x)) \Rightarrow Bel(G, (\forall x)P(x))$

By providing appropriate knowledge conditions, these formulas may be extended to cover the case of the relativized universal quantifier: $(\forall x \in X)$.[8] For example, P5 below extends formula B1 using the knowledge condition K_1. K_1 requires that whenever x is in X, the agent G *believes* x is in X (i.e., G's beliefs about x being in X are *complete*). Similarly, P6 below extends formula B2 using the knowledge condition K_2. K_2 requires that G believe x is in X only when x actually is in X (i.e., G's beliefs about x being in X are *correct*).

(P5) $Bel(G, (\forall x \in X)P(x)) \wedge K_1 \models (\forall x \in X)Bel(G, P(x))$,
      where $K_1 \equiv (\forall x \in X)Bel(G, x \in X)$.

(P6) $(\forall x \in X)Bel(G, P(x)) \wedge K_2 \models Bel(G, (\forall x \in X)P(x))$,
      where $K_2 \equiv (\forall x)(Bel(G, x \in X) \Rightarrow (x \in X))$.

Furthermore, these results have mutual belief analogues, as follows.

(P7) $MB(GR, (\forall x \in X)P(x)) \wedge K_3 \models (\forall x \in X)MB(GR, P(x))$,
      where $K_3 \equiv (\forall x \in X)MB(GR, x \in X)$.

(P8) $(\forall x \in X)MB(GR, P(x)) \wedge K_4 \models MB(GR, (\forall x \in X)P(x))$,
      where $K_4 \equiv (\forall x)(MB(GR, x \in X) \Rightarrow (x \in X))$.

Finally, agents are assumed to have correct and complete beliefs about whether actions are basic or complex, and about their individual commitments to do actions and their individual intentions-that propositions hold.[9]

(A1) $Bel(G, Basic(A)) \Leftrightarrow Basic(A)$
(A2) $Bel(G, Complex(A)) \Leftrightarrow Complex(A)$
(A3) $Bel(G, Commit(G, A)) \Leftrightarrow Commit(G, A)$
(A4) $Bel(G, Int.Th(G, \phi)) \Leftrightarrow Int.Th(G, \phi)$

4.2 Theorems

Theorem 1 states that an agent G has an intention to do some basic action A if and only if G *believes* it has such an intention. Note that an analogous result does *not* hold for $B.CBA$, since an agent may be mistaken about its ability to do some basic action.

Theorem 1. $B.Int.To(G, A) \Leftrightarrow Bel(G, B.Int.To(G, A))$

---

[8] $(\forall x \in X)\psi(x)$ is an abbreviation for $(\forall x)((x \in X) \Rightarrow \psi(x))$.
[9] Assumptions A1 and A2 are made by Grosz & Kraus, assumption A3 ($\Rightarrow$) follows from Axiom 2 in V_1, and assumption A4 ($\Rightarrow$) is Axiom 3 in V_1 [5].

Proof of Theorem 1. Theorem 1 follows directly from the definition of $B.Int.To$, preliminary results P1 and P2, and assumption A3. If A3 is weakened to only a single direction of implication, then Theorem 1 must be similarly weakened. □

The rest of the theorems in this section specify the knowledge conditions sufficient to ensure that a group of agents hold a SharedPlan if (or only if) they hold a specified set of mutual beliefs. For example, Theorem 2 states that under the knowledge conditions given by $GrKnowFPT$, if a group of agents hold the set of mutual beliefs given by $RMB.FSP$, then they necessarily have a Full SharedPlan. $GrKnowFPT$ and $RMB.FSP$ are defined in Fig. 3.

Theorem 2. $RMB.FSP(PT_\alpha) \wedge GrKnowFPT(PT_\alpha) \models FSP(PT_\alpha)$

$GrKnowFPT(PT_\alpha)$ represents that the group of agents GR_α know the structure and contents of the plan tree PT_α with the caveat that for the action associated with any given κ node, only the group of agents GR_κ selected to work on that action are required to know anything about the structure and contents of the plan subtree PT_κ being used to do that action. Similarly, $RMB.FSP(PT_\alpha)$ represents that the group GR_α mutually believe that they have a Full Shared-Plan using PT_α with the caveat that for the action associated with any given κ

(Group) Know Full Plan Tree
$GrKnowFPT(PT_\alpha) \equiv GrKnowFPT.Top(PT_\alpha) \wedge GrKnowFPT.Rec(PT_\alpha),$
where

    (Group) Know-Full-Plan-Tree: Top-Level Portion
    $GrKnowFPT.Top(PT_\alpha) \equiv K_1 \wedge K_2 \wedge K_3 \wedge K_4 \wedge K_\beta \wedge K_\kappa$
    where
$$K_1 \equiv MB_\alpha(PT_\alpha^{Elab} = \text{NIL}) \Rightarrow PT_\alpha^{Elab} = \text{NIL}$$
$$K_2 \equiv MB_\alpha(PT_\alpha^{SelRec} = \text{NIL}) \Rightarrow PT_\alpha^{SelRec} = \text{NIL}$$
$$K_3 \equiv MB_\alpha(\epsilon set_\alpha = \emptyset) \Rightarrow \epsilon set_\alpha = \emptyset$$
$$K_4 \equiv MB_\alpha(\mu set_\alpha = \emptyset) \Rightarrow \mu set_\alpha = \emptyset$$
$$K_\beta \equiv \begin{cases} (\forall \langle I_\beta, G_\beta, A_\beta \rangle \in \beta set_\alpha) MB_\alpha(\langle I_\beta, G_\beta, A_\beta \rangle \in \beta set_\alpha) \\ \wedge \\ (\forall \langle I_\beta, G_\beta, A_\beta \rangle \in \beta set_\alpha)(MB_\alpha(G_\beta \in GR_\alpha) \Rightarrow (G_\beta \in GR_\alpha)) \end{cases}$$
$$K_\kappa \equiv \begin{cases} (\forall \langle I_\kappa, GR_\kappa, A_\kappa \rangle \in \kappa set_\alpha) MB_\alpha(\langle I_\kappa, GR_\kappa, A_\kappa \rangle \in \kappa set_\alpha) \\ \wedge \\ (\forall \langle I_\kappa, GR_\kappa, A_\kappa \rangle \in \kappa set_\alpha)(MB_\alpha(GR_\kappa \subseteq GR_\alpha) \Rightarrow (GR_\kappa \subseteq GR_\alpha)) \end{cases}$$

(Group) Know-Full-Plan-Tree: Recursive Portion
$GrKnowFPT.Rec(PT_\alpha) \equiv (\forall \langle I_\kappa, GR_\kappa, A_\kappa \rangle \in \kappa set_\alpha) GrKnowFPT(PT_\kappa(GR_\kappa))$

Restricted Mutual Belief in a Full SharedPlan
$$RMB.FSP(PT_\alpha) \equiv \begin{cases} MB_\alpha(FSP.Top(PT_\alpha)) \\ \wedge \\ (\forall \langle I_\kappa, GR_\kappa, A_\kappa \rangle \in \kappa set_\alpha) RMB.FSP(PT_\kappa(GR_\kappa)) \end{cases}$$

Fig. 3. Definitions of $GrKnowFPT$ and $RMB.FSP$

node, only the agents selected to work on that action are required to participate in the mutual beliefs pertaining to the subplan for that action. More formally, the first part of the $RMB.FSP$ definition requires that the parent group GR_α mutually believe that the top level of their plan satisfies the top-level requirements of an FSP, while the second part recursively requires, for each κ node child of the root node, that the selected subgroup GR_κ holds the mutual beliefs specified by $RMB.FSP$ with respect to the plan subtree PT_κ.

If, instead of satisfying the comparatively weak requirements of $GrKnowFPT$ and $RMB.FSP$, the agents in GR_α had knowledge of the structure and contents of the *entire* plan tree PT_α and, furthermore, they mutually believed that their plan satisfied the requirements of an *FSP at every level of the action decomposition hierarchy* (i.e., $MB_\alpha(FSP(PT_\alpha))$), then the following would be entailed:[10]

$$MB_\alpha(FSP.Top(PT_\alpha))$$
$$\wedge$$
$$(\forall \langle I_\kappa, GR_\kappa, A_\kappa \rangle \in \kappa set_\alpha)MB_\alpha(FSP(PT_\kappa(GR_\kappa)))$$

The top-level portion of the above expression is identical to the top-level portion of the $RMB.FSP$ definition; but the recursive portion of the above expression is much stronger than its $RMB.FSP$ counterpart. In particular, for each κ node child of the root node, it requires that the *entire* group GR_α mutually believe that the selected subgroup GR_κ has a Full SharedPlan using the specified plan subtree PT_κ, whereas the recursive portion of $RMB.FSP$ only requires that the *subgroup* GR_κ participate in mutual beliefs pertaining to that subplan.

Proof of Theorem 2. Given the definitions of $RMB.FSP$, $GrKnowFPT$ and FSP, it suffices to show the following:

(2a) $MB_\alpha(FSP.Top(PT_\alpha)) \wedge GrKnowFPT.Top(PT_\alpha) \models FSP.Top(PT_\alpha)$

(2b) $(\forall \langle I_\kappa, GR_\kappa, A_\kappa \rangle \in \kappa set_\alpha)(RMB.FSP(PT_\kappa(GR_\kappa))$
$\qquad\qquad \wedge GrKnowFPT(PT_\kappa(GR_\kappa))) \models FSP.Rec(PT_\alpha)$

First, consider (2a), which involves only the top level of the plan tree PT_α. Since $FSP.Top(PT_\alpha)$ is the conjunction of several clauses, preliminary result P3 gives that it is sufficient to find, for each conjunct C, the knowledge condition, K, such that $MB_\alpha(C) \wedge K \models C$. The conjunction of these knowledge conditions defines $GrKnowFPT.Top(PT_\alpha)$ in Fig. 3.

For C of the form, $MB_\alpha(\phi)$, for some ϕ, no knowledge condition is necessary, since $MB_\alpha(MB_\alpha(\phi)) \models MB_\alpha(\phi)$ by preliminary result P4. For C a statement that PT_α^{Elab} or PT_α^{SelRec} is NIL, or that $eset_\alpha$ or μset_α is empty, K is given by: $MB_\alpha(C) \Rightarrow C$. (See clauses K_1 through K_4 in the $GrKnowFPT.Top$ definition.)

For C of the form, $(\forall x \in X)P(x)$, as in the F_β and F_κ clauses in the FSP definition (where X, a set of nodes, is either βset_α or κset_α), it is sufficient to show that $MB_\alpha((\forall x \in X)P(x)) \models (\forall x \in X)MB_\alpha(P(x)) \models (\forall x \in X)P(x)$.

---

[10] From the definition of FSP and preliminary results P3 and P7.

The first entailment follows from preliminary result P7, given the knowledge condition, $K' \equiv (\forall x \in X) MB_\alpha(x \in X)$. (See the first conjuncts in the K_β and K_κ clauses in the $GrKnowFPT.Top$ definition.) To get the second entailment, note that $P(x)$ is itself a conjunction: $P(x) \equiv P_1(x) \wedge \ldots \wedge P_n(x)$. Thus, by preliminary result P3, it is sufficient to find, for each conjunct $P_i(x)$, the knowledge condition $K_i(x)$ such that $(\forall x \in X)(MB_\alpha(P_i(x)) \wedge K_i(x)) \models (\forall x \in X)P_i(x)$. The knowledge condition for the second entailment is the conjunction of the individual $K_i(x)$. For $P_i(x)$ being either $(G_\beta \in GR_\alpha)$ or $(GR_\kappa \subseteq GR_\alpha)$, $K_i(x)$ is $MB_\alpha(P_i(x)) \Rightarrow P_i(x)$. (See the second conjuncts in the K_β and K_κ clauses of $GrKnowFPT.Top$.) For $P_i(x)$ being $B.Int.To(G_\beta, A_\beta)$ or $MB_\alpha(\ldots)$, no knowledge conditions are required, given Theorem 1 and preliminary result P4, respectively. This exhausts the cases for (2a). Hence, (2a) holds for any PT_α.

Next, (2b) is proved by induction on the depth of PT_α. In the base case, PT_α has depth 0 (i.e., the root node is the only node in the tree). In particular, κset_α is empty and (2b) is vacuously true. For the recursive case, assume that (2b) holds for all plan trees with depth at most k and suppose that PT_α is some plan tree with depth $k + 1$. For each κ child of the root node of PT_α, the plan subtree PT_κ rooted at that node is of depth at most k. Hence, (2b) holds for each such PT_κ. But (2a) also holds for each such PT_κ. Hence, Theorem 2 holds for each such PT_κ, which, given the definition of $FSP.Rec$, is equivalent to (2b) holding for PT_α. $\square$

Theorem 3. $RMB.PSP(PT_\alpha) \wedge GrKnowPPT(PT_\alpha) \models PSP(PT_\alpha)$

Theorem 4. $RMB.SP(PT_\alpha) \wedge GrKnowPT(PT_\alpha) \models SP(PT_\alpha)$

Theorems 3 and 4 are the PSP and SP analogues of Theorem 2. Their proofs (omitted due to space limitations) are intertwined by the presence of the clause, $(\forall \langle I_\kappa, GR_\kappa, A_\kappa \rangle \in \kappa set_\alpha) SP(PT_\kappa(GR_\kappa))$, in the definition of $PSP.Top$. (Recall that $SP \equiv FSP \otimes PSP$.) Furthermore, the presence of associate plan trees complicates the definitions of $GrKnowPPT$ and $RMB.PSP$ (definitions omitted). Nonetheless, the proof of Theorem 3 is similar to that of Theorem 2. (Since the associate plans must be full plans, they are handled by appeals to Theorem 2.) For Theorem 4, the group's knowledge of whether the $Elab$ plan tree associated with the root node is NIL or not is used to distinguish the FSP and PSP cases, followed by appeals to Theorems 2 and 3.

Theorems 2, 3 and 4 specify knowledge conditions sufficient to ensure that if a group of agents hold a specified set of mutual beliefs, then they necessarily have a SharedPlan. By altering the knowledge conditions, it is fairly straightforward to come up with theorems that are, in spirit, the converses of Theorems 2, 3 and 4.[11] For example, given slightly different knowledge conditions, having an FSP entails restricted mutual belief in that FSP (i.e., $RMB.FSP$).

---

[11] The different knowledge conditions are due in part to the proofs of these *quasi-converses* using preliminary result P8 where Theorems 2, 3 and 4 use P7.

The theorems presented so far involve the RMB meta-predicates that capture the intuitively appealing idea that only the agents working on any given action need participate in the mutual beliefs pertaining to how that action is being done. Next, some theorems are presented that restrict attention to mutual beliefs held by the entire group. The meta-predicates in these theorems are not recursive, dealing only with the top level of the plan tree. The consequents of such theorems are necessarily weaker, stipulating mutual belief in the mere *existence* of a SharedPlan rather than mutual belief in a SharedPlan using a *particular* plan tree. For example, Theorem 5 states that if the top level of a group's plan meets the requirements of $FSP.Top$ (see Fig. 1), then, given the knowledge conditions modelled by $GrKnowFPT.Top_2$, they necessarily mutually believe that they have *some* Full SharedPlan, as modelled by the $ExistsFSP$ meta-predicate.[12]

Theorem 5. $FSP.Top(PT_\alpha) \wedge GrKnowFPT.Top_2(PT_\alpha) \models MB_\alpha(ExistsFSP(PT_\alpha))$

$GrKnowFPT.Top_2$ and $ExistsFSP$ are defined in Fig. 4. $ExistsFSP$ represents that the top-level of the group's plan meets the requirements of $FSP.Top$ and, in addition, for each κ child of the root node, the selected subgroup has an FSP to do the corresponding action using *some* (existentially quantified) plan tree. Aside from the existentially quantified plan trees in the recursive clause, the definition of $ExistsFSP$ is identical to that of FSP (in Fig. 1).

(Group) Know-Full-Plan-Tree: Top-Level Portion (Version 2)

$GrKnowFPT.Top_2(PT_\alpha) \equiv K_1 \wedge K_2 \wedge K_3 \wedge K_4 \wedge K_\beta \wedge K_\kappa$, where

$K_1 \equiv (PT_\alpha^{Elab} = \text{NIL}) \Rightarrow MB_\alpha(PT_\alpha^{Elab} = \text{NIL})$

$K_2 \equiv (PT_\alpha^{SelRec} = \text{NIL}) \Rightarrow MB_\alpha(PT_\alpha^{SelRec} = \text{NIL})$

$K_3 \equiv (\epsilon set_\alpha = \emptyset) \Rightarrow MB_\alpha(\epsilon set_\alpha = \emptyset)$

$K_4 \equiv (\mu set_\alpha = \emptyset) \Rightarrow MB_\alpha(\mu set_\alpha = \emptyset)$

$$K_\beta \equiv \begin{cases} (\forall \langle I_\beta, G_\beta, A_\beta \rangle)(MB_\alpha(\langle I_\beta, G_\beta, A_\beta \rangle \in \beta set_\alpha) \Rightarrow (\langle I_\beta, G_\beta, A_\beta \rangle \in \beta set_\alpha)) \\ \wedge \\ (\forall \langle I_\beta, G_\beta, A_\beta \rangle \in \beta set_\alpha)(G_\beta \in GR_\alpha) \Rightarrow MB_\alpha(G_\beta \in GR_\alpha) \end{cases}$$

$$K_\kappa \equiv \begin{cases} (\forall \langle I_\kappa, GR_\kappa, A_\kappa \rangle) \\ \quad (MB_\alpha(\langle I_\kappa, GR_\kappa, A_\kappa \rangle \in \kappa set_\alpha) \Rightarrow (\langle I_\kappa, GR_\kappa, A_\kappa \rangle \in \kappa set_\alpha)) \\ \wedge \\ (\forall \langle I_\kappa, GR_\kappa, A_\kappa \rangle \in \kappa set_\alpha)(GR_\kappa \subseteq GR_\alpha) \Rightarrow MB_\alpha(GR_\kappa \subseteq GR_\alpha) \end{cases}$$

There Exists a Full SharedPlan

$$ExistsFSP(PT_\alpha) \equiv \begin{cases} FSP.Top(PT_\alpha) \\ \wedge \\ (\forall \langle I_\kappa, GR_\kappa, A_\kappa \rangle \in \kappa set_\alpha)(\exists PT)FSP(PT(GR_\kappa, A_\kappa)) \end{cases}$$

Fig. 4. Definitions of $GrKnowFPT.Top_2$ and $ExistsFSP$

---

[12] $ExistsFSP$ is used instead of $(\exists PT)FSP(PT(GR_\alpha, A_\alpha))$ because the latter involves second-order problems of existential quantification over an object partially defined using functions.

Proof of Theorem 5. As in the proof of Theorem 2, it is sufficient to deal with each conjunct, C, of $FSP.Top$ individually. For each such conjunct, the corresponding knowledge condition, K, gives that $C \wedge K \models MB_\alpha(C)$.

For C stating that PT_α^{Elab} or PT_α^{SelRec} is NIL, or that ϵset_α or μset_α is empty, K is of the form, $C \Rightarrow MB_\alpha(C)$. (See clauses K_1 through K_4 in the definition of $GrKnowFPT.Top_2$.) For C of the form, $MB_\alpha(\phi)$ for some ϕ, no knowledge conditions are required, by preliminary result P4.

For C of the form, $(\forall x \in X)P(x)$, as in the F_β and F_κ clauses of the $FSP.Top$ definition, it is sufficient to show that

$$(\forall x \in X)P(x) \models (\forall x \in X)MB_\alpha(P(x)) \models MB_\alpha((\forall x \in X)P(x)).$$

For the first entailment, since $P(x)$ is a conjunction of clauses, $P_i(x)$, it is sufficient to give a conjunction of knowledge conditions, $K_i(x)$, such that for each i, $(\forall x \in X)(P_i(x) \wedge K_i(x)) \models (\forall x \in X)MB_\alpha(P_i(x))$. For $P_i(x)$ of the form, $MB_\alpha(\ldots)$ or $B.Int.To(G_\beta, A_\beta)$, no knowledge conditions are required, by preliminary result P4 and Theorem 1, respectively. For $P_i(x) \equiv (G_\beta \in GR_\alpha)$, $K_i(x) \equiv (G_\beta \in GR_\alpha) \Rightarrow MB_\alpha(G_\beta \in GR_\alpha)$. For $P_i(x) \equiv (GR_\kappa \subseteq GR_\alpha)$, $K_i(x) \equiv (GR_\kappa \subseteq GR_\alpha) \Rightarrow MB_\alpha(GR_\kappa \subseteq GR_\alpha)$.

The second entailment follows from preliminary result P8, given the knowledge condition, $K' \equiv (\forall x)(MB_\alpha(x \in X) \Rightarrow x \in X)$.

Thus, $FSP.Top(PT_\alpha) \wedge GrKnowFPT.Top_2(PT_\alpha) \models MB_\alpha(FSP.Top(PT_\alpha))$. To conclude the proof, observe that $FSP.Top$ contains the clause,

$$C \equiv (\forall \langle I_\kappa, GR_\kappa, A_\kappa \rangle \in \kappa set_\alpha)MB_\alpha((\exists PT)FSP(PT(GR_\kappa, A_\kappa))).$$

But using K' above, under appropriate substitutions, P8 gives the following:

$$C \wedge K' \models MB_\alpha((\forall \langle I_\kappa, GR_\kappa, A_\kappa \rangle \in \kappa set_\alpha)(\exists PT)FSP(PT(GR_\kappa, A_\kappa))). \quad \square$$

Theorem 6. $PSP.Top(PT_\alpha) \wedge GrKnowPPT.Top_2(PT_\alpha) \models MB_\alpha(ExistsPSP(PT_\alpha))$

Theorem 7. $SP.Top(PT_\alpha) \wedge GrKnowPT.Top_2(PT_\alpha) \models MB_\alpha(ExistsSP(PT_\alpha))$

Theorems 6 and 7 are the PSP and SP analogues of Theorem 5. The meta-predicate $GrKnowPPT.Top_2$ (definition omitted), is more complex than its FSP counterpart. For example, it requires that the group know the "tops" of the associate plan trees, PT_α^{Elab} and PT_α^{SelRec}. Thus, the proof of Theorem 6, while similar to that of Theorem 5, is more complicated, including appeals to Theorem 5 to get that $ExistsFSP$ holds for the $Elab$ and $SelRec$ plan trees. In addition, because the PSP clauses, $P_{\beta_2\ 2_p}$ and $P_{\kappa_2.2_p}$, are not embedded in mutual belief contexts, Theorem 6 requires an additional (strong) condition, namely, that the group's mutual beliefs about the intentions-that specified in these clauses must be *correct*. For Theorem 7, $GrKnowPT.Top_2$ (definition also omitted) only requires that the group be able to distinguish the FSP and PSP cases. The proof then appeals to Theorems 5 and 6, as appropriate.

The Case of Single-Agent Groups. As noted in the previous section, an Individual Plan in V_2 is simply a SharedPlan of a single-agent group. However, a single-agent group is special because that single agent must be the responsible agent for each action in the hierarchy. Consequently, the theorems presented above become simpler in the case of a single-agent group. For example, since

$$Bel(G, FSP(PT_\alpha(\{G\}))) \wedge GrKnowFPT(PT_\alpha(\{G\}))$$
$$\models RMB.FSP(PT_\alpha(\{G\})),$$

the single-agent version of Theorem 2 may be stated as

$$Bel(G, FSP(PT_\alpha(\{G\}))) \wedge GrKnowFPT(PT_\alpha(\{G\})) \models FSP(PT_\alpha(\{G\})),$$

where $MB(\{G\}, \phi) \equiv Bel(G, \phi)$ by preliminary result P2. Similarly, the single-agent version of the quasi-converse of Theorem 2 may be stated as

$$FSP(PT_\alpha(\{G\})) \wedge GrKnowFPT_2(PT_\alpha(\{G\})) \models Bel(G, FSP(PT_\alpha(\{G\}))),$$

where $GrKnowFPT_2$ (definition omitted) represents slightly different knowledge conditions than $GrKnowFPT$. This result obviates the need for a single-agent version of Theorem 5, the whole point of which was that some agents in the group were likely to be unaware of what others were doing. Similar remarks apply to the single-agent versions of Theorems 3, 4, 6 and 7.

5 Related Work

Many researchers are actively investigating frameworks for reasoning about collaborative activity in multi-agent systems. Although they address similar issues, their different frameworks and perspectives lead to consideration of different technical problems.

Kinny et al. [8] present a framework in which a *joint plan* specifies (1) a recipe for a group action, and (2) an abstract team structure onto which the group doing the action must be mapped. While their joint plan representation implicitly allows abstract plans to be only partially specified, their definition of a *joint intention* requires a fully specified plan and a hierarchy of subordinate intentions analogous to a Full SharedPlan. Kinny et al. do not formally model the group's commitment to elaborate a partial plan into a full plan; but they do provide algorithms for team formation and role assignment that enable agents to simultaneously adopt a fully instantiated plan. The representation allows agents to reason in advance about whether or not a given unstructured group of agents "has the skills to execute" some abstract joint plan, but the question of precisely which knowledge conditions and mutual beliefs are sufficient to ensure that a team actually has a joint intention to do some action is not addressed.

More recently, some of the same authors (Rao et al. [9]) have presented an axiomatization of team knowledge in which teams are treated as first class entities to which team knowledge is directly ascribed. They claim that this *team-oriented approach*, which employs a separate team knowledge modal operator for each team, might enable the designer of a multi-agent system to focus on knowledge relationships between teams without necessarily having to consider in detail the knowledge of individual agents. They plan to "extend the team-oriented model to include the mental attitudes of mutual belief, joint goals, and joint intentions."

Cavedon and Sonenberg [2] focus on *roles* to which the goals "required of a socially committed agent" may be attached. Eschewing "the commitment to joint intention, [they instead] see participation in a team-plan as socially committing [an] agent to the role it adopts in that plan as well as to the other agents involved in the plan." They see roles as providing a way "to specify how the agent should balance competing obligations." In future work, they plan to tie these concepts "more completely to team plans and the process of their selection and execution."

Tambe [13] presents STEAM, an implemented model of teamwork based primarily on Cohen et al.'s theory of Joint Intentions, but informed by key concepts from SharedPlans. Following Cohen et al., a team initially adopts "a joint intention for a high-level team goal" that includes commitments to maintain the goal until it is deemed already achieved, unachievable or irrelevant. The agents then construct a hierarchy of individual and joint intentions "analogous to partial SharedPlans." Tambe notes that as the hierarchy evolves, "if a step involves only a subteam then that subteam must form a joint intention to perform that step", and the remaining team members need only *track* the subteam's joint intention, requiring that they be able to infer whether or not the subteam intends to, or is able to, execute that step. Thus, Tambe informally addresses some of the central issues in this paper.

Stone and Veloso [11] use *locker room agreements* (i.e., pre-determined sets of fixed protocols and *flexible teamwork structures*) to allow teams of agents operating in dynamic domains (e.g., robotic soccer) to avoid much of the negotiation and communication that might otherwise be required to establish and maintain the network of intentions and mutual beliefs that are essential for the collaboration. Rather than hierarchically decomposing the task space in terms of *actions*, the teamwork structures hierarchically decompose the task space in terms of *formations, sub-formations* and *roles*, where each role has an associated set of behaviors. Locker room agreements may stipulate that certain events shall trigger the adoption of new formations and may specify efficient protocols to allow subsets of agents to flexibly switch roles within a formation. The primary concern is to avoid periods of uncoordinated activity arising from inconsistent beliefs about which formation the team is using and which agents are filling which roles. The theorems in this paper apply directly to such concerns.

6   Conclusions

A reformulation of the theory of SharedPlans has been presented that makes the theory more concise and that enables a set of important theorems about agents and their SharedPlans to be formulated and proven. The theorems specify knowledge conditions sufficient to ensure that a group of agents have a SharedPlan if (or only if) they hold a specified set of mutual beliefs. Thus, the theorems may be used to guide the designer of a multi-agent system by clearly specifying the mutual beliefs agents need to establish and the knowledge conditions they need to satisfy as they construct their SharedPlans. The theorems also indicate the potential cost of weakening any of the underlying assumptions. SharedPlan Trees were introduced to make the meta-predicate definitions from the original formulation more concise and to enable precise specification of the knowledge conditions and mutual beliefs appearing in the theorems.

References

1. *Third International Conference on Multi-Agent Systems (ICMAS-98)*. IEEE Computer Society, 1998.
2. Lawrence Cavedon and Elizabeth Sonenberg. On social commitment, roles and preferred goals. [1], pages 80–87.
3. D.M. Gabbay, C.J. Hogger, and J.A. Robinson, editors. *Handbook of Logic in Artificial Intelligence and Logic Programming*. Clarendon Press, Oxford, 1993.
4. Barbara J. Grosz. AAAI-94 Presidential Address: Collaborative systems. *AI Magazine*, pages 67–85, Summer 1996.
5. Barbara J. Grosz and Sarit Kraus. Collaborative plans for complex group action. *Artificial Intelligence*, 86:269–357, 1996.
6. Barbara J. Grosz and Sarit Kraus. The evolution of SharedPlans. In A.S. Rao and M. Wooldridge, editors, *Foundations and Theories of Rational Agencies*. 1997. To appear.
7. Merav Hadad. Using SharedPlan model in electronic commerce environment. Master's thesis, Bar Ilan University, Ramat-Gan, Israel, 1997.
8. D. Kinny, M. Ljungberg, A.S. Rao, E. Sonenberg, G. Tidhar, and E. Werner. Planned team activity. In C. Castelfranchi and E. Werner, editors, *Artificial Social Systems*, Lecture Notes in Artificial Intelligence. Springer Verlag, Amsterdam, 1994. Volume 830.
9. A.S. Rao, E. Sonenberg, and G. Tidhar. On team knowledge and common knowledge. [1], pages 301–308.
10. Charles Rich and Candace L. Sidner. Collagen: When agents collaborate with people. In *First International Conference on Autonomous Agents*. Marina del Ray, CA, Feb. 1997.
11. P. Stone and M. Veloso. Task decomposition and dynamic role assignment for real-time strategic teamwork. In J. P. Müller, M. P. Singh, and A. S. Rao, editors, *Intelligent Agents V — Proceedings of the Fifth International Workshop on Agent Theories, Architectures, and Languages (ATAL-98)*, Lecture Notes in Artificial Intelligence. Springer-Verlag, Heidelberg, 1999. In this volume.
12. Milind Tambe. Agent architectures for flexible, practical teamwork. In *Proceedings of the Fourteenth National Conference on Artificial Intelligence*. 1997.
13. Milind Tambe. Towards flexible teamwork. *Journal of Artificial Intelligence Research*, 7:83–124, 1997.

Autonomous Norm Acceptance

Rosaria Conte [1], Cristiano Castelfranchi [1], Frank Dignum[2]

[1]Division of AI, Cognitive and Interaction Modelling - IP/Cnr - Rome, Italy - email:
rosaria@pscs2.irmkant.rm.cnr.it

[2] Eindhoven University of Technology - The Netherlands -
e-mail: dignum@win.tue.nl

Abstract. It is generally acknowledged that norms and normative action emphasize autonomy on the side of *decision*. But what about the autonomous *formation* of normative goals? This paper is intended to contribute to a theory of how agents form normative beliefs and goals, and to formulate general but *non* exhaustive principles of norm based autonomous agent-hood – namely goal generation and decision making- upon which to construct software agents.

1 Norms as inputs to goals

It is generally acknowledged that norms and normative action emphasize autonomy on the side of *decision*. But what about the autonomous *formation* of normative goals?

In a recent paper (Dignum & Conte 1997), the treatment of goal acquisition in the Agent Theory (AT) literature was found inadequate, some formal rules for goal generation have been proposed, and the role of social inputs in the acquisition of new goals has been emphasized. Here, we intend to continue that work, by including norms among the social inputs to one's goals, and by extending the goal generation rule to the case of normative goals. The general question then is, how and why do autonomous agents form normative goals? The answer to this question goes back to a former paper by some of the authors (Conte & Castelfranchi 1995), where a typology of reasons for accepting norms has been explored in analogy with goal adoption. Here, however, the formal instruments worked out with regard to the general rules for goal generation will be applied to the special case of normative goals. In the next section we will describe other work related to norms in the multi-agent field. In Section 3 the objectives of this work will be described. In Section 4, the main concepts necessary for the description of norm acceptance will be introduced, and in Section 5 the rules for goal formation will be summarized to serve as a basis for the rules for norm acceptance. Finally, in Section 6, we will give a (formal) treatment of norm acceptance in which several aspects of autonomy in norm acceptance will be distinguished and characterized. Section 7 will conclude and indicate areas for further research.

2 The main issues

Many mechanisms have been proposed to regulate social relationships between agents in multi-agent systems. The interesting new concept of emotion was introduced in another paper in these proceedings (Bazzan *et al.* 1998). Through simulations of societies of agents in which some were altruistic and others egoistic they showed that altruistic behavior is beneficial for the whole society. Unfortunately, they did not indicate how altruistic behavior could evolve. Their agents were either altruistic or egoistic. Both emotions were hardwired into the behavior of the agents. In this paper we actually want to show how self-interested agents change their social behavior under the influence of their experiences (through the use of norms and norm violations).

Legal and social norms also have received a considerable attention in the social sciences, in logical and social philosophy, in some AI sub-fields (legal expert systems, norm-based reasoners, etc.), and more recently in the MAS domain. Nonetheless, they have not yet received a satisfactory explanation.

As for the social sciences, no theory of autonomous normative decision as grounded upon agents' internal representations has been provided. Norms are often viewed as *emergent* properties of utilitarian agents' behavior, independent of their beliefs and goals (Binmore 1994).

As for the logical models of obligations, the connections between obligations and mental states are usually not formalized (Shoham & Cousins 1994).

In the Multi-Agent Systems field, social norms are perceived to help improve coordination and cooperation (Shoham & Tennenholtz 1992; Jennings and Mamdani 1992; Conte & Castelfranchi 1995; Walker & Wooldridge 1995). Furthermore, the advent of large communication networks, civic networks, as well as the spread of electronic commerce, contributed dramatically to draw the attention of the AI scientific community to issues such as *authorization*, *access* regulation, *privacy* maintenance, respect of *decency*, etc. not to mention the more obvious problems associated with the regulation of the *use* and *purposes* of networks.

Indeed, the efforts done by MAS researchers and designers to construct *autonomous* agents (Wooldrige & Jennings 1995) carry with themselves a number of interesting but difficult tasks:

1. how to avoid interference and collisions (also metaphorical) among agents autonomously acting in a common space?
2. How to ensure that negotiations and transactions fulfil the norm of reciprocity? Imagine a software assistant delegated to conduct transactions on behalf of its user. In principle, due to its loyalty (benevolence), the assistant will behave as a shark

with regard to potential partners, always looking for the transaction most convenient for its user, and thereby infringing existing commitments.

3. More generally, how to obtain robust performance in team work (Cohen & Levesque 1990)? How to prevent agents from dropping their commitments, or better, how to prevent agents from disrupting the common activity (cf. Jennings 1994; Kinny & Georgeff 1994; Tambe 1996; Singh 1995)?

These questions have become central research issues within the MAS field. Other problems are perhaps less obvious. For example, the existence of so-called virtual *representatives* brings about the question of delegation. Software assistants, mobile agents are intended to act as virtual representatives of network clients. But the role of representatives implies that some normative mechanism is at work, such as *responsibility* (Jennings 1995) and *delegation* (Santos & Carmo 1996). Analogously, the concept of role (Werner 1990) and role-tasks - which is so crucial for the implementation of organizational work - requires a model of *authorization* and (institutional) *empowerment* (Jones & Sergot 1995).

These concepts explicitly or implicitly point to at least two questions, of vital importance:

1. how do agents acquire norms? In the formal social scientific field[1], the spread of norms and other cooperative behaviors is usually not explained by means of models of internal representations of norms. The object of inquiry usually consists of the conditions under which agents converge on behaviors which prove efficient in solving problems of coordination (Lewis 1969) or cooperation (Axelrod 1987). In the multi-agent field, norms are represented in the agents, but they are treated as built-in constraints. Therefore, what about the acquisition of new norms? This question is crucial with regard to all the problems listed above. If agents are enabled to acquire new norms, there is no need for expanding exceedingly the individual agents' knowledge base. Consequently, the multi-agent system may be optimized when it is *on-line*, while multi-agent systems where norms have been actually implemented allow for a modification of norms only when the system is *off-line* (Shoham & Tennenholz 1992).

2. How can agents violate norms? So far, norms are treated as constraints to either the agent's action repertoire (Shoham & Tenneholz 1992) or its evaluation module (Boman 1996). Norms operate by reducing the set of available or convenient actions to those that meet the existing constraints. Therefore, norms apply unfailingly. Agents cannot violate them. However, the possibility to violate norms is crucial for solving possible conflicts of norms, which often arise among tasks associated with different roles, or among norms belonging to different domains of

---

[1] That is, in utility theory and in game theory. Social (psychological) theorists have attempted behavioral explanations of normative influence. However, these theories cannot be immediately translated into computational models of autonomous norm-acceptance, since poor attention is paid within behavioral social science to the internal representations and processing of norms. On the other hand, cognitive social psychologists pay attention to rules of reasoning (natural vs. formal logics) rather than to moral and social norms. Generally speaking, the role of cognition for social action is still relatively poorly explored.

activity. This question is crucial with regard to both legal expert systems and autonomous agents interacting in a common world.

Both questions bring into play autonomy: the capacity for acquiring and the capacity for violating them are direct consequences of the agents' autonomy and bear crucial application consequences. If we need autonomous agents, we also need autonomous normative agents. One advantage of autonomous agents is their capacity to select the external requests, which it is necessary or convenient for them to fulfil. This selective capacity affects not only the agents' normative *decisions*, but also their *acquiring* new norms. Indeed, agents take a decision even when they decide to form a "normative belief", and then to form a new (normative) goal, and not only when they decide whether to execute it or not. The decision to form a normative goal will be called here norm *acceptance;* the decision to execute a norm will be called norm compliance. Obviously, this depend on a radical divorce of goals from intentions (see again Dignum & Conte 1997). Although we will not provide examples of implementation in this paper, computational applications of autonomous norm compliance do exist (think of the systems in which norms are treated as inputs for decision making; for a reference to these systems, see Boman, 1996). As was observed by Shoham and Tennenholtz (Shoham & Tennenholtz 1992), computational models of autonomous norm acceptance are lacking in the field of multi-agent systems. In our view, a capacity for autonomous norm acceptance would greatly enhance multi-agent systems' flexibility and dynamic potentials. To implement such a capacity it is necessary to model and implement the recognition of norms and the formation of normative beliefs.

Here, we will primarily deal with autonomous formation of new *normative* beliefs and goals. To do so, the more general property of *social* autonomy must be characterized.

3 Objectives

This paper is not intended to provide a descriptive theory of human agents' normative behavior. Instead, we intend to

1. contribute to a theory of autonomous normative decision as grounded upon agents' internal representations, and

2. formulate general but *non* exhaustive principles of norm based autonomous agenthood, namely goal generation and decision making. These principles should be seen as applicable to both natural and artificial systems. Whether they are necessary and sufficient to describe the behavior of real natural systems is of no concern here. We aim at identifying mechanisms such that, if implemented into some artificial systems, will give rise to autonomous norm acceptance and compliance.

3. A sub-goal is to design principles for how software agents should be constructed in order to exhibit autonomous normative action. Empirical claims about the behavior of software agents that are designed according to these principles will be specified.

However, the empirical control of the validity of the present model is beyond the scope of this paper. Possible experimental controls through computer simulation are under study.

4 Concepts for dealing with normative agents

In this section we will introduce the concepts necessary to define norm acceptance by agents.

An *agent* is a system whose behavior is neither *accidental* nor strictly *causal*, but oriented to achieve a given state of the world.

Goal-governed agents are able to achieve goals by themselves, by planning, executing, adapting and correcting actions. A goal-governed or purposive behavior (Miller et al. 1960; Rosenblueth & Wiener 1968) is controlled by goals. Agents that contain explicit representations for goals, intentions and beliefs are called *cognitive* agents.

Goals are internal explicit representations of world states which agents want to be realized.

Beliefs are those propositions about the world that agents hold to be true. In the rest of this paper we assume our agents to be cognitive agents.

Intentions are those goals that agents intend to reach, and intentional actions are those actions that agents intend to perform (Castelfranchi, 1995). Cognitive agents are not necessarily *autonomous*. Autonomy requires autonomous goals (Covrigaru & Lindsay 1991). It is a relational concept: a system is defined as autonomous always with regard to another system. An agent is autonomous only relative to other agents in a common world: *x is autonomous from y as for a goal p* where *p* is a behavior of *x* (for a cognitive agent, *p* is a goal). Here, we will consider only social autonomy, that is to say, *autonomy from other agents.* To be noted, autonomy is not a none-or-all notion. There are different levels and kinds of autonomy. With goal-governed agents, the most important distinction is relative to their level of autonomy. Here we will focus on goal autonomy and norm autonomy.

An agent x is *goal-autonomous* if and only if whatever new goal q it comes to adopt, there is at least a goal p of x's to which q is believed by that agent to be instrumental. More precisely, a socially autonomous agent adopts other agents' goals only if this adoption is conceived of as a way to achieve one or more further goals. As shown in (Dignum & Conte 1997), to adopt a goal does not imply to generate the relative intention and perform the relative action. It is also possible that an agent *adopts a given goal* but will not eventually pursue it; this does not become an intention, because, for example, *it is not preferred* to other more important goals.

A *norm* is an obligation on a given set of agents to accomplish (active norm), or abstain (passive norm) from, a given action. A norm is only external, when its subject agents have no mental representation, neither goal nor belief that corresponds to it. To be noted, norms are not meant here in the restrictive sense of laws, but in the more general sense of social obligations and conventions. Phenomena such as that of reciprocity imply obligations and permissions even though they may not allow for a strictly juridical treatment.

4.1 Empirical criteria for autonomous normative agents

An agent is *norm-autonomous* if it can:
1. recognize a norm as a norm (normative belief formation);
2. argue whether a given norm does or does not concern its case; decide to accept the norm or not;
3. decide to comply with it or not (obey or violate);
4. take the initiative of re-issuing (prescribing) the norm, monitoring, evaluating and sanctioning the others' behavior relatively to the norm.

In this paper we will examine the main aspects of norm-autonomous agents. Whenever we use the word agent, we will therefore mean norm-autonomous agent.

5 Previous work: goal generation and the role of social inputs

In this section, we will summarize the work done in (Dignum & Conte 1997) in which a formal model was developed for goal formation. In the next section we will apply the model there developed to the case of norms.

The general intuitive idea on goal formation is that an agent might form a goal p *if* it already has a goal q and achieving p is in some way *instrumental* to achieving q. We say that p is instrumental for q, denoted by INSTR(p,q), if achieving p contributes to achieving q. This notion of instrumentality can be seen as a generalization of the idea of sub-goals. In the next section we will say something more about different types of instrumentality in the context of normative goals.

The general goal generation rule is formalized as follows:

$$GOAL_x(q|r \land BEL_x(INSTR(p,q)) \rightarrow C\text{-}GOAL_x(p|GOAL_x(q|r) \land r) \qquad (1)$$

I.e. if an agent x has a goal q as long as r is true and it believes that p is instrumental to achieving q then agent x has a candidate goal p as long as it has the goal q and r is true. If x's beliefs about the instrumentality are given and do not change, the above rule is completely endogenous. I.e. it does not depend on any external situation or change of circumstances. However, the goal generation rules can also be used to react to the environment. To effect this, the agent should have some beliefs about the benefits of reacting to other agents. I.e. how the generation of a goal in response to an event contributes to some overall goal of itself. In (Dignum & Conte 1997) three possible behaviors were given as input for goal formation:
1. behavioral conformity
2. goal conformity
3. goal adoption

Behavioral conformity is effected through the following two formulas:

$$GOAL_x(be\text{-}like(x,y)|true) \qquad (2)$$
$$BEL_x[DONE(y,\alpha) \rightarrow INSTR(DONE(x,\alpha), be\_like(x,y))] \qquad (3)$$

It is easy to see that, with the goal generation rule, we can derive that x will do whatever y does as long as x wants to be like y. Or formally:

$$C\text{-}GOAL_x(DONE(x,\alpha)|GOAL_x(be\_like(x,y))) \qquad (4)$$

The idea of goal conformity is similar to that of behavioral conformity, except that x will now mimic the goals of y. This is formalized by the following:

$$GOAL_x(be\text{-}like(x,y)|true) \qquad (5)$$

$$BEL_x[GOAL_y(p|r) \wedge r \rightarrow INSTR(p,be\_like(x,y))] \qquad (6)$$

And again with the goal generation rule we can derive:

$$C\text{-}GOAL_x(p|GOAL_x(be\_like(x,y))) \qquad (7)$$

The idea of goal adoption is slightly different from the previous two. In this case, x not only takes over a goal, but it also tries to help y to obtain its goal. The formulas to describe this are as follows:

$$GOAL_x(help(x,y)|true) \qquad (8)$$

$$BEL_x[GOAL_y(p|r) \wedge r \rightarrow INSTR(help(x,y),OBT_y(p))] \qquad (9)$$

Therefore, whenever x believes that y has a goal p it will try to help y to obtain p.

As can be seen from the above, all types of goal formation follow the same pattern. Given some overall goal of x's, x believes that in some circumstances (y has performed some action or has some goal) it is instrumental for x to have some (candidate) goal that helps achieve the overall one. The (candidate) goal that will be generated depends on the type of behavioral rules that the agent follows.

In (Dignum & Conte 1997) a sketch of the semantics of the logic that is used above is given. Due to space limitations we will leave such formalization out of the present paper. In the next section we will explore whether similar rules as were given for goal formation can be used for autonomous norm acceptance.

6 Normative inputs to one's goals

Norms are an important device for some agents to influence and control the behaviors of other social agents, and thereby make the whole social behavior more predictable. In order to influence the behavior of the agent, a norm itself must generate a corresponding intention; and in order to generate an intention it must be adopted by the agent, and become one of its goals. First, the agent x must be aware that the norm is in force (belief) and concerns (belief) the agent itself; secondly, x must have some motive of its own to obey the norm, since in general x must have reasons for adopting goals from outside. Which are the motives for norm acceptance? What kind of autonomy is brought about by norm acceptance and by normative agents?

6.1 Forms of autonomy in norm acceptance

There are two decisions to be taken in the process from a normative input to a conforming normative behavior (norm compliance): *the acceptance of the norm as a norm*; and *the decision to conform to it*.

Norm recognition as presupposition of norm acceptance

The issue is whether the agent will accept the candidate norm *as a norm*, and why it will accept it. For the purpose of this paper we will take the candidate norms to be external norms that are somehow observed by the agent but in reality several things can operate as candidate norms.

We will denote candidate norms as obligations: $O_yX(q)$, where q stands for the norm, y is the authority that issues the norm and X is the set of intended addressees of the norm (the norm subjects). An autonomous agent is able to evaluate a candidate norm against several criteria. It can reject it for several reasons:

1. *evaluation of the candidate norm;* if it is based upon [2] an already recognized norm, the norm is recognized as a norm itself ; if not
2. *evaluation of the source;* if the norm is not based upon a recognized norm, the entity y that has issued the norm is evaluated. If y is perceived to be entitled to issue some norms (it is a normative authority), $O_yX(q)$ can be accepted as a norm; this belief entails or is supported by other more specific beliefs relative to several of y's features:
   - (i)   q is (not) within y's domain of normative competence;
   - (ii)   the current context is (not) the proper context in which y is entitled to issue q ;
   - (iii)   y is addressing a set of agents that is (not) within the scope of its authority.
3. *evaluation of the motives;* $O_yX(q)$ is issued for y's personal/private interest, rather than for the interest y is held to protect: if x believes that y's prescription is only due to some private desire, etc. x will not take it as a norm. x might ignore what the norm is for, what its utility is for the group or its institutions, but may expect that the norm is aimed at having a positive influence for the group; at least, it is necessary that x does not have the opposite belief, that is, that the norm is not aimed to be "good for" the group at large, but only for y. This is so crucial of a norm that one could even conceive it as implied by the first belief: y is entitled only to deliver prescriptions and permissions that are aimed at the general rather than at its own private interest.

The agent subject to $O_yX(q)$ is an *evaluator* of $O_yX(q)$. The output of its evaluation is a normative belief: the belief about the existence of a norm[3] (rather than of a simple request or expectation). We can formalize the evaluation process with the following two formulas:

(a) $BEL_x(O_zU(r)) \wedge BEL_x(O_zU(r) \rightarrow O_yX(q))$ (10)

(b-c) $(O_yX(q) \wedge BEL_x(auth(y,X,q,C)) \wedge BEL_x(mot(y,OK)))$
$$\rightarrow BEL_x(O_yX(q))   (11)$$

Both formulas lead to $BEL_x(O_yX(q))$. The first through simple modus ponens and the second directly from its fulfilled premises. Many things can be said about when one norm implies another (see e.g. (Royakkers 1996 and Herrestad & Krogh 1996)),

---

[2] The new norm is just an instantiation, application, or interpretation of the former one.

[3] Notice that such an evaluation and recognition plays a very active role as one step of the process of collective norms *creation*: to recognize that a given norm exists as a norm puts it into existence (see later).

but to go into this subject is beyond the scope of this paper. The relation "auth" introduced above stands for: y is authorized to issue the norm q to the set of agents X in context C. The relation "mot" indicates that the motives of y are indeed correct. Both relations are of course very complex. More about the authorization can be found in (Dignum & Weigand 1995).

The acceptance of the norm as a norm is an act that contributes both to spreading around the norm in question as well as to constructing/creating/forming the norm at the social level.

Norm acceptance

Once a norm has been recognized as a norm, a normative belief has been formed. x has an additional belief. Is such a belief sufficient for the formation of a new goal? The answer to this question that we can derive from our postulate of social autonomy is: No! A normative belief is never sufficient for the formation of a new goal. Another ingredient is needed, that is, a goal already formed in x's mind for which x believes that complying with the norm n is instrumental.

Social autonomy has a normative corollary: *A norm-autonomous agent accepts a norm q, only if it sees accepting q as a way of achieving (one of) its own further goal(s).*

$$BEL_x(O_yX(q) \wedge INSTR(OBT_X(q),p) \wedge GOAL_x(p|r))$$
$$\rightarrow N\text{-}GOAL_x(OBT_X(q)|GOAL_x(p|r) \wedge r) \quad (12)$$

Intuitively, the above formula states that x forms a normative goal $OBT_X(q)$ (i.e. accepts the norm q) if x believes that the norm exists (for agents in set X) and that fulfilling the norm (i.e. $OBT_X(q)$) is instrumental to one of its own goals. Although the rule for norm acceptance resembles the one for goal formation there are a few important differences. The first difference with the goal formation rule is that in the premises we included a belief of an existing norm. I.e. a normative goal is only derived with this rule if there exists some norm outside the agent to start with. Note that the implication in the rule is only a one-way implication. This means that not every normative goal has to be derived through this rule! We can imagine that agents can also autonomously form new norms. We could describe this by saying that the agent believes that a certain norm should exist, which leads to the following rule:

$$BEL_x(O(O_yX(q)) \wedge INSTR(OBT_X(q),p) \wedge GOAL_x(p|r))$$
$$\rightarrow N\text{-}GOAL_x(OBT_X(q)|GOAL_x(p|r) \wedge r) \quad (13)$$

Where O(x) stands for a general obligation that holds for the set of all agents for which the issuer is a standard (central) authority. However, this is only one possible way in which new norms can be formed. We leave further discussion of this topic for another paper.

The other, less conspicuous, difference with the goal formation rule is the fact that we do not require q to be instrumental for the goal p, but rather $OBT_X(q)$. With $OBT_X(q)$ in this context we mean the fulfillment of the norm q by all members of X. The difference is that in this case we only try to fulfil the norm, because it is a norm. A much stronger case is when the norm itself is believed to act to the benefit of our goal p. This corresponds to "internalizing" the norm, making it our own goal, and would formally be described by:

$BEL_x(O_yX(q) \wedge INSTR(q,p) \wedge GOAL_x(p|r))$

$$\rightarrow C\text{-}GOAL_x(q|GOAL_x(p|r) \wedge r) \qquad (14)$$

This follows directly from the goal formation rule, because we have only strengthened the antecedent by adding a normative belief.

Given the above rule(s) for norm acceptance, it seems reasonable to see whether there are similar rules for norm conformity and norm adoption as were defined for goals. Obviously, we cannot define the same type of rules for norms, because an independent belief in the existence of some external norm is required before a normative goal is derived. x cannot deduce the existence of a norm by y performing a given action. Therefore we need at least the following two implications:

$$BEL_x(BEL_y(O_zX(q))) \rightarrow BEL_x(O_zX(q)) \qquad (15)$$
$$BEL_x(N\text{-}GOAL_y(OBT_X(q)| r) \rightarrow INSTR(OBT_X(q),be\_like(x,y))) \qquad (16)$$

plus of course:

$$GOAL_x(be\_like(x,y)|true) \qquad (17)$$

From the above, only norm adoption but no norm conformity is derived. It is not possible to mimic only the norms that were accepted by another agent! They should also be accepted in some way. Therefore we do have norm adoption, but no conformity. Of course, we can have "apparent" norm adoption in case an agent x adopts all the goals of an agent y that follow from a certain norm. In that case, if agent y fulfils the norm then agent x will follow it and fulfil the norm!

6.2 Norm compliance

Once accepted, a norm becomes a normative goal. We distinguish normative goals from candidate goals primarily because the agent has different motivations to either choose a candidate or a normative goal as the goal it will actually try to achieve. The decision of normative compliance is influenced by the type of instrumentality of the norm, which is always related to some external source (the external norm). The candidate goals have an instrumentality that is determined by the inner motives of the agent. This difference becomes clear if we look at the reasons to give up a goal. If it is a normative goal it can be dropped at the moment the norm is changed or is no longer applicable. Candidate goals are only dropped when the agent knows they can no longer be achieved or a more urgent goal has become active.

Below, some reasons for non-conforming behaviors are summarized based on the different instrumentality evaluations described in the previous section:

1. *Norm responsibility;:* the agent has accepted the norm $O_yX(q)$, but is only prepared to try to fulfil this norm itself. It will not try to "help" other agents to fulfil the norm. Formally:

2. $N\text{-}GOAL_x(OBT_X(q)| r) \rightarrow C\text{-}GOAL_x(OBT_X(q)| r) \qquad (18).$

3. *Goal conflict:* the normative goal contrasts with goals that are more urgent than the goal of complying with the norm. The expected value of norm violation depends on factors that vary with different kinds of agents, societies, or situations; such factors include

1. the importance of the goal or *value* of respecting the norms, of being a good citizen, etc.;
2. the importance of possible *feelings* related to norm violation (guilt, indignity, etc.);
3. the importance of foreseen *negative consequences of the violation for the global interest* that the norm claims to protect, or for other important societal goals (e.g., to violate norms will destroy respect, trust, and solidarity in the society).
4. the probability and weight of *punishment* (including social approval and its consequences);
5. *Norm conflict* (ubi major...): these may include provocation and rebellion, or other normative goals prescribing opposite norms (e.g., pacifist vs. military norms).
6. *Impertinence*: x does not believe to be a member of the set of agents mentioned by the norm; for example, x strongly supports the norms regulating the car traffic, but has no driving license. Obviously, x can be said to execute the norm at a higher level: it will probably support the norms in question by monitoring the drivers' behaviors any time it happens to have the possibility to do so. However, x will not execute the norm on its own.
7. *Material impossibility*: obviously when the norm prescribes an action which cannot be executed, x will not comply with it although it has recognized it as a norm and no conflict holds between the norm and other goals of x's; consider, for example, the case in which x finds itself trapped in a traffic jam. The traffic light turns red while x is in the middle of the crossing. x knows that it is violating the norm; it has recognized the norm, and has accepted it; x may even have formed a corresponding intention. Still, its behavior does not, and cannot correspond to what the norm prescribes.
8. If x accepts and executes a norm, it will monitor and check that people (subject to the same norm) respect it, and will implicitly or explicitly prescribe this, probably reacting to any violation of it, since this also turns into a frustration of a goal and expectation of x's.

Therefore, acceptance contributes to the *spreading* of the norm. Indeed norm spreading:

1. is not primarily behavioral but mentalistic: norms spread among minds through recognition (normative beliefs), acceptance (normative goals) and possibly, through *norm sharing* (see below);
2. the mental spread of norms will determine conforming behaviors which will influence the others and enhance the general acceptance and conformity.

Unlike current social scientific theories of norms, the hypothesis presented in this paper states that agents converge on norms if, and only if, these norms spread through their minds, and that there is a continuous feedback from some agents' norm compliance to the observation of this behavior by other agents, their forming new normative beliefs and goals, and their possible consequent norm compliance. While in current social scientific theories, the mental processing of norms is essentially overlooked for the emergence and diffusion of conventions, here it is considered as a crucial segment in the process leading to the emergence and spread of norms as a specific social cognitive artifact.

7 Concluding remarks and computational applications

Here, we have endeavored to account for a process of autonomous normative decision, which includes two fundamental steps: the formation of a normative belief, and the decision to accept a norm. Indeed, not only to comply with a norm, but also to believe that something *is* a norm, are outputs of a complex decision making of an autonomous agent.

But the analysis described so far shows that a lot is yet to be done. In particular, two further aspects, mentioned throughout the paper, seem to play a fundamental role in norm spreading and emergence, especially in the case of social norms:

1. norm sharing: in some circumstances, agents come to share for some reason the utility, convenience or functionality of the norms. Under which circumstances does norm sharing occur? What are its effects?

2. autonomous norm formation: norms come into existence not only when they are "issued" by some "legislator", but also when they emerge from agents' implicit or explicit agreements. How is this possible? In which moment does a social (non-institutional) norm start to exist and why?

The comprehension of both phenomena would largely benefit from the view presented in this paper: norms cannot be shared, without a mental representation of them. Analogously, while habits, routines, etc. emerge from a mere behavioral convergence, norms an only come into existence if agents start to believe that some given behaviors are obligatory and legitimate, that is, normative. The question is, how and why do agents form such beliefs. Both norm sharing and norm formation will be addressed in future studies.

Three types of computational applications of the model presented in this paper are under study:

1. in the area of legal expert systems, the implementation of (aspects of) the present model would allow for detection of
   - violations, which will be distinguished from other behaviors that do not correspond to norms; this would be of special interest in applications of expert systems to legal "diagnostic" reasoning and certification;
   - norm conflict; this is particularly relevant for the automatic advice to legal interpretation.

2. In the MAS field, the implementation of rules of norm acceptance would allow for
   - the acquisition of norms when the system is on-line, and consequently
   - greater flexibility of the system
   - a reduced load at the level of the agents' knowledge bases.

3. In the area of computer simulation, the hypothesis formulated in this paper can be experimentally tested; in particular, the advantages of autonomous norm acceptance and compliance in agents' monitoring others' behaviors should be tested and compared with models of convergence among autonomous but non-normative agents.

Acknowledgements

We would like to thank Harko Verhagen for convincing us about the opportunity and importance to make the level of autonomy postulated in our theory of norm- and goal adoption more explicit.

References

Axelrod, R. (1987). The Evolution of Strategies in the Iterated Prisoner's Dilemma. In L.D. Davis (ed) *Genetic Algorithms and simulated annealing.* Los Altos, CA: Kaufmann, 32-41.

Bazzan, A.L.C., Bordini, R.H., Campbell, J.A. (1998). Moral sentiments in multi-agent systems. In this volume.

Binmore, K. (1994). *Game-theory and Social Contract.* Vol. 1: Fair Playing. Cambridge: Clarendon.

Boman, M. (1996). Implementing Norms through Normative Advice, in R. Conte & R. Falcone (eds) *ICMAS '96 WS5 on "Norms, Obligations, and Conventions",* Kyoto, Keihanna Plaza 10 Dec. 1996.

Cohen, Ph. & Levesque, H. (1990). Intention is Choice with Commitment. *Artificial Intelligence,* 42(3), 213-261.

Conte, R. & Castelfranchi, C. (1995). *Cognitive and Social Action.* London: UCL Press.

Covrigaru, A. A. & Lindsay, R.K. (1991). Deterministic Autonomous Systems. *AI Magazine,* Fall, 110-17.

Dignum, F. & Conte, R. (1997). Intentional Agents and Goal Formation. In M.P. Singh et.al. (ed) *Proceedings of the 4th International Workshop on Agent Theories Architectures and Languages,* Providence, USA.

Dignum, F. & Weigand, H. (1995). Communication and Deontic Logic. In R. Wieringa & R. Feenstra (eds) *Information Systems, Correctness and Reusability.* Singapore: World Scientific, 242--260.

Herrestad, H. & Krogh, C. (1996). Deontic Logic Relativised to Bearers and Counterparties. In J. Bing & O. Torrund (eds), *Anniversary Anthology in Computers and Law,* , Tano A.S, 453-522.

Jennings N.R. (1995). Commitment and Conventions: the Foundation of Coordination in Multi-Agent Systems. *The Knowledge Engineering Review* , 8, 223-250.

Jennings, N.R. (1992). On Being Responsible, in Y. Demazeau & E. Werner (eds) *Decentralized Artificial Intelligence 3,* Amsterdam: Elsevier Science Publisher, 93-102.

Jennings, N.R. & Mamdani, E.H. (1992). Using Joint Responsibility to Coordinate Collaborative Problem Solving in Dynamic Environments. In *Proceedings of the 10th National Conference on Artificial Intelligence,* San Mateo, CA: Kaufmann, 269-275.

Jones, A.J.I. & Sergot, M. (1995). Norm-Governed and Institutionalised Agent Interaction, *Proceedings of ModelAge'95: general meeting of ESPRIT wg* 8319, Sophia Antipolis: France, January, 22-24.

Lewis, D. (1969).*Convention.* Cambridge, MA: Harvard University Press.

Kinny, D. & Georgeff, M. (1994). Commitment and Effectiveness of Situated Agents. In *Proceedings of the 13th International Joint Conference on Artificial Intelligence*, IJCAI-93, Sydney, 82-88.

Miller, G., Galanter, E., & Pribram, K.H. (1960). *Plans and the Structure of Behavior*, New York: Holt, Rinehart & Winston.

Rao, A.S. & Georgeff, M.P. (1991). Modelling Rational Agents within a BDI Architecture. In J. Allen, R. Fikes, & E. Sandewall (eds), *Proceedings of the International Conference on Principles of Knowledge Representation and Reasoning*, San Mateo, CA: Kaufmann, 473-485.

Rosenblueth, A. & Wiener, N. (1968). Purposeful and Non-Purposeful Behavior. In W. Buckley (ed.) *Modern Systems Research for the Behavioral Scientist*. Chicago: Aldine.

Royakkers, L. (1996). *Representing Legal Rules in Deontic Logic*. Ph.D. Thesis, Tilburg University, The Netherlands.

Santos, F. & Carmo, J. (1996). Indirect Action, Influence and Responsibility, in Brown, M. & Carmo, J. (eds), *Deontic Logic, Agency and Normative Systems*, Berlin: Springer, 194-215.

Shoham, Y. & Cousins, S.B. (1994). Logics of Mental Attitudes in AI. In G. Lakemeyer & B. Nebel (eds) *Foundations of Knowledge Representation and Reasoning*, Berlin: Springer.

Shoham, Y. & Tennenholtz M. (1992). On the Synthesis of Useful Social Laws in Artificial Societies. *Proceedings of the 10th National Conference on Artificial Intelligence*, San Mateo, CA: Kaufmann, 276-282.

Singh, M.P. (1995). *Multi-Agent Systems: A Theoretical Framework for Intentions, Know-how, and Communications*. Berlin: Springer.

Tambe, M. (1996). Teamwork in Real-World, Dynamic Environments. In *Proceedings of ICMAS 1996*, Menlo Park, CA: AAAI.

Verhagen, H.J.E. & Smit, R.A. (1996). Modeling Social Agents in a Multi-Agent World, Eindhoven: Working Notes MAAMAW 1996.

Walker, A. & Wooldridge, M. (1995). Understanding the Emergence of Conventions in Multi-Agent Systems, *Proceedings of the First International Conference on Multi-Agent Systems*, the MIT Press, 384-389.

Werner, E. (1990). Cooperating Agents: A Unified Theory of Communication and Social Structure. In L.Gasser and M.N.Huhns (eds), Distributed Artificial Intelligence: Volume II. Kaufmann.

Wooldridge, M. & Jennings, N.R. (1995) (eds). *Intelligent Agents (LNAI Volume, 890)*. Berlin: Springer.

Moral Sentiments in Multi-agent Systems

Ana L. C. Bazzan[1], Rafael H. Bordini[2], and John A. Campbell[2]

[1] Department of Computer Science
University of Massachusetts at Amherst
Amherst, MA 01003-4610, USA
bazzan@cs.umass.edu
[2] Department of Computer Science
University College London
Gower Street, London WC1E 6BT, U.K.
{R.Bordini, J.Campbell}@cs.ucl.ac.uk

Abstract. We present a simulation of a society of agents where some of them have "moral sentiments" towards the agents that belong to the same social group, using the Iterated Prisoner's Dilemma as a metaphor for the social interactions. Besides the well-understood phenomenon of short-sighted, self-interested agents performing well in the short-term but ruining their chances of such performance in the long run in a world of reciprocators, the results suggest that, where some agents are more generous than that, these agents have a positive impact on the social group to which they belong, without compromising too much their individual performance (i.e., the group performance improves). The inspiration for this project comes from a discussion on Moral Sentiments by M.Ridley. We describe various simulations where conditions and parameters over determined dimensions were arranged to account for different types and compositions of societies. Further, we indicate several lessons that arise from the analysis of the results and comparison of the different experiments. We also relate this work to our previous anthropological approach to the adaptation of migrant agents, and argue that allowing agents to possess suitably-chosen emotions can have a decisive impact on Multi-Agent Systems. This implies that some common notions of agent autonomy (and related concepts) should be reexamined.

1 Introduction

We have been concerned with the problem of adapting agents to different artificial cultures (Bordini and Campbell 1995; Bordini, Campbell, and Vieira 1997; Bordini 1998); in other words, the problem of interoperability of Multi-Agent Systems (MAS). We have recently come to appreciate the importance, for this project, of including issues of *emotions* or *sentiments* (we use these words interchangeably here) in the modelling of MAS in general, as we shall discuss later. Inspired by Ridley's ideas on Moral Sentiments (1996) we also wish to argue here that emotions are a missing factor for agents to display social behaviour; it indicates why autonomous agents do not have to be necessarily selfish (as claimed, e.g., in (d'Inverno and Luck 1996)). Further, notions of goal adoption and social norms (Conte and Castelfranchi 1995) also need to be revisited, based on the *emotional stance* that we propose informally for MAS. We began the work reported here, whose initial result were presented in (Bazzan, Bordini, and Campbell 1997), by introducing (metaphorically) an emotional aspect into simulations using the Iterated Prisoner's Dilemma (IPD). Ironically, IPD originated in the field of Game Theory, an area concerned with *rational* decisions and self-interest.

It is known that in the IPD, mutual defection is not the only solution, unlike the situation for the one-shot Prisoner's Dilemma (PD), where it is the rational one (Brembs 1996). This was verified in Axelrod's computer tournament (1984), by the use of a tactic referred to as Tit-For-Tat (TFT), whose success is due to its being, in Axelrod's words, nice, retaliatory, forgiving, and clear. These ideas have been employed in the field of MAS in order to explain the achievement of cooperation and coordination (e.g. in (Rosenschein and Zlotkin 1994)). Nevertheless, little work has been devoted to the IPD for social agents, particularly agents with emotions. One reason for this may be the failure of theories based on rational choice to account for *social* action and choice as claimed by Conte and Castelfranchi (1995). Game theory tends to treat social agents' goals in a process of choice for each agent in isolation and exclusively from its own point of view. For instance, agents do not attempt to modify the mental state of an opponent.

There has been marked opposition from game theorists to the widespread use of IPD and TFT as the basis for explaining complex social interactions among humans (Binmore 1998). We have extended the rules of the game so that it can relate to various issues of social agents, including moral and philosophical aspects such as why people are able to keep their promises once they agree to cooperate and why people behave altruistically. We have used the PD simply as a metaphor for social interaction, without the intention of further colonisation of game theorists' territory.

The ideas on moral sentiments that inspired this work are presented in the next section. We then describe in Section 3 the simulation that assesses those ideas, and show the results and some analysis in Section 4. Section 5 discusses these results in the light of our anthropological approach to agent adaptation and contrasts it with some widespread conceptions of agent autonomy and related notions. In the final section we summarise the lessons from the present work and mention possible extensions to it.

2 Moral Sentiments: a Prolific Source of Ideas

In a recent publication on "The Origins of Virtue" (Ridley 1996), particularly in its Chapter 7 entitled "Theories of Moral Sentiments"[1], Ridley makes the

---

[1] The reader will notice that this is an important influence on our work. This does not mean, of course, that we share all the views expressed in that book, in particular the political implications drawn towards the end of the text.

point that *moral sentiments* (emotions like compassion towards others and guilt for not having played fair with someone) prevent us from being *rational fools*. These are short-sighted, self-interested people who fail to consider the effects that their actions have on others. They act to maximise their earnings in the short term but spoil their chances of doing well in the long run because people do not reciprocate with those who have proven selfish in the past.

Moral sentiments lead us to sacrifice rational decisions, yet they are of fundamental importance to social relations inasmuch as they allow us to create a reputation as altruistic people. Altruism, which most people praise as a virtue, will lead a kind person to have a good reputation, hence paying off in future interactions (see comments below on the role of trust in PD situations). However, these same emotions drive us to want those who belong to the same social group to be somewhat self-interested, which is better for the group too: we are particularly concerned with the welfare of people from the same social group or those who "share our genes."

In other words, moral sentiments are decisive in the dilemma between getting the maximum out of an opportunity and being cautious about the future. They are instinctive[2], an intrinsic part of our highly social nature (remarkably, distinct sciences have arrived at this conclusion from completely different sources of evidence). In effect, they are the *guarantee of our commitments*, which makes complex, stable social relations possible, and this stands to our long-term advantage. They alter the reward of problems in which one must be committed to cooperation (like the PD) and somehow bring to the present distant costs that would not have arisen in a rational calculation. Furthermore, the fact that emotions are *universally recognisable* allows the virtuous to get together and take advantage of cooperation (thinking in terms of the PD helps here too), isolating the selfish rationalists: people can actually avoid "playing" with those who do not reciprocate in real life. To summarise the workings of emotions in social life: "Rage deters transgressors; guilt makes cheating painful for the cheat; envy represents self-interest; contempt earns respect; shame punishes; compassion elicits reciprocal compassion. And love commits us to a relationship."(Ridley 1996).

When, however, people perform altruistic acts that are not rational and do not pay off even in the long run (which we shall refer to as *true altruism*), they are falling prey to sentiments originally designed (through natural selection) to obtain other people's trust, which is convenient for "real life's prisoner's dilemmas"[3]. This is a remarkable insight, as it admits some light into the discussion on altruism, which has become so paradoxical and with dangerous consequences since the wide acceptance (followed by misinterpretations) of the "selfish gene" theory (Dawkins 1989).

In terms of MAS, we expect that the representation of emotions in agents' architectures, leading agents to have moral sentiments, could account for a type

---

[2] This is not to say that we are not self-interested and that we do not have other "darker" instincts too.

[3] It should be noted that, as Ridley puts it, this is only a dilemma if one does not know whether one can trust one's accomplice.

of long-term coordination which would not be possible otherwise. The nature of the beneficial effect of altruism is such that *it cannot be calculated in advance*: not by human beings, let alone computational agents. This is a direct consequence of the principle of bounded rationality, and MAS should borrow from the ingenious mechanism designed by natural selection to solve this problem (i.e., our innate ability to empathise, to feel guilty, etc.; in other words, our moral sentiments). In more practical terms, agents who seek only to maximise a utility function or are overconcerned with self-interest (Rosenschein and Zlotkin 1994) can miss good opportunities for themselves that they cannot foresee. In order to make our point clearer, it is important to emphasise the characterisation of altruism: *an altruist acts without an anticipation of increased payoff at any time* even if such reward is likely to happen. This concept also relates to the type of altruism that is an investment in trustworthiness which eventually repays itself, and can, therefore, be considered ultimately as selfish, according to some schools of thought; it is not necessarily the "misuse" of sentiments that allows what we referred to earlier as true altruism.

To all this, a utilitarian MAS researcher might well counterargue that, if humans fall prey to these sentiments and end up doing things that are not to their own advantage even in the long run, then surely there is the chance of the same problem befalling agents if they are endowed with emotions. To show that, even if this happened, it would not be a "problem", is the whole point of the present work. The results of our experiments clearly show that even this type of truly altruistic behaviour has an indirect, unwitting benefit if a *group* of agents is considered.

In brief, the main lessons drawn from Ridley's book are that we keep our *commitments* (or break them) and are capable of living in complex, stable social environments because of our emotional *decisions* (based on our instinctive virtue), not because of our rationality alone. This is enough support in favour of an emotional stance for MAS, given that the whole point of this area is to profit from social action that enriches individual capabilities. If this is so, it means that we need to revisit several notions in MAS, particularly the concept of agents' *autonomy*. We concentrate, briefly and informally, on these issues in Section 5.

These are the general ideas that have inspired the conception of the simulations we describe below. The discussions are much more elaborate in (Ridley 1996, Chapter 7), so we advise the reading of that material for a complete account. Similar motivations are also seen behind the ideas discussed in (Simon 1990) and (Cesta, Miceli, and Rizzo 1996), although these motivations were explored there in rather different contexts and not with this particular issue of emotions in mind.

3 Description of the Experiments: Agents with Moral Sentiments in an IPD Exercise

In this paper we extend the initial results in (Bazzan, Bordini, and Campbell 1997) to other configurations of the simulations, in which agents interact by playing the IPD. Unlike other experiments reported in the literature, the overall population of agents here is divided into groups. We design them to reflect different characteristics of social groups, as we want to investigate Ridley's point about the effects of altruism. We analyse the effects of parameters such as population size, organisation, percentage of agents playing, number of egoists and altruists present in the groups.

At each step of the simulation the characteristics of an agent are assigned: whether it plays or not, a random opponent, its state, etc. Once this is known, each agent decides how to play according to the tactics we introduce later. The points they earn by playing are the standard amounts for the PD payoff matrix: $T = 5$, $R = 3$, $P = 1$, and $S = 0$. After each move, individuals collect the points earned (as in some sort of bank account). The average value of points earned in a certain number of simulation steps is used to determine the *wealth state* of the individual, which influences how it will play. According to two thresholds (T_W and T_S) on this average, an agent's state in each simulation step can be *Wealthy* (W), *Medium* (M), or *Straitened* (S). These thresholds vary in the different types of societies we study, and are better detailed next when we explain these differences. To represent the effort one puts into interacting socially, agents pay P points to play.

In all experiments conducted, individuals can be either egoistic or altruistic. The former type of agent defects in all interactions (ALLD), and the latter plays either Tit-for-Tat (TFT) when the opponent is an agent from another group, hence displaying a fair (reciprocating) behaviour, or plays with Moral Sentiments (MS) when interacting with agents from the same social group (the truly altruistic behaviour). We use the word *partner* to refer to an agent who belongs to the *same social group* as another. Pairs of agents are chosen randomly from all groups to play each round of the game.

The MS strategy for an altruistic agent means that it cooperates with its partners unless it is in a straitened state and the opponent is wealthy. To understand this, we must first think of the most altruistic strategy that is possible in the IPD, namely ALLC (always cooperate). Our MS strategy is close to that, apart from the fact that the altruistic behaviour is dropped when the agent is itself in need of help. Note that the straitened altruist will only defect from a wealthy partner, so its defection will not be too harmful for the other agent; the straitened altruist does not try to recover by taking advantage of a partner who is not in a wealthy state. It is important to emphasise that, when using the MS strategy, the opponent (in terms of the PD) is necessarily a partner (i.e., from the same group), but may be an egoistic agent. In this case, the straitened altruist avoids being exploited by its partner since it cannot afford this. If the opponent is an altruistic partner agent (and, recall, wealthy), then the straitened altruist will clearly be helped (as it will get T points). In the perspective of the wealthy altruistic agent, there is nothing wrong with this: remember that by the fact that they both belong to the same social group we mean that there is an emotional liaison between them.

As usual in IPD experiments, agents have the means of remembering the last move of any opponents they have met in the past. This has no meaning for "pure" egoists since in our design they always defect. However, if they are to learn from past experiences (e.g. that this behaviour does not pay off and that egoistic may not mean "always defect" but rather "only defect while others still cooperate with you"), then that capacity to remember may be useful for egoists as well as others. For altruistic individuals, the memory of the past move influences their current one in the following way: if the opponent is not a partner and has defected in the last move, TFT will lead to defection as well. If the opponent is a partner, the determining factor here is the wealth of both individuals.

We have investigated many scenarios by combining specific values for the parameters mentioned earlier. We design each situation to model characteristics that we can relate to human societies, and report here about the most significant ones.

There are four type of societies[4]: *Long Memory* (LM), *Generous Middle Class* (GM), *Polarised Society* (PS), and *Fair Shares* (FS). In the LM the strong characteristic is that the whole history of agents' performance in their past plays is remembered when classifying them as W, M or P. On the other hand, in the other three types of society, the states of the agents are a function of their performance over a fraction of this time. We have experimentally set this *History Length* to be $HL = 10$ steps for the societies with a limited length of history[5].

As for the GM society, the aim is to check the performance of the groups when agents in state S also take advantage of the MS strategy when playing with agents in state M. In fact, the role of agents in state M is not the one of the middle class, but the role of the wealthy altruists of the society (one may think of them as compassionate: they help even though they cannot afford it as much as the wealthy ones). Therefore, in practice there are only two states of wealth in this society. The PS has been designed so that only a small proportion of agents can be considered to belong to the middle class of the society, but again straitened altruistic partners do not borrow from the middle class.

In the FS the wealth classification of each individual agent depends on the points earned by every agent in the group in the recent history. Each group has its own thresholds which vary at each simulation step. Let $k_1 = P/2$ and $k_2 = T/2$ be two constants (defined experimentally). We identify the wealthiest agent and the poorest agent in the group (Gr), so as to calculate a *difference of wealth* (DW) in that group according to $DW_{Gr} = max(AvgScs_{HL}(Gr)) - min(AvgScs_{HL}(Gr))$, where $AvgScs_{HL}(Gr)$ are the average scores for each of the agents in group Gr in the last HL steps.

If the difference of wealth in the group is substantial, i.e. $DW_{Gr} > (P - k_1)$, then there will be three different classes of agents (as described above) and MS

---

[4] We have used brief illustrative names to characterise the types of societies we have simulated, so that the reader can interpret them easily in the text.

[5] We have also performed simulations with smaller values of HL, which did not introduce significant changes in the results. A detailed study of the effect of the value of HL in the computation of agents' states is envisaged.

is played when an altruistic straitened agent and a wealthy partner are chosen to interact. If DW_{Gr} is not substantial, no agent plays MS (altruists cooperate). When there is a considerable difference in the recent earnings of the agents in the group being analysed, new thresholds are calculated for that group at this simulation step. For this, we employ a factor that reflects the difference of wealth (DWf) in the agents of the particular group (Gr): $DWf_{Gr} = DW_{Gr}/k_2$. The thresholds for the current group (Gr) are then defined as: $T_{W_{Gr}} = max(AvgScs_{HL}(Gr)) - DWf_{Gr}$ and $T_{S_{Gr}} = min(AvgScs_{HL}(Gr)) + DWf_{Gr}$, where T_W and T_S are as described previously.

Each of the above types of societies was tested under the following conditions:

Bankrupt-Excluded (BE): if an agent runs too low in points it is said to be *bankrupt*, in which case neither itself nor its opponent is allowed to play; instead the bankrupt agent is awarded P points so that it can at least afford the price to play in the next step of simulation. Another important characteristic here is that all agents are scheduled to play.

Some-Play (SP): in this version, agents are not given points to recover but are allowed to play even with negative balances in their accounts. Also, only a variable percentage of the agents are selected to play at each time. This aims at representing societies with different opportunities for agents to do "business". The selection of agents to play does not discriminate among their states: even agents in a straitened state can play and in this case they can only hope that the opponent is a wealthy partner playing the MS strategy to help it to recover. Another peculiarity here is that agents that are not selected to play pay $P/2$ points. This represents the costs for "living".

We have simulated the SP cases with $p = 60\%$ and $p = 80\%$ of agents playing. Finally, each one of the twelve combinations above (i.e. the four types of societies in each of the three conditions) was simulated for the following combinations of parameters:

- 3 groups of either 4, 20, 40, 80, or 100 agents; group G1 is formed by altruists only, G3 by egoists only, while G2 is mixed (with variable proportions of egoists and altruists);
- 15 groups of either 4, 20, or 60 agents; more specifically, there are 5 groups of altruists only, 5 mixed groups (i.e., each composed of 50% of egoists), and 5 groups of egoists only.

Each case was repeated 1000 times, enough to nullify variations in individual runs of the simulation. The simulation horizon was $t = 500$ steps for populations of 12 agents; $t = 1000$ for 60 agents; $t = 2000$ for 120, 240, and 300 agents; and $t = 5000$ for more than 300 agents in the society.

Altogether 168 cases were studied, from which we were able to verify the effects of the relevant parameters and draw several conclusions. These appear to be significant for MAS in general, in the quest to use human societies as a model for designing more efficient societies of agents, as we discuss in Section 5. The most significant of these conclusions are presented next.

4 Results and Analysis: the Unwitting Benefit of Altruism

Our main measure of performance is whether the *altruists* perform better than the *egoists*. This can be translated, initially, into whether the group G1 accumulates more points than G3 and, if it does, how long it takes for this to happen (normally the performance of G1 is poor near the beginning of the simulation, whilst G3 has a bad performance by the end). Since G2 is not an homogeneous group, we have to distinguish the two types of agents belonging to it, namely altruists and egoists, who clearly have different levels of performance. We call AM the subgroup of altruists and EM the subgroup of egoists in G2. The homogeneous groups G1 and G3 are called here AH and EH respectively. We then compare the performance of AH to those of the AM and EM subgroups and examine the time needed for AH to surpass AM and EM in performance.

There are two basic types of graphs, the first showing the performance of each of the social groups. We were able to observe the behaviour of each individual agent in every case in which the number of agents was less than 20. Otherwise, for the second type of graph, we only depict the behaviours of the AH, AM, EM, EH types. Another important comparison is between AM and EM. We present only a small number of graphs and reduced quantitative analysis due to the lack of space. We provide a lookup table (see Table 1) with the abbreviation we have introduced so far, to facilitate the reading of the analysis of the results presented in this section.

Ab.	Definition	Ab.	Definition
G1	A homogeneous group of altruists	MS	Moral Sentiments (the strategy we have introduced)
G2	A mixed group (i.e., one that has both egoists and altruists)	LM	Long Memory (all past earnings count in wealth classification)
G3	A homogeneous group of egoists	GM	Generous Middle Class (agents in state M also play MS)
AH	Altruist agents in a Homogeneous group	PS	Polarised Society (society with an attenuated middle class)
AM	Altruist agents in a Mixed group	FS	Fair Shares (society with variable wealth classification thresholds)
EM	Egoist agents in a Mixed group	BE	Bankrupt-Excluded
EH	Egoist agents in a Homogeneous group	SP	Same-Play (not all agents are chosen to play the IPD each step)

Table 1. A Lookup Table with the Abbreviations Used Below

Besides the time it takes for altruists to overtake the egoists, other measurements of performance were made using a snapshot in the simulation regarding the amount of points (per capita, so as to account for differences in the size of the groups) accumulated by the best group at that moment. This gives us a measure of the wealth of the society. Finally, we have also measured the number of times the MS strategy was selected and look at the effect this has on the wealth of the group and on the performance of the altruists. The general results can be seen in Figure 1 (the performance of social groups and types of agents are depicted in Graphs 1(c) and 1(d), respectively). The notation $G_n(a/e)$ means that group n has a agents of which e are egoists.

Despite the various configurations of conditions and parameters introduced in the present set of simulations, we were able to confirm the conclusions previously reported (Bazzan, Bordini, and Campbell 1997). These major lessons are:

1. The more egoists in a group, the faster the group collects points initially, but the worse is its performance after some time—which means that rational fools maximise their earnings in the short term but compromise their future performance (a consequence of the reciprocating character of TFT). Groups of altruists accumulate more points than the others in the long run.
2. The more egoists in the society:
   (a) the less time it takes for G1 to surpass G2, no matter what percentage of agents is playing; in most cases studied, this is also valid regarding the time for AM to surpass EM;
   (b) the fewer points it collects as a whole (regardless of the percentage of agents playing).

Thus, the presence of the egoists is harmful for all members of the group in the long run, since they would all be performing better if the egoists would stop being rational fools.

Next, we enumerate more recent conclusions, considering the whole range of parameters and types of simulations. One important observation which we have not made explicit before is that:

3. The generosity of the MS strategy yields a better performance for the group than mere reciprocity—recall that reciprocity is what accounts for the long-term success of individual agents; ultimately, the reason for the conclusions above.

In Figure 1 we have added a fourth line to the group graphs (a) and (c) which is the average of the performance of G1 and G3 (**Avg(G1,G3)**, in the figure). This is to make it easier to visualise how much better G2 is doing because of the generosity of its altruists. Note that if the altruists in G2 were playing TFT instead of MS within the group, the performance of G2 would be exactly that of the average of G1 and G3's performances, rather than what it is in the figure[6]. This is a remarkable finding, whose message can be understood better in terms of an analogy. If one gives money to a homeless person and nobody else gets to know about it, this is clearly the case where altruism has no personal reward. It is the situation that we mention in Section 2 where one is falling prey to the sentiments that are an important mechanism in social life, and it happens that they bring great personal rewards in normal circumstances through trustworthiness. In circumstances where no personal reward ensues, one interesting

---

[6] This is so because, if a group has half of its agents performing as well as agents in G1 and the other half performing as badly as the ones in G3, the group as a whole has the exact average of G1 and G3.

side-effect occurs: the improvement of the social group! In the homeless analogy, it is as if one is not better off by one's altruistic act, but one's city as a whole is doing much better (compare, in Graph 1(c), G2 with Avg(G1,G3)), without reducing significantly one's own performance (compare, in Graph 1(d), AM with AH). Regarding MAS, this implies a better performance of the overall system, which is important. In terms of the PD, this happens because, for the group, a joint reward of $T + S$ earned when an egoist plays against a wealthy/medium altruist partner, is better than $P + P$, received when TFT is played against ALLD. It is a similar effect to the Smithian finding that the division of labour leads to society being *more than the sum of its parts*. The lesson here is: even the individual drawback of being driven by an emotional response when it will not repay itself allows a group that is encumbered with rational fools to perform much better than it would if emotions were used only for the purpose for which they evolved in our species (i.e., the virtuous purely maximising their individual earnings in the long run).

Figure 1 also shows the effect of the use of the MS strategy. Graphs (a) and (b) are from the LM type of society, where MS was not used (ALLC was used instead). On the other hand, graphs (c) and (d) are from the FS society, where the use of MS is best managed (recall that the thresholds were variable there). A very interesting effect is seen here. Although the graphs for the groups (1(a) and 1(c)) have very similar shapes, one can see easily that this is not so in the graphs for the types of agents (1(b) and 1(d)). While in the LM society EM agents are doing consistently better than AM, the same does not happen in the society FS, where MS is being used! The reason is that with ALLC the altruists are being too much exploited by their selfish partners. The MS strategy is "kind" enough to keep the performance of the mixed group higher than with pure reciprocation (remember the similarity of the curves for G2 in (a) and (c)), yet being fairer to those who are actually responsible for the good performance of the group.

Concerning the various sizes of populations and their compositions, for both the BE and SP conditions, we conclude that:

4. The larger the number of agents in the groups:
   (a) the longer it takes for G1 to surpass G2 and for AM to surpass EM (although, in some cases of LM, G1 already begins by performing better than G2);
   (b) the greater the total use of MS (though this is not always true regarding its use per capita).
5. The reverse of items 4a and 4b is true if the number of agents is kept fixed but distributed in a larger number of groups.
6. In general, the larger the number of agents in the groups, the more points the group collects, no matter what number of groups is involved.
7. The effect of the number of egoists on the amount of use of the MS strategy is not coherent among the different types of societies. While the latter increases with the former for the society FS, it decreases for GM, and has no monotonic relation in PS.

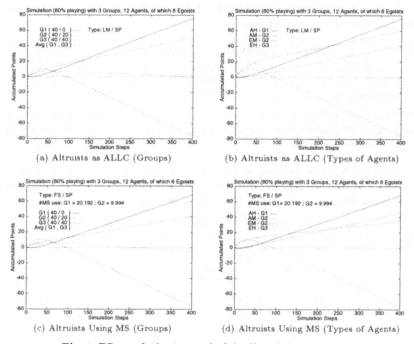

Fig. 1. Effects of Altruism and of the Use of the MS Strategy

8. For the case where there is more use of MS (society GM), the time for AM to overtake EM is lower. However, the use of the MS strategy slightly decreases the number of points that are accumulated. (See discussion near the end of this section.)

9. The more groups, the fairer the picture is: the EM subgroups in the mixed groups perform closer to their homogeneous counterparts, as do AM subgroups with respect to groups of altruists only (so the surplus performance of mixed groups is not as conspicuous here).

From items 4b, 5, and 9, we can conclude that the effect of the MS strategy is more conspicuous in societies with few but large groups, where partners have more chance to interact.

By comparing the BE and SP conditions, we can conclude that:

10. Irrespective of the other parameters, when agents are playing under BE, the altruists outperform the egoists by an even greater margin and the society as a whole collects more points. This is explained by the fact that in BE all agents play (except the small proportion that is bankrupt): the more opportunities for "business" exist at each instant in the society, the more rapidly the simulation stabilises.

11. Under SP, agents use the MS more often, and this helps the altruists.

As for the comparison of the different types of societies and conditions concerning the use of the MS strategy:

12. Visual comparison of the graphs for GM and FS show that they are very similar; sometimes AM overtakes EM faster in GM, but FS has slightly greater accumulated points. We believe this is due to the use of MS being better managed in FS (i.e., it happens only when it is really necessary).

Finally, comparing the cases for which we have defined three variations on the number of egoists in the mixed group (keeping the other parameters fixed) we conclude that:

13. Every increase in the number of egoists in G2 by 25% causes the performance of those egoists to decrease by 36% of what it was before (in terms of accumulated points by the end of the simulation).

The numbers in the item above are averages of the ratios for all types of societies. There are variations for each type but the ratios are very similar when, in the same type of society, the total number of agents is increased. Based on this and other parameters still to be considered (e.g. length of stay), one could create heuristics for an egoist agent deciding which group to join and seeking the one where its attitude would be most profitable. The effect of increasing the number of egoists in the mixed group (G2) is seen in Figure 2. G2 is composed of $\frac{1}{4}$ and $\frac{3}{4}$ of egoists in graphs (a) and (b), respectively.

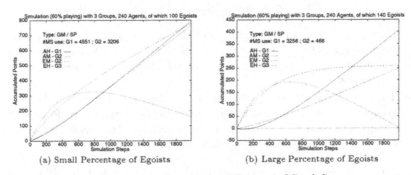

(a) Small Percentage of Egoists   (b) Large Percentage of Egoists

Fig. 2. Effects of the Percentage of Egoists in Mixed Groups

The horizon of the simulations shown in some of the graphs in this paper is not always sufficient for AH and AM to perform better than EM. Nevertheless, the trend in those graphs (e.g., Figure 2(a) and 2(b)) shows clearly that this would happen soon afterwards. In some cases with few EM, these really have the best performance of all (and in some cases when MS was not being used, they performed better than AM). This is because the few egoists can count on the generosity of the (many) altruists in their group, who cooperate with them despite the fact that they are selfish, for the sake of group welfare.

A current drawback is the fact that the use of MS slightly decreases the amount of accumulated points in comparison with ALLC (see Figure 1), because this "defect to be cared for" mechanism results in a lower total of points to the group than a mutual cooperation. Recall that for the group, $S + T$ was better than $P + P$, but not better than $R + R$ (due to the condition of the PD that $R > (S + T)/2$ must hold) which could happen between two partner altruists playing ALLC. However, it is important to remember too that this mechanism is essential to allow the altruists to discern when they can afford to cooperate with partners (who may be egoists); we have discussed this in our comments on Figure 1. Therefore, future extensions should also include some sort of penalty for societies with straitened agents, which would reverse the current side-effect of decreased accumulated points due to agents helping their partners. This is not just artificial modelling, for we see this phenomenon in human societies: the more capital a group has, the greater the amount of money that can be earned from the financial interactions in which they engage. Note that, if we decided that altruists would always cooperate among themselves (even when not wealthy) in order to prevent the drawback, there would not be a clear way of distinguishing altruist and egoist partners without changing the rules of the PD and agents being informed of the opponents' strategy artificially. (Interestingly, it is not possible to distinguish these strategies through behaviour.)

In short, the results show clearly that, in the long run, groups of altruistic agents (G1 and AM) accumulate more points than any other. The altruists are not rational fools: they compromise their present possibilities of gain to make sure they will do well in the future. The whole group performs well because individual failures are compensated by the generosity of those doing well, avoiding bankruptcy. In other words, to reciprocate pays off in the long run and altruism improves the performance of the group! Also, restrained altruism (rather than unconditional) produces more sensible results as far as the altruists are concerned (they at least perform better than their egoistic partners, while still keeping an improved group performance). We have also verified that homogeneous groups of egoists (G3) perform very well only in the short term. Their selfishness in the game compromises their reputation: once the agents in a society have found out about their character, they suffer retaliation (characteristic of the TFT). At this point, egoists either only earn enough points to survive, that is, pay to play in the next step (in the BE condition), or go to complete bankruptcy (in SP). Mixed groups (G2) have an intermediate performance, but they do not exhibit the "catastrophic" effect seen in a group where there are no altruists. The presence of some altruists there assures the relative development of the group.

5 Discussion: Let Agents be Benevolent

As part of our anthropological approach to interoperability of Multi-Agent Systems (Bordini and Campbell 1995; Bordini, Campbell, and Vieira 1997; Bordini 1998) we are now concerned with agents' emotions or sentiments. We believe that, in future, agreement on emotions (and perhaps perceptions) would avoid the need to standardise on other aspects of agency while still allowing interoperability of MAS (through our anthropological approach). We draw this lesson from social anthropology: one of the things that an anthropologist can be sure is present in all cultures is the whole spectrum of human emotions; Ridley (1996) says that they are *universally recognisable*, and even motives such as avoiding guilt are common across all cultures. An *anthropologist agent* (i.e., an agent responsible for supporting migrant agents in their adaptation to "strange" societies) needs, thus, to study the "culture" present in *target societies*. "But our cultures are not random collections of arbitrary habits. They are canalized expressions of our instincts. ... That is why, for all their superficial differences of language and custom, foreign cultures are still immediately comprehensible at the deeper level of motives, emotions and social habits." (Ridley 1996).

Further, our view is that an *emotional stance* is yet another "missing point" (Castelfranchi 1990) in present MAS. It should not be considered only for its role in believability, which is the point that most works that consider emotions as being relevant to agents make (see, for example, (Rizzo *et al.* 1997; Bates 1994; Hayes-Roth, Brownston, and van Gent 1995)). It is evident from the results shown here that to behave altruistically (even in a prisoner's dilemma context, where *rationality* has always been paramount) can prevent agents (of whatever paradigm) being *rational fools*, for it secures a good performance in the long run for the agents and in the more extreme cases for their social groups, at least (metaphorically, a social group can be seen as a complete MAS, wherever the notion of group is not available). This leads us to question the current widespread idea in MAS that autonomous agents should necessarily be selfish. Ridley wittily says that sociobiology "caught the self-interest virus" in the 1960s. It can be said that MAS has caught the same virus too.

Apart from the whole tradition of work on utility maximisation in the game-theoretic approach (Rosenschein and Genesereth 1985; Rosenschein and Zlotkin 1994) where agents are by definition self-interested, among the representatives of the "autonomy as selfishness" outlook in MAS are d'Inverno and Luck (1996) who have claimed:

> Cooperation will occur between two parties only when it is considered advantageous to each party to do so. Autonomous agents are thus selfish agents. A goal (whether traditionally viewed as 'selfish' or 'altruistic') will always be adopted so as to satisfy a 'selfish' motivation. (page 529)
>
> The effects of benevolence are possible, but only through self-serving motivations. (page 533)

In terms of the history of MAS, this line of thought seems to have started with the the discussion on social power in (Castelfranchi 1990). The paper was in the right direction at that stage, when benevolence was being taken for granted. It is time now to relocate benevolence, not as something taken for granted, but as an important phenomenon which may *evolve* in societies of autonomous intelligent agents from explorations of agent emotions. This issue should be of interest for those concerned with agent autonomy via the cognitive (as opposed to utilitarian) view of the field (c.f. (Conte and Castelfranchi 1995)).

The misconception about autonomy and benevolence goes together with the absence of an explicit emotional component in present MAS theories. Motivations do not have to be necessarily self-serving. Consider, e.g., the idea of terminal interest adoption defined by Conte and Castelfranchi (1995). They mention the possibility of autonomous agents adopting others' interests out of affection, although they do not concentrate on the emotional aspects of agents in that book. On the other hand, they say that the usual means by which an agent can act in a selfless way, i.e. adopt a goal of another agent, is through an individual (personal) goal of being benevolent (compassionate) towards that agent. Further, they state that truly benevolent agents are those who undertake a mode of goal adoption they call *terminal*, which they claim to be the type of adoption common since the early days of MAS (i.e., it is *assumed* that agents will adopt each other's goals; essentially, these agents are not fully autonomous). This is, therefore, the perfect ground for d'Inverno and Luck's definition (quoted above). So in this context there is a point in saying that when an agent is being benevolent, either it is not autonomous or it is pursuing an individual goal and thus its motivation is ultimately selfish. The problem is exactly in the artificial mechanism of modelling benevolence as an individual goal *per se*, due to the lack of representation and processing of "emotion". Recall that the important consequence of the emotional stance is the ability to truly exploit societal interaction in MAS, according to our discussion on the role of emotions in human social nature. In brief, emotional processing should be balanced with rational processing in the decision-making process in autonomous agents.

To round off the argument, agent autonomy is not necessarily concerned with fulfilling an agent's own selfish motivations; it has to do with its freedom to *choose* how to behave (or to have the resources to do something by itself, depending on the context)—even if that means choosing what is not best for its own goals, e.g. under the influence of emotional decisions (as we have remarked, this requires a specific part of the agent's architecture to deal with emotions). We observe in the results of our simulation that altruism prevents agents from being rational fools. As Ridley puts it, when being truly altruistic (i.e., doing something in the interests of others at one's own expense and even with no future reward at all), we are giving way to emotions which are an important mechanism behind the complex brand of social interactions that humans experience. It is certainly worth recovering this notion for the benefit of MAS.

The main advantage of the simulations we present here is that it allows us to verify some of Ridley's propositions; it also yields some insights into the issues discussed above. Note that, whilst the quantitative results of the simulations presented here apply to MAS where the IPD metaphor (with the further assumptions we have made here, e.g., the existence of groups) makes sense, Ridley's line of argument, presented in Section 2, seems to apply quite generally; it is a high-level argument in support of our suggestion that designers of general[7] MAS architecture should consider an emotional aspect as well as the traditional rational

---

[7] By general we mean architecture for all sorts of agents and not only those that have a specific relation to "believability"; see references for this area given above.

one, as we assert in this paper. We do not aim at proposing a specific implementation of emotions in an agent architecture. There have been only a few attempts to do so in general agent architectures so far, but see (Aubé and Senteni 1996; Sloman and Poli 1996). (Sloman and Poli's SIM_AGENT and Tok, an architecture for believable agents, are mentioned in (Müller 1999), in this volume.)

Our ideas on moral sentiments relate closely to at least two papers in this volume. First, emotions in agents are undoubtedly related to issues of *formation* of norms (conventions) among autonomous agents (Conte, Castelfranchi, and Dignum 1999). It is easy to see that emotions are important in attaching agents to social norms—Doran mentioned in (1998b) that emotions may be an important mechanism for designers of society to "manipulate" agents, e.g., to maintain their collective misbelief in "cults" (Doran 1998a). However, in a contrary view, it is plausible that just as emotions are the right basis for seeing that autonomous agents can be *autonomous* and still behave (truly) altruistically as we have argued above, studying emotions in agent architectures can help us understand how autonomous agents form and perpetuate conventions, which are essential for social behaviour. These are interesting issues to be addressed in further research.

Second, similar motivations to (Conte, Castelfranchi, and Dignum 1999) can be found in (Ossowski and García-Serrano 1999), which relies on both a sociologic and an economic approach. They use the former to define what they call structural cooperation, a coordination mechanism in which a social structure biases autonomous agent behaviour. The economic approach is then used to determine the outcome of the process of social coordination. Their main point is that the apparent "irrational" social actions of individuals in a certain society can be seen as a reflection of the society's social structure (e.g. norms, values, and behaviour rules). Respecting such social structure constrains the individuals' choices as it prescribes what one has to do as a member, while also biasing their behaviours so as to ensure the necessary conditions for the survival of that society. As in the case of (Conte, Castelfranchi, and Dignum 1999), they are concerned with social action without compromising on agents' autonomy; this seems to be connected intrinsically to some notions of emotions or moral sentiments.

In a recent paper, Castelfranchi, de Rosis, and Falcone (1997) recognise the importance of emotions in domains other than the usual believable-agents one, which seems to support our argument. When commenting on the several reasons for agents needing personalities they include *Social/Cognitive Modelling*, as follows:

> Since in nature and in society agents have personality and this seems
> an important construct in psychology, one might aim at modelling personality in agents (or emotions or cognitive biases) to reproduce relevant
> features of human interaction. (page 16)

We believe this should be a new source of guidance for the work on MAS as originally defined as the field of Distributed Artificial Intelligence concerned with coordinated intelligent behaviour among a collection of autonomous intelligent agents (Gasser 1987). In other words, if we build agents' rationality inspired by the human counterpart but fail to provide them with other important human mechanisms like emotions, we shall find that we have built rationally foolish agents, which will be no more useful to their collaborators than rational fools are to human societies (with analogues of all the undesirable consequences to individuals too).

6 Conclusions

Our results suggest strongly that rational fools maximise their earnings in the short term but compromise their performance in the long run, while altruists may not have the best performance at the beginning of the simulations, but normally end up much better than the others. The results also show clearly that the more altruists there are in a group, the better they, and the group as a whole, perform; more importantly, their generosity, although somewhat "irrational" from an individual point of view, implies that the group as a whole performs significantly better than when pure reciprocation is used. Accordingly, we conclude that to behave rationally (in the classical sense in game theory) may not be the best attitude in the long run or as far as the group is concerned. We believe that a present "missing point" in MAS that would yield societal surplus (in a sense resembling the Smithian notion of the society being more than the sum of its individuals), as well as agent-level improvement, is an emotional stance to be amalgamated with the present rational/intentional one. Further, we have related this present work to our anthropological approach to MAS, and remarked on the consequential view that the notion of agent autonomy and others related to it deserve reevaluation.

There are various other hypotheses to be tested and many variations and extensions of these simulations to consider. We shall comment on these in future papers. One example we mentioned earlier was the strategy for egoists attempting to join the group that maximises their own earnings. Also, we have mentioned in Section 4 that future extensions should also account for the burden that it is to have straitened agents in a social group, which would reverse the current side-effect of decreased accumulated points in the use of the MS strategy. Further, we plan to investigate the robustness of our strategy in an "artificial life" type of simulation (with a group-related fitness functions, which is not usual). Further, egoistic agents could learn by reinforcement that their behaviour is not appropriate and try to reverse it, if they could regain trustworthiness in the society. We also plan to introduce some mechanism to allow agents to discover the characters of others and eventually exercise a freedom to refuse them as partners in future social interactions, as Ridley argues to be the case among humans.

Acknowledgements

We would like to acknowledge the valuable comments from the anonymous referees and reviewer for this paper and another related one. Rafael H. Bordini gratefully acknowledges CAPES (Brazilian government agency for postgraduate studies) for the grant for his PhD at University College London.

References

Aubé, M., and Senteni, A. 1996. Emotions as commitements operators: a foundation for control structure in multi-agents systems. In Van de Velde, W., and Perram, J., eds., *Proceedings of the Seventh Workshop on Modelling Autonomous Agents in a Multi-Agent World (MAAMAW'96), 22 25 January, Eindhoven, The Netherlands,* number 1038 in Lecture Notes in Artificial Intelligence, 13 25. London: Springer-Verlag.

Axelrod, R. 1984. *The Evolution of Cooperation.* New York: Basic Books.

Bates, J. 1994. The role of emotion in believable agents. *Communications of the ACM* 37(7):122 125.

Bazzan, A. L. C., Bordini, R. H., and Campbell, J. A. 1997. Agents with moral sentiments in an iterated prisoner's dilemma exercise. In Dautenhahn, K., Masthoff, J., and Numaoka, C., eds., *Proceedings of the AAAI Fall Symposium on Socially Intelligent Agents, 8 10 November, Cambridge, MA,* 4 6. Menlo Park, CA: AAAI Press. AAAI Press Technical Report FS-97-02. UCL-CS [RN/97/74]. URL: http://www.cs.ucl.ac.uk/staff/R.Bordini.

Binmore, K. 1998. Review of R. Axelrod's "The complexity of cooperation: Agent-based models of competition and collaboration". *Journal of Artificial Societies and Social Simulation* 1(1). <http://www.soc.surrey.ac.uk/JASSS/1/1/review1.html>.

Bordini, R. H., and Campbell, J. A. 1995. Towards an anthropological approach to agent adaptation. In *Proceedings of the First International Workshop on Decentralized Intelligent and Multi-Agent Systems (DIMAS'95),* II/74 II/83. Krakow, Poland: Dom Wydawnictwa Naukowych, 22 24 November, 1995. UCL-CS [RN/95/78]. URL: http://www.cs.ucl.ac.uk/staff/R.Bordini.

Bordini, R. H., Campbell, J. A., and Vieira, R. 1997. Ascription of intensional ontologies in anthropological descriptions of multi-agent systems. In Kandzia, P., and Klusch, M., eds., *Proceedings of the First International Workshop on Cooperative Information Agents (CIA'97), 26-28 February, Kiel, Germany,* volume 1202 of *Lecture Notes in Artificial Intelligence,* 235 247. Berlin: Springer-Verlag. UCL-CS [RN/97/1]. URL: http://www.cs.ucl.ac.uk/staff/R.Bordini.

Bordini, R. H. 1998. *Contributions to an Anthropological Approach to the Cultural Adaptation of Migran Agents.* Ph.D. Dissertation, University of London. To appear.

Brembs, B. 1996. Chaos, cheating and cooperation: Potential solutions to the prisoner's dilemma. *Oikos* 76(1):14 24.

Castelfranchi, C., de Rosis, F., and Falcone, R. 1997. Social attitudes and personalities in agents. In *Proceedings of the AAAI Fall Symposium on Socially Intelligent Agents.* Cambridge, Massachusetts, 8 10 November, 1997.

Castelfranchi, C. 1990. Social power: a point missed in multi-agent DAI and HCI. In Demazeau, Y., and Müller, J.-P., eds., *Decentralized A.I. Proceedings of the First European Workshop on Modelling Autonomous Agents in a Multi-Agent World (MAAMAW'89), 16 18 August, Cambridge, 1989.* Amsterdam: Elsevier Science B.V. 49 62.

Cesta, A., Miceli, M., and Rizzo, P. 1996. Help under risky conditions: Robustness of the social attitude and system performance. In Durfee, E., ed., *Proceedings of the Second International Conference on Multi-Agent Systems (ICMAS'96), 11 13 December, Kyoto, Japan,* 18 25. Menlo Park, CA: AAAI Press.

Conte, R., and Castelfranchi, C. 1995. *Cognitive and Social Action*. London: UCL Press.

Conte, R., Castelfranchi, C., and Dignum, F. 1999. Autonomous norm-acceptance. In Müller, J. P., Singh, M. P., and Rao, A. S., eds., *Intelligent Agents V Proceedings of the Fifth International Workshop on Agent Theories, Architectures, and Languages (ATAL-98)*, Lecture Notes in Artificial Intelligence. Heidelberg: Springer-Verlag. In this volume.

Dawkins, R. 1989. *The Selfish Gene*. Oxford: Oxford University Press, new edition.

d'Inverno, M., and Luck, M. 1996. Understanding autonomous interaction. In Wahlster, W., ed., *Proceedings of the 12th European Conference on Artificial Intelligence (ECAI'96)*.

Doran, J. 1998a. Simulating collective misbelief. *Journal of Artificial Societies and Social Simulation* 1(1). <http://www.soc.surrey.ac.uk/JASSS/1/1/3.html>.

Doran, J. 1998b. Social simulation, agents and artificial societies. In Demazeau, Y., ed., *Proceedings of the Third International Conference on Multi-Agent Systems (ICMAS'98), Agents' World, 4 7 July, Paris*, 4 5. Washington: IEEE Computer Society Press. Extended Abstract for an Invited Talk.

Gasser, L. 1987. Distribution and coordination of tasks among intelligent agents. In *Proceedings of the First Scandinavian Conference on Artificial Intelligence*. Tromsö, Norway, March, 1987.

Hayes-Roth, B., Brownston, L., and van Gent, R. 1995. Multiagent collaboration in directed improvisation. In Lesser, V., and Gasser, L., eds., *Proceedings of the First International Conference on Multi-Agent Systems (ICMAS'95), 12 14 June, San Francisco, CA*, 148 154. Menlo Park, CA: AAAI Press / MIT Press.

Müller, J. P. 1999. The right agent (architecture) to do the right thing. In Müller, J. P., Singh, M. P., and Rao, A. S., eds., *Intelligent Agents V Proceedings of the Fifth International Workshop on Agent Theories, Architectures, and Languages (ATAL-98)*, Lecture Notes in Artificial Intelligence. Heidelberg: Springer-Verlag. In this volume.

Ossowski, S., and García-Serrano, A. 1999. Social structure in artificial agent societies: Implications for autonomous problem-solving agents. In Müller, J. P., Singh, M. P., and Rao, A. S., eds., *Intelligent Agents V Proceedings of the Fifth International Workshop on Agent Theories, Architectures, and Languages (ATAL-98)*, Lecture Notes in Artificial Intelligence. Heidelberg: Springer-Verlag. In this volume.

Ridley, M. 1996. *The Origins of Virtue*. London: Viking Press.

Rizzo, P., Veloso, M., Miceli, M., and Cesta, A. 1997. Personality-driven social behaviors in believable agents. In *Proceedings of the AAAI Fall Symposium on Socially Intelligent Agents*. Cambridge, Massachusetts, 8 10 November, 1997.

Rosenschein, J., and Genesereth, M. 1985. Deals among rational agents. In Joshi, A., ed., *Proceedings of the Ninth International Joint Conference on Artificial Intelligence (IJCAI-85)*. Los Angeles, CA: AAAI Press / Morgan Kaufmann. 91 99.

Rosenschein, J., and Zlotkin, G. 1994. *Rules of Encounter*. Cambridge, MA: MIT Press.

Simon, H. A. 1990. A mechanism for social selection and successful altruism. *Science* 250(4988):1665 1668.

Sloman, A., and Poli, R. 1996. SIM_AGENT: A toolkit for exploring agent designs. In Wooldridge, M., Müller, J. P., and Tambe, M., eds., *Intelligent Agents II Proceedings of the Second Internation Workshop on Agent Theories, Architectures, and Languages (ATAL'95), held as part of IJCAI'95, Montréal, Canada, August 1995*, number 1037 in Lecture Notes In Artificial Intelligence, 392 407. Berlin: Springer-Verlag.

Social Structure in Artificial Agent Societies: Implications for Autonomous Problem-Solving Agents[*]

Sascha Ossowski [1] and Ana García-Serrano [2]

[1] School of Engineering, Rey Juan Carlos University at Madrid,
Campus de Móstoles s/n, 28933 Móstoles (Madrid), Spain
S.Ossowski@escet.urjc.es

[2] Department of Artificial Intelligence, Technical University of Madrid,
Campus de Montegancedo s/n, 28660 Boadilla del Monte (Madrid), Spain
agarcia@dia.fi.upm.es

Abstract. In Distributed Problem-solving systems a group of purposefully designed computational agents interact and co-ordinate their activities so as to jointly achieve a global task. Social co-ordination is a decentralised mechanism, that sets out from autonomous, non-benevolent agents that interact primarily to improve the degree of attainment of their local goals. One way of ensuring the effectiveness of social co-ordination with respect to global problem solving is to rely on self-interested agents and to coerce their behaviour in a desired direction. In this paper we model the notion of social structure for a particular class of multiagent domains, and determine its functionality with respect to social co-ordination. We show how social structure can be used to bias macro-level properties in the frame of multiagent system design, and discuss micro-level implications respecting the architecture of autonomous problem-solving agents.

1. Introduction

Distributed Problem-Solving (DPS) relies on a purposefully designed architecture of computational agents that interact in order to achieve jointly a desired global functionality. The traditional DPS design philosophy of *reductionism*, that relies on a top-down decomposition of the global task, the assignment of subtasks to agents and co-ordination based on pre-established interaction patterns among *benevolent* agents, often turns out to be too rigid for large-scale agent systems [8]. Instead, a *constructionist* approach, based on the metaphor of societies of *autonomous problem-solving agents*, has become popular: agents are primarily interested in their local goals and interact to increase the degree of their attainment. This *decentralised* interaction [5] is termed *social co-ordination*. In order that the DPS system copes with the global task,

---

[*] This work was partially supported by the Human Capital and Mobility Program (HCM) of the European Union, contract ERBCHBICT941611.

social co-ordination must be based on agent behaviour that lies between benevolence and self-interest [11].

Two paradigms exist respecting social co-ordination. The first influences self-interested agent behaviour *directly*, by modifying its *internal* concept of rationality. Jennings and Campos, for instance, introduce the concept of "social rationality", according to which an agent selects certain behaviour only if it is either beneficial for itself *or* for society [8]. Brainov's notion of *altruism* is another representative of this current [2]. The second class of approaches, exemplified by Shoham and Tennenholz's notion of social laws [16], provides a higher degree of cognitive plausibility as it changes the agents' behaviour *indirectly* through a coercive *external* context.

The latter approach requires a model of self-interested action in a multiagent world. Again, two major approaches exist [11]. The *sociological* approach expresses the agents' positions in society through qualitative relations of dependence [3], which determine how they can help (or harm) each other. Sichman and Demazeau present a framework that models agent interactions on this basis [17]. By contrast, the *economic* approach [14] models an agent's self-interested action by means of a utility function, which quantitatively measures the "benefits" that it obtains from different ways of co-ordinating its behaviour with the group. On the one hand, the latter approach overcomes the problems of conceptual fuzziness of the former, as it is grounded in the well-developed mathematical framework of game theory. On the other, the sociological approach makes the structural relations in society explicit. These relations turn out to be crucial for social co-ordination, but are entirely hidden in the utility function of the economic approach.

In this paper, we present the co-ordination mechanism of *structural co-operation*, in which *social structure* biases autonomous agent behaviour, so as to make it instrumental for problem solving. We rely on the sociological approach to define *structural* notions within an agent society, while the economic approach is used to determine the outcome of the *process* of social co-ordination.

Section 2 describes our model of societies of autonomous problem-solving agents, and outlines our notion of social structure and its effects. Section 3 maps it to a bargaining framework, in order to develop an operational model of structural co-operation. Section 4 discusses the repercussions of our findings on the micro-level, while concluding remarks are presented in Section 5.

2. Social Structure and its Functionality

The model of social co-ordination that will be presented in this section goes back to Sociology, and in particular to the school of *structural functionalism* that was popular in the first part of this century. Apparently "irrational" social actions of individuals in a certain society (e.g. rituals) are seen as a reflections of the society's *social structure* (e.g. its norm, values and behaviour rules). Respecting an individual, social structure constrains its choice as it prescribes what "one has to do" as member of society. Still, with respect to society, a *function* is ascribed to social structure: it biases the individuals (potentially self-interested) behaviour so as to ensure the necessary conditions for the existence and the reproduction (or "survival") of society [13].

In the sequel, structural functionalist *explanations* are put upside down: we aim to *design* a social structure, that biases the self-interested behaviour of computational social agents, in order that the result of social co-ordination be instrumental with respect to a desired global functionality. We will call this mechanism *structural co-operation*.

2.1 Domain Model

In this section we present a formal description of the class of multiagent worlds that we are interested in: societies of cognitive agents that reactively develop short-term plans. Elsewhere [4], we have argued that such a stance is appropriate for a variety of real world scenarios, such as many decisions support domains.

Let S be a set of *world states* and Π a finite set of *plans*. The execution of a plan π changes the state of the world, which is modelled as a partially defined mapping

$$res: \Pi \times S \to S.$$

A plan is *executable* in s, if only if *res* is defined for a certain world state s. We express this formally by means of the predicate $exec(\pi,s)$. At least one *empty plan* π_ε is required to be included in the set of plans Π; it is modelled as identity.

There is a set of agents A, each of which can act in the world thereby modifying its state. An agent $\alpha \in A$ is characterised by the following notions:

- a predicate $can(\alpha,\pi)$, determining the *individual plans* $\pi \in \Pi$ that α is able to execute. An agent α is always capable of executing the empty plan π_ε;
- a predicate $ideal(\alpha,s)$, expressing the states $s \in S$ that the agent $\alpha \in A$ would ideally like to bring about;
- a metric function d_α, which maps two states to a real number, representing agent α's estimation of "how far" one state is away from another. It usually models the notion of (relative) "difficulty" to bring about changes between world states.

In the scenarios that we are interested in, an agent usually cannot fully reach an ideal state. So, we will use the notion of ideal states together with the distance measure d_α to describe an agent's preferences respecting world states. Note that the agents in A may have different (partially conflicting) ideal states and may even measure the distance between states in different scales.

We now introduce a notion of interdependent action. The set M of *multiplans* comprises all multisets over the individual plans Π, i.e. $M = bagof(\Pi)$. A multiplan $\mu \in M$ models the simultaneous execution of all its component plans, i.e. of the individual plans $\pi \in \mu$ that are contained in the multiset μ. The commutative operator $\circ$ denotes multiset union and hence states that its operands are executed together[1].

---

[1] In the sequel, we will use a set of cardinality one and its only element indiscriminately. So, for instance, we write $\mu = \pi \circ \pi' = \pi' \circ \pi = \{\pi,\pi'\}$ and $\mu \circ \pi = \pi \circ \mu = \{\pi,\pi,\pi'\}$.

By identifying an individual plan with a multiplan that contains it as its only element, the partial function *res* is extended to multiplans:

$$res : M \times S \to S \; .$$

The function *res* is undefined for a multiplan μ and a state s, if some of the individual plans that it contains are *incompatible*, i.e. in case that in a state s of a modelled domain it is impossible to execute them simultaneously. Otherwise, μ is said to be *executable* in s (formally: $exec(\mu,s)$). The empty plan π_ε is compatible with every multiplan and does not affect its outcome.

The notion of capability for executing a multiplan is also a natural extension of the single agent case. We define the set of groups Γ as the powerset of the set of agents, i.e. $\Gamma = \wp(A)$. A group $\gamma \in \Gamma$ is capable of executing a multiplan μ, if there is an assignment such that every agent is to execute exactly one individual plan and this agent is capable of doing so, i.e. there is a bijective mapping ψ from individual plans to agents, such that

$$can(\gamma, \mu) \equiv \forall \pi \in \mu. \; can(\psi(\pi), \pi) \; .$$

Definition 1. A social co-ordination setting D is defined by the sets of individuals S, Π, A, M and Γ, the functions *res*, d_α and $\circ$ as well as the predicates *exec*, *can* and *ideal*.

2.2 The Dependence Structure

2.2.1 Plan Relations

In a setting of the above type different relations between plans arise. In a situation s a plan π can be in four mutually exclusive qualitative relations to a multiplan μ:

Definition 2. Relations between plans

$$indifferent_s(\pi, \mu) \quad \Leftrightarrow \quad (exec(\pi, s) \wedge exec(\pi \circ \mu, s) \wedge res(\pi \circ \mu, s) = res(\pi, s))$$
$$\vee \; (\neg exec(\pi, s) \wedge \neg exec(\pi \circ \mu, s))$$
$$interferent_s(\pi, \mu) \quad \Leftrightarrow \quad exec(\pi, s) \wedge exec(\pi \circ \mu, s) \wedge res(\pi \circ \mu, s) \neq res(\pi, s) \quad (A_1)$$
$$complementary_s(\pi, \mu) \quad \Leftrightarrow \quad \neg exec(\pi, s) \wedge exec(\pi \circ \mu, s)$$
$$inconsistent_s(\pi, \mu) \quad \Leftrightarrow \quad exec(\pi, s) \wedge \neg exec(\pi \circ \mu, s)$$

The multiplan μ is *indifferent* with respect to π if the execution of μ does not affect π at all. It is *interferent* with π if π is executable alone as well as in conjunction with μ, but the two alternatives lead to different world states. Complementarity of μ with respect to π is given, when π is not executable alone, but in conjunction with μ it is. Finally, the plan μ is *incompatible* with π if π is executable alone but not in conjunction with μ.

2.2.2 Agent Relations

From the point of view of an agent, a world state s is preferred to s', if it is closer to some ideal state than s'. Formally:

$$s' \prec_\alpha s \; \Leftrightarrow \; \exists \bar{s} \, \forall \bar{s}' \, ideal(\alpha, \bar{s}) \wedge ideal(\alpha, \bar{s}') \wedge d_\alpha(s, \bar{s}) < d_\alpha(s', \bar{s}') \qquad (S)$$

Different relations between agents arise when plan relations are judged from this stance. An agent is in a social relation with others, if the outcome of its plans is influenced by the options that others are "prepared" to choose. This distinction between capability and preparedness will be used in Section 2.3. For the time being, we state that capability implies preparedness

$$can(\gamma,\mu) \implies prep_s(\gamma,\mu) \tag{P}$$

Four mutually exclusive social relations of an agent α and its individual plan π with respect to a group of agents γ and their multiplan μ are relevant for our purposes:

Definition 3. Dependence relations between agents

$$prevents_s(\alpha,\pi,\gamma,\mu) \iff prep_s(\alpha,\pi) \wedge prep_s(\gamma,\mu) \wedge inconsistent_s(\pi,\mu)$$

$$enables_s(\alpha,\pi,\gamma,\mu) \iff prep_s(\alpha,\pi) \wedge prep_s(\gamma,\mu) \wedge complementary_s(\pi,\mu)$$

$$hinders_s(\alpha,\pi,\gamma,\mu) \iff prep_s(\alpha,\pi) \wedge prep_s(\gamma,\mu) \wedge interferent_s(\pi,\mu) \wedge$$
$$res(\pi \circ \mu, s) \prec_\alpha res(\pi,s) \tag{A_2}$$

$$favours_s(\alpha,\pi,\gamma,\mu) \iff prep_s(\alpha,\pi) \wedge prep_s(\gamma,\mu) \wedge interferent_s(\pi,\mu) \wedge$$
$$res(\pi,s) \prec_\alpha res(\pi \circ \mu, s)$$

Both, agent α and the group γ, need to be prepared to execute their plans in order that a social relation exists between them. Under this condition, the execution of agent α's plan π is related to the concurrent execution of the multiplan μ by the group γ in four different ways. A *prevents* relation exists, if decisions of the agents in γ can turn down α's individual plan π. An *enables* relation is present, if decisions of the agents in γ can make it possible for α to enact its individual plan π, which is impossible for it individually. The *hinders* relation expresses that γ can hamper π in being fully effective in the eyes of α. Finally, a *favour* relation indicates that γ's choice can influence positively in the effectiveness of π.

2.2.3 Type and Degree of Agent Dependence

By abstracting from the concrete actions that an agent's acquaintances may take, we obtain the following classes or types of relations.

Definition 4. Types of dependence relations

$$feas\text{-}dep_s(\alpha,\pi,\gamma) \iff \exists\mu.\,enables_s(\alpha,\pi,\gamma,\mu) \vee prevents_s(\alpha,\pi,\gamma,\mu)$$

$$neg\text{-}dep_s(\alpha,\pi,\gamma) \iff \exists\mu.\,hinders_s(\alpha,\pi,\gamma,\mu) \tag{A_3}$$

$$pos\text{-}dep_s(\alpha,\pi,\gamma) \iff \exists\mu.\,favours_s(\alpha,\pi,\gamma,\mu)$$

There is a feasibility dependence (*feas-dep*) of agent α for a plan π with respect to a set of agents γ, if γ can invalidate the plan, i.e. if they can turn down the execution of π. Agent α is negatively dependent (*neg-dep*) for a plan π with respect to γ, if γ can deviate the outcome of the plan to a state that is less preferred by α. If γ can bring about a change in the outcome of α's plan π that α welcomes, then α is positively dependent (*pos-dep*) on γ. Note that we do not distinguish between enabling and preventing dependence, because in both cases the group γ can decide to make it impossible for α to execute π.

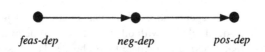

feas-dep   *neg-dep*   *pos-dep*

Figure 1. Degrees of agent dependence

These *types* imply different *degrees* of social dependence as depicted by Figure 1. Feasibility dependence is the strongest relation as the agents in γ can turn down the execution of π; *neg-dep* implies a social dependence of medium level, because the acquaintances can do something "bad" to the effectiveness of the plan; finally, positive dependence is the weakest, as the worst option that the acquaintances can choose is *not* to do something "good" to the effectiveness of the plan. The dependence structure comprises all three types and degrees of dependence.

Definition 5. The *dependence structure* in a situation s is defined as

$$A_1, A_2, A_3, S, P \models_D \ feas\text{-}dep_s(\alpha, \pi, \gamma) \wedge neg\text{-}dep_s(\alpha', \pi', \gamma') \wedge pos\text{-}dep_s(\alpha'', \pi'', \gamma'')$$

2.2.4 Dependence structure and the outcome of social co-ordination

In order to model self-interested choice in a multiagent world, we would like to rely on the notion of the "social position" of an agent: the less others can influence the outcome of an agent's plan, the better is its position in society. Respecting social co-ordination this means that when discussing a potential agreement concerning the co-ordination of individual plans, the preferences of an agent in a better position will have more weight; if an agreement is reached, it will be biased towards that agent.

The above liability to be influenced is captured by type and degree of social dependence. Still, it remains to be shown what will be the sequence of *social exchanges* among agents in situations of reciprocal dependence, where all involved agents have the potential to influence the outcome of the others' plans [3, 18]. The result of this process constitutes the outcome of social co-ordination.

As in resource-bounded domains it is hardly possible to model this process on the basis of merely qualitative notions, in Section 3 we will present a formalism to determine the outcome of social co-ordination based on the quantitative "economic" approach. But let us first introduce the notion of social structure on the basis of the above informal characterisation of the co-ordination process.

2.3 The Social Structure

Social co-ordination on the basis of the "natural strength" of the agents need not contribute to the "welfare of society" (i.e. the global task of the DPS system). The normative structure modifies the dependence structure, so as to make it instrumental for the global functionality to be achieved. For the purpose of this paper, we consider the normative structure to be a set of *prohibitions*: if in a situation s it is forbidden for a group of agents γ to enact a multiplan μ we write

$$forbidden_s(\gamma, \mu) \tag{N}$$

Our *social* agents are norm abiding, i.e. they do what "is to be done". So, the notion of preparedness is extended to capability plus the absence of prohibitions

$$prep_s(\gamma,\mu) \Leftrightarrow can(\gamma,\mu) \wedge \neg forbidden_s(\gamma,\mu) \qquad \text{(P')}$$

By recalling the role of preparedness in Definition 3, it becomes apparent that normative prescriptions actually "switch off" certain dependence relations between agents. The social structure is a transformation of the original dependence structure by norms within a society of social agents:

Definition 6. The *social structure* in a situation s is defined as

$$A_1, A_2, A_3, S, P', N \models_{D} feas\text{-}dep_s(\alpha,\pi,\gamma) \wedge neg\text{-}dep_s(\alpha',\pi',\gamma') \wedge pos\text{-}dep_s(\alpha'',\pi'',\gamma'')$$

Normative prescriptions comprise a "structural" aspect, as a set of prohibitions for certain agents may imply a *qualitative* change in their relative positions. We say that α is permitted to execute π if all plans μ that are incompatible with π and that a group γ may enact are forbidden for that group:

$$permitted_s(\alpha,\pi) \equiv \forall\gamma\forall\mu.(can(\gamma,\mu) \wedge prevents_s(\alpha,\pi,\gamma,\mu) \rightarrow forbidden_s(\gamma,\mu))$$

By means of the normative structure a DPS system designer can modify the "natural" dependence structure as implied by the co-ordination setting, so as to have a desired global functionality *emerge* from the self-interested choice of autonomous agents, which is determined by the resulting social structure.

3. Social Structure and Social Co-ordination

In this section we model the effect of social structure on social co-ordination within a quantitative framework. We develop a mapping from our problem domain to a bargaining scenario, in order to determine the outcome of social co-ordination, sketch an asynchronous distributed algorithm for computing this outcome and illustrate the approach by an example.

3.1 Social Co-ordination as a Bargaining Scenario

3.1.1 Modelling Co-operation

We first need to introduce a quantitative notion of preference over *agreements*. Agent α's preference for a world state s is expressed by its distance to some ideal state:

$$|s|_\alpha = min\{d_\alpha(s,\bar{s}) \mid ideal(\alpha,\bar{s})\}.$$

Furthermore, we introduce the set X of *legally enactable* multiplans in a situation s. It comprises all plans that are executable in s and for which there is a group of agents prepared to do so:

$$X = \{\mu \in M \mid exec(\mu,s) \wedge \exists\gamma \in \Gamma. prep_s(\gamma,\mu)\}$$

On this basis we can define a quantitative preference over multiplans.

Definition 7. In a state s, the *utility* of a legally enactable multiplan $\mu \in X$ for an agent α_i is

$$U_i(\mu) = \left| s \right|_{\alpha_i} - \left| res(\mu, s) \right|_{\alpha_i} .$$

The utilities that each agent obtains from a multiplan can be comprised in a vector. The set of utility vectors that are realisable over X is denoted by $U(X)$.

When agents have different points of view respecting which multiplan to agree upon, they may "flip a coin" in order to choose between alternative agreements. A probability distribution over the set of compatible multiplans is called a *mixed multiplan*. Let m be the cardinality of X, then a mixed multiplan is a m-dimensional vector

$$\sigma = (p_1, ..., p_m), 0 \le p_i \le 1, \sum_{i=1}^{m} p_i = 1 .$$

The set of mixed multiplans is denoted by Σ. The *expected* utility of a mixed multiplan is given by the sum of each legally enactable multiplan's utility weighed by its probability[2]:

Definition 8. In a state s, the utility of a mixed multiplan $\sigma \in \Sigma$ for an agent α_i is

$$U_i(\sigma) = \sum_{k=1}^{m} p_k U_i(\mu_k)$$

The set of expected utility vectors that are realisable over Σ is denoted by $U(\Sigma)$.

3.1.2 Modelling Conflict

When agents co-ordinate their strategies and agree on some mixed multiplan, the corresponding vector of utilities is what each agent expects to obtain. Still, agents are autonomous and not forced to co-operate. So, it remains to model what happens in case of conflict.

In a conflict situation we define the *response* of the set of agents γ to a single agent α's plan π to be the multiplan μ that they are capable of executing and that minimises α's utility from $\pi \circ \mu$, i.e.

$$response_s(\pi, \alpha_i, \mu, \gamma) \quad \Leftrightarrow \quad \mu = \min_{U_i(\pi \circ \mu')} \{ \mu' \in X \mid prep_s(\mu', \gamma) \} .$$

This models that in case of disagreement an agent must account for the unpleasant situation that all its acquaintances jointly try to harm it. As the possibility of reaching an incompatible multiplan has to be excluded, α can only choose from the set $FEAS_s(\alpha)$ of plans that are feasible regardless what others do:

$$FEAS_s(\alpha) \equiv \{ \pi \in \Pi \mid \forall \gamma. \neg feas\text{-}dep(\alpha, \pi, \gamma) \}$$

The empty plan π_ε is contained in $FEAS_s(\alpha)$ by definition. Agent α will choose the plan π out of $FEAS_s(\alpha)$, that maximises its individual utility value when combined with the response of its acquaintances.

Definition 9. The *conflict utility* of the agent α is

$$U_i^d = \max \{ U_i(\pi \circ \mu) \in \Re \mid \pi \in FEAS_s(\alpha_i) \wedge response_s(\pi, \alpha_i, \mu, \gamma) \} .$$

---

[2] The definition assumes a neutral attitude towards risk.

3.1.3 The Associated Bargaining Scenario

We now outline how a bargaining scenario can be defined on the basis of the above notions. For this purpose, we define the conflict utility within a society of agents as

$$\vec{d} = \left(U_1^d, \ldots, U_n^d \right)$$

and treat the conflict utility vector as an effectively reachable agreement, defining a set S to be the convex and comprehensive hull (*cch*) of the legally enactable multi-plans plus the conflict utility vector

$$S = cch\left(U(X) \cup \{\vec{d}\} \right).$$

The set S usually equals $U(\Sigma)$, but may also be a (convex) superset of the latter.

Definition 10. The *bargaining scenario B* associated with a social co-ordination problem is a pair $B = (S, \vec{d})$

S is called the *bargaining set* and $\vec{d}$ the *disagreement point*. B complies with the formal properties of bargaining models, so the whole mathematical apparatus of bargaining theory becomes applicable [19].

3.2 The Outcome of Social Co-ordination

3.2.1 Applying the Nash solution

In this section we rely on Bargaining Theory to find a solution to the associated bargaining scenario $(S, \vec{d})$: a vector $\vec{\varphi} \in S$ needs to be singled out upon which a bargaining process – and the social co-ordination that it models – is supposed to converge. Strategic bargaining theory relies on a sequential setting where agents alternate in making offers to each other in a pre-specified order and eventually converge on an agreement. By contrast, the axiomatic models of bargaining that we will use in the sequel first postulate desirable properties of a bargaining solution, and then seek the solution concept that satisfies them.

The five requirements of *individual rationality, Pareto-optimality, symmetry, scale invariance* and *contraction independence* that Nash bargaining models state for "fair" solutions to a bargaining scenario [19] provide an adequate model for our purposes.

Theorem 1 (due to Nash [9]). A utility vector $\vec{\varphi}$ that complies with the above axioms, maximises the function

$$N(\vec{x}) = \prod_{i=1}^{n} (x_i - d_i)$$

So, a solution $\vec{\varphi}$ maximises the *product* of gains from the disagreement point. It always exists and is unique [19].

3.2.2 Effects of the dependence structure

We now observe how the associated bargaining scenario relates to the notion of social structure. First, it has to be noticed that the shape of the bargaining set is only correlated with the notions of executability and preparedness. A point in the bargaining set is not endowed with any "contextual attachment" that states which agents can actually

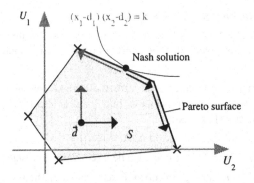

Figure 2. Disagreement point monotonicity

decide whether it is reached or not. For instance, a utility vector $U(\pi \circ \pi') \in S$ may be the result of either an *enables-* or an *indifferent*-relation between π and π'.

Still, social relations *do* influence the choice of the disagreement point. The conflict utility d_i for an agent α_i is affected by social dependence relations as follows:

- *feas-dep$_s$(α_i,π,γ)*: neither $U_i(\pi)$ nor any other $U_i(\pi \circ \mu) < U_i(\pi)$ can be used as conflict utility.
- *neg-dep$_s$(α_i,π,γ)*: any $U_i(\pi \circ \mu) < U_i(\pi)$ can be used as conflict utility.
- *pos-dep$_s$(α_i,π,γ)*: $U_i(\pi)$ can be used as conflict utility.

So, the potential conflict utility of a plan reflects precisely the degree of social dependence as depicted in Figure 1.

3.2.3 Effects of the normative structure

In remains to be shown that the solution concept also captures the nature of the normative structure. A permission should makes an agent less vulnerable. In consequence, its social position must be strengthened and it is supposed to obtain a larger compensation in a potential compromise. In the associated bargaining scenario, this is expressed by the fact that the normative structure influences the disagreement point $\bar{d}$. So, when the disagreement point changes in favour of a certain agent, the utility that this agent gets from the solution should increase.

Still, this is precisely the property of *disagreement point monotonicity* of the Nash solution: if $\bar{d}$ and $\bar{d}'$ are two arbitrary disagreement points for the same bargaining set S, and $\bar{\varphi}$ and $\bar{\varphi}'$ denote the solutions to the corresponding bargaining scenarios, then

$$d_i' \geq d_i, \quad \forall j \neq i \; d_j' = d_j \; \Rightarrow \; \varphi_i' \geq \varphi_i \quad [19]$$

Figure 2 illustrates this: the bargaining solution moves on the Pareto surface in the direction of the agent that strengthens its fallback position. By adequately designing a normative structure, a designer can thus bias the solution towards an agent while maintaining its "effectiveness".

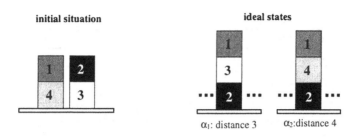

Figure 3. A scenario in the synchronous blocks domain

3.2.4 Computing the Outcome

We are now endowed with a characterisation of the *outcome* of social co-ordination. So, there is no need to explicitly "simulate" the co-ordination process among norm-abiding autonomous agents. Instead, we use a distributed multistage algorithm that *directly* computes the solution [10]:

- Stage 1 performs an asynchronous distributed search for Pareto-optimal multiplans.
- Stage 2 determines the *mixed* multiplan that constitutes the solution to the associated bargaining scenario.
- Finally, in Stage 3 a specific multiplan is chosen by means of a lottery and the corresponding individual plans are assigned to the agents.

Note that on the micro-level this algorithm requires agents to follow strict behaviour rules. Still, although this behaviour is rather benevolent, we can assure that its outcome corresponds to the result of social co-ordination among autonomous agents.

3.3 An Example

We will illustrate the above model by a scenario within the *synchronous blocks domain* [10], which is an extension of the well-known blocks world. There is a table of unlimited size and a fixed amount of numbered blocks. Blocks can be placed either directly on the table or on top of another block. The only operation that can be performed is to place a block x on top of some block y or on the table (formally: *move(x,y)* or *move(x,table)*). In the former case, the blocks x and y are required to be clear. There is a clock that marks each instant of time by a tic. A *plan* of length k is a sequence of k operations performed successively at tics. Instead of an operation, a plan may contain a NOP, indicating that nothing is done at a certain tic.

We define the result of a multiplan μ to be the "sum" of the effects of its component plans. Still, if the component plans "interact" the following rules apply:

Plan	Operations	$can(\alpha,\pi)$	$exec(\pi,s)$
π_1	[*move*(2,*table*),*move*(3,2)]	α_1	true
π_3	[*move*(2,*table*),*NOP*]	α_1, α_2	true
π_4	[*move*(1,*table*),*NOP*]	α_1, α_2	true
π_9	[*move*(2,*table*),*move*(4,2)]	α_2	false
π_{10}	[*move*(1,2),*move*(4,1)]	α_2	true
π_{11}	[*move*(2,1), *move*(3,2)]	α_1	true
π_ε	[*NOP*,*NOP*]	α_1, α_2	true

Table 1. Some individual plans

- A multiplan μ is *not* executable if some component plans *access* the same block at one tic in different ways, or if they *obstruct* a block that another component plan uses at a later tic.
- A multiplan μ *is* executable despite a non-executable component plan, if other component plans "complement" it, e.g. by providing a missing action.

Suppose a scenario as depicted in Figure 3: it shows the configuration of four blocks in an initial situation. There are two agents α_1 and α_2 both capable of executing plans of length 2. Still, while the former can move all blocks but Block 4, the latter is capable of manipulating all blocks but Block 3. The agents' ideal states correspond to the configurations of blocks shown in Figure 3. They both measure the distance between two states s_1 and s_2 by the length of the shortest plan that transforms s_1 into s_2.

Table 1 shows some plans in this scenario, the capability of the agents to enact them and their executability in the initial situation s. The following predicates constitute examples of the existing plan relations:

$indifferent_s(\pi_\varepsilon,\pi_9)$, $interferent_s(\pi_3,\pi_4)$, $complementary_s(\pi_9,\pi_4)$ and $incompatible_s(\pi_{10},\pi_{11})$

Without any normative prescriptions, the social relations between agents include:

$prevents_s(\alpha_2,\pi_{10},\alpha_1,\pi_{11})$, $enables_s(\alpha_2,\pi_9,\alpha_1,\pi_4)$ and $favours_s(\alpha_2,\pi_3,\alpha_1,\pi_4)$

In the example each agent is in a feasibility dependence relationship with the other for all plans but π_ε. Just two examples of types of social relations:

$feas\text{-}dep_s(\alpha_2,\pi_{10},\alpha_1)$ and $pos\text{-}dep_s(\alpha_2,\pi_3,\alpha_1)$

Stage 1 of the distributed asynchronous algorithm sketched previously determines that there are three Pareto-optimal (pure) multiplans (π_1,π_4), (π_4,π_9) and (π_3,π_4). Their execution leads to the world states depicted in Figure 4, which comes down to utility vectors of $(2,1)$, $(0,3)$ and $(1,2)$ respectively.

Stage 2 now calculates the solution in Pareto-optimal mixed multiplans, which are obtained by randomising among (π_1,π_4), (π_4,π_9) and (π_3,π_4). First, the disagreement point is to be determined. The only plan that α_1 can execute and which is guaranteed not to become incompatible is π_ε, which α_2 counters by π_{10}, resulting in a conflict utility of -2 for α_1. Agent α_2 also needs to choose π_ε in case of disagreement, to which α_1's most malicious response is to enact π_{11}, giving rise to a conflict utility of -1 for α_2, i.e.

$$\vec{d} = (-2,-1).$$

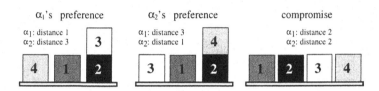

Figure 4. Efficient outcomes of the example scenario

In accordance with Theorem 1 this leads to a solution vector of
$$\vec{\varphi} = (1,2) \ .$$
Consequently, the outcome of stage 2 is to choose the "compromise" multiplan (π_3,π_4) with probability 1, so that in stage 3 just π_3 is assigned to α_1 and π_4 is assigned to α_2.

Suppose now a normative structure in which it is *forbidden* for all agents to put Block 1 on Block 2. As a result, agent α_2 is no longer *prepared* to execute plan π_{10} and it is *permitted* for α_1 to enact π_4. So, the worst situation that α_2 can bring about in the eyes of α_1 is to put the light grey Block 4 on top of Block 2. The conflict utility of α_2 remains unchanged so that the disagreement point changes in favour of α_1 to
$$\vec{d} = (-1,-1).$$
Because of the change in $\vec{d}$, stage 2 of the algorithm produces
$$\vec{\varphi} = \left(1\tfrac{1}{2},1\tfrac{1}{2}\right),$$
which is reached by randomising equally between "compromise" (π_3,π_4) and α_1's favourite (π_1,π_4). Stage 3 tosses an equally weighed coin, selects one of the above multiplans accordingly, and assigns the corresponding component plans to α_1 and α_2.

Imagine now another normative structure where it is *permitted* for agent α_2 to unstack Block 1 at the first tic (e.g. by executing plan π_4). So, all plans that manipulate the left stack in the first step are *forbidden* for α_1. Consequently, the worst thing that α_1 can still do is to obstruct Block 2 for α_2 by putting Block 4 on it in the second step. Now the disagreement point moves towards α_2:
$$\vec{d} = (-2,0).$$
The solution utility vector computed in stage two becomes
$$\vec{\varphi} = \left(\tfrac{1}{2},2\tfrac{1}{2}\right)$$
This is reached by selecting α_2's favourite (π_4,π_9) and compromise (π_3,π_4) both with probability $p = \tfrac{1}{2}$. Again, a coin is tossed and the winning multiplan enacted.

4. Social Structure and the Micro-level

The mechanism of structural co-operation, and the notion of the functionality of social structure in particular, have important repercussions on both, the architecture and the design strategy for autonomous problem-solving agents. It requires an agent to be endowed with three types of knowledge: individual knowledge in order to come up with alternative individual plans in every situation; social knowledge concerning its

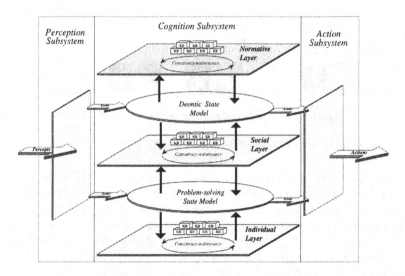

Figure 5. The ProsA$_2$ agent architecture

acquaintances, so as to determine the outcome of social co-ordination on the basis of the dependence structure; and normative knowledge which issues normative prescriptions, thus biasing the outcome of social co-ordination.

We have developed the ProsA$_2$ (<u>Pro</u>blem-<u>s</u>olving <u>A</u>utonomous <u>A</u>gent) agent architecture which reflects these insights [10]. ProsA$_2$ is a vertically layered architecture, comprising an individual, a social and a normative layer, which put to use the above knowledge types. The layers communicate via shared information models (deontic state model and problem-solving state model), which are also accessed by the perception and action subsystems (see Figure 5).

In consequence, we conceive the design of autonomous problem-solving agents as a three-step process:

1. Design of local problem-solving within the individual layer: Agents are endowed with a "motivation" on the basis of which they create individual goals depending on the current situation of the world; they are provided with problem-solving mechanisms by means of which *individual plans* are generated so as to attain (or: "head towards") these goals.

2. Modelling of autonomous agent interaction within the social layer: ProsA$_2$ agents realise the individual behaviour strategies implied by the algorithm sketched in Section 3.2.4. In order to do so, they maintain acquaintance models, containing knowledge about plan relations and the capabilities of other agents in society.

3. Design of a functional normative bias within the normative layer: depending on the characteristics of the current world state, a set of normative prescriptions is issued and stored in the information models, from where they influence the interaction behaviour generated by the social layer.

Each layer can be designed and tested separately.

5. Discussion

In this paper, we have introduced the notion of social structure as an instrument for making social co-ordination functional for the attainment of global tasks in DPS systems. Our work is inspired by Conte and Castelfranchi's Dependence Theory [3] and draws on Sichman and Demazeau's computational approach to social exchange [17]. It complements the latter as it accounts for *resource limitations* and *normative biasing*. Bazzan et al. [1] use metaphors from social anthropology just as we do. However, they consider agent behaviour to be influenced *internally* by "moral sentiments", while we conceive social structure as an *external* factor, which biases the self-interested (but norm abiding) behaviour of autonomous agents.

The formalisation of our work is similar to Rosenschein and Zlotkin's approach [14], as both set out from classical bargaining theory. Still, the latter aims at designing conventions in *heterogeneous* agent societies that avoid strategic manipulation, while we are concerned with problem solving among *homogeneous* (centrally designed) DPS agents.

Still, choosing classical bargaining theory as a vehicle to formalise social structure entails a "price to be paid". Firstly, we assume that agents make joint *binding* agreements. Secondly, we do not account for the formation of coalitions. Finally, we assume agents to be perfectly rational. However, as we are concerned with *homogeneous* societies of problem-solving agents, these assumptions become less severe: law abidance can just be "build into" our artificial agents; by ignoring coalition formation, we have sacrificed some plausibility of our model in favour of efficiency, as coalition formation is a computationally complex process [15]. The assumption of perfect rationality is justified by the fact that there exists a sound axiomatic characterisation of a solution, which allows for its direct computation without an extensive "simulation" of the bargaining process.

The approach is currently being evaluated for real-world problems such as decentralised multiagent road traffic management.

References

1. Bazzan, A.; Bordini, R.; Campbell, J.: "Moral Sentiments in Multi-agent Systems". *Intelligent Agents V — Proc. 5th Int. Workshop on Agent Theories, Architectures, and Languages* (Müller, Singh & Rao, eds.). Springer-Verlag, 1999, in this volume
2. Brainov, S.: "Altruistic Cooperation Between Self-interested Agents". *Proc. 12th Europ. Conf. on Artificial Intelligence (ECAI)*, 1996, pp. 519-523
3. Conte, R.; Castelfranchi, C.: *Cognitive and Social Action*, UCL Press, 1995
4. Cuena, J.; Ossowski, S.: "Distributed Models for Decision Support". *Multiagent Systems — A Modern Approach to Distributed Artificial Intelligence* (Weiß & Sen, eds.), AAAI/MIT Press, 1998, pp. 459-504
5. Demazeau, Y.: *Decentralised A.I. 2*. North Holland, 1991
6. Durfee, E.: "Planning in Distributed Artificial Intelligence". *Foundations of Distributed Artificial Intelligence* (O'Hare & Jennings, eds.). John Wiley, 1996, pp. 231-246
7. Durfee, E.; Rosenschein, J.: "Distributed Problem Solving and Multiagent Systems: Comparisons and Examples". *Proc. 13th Int. DAI Workshop*, 1994, pp. 94-104

8. Jennings, N.; Campos, J.: "Towards a Social Level Characterisation of Socially Responsible Agents". *IEE Proc. on Software Engineering, 144(1)*, 1997

9. Nash, J.: "The bargaining problem". *Econometrica 20*, 1950, pp. 155-162

10. Ossowski, S.: *Co-ordination in Artificial Agent Societies*. Lecture Notes in Artificial Intelligence No. 1535, Springer-Verlag, 1998

11. Ossowski, S.; García-Serrano, A.: "Social Co-ordination Among Autonomous Problem-solving Agents". *Agents and Multi-agent Systems* (Wobcke, Pagnucco & Zhang, eds.). Lecture Notes in Artificial Intelligence No. 1441, Springer-Verlag, 1997, pp. 134-148

12. Ossowski, S.; García-Serrano, A.; Cuena, J.: "Emergent Co-ordination of Flow Control Actions Through Functional Co-operation of Social Agents". *Proc. 12th Europ. Conf. on Artificial Intelligence*, 1996, pp. 539-543

13. Radcliffe-Brown, A.: *Structure and Function in Primitive Society*. Cohen & West Ltd., 1952

14. Rosenschein, J.; Zlotkin, G.: *Rules of Encounter: Designing Conventions for Automated Negotiation among Computers*. AAAI/MIT Press, 1994

15. Shehory, O.; Kraus, S.: "A Kernel-Oriented Model for Autonomous-Agent Coalition Formation in General Environments" *Distributed Artificial Intelligence: Architecture and Modelling* (Zhang & Lukose, eds.). Lecture Notes in Artificial Intelligence No. 1087, Springer-Verlag, 1995, pp. 31-45

16. Shoham, Y.; Tennenholz, M.: "On Social Laws for Artificial Agent Societies: Off-line Design". *Artificial Intelligence 73*, 1995, pp. 231-252

17. Sichman, J.: *Du Raisonnement Social Chez des Agents*. Ph.D. Thesis, Institut Polytechnique de Grenoble, 1995

18. Sichman, J.; Demazeau, Y.; Conte, R.; Castelfranchi, C.: "A Social Reasoning Mechanism Based On Dependence Networks". *Proc. 11th Europ. Conf. on Artificial Intelligence*, 1994, pp. 188-192

19. Thomson, W.: "Cooperative Models of Bargaining". *Handbook of Game Theory* (Auman & Hart, eds.), 1994, pp. 1238-1284

20. Von Martial, F.: *Coordinating Plans of Autonomous Agents*. Lecture Notes in Artificial Intelligence No. 610, Springer-Verlag, 1992

The Bases of Effective Coordination in Decentralized Multi-agent Systems[*]

Sudhir K. Rustogi and Munindar P. Singh[**]

Department of Computer Science
North Carolina State University
Raleigh, NC 27695-7534, USA

skrustog@eos.ncsu.edu, singh@ncsu.edu

Abstract

Coordination is a recurring theme in multiagent systems design. We consider the problem of achieving coordination in a system where the agents make autonomous decisions based solely on local knowledge. An open theoretical issue is what goes into achieving effective coordination? There is some folklore about the importance of the knowledge held by the different agents, but the rest of the rich agent landscape has not been explored in depth. The present paper seeks to delineate the different components of an abstract architecture for agents that influence the effectiveness of coordination. Specifically, it proposes that the extent of the choices available to the agents as well as the extent of the knowledge shared by them are both important for understanding coordination in general. These lead to a richer view of coordination that supports a more intuitive set of claims. This paper supports its conceptual conclusions with experimental results based on simulation.

1 Introduction

The coordination of agents is a crucial problem in the study of multiagent systems. Consequently, the challenge of understanding the various bases of coordination is important. Although a number of strategies have been considered and applied on a variety of problems, there is little domain-independent agreement on the phenomena that affect coordination. A particularly interesting class of coordination problems arises in multiagent systems in which the decision processes are fully decentralized. Each agent decides its actions purely locally.

A number of interesting research questions arise in this context. In particular, we address the following questions, which emerge at the interface between agent theory and architecture.

[*] We are indebted to Sandip Sen for explaining his previous efforts on this topic, and to Jie Xing for useful discussions. We would also like to thank the anonymous reviewers for comments on a previous version.

[**] Munindar Singh is supported by the NCSU College of Engineering, the National Science Foundation under grants IRI-9529179 and IRI-9624425 (Career Award), and IBM corporation.

- What are the main concepts involved in achieving coordination in decentralized, i.e., locally autonomous, multiagent systems?
- What are the trade-offs involved in terms of these concepts from the standpoint of achieving coordination effectively?

The answers to the above questions are, inevitably, interleaved. Also, since multiagent systems are a new area of investigation, we follow Simon's advice to study carefully designed simulations to develop a clearer understanding of the theoretical concepts [16, p. 15].

Knowledge is a key component of several abstract agent architectures, e.g., the family of BDI architectures [6, 18]. The MAS folklore identifies the importance of the relationship of knowledge and coordination [4]. Previous studies indicate informally that knowledge helps, but the notion of knowledge is not formalized or quantified in an obvious manner. Sen *et al.* recently introduced a simple experimental setup in which coordination arises among agents (optimally) exploiting shared resources [14]. The agents decide locally, and coordination corresponds to their achieving equilibrium. Sen *et al.* argued that, contrary to what one might naively believe, giving the interacting agents additional knowledge can cause their coordination, i.e., the achievement of equilibrium, to slow down.

1.1 Key Concepts

Thus, it appears that the traditional answers to our two research questions are (a) only knowledge—howsoever formalized—matters for coordination, and (b) the trade-offs involving knowledge are not universally agreed upon.

We find both the above answers intuitively unsatisfactory. First, we believe that knowledge is not the only relevant concept influencing coordination. The following concepts are also potentially important. (We describe these terms technically below.)

- The inertia that the agents exhibit in updating their decisions in response to changes in the state of the world brought about by others' actions. A system whose agents have low inertia may exhibit chaotic behavior, and never achieve coordination.
- The choices that are available to the agents. Too many choices may also lead to chaotic behavior.
- The amount of shared knowledge among the agents. If the agents follow a homogeneous strategy, shared knowledge would tend to lead to similar decisions by all. Similar decisions could lead to more or less effective coordination depending on whether the setting requires the same or complementary decisions. In general, complementary decisions are more interesting, because they cannot be hardwired in some trivial mechanism.
- The extent of the precision in the coordination required. Potentially, the above factors may have a different kind of influence on effectiveness depending on whether we were considering coarse-grained coordination.

When these concepts are factored in, we obtain a richer understanding of the terrain of coordination.

1.2 Main Results

We developed an experimental framework that generalized over the one used by Sen *et al.* Whereas they considered only knowledge (which we find is coupled in their setup with choice), we considered the other important concepts mentioned above. When the enhancements were eliminated, we did indeed achieve results similar to those of Sen *et al.*, but in light of our more extensive exploration, were forced to different conclusions.

When we increased the choices available to an agent independently of its knowledge, we found as we had suspected that it took longer and longer to converge. More choices lead the agents to coordinate slowly.

However, we found that holding the extent of the choices constant and increasing the knowledge also led to increased times for convergence. This was a big surprise! But it was still good news, because surprises are what make empirical research, especially simulations, worthwhile [16, p. 14]! We conjectured that the inherent symmetry in our problem might be causing this. When we tried to break it by offsetting the agents' choices and knowledge, however, it had no substantial effect on the above behavior. So we discarded that conjecture.

We made another interesting observation. When the local knowledge of the agents is increased, another hidden effect is obtained. This is the amount of *sharing* that the agent has with other agents. Intuitively, as the agents share more and more knowledge, their decisions can become more and more similar, resulting in greater instability. We attempted to characterize the sharing of knowledge among the agents. When the sharing was factored in, we found that it appears to explain the decreased effectiveness of coordination when the extent of choices are held constant.

1.3 Organization

Section 2 describes our experimental setup. Section 3 describes the main experimental results we obtained. Section 4 discusses some relevant conceptual issues, mentions some related literature, and concludes with a description of some open problems.

2 Experimental Setup

The setup consists of an array, each of whose elements is thought of as a resource. Figure 1 shows the array—accessed as a ring—that captures the resources available in the experiment. A number of agents are given. The agents use a given resource by being in the array index corresponding to that resource. There can be multiple agents using a resource; each agent uses exactly one resource. It is tacitly assumed that the quality of a resource received by an agent varies inversely in some way with the number of agents using that resource. Thus—although the utility accruing to an agent is not explicitly modeled in the present version of the experiments—each agent would like to be using a resource that is used by as few agents as possible.

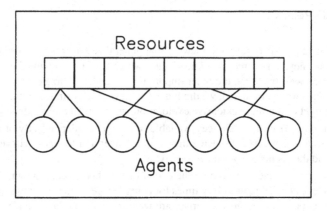

Fig. 1. Resources and Agents

2.1 Knowledge and Choice

As motivated above, it is crucial to distinguish between *knowledge* and *choice*. Knowledge refers to a reduction in uncertainty perceived by the agent. The amount of knowledge available to an agent is given by the number of resources whose occupancy is known to the agent. Thus, the knowledge of an agent increases as the agent is given information about an increasing number of resources.

Choice has to do with the number of actions that an agent is allowed to choose among. In other words, by choice, we mean raw physical choice. Note that a rational agent may find it has fewer realistic choices when it comes to know more facts, but that aspect is not directly measured here.

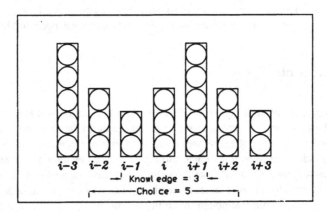

Fig. 2. Knowledge and Choice Windows

Intuitively, knowledge and choice are orthogonal properties. Figure 2 illustrates the knowledge and choice windows for an agent at location i. In the initial experiment, the knowledge and choice windows of an agent were symmetrically distributed around its current location. In later experiments, we allowed for the knowledge and choice windows to be skewed with respect to each other and the agent's current location. This had no significant bearing on the trends observed. For this reason, we report results from the simplest case, where the knowledge and choice windows are placed symmetrically around the agent, just as shown in Figure 2.

2.2 The Protocol

It is postulated that each agent has knowledge of a limited number of the available resources. This knowledge is in terms of the occupancy at a given resource. Using this knowledge, each agent fires a simple rule (the same for all agents) to stochastically decide whether to move to a new (less occupied) location, and if so, which one. In this scheme, the agents gradually disperse from the more crowded locations toward the less crowded ones. The system as a whole stabilizes when all of the resources are equally occupied. This convergent situation represents coordination, because it corresponds to the agents having achieved a sharing of resources that maximizes the performance or utility for each of them. Typically, to facilitate convergence, we set an integral ratio of agents to resources. However, when the convergence condition is liberalized, so that the systems stops even when an exact match is not obtained, the integral ratio requirement can also be safely relaxed.

The expressions used by an agent to compute the probability of moving from current resource i to another resource j in its choice window are given as follows. The f_{ij} are treated as weights.

$$
f_{ij} = \begin{cases} 1 & \text{if } i = j \\ 0 & \text{if } i \neq j \text{ and } r_i \leq r_j \\ 1 - \dfrac{1}{1 + \tau \exp(\frac{r_i - r_j - \alpha}{\beta})} & \text{otherwise} \end{cases}
$$

where α, β and τ are control parameters, r_i the number of agents at resource i, and r_j the number of agents at resource j. In our experiments, we set $\alpha = 5$, $\beta = 2$, and $\tau = 1$.

The weights are normalized so they are guaranteed to add to 1, and are then treated as probabilities. Thus, the probability of moving from resource i to resource j is given by

$$
p_{ij} = \frac{f_{ij}}{\sum_j f_{ij}}
$$

The variables r_i and r_j, which refer to the number of agents at a resource are based on what the given agent knows about the environment. If location j is within the agent's knowledge window (thus it is in the intersection of its knowledge and choice windows), then r_j is the actual value of resource occupancy. If j is not in the agent's knowledge window, then we use an estimated value for it based on the total number of agents and the occupancy of the known part of the world. If location j is not in the choice window, then r_j is not used.

$$r_j = \begin{cases} \text{occupancy of } j & \text{if } j \text{ is in knowledge window} \\ (N - K)/u & \text{otherwise} \end{cases}$$

where N is the total number of agents in the system, K is the number of agents in the knowledge window, u is the number of locations that are not known about. Thus, N and u are a form of global knowledge in the system. Since eliminating them would complicate the present experiment considerably, that aspect is deferred to future work.

2.3 Inertia

Inertia refers to the tendency of an agent to stay in its location even if preferable alternatives are available. This is reflected in the probability p_{ii}. It turns out that the above protocol used by the agents in deciding their actions maximizes the agents' inertia for problems of small dimensions. With small dimensions, especially when the choices are limited, the agent typically has only a few good alternatives. Each good alternative gets a small positive weight; each undesirable alternative gets a weight of 0. Thus, the value of p_{ii} comes out fairly high. As the distribution of the agents becomes more uniform, the inertia of each of them goes up, resulting in an inertia of 1 at equilibrium. An inertia of 1 for all agents denotes convergence, because then none of them move.

From our experiments, we can safely state that inertia is crucial to coordination. Without substantial inertia, the system can become highly unstable leading to situations in which convergence never occurs. We revisit inertia below, but suffice it to state here that we used high inertia just for our simulations to terminate.

3 Analysis

The hypotheses we wished to test were based on the idea that in the original formulation the knowledge and choice are tied together as a single variable, whereas they could be orthogonal in principle. Our hypotheses were

H1. Increasing the choice and the knowledge simultaneously would increase the time taken to coordinate—in our opinion, this is essentially Sen *et al.*'s main result.
H2. Increasing the choice while holding the knowledge constant would increase the time taken to coordinate.
H3. Increasing the knowledge while holding the choice constant would not increase, and may even decrease, the time taken to coordinate.

3.1 Error Tolerance

Instead of defining convergence as precise convergence, we found it convenient to allow a small band of tolerance of error. Thus, a state would be deemed acceptable (and the simulation would halt) if the number of agents occupying each resource were within a certain range of the optimal. By reducing the time taken to converge, this enabled us to test configurations involving a larger number of agents and resources than otherwise possible.

We discovered that including some tolerance for error made the system more robust in that the trends were more reliable than otherwise. Intuitively, this is because it reduces the chance that the system would be stuck in a suboptimal state that was several moves away from the optimal, e.g., if almost all of the resources were being used optimally, but one of the resources was under-used and another, faraway resource was over-used.

3.2 Results

		Choice						
		3	5	7	9	11	13	15
Knowledge	3	7	9	20	45	59	100	180
	5		9	20	50	102	117	246
	7			37	65	144	237	335
	9				151	205	519	831
	11					790	901	1563
	13						2974	5023
	15							7520

Table 1. Summary of Number of Iterations to Convergence $\langle 15, 45, \pm 1, 50 \rangle$

		Choice			
		3	5	7	9
Knowledge	3	40	136	749	2336
	5		194	837	4622
	7			977	4759
	9				6766

Table 2. Summary of Number of Iterations to Convergence $\langle 9, 27, \pm 0, 50 \rangle$

Some of our experimental results are displayed in Tables 1 and 2. The tuple in each caption indicates, respectively, the number of agents, the number of resources, the error tolerance, and the number of simulation runs over which the results are averaged.

We always average the results over several runs, but it takes more runs for the results to be reliably duplicated if the tolerance is set low. However, the interesting aspect of the trends is not the exact number of steps taken to converge, but the qualitative relationships among them, such as whether the number of steps is increasing or decreasing and if so at what polynomial order. For this reason, Table 1, which has more data points and a larger error tolerance, is taken as the more important one. Table 2, in which the error is limited to 0, should be treated mostly as a corroboration of Table 1.

We compute the tables only for the upper triangular submatrix, because the lower triangular submatrix is readily determined from it. The lower triangular submatrix corresponds to the knowledge window being a superset of the choice window. In our reasoning protocol, this extra knowledge is useless and harmless, because it does not affect the agent's decisions. Thus, the values are essentially constant along each column below the principal diagonal. (In an actual simulation, they would not be exactly constant because of randomization, but they are reliably approximately equal.)

3.3 Initial Hypotheses

Tables 1 and 2 show that we had mixed success in establishing our initial hypotheses. Hypothesis H1 corresponds to the principal diagonals of Tables 1 and 2. This hypothesis is clearly supported by the evidence. In this respect, by restricting our system, we were able to reconstruct the numerical trends exhibited in [14]. However, because of the above case corresponds to increasing knowledge and choice simultaneously, we do *not* support the conclusion that increasing knowledge *alone* causes a loss of the effectiveness of coordination.

Hypothesis H2 corresponds to rows of Tables 1 and 2. Reading to the right, the time to convergence increases as the choices increases, if the knowledge is held constant. Thus this hypothesis is supported.

Hypothesis H3 corresponds to the columns of Tables 1 and 2. Reading downwards, the time to convergence increases as knowledge increases, even as choices are held constant. Thus this hypothesis is not supported! We explain why next.

3.4 Sharing of Knowledge

We define a metric to estimate the extent of sharing of knowledge among the agents. This metric estimates the "amount" of knowledge of a given agent that is also available to others. This metric obviously depends on the size of the knowledge window. As the windows for the agents increase, the windows overlap to a greater degree with more agents, resulting in higher effective sharing.

To define our metric, let the window size available to all agents be k. The given agent's window overlaps to the extent of $(k-1)$ with agents one slot to the right or left of it, $(k-2)$ with those two slots away, and so on. Thus each agent has a sharing of $\Theta(k^2)$. The sharing in the entire system is $\Theta(Nk^2)$, for a total of N agents. When k is large, we can treat this as $\Theta(k^3)$. In fact, the interesting results are the rightmost column (where choice equals N, and k increases toward N). Now we have the following hypothesis.

H4. Increasing the knowledge while holding the choice constant increases the convergence time proportional to the sharing metric defined above.

Figure 3 is based on the last column of Table 1. (We do not pursue Table 2 further, because it has too few data points. Suffice it to state here that the results are essential alike.) Figure 3 shows that the time to convergence has the same order as the sharing metric. To reduce clutter, we only show the graphs for a cubic polynomial that was

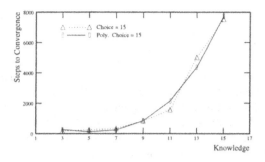

Fig. 3. Relating Sharing of Knowledge and Time to Coordinate $\langle 15, 45, \pm 1, 50 \rangle$

fit to the data, and data corresponding to the last column (constant, maximal choice) of Table 1. This does not prove that the sharing of knowledge is the real reason for the delay in convergence. It does, however, give an indication that sharing may have a significant role to play in the final understanding of coordination in decentralized systems where the agents are homogeneous and coordination calls for complementary decisions, as here.

3.5 Inertia Revisited

Recall that inertia refers to the tendency (or probability) of an agent to stay in its present location even in the face of available alternative locations. From the probability calculations of section 2, it should be clear that, in general, as the number of choices increase, $\sum_j f_{ij}$ increases, and consequently the inertia (i.e., p_{ii}) decreases. This reason, especially when coupled with a band of 0 tolerance, can prevent convergence for moderately large dimensions.

We considered an alternative formulation of inertia, in which inertia is given directly in terms of a constant probability. An agent decides among its choices to move by normalizing the probabilities as before. The probability for moving to an undesirable alternative is still set to 0; however, the sum of the probabilities of moving to good alternatives are limited to $(1 - p_{ii})$. We discovered in preliminary experiments that going from a high inertia (0.9) to a medium inertia (0.7 or 0.5) can cause significant variations in the trends observed. Those results are not yet suitable for reporting.

4 Discussion

This paper developed some experimental results about coordination in a simple setting involving multiple, potentially conflicting, autonomous agents. Despite its simplicity, it led to nontrivial and surprising results. By using an experimental framework more general than that of Sen *et al.*, we were able to reproduce their numeric results as a special case, yet also show how their conclusions were not supported.

There are some limitations of the present experimental setup. It focuses on cases where the resource conflicts are direct and immediately perceived, the resources are homogeneous, the agents all use the same decision-making protocol, and the agents do not communicate directly. Further, there are well-known limitations of reinforcement learning in terms of time taken to learn even simple concepts. The present experiments leave open the possibility that more sophisticated agents in more flexible environments, where their learning is supervised in certain ways might discover better ways of coordination, which may turn out to have different characteristics in terms of the influence of knowledge and choice.

Our contribution, however, is not only in developing the results we presented, but in identifying some of the several factors that play a role in determining the coordination of autonomous agents. We also made some progress in delineating the trade-offs among these factors. In general, in making claims about an intuitively interesting concept, we must avoid the risk that other factors may intrude into our representation, processing, or measurement and collation. This is a difficult task where theoretical development must be interleaved with controlled experimentation or simulation. We have only taken the initial steps of such a systematic study.

Although the present results should not be taken as final, it is essential to report and discuss them. This is because of two major reasons. One, the problem of learning to coordinate and its relationship to other concepts is crucial to theories and architectures of agents and multiagent systems. Two, the present kinds of studies are of the category of *exploratory research*, which Cohen [3] eloquently argues is key to empirical research and must occur prior to the formulation of more precise questions and experimental protocols that are ultimately the core of experimental science.

4.1 Literature

In addition to the works mentioned above, some interesting relevant approaches are known in the literature. For instance, Kuwabara *et al.* present a market-based approach in which agents controlling different resources set their prices based on previous usage, and buyer agents choose which resources to use [9]. The buyer agent can use more than one resource concurrently, and seeks to minimize its total price it has to pay. As in our approach, the buyer's decision-making is probabilistic. Although their model is similar to ours, they do not study the reasons for achieving effective coordination.

Often an agent takes an action that appears to be the best action based on its knowledge. It is well known, however, that what appears to be the best action may in fact lead to a lower return for the agent. Therefore, an agent must not always exploit the seemingly best action but must explore other actions as well. The notion of inertia allows an agent to resist the temptation of always exploiting the best action based on its knowledge which is to move to the least utilized resource. Schaerf *et al.* have treated this issue of exploitation versus exploration in some detail in their study on multiagent reinforcement learning in the context of load balancing in distributed systems [13]. Their framework consists of a multiagent multiresource stochastic system which involves a set of agents, a set of resources, probabilistically changing resource capacities, probabilistic assignment of new jobs to each agent, probabilistic job sizes and a resource selection rule for each agent. Schaerf *et al.* show that when all agents are noncooperative by always selecting the best resources, they all stand to lose. However, when individuals sometimes select the less desirable resources, the entire population benefits. This is an illuminating instance of the well-known prisoner's dilemma [1]. Schaerf *et al.* also rely on the limited information available to agents to achieve coordination without explicit communication. They show that communication may not be useful in improving the performance of the population and may in fact be detrimental.

Rachlin *et al.* show how agents can achieve coordination without explicit communication using their A-Team architecture [12]. An A-Team is an asynchronous team of agents that shares a population of solutions that evolve over time into an optimal set of solutions. Through sharing of the solution population, cooperative behavior between agents may emerge leading to better solutions than any one agent could produce. Often, however, a human agent may be necessary to help achieve coordination by imparting domain-specific knowledge. In another MAS approach, namely the Agentis framework due to Kinny, coordination is achieved by organizing agents into a communications hierarchy that constrains and controls relationships between agents interacting using explicit notions of request and provision of services and tasks [7].

Shehory *et al.* present an approach to load balancing based on agent cloning [15]. They treat load balancing problems by considering that agents are overloaded with tasks while the resources that the agents use may be idle. They implement agent cloning mechanism in their RETSINA infrastructure to remedy local agent overloads. Overloaded agents create new agents or clones to perform excess tasks using the unused resources on the system. To decide when to clone, a stochastic model of decision making based on dynamic programming is used.

Results by Hogg & Huberman indicate the potential benefits of introducing heterogeneity of different forms [5]. These agree with the intuition that in homogeneous settings, the sharing of knowledge may have an undesirable effect on coordination. This is especially so when the agents must make complementary decisions so as to coordinate, i.e., move to different locations. This problem is closely related to the emergence of conventions for resource sharing [10].

4.2 Future Work

Although we introduced some interesting considerations, a lot remains to be done. Choice bears an interesting relationship to the notion of commitments. It appears that the two are complementary in that the greater the agent's choice the lower its commitment to a particular decision. Previous experimental work by Kinny & Georgeff [8] and Pollack *et al.* [11] appears especially relevant. However, there is more structure to commitments that the present setup does not capture; some of this is discussed in [17].

We mention some high-level open issues that would extend the experiments described above. Although not as detailed as hypotheses, they can be studied in variations of the present experiments.

11. The improvement in speed with a nonzero band suggests a natural trade-off between the time taken and the quality of the solution. We conjecture that the time required increases exponentially as the tolerance is reduced to zero.

12. In settings where the agents coordinate by making the similar, but noncomplementary, decisions, increasing the sharing of knowledge will improve coordination.

13. A large class of strategies leading to adaptive behavior may be approximated by varying the inertia of the agents dynamically.

Our programs and data are available (for educational and research purposes) from http://www4.ncsu.edu/eos/info/dblab/agents/learning/data/.

References

1. Robert Axelrod. *The Evolution of Cooperation*. Basic Books, New York, 1985.
2. Scott Clearwater, editor. *Market-Based Control: A Paradigm for Distributed Resource Allocation*. World Scientific, 1996.
3. Paul R. Cohen. *Empirical Methods for Artificial Intelligence*. MIT Press, Cambridge, MA, 1995.
4. Edmund H. Durfee. *Coordination of Distributed Problem Solvers*. Kluwer, 1988.
5. Tad Hogg and Bernardo A. Huberman. Controlling chaos in distributed systems. *IEEE Transactions on Systems, Man, and Cybernetics*, 21(6):1325–1332, 1991.
6. F. Felix Ingrand, Michael P. Georgeff, and Anand S. Rao. An architecture for real-time reasoning and system control. *IEEE Expert*, 7(6), 1992.
7. D. Kinny. The AGENTIS agent interaction model. In J. P. Müller, M. P. Singh, and A. S. Rao, editors, *Intelligent Agents V — Proceedings of the Fifth International Workshop on Agent Theories, Architectures, and Languages (ATAL-98)*, Lecture Notes in Artificial Intelligence. Springer-Verlag, Heidelberg, 1999. In this volume.
8. David N. Kinny and Michael P. Georgeff. Commitment and effectiveness of situated agents. In *Proceedings of the International Joint Conference on Artificial Intelligence (IJCAI)*, pages 82–88, 1991.
9. Kazuhiro Kuwabara, Toru Ishida, Yoshiyasu Nishibe, and Tatsuya Suda. An equilibratory market-based approach for distributed resource allocation and its applications to communication network control. In *[2]*. 1996.
10. David K. Lewis. *Convention: A Philosophical Study*. Harvard University Press, Cambridge, MA, 1969.
11. Martha E. Pollack, David Joslin, Arthur Nunes, Sigalit Ur, and Eithan Ephrati. Experimental investigation of an agent commitment strategy. TR 94-13, Computer Science, University of Pittsburgh, Pittsburgh, June 1994.
12. J. Rachlin, R. Goodwin, S. Murthy, R. Akkiraju, F. Wu, S. Kumaran, and R. Das. A-Teams: An agent architecture for optimization and decision-support. In J. P. Müller, M. P. Singh, and A. S. Rao, editors, *Intelligent Agents V — Proceedings of the Fifth International Workshop on Agent Theories, Architectures, and Languages (ATAL-98)*, Lecture Notes in Artificial Intelligence. Springer-Verlag, Heidelberg, 1999. In this volume.
13. Andrea Schaerf, Yoav Shoham, and Moshe Tennenholtz. Adaptive load balancing: A study in multi-agent learning. *Journal of Artificial Intelligence Research*, 2:475–500, 1995.
14. Sandip Sen, Shounak Roychoudhury, and Neeraj Arora. Effect of local information on group behavior. In *Proceedings of the International Conference on Multiagent Systems*, pages 315–321, 1996.

15. O. Shehory, K. Sycara, P. Chalasani, and S. Jha. Increasing resource utilization and task performance by agent cloning. In J. P. Müller, M. P. Singh, and A. S. Rao, editors, *Intelligent Agents V — Proceedings of the Fifth International Workshop on Agent Theories, Architectures, and Languages (ATAL-98)*, Lecture Notes in Artificial Intelligence. Springer-Verlag, Heidelberg, 1999. In this volume.

16. Herbert Simon. *The Sciences of the Artificial*. MIT Press, Cambridge, MA, third edition, 1996.

17. Munindar P. Singh. Commitments in the architecture of a limited, rational agent. In *Proceedings of the Workshop on Theoretical and Practical Foundations of Intelligent Agents*, pages 72–87. Springer-Verlag, 1997.

18. Munindar P. Singh, Anand S. Rao, and Michael P. Georgeff. Formal methods in DAI: Logic-based representation and reasoning. In *[19]*, chapter 8. 1998. www.csc.ncsu.edu/ faculty/ mpsingh/ papers/ mas/ formal-DAI.ps.

19. Gerhard Weiß, editor. *Multiagent Systems: A Modern Approach to Distributed Artificial Intelligence*. MIT Press, Cambridge, MA, 1998.

A Model Checking Algorithm for Multi-agent Systems

Massimo Benerecetti[1], Fausto Giunchiglia[1,2], Luciano Serafini[2]

[1] DISA - University of Trento,
Via Inama 5, 38050 Trento, Italy
[2] IRST - Istituto Trentino di Cultura,
38050 Povo, Trento, Italy
bene@cs.unitn.it {fausto,serafini}@irst.itc.it

Abstract. Model checking is a very successful technique which has been applied in the design and verification of finite state concurrent reactive processes. In this paper we show how this technique can be lifted to be applicable to multiagent systems. Our approach allows us to reuse the technology and tools developed in model checking, to design and verify multiagent systems in a modular and incremental way, and also to have a very efficient model checking algorithm.

Keywords: Model Checking, BDI Logics, Engineering Methodologies for Multiagent Systems, Verification and Validation, Formal Methods.

1 Introduction

Model checking is a very successful automatic technique which has been devised for the design and verification of finite state reactive systems, e.g., sequential circuit designs, communication protocols, and safety critical control systems (see, e.g., [2]). There is evidence that model checking, when applicable, is far more successful than the other approaches to formal methods and verification (e.g., first order or inductive theorem proving, tableau based reasoning about modal satisfiability). Nowadays many very efficient and well developed tools implementing model checking, so-called "model checkers", are available (for instance: SPIN [7] and, SMV [8]). Some of these tools have been successfully applied to real case studies, and are currently in use in industry (see, e.g., [6]).

In this paper we show how model checking can be "lifted" to become applicable to multiagent systems in a way to *(i)* reuse with almost no variations all the technology and tools developed in model checking; and *(ii)* allow for a modular design and verification of multiagent systems. The first feature allows us to exploit the huge amount of expertise, technology and tools developed in model checking. The second feature is necessary in order to deal with real world complex systems (see [5] for a discussion of this topic).

Model checking allows us to model concurrent reactive finite state *processes*. We model *agents* as concurrent reactive non-terminating finite state processes able to have what we call BDI attitudes, i.e., beliefs, desires and intentions. (see, e.g., [1,9] for more details about BDI architectures). The specification of an agent has therefore two orthogonal aspects: a temporal aspect and a "mental attitudes" aspect. The key idea

SENDER:
initial state
 all propositions are false
loop
 read(p)
 if $p \wedge \neg B_r p$ **then**
  put-msg(inform(s, r, p))
 if $\neg p \wedge \neg B_r \neg p$ **then**
  put-msg(inform($s, r, \neg p$))
 get-msg(m)
 if $m =$inform($r, s, B_r p$) **then**
  $B_r p := True$; $B_r \neg p := False$;
 if $m =$inform($r, s, B_r \neg p$) **then**
  $B_r \neg p := True$; $B_r p := False$;
endloop

RECEIVER:
Initial state
 $p = False$; $m = \langle null \rangle$
loop
 get-msg(m)
 if $m =$inform(s, r, p) **then**
  $p := True$;
  put-msg(inform($r, s, B_r p$))
 if $m =$inform($s, r, \neg p$) **then**
  $p := False$;
  put-msg(inform($r, s, B_r \neg p$))
endloop

Fig. 1. The s and r's algorithms.

underlying our approach is to keep these two aspects separated. In practice things work as follows:

- when we consider the temporal evolution of an agent we treat BDI atoms (i.e. atomic formulas expressing belief, desire, or intention) as atomic propositions. The fact that these formulas talk about BDI attitudes is not taken into consideration.
- We deal with BDI attitudes as follows. The fact that an agent a_1 has BDI attitudes about another agent a_2 is modeled as the fact that a_1 has access to a representation of a_2 as a process (one representation for each BDI attitude). Then, any time it needs to verify the truth value of some BDI atom about a_2, e.g., $B_2 AF \phi$, a_1 simply tests whether, e.g., $AF \phi$ holds in its (appropriate) representation of a_2. BDI attitudes are essentially used to control the "jumping" among processes. This operation is iterated in the obvious way in case of nested BDI attitudes.

The paper is structured as follows. In Section 2 we describe a motivating example which we then formalize and study throughout the rest of the paper. The basic ingredients of model checking are: (i) a propositional temporal logic used to write specifications; (ii) a language for describing the system (i.e., the set of processes) to be verified as a finite state automaton; and (iii) a model checking procedure which efficiently and automatically determines whether the specifications are satisfied by the state-transition graph generated by the system automaton. Sections 3, 4 and 5 describe these three ingredients for multiagent model checking. The description is given incrementally over the standard model checking notions. In particular, we adopt CTL [2] as the propositional temporal logic used to state specifications. We conclude with a discussion of an achievement and the related work (Section 6).

PROTOCOL:
initial state
  all propositions are false
loop
  set all propositions to false
  do-one-of
    begin
      B_sAF Do(put-msg(inform(s, r, p))) $= True$;
      B_rAF Do(get-msg(inform(s, r, p))) $= True$;
    end
    begin
      B_sAF Do(put-msg(inform($s, r, \neg p$))) $= True$;
      B_rAF Do(get-msg(inform($s, r, \neg p$))) $= True$;
    end
  end
  set all propositions to false
  do-one-of
    begin
      B_rAF Do(put-msg(inform($r, s, B_r p$))) $= True$;
      B_sAF Do(get-msg(inform($r, s, B_r p$))) $= True$;
    end
    begin
      B_rAF Do(put-msg(inform($r, s, B_r \neg p$))) $= True$;
      B_sAF Do(get-msg(inform($r, s, B_r \neg p$))) $= True$;
    end
endloop

Fig. 2. The communication protocol algorithm.

2 A Motivating Example

Let us consider the following scenario involving two agents: a receiver r and a sender s. s continuously reads news on a certain subject from its sensors. Once it has read the news, s informs r only if it believes that r does not have the correct knowledge about that subject (this in order to minimize the traffic over the network). Once it has received the news, r acknowledges this fact back to s.

We implement this scenario using a FIPA compliant [4] architecture. We have therefore three agents: s, r, and a network (communication protocol) which allows them to interact. Figures 1 and 2 give the algorithmic descriptions of s, r and the communication protocol, respectively, in a `Promela`-like [1] language [7]. In these algorithms, the news subject of the information exchange is the truth value of the propositional atom p. inform(s,r, p) returns a message with sender s, receiver r, and content p (inform is a FIPA primitive). put-msg and get-msg are the primitives for putting and getting a message from the communication channel. read allows for reading from the standard input. B_r is the operator used to represent the beliefs of r as perceived by the other agents, and dually for B_s. Notice that the communication protocol has beliefs about r and s and

---
[1] `Promela` is the input language of SPIN and, indirectly, also of other model checkers.

therefore must have a representation of how they behave. We suppose that this representation coincides with what r and s actually are, as described in Figure 1. This allows us to model the fact that the communication protocol behaves correctly following what s and r do. There is no nesting of belief operators and, therefore, there is no need of further representations. s also has beliefs about r. We suppose that s (which in principle does not know anything about how r works) only knows that r can be in one of two states, with p being either true or false. In Figure 2, $B_s\mathbf{AF}\,Do(\texttt{<statement>})$ ($B_r\mathbf{AF}\,Do(\texttt{<statement>})$) intuitively means that s (r) will necessarily reach a state in which it will have just performed the action corresponding to $\texttt{<statement>}$. The algorithm in Figure 2 codifies the fact that the protocol implements the information flow between s and r, and the fact that it always delivers the messages it is asked to deliver.

3 Background Concepts

Finite state processes can be modeled as finite state machines. In order to model processes we will employ the logic CTL, a propositional branching-time temporal logic which has been widely used in modeling finite state processes [2]. Let us consider in turn the language and semantics. Given a set P of propositional atoms, the set of CTL formulas ϕ is defined inductively as follows:

$$\phi, \psi ::= p \mid \neg\phi \mid \phi \wedge \psi \mid \mathsf{EX}\,\phi \mid \mathsf{A}\,(\phi\,\mathcal{U}\,\psi) \mid \mathsf{E}\,(\phi\,\mathcal{U}\,\psi)$$

where $p \in P$. $\mathsf{EX}\,\phi$ intuitively means that there is a path such that ϕ will be true in the next step; $\mathsf{A}\,(\phi\,\mathcal{U}\,\psi)$ means that ψ will be true in a state in the future and that ϕ will be true in all the states before, for all paths; $\mathsf{E}\,(\phi\,\mathcal{U}\,\psi)$ means that there exists a path such that ψ will be true in a state in the future and that ϕ will be true in all the states before. The following abbreviations are used:

$$\perp \stackrel{\text{def}}{=} p \wedge \neg p \qquad\qquad \top \stackrel{\text{def}}{=} \neg\perp$$
$$\phi \supset \psi \stackrel{\text{def}}{=} \neg(\phi \wedge \neg\psi) \qquad\qquad \mathsf{AF}\,\phi \stackrel{\text{def}}{=} \mathsf{A}\,(\top\,\mathcal{U}\,\phi)$$
$$\mathsf{EF}\,\phi \stackrel{\text{def}}{=} \mathsf{E}\,(\top\,\mathcal{U}\,\phi) \qquad\qquad \mathsf{AG}\,\phi \stackrel{\text{def}}{=} \neg\mathsf{E}\,(\top\,\mathcal{U}\,\neg\phi)$$
$$\mathsf{EG}\,\phi \stackrel{\text{def}}{=} \neg\mathsf{A}\,(\top\,\mathcal{U}\,\neg\phi) \qquad\qquad \mathsf{AX}\,\phi \stackrel{\text{def}}{=} \neg\mathsf{EX}\,\neg\phi$$

The semantics for CTL formulas is the standard branching-time temporal semantics based on Kripke-structures. A CTL structure is a tuple $m = \langle S, s_0, R, L \rangle$, where S is a set states, $s_0 \in S$ is the *initial state*, R is a total binary relation on S, and $L : S \to \mathcal{P}(P)$ is a *labeling function*, which associates to each state $s \in S$ the set $L(s)$ of propositional atoms true at s. A *path* x in m is an infinite sequence of states $s_1, s_2, \cdots$ such that for every $i \geq 1$, $s_i R s_{i+1}$. Satisfiability of a formula ϕ in a CTL structure m at a state s is defined as follows:

- $m, s \models p$ iff $p \in L(s)$;
- $m, s \models \neg\phi$ iff $m, s \not\models \phi$;
- $m, s \models \phi \wedge \psi$ iff $m, s \models \phi$ and $m, s \models \psi$;
- $m, s \models \mathsf{EX}\,\phi$ iff there is an s' with sRs', such that $m, s' \models \phi$;

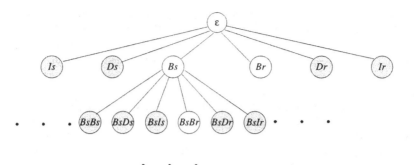

Fig. 3. The set of views for the example of Section 2.

- $m, s \models \mathsf{A} (\phi \, \mathcal{U} \, \psi)$ iff for every path $x = (s = s_1, s_2, \cdots)$ there's a $k \geq 1$ such that $m, s_k \models \psi$ and, for every j such that $1 \leq j < k, m, s_j \models \phi$;
- $m, s \models \mathsf{E} (\phi \, \mathcal{U} \, \psi)$ iff there is a path $x = (s = s_1, s_2, \cdots)$ and a $k \geq 1$ such that $m, s_k \models \psi$ and for every j such that $1 \leq j < k, m, s_j \models \phi$.
- $m \models \phi$ iff $m, s_0 \models \phi$.

We build the notion of agent incrementally over the notion of process. Suppose that we have a set I of agents. Each agent has its own beliefs, desires, and intentions about itself and the other agents. We adopt the usual syntax for propositional attitudes: $B_i \phi$, $D_i \phi$ and $I_i \phi$ mean that agent i believes, desires and intends (to bring about) ϕ, respectively. B_i, D_i and I_i are called BDI operators for agent i (or simply BDI operators). O_i denotes any BDI operator for agent i. The idea is to model each nesting of BDI operators as a different process evolving over time. For example, the beliefs of agent s evolving over time in our example can be modeled by the process whose algorithm *SENDER* is given in Figure 1.

Formally, let $O = \{B, D, I\}$ be a set of symbols, one for each BDI attitude. OI^* denotes the set $(O \times I)^*$, i.e., the set of finite (possibly empty) strings of the form $o_1 i_1 \ldots o_n i_n$ with $o_k \in O$ and $i_k \in I$. We call any $\alpha \in OI^*$, a *view*. Intuitively, each view in OI^* represents a possible nesting of BDI attitudes. We also allow for the empty string, ϵ. The intuition is that ϵ represents the view of an external observer which, from the outside, "sees" the behavior of the overall multiagent system. Depending on the goals, the external observer can represent the person designing the system, or a selected process of the multiagent system which is given this privileged status.

Consider the example in Section 2. We take the external observer to be the point of view of the communication protocol. Therefore, there is a view ϵ corresponding to the beliefs of the communication protocol, and also two views Bs, Br corresponding to the beliefs of the two agents s and r. Finally s has beliefs about the beliefs of r.

Figure 3 graphically represents this situation. The dark circles represent the views which exist in principle, the white ones represent those which are actually needed.

An agent, e.g., s, is thus a tree of views rooted in the view that the external observer has of it, e.g., Bs. Notice also that the view that an agent has of another agent is in general different from the agent itself. This allows us for instance, in the example of Section 2, to model the fact that s might have false beliefs about r.

The final step is to associate a logical language $\mathcal{L}_\alpha$ to each view $\alpha \in OI^*$. Intuitively, each $\mathcal{L}_\alpha$ is the language used to express what is true (and false) in the representation corresponding to α. Let $\{P_\alpha\}$ be a family of sets of propositional atoms. Each P_α allows for the definition of a different language (also called an MATL language (on $\{P_\alpha\}$)). The family of MATL languages on $\{P_\alpha\}$ is the family of CTL languages $\{\mathcal{L}_\alpha\}$ where $\mathcal{L}_\alpha$ is the smallest CTL language containing the set of propositional atoms P_α and the BDI atoms $O_i\phi$ for any formula ϕ of $\mathcal{L}_{\alpha O i}$. In particular, $\mathcal{L}_\epsilon$ is used to speak about the whole multiagent system. Thus, intuitively, a formula $p \wedge B_i \mathsf{AG} \neg p \in \mathcal{L}_\epsilon$, (denoted by $\epsilon : p \wedge B_i \mathsf{AG} \neg p$) means that p is true and that i believes that in every future state p will be false. The languages $\mathcal{L}_{Bi}$ $\mathcal{L}_{Di}$, and $\mathcal{L}_{Ii}$ are the languages that i adopts to represent its beliefs, desires and intentions, respectively. The language $\mathcal{L}_{Bilj}$ is used to specify i's beliefs about j's intentions, and so on. Note that the only restriction on the languages is that $O_i\phi$ must be an atomic formula of $\mathcal{L}_\alpha$ if and only if ϕ is a formula of $\mathcal{L}_{\alpha O i}$ (see [5] for a study of how this condition can be modified in order to capture various interesting properties). We allow also for empty languages. However $\mathcal{L}_\epsilon$ cannot be empty as we need to be able to talk about the whole multiagent system.

4 Multiagent Finite State Machines

We are interested in extending model checking to multiagent model checking. In model checking we deal with *finite CTL structures*, i.e., those CTL structures which have a finite set of states, and also a labeling function mapping to a finite number of atoms. The crucial observation is that finite CTL structures can be seen as *finite state machines* (FSMs), an FSM being an object $f = \langle S, s_0, R, L \rangle$ (with everything finite). Our solution is to extend the notion of FSM to that of *MultiAgent Finite State Machine (MAFSM)*, where, roughly speaking, a MAFSM is a finite set of FSMs.

A first step in this direction is to restrict ourselves to a finite number of views α. Thus, let OI^n denote a finite subset of OI^* obtained by taking the views in any finite subtree of OI^* rooted at view ϵ. However this is not enough as also a finite set of views allows for an infinite number of BDI atoms. Even if we have a finite number of processes we cannot model them as FSMs. We solve this problem by introducing the notion of explicit BDI atom. Formally if $\{\mathcal{L}_\alpha\}$ is a family of MATL languages, then $Expl(oi, \alpha)$ is a (possibly empty) *finite* subset of the BDI atoms of $\mathcal{L}_\alpha$. The elements of $Expl(oi, \alpha)$ are called *explicit BDI atoms*. We have the following.

Definition 1. *Let $\{\mathcal{L}_\alpha\}$ be a family of MATL languages on $\{P_\alpha\}$. A MultiAgent Finite State Machine (MAFSM) $F = \{F_\alpha\}$ for $\{\mathcal{L}_\alpha\}$ is a recursive total function such that:*

1. *$F_\epsilon \neq \emptyset$;*
2. *for all views $\alpha \in OI^n \subset OI^*$ with OI^n finite, it associates a finite set F_α of FSMs on the MATL language on the following atoms: P_α, $Expl(\mathtt{B}i, \alpha)$, $Expl(\mathtt{D}i, \alpha)$ and $Expl(\mathtt{I}i, \alpha)$, for all $i \in I$;*
3. *for all the views $\alpha \in OI^* \setminus OI^n$, $F_\alpha = \emptyset$.*

The first condition is needed as otherwise there is nothing we can reason about; the second allows us to deal with finite views, and the third allows us to deal with finite sets of atoms.

Example 1. Let us construct the MAFSM of the example in Section 2. Let us concentrate on a process and the corresponding view. The propositional atoms are all the propositional atoms which appear in the Promela-like specification. $O_i\phi$ is a BDI atom of $\mathcal{L}_\alpha$ if and only if ϕ is a formula of $\mathcal{L}_{\alpha O i}$. The set of explicit BDI atoms contains all the BDI atoms which are set in the Promela-like specification. The intuition is that explicit BDI atoms can change independently, while the value of implicit BDI atoms can only change as a consequence of changes of value of explicit BDI atoms. This identifies the set of state variables and therefore the space of possible states. The value of the state variables in the initial state can be extracted from the top part of the Promela-like specification.

Let us detail the FSMs corresponding to the processes of our example. Notice that any Promela-like construct can be directly translated, with a one-to-one mapping, into transitions of a finite state automaton. We leave to the reader the definition of the state transitions of the FSMs in the views ϵ, Bs, Br. Since the initial state is completely defined, there is only one FSM per view. The propositional atoms of all the views can be easily extracted from the algorithms given in Section 2. We concentrate therefore on the explicit BDI atoms.

FSMs in ϵ: F_ϵ contains only one FSM generated from *PROTOCOL.*[2]

$$Expl(Br, \epsilon) = \left\{ \begin{array}{l} B_r\text{AF}\,Do(\text{put-msg(inform}(s, r, B_r p))), \\ B_r\text{AF}\,Do(\text{put-msg(inform}(s, r, B_r\neg p))), \\ B_r\text{AF}\,Do(\text{get-msg(inform}(r, s, p))), \\ B_r\text{AF}\,Do(\text{get-msg(inform}(r, s, \neg p))) \end{array} \right\}$$

$$Expl(Bs, \epsilon) = \left\{ \begin{array}{l} B_s\text{AF}\,Do(\text{get-msg(inform}(r, s, B_r\neg p))), \\ B_s\text{AF}\,Do(\text{put-msg(inform}(s, r, p))), \\ B_s\text{AF}\,Do(\text{put-msg(inform}(s, r, \neg p))), \\ B_s\text{AF}\,Do(\text{get-msg(inform}(r, s, B_r p))) \end{array} \right\}$$

and $Expl(Ds, \epsilon) = Expl(Dr, \epsilon) = Expl(Is, \epsilon) = Expl(Ir, \epsilon) = \emptyset$.

FSMs in Bs: F_{Bs} contains only one FSM generated from *SENDER*. $Expl(Br, Bs) = \{B_r p, B_r\neg p\}$. All the other sets of explicit BDI atoms are empty.

FSMs in Br: F_{Br} contains only one FSM generated from *RECEIVER*. $Expl(oi, Br)$ is the empty set.

FSMs in $BsBr$: Section 2 does not give an algorithmic specification of this view. It only says that "... s ... only knows that r can be in one of two states, with p being either true or false". This tells us that there is only one state variable p, and that F_{BsBr} will contain all the FSMs with only one state variable (which are sixteen). This formalizes the fact that s knows nothing of the initial state and state transitions of r.

---

[2] Note that $Do(\text{put-msg(inform}(s, r, p)))$ is a propositional atom of the language of s which is true only if s is in a state in which it has just performed the action "put-msg(inform(s, r, p))". The other atoms have a similar intuitive meaning.

Given the notion of MAFSM, the next step is give a notion of satisfiability in a MAFSM. We start from the notion of satisfiability of CTL formulas in an FSM at a state. This notion is defined as in CTL structures. This allows us to determine the satisfiability of all the propositional and explicit BDI atoms (and all the formulas belonging to the corresponding MATL language). For these formulas we do not need to use the machinery associated to BDI attitudes. However, this machinery is needed in order to deal with the (infinite) number of BDI atoms which are not memorized anywhere in MAFSM.

Let the set of *implicit BDI atoms* of a view α, written $Impl(oi, \alpha)$, be defined as the (infinite) subset of all BDI atoms of $\mathcal{L}_\alpha$ which are not explicit BDI atoms, i.e. $Impl(oi, \alpha) = \{O_i\phi \in \mathcal{L}_\alpha \setminus Expl(oi, \alpha)\}$. Let $ArgExpl(oi, \alpha, s)$ be defined as follows.

$$ArgExpl(oi, \alpha, s) = \{\phi \in \mathcal{L}_{\alpha Oi} \mid O_i\phi \in L(s) \cap Expl(oi, \alpha)\}$$

Intuitively, $ArgExpl(oi, \alpha, s)$ consists of all the formulas $\phi \in \mathcal{L}_{\alpha Oi}$ such that the explicit BDI atom $O_i\phi$ is true in s. At this point, to define the satisfiability in a MAFSM, it is sufficient to use the fact that we know how to compute $ArgExpl(oi, \alpha, s)$ (it is sufficient to use CTL satisfiability and then to compare the results of the relevant CTL structures) and exploit $ArgExpl(oi, \alpha, s)$ to compute the implicit BDI atoms which satisfy an appropriate correctness and completeness condition.

Definition 2. (Satisfiability in a MAFSM) *Let F be a MAFSM, α a view in OI^*, $f = \langle S, s_0, R, L \rangle \in F_\alpha$ an FSM, and $s \in S$ a state. Then, for any formula ϕ of $\mathcal{L}_\alpha$, the satisfiability relation $F, \alpha, f, s \models \phi$ is defined as follows:*

1. *$F, \alpha, f, s \models p$, where p is a propositional atom or an explicit BDI atom: the same as FSM satisfiability;*
2. *satisfiability of propositional connectives and CTL operators: the same as FSM satisfiability;*
3. *$F, \alpha, f, s \models O_i\phi$, where $O_i\phi$ is an implicit BDI atom, iff for all $f' \in F_{\alpha Oi}$ and s' state of f', $F, \alpha oi, f', s' \models \bigwedge ArgExpl(oi, \alpha, s) \supset \phi$*

We have furthermore:

4. *$F, \alpha, f \models \phi$ iff $F, \alpha, f, s_0 \models \phi$;*
5. *$F, \alpha \models \phi$ iff for all $f \in F_\alpha$, $F, \alpha, f \models \phi$;*
6. *$F \models \alpha : \phi$ iff $F, \alpha \models \phi$.*

In the definition of satisfiability above, item 3 is the crucial step. The formula $\bigwedge ArgExpl(oi, \alpha, s)$ is the conjunction of all the elements of $ArgExpl(oi, \alpha, s)$. We need to use $ArgExpl(oi, \alpha, s)$ in order to compute the formulas ϕ such that $O_i\phi$ is an implicit BDI atom. Notice that item 3 gives to BDI operators the same strength as modal $K(3m)$, where m is the number of agents. In particular, we have that if $\Gamma \supset \phi$ is a theorem in a view then $O_i\Gamma \supset O_i\phi$ is a theorem in the (appropriate) view above, where $O_i\Gamma$ is the set $\{O_i\phi \mid \phi \in \Gamma\}$.

Item 4 states that a FSM satisfies a formula if the formula is satisfied in its initial state. Item 5 states that a formula is satisfied in a view if it is satisfied by all the FSMs of that view. Finally item 6 states that a labeled formula $\alpha : \phi$ is satisfied if ϕ is satisfied in the view corresponding to the label.

5 Model Checking a MAFSM

The basic operation of a standard CTL model checking algorithm is to extend the labeling function of an FSM (which considers only propositional atoms) to all the (atomic and not atomic) subformulas of the formula being model checked. Let us call Extended FSM (or, simply, FSM when the context makes clear what we mean) the result of this operation. The generation of an extended FSM relies on the fact that the labeling function explicitly defines the truth value of all the atoms. The problem is that in the FSMs of a MAFSM the labeling function is not defined on implicit BDI atoms, whose truth value is therefore left undefined; and that we need to know the truth values of the implicit BDI atoms occurring in the formula to be model checked. The definition of satisfiability in a MAFSM (item 3 in Definition 2) tells us how to fix this problem. That is, if $O_i \psi$ is an implicit BDI atom, then $F, \alpha, f, s \models O_i \psi$ if and only if for every $f' \in F_{\alpha O i}$ and every state s' of f', we have $F, \alpha o i, f', s' \models \bigwedge ArgExpl(oi, \alpha, s) \supset \psi$.

The crucial observation is that $ArgExpl(oi, \alpha, s)$ is generated from the formulas in $Expl(oi, \alpha)$ and the labeling functions of the FSMs; that it is a finite set; and that it is a property of the MAFSM (and thus independent of the formula to be model checked). The idea, therefore, is to precompute, once for all, and store in an appropriate data structure, this information. In particular, for each BDI operator O_i, let C_{Oi}, called the *(MAFSM) compatibility relation* of O_i, be a relation defined as follows. Let $ex \subseteq Expl(oi, \alpha)$ be a subset of the explicit BDI atoms of a view α. Then:

$$C_{Oi}(\alpha, ex) = \{\langle f', s' \rangle \mid f' \in F_{\alpha Oi}, s' \text{ a state of } f' \text{ and} \\ F, \alpha oi, f', s' \models \{\phi \mid O_i \phi \in ex\}\}$$

Starting from a view α and a set of explicit BDI atoms ex of α, $C_{Oi}(\alpha, ex)$ collects all the FSMs f' and states s' of f' (in the view αoi below) which satisfy the arguments of the chosen explicit BDI atoms. We need to consider all the subsets ex of $Expl(oi, \alpha)$ as a priori we do not know which explicit BDI atoms are relevant for the computation of the truth value of an implicit BDI atom. Implicit BDI atoms evaluated at different states will need different ex's.

It can be easily seen that

$$\langle f', s' \rangle \in C_{Oi}(\alpha, L(s) \cap Expl(oi, \alpha)) \text{ iff } F, \alpha oi, f', s' \models \bigwedge ArgExpl(oi, \alpha, s)$$

and, therefore, that

$$F, \alpha, f, s \models O_i \phi \text{ iff} \\ \text{for all } \langle f', s' \rangle \in C_{Oi}(\alpha, L(s) \cap Expl(oi, \alpha)), \ F, \alpha oi, f', s' \models \phi \quad (1)$$

where $O_i \phi$ is an implicit BDI atom and $L(s) \cap Expl(oi, \alpha)$ is the set of explicit BDI atoms satisfied by state s of $f \in F_\alpha$.

The model checking algorithm relies on the following global data structures: a data structure F which contains, for each view, a set of (extended) FSMs F_α; a data structure $Expl(oi, \alpha)$ which contains for each operator and view, the set of explicit BDI atoms

$O_i\phi$; a data structure C which contains for each modal operator O_i, a compatibility relation $C_{Oi} = \langle \alpha, ex, f', s' \rangle$.

Global Variables

$Expl(oi, \alpha) = \{O_i\phi\}$ with $O_i\phi$ an explicit BDI atom of α;

$F = \{F_\alpha\}$ with F_α a set of FSMs on $\mathcal{L}_\alpha$;

$C_{Oi} = \{\langle \alpha, ex, f', s' \rangle\}$ with $ex \subseteq Expl(oi, \alpha)$, f' an FSM in $F_{\alpha Oi}$ and s' a state of f'.

Algorithm MAMC(α, ϕ)

MAMC-View$(\alpha, \{\phi\})$
for each $f \in F_\alpha$ do
    if $\phi \notin L(s_0)$ then return$(False)$
end
return$(True)$
end

Algorithm MAMC-View(α, Γ)

$Sub := \bigcup\{sub(\phi) \mid \phi \in \Gamma\}$
for each oi do
    $ArgImpl(oi, \alpha, Sub) := \{\phi \mid O_i\phi \in Sub \setminus Expl(oi, \alpha)\}$
    if $ArgImpl(oi, \alpha, Sub) \neq \emptyset$ then
        MAMC-View$(\alpha oi, ArgImpl(oi, \alpha, Sub))$
    endif
end
for each $f \in F_\alpha$ do   /* $f = \langle S, s_0, R, L \rangle$ */
    if $\langle Sub$ contains implicit BDI atoms$\rangle$ then
        for each $s \in S$ do
            for each oi do
                $ArgImpl(oi, \alpha, Sub) := \{\phi \mid O_i\phi \in Sub \setminus Expl(oi, \alpha)\}$
                for each $\langle f', s' \rangle \in C_{Oi}(\alpha, L(s) \cap Expl(oi, \alpha))$ do
                                      /* $f' = \langle S', s'_0, R', L' \rangle$ */
                    $ArgImpl(oi, \alpha, Sub) := ArgImpl(oi, \alpha, Sub) \cap L'(s')$
                end
            $L(s) := L(s) \cup O_i ArgImpl(oi, \alpha, Sub)$
        end
        end
    endif
    CTLMC(f, Γ)
end
end

Fig. 4. The multiagent model checking algorithm.

The MultiAgent Model Checking algorithm MAMC(α, ϕ) takes two arguments, namely a view α and the MATL formula $\phi \in \mathcal{L}_\alpha$ that we want to model check. MAMC(α, ϕ) returns true if $F \models \alpha : \phi$, false otherwise. Notice that we can model check any view (and therefore any subpart of the multiagent system).

Thus, if we take α to be ϵ we model check the overall multiagent system; if we take α to be of length 1 we model check a single agent; if we take α to be of length 2 we model check the view that an agent has of another agent, and so on.

The algorithm of $MAMC(\alpha, \phi)$ is shown in Figure 4. As a first step, the algorithm $MAMC(\alpha, \phi)$ calls the algorithm MAMC-View on view α and the set of formulas $\{\phi\}$. MAMC-View(α, Γ) takes in input a view α and a set of formulas $\Gamma \in \mathcal{L}_\alpha$, and labels the MAFSM with all the subformulas of the formulas in Γ. As a result, after this step, MAMC can return the appropriate truth value simply by testing whether ϕ is contained in the label set of the initial state s_0 of all the FSMs $f \in F_\alpha$ (remember, from Section 3 that an FSM satisfies a formula if and only if its initial state satisfies it).

Notationally, let $sub(\phi)$ denote the set of subformulas of ϕ (remember that $O_i\phi$ is atomic and that, therefore, it is the only subformula of itself). Then, inside MAMC-View, we can distinguish three main phases.

Phase 1: Initialization. This phase, corresponding to the first line of the algorithm, collects in Sub all the subformulas of the formulas in Γ.

Phase 2: Model Checking implicit BDI atoms. This phase corresponds to the first loop. This loop considers in turn all the pairs oi. For each of them, the first step is to compute the set $ArgImpl(oi, \alpha, Sub)$, i.e., the set of all the formulas ϕ which are arguments of the implicit BDI atoms $O_i\phi$ which are subformulas of Γ. Notice that this step is performed using the set of explicit BDI atoms $Expl(oi, \alpha)$ and not the set of implicit BDI atoms $Impl(oi, \alpha)$, the latter set being infinite. Notice also that the knowledge of the formulas to be model checked allows us to restrict ourselves to the *finite* set of implicit BDI atoms $Sub \setminus Expl(oi, \alpha)$ which are relevant to the satisfiability of these formulas.

Then, the second step is to call recursively MAMC-View on the view below and on the set $\Gamma = ArgImpl(oi, \alpha, Sub)$. In this phase MAMC-View visits the tree structure which needs to be model checked, extending the labeling functions of the visited FSMs. The leaves of this tree are the views for which there is no need to model check implicit BDI atoms, due to the fact that no more implicit BDI atoms occur in the set of formulas Γ in input.

Notice that the tree which is visited is usually a subtree of the tree constituent the MAFSM, in particular it is the subtree which contains all and only the views which are necessary to compute the implicit BDI atoms mentioned in the top level goal formula given in input to MAMC.

Phase 3: This phase is a loop over all the FSMs f of the current view α. This loop iteratively performs the following two phases:

Phase 3.1: Labeling f with the implicit BDI atoms. This phase corresponds to the second level loop. It is entered only if we are at a view for which some implicit BDI atom occurs in the input formulas Γ. Here the algorithm extends the labeling function of f with the true implicit BDI atoms $O_i\phi$ occurring in Γ. This step is computed according to Definition (1) of satisfiability of implicit BDI atoms. Thus $L(s) \cap Expl(oi, \alpha)$ is the set of true explicit BDI atoms in a state s of the FSM f of view α. $\langle f', s' \rangle$ is any FSM f' and state s', where f' in view αoi is compatible with the true explicit BDI atoms computed before. The innermost loop computes and stores in $ArgImpl(oi, \alpha, Sub)$ the arguments of the implicit BDI atoms which occur in Sub and which are true in all the pairs $\langle f', s' \rangle$. $O_i ArgImpl(oi, \alpha, Sub)$ at the end of the loop is the set of implicit BDI atoms true in the current state s. This set is therefore used to extend the labeling of s.

Phase 3.2: Model checking f. At this point every state s in the current f has been labeled with all the atoms (i.e, propositional atoms, explicit and implicit BDI atoms) occurring in Γ. Therefore, it is sufficient to apply the usual CTL model checking algorithm CTLMC(f, Γ). CTLMC(f, Γ) takes in input an (Extended) FSM f and a set of formulas Γ and extends the labeling function of f to all the subformulas of Γ (see for instance [2]). Notice that we can call any state-of-the-art model checker as a black box.

The following result states that MAMC-View actually solves the model checking problem for MATL.

Theorem 1 (Correctness of MAMC-View). *Let* $f = \langle S, s_0, R, L \rangle \in F_\alpha$, *with* α *any view, and* s *a state in* S. $F, \alpha, f, s \models \phi$ *iff MAMC-View*$(\alpha, \{\phi\})$ *applied to* F *constructs a new* F *such that* $\phi \in L(s)$, *with* s *state of* f.

Proof. We proceed by induction on the maximum number n of nested BDI operators occurring in ϕ.

[Base case] If $n = 0$, ϕ is a CTL formula and no subformula of ϕ is a BDI atom. In this case, phases 2 and 3.1 of MAMC-View leave everything unchanged. In fact neither any recursive call to MAMC-View nor any iteration in the first loop of phase 3 is performed. The correctness of MAMC-View is therefore a consequence of the correctness of CTLMC.

[Step case] Assume now that the thesis holds for every $m < n$ and that n is the maximum number of nested BDI operators in $Sub(\phi)$. Let $O_i\psi$ be a BDI atom in $Sub(\phi)$. By equation (1), for every state s of f, $F, \alpha, f, s \models O_i\psi$ iff for every $\langle f', s' \rangle \in C_{Oi}(\alpha, L(s) \cap Expl(oi, \alpha))$, $F, \alpha oi, f', s' \models \psi$. For the induction hypothesis, after phase 2 of the algorithm, we have that in the new F, for any (Extended) FSM $f' = \langle S', s'_0, R', L' \rangle$ of view αoi, $F, \alpha oi, f', s' \models \psi$ if and only if $\psi \in L'(s')$. In phase 3.1, the algorithm extends the label set of each state s of $f \in F_\alpha$ with the BDI atom $O_i\psi$ if and only if for every pair $\langle f', s' \rangle \in C_{Oi}(\alpha, L(s) \cap Expl(oi, \alpha))$, $\psi \in L'(s')$, that is iff $F, \alpha oi, f', s' \models \psi$. Thus, after phase 3.1, the labeling function of f has been extended to all the atoms of $Sub(\phi)$. Phase 3.2 just applies CTL model checking, which extends the labeling function of f to all the subformulas of ϕ. Again, the thesis follows from the correctness of the CTL model checking algorithm.

6 Conclusion

In this paper we have defined a model-checking based decision procedure for multiagent systems. Our approach allows us to reuse the technology and tools developed in model checking and to specify multiagent systems incrementally.

The closest work to ours is the work by Rao & Georgeff [10]. Similarly to us, they employ a class of logics obtained by combining branching-time temporal logics (e.g., CTL), with logics for BDI attitudes. The resulting logics are similar to ours. The essential difference is that, in their approach, a multiagent system is specified by using a unique language. Similarly, their semantics consists of a unique Kripke structure with a temporal accessibility relation and one accessibility relation for each BDI attitude. This "having everything in a single pot" makes them lose some of our properties, in particular: the modularity and incrementality of the specification, but also the structural correspondence we have between the agents' specification and the structure of the model. These two features give us important advantages in the definition of the model checking algorithm. In particular: we can deal very naturally with the case of bounded nesting; we can implement multiagent model checking by directly calling, as a subroutine, the standard model checking algorithm; and we can implement an algorithm which visits the smallest possible submodel (this last property does not seem to be possessed by the algorithm in [10] — as they need to label all the worlds in the model). Finally, we also improve on their work as they don't face the problem of the automatic generation of a model starting from the specification of a multiagent system. Notice that, at the current state-of-the-art, we can take a standard model checking language (e.g., Promela) and compiler, and extend them so that it becomes possible to generate models of multiagent systems.

Another approach to verification of BDI agents is envisaged in [11], where the author shows how BDI logics can be phrased in μ–calculus terms, for which model checking algorithms already exist. Even though the author's concern is not MAS verification, the approach, suggesting to employ a unique language to specify MAS, is prone to the same criticism as Rao & Georgeff approach when modularity and incrementality of specification/verification are concerned.

A different approach to verification of MAS can be found in [3], where the authors propose a compositional methodology for verifying MAS. Their methodology is based on specifying systems at different abstraction levels and verifying each level against the others. Similarly to us they partition a MAS into subcomponents in order to cope with complex and potentially big systems. They also allow for multiple languages to describe each component independently of the others. The main difference rely on the fact that they employ a deduction-based process, mainly dependent on the user's ability to guess assumptions about lower level components that enable them to prove a property at a higher level. Therefore, their methodology seems basically heuristic-based (if not fully interactive). Our approach, on the other hand, is model-based and is completely automatic. Once specified the system, verification of a property does not involve any user intervention.

This is only the beginning and a lot of work remains to be done, in particular: individuate a class of interesting applications, define interesting subclasses of the logics defined in this paper, implement these logics into a system constructed as an extension of a state-of-the-art model checker (e.g., SMV), and test the resulting system on the applications of interest.

References

1. M. E. Bratman. *Intention, plan and practical reason*. Harvard University Press, 1990.
2. E. Clarke, O. Grumberg, and D. Long. Model Checking. In *Deductive Program Design* (Manfred Broy, ed.), NATO ASI Series, Springer-Verlag (1995), pages 305–349. Proceedings of the NATO Advanced Study Institute on Deductive Program Design, held in Marktoberdorf, Germany (1994).

3. J. Engelfriet, C. M. Jonker, and J. Treur. Compositional verification of multi-agent systems in temporal multi-epistemic logic. In J. P. Müller, M. P. Singh, and A. S. Rao, editors, *Intelligent Agents V — Proceedings of the Fifth International Workshop on Agent Theories, Architectures, and Languages (ATAL-98)*, Lecture Notes in Artificial Intelligence. Springer-Verlag, Heidelberg, 1999. In this volume.

4. FIPA Foundation for Intelligent Physical Agents. Fipa '97 draft specification, 1997. Revision 2.0 available at http://drogo.cselt.stet.it/fipa/.

5. E. Giunchiglia and F. Giunchiglia. Ideal and Real Belief about Belief. In *Practical Reasoning, International Conference on Formal and Applied Practical Reasoning, FAPR'96*, number 1085 in Lecture Notes in Artificial Intelligence, pages 261–275. Springer Verlag, 1996.

6. O. Grumberg, editor. *Proceedings of the 9th International Conference on Computer-Aided Verification, CAV'97*, Haifa, Israel, 1997. Springer Verlag.

7. G.J. Holzmann. *Design and Validation of Computer Protocols.* Prentice Hall, 1991.

8. K.L. McMillan. *Symbolic Model Checking.* Kluwer Academic, 1993.

9. A. S. Rao and M. P. Georgeff. Modeling rational agents within a BDI architecture. In J. Allen, R. Fikes, and E. Sandewall, editors, *Proceedings of the 2nd International Conference on Principle of Knowledge Representation and Reasoning*, pages 473–484. Morgan Kaufmann, 1991.

10. A. S. Rao and M. P. Georgeff. A model-theoretic approach to the verification of situated reasoning systems. In *Proceedings of the Thirteenth International Joint Conference on Artificial Intelligence (IJCAI-93)*, pages 318–324, Chambéry, France, 1993.

11. K. Schild. On the relationship between BDI logics and standard logics of concurrency. In J. P. Müller, M. P. Singh, and A. S. Rao, editors, *Intelligent Agents V — Proceedings of the Fifth International Workshop on Agent Theories, Architectures, and Languages (ATAL-98)*, Lecture Notes in Artificial Intelligence. Springer-Verlag, Heidelberg, 1999. In this volume.

Compositional Verification of Multi-agent Systems in Temporal Multi-epistemic Logic

Joeri Engelfriet, Catholijn M. Jonker, Jan Treur

Vrije Universiteit Amsterdam
Department of Mathematics and Computer Science, Artificial Intelligence Group
De Boelelaan 1081a, 1081 HV Amsterdam, The Netherlands
Email: {joeri,jonker,treur}@cs.vu.nl

Abstract. Compositional verification aims at managing the complexity of the verification process by exploiting compositionality of the system architecture. In this paper we explore the use of a temporal epistemic logic to formalize the process of verification of compositional multi-agent systems. The specification of a system, its properties and their proofs are of a compositional nature, and areformalized within a compositional temporal logic: Temporal Multi-Epistemic Logic. It is shown that compositional proofs are valid under certain conditions. Finally, the possibility of incorporating default persistence of information in a system, is explored.

1 Introduction

It is a recent trend in the literature on verification to study the use of compositionality and abstraction to structure the process of verification; for example, see [1, 9, 19]. In [20] a compositional verification method was introduced for (formal specifications of) multi-agent systems. In that paper, properties to be verified were formalized semantically in terms of temporal epistemic models, and proofs were constructed by hand. The current paper focuses on the requirements for the choice and use of a suitable logic within which both the properties to be verified and their proofs can be formalized. For the particular application of the logic the following requirements for the logic itself and for the use of the logic are of importance:
- compositional structure: properties and proofs can be structured in a compositional manner, in accordance with the compositional structure of the system design.
- dynamics and time: dynamic properties can be expressed, reasoning and induction over time is possible.
- incomplete information states can be expressed.
- transparency: the proof system and the semantics are transparent and not unnecessarily complicated.

In the following sections, *Temporal Multi-Epistemic Logic* (TMEL) is introduced and shown to be a suitable logic; this logic is a generalization of the Temporal Epistemic Logic TEL introduced in [11, 12]; see also [10, 13]. The generalization is made by adding multiple epistemic operators according to the hierarchical compositional structure of the system to be verified. This generalization was inspired by [18], were multiple modal operators were introduced (in their case without hierarchical compositional structure) to verify multi-agent systems specified in Concurrent METATEM. By choosing temporal epistemic logic as a point of departure, a choice was made for a discrete and linear time structure and for time to be global.

The structure of the paper is as follows. In Section 2 the compositional verification method for multi-agent systems is briefly described and an example is given. In Section 3 the temporal multi-epistemic logic is defined. Section 4 discusses compositional temporal theories, Section 5 compositional proof structures, and Section 6 focuses on how to treat non-classical semantics related to default persistence of information.

2   Compositional Verification

The purpose of verification is to prove that, under a certain set of assumptions, a system satisfies a certain set of properties, for example, the design requirements. In the approach introduced in [20], this is done by mathematical proof (i.e., a proof in the form mathematicians are accustomed to), which proves that the specification of the system together with the assumptions implies the properties that the system needs to fulfill. A compositional multi-agent system can be viewed and specified at different levels of abstraction. Viewed from the top level, denoted by L_0, the complete multi-agent system is one component S, where internal information and processes are left unspecified at this level of abstraction (information and process hiding). At the next level of abstraction, L_1, the internal structure of the system is given in terms of its components (as an example, see the agents A and B and the external world EW in Figure 1), but the details of the components are hidden. At the next lower level of abstraction, L_2, (for example) the agent A is specified as a composition of sub-components (see Figure 2). Some components may not be composed of sub-components; such components are called *primitive*. The example has been designed using the compositional development method DESIRE, see [7]. This is a method to develop multi-agent systems according to a compositional structure. The approach to compositional verification addressed in this paper can be used for multi-agent systems designed on the basis of DESIRE, but also for systems designed on the basis of any other method using compositionality as a design principle.

Compositional verification takes into account this compositional structure during the verification process. Properties of a component are only to be expressed using the language specified for the component's interfaces (and not the languages specified for sub-components or super-components); this drastically restricts the space of the properties that can be formulated. Verification of a composed component is done using properties of the sub-components it embeds and the component's specification (which specifies how it is composed of its sub-components). The assumptions on its sub-components under which the component functions properly, are properties to be proven for these sub-components. This implies that properties at different levels of abstraction are involved in the verification process. These properties have hierarchical logical relations in the sense that at each level, given the component's specification, a property is logically implied by (a conjunction of) the lower level properties that relate to it in the hierarchy (see Figure 3); of course, also logical relations between properties within one abstraction level may exist.

The example multi-agent model used in this paper is composed of two co-operative information gathering agents, A and B, and a component EW representing the external world (see Figure 1). Each of the agents is able to acquire partial information about the external world (by observation). Each agent's own observations are insufficient to draw conclusions of a desired type, but the combined information of both agents is sufficient. Therefore communication is required to be able to draw conclusions. The agents can communicate their own observation results and requests for observation information of the other agent. This quite common situation is simplified to the following materialized form. The world situation consists of an object that has to be classified. One agent can only observe the bottom view of the object (e.g., a circle), the other agent the side view (e.g., a square). By exchanging and combining observation information they are able to classify the object (e.g., a cylinder, expressed by the atom object_type(cylinder)).

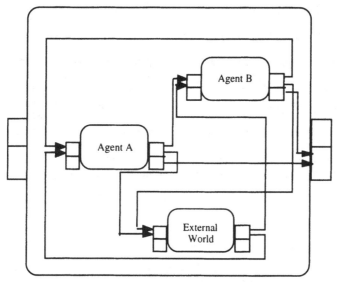

Fig. 1. Example multi-agent system for co-operative information gathering

Communication from the agent A to B takes place in the following manner:
- the agent A generates at its output interface a statement of the form:
  to_be_communicated_to(*<type>*, *<atom>*, *<sign>*, B)
- the information is transferred to B; thereby it translated into
  communicated_by(*<type>*, *<atom>*, *<sign>*, A)

In the example *<type>* can be filled with a label request or world_info, *<atom>* is an atom expressing information on the world, and *<sign>*, is one of pos or neg, to indicate truth or falsity.

Interaction between agent A and the world takes place as follows:
- the agent A generates at its output interface a statement of the form:
  to_be_observed(*<atom>*)
- the information is transferred to EW; thereby it is translated into
  to_be_observed_by(*<atom>*, A)
- the external world EW generates at its output interface a statement of the form:
  observation_result_for(*<atom>*, *<sign>*, A)

- the information is transferred to A; thereby it is translated into
  observation_result(<*atom*>, <*sign*>)

Part of the output of an agent are conclusions about the classification of the object of the form object_type(ot); these are transferred to the output of the system.

To be able to perform its tasks, each agent is composed of four components, see Figure 2: three for generic agent tasks (world interaction management, or WIM for short, which reasons about the interaction with the outside world, agent interaction management, or AIM, which reasons about the interaction with other agents, and own process control, or OPC, which reasons about the control of the agent itself; in this example it determines the agent characteristics, for example whether the agent is pro-active or reactive), and one for an agent specific task (object classification, or OC). Since the two agents have a similar architecture, the notation A.WIM is used, for example, to denote component WIM of agent A. As an example of how this agent model works, information describing communication by the agent B to the agent A is transferred to the (input interface of the) component AIM within A (in the form of an atom communicated_by(<*type*>, <*atom*>, <*sign*>, A)). In the component AIM the communicated information is identified (by a meta-reasoning process that interprets the communication) and athe outputinterface of AIM the atom new_world_info(<*atom*>, <*sign*>) is generated. From this output interface the information is transferred to the component OC, where it is stored as object level information in the form <*atom*> or not <*atom*>, depending on whether <*sign*> is pos or neg. A similar process takes place when observation information is received by the agent, this time through the component WIM.

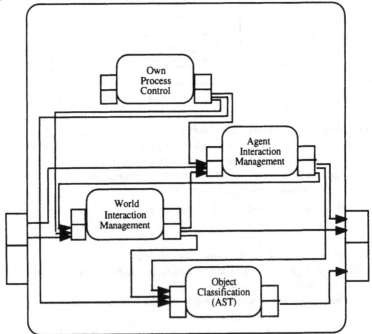

Fig. 2. Composition of an agent

This example multi-agent system has been verified for all 64 cases where each of the two agents may be pro-active or reactive with respect to observation, communication and/or reasoning in any combination (see [20]; in Figure 3 a small part of the properties and logical relations found is depicted). The example used to illustrate the formalization in the current paper is restricted to a pro-active agent A and a reactive agent The *compositional verification method* can be formulated informally as follows (for a formalization, see Section 5 below):

A. Verifying one abstraction level against the other

For each abstraction level the following procedure is followed:

1. Determine which properties are of interest for the (higher level) component D; these properties can be expressed only in terms of the vocabulary defined for the interfaces of D.
2. Determine assumed properties for the lower level components (expressed in terms of their interface languages) that guarantee D's properties.
3. Prove D's properties on the basis of the properties of its sub-components, using the system specification that defines how D is composed.

B. Verifying a primitive component

For primitive knowledge-based components a number of verification techniques exist in the literature, for example, [21].

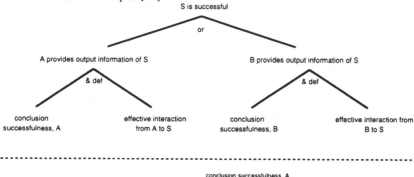

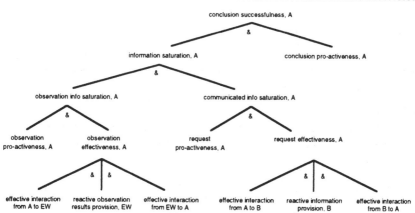

Fig. 3. Logical relations between a number of properties at different levels of abstraction for the example multi-agent model

C. The overall verification process

To verify the complete system:

1. Determine the properties are that are desired for the whole system.
2. Apply the above procedure **A** iteratively.
   In the iteration the desired properties of abstraction level L_i are either:
   - those determined in step 1, if i = 0, or
   - the assumptions made for the higher level L_{i+1}, if i > 0
3. Verify the primitive components according to **B**.

The results of verification are:

- Properties and assumptions at the different abstraction levels.
- Logical relations between the properties of different process abstraction levels (cf. Figure 3).

Note that both static and dynamic properties and connections between them are covered. Furthermore, process and information hiding limits the complexity of the verification per abstraction level.

3 Temporal Multi-Epistemic Logic

In this section we introduce a logic that can be used to formalize the dynamic aspects of reasoning and the incomplete information states that play a role: temporal multi-epistemic logic. Our approach is in line with what in [16] is called *temporalizing* a given logic; in our case the given logic is a multi-modal epistemic logic based on the component hierarchy of a multi-agent system to be verified. As the base language in which the multi-agent system can express its knowledge and conclusions, we will take a propositional language. Let **COMP** be a given set of component names with a hierarchical relation **sub** between them, defining a finite tree structure. The following definition formalizes information states and a temporalization of these states, using linear discrete time with a starting point. For convenience we will take the set of natural numbers $\mathbb{N} = \{0, 1, 2, ...\}$ as the time frame.

Definition 3.1 (compositional temporal epistemic model)

a) A *signature* Σ is an ordered sequence of (propositional) atom names. A *compositional epistemic state*, or *compositional information state*, based on Σ, is a collection $(Min_X, Mint_X, Mout_X)_{X \in COMP}$ of triples of sets Min_X, $Mint_X$, $Mout_X$ of propositional models of signature Σ for each of the components X in **COMP**.
The set of compositional information states based on Σ is denoted by **CIS(Σ)**, or shortly **CIS**.
b) Let Σ be a signature. A (propositional) *compositional temporal epistemic model* M of signature Σ is a mapping M: $\mathbb{N} \rightarrow$ **CIS(Σ)**. We will sometimes use the notation $(M_t)_{t \in \mathbb{N}}$ for M.

In the language we introduce modal operators Cin_X, $Cint_X$, $Cout_X$ for each component X in **COMP**, expressing the input, internal, and output knowledge of the component. We call these operators the *epistemic operators*. Modal formulae can be evaluated in compositional epistemic states at any point in time: a modal formula $Cout_X \, \alpha$ (where

α is propositional) is true in a compositional epistemic state M, denoted M ⊢ Cout$_X$ α, if m ⊢ α for all m ∈ Mout$_X$ (and similarly for Cin$_X$ and Cint$_X$). The operators Cin$_X$, Cint$_X$, Cout$_X$ are very similar to the modal K operator, so for instance the formula ¬ Cout$_X$ α ∧ ¬ Cout$_X$ ¬ α denotes that α is unknown in the output state of component X (i.e., neither known to be true nor known to be false).

We need a language to express changes over time. To this end in [11, 12] the temporal (uni-modal) epistemic language TEL and its semantics were introduced. To obtain a compositional temporal logic, this logic TEL is generalized in the following manner (the result is called Temporal Multi-Epistemic Logic, or TMEL). Formulae of the form Cin$_X$ α, Cint$_X$ α and Cout$_X$ α play the role of atomic propositions. The temporal operators X, Y, F and G are used. Intuitively, the temporal formula Fα is true at time t means that viewed from time point t, the formula α will be true at *some* time in the future (in *some* future information state), Gα is true at time t means that viewed from time point t, the formula α will be true at *all* time points in the future, and Xα is true at time t means that α will be true in the next information state. The operator Y means "true at the previous time point". Some examples of temporal formulae will be given in the next section. For more details of TEL, see [11, 12]. For temporal epistemic logic different entailment relations can be used, both classical and non-classical; see e.g., [10, 13].

4 Compositional Temporal Theories

In order to embed the compositional verification proofs in temporal multi-epistemic logic, a multi-agent system specification is translated into a temporal theory. We require of this translation that the compositional structure is preserved. This means that instead of one global temporal theory, each component in the hierarchy is translated into a separate temporal theory for this component. Therefore, we introduce collections of sub-languages and collections of temporal theories that are labelled by the set of components COMP. A language for a component defines the terms in which its internal information, as well as the information in its input and output interface can be expressed.

Definition 4.1 (language composition)
Let COMP be a set of component names with a binary sub-component relation sub. *Primitive* components are elements D ∈ COMP for which no C ∈ COMP exists with C sub D. The other components are called *composed*.
A *language composition* is a collection of sub-languages (L$_C$)$_{C ∈ COMP}$, where in each language L$_C$ only the epistemic operators Cin$_C$, Cint$_C$ and Cout$_C$ are used (and no epistemic operators for other components).
The collection of *interface languages* for the language composition (L$_C$)$_{C ∈ COMP}$ is the collection (L$^{if}_C$)$_{C ∈ COMP}$ where for any component D, the language L$^{if}_D$ is the restriction of L$_D$ to formulae in which the epistemic operator Cint$_D$ does not occur.
The collection of *bridge languages* for the language composition (L$_C$)$_{C ∈ COMP}$ is the collection (L^+_C)$_{C ∈ COMP}$ defined for any component D by

$$L^+_D = L_D \cup \bigcup_{C \text{ sub } D} L^{if}_C$$

The *cumulative language composition* for the language composition (L$_C$)$_{C ∈ COMP}$ is the collection

$(L^*_C)_{C \in COMP}$ defined for any component D by

$$L^*_D = L_D \cup \bigcup_{C \, sub \, D} L^*_C \qquad \text{if D is a composed component}$$
$$L^*_D = L_D \qquad \text{if D is a primitive component}$$

Example 4.2 (language composition)

We give part of the languages of some of the components of the example multi-agent system (for ot varying over the object types, r over shapes, X is the agent A or B, sign is pos or neg):

L_S	$Cout_S$	object_type(ot)
----	----	----
L_A	$Cout_A$	to_be_observed(view(A, r)),
	$Cout_A$	to_be_communicated_to(request, view(B, r), pos, B)
	Cin_A	observation_result(view(A, r), pos)
	Cin_A	communicated_by(world_info, view(B, r), pos, B)
L_{EW}	Cin_{EW}	to_be_observed_by(view(X, r), X),
	$Cout_{EW}$	observation_result_for(view(X, r), sign, X)

Definition 4.3 (theory composition)

Let $(L_C)_{C \in COMP}$ be a language composition. A *compositional temporal theory* for $(L_C)_{C \in COMP}$ is a collection $(T_C)_{C \in COMP}$ where each temporal theory T_C is a theory in the language L^+_C.

Let $(T_C)_{C \in COMP}$ be a compositional temporal theory. The *collection of cumulative theories* $(T^*_C)_{C \in COMP}$ is defined for any component D as:

$$T^*_D = T_D \cup \bigcup_{C \, sub \, D} T^*_C \qquad \text{if D is a composed component}$$
$$T^*_D = T_D \qquad \text{if D is a primitive component}$$

Example 4.4 (partial compositional theory; a composed component)

For each of the components of the multi-agent system its specifcation can be translated into a temporal theory. The part of the theory for the top level component that is relevant to prove success of the system is the following (again, ot ranges over the object types, r over shapes, X is the agent A or B, sign is pos or neg):

T_S: Y $Cout_X$ to_be_observed(view(X,r))
　　　　→ Cin_{EW} to_be_observed_by(view(X,r), X)
　　Y $Cout_A$ to_be_communicated_to(request, view(B,r), pos, B)
　　　　→ Cin_B communicated_by(request, view(B,r), pos, A)
　　Y $Cout_B$ to_be_communicated_to(world_info, view(B,r), sign, A)
　　　　→ Cin_A communicated_by(world_info, view(B,r), sign, B)
　　Y $Cout_X$ object_type(ot)　　　→ $Cout_S$ object_type(ot)
　　Y $Cout_X$ ¬ object_type(ot)　　→ $Cout_S$ ¬ object_type(ot)
　　Y $Cout_{EW}$ observation_result_for(view(X,r), sign, X)
　　　　→ Cin_X observation_result(view(X,r), sign, X)

For example, the last formula is part of the description of the information links from EW to A and from EW to B. This formula expresses that the information previously in the output of EW is currently contained in the input interface of the agent A (under a simple translation). The part of the theory for agent A that is relevant to prove successfulness of the system is the following:

T_A :
Y Cin$_A$ observation_result(view(A,r), sign)
$\rightarrow$ Cin$_{A.WIM}$ observation_result(view(A,r), sign)
Y Cin$_A$ communicated_by(world_info, view(B,r), sign, B)
$\rightarrow$ Cin$_{A.AIM}$ communicated_by(world_info, view(B,r), sign, B)
Y Cout$_{A.WIM}$ to_be_observed(view(A,r), sign)
$\rightarrow$ Cout$_A$ to_be_observed(view(A,r), sign)
Y Cout$_{A.AIM}$ to_be_communicated_to(request, view(B,r), pos, B)
$\rightarrow$ Cout$_A$ to_be_communicated_to(request, view(B,r), pos, B)
Y Cout$_{A.OC}$ object_type(ot) $\rightarrow$ Cout$_A$ object_type(ot)
Y Cout$_{A.OC}$ ¬ object_type(ot) $\rightarrow$ Cout$_A$ ¬ object_type(ot)
Y Cout$_{A.AIM}$ communicated_by(request, view(A,r), sign, B)
$\rightarrow$ Cin$_{A.WIM}$ requested(view(A,r))
Y Cout$_{A.AIM}$ new_world_info(view(B,r), pos)
$\rightarrow$ Cin$_{A.OC}$ view(B,r)
Y Cout$_{A.AIM}$ new_world_info(view(B,r), neg)
$\rightarrow$ Cin$_{A.OC}$ ¬view(B,r)
Y Cout$_{A.WIM}$ new_world_info(view(A,r), pos)
$\rightarrow$ Cin$_{A.OC}$ view(B,r)
Y Cout$_{A.WIM}$ new_world_info(view(A,r), neg)
$\rightarrow$ Cin$_{A.OC}$ ¬view(B,r)

Example 4.5 (partial compositional theory; a primitive component)
Primitive components can, for example, be specified by logical rules of the form
'conjunction of literals' implies 'literal'), as is the case in DESIRE. Consider the
following rule of the knowledge base of the primitive component object classification:

if view(A, circle) and view(B, square) then object_type(cylinder)

This rule can be formalized in TMEL by:

$\phi \wedge$ Y Cin$_{X.OC}$ **view(A, circle)** $\wedge$ Y Cin$_{X.OC}$ **view(B, square)** $\rightarrow$ Cout$_{X.OC}$ **object_type(cylinder)**

where ϕ is a formula expressing control information that allows the rule to be used
(for example, the component should be active).

5 Compositional Proof Structures

Verification proofs are composed of proofs at different levels of abstraction (see
Figure 3). These proofs involve properties of the components at these abstraction
levels.

Definition 5.1 (composition of properties)
A *composition of properties* for a language composition $(L_C)_{C \in COMP}$ is a collection
$(P_C)_{C \in COMP}$ where for each C the set P_C is a set of temporal statements in the
language L^{if}_C.

Note that in our approach it is not allowed to phrase properties of a component in
terms other than those of its interface language.

Example 5.2
In the proof of the success property of S (a small part of which is depicted in Figure 3)
the following composition of properties is used (see also Example 4.2):

System S as a whole

P_S : $\bigwedge_{ot}$ (F Cout$_S$ object_type(ot) ∨ F Cout$_S$ ¬ object_type(ot))

Agent A (the pro-active agent)

P_A :   [$\bigwedge_r$ (Cin$_A$ observation_result(view(A,r), pos) ∨
                    Cin$_A$ observation_result(view(A,r), neg))]
       ∧ [$\bigwedge_r$ (Cin$_A$ communicated_by(world_info, view(B,r), pos, B) ∨
                    Cin$_A$ communicated_by(world_info, view(B,r), neg, B))]
       → $\bigwedge_{ot}$ (F Cout$_A$ object_type(ot) ∨ F Cout$_A$ ¬ object_type(ot))
           (conclusion pro-activeness, A)

       $\bigwedge_r$ F Cout$_A$ to_be_observed(view(A,r))
           (observation pro-activeness, A)

       $\bigwedge_r$ F Cout$_A$ to_be_communicated_to(request, view(B,r), pos, B),
           (request pro-activeness, A)

Agent B (the reactive agent)

P_B : $\bigwedge_r$ [Cin$_B$ communicated_by(request, view(B,r), pos, A)
       → (F Cout$_B$ to_be_communicated_to(world_info, view(B,r), pos) ∨
           F Cout$_B$ to_be_communicated_to(world_info, view(B,r), neg))]
           (reactive information provision, B)

External World EW

P_{EW} : $\bigwedge_r$ [Cin$_{EW}$ to_be_observed_by(view(X,r), X)
                    → (F Cout$_{EW}$ observation_result_for(view(X,r), pos) ∨
                        F Cout$_{EW}$ observation_result_for(view(X,r), neg))]
           (reactive observation results provision, EW)

Components within A

$P_{A.OPC}$: F Cout$_{A.OPC}$ pro-active
                    (pro-activeness, OPC)

$P_{A.AIM}$: [Cin$_{A.AIM}$ pro-active
             → $\bigwedge_r$ F Cout$_{A.AIM}$ to_be_communicated_to(request, view(B,r), pos, B)],
                    (conditional request pro-activeness, AIM)

       [$\bigwedge_r$ Cin$_{A.AIM}$ communicated_by(world_info, view(B,r), sign, B)
       → F Cout$_{A.AIM}$ new_world_info(view(B,r), sign)]

$P_{A.WIM}$: [Cin$_{A.WIM}$ pro-active → $\bigwedge_r$ F Cout$_{A.WIM}$ to_be_observed(view(A,r))],
                    (conditional observation pro-activeness, WIM)

       [$\bigwedge_r$ Cin$_{A.WIM}$ observation_result(view(A,r), sign)
       → F Cout$_{A.WIM}$ new_world_info(view(A,r), sign)]

$$P_{A,OC} : \quad \bigwedge_{r,X} (\text{Cin}_{A,OC} \text{ view}(X,r) \vee \text{Cin}_{A,OC} \neg \text{ view}(X,r))$$
$$\rightarrow \bigwedge_{\text{st}} (\text{ F Cout}_{A,OC} \text{ object\_type}(ot) \vee \text{F Cout}_{A,OC} \neg \text{ object\_type}(ot))$$

In the proof of the properties shown in Example 5.2, the theories shown in Example 4.4 and 4.5 are used.

Definition 5.3 (compositional and global provability)

For the language composition $(L_C)_{C \in \text{COMP}}$, let a composition of properties $(P_C)_{C \in \text{COMP}}$ and a compositional temporal theory $(T_C)_{C \in \text{COMP}}$ be given. Let $\vdash$ be an entailment relation for temporal multi-epistemic logic.

a) The composition of properties $(P_C)_{C \in \text{COMP}}$ is *compositionally provable* with respect to $\vdash$ from the compositional temporal theory $(T_C)_{C \in \text{COMP}}$ if for each component D the following holds:

$$T_D \cup \bigcup_{C \text{ sub } D} P_C \vdash P_D \qquad \qquad \text{if D is composed}$$
$$T_D \vdash P_D \qquad \qquad \text{if D is primitive}$$

b) The composition of properties is *globally provable* with respect to $\vdash$ from the compositional temporal theory $(T_C)_{C \in \text{COMP}}$ if for each component D the following holds:

$$T^*_D \vdash P_D$$

For example, the collection of success properties of Example 5.2 turns out to be globally provable from the compositional temporal theory $(T_C)_{C \in \text{COMP}}$, with respect to the provability relation of classical entailment in TMEL, augmented with a default persistence assumption (see the next section).

Compositional provability does not necessarily imply global provability. However, the implication holds if the entailment relation satisfies, apart from reflexivity (if $V \subseteq W$, then $W \vdash V$), the property of transitivity:

$$T \vdash U \ \& \ U \vdash W \Rightarrow T \vdash W \qquad \qquad \qquad (Transitivity)$$

for all sets of formulae T, U, W. It is well-known that transitivity and reflexivity imply monotonicity.

Proposition 5.4

If the entailment relation $\vdash$ satisfies, in addition to reflexivity, transitivity, then compositional provability with respect to $\vdash$ implies global provability with respect to $\vdash$. In particular, if $\vdash$ is a classical provability relation for temporal multi-epistemic logic, then compositional provability with respect to $\vdash$ implies global provability with respect to $\vdash$.

This proposition shows that for classical entailment the implication holds. But, for example, for an entailment relation taking into account minimal change the implication does not hold. In the light of these results, for compositional verification a classical proof system is the best choice.

6 Default Persistence and Revision

The conditions under which a classical inference relation can be used depend on the specific form of semantics. For example, in DESIRE a default persistence assumption has been made: it is only specified what has to be changed; all other information is meant to persist in time. An exception is made for information that has to be retracted because it was derived from information that does not hold any more. We now discuss a manner in which default persistence and revision can be treated within temporal multi-epistemic logic.

In principle, a compositional specification can be formalized using executable temporal formulae. Roughly, executable temporal formulae are temporal formulae of the form

$$\text{declarative past} \quad \Rightarrow \quad \text{imperative future}$$

For more details on this paradigm, and the different variants within, see [2, 3]. For our purposes the following definition is chosen. *Simplified executable temporal formulae* are formulae of the form

$$\text{past and present} \quad \Rightarrow \quad \text{present}$$

The right hand side of these formulae F are called *heads*, denoted by head(F); they are taken from the set

$$\text{HEADS} = \quad \{ \text{CL} \mid \text{L propositional literal, C epistemic operator} \} \cup$$
$$\{ \neg \text{CA} \wedge \neg \text{ C} \neg \text{A} \mid \text{A propositional atom, C epistemic operator} \}$$

The left hand side of F is called *body*, denoted by body(F). Within the body, the 'past' part is a formula that refers strictly to the past. The 'present' part is a conjunction of temporal literals that are either of the form CL or $\neg$CL.

These formulae only specify what has to be changed. All other information is meant to persist (default persistence) in time, with an exception for information that has to be revised because it was derived from information that does not hold anymore. In principle this entails non-classical semantics. However, a translation is possible into temporal theories with classical semantics if a form of temporal completion (similar to Clark's completion in logic programming) is applied:

Let T be a temporal theory consisting of simplified executable temporal formulae. For each $H \in \text{HEADS}$ define

$$T_H \quad = \quad \{ F \in T \mid \text{head}(F) = H \}$$

Let L be a literal and C an epistemic operator; define

$$tc(T_{CL}) \quad = \quad [\bigvee \{\text{body}(F) \mid F \in T_{CL} \} \vee$$
$$(\neg \bigvee \{\text{body}(F) \mid F \in T_{C\text{-}L} \} \wedge$$
$$\neg \bigvee \{\text{body}(F) \mid F \in T_{\neg CL \wedge \neg C\text{-}L} \} \wedge$$
$$YCL)]$$

$$\leftrightarrow CL$$

$$tc(T_{\neg\, CL\, \wedge\, \neg C\, -L}) = [\, \bigvee \{body(F) \mid F \in T_{\neg\, CL\, \wedge\, \neg C\, -L}\} \vee$$

$$(\neg\, \bigvee \{body(F) \mid F \in T_{C-L}\} \wedge$$

$$\neg\, \bigvee \{body(F) \mid F \in T_{CL}\} \wedge$$

$$\neg\, YCL \wedge \neg YC\, -L\,)\,]$$

$$\leftrightarrow \neg\, CL \wedge \neg C\, -L$$

Here -L denotes the complementary literal of L. The intuition behind these formulae is the following: a literal is (known to be) true in a component exactly when either there is an applicable rule making it true, or it was true before, and no rule making the literal false or unknown, is applicable.

The *temporal completion* of T is defined by

$$tc(T) = \{\, tc(T_{CL}) \mid L \text{ literal, C epistemic operator } \} \cup$$
$$\{\, tc(T_{\neg\, CL\, \wedge\, \neg C\, -L}) \mid L \text{ literal, C epistemic operator } \}$$

Under a consistency assumption the right part $\{\, tc(T_{\neg\, CL\, \wedge\, \neg C\, -L}) \mid L$ literal, C epistemic operator $\}$ of the above union is already implied by the left part $\{\, tc(T_{CL}) \mid L$ literal, C epistemic operator $\}$.

Example 6.1 (temporal completion of a link formalization)
Let T be the temporal theory (a subset of T_S) that formalizes the information link from EW to the agent X; see Example 4.4. The temporal completion of T contains the set of formulae:

[Y Cout$_{EW}$ observation_result_for(view(X,r), sign, X)) ∨
(¬Y Cout$_{EW}$ ¬ observation_result_for(view(X,r), sign, X)) ∧
     Y Cin$_X$ observation_result(view(X,r), sign, X))]

↔   Cin$_X$ observation_result(view(X,r), sign, X)

[Y Cout$_{EW}$ ¬ observation_result_for(view(X,r), sign, X)) ∨
(¬Y Cout$_{EW}$ observation_result_for(view(X,r), sign, X)) ∧
     Y Cin$_X$ ¬ observation_result(view(X,r), sign, X))]

↔   Cin$_X$ ¬ observation_result(view(X,r), sign, X)

Note that the result of temporal completion is a temporal theory that is not any more in executable format.

The temporal completion allows to formalize proofs in a classical proof system. This means that, given a compositional theory $(T_C)_{C\,\epsilon\,COMP}$, we should consider the completion of the union of these theories, i.e., $tc(T^*_S)$ where S is the component of the entire system, for global provability. On the other hand, for compositional provability, we have to consider $(tc(T_C))_{C\,\epsilon\,COMP}$. In general, however, $tc(T^*_S)$ need not be identical to the union of $(tc(T_C))_{C\,\epsilon\,COMP}$. This may occur when a literal occurs in the head of two rules belonging to different components. Then there will be one formula $tc(T_{CL})$ in $tc(T^*_S)$, combining the two rules (and this is intended), but there will be two in the union of $(tc(T_C))_{C\,\epsilon\,COMP}$, one for each component (and this is not intended). In the case of simplified executable temporal formulae we can give a simple criterion which ensures that $tc(T^*_S)$ is equal to the union of $(tc(T_C))_C \in COMP$. The only thing that is required is that for each formula CL, the temporal formulae defining it, are all in one component, i.e., $T_{CL} \subseteq T_D$ for some component D. It is easy to see that this requirement is sufficient, and it is a requirement satisfied at least by all theories describing components in DESIRE.

Given that this requirement is satisfied, we can of course apply Proposition 5.4 to the compositional theory $(tc(T_C))_C \in COMP$:

Corollary 6.2

For the language composition $(L_C)_C \in COMP$, let a composition of properties $(P_C)_C \in COMP$ and a compositional temporal theory $(T_C)_C \in COMP$ be given. Let $\vdash$ be a classical provability relation for temporal multi-epistemic logic.

If $(P_C)_C \in COMP$ is compositionally provable with respect to $\vdash$ from the compositional temporal theory $(tc(T_C))_C \in COMP$ then $(P_C)_C \in COMP$ is globally provable with respect to $\vdash$ from the compositional theory $(tc(T_C))_C \in COMP$.

The notion of temporal completion defined above expresses default persistence for all information in the system. This implies that in all cases where no default persistence is intended, explicit temporal rules are required that prohibit the persistence. For example, to describe retraction of information that deductively depends on other information that was revised (such as occurs, for example, in the truth maintenance process of primitive components in DESIRE), it is needed in addition to explicitly express a temporal rule, e.g., (for the Example 4.5) of the form:

$$\phi \wedge \neg (Y\ Cin_{x.oc}\ \textbf{view(A, circle)} \wedge Y\ Cin_{x.oc}\ \textbf{view(B, circle)}) \rightarrow$$
$$\neg\ Cout_{x.oc}\ \textbf{object\_type(sphere)} \wedge \neg\ Cout_{x.oc} \neg\ \textbf{object\_type(sphere)}$$

where ϕ is again a formula expressing control information that allows the rule to be used (for example, the component should be active). Another approach is to define a more sensitive form of temporal completion already taking this into account, in which case these separate rules for retraction are not needed.

7 Conclusions

The compositional verification method formalized in this paper can be applied to a broad class of multi-agent systems. Compositional verification for one process abstraction level deep is based on the following very general assumptions:
- a multi-agent system consists of a number of agents and external world components.
- agents and components have explicitly defined input and output interface languages; all other information is hidden; information exchange between components can only take place via the interfaces (*information hiding*).
- a formal description exists of the manner in which agents and world components are composed to form the whole multi-agent system (*composition relation*).
- the semantics of the system can be described by the evolution of states of the agents and components at the different levels of abstraction (*state-based semantics*).

This non-iterative form of compositional verification can be applied to many existing approaches, for example, to systems designed using Concurrent METATEM [17, 18]. Compositional verification involving more abstraction levels assumes, in addition:

- some of the agents and components are composed of sub-components.
- a formal description exists of the manner in which agents or components are composed of sub-components (*composition relation*).
- information exchange between components is only possible between two components at the same or adjacent levels (*information hiding*).

Currently not many approaches to multi-agent system design exist that exploit iterative compositionality. One approach that does is the compositional development method DESIRE. The compositional verification method formalized in this paper fits well to DESIRE, but not exclusively.

Two main advantages of a compositional approach to modelling are the transparent structure of the design and support for reuse of components and generic models. The compositional verification method extends these main advantages to (1) a well-structured verification process, and (2) the reusability of proofs for properties of components that are reused.

The first advantage entails that both conceptually and computationally the complexity of the verification process can be handled by compositionality at different levels of abstraction. Apart from the work reported in [20], a generic model for diagnosis has been verified [8] and a multi-agent system with agents negotiating about load-balancing of electricity use [6]. The second advantage entails: if a modified component satisfies the same properties as the previous one, the proof of the properties at the higher levels of abstraction can be reused to show that the new system has the same properties as the original. This has high value for a library of reusable generic models and components. The verification of generic models forces one to find the assumptions under which the generic model is applicable for the considered domain, as is also discussed in [14]. A library of reusable components and generic models may consist of both specifications of the components and models, and their design rationale. As part of the design rationale, at least the properties of the components and their logical relations can be documented.

The usefulness of a temporal multi-epistemic logic, TMEL, a generalization of temporal epistemic logic was investigated to formalize verification proofs. As a test, the properties and proofs for verification of an example multi-agent system for co-operative information gathering [20] were successfully formalized within the logic TMEL. Our study shows that TMEL provides enough expressivity for dynamics and reasoning about time, and formalizes incomplete information states in an adequate manner. To obtain the right structure in accordance with the compositional system design, the logic is equipped with a number of compositional structures: compositions of sub-languages, compositional theories, and compositional provability. It was established that under the assumption that the provability relation is reflexive and transitive, compositional provability implies global provability. Therefore this logic is adequate if the executable temporal theories formalizing a specification are temporally completed, a temporal variant of Clark's completion for logic programs. In this case classical provability can be used, which is much more transparent than the more complicated non-classical provability relations that are possible.

In [18] a temporal belief logic, TBL, was introduced to define semantics and verify properties for systems specified in Concurrent METATEM [17]. A similarity with our approach as introduced above is that in both cases modal operators are used to distinguish knowledge of different agents, and a discrete linear time temporal logic is built on top of the multi-modal logic. A main difference in comparison to [18] is that our approach exploits compositionality. In Concurrent METATEM no iterated compositional structures can be defined, as is the case in DESIRE. Therefore verification in TBL always takes place at the global level, instead of the iterated compositional approach to verification in TMEL. Another difference is that in our approach the states in the base logic are in principle three-valued, whereas the states in Concurrent METATEM are two-valued: an atom in a state that is not true is assumed false in this state.

A similarity between our approach and the approach introduced in [4] is that both employ a combination of temporal logic and modal logic, and exploit modular system structures to limit complexity. A difference is that in [4] branching time logic is used and the agent architecture is restricted to the BDI-architecture. Another difference is that they use model checking as the verification approach, whereas our approach is based on proofs. In our case it is easier to include a description of a verification proof as part of the design rationale documentation.

A future continuation of this work will consider the development of tools for compositional verification.

References

1. Abadi, M. and L. Lamport (1993). Composing specifications, *ACM Transactions on Programming Languages and Systems*, Vol. 15, No. 1, pp. 73–132.

2. Barringer, H., M. Fisher, D. Gabbay, and A. Hunter (1991). Meta-reasoning in executable temporal logic. In: J. Allen, R. Fikes, E. Sandewall, *Proceedings of the 2nd International Conference on Principles of Knowledge Representation and Reasoning*, KR'91.

3. Barringer, H., M. Fisher, D. Gabbay, R. Owens, and M. Reynolds (1996). *The Imperative Future: Principles of Executable Temporal Logic*, Research Studies Press Ltd. and John Wiley & Sons.

4. M. Benerecetti, F. Giunchiglia, and L. Serafini (1999). A model-checking algorithm for multiagent systems. In this volume.

5. Benthem, J.F.A.K. van (1983). *The Logic of Time : a Model-theoretic Investigation into the Varieties of Temporal Ontology and Temporal Discourse*, Reidel, Dordrecht.

6. Brazier, F.M.T., F. Cornelissen, R. Gustavsson, C.M. Jonker, O. Lindeberg, B. Polak, and J. Treur, (1998). Compositional design and verification of a multi-agent system for one-to-many negotiation. In: *Proceedings of the Third International Conference on Multi-Agent Systems*, IEEE Computer Society Press.

7. Brazier, F.M.T., B.M. Dunin-Keplicz, N.R. Jennings, and J. Treur, (1995) Formal specification of multi-agent systems: a real world case. In: Lesser, V. (ed.), *Proceedings of the First International Conference on Multi-Agent Systems*, MIT Press, pp. 25-32. Extended version in: Huhns, M. and Singh, M. (eds.), *International Journal of Co-operative Information Systems*, IJCIS vol. 6 (1), special issue on Formal Methods in Co-operative Information Systems: Multi-Agent Systems, pp. 67–94.

8. Cornelissen, F., C.M. Jonker, and J. Treur (1997). Compositional verification of knowledge-based systems: a case study for diagnostic reasoning. In: E. Plaza, R. Benjamins (eds.), *Knowledge Acquisition, Modelling and Management, Proceedings of the 10th EKAW*, Lecture Notes in AI, vol. 1319, Springer Verlag, pp. 65–80.

9. Dams, D., R. Gerth, and P. Kelb (1996). *Practical symbolic model checking of the full μ-calculus using compositional abstractions.* Report, Eindhoven University of Technology, Department of Mathematics and Computer Science.

10. Engelfriet, J. (1996). Minimal temporal epistemic logic, *Notre Dame Journal of Formal Logic*, vol. 37, pp. 233–259 (special issue on Combining Logics).

11. Engelfriet, J., and J. Treur (1996). Specification of nonmonotonic reasoning. In: *Proceedings International Conference on Formal and Applied Practical Reasoning.* Springer-Verlag, Lecture Notes in Artificial Intelligence, vol. 1085, pp. 111–125.

12. Engelfriet, J., and J. Treur (1996). Executable temporal logic for nonmonotonic reasoning; *Journal of Symbolic Computation*, vol. 22, no. 5&6, pp. 615–625.

13. Engelfriet, J., and J. Treur (1997). An interpretation of default logic in temporal epistemic logic. *Journal of Logic, Language and Information*, vol. 7, no. 3, pp. 369–388.

14. Fensel, D., and R. Benjamins (1996). Assumptions in model-based diagnosis. In: B.R. Gaines, M.A. Musen (eds.), *Proceedings of the 10th Banff Knowledge Acquisition for Knowledge-basedSystems workshop,* Calgary: SRDG Publications, Department of Computer Science, University of Calgary, pp. 5/1–5/18.

15. Fensel, D., A. Schonegge, R. Groenboom, and B. Wielinga (1996). Specification and verification of knowledge-based systems. In: B.R. Gaines, M.A. Musen (eds.), *Proceedings of the 10th Banff Knowledge Acquisition for Knowledge-based Systems workshop,* Calgary: SRDG Publications, Department of Computer Science, University of Calgary, pp. 4/1–4/20.

16. Finger, M. and D. Gabbay (1992). Adding a temporal dimension to a logic system. *Journal of Logic, Language and Information* 1, pp. 203–233.

17. Fisher, M. (1994). A survey of Concurrent METATEM — the language and its applications. In: D.M. Gabbay, H.J. Ohlbach (eds.), Temporal Logic — Proceedings of the First International Conference, Lecture Notes in AI, vol. 827, pp. 480–505.

18. Fisher, M., and M. Wooldridge (1997). On the formal specification and verification of multi-agent systems. In: Huhns, M. and Singh, M. (eds.), *International Journal of Co-operative Information Systems, IJCIS* vol. 6 (1), special issue on Formal Methods in Co-operative Information Systems: Multi-Agent Systems, pp. 37–65.

19. Hooman, J. (1994). Compositional verification of a distributed real-time arbitration protocol. *Real-Time Systems*, vol. 6, pp. 173–206.

20. Jonker, C.M. and J. Treur (1998). Compositional verification of multi-agent Systems: a formal analysis of pro-activeness and reactiveness. In: W.P. De Roever, H. Langmaack, A. Pnueli, (eds.). *Proceedings of the International Symposium on Compositionality,* Springer Verlag, to appear.

21. Treur, J., and M. Willems (1994). A logical foundation for verification. In: *Proceedings of the Eleventh European Conference on Artificial Intelligence, ECAI'94,* A.G. Cohn (ed.), John Wiley & Sons, Ltd., pp. 745–749.

Emergent Mental Attitudes in Layered Agents

Christoph G. Jung*

GK Kogwiss. & MAS Group, FB Inform., Univ. des Saarlandes & DFKI GmbH
Im Stadtwald, D-66123 Saarbrücken, Germany
jung@dfki.de

Abstract. One crucial milestone towards an advanced and mature agent technology is the exploration of relationships between nowadays settled theories and architectures. This requires the formal specification of computational aspects by reasonable software-engineering approaches. Complementary, this also requires carefully investigating the practical (and cognitive) relevance of normative presumptions which are theoretically ascribed to the "mental" states of agents. Especially for *hybrid* architectures which reconcile the radical changes of paradigms in Artificial Intelligence over the past decades, a corresponding theoretical foundation has still not been found. The present work is a first attempt to capture such forms of practical rationality. Focusing on layered agents, such as those following the InteRRaP model, our proposal upholds the benefits of the established *Belief, Desire,* and *Intention* (BDI) theory. To this end, we describe the layered agent as a *holon,* i.e., a structured group of traditional BDI agents, and explore how its attitudes emerge from the dynamic interplay of its normative parts.

1 Introduction

Some time in the not-so-distant future, you advise your new household robot, Heinz, to bring the last bottle of beer out of the cellar. Heinz is a hybrid system that has been sold off because he is not equipped with the popular PROVABLY RATIONAL™ certificate. On his way back up the stairs, he unfortunately slips on a puddle of liquid. Fighting to retain his foothold, he drops the bottle and it crashes. You stay calm— still happy with your decision to buy Heinz —because you know that the puddle has resulted from last week's expensive dismantlement of certified Willie, the predecessor of Heinz. After much re-engineering, the manufacturers had reconstructed Willie following a unified architecture and logical specification. While slipping on a piece of chewing gum, but, Willie was so busy computing his "rational balance" that he could not come up with an idea about how to retain his physical balance in time. Now you only wish that Heinz could be PROVABLY RATIONAL™, too!

This tiny episode could be the continuation to the famous introduction of Cohen & Levesque [6], a story which impressively motivates their logical specification of the rational balance of agents. Backed by investigations of Bratman [2], the realised distinction of separate "mental attitudes" (*Beliefs, Desires* ≅ goals, *Intentions*), each playing a different functional role in the perception-action-cycle, has had a wide and fundamental impact on BDI theories, e.g., the work of Rao & Georgeff [24]. BDI has been able to

---

* supported by a grant from the "Deutsche Forschungsgemeinschaft" (DFG).

improve some flaws of Cohen & Levesque [6]. It is close to formally bridge the gap to the corresponding architectural design of *Procedural Reasoning Systems* (PRS) [12, 8].

The *unified* agent perspective, however, sacrifices many computational aspects for the sake of theoretical declarativeness and conciseness. Current agent applications in flexible manufacturing, telematics, robotics, and virtual reality focus on broad and situated systems like Heinz and Willie. These are systems that exhibit a variety of (sub-) cognitive abilities, including reactive behaviour, deliberative problem solving, and social coordination, each in a satisficing[1] manner. Hence, broad agents have to represent and arbitrate between a wide range of goals on various levels of abstraction.

In this context, unified agent descriptions tend to be overloaded, because they rely on a single state and a corresponding rational computation. It is an overload for the agent's designer or instructor who has the burden of fussily modelling interactions of representations based on the most primitive level of abstraction. Subsequently, it is a particular overload for any applied reasoning procedure bombarded with a vast amount of heterogeneous information. Whether such a unified agent will ever find an appropriate solution before completely failing by system disintegration **and** smashing your last bottle of beer[2] cannot be predicted, e.g., from a BDI specification.

Such insights have rendered the appropriate notion of rationality a highly controversial subject in Artificial Intelligence (AI) over the past decades. While early symbolists concentrated on perfect, deliberative intelligence for making optimal decisions, the *Reactive AI* community has argued against any expensive representation and reasoning (see, e.g., Brooks [3]). Today, there is an increasing concordance on *bounded rationality* which is measured by a combined utility of decision quality and computation costs. With respect to bounded rationality, the deliberative and the reactive approaches can be seen as extreme instances.

Indeed, *hybrid* agent architectures provide a special and practical trade-off between computation cost and solution quality because they combine myopic, but reactive mechanisms with optimal, but expensive deliberation facilities. For example, the InteRRaP architecture [21] introduces a layered scheme for the combination of the respective *modules*: the reactive *Behaviour-Based Layer*, the deliberative *Local Planning Layer*, and the *Social Planning Layer*. Each layer is associated with reasoning on a particular level of abstraction and each layer controls its subordinate layer in order to put through more abstract goals. Hybrid models, such as InteRRaP, are particularly successful in constructing broad agents for sophisticated real-world and virtual-world domains [22].

Along with current formalisations of hybrid agents [9, 17], we have observed that all functional modules in InteRRaP can be reasonably described by identifying appropriate sub-languages and sub-inferences of a unified logic [15]. However, a theoretical foundation of hybrid rationality has not yet been found, because it is not obvious how to cater to the differences among the modules: partial inconsistencies, different styles of computation, encapsulation, and meta-control. Although these are practical features that ease the designer's task in specifying a broad range of reactiveness and abstraction, a clear and declarative model of system performance is still desirable and necessary.

---

[1] This extends the weaker requirement of *shallow* abilities in Bates et al. [1]

[2] May the reader decide which condition appears to be the most fatal.

Contribution. The aim of the present paper is to give a first, theoretical account of hybrid systems focused on layered approaches, such as InteRRaP [21]. We do **not** claim any cognitive relevance, hence the unquoted mentalistic vocabulary is used for **illustrating a specification**. We largely keep with the established BDI framework [24] (Section 2) to reductionistically decompose the rationality of each single layer into the balanced interplay of its mental attitudes. Complementarily, we develop a constructive, *holonic* definition of the complete InteRRaP agent whose mental state emerges from the dynamic interaction of its normative layers. Section 3 motivates our approach in detail using a typical, real-world application scenario of InteRRaP.

The idea of describing complex systems as *holons*, i.e., self-similar structures, goes back to Koestler [19] and has already been put into multi-agent practice [4]. Up to now, the respective theoretical foundations are unclear. Fisher [11], for example, uses temporal logic to represent architectures as groups of agents, but does not derive any implications from that. In Section 4, we present an extended BDI logic for such holonic and, in particular, layered systems which enables a re-investigation of consistency, commitment, and persistence within the hybrid InteRRaP scheme. Contrasting the claim of Piaggio [23], these theoretical results emphasise the importance of hierarchical structures. Opposed to collaborative team cases [7], our structured group of BDI layers does not primarily focus on joint attitudes, but on emergent, possibly conflicting mental states. Since InteRRaP uses shared memory, a safe communication channel and introspection mechanisms are plausible assumptions.

2 The Normative BDI Theory

The following section shortly summarises the basics of the established *Belief, Desire,* and *Intention* theory (BDI) [24]. Because of the focus of the present paper and due to space constraints, we assume that the reader is familiar with sorted epistemic logics (see the tutorial of Meyer [5]) to model a dynamic environment and the mental states of situated agents. We stay with syntactic constraints rather than giving lengthy semantics.

Our variant of the formalism relies on reasonable properties of the original, e.g., consistency, realism, no over-commitment, and competence for own actions, but introduces some minor ontological changes. We provide for multiple agents executing simultaneous (instantaneous) actions. We do not distinguish success and failure of events, because these notions are, in our opinion, not manifested in the "real world" and are evaluated rather with respect to the mental attitudes of the performing agent.

Figure 1 defines the pretty-much standard syntax with well-formed formulae ($\langle$Wff$\rangle$, in the following also denoted by $\omega_1, \omega_2, \ldots$) operating on a particular, static state of the world. Path formulae ($\langle$Path-Wff$\rangle$, also $\pi_1, \pi_2, \ldots$) operate with temporal modalities (next $\bigcirc$, eventually $\Diamond$, and weak until $\bigcup$) on dynamic state transitions caused by combinations of simultaneous, primitive actions ("Happened"). From non-deterministic transitions, histories are selected via "optional". Finally, the mental modalities "Bel", "Goal", and "Intend" ascribe propositions to the attitudes of the respective agent.

The temporal semantics follows the standard CTL* [10] interpretation. Accessibility relations discriminate worlds with respect to the attitudes of agents. Whenever the agent has no attitude towards a proposition, it does not discriminate access to worlds

$\langle$Obj-Var$\rangle$ ::= $X, X_1, X_2, X_3, \ldots$	$\langle$Var$\rangle$ ::= $\langle$Obj-Var$\rangle$ | $\langle$Ag-Var$\rangle$ | $\langle$Ev-Var$\rangle$
$\langle$Ag-Var$\rangle$ ::= $A, A_1, A_2, A_3, \ldots$	$\langle$Predicate$\rangle$ ::= $\langle$Pred$\rangle(\langle$Var$\rangle, \ldots, \langle$Var$\rangle)$
$\langle$Ev-Var$\rangle$ ::= $E, E_1, E_2, E_3, \ldots$	$\langle$Wff$\rangle$ ::= $\langle$Predicate$\rangle$ | $\langle$Wff$\rangle \wedge \langle$Wff$\rangle$ |
$\langle$Pred$\rangle$ ::= $P, P_1, P_2, P_3, \ldots$	$\neg\langle$Wff$\rangle$ | $\exists\langle$Var$\rangle.\langle$Wff$\rangle$ |
$\langle$Path-Wff$\rangle$ ::= $\langle$Wff$\rangle$ | $\neg\langle$Path-Wff$\rangle$ |	Happened($\langle$Ag-Var$\rangle, \langle$Ev-Var$\rangle)$ |
$\langle$Path-Wff$\rangle \wedge \langle$Path-Wff$\rangle$ |	Bel($\langle$Ag-Var$\rangle, \langle$Wff$\rangle)$ |
$\langle$Path-Wff$\rangle \bigcup \langle$Path-Wff$\rangle$ |	Goal($\langle$Ag-Var$\rangle, \langle$Wff$\rangle)$ |
$\Diamond\langle$Path-Wff$\rangle$ |	Intend($\langle$Ag-Var$\rangle, \langle$Wff$\rangle)$ |
$\bigcirc\langle$Path-Wff$\rangle$	optional$\langle$Path-Wff$\rangle$

Fig. 1. BDI Syntax

that differ in the validity of the proposition. Hence, a particular attitude amounts to the validity of the proposition in all accessible worlds. Happens(A, E) ::= inevitable $\bigcirc$ Happened(A, E) and dual operators $\vee, \forall$, *inevitable*, and $\square$ are defined with respect to to the already introduced constructs.

Definition 1 (Basic BDI Interpretation). *A basic BDI interpretation M is a tuple $\langle U, W, T, \succ, \mathcal{B}, \mathcal{G}, \mathcal{I}, \Phi \rangle$. The universe $U \supseteq \mathcal{A} \uplus \mathcal{E}$ includes agents $\mathcal{A}$ and their respective actions $\mathcal{E} = \uplus_{a \in \mathcal{A}} \mathcal{E}_a$. There are time points T ordered by the partial "immediate predecessor" function $\succ: T \twoheadrightarrow T$ s.t. for all $t \in T : t \not\succ^* t$. Each world $\langle T_w, A_w \rangle = w \in W$ with $T_w \subseteq T$ implements a partial transition $A_w : (T_w \times F) \twoheadrightarrow T_w$ s.t. $A_w(t_1, f_1) = t_2$ only if $t_2 \succ t_1$. Hereby, F is the set of total agent-event mappings $f : \mathcal{A} \mapsto \mathcal{E}$ s.t. for all $f(a) = e$ it holds $e \in \mathcal{E}_a$. A state w_t is the combination of a world $w \in W$ and a corresponding time point $t \in T_w$. It is associated with relations on U which interpret predicates $\Phi : W \times T \to (\langle Pred \rangle \mapsto \mathcal{P}(U^*))$. $\mathcal{B}, \mathcal{G}, \mathcal{I} : (W \times T \times \mathcal{A}) \times W$ describe the worlds that are accessible with respect to to an agent's mental attitudes of belief, goal, and intention in a particular state. Let M be a basic BDI interpretation, $\sigma : \langle Var \rangle \to U$ be a sort-preserving variable assignment, and w_t be a selected world state. Entailment $M, w_t, \sigma \models$ is then defined by slightly adapting the framework of [24].*

The basic interpretation does not cover any normative rational balance. Definition 2 thus further restricts the general accessibility relations. Constraints C1–C4 are to establish consistency, closure under consequence, and appropriate nesting. They make use of the traditional $K_{(m)}$, D, A4, and A5 axioms of epistemic logic [14]. Mental attitudes should be realistic; C5 and C6 demand each goal (intention) towards an option to be also believed (desired) to be optional. Semantically characterised by a *sub-world* relationship [24], this construction attacks the problem of over-committed agents: a goal's believed side-effects and irremediable situations are not necessarily adopted as further goals. Finally, each agent should be competent with respect to its own actions (C7,C8) and eventually work on its intentions which is called "no infinite deferral" (C9).

Definition 2 (Normative BDI Interpretation). *A basic BDI interpretation M is a normative BDI interpretation iff the following constraints hold:*

(C1) $\mathcal{B}, \mathcal{G}$, *and* $\mathcal{I}$ *obey the axioms* $K_{(m)}$ *and D.* $\mathcal{B}$ *satisfies the axioms A4 and A5.*

(C2) $M \models \text{Goal}(A, \omega) \supset \text{Bel}(A, \text{Goal}(A, \omega))$

(C3) $M \models \text{Intend}(A, \omega) \supset \text{Goal}(A, \text{Intend}(A, \omega))$

(C4) $M \models \text{Intend}(A, \omega) \supset \text{Bel}(A, \text{Intend}(A, \omega))$

(C5) $M \models \text{Goal}(A, \text{optional}\pi) \supset \text{Bel}(A, \text{optional}\pi)$

(C6) $M \models \text{Intend}(A, \text{optional}\pi) \supset \text{Goal}(A, \text{optional}\pi)$

(C7) $M \models \text{Intend}(A, \text{Happens}(A, E)) \supset \text{Happens}(A, E)$

(C8) $M \models \text{Happened}(A, E) \supset \text{Bel}(A, \text{Happened}(A, E))$

(C9) $M \models \text{Intend}(A, \omega) \supset \text{inevitable}\Diamond\neg\text{Intend}(A, \omega)$

3 The Layered Agent as a BDI Holon: Motivating Example

Hybrid systems, such as InteRRaP agents [21] (Figure 2), represent a special form of boundedly rational intelligence by integrating and mediating between different styles of computation, i.e., deliberative, goal-oriented reasoning versus reactive, situation-driven reasoning. While this is also claimed for unified logical approaches, such as [20], the layered attempt of InteRRaP does not restrict to a co-existence of the inferences. Rather, it is a cooperative and structured form of integration in order to make higher-level reasoning feasible: In InteRRaP, each layer encapsulates the reasoning on a particular level of abstraction and controls its subordinate layer in order to obey its more abstract (thus more important) decisions.

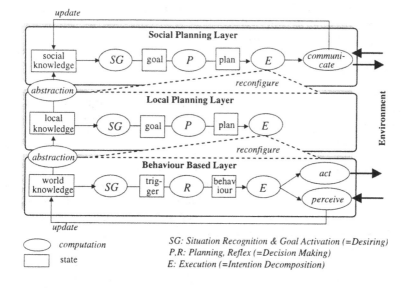

Fig. 2. The InteRRaP Architecture

The most concrete layer, the *Behaviour-Based Layer* (BBL), provides immediate feedback with the environment. It applies procedural knowledge, so-called patterns of behaviour, to turn the sensor stimuli (input) into motor commands (output). On top of the BBL, the *Local Planning Layer* (LPL) (meta-)reasons about the state of the BBL rather than about the state of the external world in order to perform deliberative tasks. Accordingly, the LPL's means to achieve these tasks are not external actions, but internal *reconfigurations* of the computational activities in the BBL, such as (de-)activation, suppression, parameter changes, etc. This decouples the perception-action-cycle of the LPL from the hard timing constraints of a dynamic environment. Furthermore, the LPL's representations are more abstract and persistent which renders the applied symbolic planning tractable. Similarly, the *Social Planning Layer* (SPL) reasons on top of the LPL about communicative and social actions that have the state of the LPL as their topic, e.g., communicating a goal or committing to a joint plan. The results of SPL negotiations have the adaption of the LPL as a consequence, for example by adding or removing a goal in the LPL.

A fine-grained process model is developed to practically implement the described architecture [17, 15]. However, the present paper does not address the proposed inner-layer modularisation. InteRRaP processes can be uniquely assigned to the typical functional roles in BDI: belief update, goal activation, decision making, and execution (see Figure 2). Thus, we assume an idealised architecture for the moment, while Section 5 outlines issues related to ultra-hybrid InteRRaP. But still, there are problems for employing unified theories:

1. The layers' different computational styles, especially deliberative versus reactive, has to be represented. Computation is implicit in the original BDI model.
2. BDI preserves only a single, logically self-contained belief modality while InteRRaP introduces three knowledge bases with a special access policy.
3. Encapsulated inferences in InteRRaP interleave action, deliberation, and negotiation which leads to temporarily inconsistent goals and intentions.
4. The meta-object relationship between layers including reconfigurations represents a highly non-monotonic scheme in the BDI sense.

As the idealised design in Figure 2 suggests, each layer itself can be described as a BDI machine following the normative notion of rationality. This approach is now motivated and exemplified using the sophisticated test-bed of InteRRaP: the automated loading dock (Figure 3).

Herein forklift robots (type Khepera) are faced with tasks to (un-)load boxes of different categories to (from) a truck from (to) respective shelves. Their sensor-motor-loop is implemented by procedural behaviour processes that translate the incoming (sub-symbolic) readings from infrared sensors, optical gripper sensors, and motor registers into commands for controlling the two wheels and an attached gripper device. For example, the "avoid-collision" reflex triggers upon obstacles being recognised in the sensor data. It spawns a "move" behaviour to dodge.

Task and path planning is performed within the LPL based on deduced symbolic data, e.g., spatial representations of connected regions, and based on plan-operators whose execution parameterises the underlying behaviour layer. Among other things, the operator "approach shelf" suppresses the output of the avoid-collision reflex.

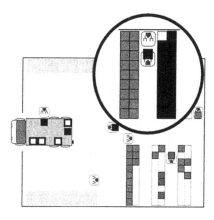

Fig. 3. The Automated Loading Dock

Figure 3 shows a situation where the robot delivering the black box to the shelf is in conflict with another forklift intending to move out of the corridor. Such conflicts require the SPL to negotiate a joint solution— here, the exchange of the box. The exchange is then initiated by the SPL informing the LPL that the delivery task can be fulfilled by an agreed two-agent plan. Computation of the delivering robot will now be outlined in terms of a BDI model[3] in which layers are described as traditional BDI agents.

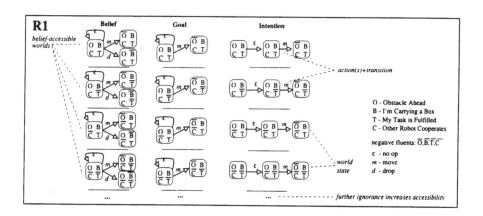

Fig. 4. The BBL as a BDI Agent: **R1**

---

[3] For the sake of simplicity, we use graphical, propositional descriptions which abstract from realistic representations and timing. States omit temporal uniqueness which is used to denote loops. Partially annotated transitions represent all transitions in which the respective actions occur.

Scheme **R1** in Figure 4 shows the initial mental state of the robot's BBL. Its belief, or world knowledge, comprises such basics as the existence of an obstacle (O) and whether the robot is carrying a box (B). The BBL is ignorant about the successful fulfilment of a delivery task (T) and the other agent being cooperative (C). Thus, all alterations of T and C are belief-accessible. Similarly, the BBL's belief is also restricted with respect to the effects of its actions no-op (ϵ), move (m), and drop (d) in combination with actions of other agents and layers. **R1** also shows that activity of the avoid-collision reflex has been already triggered by the "dodge" goal ($\Diamond\neg$O) and spawned the behaviour (intention) to move away from the obstacle at the next step in time: Intend(BBL, inevitable $\bigcirc$ Happens(BBL, m)).

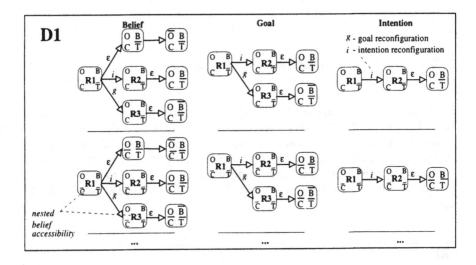

Fig. 5. The LPL as a BDI Agent: **D1**

With a tight deadline, dodging makes the on-time delivery no longer achievable. In the loading dock, it is safe and even necessary to approach particular objects. The layered approach releases the BBL from the expensive reasoning to handle such situations. Instead, the LPL, as depicted in Figure 5, meta-reasons about the situation including the BBL's state — **R1** is nestedly accessible. Additional local knowledge allows to infer the task's state ($\overline{T}$) and the effects of reconfiguring the BBL, e.g., intention reconfiguration (i) and goal reconfiguration (g). The LPL predicts that i suppresses the undesirable collision-avoidance reflex, hence delays the m action of the BBL (**R2** in Figure 6). If doing nothing (ϵ), the LPL knows furthermore that the BBL would immediately trigger m which renders T unachievable due to the deadline. Hence, the LPL adopts the goal "inevitable $\bigcirc$ $\bigcirc$O" and subsequently intends to perform i to maintain its option for T.

The LPL does not know that it can fulfil its task by persuading (with g) the BBL to adopt state **R3** (Figure 6), hence the goal Happens(BBL, d) to drop or exchange the box. This is because neither the cooperative attitude of the other agent willing to put

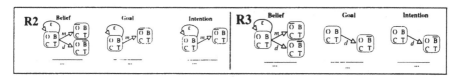

Fig. 6. Further States of the BBL: **R2** and **R3**

the box on the shelf, nor its implications for the task are present. Therefore, Figure 7 introduces the BDI model of the SPL in which these relations are reasoned about. The SPL could have performed a communicative action and thus believe in C. Furthermore, it has access to the state **D1** of the LPL and predicts that performing b (belief reconfiguration) forces the LPL to state **D2** (Figure 8). In **D2**, the LPL still does not know about C, but believes that T is reachable by performing g. The SPL thus adopts the mentioned option as goal and intention, because it infers, e.g., from conflicting goals with the other robot, that T cannot be achieved in any other way. As a result in the real-world, provided a certain competence[4], first BBL (suppressing the avoid-collision reflex) and LPL (getting to know the effects of the multi-agent plan) are reconfigured ($\epsilon\&i\&b$). Afterwards ($\epsilon\&g\&\epsilon$) the LPL activates the drop behaviour in order to exchange the box with the partner robot in the next step ($\epsilon\&\epsilon\&d$).

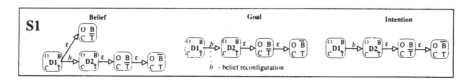

Fig. 7. The SPL as a BDI Agent: **S1**

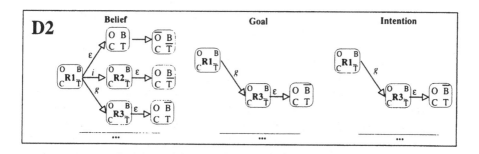

Fig. 8. Further State of the LPL: **D2**

---

[4] Reconfigurations can fail quite similar to real actions. They could conflict with vital changes in the mental state of the subordinate layer which prohibits the desired change in attitude. Our theory in Section 4 reflects this by mentally grounding reconfigurations in the super-layer. In practice, this means that failure handling is never obsolete, even in layered agents.

4 A Holonic and Layered BDI Theory

This section develops an extension of the BDI theory to represent structured, especially layered *holons* which allows the specification and investigation of InteRRaP agents, such as the forklifts discussed in the preceding example. The Hungarian philosopher Arthur Koestler has proposed the term *holon* to describe a basic organisational unit in biological and social systems [19]. This term is a combination of the Greek word *holos*, meaning *whole* and the suffix *on* meaning *particle*. Koestler elaborated that in living organisms as in social organisations entirely self-supporting, non-interacting entities did not exist. Every identifiable unit, e.g., a single cell in an animal or a family in the society, comprises more basic units (plasma and nucleus, parents and siblings) at the same time forming a part of a larger unit (a muscle tissue, a community). Generalised to the notion of a complex agent, it is reasonable to employ a holonic approach, i.e., to regard the agent as a fractal, self-similar concept.

$$
\begin{array}{ll}
\langle\text{Ho-Var}\rangle & ::= H, H_1, H_2, H_3, \ldots \\
\langle\text{Var}\rangle & ::= \ldots \mid \langle\text{Ho-Var}\rangle \\
\langle\text{Predicate}\rangle & ::= \ldots \mid \langle\text{Ho-Var}\rangle \vartriangleleft \langle\text{Ho-Var}\rangle \mid \\
 & \quad \langle\text{Ag-Var}\rangle \vartriangleleft \langle\text{Ho-Var}\rangle \mid \\
 & \quad \langle\text{Ag-Var}\rangle \blacktriangleleft \langle\text{Ag-Var}\rangle \\
\langle\text{Wff}\rangle & ::= \ldots \mid \text{Bel}^*(\langle\text{Ho-Var}\rangle, \langle\text{Wff}\rangle) \mid \\
 & \quad \text{Goal}^*(\langle\text{Ho-Var}\rangle, \langle\text{Wff}\rangle) \mid \\
 & \quad \text{Intend}^*(\langle\text{Ho-Var}\rangle, \langle\text{Wff}\rangle) \mid \\
 & \quad \text{Happened}^*(\langle\text{Ho-Var}\rangle, \langle\text{Ev-Var}\rangle)
\end{array}
$$

Fig. 9. HLBDI Syntax Extensions

Figure 9 extends the vocabulary of BDI with the new sort of holons which in turn consist of holons or primitive BDI agents (the *sub-holon* relation ◁). Structure is imposed by layering normative agents (◀: the immediate sub-layer of). We introduce new mental modalities for holons which emerge from the mental states of their respective parts. Much work has been done in research on common or mutual knowledge [13] and joint intentions [7] which use the intersection of primitive attitudes to explain the holon. These approaches are able to lift the normative properties to the group level.

We object that such an attempt is not desirable for describing hybrid systems. Conflicts as present between InteRRaP layers would lead to neutral group attitudes by a broader accessibility relation. This would imply the underivability of some dispositions which are indeed manifested and could lead to observable actions. Instead of *a priori* postulating rational balance of the holon, we envisage to explicitly capture inconsistencies and dynamic interactions within the hybrid scheme by transparently joining the attitudes of subordinate holons. Although this limits the expressiveness of inference at the first sight, our investigations into the role of structural constraints in layered groups will mitigate this impression.

Definition 3 extends normative BDI to the respective holonic and layered HLBDI framework. While constraints C9, C10, C11, and C12 install the transparent shift of attitudes and actions to the group level, HLBDI also makes precise the notion of a layer as a reconfiguring and at the same time reconfigurable entity. Layers inherit the believes of their subordinates (C13). Furthermore, they are realistic (C14 to C16) with respect to their reconfiguration options, i.e., they cannot desire attitudes of their controlled partner that they do not have themselves. This is weaker than formulating real-world constraints, but it is more reasonable in that reconfigurations do not always succeed due to the environmental dynamics (see Section 3). In Lemma 1, we will then state a few properties of HLBDI, such as layered introspection (a), limited inference (c), and the ability to represent inconsistencies (d).

Definition 3 (Holonic and Layered BDI Interpretation). *A normative BDI interpretation M is holonic and layered iff there are holons $\mathcal{H} \subseteq U$, $\mathcal{H} \cap (\mathcal{A} \cup \mathcal{E}) = \{\}$, a partial-order relation $\mathcal{S} : (A \uplus H) \times H$ and a partial injection $\mathcal{L} : A \rightarrowtail A$ with $a \notin \mathcal{L}^*(a)$. We define $M, w_t, \sigma \models V \lhd H$ iff $(\sigma(V), \sigma(H)) \in \mathcal{S}$, and $M, w_t, \sigma \models A_1 \blacktriangleleft A_2$ iff $(\sigma(A_1), \sigma(A_2)) \in \mathcal{L}$. Additionally, the following constraints are satisfied:*

(C9) $M \models \text{Bel}^*(H, \omega) \equiv \exists A. A \lhd H \land \text{Bel}(A, \omega)$
(C10) $M \models \text{Goal}^*(H, \omega) \equiv \exists A. A \lhd H \land \text{Goal}(A, \omega)$
(C11) $M \models \text{Intend}^*(H, \omega) \equiv \exists A. A \lhd H \land \text{Intend}(A, \omega)$
(C12) $M \models \text{Happened}^*(H, E) \equiv \exists A. A \lhd H \land \text{Happened}(A, E)$
(C13) $M \models A_1 \blacktriangleleft A_2 \supset (\text{Bel}(A_1, \omega) \supset \text{Bel}(A_2, \omega))$
(C14) $M \models A_1 \blacktriangleleft A_2 \supset (\neg\text{Bel}(A_2, \omega) \supset \neg\text{Goal}(A_2, \text{optional}\lozenge\text{Bel}(A_1, \omega)))$
(C15) $M \models A_1 \blacktriangleleft A_2 \supset (\neg\text{Goal}(A_2, \omega) \supset \neg\text{Goal}(A_2, \text{optional}\lozenge\text{Goal}(A_1, \omega)))$
(C16) $M \models A_1 \blacktriangleleft A_2 \supset (\neg\text{Intend}(A_2, \omega) \supset \neg\text{Goal}(A_2, \text{optional}\lozenge\text{Intend}(A_1, \omega)))$

Lemma 1 (Some Properties of HLBDI). *Let M be a HLBDI interpretation. It holds:*
(a) $M \models A_1 \blacktriangleleft A_2 \supset (\text{Intend}(A_1, \omega) \supset \text{Bel}(A_2, \text{Intend}(A_1, \omega))$
(b) $M \models A_1 \blacktriangleleft A_2 \supset (\text{Intend}(A_2, \text{optional}\lozenge\text{Intend}(A_1, \omega)) \supset \text{Intend}(A_2, \omega))$
(c) $\text{Intend}^*(H, P) \land \text{Intend}^*(H, P \supset Q) \not\models \text{Intend}^*(H, P)$
(d) $\text{Goal}^*(H, \omega) \land \text{Goal}^*(H, \neg\omega)$ *is satisfiable*
(e) $M \models \text{Goal}^*(H, \text{optional}\pi) \supset \text{Bel}^*(H, \text{optional}\pi)$
(f) $M \models \text{Intend}^*(H, \text{Happens}^*(H, E)) \supset \text{Happens}^*(H, E)$

Proof. We restrict to property (b). The rest is easy to verify. From C5, it follows that $\text{Intend}(A_2, \text{optional}\lozenge\text{Intend}(A_1, \omega)) \supset \text{Goal}(A_2, \text{optional}\lozenge\text{Intend}(A_1, \omega))$. C16 then derives (b) $\text{Goal}(A_2, \text{optional}\lozenge\text{Intend}(A_1, \omega)) \supset \text{Intend}(A_2, \omega)$.

We are now able to express the layered InteRRaP holon in Definition 4 and to investigate the resulting knowledge base. Theorem 1 states that it is equivalent to the belief of the social planning layer (A_3), hence has the same quality as a normative attitude.

Definition 4 (InteRRaP holon).

$$\text{InteRRaP}(H, A_1, A_2, A_3) ::= A_1 \lhd H \land A_2 \lhd H \land A_3 \lhd H \land$$

$$\forall V. V \lhd H \supset (V = A_1 \lor V = A_2 \lor V = A_3) \land A_1 \blacktriangleleft A_2 \blacktriangleleft A_3 \land \neg\exists A. A_3 \blacktriangleleft A$$

Theorem 1 (InteRRaP KB). *Let M be a HLBDI interpretation. It holds:*

$$M \models \forall H, A_1, A_2, A_3.(\text{InteRRaP}(H, A_1, A_2, A_3) \supset (\text{Bel}^*(H, \omega) \equiv \text{Bel}(A_3, \omega)))$$

Proof. By Definition 4, the InteRRaP holon is the exhaustive combination of its three layers; with C9 it follows $\text{Bel}^*(H,\omega) \equiv (\text{Bel}(A_1,\omega) \vee \text{Bel}(A_2,\omega) \vee \text{Bel}(A_3,\omega))$. Because of C13 from Definition 3, the belief of BBL and LPL is subsumed by the SPL's KB, thus the theorem follows.

In contrast to the InteRRaP knowledge base, the possibly conflicting, holonic combination of goals and intentions is in general not to be found within a single layer. If we speak of emergent attitudes in this respect, this does not mean any sudden appearance of properties not grounded in the parts of the holon. We regard emergent functionality to arise from the ability of the members of a group to reflect the group as a whole and their status within. By changing their mind or influencing other members in interaction and communication, the group eventually evolves towards a homogeneous state. This self-organisation has a static component in social reflection, such as the postulated selection of realistic reconfigurations, and a dynamic component in acting upon this reflection.

In the remainder of this section, we explore this dynamic component by reconsidering commitment strategies [24]. These are characterisations of mental attitudes that persist under specified circumstances over periods of time. For example, the blindly committed agent keeps a strong (inevitable) intention at least as long as it does not believe in its coming into existence. Simple-minded agents can additionally drop intentions if they believe that success is not possible. Finally, open-minded agents even allow a change of goals to influence persistence of intentions. The empirical results of [18] attest that the more sophisticated strategies, especially those of open-minded agents, are more efficient in dynamic settings.

For our purposes, we have to slightly modify the original definitions in order to be compatible with our notion of a layer, i.e., a reconfigurable module. The intention of a superior layer to interrupt could always be a reason to drop an intention (Definition 5). Although we will not be able to observe convergence of the complete InteRRaP agent towards a stable, normative state in highly dynamic settings, Theorem 2 states that, if all layers follow a joint commitment strategy, the holon will exhibit a similar persistence. In addition, this persistence reasonably mirrors the hybrid context of possible conflicts. In the following, let $\overline{\text{Bel}}^*(H,\omega) ::= \exists A.A \vartriangleleft H \wedge \neg\text{Bel}(A,\omega)$ and $\overline{\text{Goal}}^*(H,\omega) ::= \exists A.A \vartriangleleft H \wedge \neg\text{Goal}(A,\omega)$.

Definition 5 (Committed InteRRaP Layers).

(C17) $\text{Blind}(A) ::= \text{Intend}(A, \text{inevitable}\Diamond\omega) \supset \text{inevitable}(\text{Intend}(A, \text{inevitable}\Diamond\omega) \cup$
$\quad (\text{Bel}(A,\omega) \vee \exists A_2.A \blacktriangleleft A_2 \wedge \text{Intend}(A_2, \text{optional}\Diamond\text{Intend}(A, \text{optional}\Box\neg\omega)))$

(C18) $\text{BlindInteRRaP}(H) ::= \exists A_1, A_2, A_3.\text{InteRRaP}(H, A_1, A_2, A_3)\wedge$
$\quad \text{Blind}(A_1) \wedge \text{Blind}(A_2) \wedge \text{Blind}(A_3)$

(C19) $\text{Simple}(A) ::= \text{Intend}(A, \text{inevitable}\Diamond\omega) \supset \text{inevitable}(\text{Intend}(A, \text{inevitable}\Diamond\omega) \cup$
$\quad (\text{Bel}(A,\omega) \vee \neg\text{Bel}(A, \text{optional}\Diamond\omega)\vee$
$\quad \exists A_2.A \blacktriangleleft A_2 \wedge \text{Intend}(A_2, \text{optional}\Diamond\text{Intend}(A, \text{optional}\Box\neg\omega))$

(C20) $\text{SimpleInteRRaP}(H) ::= \exists A_1, A_2, A_3.\text{InteRRaP}(H, A_1, A_2, A_3)\wedge$
$\quad \text{Simple}(A_1) \wedge \text{Simple}(A_2) \wedge \text{Simple}(A_3)$

(C21) $\text{Open}(A) ::= \text{Intend}(A, \text{inevitable}\Diamond\omega) \supset \text{inevitable}(\text{Intend}(A, \text{inevitable}\Diamond\omega) \cup$
$\quad (\text{Bel}(A,\omega) \vee \neg\text{Goal}(A, \text{optional}\Diamond\omega)\vee$
$\quad \exists A_2.A \blacktriangleleft A_2 \wedge \text{Intend}(A_2, \text{optional}\Diamond\text{Intend}(A, \text{optional}\Box\neg\omega)))$

(C22) OpenInteRRaP(H) ::= $\exists A_1, A_2, A_3.$InteRRaP$(H, A_1, A_2, A_3) \wedge$
$\quad$ Open$(A_1) \wedge$ Open$(A_2) \wedge$ Open(A_3)

Theorem 2 (Committed InteRRaP Agents). *Let M be a HLBDI interpretation. It holds:*

(g) $M \models$ BlindInteRRaP$(H) \supset$
$\quad$ (Intend$^*(H,$ inevitable$\Diamond\omega) \supset$ inevitable(Intend$^*(H,$ inevitable$\Diamond\omega) \bigcup$
$\quad$ (Bel$^*(H, \omega) \vee$ Intend$^*(H,$ optional$\square\neg\omega)$)))
(h) $M \models$ SimpleInteRRaP$(H, A) \supset$
$\quad$ (Intend$^*(H,$ inevitable$\Diamond\omega) \supset$ inevitable(Intend$^*(H,$ inevitable$\Diamond\omega) \bigcup$
$\quad$ (Bel$^*(H, \omega) \vee \overline{\text{Bel}}^*(H,$ optional$\Diamond\omega) \vee$ Intend$^*(H,$ optional$\square\neg\omega)$)))
(i) $M \models$ OpenInteRRaP$(H) \supset$
$\quad$ (Intend$^*(H,$ inevitable$\Diamond\omega) \supset$ inevitable(Intend$^*(H,$ inevitable$\Diamond\omega) \bigcup$
$\quad$ (Bel$^*(H, \omega) \vee \overline{\text{Goal}}^*(H,$ optional$\Diamond\omega) \vee$ Intend$^*(H,$ optional$\square\neg\omega)$)))

Proof. While we outline the proof of (h), (g) and (i) are analogue. From C20 in Definition 5, Definition 4, and C11 in Definition 3 we can derive that there is some simple-minded layer A s.t.

$$\text{Intend}^*(H, \text{inevitable}\Diamond\omega) \supset \exists A..A \triangleleft H \wedge \text{Intend}(A, \text{inevitable}\Diamond\omega)$$

Because of C19 in Definition 5, the intention of A, and hence the one of H (C11), persists until

$$\text{Bel}(A, \omega) \models_{C9} \text{Bel}^*(H, \omega) \quad \text{or} \quad \neg\text{Bel}(A, \text{optional}\Diamond\omega) \models \overline{\text{Bel}}^*(H, \text{optional}\Diamond\omega)$$

or the third condition. This requires

$$\exists A_2.A \blacktriangleleft A_2 \wedge \text{Intend}(A_2, \text{optional}\Diamond\text{Intend}(A, \text{optional}\square\neg\omega))$$

from which, because of property (b) in Lemma 1, we can infer Intend$(A_2,$ optional$\square\neg\omega)$. From Definition 4, the existence of such an A_2 implies its being a layer in H and thus Intend$(A_2,$ optional$\square\neg\omega) \models_{C11}$ Intend$^*(H,$ optional$\square\neg\omega)$. Because of weak until supporting $(\pi_1 \supset \pi_2) \supset ((\omega \bigcup \pi_1) \supset (\omega \bigcup \pi_2))$, we derive the theorem.

5 Discussion

Along with the practical success of hybrid agent architectures, the need for their theoretical understanding has become highly important. We motivated and presented an approach to formalising layered architectures, such as InteRRaP, based on the established, normative BDI framework. Our encouraging results, e.g., the reasonable emergence of commitment strategies, will hopefully initiate an ongoing— *holonic* —effort that tries to explain practical forms of rationality which arise from the interaction of simpler, but possibly normative and unified entities.

Such a perspective complements the traditional, reductionistic attempt to decompose intelligence into dumb functionalities. Hence it could be relevant in cognitive and social sciences as well. While our choice of mental modalities for holons has been pragmatic, it is necessary to compare them with state-of-the-art semantics, e.g., prioritised conflict handling, to come up with more expressive operators. Similarly, a stronger formalisation of reconfigurations which clearly distinguishes them from the domain-specific external actions has to be found.

As discussed in Section 3, an important topic remains to be addressed to formally relate this theoretical InteRRaP model to the operational specifications of [17, 15]: the idealised inner-layer computation. Indeed, the modularisation of the InteRRaP agent has been refined down to the level of concurrent processes, e.g., desires, reflexes, planning, and plan execution. Thus inconsistency, encapsulation, and control also appear within a particular layer. To reconcile such a design with the normative BDI model requires further thought. Additionally, processes in InteRRaP, especially planning, have been mainly connected to an abductive, first-order temporal logic [16] whose relation to modal and dynamic logic is still unclear.

Research of this type gives rise to more issues, such as open-mindness in the presence of undecidable planning or the representation of resource-adaptive mechanisms in the BDI model. The ongoing work on InteRRaP, for example, attempts to enhance the layered scheme towards a boundedly rational architecture by explicit representation and management of resources. Within the present theory, this is already expressible: A layer is forced to drop a goal, because its supervising layer estimates that the decision making costs are higher than the goal utility. In general, extensions of BDI with respect to such computational properties will offer much insight into bounded rationality as the up-to-date paradigm of AI.

Acknowledgements

The author is grateful for the stimulating discussions with Klaus Fischer, Hans-Jürgen Bürckert, Gero Vierke, Christian Gerber, Alistair Burt, and David Pearce. The work of Jörg Müller on InteRRaP has been a constant source of inspiration. Thanks to Munindar P. Singh and to the anonymous reviewers of ATAL'98 for most valuable comments.

References

1. J. Bates, A. B. Loyall, and W. S. Reilly. Broad agents. *SIGART Bulletin*, 2(4), August 1992.
2. M. E. Bratman. *Intentions, Plans, and Practical Reason*. Harvard University Press, 1987.
3. R. A. Brooks. Intelligence without reason. Technical Report 1293, MIT AI Laboratory, April 1991.
4. H. J. Bürckert, G. Vierke, and K. Fischer. TELETRUCK: A Holonic Fleet Management System. In *Cybernetics And Systems'98 — Proceedings of the 14th European Meeting on Cybernetics and System Research*, pages 695–700, Vienna, 1998. Austrian Society for Cybernetic Studies.
5. J.-J. Ch. Meyer, W. van der Hoek, and G. A. W. Vreeswijk. Epistemic logic for computer science (part 1). *Bulletin of the European Association for Theoretical Computer Science*, (44):242–270, 1991.

6. P.R. Cohen and H.J. Levesque. Intention is choice with commitment. *Artificial Intelligence*, 42(3):213–261, 1990.

7. P.R. Cohen and H.J. Levesque. Teamwork. *Nous*, 35, 1991.

8. M. d'Inverno, D. Kinny, M. Luck, and M. Wooldridge. A Formal Specification of dMars. In *Intelligent Agents IV*, volume 1365 of *Lecture Notes in Artificial Intelligence*, pages 155–174. Springer, 1998.

9. B. Dunin-Keplicz and J. Treur. Compositional formal specification of multi-agent systems. In *Intelligent Agents*, volume 890 of *Lecture Notes in Artificial Intelligence*, pages 102–117. Springer, 1994.

10. E. A. Emerson and J. Srinivasan. Branching Time Temporal Logic. In J. W. deBakker, W. P.deRoever, and G.Rozenberg, editors, *Linear Time, Branching Time and Partial Order in Logics and Models for Concurrency*, pages 123–172. Springer-Verlag, Berlin, 1989.

11. M. Fisher. Representing abstract agent architectures. In J. P. Müller, M. P. Singh, and A. S. Rao, editors, *Intelligent Agents V — Proceedings of the Fifth International Workshop on Agent Theories, Architectures, and Languages (ATAL-98)*, Lecture Notes in Artificial Intelligence. Springer-Verlag, Heidelberg, 1999. In this volume.

12. M. P. Georgeff and A. L. Lansky. Reactive reasoning and planning. In *Proc. of the 6th National Conference on Artificial Intelligence*, 1987.

13. J. Y. Halpern and Y. O. Moses. Knowledge and Common Knowledge in a Distributed Environment. *Journal of the the ACM*, 37(3):549–587, 1990.

14. G. E. Hughes and M. J. Creswell. *A Companion to Modal Logic*. Methuen & Co. Ltd., London, 1984.

15. C. G. Jung. On the Role of Computational Models for Specicying Hybrid Agents. In *Cybernetics And Systems '98 — Proceedings of the 14th European Meeting on Cybernetics and System Research*, pages 749–754, Vienna, 1998. Austrian Society for Cybernetic Studies.

16. C. G. Jung. Situated abstraction planning by abductive temporal reasoning. In *Proc. of the 13th European Conference on Artificial Intelligence ECAI'98*, pages 383–387. Wiley, 1998.

17. C. G. Jung and K. Fischer. A Layered Agent Calculus with Concurrent, Continuous Processes. In *Intelligent Agents IV*, volume 1365 of *Lecture Notes in Artificial Intelligence*, pages 245–258. Springer, 1998.

18. D. Kinny and M. P. Georgeff. Commitment and effectiveness of situated agents. In *Proc. of the Twelfth International Joint Conference on Artificial Intelligence (IJCAI-91)*, pages 82–88, Sydney, Australia, 1991.

19. A. Koestler. *The Ghost in the Machine*. Arkana Books, 1989.

20. R. Kowalski and F. Sadri. Towards a unified agent architecture that combines rationality with reactivity. In D. Pedreschi and C. Zaniolo, editors, *Logic in Databases*, volume 1154 of *Lecture Notes in Computer Science*. Springer-Verlag, 1996.

21. J. P. Müller. *The Design of Intelligent Agents: A Layered Approach*, volume 1177 of *Lecture Notes in Artificial Intelligence*. Springer-Verlag, December 1996.

22. J. P. Müller. The right agent (architecture) to do the right thing. In J. P. Müller, M. P. Singh, and A. S. Rao, editors, *Intelligent Agents V — Proceedings of the Fifth International Workshop on Agent Theories, Architectures, and Languages (ATAL-98)*, Lecture Notes in Artificial Intelligence. Springer-Verlag, Heidelberg, 1999. In this volume.

23. M. Piaggio. HEIR — a non-hierarchical hybrid architecture for intelligent robots. In J. P. Müller, M. P. Singh, and A. S. Rao, editors, *Intelligent Agents V — Proceedings of the Fifth International Workshop on Agent Theories, Architectures, and Languages (ATAL-98)*, Lecture Notes in Artificial Intelligence. Springer-Verlag, Heidelberg, 1999. In this volume.

24. A. S. Rao and M. P. Georgeff. Modeling Agents Within a BDI-Architecture. In R. Fikes and E. Sandewall, editors, *Proc. of the 2rd International Conference on Principles of Knowledge Representation and Reasoning (KR'91)*, pages 473–484, Cambridge, Mass., April 1991. Morgan Kaufmann.

The Right Agent (Architecture) to Do the Right Thing

Jörg P. Müller*

John Wiley & Sons, Inc.

Abstract. Academic and industrial system designers who consider using agent technology to solve an application problem are faced with a wide variety of agent paradigms: There are deliberative agents, reactive agents, interacting agents, hybrid agents, layered agents, believable agents, mobile agents, software agents, softbots — the list could well be prolonged. Also, within each paradigm, the user can select between different architectures and systems, making the actual choice a complex and difficult endeavor.

The objective of this paper is to assist readers in deciding which agent architecture to choose for a specific *application*. We approach this objective in three steps. First, we identify application areas for agent technology starting from the examples presented in the first part of this paper. Then, based on the characteristics of different classes of applications identified in the first step, we propose a classification of agents according to different classes of applications. Based on this classification, the third step is to provide rules of thumb to help a software engineer or system designer decide which agent architecture (or which class thereof) is likely to be appropriate for a certain class of applications.

1 Introduction

An important research branch in AI in the early nineties has investigated control architectures for intelligent agents. An agent architecture describes the functional components of an agent and how they work together. Over the past few years, numerous architectures have been proposed in the literature, addressing different key features an agent should have, and building on a wide variety of research disciplines. Indeed the variety of agent architectures and systems is so wide that system designers in academia and industry, who are willing to "try" intelligent agents technology to solve an application problem, are often lost when it comes to decide what is the most suitable agent architecture for their specific problem.

In this paper, we address the question as to what agent architectures are most suitable for building different types of agent applications. While no complete and undebatable answer to this question can be given so far, our aim is to provide a set of guidelines that help the system designer select the right — i.e., most appropriate — architecture for a given problem domain. Thus, this paper is intended for system designers and software engineers interested in agent technology as a software-engineering paradigm.

Our approach in this paper is based on empirical evidence: we study existing agent architectures and the applications that were built using these architectures, as far as known from the literature. Based on this test set, we try to derive a taxonomy that

---

* Email: jpm@wis-dev.wiley.co.uk

classifies agents in terms of the classes of applications they appear in, and we define a set of guidelines that we hope will help system designers in identifying what is *the right agent to do the right thing*.

The paper is organized as follows: Section 2 presents the test set that we use, i.e., the set of example agent architectures. Section 3 identifies the core application for the architectures in the test set. In Section 4, we propose a taxonomy for agents based on the classes of applications identified in Section 3. A set of guidelines for choosing agent architectures is presented in Section 5. In Section 6, we discuss these guidelines and how to use them. The paper finishes with some concluding remarks in Section 7. Table 6 in Appendix A summarizes the analysis of the test set.

2 The Test Set

The test set used in this paper consists of ca. 30 agent architectures. It is an updated and extended version of the architectures described in an earlier review [26]. The architectures discussed vary widely in underlying models, approaches, and features. Available implementations range from proof-of-concept prototypes over research implementations to semi-commercial or commercial systems.

In accordance with [26] we classify our test set into five categories, i.e., *reactive agents*, *deliberative agents*, *interacting agents*, *layered approaches*, and *others*. The former four categories reflect different architectural paradigms (see [25] for a detailed discussion). The latter category serves as a container for various more recent approaches that do not fit nicely in any of the former, such as believable agents, softbots, and a variety of commercial agent-based systems.

A detailed description of the architectures in the test set would exceed the boundaries of this paper. We refer to the original article. In the remainder of this section, we provide a brief characterization of each category and its instances. For a complete list of the architectures contained in the test set, we refer to Table 6 in Appendix A.

The first category, *reactive agents*, include examples such as Brooks's subsumption architecture. Research on reactive agents is strongly influenced by behaviorist psychology and Artificial Life. Reactive agents make decisions based on a very limited amount of information, and simple situation-action rules. Some researchers denied the need of any symbolic representation of the world; instead, reactive agents make decisions directly based on sensory input. The focus of this class of system is directed towards achieving *robust* behavior instead of *correct* or *optimal* behavior. Table 1 shows the instances of reactive agents that we consider in this paper.

Deliberative agents are based on Simon and Newell's physical symbol system hypothesis in their assumption that agents maintain an internal representation of their world, and that there is an explicit mental state which can be modified by some form of symbolic reasoning. AI planning systems and BDI agents are the classical representatives of this category (see Table 2).

The third category, *interacting agents*, have their origin in Distributed Artificial Intelligence (DAI). DAI deals with coordination and cooperation among distributed intelligent agents. While the focus of this research discipline has been on the coordination process itself and on mechanisms for cooperation among autonomous agents rather

Architecture	Reference
Subsumption architecture	[6]
Self-organizing agents	[38]
AuRA	[2]
Dynamic action selection	[23]
PENGI	[1]
ECO model	[9]

Table 1. Reactive agents

Architecture	Reference
IRMA	[5]
PRS	[15]
dMARS	[33]
SOAR	[21] [41]
Cypress	[43]
Agent0 / PLACA	[35] [42]

Table 2. Deliberative agents

than on the structure of these agents, we have selected some approaches for the test set that deal with the incorporation of cooperative abilities into an agent framework (see Table 3).

Architecture	Reference
MAGSY	[12]
GRATE*	[18] [27]
MECCA	[39]
COSY	[7]

Table 3. Interactive agents

The three categories discussed so far suffer from different shortcomings: whereas purely reactive systems have a limited scope insofar as they can hardly implement goal-directed behavior, most deliberative systems are based on general-purpose reasoning mechanisms which are not tractable, and which are much less reactive. One way to overcome these limitations in practice, are layered architectures. The main idea is to structure the functions of an agent into two or more hierarchically organized layers that interact with each other in order to achieve coherent behavior of the agent as a whole.

Table 4 shows the layered architectures that we consider in this paper.

Architecture	Reference
RAPs, ATLANTIS, 3T	[11] [14] [4]
Lyons & Hendriks	[22]
TouringMachines	[10]
INTERRAP	[25]
SIM_AGENT	[37]
NMRA	[30]

Table 4. Layered approaches

The last category, others, is a collection of miscellaneous agent systems, including three sub-areas, i.e., *believable agents*, *softbots*, and various Internet software agents. The instances under consideration are shown in Table 5.

Architecture	Reference
Tok	[34]
VET	[19]
ShopBot	[16]
Zuno VRISKO, QuarterDeck Web-Compass, AgentSoft LifeAgent Pro, FireFly ...	—

Table 5. Other approaches

In the remainder of this paper, we will identify and classify the core application areas of each architecture in the test set, and establish some guidelines to assist a system designer in selecting an architecture for a specific application.

3 Application Areas for Intelligent Agents

In the absence of theories to determine which agent paradigm is most useful for which class of applications, we take an empirical approach: we analyze the main areas of application known from the literature for each of the agent architectures described in Section 2. The first two columns of Table 6 in Appendix A summarize the main application areas for the architectures under consideration. While we refer to the appendix for details, in this section we discuss some interesting observations relating to Table 6.

Observation 1 Most architectures discussed are used for autonomous control systems. The first striking observation is that a large percentage of applications (approximately half of them) are in the area of mobile robots or, more broadly speaking, autonomous control systems (ACS). While this is likely to be explained as a historical coincidence, it is striking to what degree this also affects the more recent hybrid architectures, such as NMRA, 3T, INTERRAP, or SIM_AGENT.

Observation 2 There is only a limited number of examples of cooperating hardware agents.
The second, and maybe more surprising observation is that while few researchers will doubt the role of cooperation and agent interaction, our list of applications contains only a few examples that actually use interaction among ACSs as a core ingredient. Where these systems can be found (most notably production planning and flexible transport system applications), in most cases the individual agents have limited autonomy, and the interactions among them are simple (e.g., a decentralized material flow where two machines are fed by a transport robot using material buffers, thus eliminating the nitty-gritty details of real-time interaction). One possible explanation for the small number of applications for cooperating ACSs is that there are still a number of fundamental problems in the modeling of an individual ACS (e.g., at the level of sensorimotor control and the abstraction of input sensor data), that need to be solved before the use of cooperating ACSs in real-world applications becomes practical.

Observation 3 Distributed resource allocation is a core area for interacting agents.
The third observation is that a considerable class of applications found in Table 6 deals with distributed resource allocation, routing, and scheduling problems. Examples are logistics and transport planning, production planning systems, workflow management, and business process enactment and monitoring systems.

Observation 4 Cooperative expert systems are a core area for interacting agents.
A fourth observation is that some of the traditional areas of use of expert systems reappear as application areas of agent technology. Again, this is not very surprising as a significant part of the momentum behind developing multiagent systems originated from the need to build cooperating expert systems. The most prominent example of this class of applications are diagnosis problems that require systems capable to deal with fuzzy and possibly inconsistent knowledge (e.g., GRATE* as used in ARCHON, or the spacecraft health management component of the NMRA architecture).

Observation 5 Mainstream architectures do not sufficiently account for HCI requirements.
A fifth observation is that a small class of applications addresses the design of agents that interact with humans. Given that user modeling is a well-established discipline in AI and that many of its aspects have been revived by research areas such as *Computer-Supported Cooperative Work* (CSCW) and *Human Computer Interaction* (HCI), it is surprising how little effect the requirements of dealing with "human agents" have had on the design of mainstream agent architectures. Those applications in Table 6 that require the ability to deal with human agents are mostly software agent applications,

such as entertainment, art, education, personal assistants (meeting scheduling, traffic guidance, secretarial functions) and process monitoring agents. However, there seems to be a potential for robots interacting with or assisting humans (e.g., robotic wheelchair, errand-running, robots "working" with humans in factories or offices).

Observation 6 Designers of software agents tend to use other architectures than their hardware colleagues.

The final observation we would like to make in this subsection concerns the wide variety of application areas created by the advent of global computer networks, and, in particular, the World Wide Web. These areas require software agents to perform information retrieval, information filtering, and resource discovery tasks in a real-world software environment. Requirements that are imposed by these applications are the need for interoperability (legacy systems), user profiling capabilities to provide personalized services, and robustness to cope with ever-changing conditions in the environment (e.g., availability of WWW resources) and with changing or context-dependent user preferences. Looking at Table 6, it is striking that the architectures used to build softbot applications seem to differ largely from those developed to build autonomous robots. This is particularly surprising as the notion of a softbot has been derived from a software program being faced with conditions similar to those a mobile robot is likely to encounter, e.g., uncertainty, huge amounts of information, change. We shall get back to this observation in Section 5.

4 An Taxonomy of Agent Applications

Based on the observations made in Section 3, we propose a taxonomy of intelligent agents that reflects the different application areas identified above, and that can be used to classify the above agent architectures according to how suitable they are for different application problems.

We suggest a classification of agents according to two dimensions, the first of which is the material state of the agents, i.e.:

- *Hardware agents*: Agents that have a physical *gestalt* and that interact with a physical environment through effectors and sensors. Clearly, hardware agents will use software components.
- *Software agents*: Programs that interact with real or virtual software environments.

The second dimension is the primary mode of interaction between the agent and its environment:

- *Autonomous agents*: This perspective of autonomous agents concentrates on two entities and their relationship: the agent itself and its environment. Virtually all autonomous control systems fall into this category.
- *Multiagents*: The environment of multiagents is classified into two categories, i.e.: other agents and non-agents. An agent can use its knowledge about other agents to coordinate its actions, to make better predictions about the future, or to achieve goals collaboratively.

– *Assistant agents*: Assistant agents primarily interact with (and: act on behalf of) one particular type of other agents, i.e., humans.

The motivation for our choice is as follows: the first dimension (material state) is introduced to comply with Observation 6: if different architectures are used in practice to model hardware agents on the one hand and software agents on the other, the classification should reflect this.

The second dimension (mode of interaction) aims at complying with the main application areas identified above: In [45], the editors provide a similar separation between (autonomous) agents and multiagents underlying Observations 1 to 4. The fact that existing single-agent architectures were extended or new architectures were developed to cope with the requirements of multiagent applications in our view makes this distinction useful. In addition, Observation 5 suggests considering agents that primarily interact with humans as an important special case of multiagents.

This taxonomy allows us to distinguish between six different agent types:

1. *Autonomous hardware agents (HW-AU):* They are characterized by the requirement for robust control within a physical environment, interleaving higher-level control and lower-level execution, coping with the unexpected in real time, and making up for the limitations of practical sensors and effectors (incomplete, erroneous knowledge). Most autonomous control systems shown in Table 6 fall into this category, e.g., RAPs, NMRA, and AuRA. An example for an agent architecture of type HW-AU presented in this volume is HEIR [31].

2. *Autonomous software agents (SW-AU):* Software systems that act autonomously and make decisions in a software environment. An example is a software agent associated with a workflow. This agent autonomously plans and monitors the routing of the different tasks to be performed as part of the workflow. Also, autonomous software agents are often the back-end of what appears to be a software assistant agent (see below) in the front-end perspective. Thus, a system such as ShopBot could be seen as consisting of a front-end software assistant agent maintaining the user profile, pre-processing user input and presenting results, and of an autonomous software agent that goes shopping in the Internet. Wooldridge and Parson's abstract agent architecture presented in this volume [46] can be regarded as a further example of type SW-AU.

3. *Hardware assistant agents (HW-AS):* Hardware agents whose primary task it is to assist human users. One class of these agents are household robots. From the architectures in the test set, only ᴣT was used (among others) for human assistance purposes, e.g., as a wheelchair and for running errands. However, we suggest considering another group of hardware agents for this class, i.e., those agents that interact with humans for entertainment or educational purposes. We are likely to see examples of this species in the form of smarter, more human-like and more interesting Tamagotchi-like hardware pets.

4. *Software assistant agents (SW-AS):* Programs that assist a human on the computer screen or in Personal Digital Assistants (PDAs), that act on behalf of that human, or that entertain the human. As illustrated in the ShopBot example above, software assistant agents are often used as front-end to a system the back-end of which

are autonomous software agents. The main requirements software assistant agents have to satisfy are maintaining a user profile and adapting it to reflect changing user preferences, and find information that is relevant to a human according to her profile, and to present this information in a personalized way, i.e., in a way that is appropriate to the knowledge state of the user according to the profile. Note that entertainment agents (e.g., Creatures) and educational agents would fall into this category as well, according to the above definition. While there are no specific examples of architectures for assistant agents in this volume (neither HW-AS nor SW-AS), awareness of concepts such as norms [8] and moral sentiments [3] will be important for agents interacting with humans.

5. *Hardware multiagents (HW-MA):* Hardware agents that act as entities in a multi-agent system, e.g., cooperating robots in a manufacturing environment. Building hardware multiagents combines classical robotics requirements with the ability to reason about other agents, to form teams, and to perform joint plans and actions, e.g., in order to recognize and resolve goal conflicts or possibilities/necessities to cooperate to achieve a local or global goal. As an example to be found in this volume, see Stone and Veloso's team member architecture [40]; also in [31], the author points out that his approach can support agents of type HW-MA.

6. *Software multiagents (SW-MA):* Programs that act as entities in a multiagent system. The most common application areas for software multiagents are the solution of dynamic and distributed resource allocation problems, as well as cooperative expert systems applications. Numerous approaches found in this volume describe architectures for software multiagents. See e.g., A-Teams [32]; the agent architecture used by Skarmeas and Clark [36]; the model underlying Agentis [20], which provides an interaction model for dMARS; and PROSA$_2$ [29].

For each agent architecture considered in this paper, the third column of Table 6 shows what types of agents were built using this architecture.

5 Agent Architectures and Applications: Some Guidelines

So far, we have described a set of agent architectures and defined a taxonomy of types of agents for different applications. In this section, we address the question: *What is the right agent architecture to apply to a specific problem?*

Frankly, there is no black-or-white, algorithmic answer to this. More often than not, the answer will be pre-determined by external factors (e.g., commercial availability, availability of tools and development environments, compliance with internal information infrastructure), and the choice of the agent architecture will be one of the smaller problems to be solved. Realistically, we should not hope for more than providing useful guidelines.

Guideline 1 Check carefully whether you need agents, or whether another programming paradigm, such as (distributed) objects, will do the job to solve your application problem. Be requirements- driven rather than technology-driven. If your application problem shows some of the following properties, then you might want to consider looking at agent technologies:

- highly dynamic, necessary to be responsive and adaptable to a changing environment;
- need to deal with failure, e.g., re-scheduling, re-planning, re-allocating of resources;
- need to balance long-term goal-directed and short-term reactive behavior;
- complex and/or safety-critical, guaranteed reaction and response times;
- geographically or logically distributed, autonomous or heterogeneous nodes;
- need for reliability, robustness, and maintainability;
- complex or decentralized resource allocation problems with incomplete information;
- flexible interaction with human users.

For instance, imagine your task is to build a workflow management system to improve your company's information processes. *If* the business processes in your company are well-understood, largely involve information flow but no material flow, if there are clear and well-established ways of dealing with failure, if the services provided by different departments are static and known a priori, *then* you might as well model your workflow management system as a distributed object-oriented application.

If, however, the set of services is expected to change or service-level agreements are likely to be negotiable depending on the requester of a workflow service, if workflows are dynamic and need to be completed within a short period of time, and if your workflow system is likely to cater for the needs of offline workers and has to scale up to workflow processes beyond the control of an individual enterprise, *then* consider using agent technology, possibly based on a distributed object-oriented approach.

Guideline 2 Use Table 6 for a rough orientation. The fact that architecture A was successfully used to build applications of class P, but never used to build applications of class Q does not necessarily mean that A is not appropriate to deal with Q; however, in this case, if your problem is P, at least you have some positive evidence that A will work.

Guideline 3 If your problem requires autonomous hardware agents, then you may be well served with a hybrid architecture. A purely reactive approach may be applicable if you can find a decomposition of your system that allows you to define very simple agents. But do not underestimate the difficulty of achieving meaningful self-organizing behavior from a set of simple agents.

Guideline 4 If your problem requires autonomous software agents, then you can choose between some robust architectures such as dMARS and SOAR. dMARS is a commercial product and hence not available for free; however, there are various implementations of PRS, one of which, UM-PRS, has been developed at Michigan University.

Guideline 5 If your problem requires software assistant agents, then the agent architecture is definitely not the first thing to worry about. What is much more important is to get the domain functionality such as profiling and personalization right. These, however, are much more problems of human-computer interaction (HCI), user modeling and pattern matching.

Guideline 6 If your problem requires hardware assistant agents, then there is no off-the-shelf system available. A solution to your problem may be to select any architecture for ACSs (see also Guideline 3) and extend it by adding the required HCI functionality (see Guideline 5).

Guideline 7 If your problem requires software multiagents, then you might want to look at any of the examples presented under the *Interacting Agents* category. However, if there are high interoperability requirements on your system (e.g., communication with non-agent components within your company), then you may run into trouble as none of the systems described easily complies with interoperability standards such as CORBA. You therefore may have to modify the communication layer. When doing so, make sure that you do not do double work: there are well-established means of transporting a stream of bytes from one place to another. What is missing is a system that can deal with the semantics of these byte streams, and this is where agents can help.

Guideline 8 If your problem requires hardware multiagents, then either select one of the architectures or systems for autonomous hardware agents (see Guideline 3) and add your cooperation knowledge to these, or select one of the cooperation-centered architectures presented in Section 2 and enhance them by the necessary interface to your hardware. An architecture like INTERRAP might be of interest for you as it has been applied to the domain of interacting robots. However, its current status is that of a research prototype.

Guideline 9 Do not break a butterfly on a wheel. While it is appealing to compare an Internet search agent with a robot, this analogy must not be taken too literally. Most architectures that are used to control robots are by far too heavy-weight. If the domain you are working in is a software domain, more likely than not your architecture of choice should:

- be capable of multi-tasking;
- de-couple low-level message handling from high-level message interpretation;
- come with a service model allowing agents to vend services that are internally mapped into tasks;
- comply with interoperability standards such as CORBA to make agent services available to a wide spectrum of applications;
- have a small footprint: the empty agent should not be bigger than a few 100K.

Guideline 10 For most interesting applications, neither purely reactive nor purely deliberative architectures are useful. The odds are that you are best served with one of the hybrid architectures. Systems such as PRS, RAPS, or SOAR have been around for years and are sufficiently stable and mature to be a good choice for any type of autonomous control systems.

Guideline 11 If adaptability is crucial to solve your application problem, you will not have much choice. Most research reviewed in this paper has neglected the ability of an agent to learn and it is not clear how the architectures could support enabling an agent to deal with longer term change. A notable exception is the SOAR system, so you might want to have a look at that. Some approaches, in particular the reactive agent approaches, provide a short-term form of adaptability based on feedback. However, to our knowledge none of the described architectures offers a uniform and complete model for adaptability.

6 Discussion

The first aspect of the discussion is the taxonomy itself. The reader may wonder why we defined our own taxonomy instead of adopting e.g., either of Franklin and Graesser [13] or Nwana [28]. Also, why did we introduce two different schemes of classification in the two parts of this paper?

To answer the first part of this question: the Franklin-Graesser taxonomy has been a general, rather philosophical attempt to structure the field. As such, it does not reflect the view of a system designer who wishes to apply agent technology to a specific application domain. On the other hand, Nwana's taxonomy is restricted to software agents. Therefore, we preferred not to adopt any of the existing taxonomies.

With regard to the second part of the question, it is important to note that what we classified in the first part of this paper (reactive, deliberative, interacting, hybrid, others), were agent architectures. However, the classification proposed in Section 4 refers to agents or agent systems that were built according to an agent architecture. Thus, the two schemes classify different entities. Note that different agent types may appear in one and the same application. The most important requirement to be satisfied by the latter scheme is that it can be used to classify specific instances of agents built according to a specific agent architecture and used in a specific class of applications.

The second topic of discussion relates to the guidelines. Clearly, they are rules of thumb, and should be treated as such. They are a result of analyzing current agent architectures and the applications they were used for, as well as of our experience in designing agent architectures and agent-based systems. Guidelines 2 to 8 are more or less directly derived from Table 6. The guidelines reflect the current state of the art and are prone to changes. For instance, Guideline 9 seems to suggest to use "lighter" architectures for autonomous software agent applications than for autonomous hardware agents. In fact, what it does suggest is to make this choice *given the current state of the art in agent research*, based on observing the application areas of currently existing architectures as well as on experiences with two architectures that we developed in the past and applied to hardware and software domains alike.

Bridging the current gap, i.e., materializing the intuitive analogy between robots and softbots in terms of architectures that can be used to deal with the common aspects of both, is an interesting topic for future research.

Similarly, Guideline 11 should be understood as a requirement for future research on integrating learning mechanisms into agent architectures. There are plenty of applications that require only a limited (short-term) form of learning which is provided by at least some systems that are available today. What is lacking is longer-term adaptability.

7 Conclusion

The main contribution of this paper is threefold: Firstly, we analyzed a collection of agent architectures and systems built on the basis of these architectures with respect to what application areas they were used in. Secondly, we propose a taxonomy that allows us to classify agents with respect to types of applications they were used in. Thirdly, based on our analysis and the taxonomy, we extract guidelines as to which type of architecture is best suited for which type of application.

Clearly, the fuzzy nature of the task implies that there are a number of limitations, some of which were discussed in Section 6. For instance, the analysis of most approaches relies on information contained in the literature and to a degree on word of mouth information. In particular, our information relating to what applications were built using an architecture is prone to be somewhat incomplete. Nevertheless, we believe that the results described in this paper exceeds the scope of a traditional survey paper in that we aim at assisting system designers in finding the right agent to do the right thing.

References

1. P. E. Agre and D. Chapman. What are plans for? In *[24]*, pages 17–34. 1990.
2. R. C. Arkin. Integrating behavioral, perceptual, and world knowledge in reactive navigation. In *[24]*, pages 105–122. 1990.
3. A. L. C. Bazzan, R. H. Bordini, and J. A. Campbell. Moral sentiments in multi-agent systems. In this volume, pages 113–131.
4. R. P. Bonasso, D. Kortenkamp, D. P. Miller, and M. Slack. Experiences with an architecture for intelligent, reactive agents. In *[45]*, pages 187–202. Springer-Verlag, 1996.
5. M. E. Bratman, D. J. Israel, and M. E. Pollack. Toward an architecture for resource-bounded agents. Technical Report CSLI-87-104, Center for the Study of Language and Information, SRI and Stanford University, August 1987.
6. Rodney A. Brooks. A robust layered control system for a mobile robot. In *IEEE Journal of Robotics and Automation*, volume RA-2 (1), pages 14–23, April 1986.
7. B. Burmeister and K. Sundermeyer. Cooperative problem-solving guided by intentions and perception. In Y. Demazeau and E. Werner, eds., *Decentralized A. I.*, volume 3. North-Holland, 1992.
8. R. Conte, C. Castelfranchi, and F. Dignum. Autonomous norm-acceptance. In this volume, pages 99–112.
9. J. Ferber. Eco-problem solving: How to solve a problem by interactions. In *Proceedings of the 9th Workshop on DAI*, pages 113–128, 1989.
10. I. A. Ferguson. *TouringMachines: An Architecture for Dynamic, Rational, Mobile Agents.* PhD thesis, Computer Laboratory, University of Cambridge, UK,, 1992.
11. R. James Firby. *Adaptive Execution in Dynamic Domains.* PhD thesis, Yale University, Computer Science Department, 1989. Also published as Technical Report YALEU/CSD/RR#672.
12. K. Fischer. *Verteiltes und kooperatives Planen in einer flexiblen Fertigungsumgebung.* DISKI, Dissertationen zur Künstlichen Intelligenz. infix, 1993.
13. S. Franklin and A. Graesser. Is it an agent, or just a program?: A taxonomy for autonomous agents. In J. P. Müller, M. J. Wooldridge, and N. R. Jennings, eds., *Intelligent Agents III*,

volume 1193 of Lecture Notes in Artificial Intelligence, pages 21–36. Springer-Verlag, Heidelberg, 1997.

14. E. Gat. *Reliable Goal-directed Reactive Control for Real-World Autonomous Mobile Robots.* PhD thesis, Virginia Polytechnic and State University, Blacksburg, Virginia, 1991.

15. M. P. Georgeff and F. F. Ingrand. Decision-making in embedded reasoning systems. In *Proceedings of the 6th International Joint Conference on Artificial Intelligence*, pages 972–978, 1989.

16. S. Grand, D. Cliff, and A. Malhotra. Creatures: Artificial life autonomous software agents for home entertainment. In W. Lewis Johnson, editor, *Proceedings of the First International Conference on Autonomous Agents*, pages 22–29. ACM, 1997.

17. N. R. Jennings. Towards a cooperation knowledge level for collaborative problem solving. In *Proceedings of the 10th European Conference on Artificial Intelligence*, pages 224–228, Vienna, 1992.

18. N. R. Jennings, P. Faratin, M. J. Johnson, T. J. Norman, P. O'Brien, and M. E. Wiegand. Agent-based business process management. *International Journal of Cooperative Information Systems*, 5(2&3):105–130, 1996.

19. W. L. Johnson and J. Rickel. Integrating pedagocial capabilities in a virtual environment agent. In *Proceedings of the First International Conference on Autonomous Agents*, pages 30–38. ACM Press, 1997.

20. D. Kinny. The AGENTIS agent interaction model. In this volume, pages 331–344.

21. J. E. Laird, A. Newell, and P. S. Rosenbloom. SOAR: an architecture for general intelligence. *Artificial Intelligence*, 33(1):1–62, 1987.

22. D. M. Lyons and A. J. Hendriks. A practical approach to integrating reaction and deliberation. In *Proceedings of the 1st International Conference on AI Planning Systems (AIPS)*, pages 153–162, San Mateo, CA, June 1992. Morgan Kaufmann.

23. P. Maes. The dynamics of action selection. In *Proceedings of IJCAI-89*, pages 991–997, Detroit, Michigan, August 1989.

24. P. Maes, editor. *Designing Autonomous Agents: Theory and Practice from Biology to Engineering and Back.* MIT/Elsevier, 1990.

25. J. P. Müller. *The Design of Autonomous Agents — A Layered Approach*, volume 1177 of *Lecture Notes in Artificial Intelligence*. Springer-Verlag, Heidelberg, 1996.

26. J. P. Müller, editor. *Online Proceedings of the First International Conference on Autonomous Agents (Agents'97)*. ACM SIGART, 1997.

27. T. J. Norman, N. R. Jennings, P. Faratin, and E. H. Mamdani. Designing and implementing a multi-agent architecture for business process management. In J. P. Müller, M. J. Wooldridge, and N. R. Jennings, eds., *Intelligent Agents III*, volume 1193 of Lecture Notes in Artificial Intelligence, pages 261–276. Springer-Verlag, Heidelberg, 1997.

28. H. S. Nwana. Software agents: an overview. *Knowledge Engineering Review*, 11(3):205–244, 1996.

29. S. Ossowski and A. García-Serrano. Social structure in artificial agent societies: Implications for autonomous problem-solving agents. In this volume, pages 133–148.

30. B. Pell, D .E. Bernhard, S. A. Chien, E. Gat, N. Muscettola, P. Pandurang Nayak, M. D. Wagner, and B. C. Williams. An autonomous spacecraft agent prototype. In W. Lewis Johnson, editor, *Proceedings of the First International Conference on Autonomous Agents*, pages 253–261. ACM, 1997.

31. M. Piaggio. Heir — a non-hicrarchical hybrid architecture for intelligent robots. In this volume, pages 243–259.

32. J. Rachlin, R. Goodwin, S. Murthy, R. Akkiraju, F. Wu, S. Kumaran, and R. Das. A-teams: An agent architecture for optimization and decision-support. In this volume, pages 261–276.

33. A. S. Rao and M. P. Georgeff. BDI-agents: from theory to practice. In *Proceedings of the First Intl. Conference on Multiagent Systems*, San Francisco, 1995.

34. W. S. N. Reilly. *Believable Social and Emotional Agents*. PhD thesis, School of Computer Science, Carnegie Mellon University, 1996.

35. Y. Shoham. Agent-oriented programming. *Artificial Intelligence*, 60:51–92, 1993.

36. N. Skarmeas and K. L. Clark. Content based routing as the basis for intra-agent communication. In this volume, pages 345–362.

37. A. Sloman and R. Poli. SIM_AGENT: A toolkit for exploring agent designs. In *[45]*, pages 392–407. Springer-Verlag, 1996.

38. L. Steels. Cooperation between distributed agents through self-organization. In Y. Demazeau and J.-P. Müller, eds., *Decentralized A.I.*, pages 175–196. North-Holland, 1990.

39. D. D. Steiner, A. Burt, M. Kolb, and Ch. Lerin. The conceptual framework of MAI^{2}L. In *Pre-Proceedings of MAAMAW'93*, Neuchâtel, Switzerland, August 1993.

40. P. Stone and M. Veloso. Task decomposition and dynamic role assignment for real-time strategic teamwork. In this volume, pages 293–308.

41. M. Tambe, R. Jones, J. E. Laird, P. S. Rosenbloom, and K. B. Schwamb. Building believable agents for simulation environments. In *Proceedings of the AAAI Spring Symposium: Believable Agents*. AAAI, 1994.

42. S. R. Thomas. The PLACA agent programming language. In *[44]*, pages 355–370. 1995.

43. D. E. Wilkins, K. L. Myers, and L. P. Wesley. Cypress: Planning and reacting under uncertainty. In M. H. Burstein, editor, *ARPA/Rome Laboratory Planning and Scheduling Initiative Workshop Proceedings*, pages 111–120. Morgan Kaufmann Publishers Inc., San Mateo, CA, 1994.

44. M. J. Wooldridge and N. R. Jennings, editors. *Intelligent Agents – Theories, Architectures, and Languages*, volume 890 of *Lecture Notes in Artificial Intelligence*. Springer-Verlag, 1995.

45. M. J. Wooldridge, J. P. Müller, and M. Tambe, editors. *Intelligent Agents II*, volume 1037 of *Lecture Notes in Artificial Intelligence*. Springer-Verlag, 1996.

46. M. J. Wooldridge and S. D. Parsons. Intention reconsideration reconsidered. In this volume, pages 63–79.

A Agent architectures, types, and applications

Table 6 overviews the test set used in this paper (first column), the main types of applications that were built using these architectures (second column), and the corresponding classification of the types of agents built using these architectures according to Section 4 (third column). For each architecture mentioned, at least one reference is given in the fourth column of the table.

Architecture	Applications	Classification	Reference
Reactive agents			
Subsumption architecture	mobile robots and land vehicles	HW-AU	[6]
Self-organizing agents	mobile robots, emerging group behavior	HW-AU, (HW-MAS)	[38]
AuRA	mobile robots and land vehicles	HW-AU, (HW-MAS)	[2]
Dynamic action selection	technique has been used in mobile robots and Artificial Life applications	HW-AU	[23]
PENGI	arcade computer game	SW-AU	[1]
ECO model	distributed problem-solving	SW-MA	[9]
Deliberative agents			
IRMA	general architecture, probably robotics	HW-AU	[5]
PRS	originally: robotics	HW-AU	[15]
dMARS	air traffic control, business process enactment and monitoring	HW-AU, SW-AU, SW-AS, (SW-MA)	[33]
SOAR	general AI problem-solving architecture; mainly autonomous control systems, more recently also believable agents	HW-AU, SW-AU , SW-AS	[21] [41]
Cypress	mobile robots and vehicles	HW-AU	[43]
Agent0 / PLACA	no specific application mentioned, supports communicative acts	HW-MA (?), SW-MA (?)	[35] [42]
Interacting agents			
MAGSY	production planning, distributed resource allocation, cooperating expert systems	SW-MA, SW-AS	[12]
GRATE*	electricity network diagnosis, later: workflow management	SW-MA, SW-AS	[17] [18] [27]
MECCA	traffic control systems, personal digital assistants	SW-AS, SW-MA	[39]
COSY	production planning, transport planning	SW-MA	[7]
Layered approaches			
RAPs, ATLANTIS, 3T	mobile robots and land vehicles, robotics wheelchair, errand running (3T)	HW-AU, (HW-AS)	[11] [14], [4]
Lyons & Hendriks	mobile robots and land vehicles	HW-AU	[22]
TouringMachines	mobile robots and land vehicles	HW-AU, (SW-AU)	[10]
INTERRAP	cooperating robots, flexible transport systems, game playing agents, logistics	HW-MA, (SW-MA)	[25]
SimAgent	humanoid robots or softbots (very abstract architecture)	HW-AU (?), SW-AU (?)	[37]
NMRA	spacecraft control	HW-AU	[30]
Other approaches			
Tok	believable agents for entertainment and arts applications.	SW-AS	[34]
VET	education and training	SW-AS	[19]
ShopBot	Resource discovery, electronic commerce	SW-AS, SW-AU	[16]
Zuno VRISKO, QuarterDeck WebCompass,	information retrieval and	SW-AU, SW-AS	
AgentSoft LifeAgent Pro, FireFly ...	information filtering, personalization	SW-AU, SW-AS	—

Table 6. Agent architectures and agent applications

Representing Abstract Agent Architectures

Michael Fisher

Department of Computing and Mathematics
Manchester Metropolitan University
Manchester M1 5GD, U.K.

M.Fisher@doc.mmu.ac.uk
http://www.doc.mmu.ac.uk/STAFF/M.Fisher

Abstract. An agent's *architecture* describes not only its sub-components, but also how these elements are organised in order to provide the agent's overall behaviour. While there have been numerous different architectures developed, ranging from purely *reactive* or purely *deliberative*, through to *hybrid* and *layered* varieties, such systems have largely been developed using different frameworks, and often using ad hoc methods, thus making both comparison between architectures and the development of new architectures difficult.

In this paper we show how a high-level logical language might be utilised in order to describe both the components of an agent, which can be considered as sub-agents, and its internal organisation, which can be characterised as appropriate patterns interaction between, and structuring of, these sub-agents. In particular, we show how contemporary layered architectures, consisting of various reactive, deliberative and modelling layers, might be represented by *grouping* these sub-agents together.

This work provides an abstract framework in which the internal organisation of agents can be represented, and will also form the basis for the direct execution of these descriptions in order to prototype new architectures.

1 Introduction

The number and variety of agent-based systems continues to grow rapidly. In addition, the tasks that these agents are required to perform are becoming ever more complex, often requiring increasingly sophisticated capabilities within each agent. As the complexity of individual agents grows, so appropriate architectures for these agents must be developed [23, 24].

While early Artificial Intelligence (AI) systems tended to be monolithic, the introduction of larger *knowledge-based systems* in the 1970's led to the increased use of modularity, such as object-oriented techniques [28]. The development of agent technology not only utilised this work, but extended it further by considering real-world interaction and social ability. Not only was the *functionality* of an agent partitioned between modules, but now the behaviour of each of these modules could be inherently different. For example, each architectural element might represent some physical component (e.g a Robot's limb).

short time scale, with immediate interactions with the environment; a *deliberative* layer that deals with medium term symbolic planning; and a *modelling/cognitive/social* layer that deals with longer term elements such as manipulation of the agent's desires and the coordination of cooperative activity [18]. Each of these components potentially works on a different timescale, but must interact with each other during the agent's execution.

The aim of this paper is to show how a high-level logic-based language may be used to represent the structure of such architectures. We begin, in Section 2, with an outline of the framework in which these architectural varieties will be developed and then, in subsequent sections, consider increasingly complex scenarios. Starting with individual agents represented by monolithic logical descriptions, we show, in Section 3, how reactive, deliberative and cognitive elements can all be identified. In Section 4, we describe how modularity can be introduced into the agent descriptions simply by providing a form of procedural abstraction, whereby sub-agents are identified with particular sub-behaviours. Section 5 shows how basic layered architectures can be represented by identifying a *group* of agents with each layer. Finally, in Section 6, more sophisticated layered architectures can be developed by allowing each group of agents to have different internal execution and communication properties.

2   The Computational Model

The language we use for describing agent behaviour is Concurrent METATEM [8]. This not only provides a notation for formally representing agents, but can be seen as a programming language in that the logical representations can be directly executed [11]. The basic tenets of this approach are that

1. everything is an agent,
2. all agents are concurrently active, and,
3. the basic mechanism for communication between agents is broadcast message-passing.

Extensions to this basic model, comprising more sophisticated capabilities are

4. *groups*, which restrict the extent of broadcast message-passing and provide structure within the agent space, and,
5. *group properties*, with which the execution and communication characteristics of a group of agents can be modified.

We will consider the first four of these items below, but will leave description of the last one until it is required (in Section 6).

2.1   Agents

Agents, encapsulating both data and behaviour, are the basic entities within our model. Individual agents only act upon certain identified messages received from their environment. Thus, an agent must be able to filter out messages that it wishes to recognise, ignoring all others. The definition of which messages an agent recognises, together with a definition of the messages that an agent may itself produce, is provided by the *interface definition* for that particular agent. For example, the interface definition for a 'car' agent may be defined in the following way

```
car()
  in: go,stop,turn
  out: fuel,overheat
```

Here, {go, stop, turn} represents the set of messages the agent recognises, while {fuel, overheat} represents the set of messages the agent itself is able to produce.

2.2 Concurrency and Communication

It is fundamental to our approach that all agents are (potentially) concurrently active; by default they are asynchronously executing.

The basic communication mechanism used between agents is *broadcast* message-passing. Thus, when an agent sends a message it does not necessarily send it to a specified *destination*, it merely sends it to its environment, where it can potentially be received by *all* other agents. Although broadcast is the basic mechanism, both multicast (achieved by imposing a group structure upon the broadcasted messages — see Section 2.3) and point-to-point message-passing (achieved by adding an extra 'destination' argument to the message) can be defined in terms of this.

The default behaviour for a message is that if it is broadcast, then it will *eventually* be received at all possible receivers. In formal terms, this can be represented by[1]

$$broadcast(msg) \ \Rightarrow \ \forall a \in Agents. \ \Diamond receive(a, msg)$$

2.3 Groups

As broadcast communication can *sometimes* be inefficient and unwieldy, the notion of agent *groups* [21] is also used within Concurrent METATEM, being useful both for restricting the extent of broadcast messages and for structuring the agent space. Grouping is not only a natural structuring mechanism with diverse applications, but is also a very powerful organisation technique [9]. Groups are dynamic and open. They may contain sub-groups and each agent may be a member of several groups. The particular group structures that we will be concerned with in Section 5 and Section 6 are those with at least three groups, at least two of which overlap. For example, we might represent such groups pictorially as in Figure 1. A group is essentially a set consisting of both agents and further sub-groups. The basic properties of groups are that agents are able to broadcast a message to the members of a group (effectively achieving a form of *multicast* message passing), add an agent to a group, ascertain whether a certain agent is a member of a group, remove a specified agent from a group, and construct a new subgroup.

While the basic purpose of groups is to restrict the set of receivers for broadcast messages, and thus provide finer structure within the agent space, more complex applications can be envisaged. For example, the group might utilise an alternative model

---

[1] Note that '$\Diamond$' is the temporal operator representing "at some time in the future".

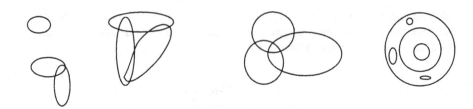

Fig. 1. Examples of grouping patterns.

of communication within that group. Thus, groups can effectively enforce their own 'meta-level' constraints on message-passing between agents, for example specifying the speed of transmission. This is exactly what we consider in Section 6.

By using groups and broadcast message-passing, we are also able to represent more complex interaction, for example cooperation and competition, amongst agents [15].

3 Inside an Agent

The language we use for describing individual agent behaviour is based on *temporal logic* [4]. This provides the expressive power necessary for describing the *dynamic* activity of an agent, yet is still simple enough to be used as the basis for a programming language for agent-based systems [9].

While the description in Section 3.1 concentrates solely on temporal representations, not only has this form of temporal logic been extended with knowledge and belief operators [5], but Concurrent METATEM itself has been refined to handle varieties of deliberation [13]. However, the internal structuring of agents described in this paper is independent of such extensions and so these architectural aspects will, for simplicity, be described with respect to purely temporal notions.

3.1 Temporal Logic and its Execution

Temporal logic can be seen as classical logic extended with various modalities representing temporal aspects of logical formulae [4]. The propositional temporal logic we use is based on a linear, discrete model of time [17]. Thus, time is modelled as an infinite sequence of discrete states, with an identified starting point, called "the beginning of time". Classical formulae are used to represent constraints *within* states, while temporal formulae represent constraints *between* states. This temporal logic extends classical logic with the '$\Diamond$', '$\Box$', and '$\bigcirc$' connectives. The intuitive meaning of these connectives is as follows: $\Diamond A$ is true now if A is true *sometime* in the future; $\Box A$ is true now if A is true *always* in the future; and $\bigcirc A$ is true now if A is true at the *next* moment in time. Similar connectives can also be introduced to enable reasoning about the *past* [20].

As an agent's behaviour is represented by a temporal formula, this can be transformed into Separated Normal Form (SNF) [12], which not only removes the majority of the temporal operators, but also translates the formula into a set of *rules* suitable for direct execution. Each of these rules is of one of the forms presented in Figure 2, where '**start**' means "at the beginning of time (i.e. execution)", and each k_i or m_j is a literal. This normal form provides a simple structure for formal temporal descriptions of agents [16].

$$\textbf{start} \Rightarrow \bigvee_{j=1}^{r} m_j \qquad \text{(an \textit{initial} rule)}$$

$$\bigwedge_{i=1}^{q} k_i \Rightarrow \bigcirc \bigvee_{j=1}^{r} m_j \qquad \text{(a \textit{step} rule)}$$

$$\bigwedge_{i=1}^{q} k_i \Rightarrow \Diamond \bigvee_{j=1}^{r} m_j \qquad \text{(a \textit{sometime} rule)}$$

Fig. 2. Separated Normal Form.

In order to animate the behaviour of an agent, we choose to execute its temporal specification directly [11]. Execution of a temporal formula corresponds to the construction of a model for that formula and, in order to execute a set of SNF rules representing the behaviour of an agent, we utilise the *imperative future* [2] approach. This evaluates the SNF rules at every moment in time, using information about the history of the object in order to constrain future execution. Thus, a *forward-chaining* process is employed to produce a model for a formula; the underlying (sequential) METATEM language [1] exactly follows this approach.

The operator used to represent the basic temporal indeterminacy within SNF rules is the *sometime* operator, '$\Diamond$'. When $\Diamond\varphi$ is executed, the system must try to ensure that φ *eventually* becomes true. As such eventualities might not be able to be satisfied immediately, it keeps a record of the unsatisfied eventualities, retrying them as execution proceeds. It should be noted that the use of temporal logic as the basis for the computation rules gives an extra level of expressive power over the corresponding classical logics. In particular, operators such as '$\Diamond$' give us the opportunity to specify future-time (temporal) indeterminacy. Transformation to SNF allows us to capture these expressive capabilities concisely.

As an example of a simple set of rules which form a fragment of an agent's description, consider the following which could be rules forming part of the behaviour of the car agent.

$$\textbf{start} \Rightarrow \neg moving$$
$$go \Rightarrow \Diamond moving$$
$$(fast \wedge go) \Rightarrow \bigcirc (overheat \vee fuel)$$

Here, we see that *moving* is false at the start of execution and, whenever *go* is true, a commitment to eventually make *moving* true is made. Similarly, whenever both *go* and *fast* are true, then either *overheat* or *fuel* must be made true in the next moment in time.

Note that, while we have introduced *propositional* temporal logic in this section, we will also use elements from *first-order* temporal logic, particularly in more complex examples. Details of the first-order framework can be found in [8].

3.2 Reactive Rules

In describing an agent in terms of a set of such rules, we can identify particular forms of rules with well known categories of behaviours. The first of these we consider is that of *reactive rules*. A typical example is

$$[hit\_object(left\_leg) \land \neg at\_limit(left\_leg)] \Rightarrow \bigcirc raise(left\_leg)$$

Thus, if a particular condition (pattern) is recognised, immediate (i.e. in the next moment) action is taken.

With such rules it is particularly important to ensure that conflicting or dangerous actions are not produced. For example, the above rule should really be

$$[hit\_object(left\_leg) \land \neg at\_limit(left\_leg) \land \neg raised(right\_leg)]$$
$$\Rightarrow \bigcirc raise(left\_leg)$$

ensuring that both legs can not be raised simultaneously.

This shows how verification of the properties of the agent's description can be useful [16]. For example, given a set of logical rules for a bipedal robotic agent, φ_{ROBOT}, we might wish to establish

$$\varphi_{ROBOT} \vdash \Box \neg [raised(left\_leg) \land raised(right\_leg)].$$

i.e. it is *never* the case that both legs are raised at the same time.

3.3 Deliberative Rules

New goals (eventualities) to be achieved can be introduced dynamically, as in:

$$go \Rightarrow \Diamond moving.$$

The execution mechanism attempts to satisfy these goals as soon as possible. However, additional rules can be used to constrain the deliberation concerned with their satisfaction. For example, consider the situation where a goal can not be achieved (using a plan) until its sub-goals have been satisfied. In this case, an additional rule such as

$$\left[\bigvee_i \neg subgoal_i\right] \Rightarrow \neg goal.$$

can be used to constrain the satisfaction of the goal. For example, in the car example above, movement might be blocked until both the hand-brake has been released and the engine started:

$$[\neg release\_handbrake \lor \neg start\_engine] \Rightarrow \bigcirc \neg moving.$$

This may, in turn, require rules that spawn further goals, such as $\Diamond start\_engine$.

An alternative approach, related to that used in many BDI architectures, is to attempt to satisfy a goal by checking if there is a pre-constructed plan for it in a *plan library*. Thus, to achieve *moving*, plans for satisfying this are collected, one is chosen and sub-goals are generated. The deliberation that occurs here is often concerned with deciding which plan is the most appropriate given the current situation.

3.4 Higher-Level Rules

Higher-level rules, variously called *cognitive* or *social* rules, appear in a number of guises. Essentially, they are concerned with manipulating and managing information about the agent's environment and its longer term aspirations. Typical examples include: rules concerning communication, such as the use of *announce* in the Contract Net [29]; rules regarding the agent's current capabilities and configuration, and maintenance of data structures used to model the agent's environment/society [15]; rules for the manipulation of the agent's longer term desires [27, 13]; rules concerning the agent's current view of other agents, e.g. rules for manipulation of *trusted* or *acquaintance* relations [18]. Concerning this last category, a typical rule concerning overtaking in the car agent might be

$$\left(\begin{array}{l} [ask(a, move(Pos)) \wedge trust(a)] \\ \vee \\ [ask(a, move(Pos)) \wedge friend(a, b) \wedge trust(b)] \end{array} \right) \Rightarrow \bigcirc move(Pos).$$

meaning that the car will only move over if the agent that requested the move is either trusted or is a friend of a trusted agent.

4 Modularising an Agent

While it is possible to represent an agent using a single monolithic set of rules, as above, it is often desirable (for clarity, if nothing else) to provide some form of modularity. In Concurrent METATEM, this can be achieved using a mechanism akin to procedural abstraction. Here, a subset of rules is extracted from the monolithic rule-set and used to form a new agent which is invoked whenever any of the extracted rules are required. To exhibit this abstraction, we consider the example below.

```
original
  in: p
  out: q,r
```
$$p(X) \Rightarrow \bigcirc q(X)$$
$$p(Y) \Rightarrow \Diamond r(Y, Y)$$
$$r(Z) \Rightarrow \bigcirc \neg q(Z)$$

The first and second rules are now extracted from this `original` agent and are encapsulated in a new agent, called `proc`:

```
proc
   in: p
   out: q,r
```
$$p(X) \Rightarrow \bigcirc q(X)$$
$$p(Y) \Rightarrow \Diamond r(Y,Y)$$

while the `original` agent is refined to be:

```
original
   in: p,r
   out: q
```
$$p(X) \Rightarrow proc(X)$$
$$r(Z) \Rightarrow \bigcirc \neg q(Z)$$

Such procedures, once invoked, are agents too. Therefore `proc` will listen for all p messages, while producing q and r messages. Consider the case where the message $p(a)$ is received by the new version of `original` above.

1. `proc` is called with the current state of `original` as its initial state (e.g. $p(a)$ is true in this initial state)
2. X is bound to a in the first rule of `proc`, while Y is bound to a in the second rule of `proc`
3. the goal $\Diamond r(a,a)$ is initiated within `proc`
4. both $r(a,a)$ and $q(a)$ are made true in `proc`
5. both $r(a,a)$ and $q(a)$ are broadcast
6. etc.....

Thus, under certain synchrony assumptions (considered in Section 6) this form of procedural abstraction will have the required semantics, i.e. that the new set of agents is equivalent to the case where the calling rule, $p(X) \Rightarrow proc(X)$, is replaced by the rules within the `proc` agent (with internal variables suitably removed). Consequently, as in procedural abstraction, inline expansion of procedure calls has equivalent semantics to the abstracted version. (For further discussion regarding the correctness of such refinements, see [14].)

Thus, in this case, we can visualise computation as an agent spawning a group of other agents to perform sub-computations as in Figure 3. The properties of groups of such agents will be considered further in Section 6, but we note that these sub-agents may either be transient (as in the above diagram) or persistent. In contrast, the above `proc` agent, once invoked, remains active until the whole system terminates.

5 Layering an Agent

In developing complex agents, layered architectures are commonly used. In many cases these architectures can been characterised as a three layer architecture comprising a *reactive* layer, dealing with real-time interactions with the environment, a *deliberative* layer, dealing with aspects of planning concerned with how to achieve immediate goals,

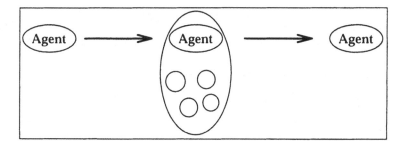

Fig. 3. Sub-computations as the spawning of sub-groups.

and a *cognitive/modelling/social* layer, dealing with more complex aspects such as communication, cooperation and selection of goals.

For example, Touring Machines [6] adopt layers very similar to these, with the reactive layer dealing with behaviour such as fast obstacle avoidance, the deliberative layer dealing with immediate goals, such as how to get in to the next street, and the social layer dealing with both communication with other vehicles and selection of goals. BDI architectures [27] can, to some extent, also be characterised in this way. Here, the reactive layer deals with the real-time issues concerning basic actions, the deliberative layer deals with identifying how to achieve current goals (intentions) using a plan library, while the social layer deals with decisions such as which goals (desires) to immediately attempt (and make into intentions). Similar structures also appear in other architectures, such as INTERRAP [22]

In our model, we can simulate this layering by grouping together similar types of behaviours. For example, relevant reactive rules can be abstracted into particular 'reactive' sub-agents. Sets of such sub-agents could then form a group in order to represent the reactive layer of the architecture. Similar structuring could be carried out for the other layers.

In order to facilitate communication between layers, it is useful to define 'linking' agents that are members of more than one group. For example, an agent linking the reactive and deliberative layers should be a member of both the reactive and deliberative groups. This leads to a common grouping structure of the form given in Figure 4.

Fig. 4. Basic group structure for layered architectures.

However, the power of the computational model, particularly the grouping aspects, allows us to represent a range of different configurations, for example the combinations represented in Figure 5. Hence, the grouping mechanism within Concurrent METATEM

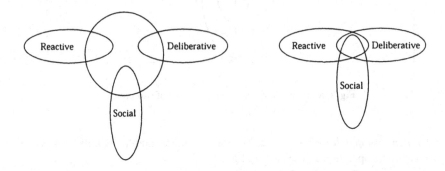

Fig. 5. Alternative group structures for layered architectures.

allows us to represent a range of alternative agent organisations.

6 Modifying Properties of Layers

While the basic structure of layered architectures such as that given in Figure 6 may be represented in terms of the grouping mechanisms described above, further sophistication is required in order to model the relative temporal activity of different elements of an agent's architecture.

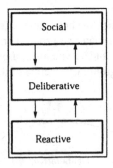

Fig. 6. Typical layered architecture.

For example, groups of sub-agents, representing reactive, deliberative, and social layers, might all have different internal properties:

- the reactive group might be synchronous, so that all the reactive components (e.g. limbs in a robot) work on exactly the same clock;
- the deliberative group might be constrained to be *relatively synchronous*[2] over a number of steps of the reactive layer;
- the social group might be purely asynchronous, so agents within it can carry out general (speculative) computation, free from constraints.

In order to represent this more complex situation, we now allow both the execution and communication properties *within* groups to be modified.

Recall that, in the basic model, agents execute asynchronously and communication satisfies the formula

$$send(msg) \Rightarrow \forall a \in Agents. \; \Diamond receive(a, msg)$$

However, we can potentially control the operational model within each group. For example, agents in a group can execute

- asynchronously
- synchronously (same clock)
- relatively synchronously (relative clocks)
- etc....

while communication in a group can be defined by

- $send(msg) \Rightarrow \forall a \in Agents. \; \Diamond receive(a, msg)$
- $send(msg) \Rightarrow \forall a \in Agents. \; receive(a, msg)$
- $send(msg) \Rightarrow \forall a \in Agents. \; \bigcirc receive(a, msg)$
- $send(msg) \Rightarrow \forall a \in Agents. \; \Diamond receive(a, msg) \lor lost(a, msg)$
- etc....

By choosing an appropriate combination of execution and communication constraints for each group, more realistic examples can be produced. Note that, at present, these constraints are *not* part of the Concurrent METATEM language and, as such, should be seen as meta-level logical conditions.

6.1 Example: Synchronous Groups

Let us consider a particular set of properties for a group of agents, namely synchronous execution and instantaneous communication.

We earlier (in Section 4) defined a form of procedural abstraction whereby a group of sub-agents is spawned to carry out a particular set of sub-computations (Figure 3). To ensure that the semantics of the abstracted version match that of the original, synchronous communication and instantaneous broadcast are required. This ensures that all rules, whether in the original agent or in a sub-agent, are activated within the same time step.

---

[2] i.e. there is a specific clock, such that ticks of clocks from all agents in the group are multiples of a tick of the common clock.

A more realistic constraint might involve execution of sub-agents occurring relatively synchronously with respect to the spawning agent. Thus, we can imagine this as the original agent working on a clock with longer 'ticks' while the sub-agents carry out their computations *between* ticks. However, such a structure can also be modelled in our framework simply by refining the properties of the groups of agents appropriately.

6.2 Example: Layered Architectures

Given that we can modify the operational properties of individual groups, we might choose to represent a typical layered architecture as three overlapping groups of sub-agents, each having the following properties outlined in Figure 7.

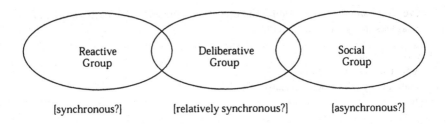

Fig. 7. Group properties for typical layered architectures.

6.3 Semantics

The semantics of each agent (and each separate group of agents), under a particular communication/execution constraint, can be given as a temporal formula [10]. An interesting question concerns the semantics of agents that are members of two groups with differing execution/communication constraints, for example an agent that is expected to act both synchronously and asynchronously. Here, all we need to do to find the constraints on the agent is to take the conjunction of the constraints from the two groups. In the examples considered above, the execution constraints are totally ordered, i.e. anything that is synchronous is also relatively synchronous and anything that is relatively synchronous is also asynchronous. Thus, if an agent is in, for example, two groups one of which is synchronous, the other asynchronous, then that agent's behaviour is given by the conjunction of 'synchronous' and 'asynchronous', which is just 'synchronous'. So, in effect, the agent must follow the tighter constraint.

However, if we consider further different constraints, it is perfectly possible that two groups have incompatible properties, and so an agent that is a member of both would be inconsistent. This is both bad (in that you probably do not want to design systems like this) and good (in that the semantics will show this inconsistency and correctness arguments will fail). Thus, we can verify that a specification of the architecture is consistent before we ever try to implement it.

7 Conclusions

In this paper, we have considered the abstract representation of agent architectures. Our view of an agent architecture is perhaps more general than most, in that we see an architecture as comprising the basic organisation (group structuring) of sub-agents, the patterns of interaction between these sub-groups, and the operational properties within such sub-groups. Many would argue that there is more to an architecture than this, particularly in its detail, but as we intend to represent only abstract architectures in this way and so such a view is sufficient (and general).

As a typical example of a class of agent architectures, we have considered layered architectures comprising reactive, deliberative and social layers. While there are a wide variety of representation techniques for each of these layers separately, it is notoriously difficult to provide a framework in which these elements can all be represented. It is even more difficult if we wish this to be logic based and so have some possibility of verification of properties.

One approach is to use a very expressive logical framework in which to specify such architectures [19]; however, both verification and execution in such a framework become difficult. By taking a simple logical approach, and enriching it with group structures, we have been able to represent basic layered architectures. By refining the internal execution and communication properties of these groups further, we are able to describe more sophisticated agent architectures where the layers work under very different operational constraints.

Why might it be beneficial to represent agent architectures in this way?

1. It is important, in developing new architectures, to be able to visualise the components and their activity — the use of an executable representation allows us to prototype new architectures.
2. As shown in Section 3.2, complex descriptions of behaviour can lead to inconsistencies — with this logical approach, verification of properties (such as the robot never raising both legs at once) is at least possible.
3. With a common framework in which a variety of different architectures can be defined, it should be possible to carry out qualitative comparisons between different architectures — something that is very rarely done.
4. The simplicity of the model, particularly the form of grouping, provides a natural modelling technique which is relatively easy to understand — this aids both the system designer and user.
5. As Concurrent METATEM has been implemented on both uni- and multi-processor architectures, these descriptions could be used as simulations of the architectures themselves.

Our future work in this area concerns: the development of a concise mechanism for specifying the properties of groups in practice; the application of this model to a wider range of architectures (e.g. [26]) and the development of comparison techniques for architectural representations; a refined semantics of groups incorporating differing execution and communication properties; and the identification of common grouping structures (corresponding to common patterns) in real-life architectures.

References

1. H. Barringer, M. Fisher, D. Gabbay, G. Gough, and R. Owens. METATEM: An Introduction. *Formal Aspects of Computing*, 7(5):533–549, 1995.

2. H. Barringer, M. Fisher, D. Gabbay, R. Owens, and M. Reynolds, editors. *The Imperative Future: Principles of Executable Temporal Logics*. Research Studies Press, Chichester, United Kingdom, 1996.

3. R. A. Brooks. A robust layered control system for a mobile robot. *IEEE Journal of Robotics and Automation*, 2(1):14–23, 1986.

4. E. A. Emerson. Temporal and Modal Logic. In J. van Leeuwen, editor, *Handbook of Theoretical Computer Science*, pages 996–1072. Elsevier, 1990.

5. R. Fagin, J. Halpern, Y. Moses, and M. Vardi. *Reasoning About Knowledge*. MIT Press, 1996.

6. I. A. Ferguson. *TouringMachines: An Architecture for Dynamic, Rational, Mobile Agents*. PhD thesis, Clare Hall, University of Cambridge, UK, November 1992. (Also available as Technical Report No. 273, University of Cambridge Computer Laboratory).

7. I. A. Ferguson. TouringMachines: Autonomous Agents with Attitudes. Technical Report 250, Computer Laboratory, University of Cambridge, Cambridge, U.K., April 1992.

8. M. Fisher. Concurrent METATEM — A Language for Modeling Reactive Systems. In *Parallel Architectures and Languages, Europe (PARLE)*, Munich, Germany, June 1993. (Published in *Lecture Notes in Computer Science*, volume 694, Springer-Verlag).

9. M. Fisher. Representing and Executing Agent-Based Systems. In M. Wooldridge and N. R. Jennings, editors, *Intelligent Agents*. Springer-Verlag, 1995.

10. M. Fisher. A Temporal Semantics for Concurrent METATEM. *Journal of Symbolic Computation*, 22(5/6), November/December 1996.

11. M. Fisher. An Introduction to Executable Temporal Logics. *Knowledge Engineering Review*, 11(1):43–56, March 1996.

12. M. Fisher. A Normal Form for Temporal Logic and its Application in Theorem-Proving and Execution. *Journal of Logic and Computation*, 7(4), August 1997.

13. M. Fisher. Implementing BDI-like Systems by Direct Execution. In *Proceedings of International joint Conference on Artificial Intelligence (IJCAI)*. Morgan-Kaufmann, 1997.

14. M. Fisher. Refining Concurrent METATEM Objects. In H. Bowman and J. Derrick, editors, *Formal Methods for Open Object-Based Distributed Systems*. Chapman & Hall, 1997.

15. M. Fisher and M. Wooldridge. A Logical Approach to the Representation of Societies of Agents. In N. Gilbert and R. Conte, editors, *Artificial Societies*. UCL Press, 1995.

16. M. Fisher and M. Wooldridge. On the Formal Specification and Verification of Multi-Agent Systems. *International Journal of Cooperative Information Systems*, 6(1), January 1997.

17. D. Gabbay, A. Pnueli, S. Shelah, and J. Stavi. The Temporal Analysis of Fairness. In *Proceedings of the Seventh ACM Symposium on the Principles of Programming Languages*, pages 163–173, Las Vegas, Nevada, January 1980.

18. N. R. Jennings. Towards a cooperation knowledge level for collaborative problem solving. In *Proceedings of the Tenth European Conference on Artificial Intelligence (ECAI-92)*, pages 224–228, Vienna, Austria, 1992.

19. C. G. Jung. Emergent mental attitudes in layered agents. In J. P. Müller, M. P. Singh, and A. S. Rao, editors, *Intelligent Agents V — Proceedings of the Fifth International Workshop on Agent Theories, Architectures, and Languages (ATAL-98)*, Lecture Notes in Artificial Intelligence. Springer-Verlag, Heidelberg, 1999. In this volume.

20. O. Lichtenstein, A. Pnueli, and L. Zuck. The Glory of the Past. *Lecture Notes in Computer Science*, 193:196–218, June 1985.

21. T. Maruichi, M. Ichikawa, and M. Tokoro. Modelling Autonomous Agents and their Groups. In Y. Demazeau and J. P. Muller, editors, *Decentralized AI 2 – Proceedings of the 2nd European Workshop on Modelling Autonomous Agents and Multi-Agent Worlds (MAA-MAW '90)*. Elsevier/North Holland, 1991.

22. J. P. Müller. *The Design of Autonomous Agents — A Layered Approach*. Springer-Verlag: Heidelberg, Germany, 1996. (LNAI 1177).

23. J. P. Müller. Control Architectures for Autonomous and Interacting Agents: A Survey. In *Intelligent Agent Systems: Theoretical and Practical Issues*. Springer-Verlag: Heidelberg, Germany, 1997. (Lecture Notes in AI 1209).

24. J. P. Müller. The right agent (architecture) to do the right thing. In J. P. Müller, M. P. Singh, and A. S. Rao, editors, *Intelligent Agents V — Proceedings of the Fifth International Workshop on Agent Theories, Architectures, and Languages (ATAL-98)*, Lecture Notes in Artificial Intelligence. Springer-Verlag, Heidelberg, 1999. In this volume.

25. J. P. Müller and M. Pischel. Modelling interacting agents in dynamic environments. In *Proceedings of the Eleventh European Conference on Artificial Intelligence (ECAI-94)*, pages 709–713, Amsterdam, The Netherlands, 1994.

26. M. Piaggio. HEIR — a non-hierarchical hybrid architecture for intelligent robots. In J. P. Müller, M. P. Singh, and A. S. Rao, editors, *Intelligent Agents V — Proceedings of the Fifth International Workshop on Agent Theories, Architectures, and Languages (ATAL-98)*, Lecture Notes in Artificial Intelligence. Springer-Verlag, Heidelberg, 1999. In this volume.

27. A. S. Rao and M. P. Georgeff. An abstract architecture for rational agents. In C. Rich, W. Swartout, and B. Nebel, editors, *Proceedings of Knowledge Representation and Reasoning (KR&R-92)*, pages 439–449, 1992.

28. S. Russell and P. Norvig. *Artificial Intelligence: A Modern Approach*. Prentice-Hall International, 1995.

29. R. G. Smith. *A Framework for Distributed Problem Solving*. UMI Research Press, 1980.

HEIR – A Non-hierarchical Hybrid Architecture for Intelligent Robots

Maurizio Piaggio

University of Genoa, Department of System Communication and Computer Science,
Via Opera Pia 13, I-16145 Genoa, ITALY

E-mail: piaggio@dist.unige.it

Abstract. In recent years different control architectures have been proposed for autonomous robots that are required to carry out service tasks robustly in civilian environments. In this paper a novel architecture is presented, which differs from the typical approaches from two main points of view: it is non hierarchical and it introduces an additional level of representation and reasoning based on image based, iconic descriptions. The paper will show how the proposed architecture has been implemented on a prototypical system, discuss its properties in detail and present our experimental experiences demonstrating the plausibility of the approach.

1. Introduction

In recent years different control architectures have been proposed for autonomous robots that are required to carry out service tasks robustly in civilian environments [1]. The common approach attempts to integrate two main classes of activities: deliberative and reactive. The former allows the robot to reason about its goals, generate plans or adapt previous ones to the current situation. The latter is capable of dealing in real time with the dynamic changes in the environment.

A typical control architecture is depicted in Figure 1. It is a three level hierarchical architecture with the following general properties. The lower levels tend to deal with numeric, analogical data whereas the higher levels manage symbolic representations. The higher levels tend to carry out complex tasks which require long lasting computations, the lower levels are normally bounded both in complexity and execution times. Many authors have suggested different intermediate boundaries between the activities and different representation paradigms. In [2], for example, we find three layers or tiers (control, sequencing and planning) in which the higher level deals with planning and lower level with execution; in [7] the planning activity is carried out by the intermediate level; the lower level still deals with execution but the upper one carries out reflective-predictive activities. Other approaches [10][14] slightly differ in the number of components but are still based the same principles.

Although I agree on the necessity of a successful integration of reactivity and deliberation with respect to the well known purely reactive approaches [3] in which explicit representation is refused at all, because of the great differences of the two paradigms, I do not think that the integration should be attempted directly. Instead, I propose an architecture with an additional, image based, level of representation (I call this diagrammatic [8][9]), which holds some characteristics of both the symbolic, deliberative component and the low-level procedural/reactive one. Moreover, partly because this component overlaps with the others both in functionality and expressiveness, it should not be considered an *intermediate level* of a hierarchical architecture, but rather a separate co-operating component.

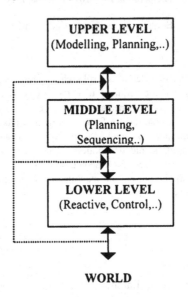

Fig. 1. The typical cognitive architecture

The proposed architecture is depicted in Figure 2. It is organised into three components characterised by the type of knowledge they deal with: a *symbolic* component (S), handling a declarative explicit propositional formalism, a *diagrammatic* component (D), dealing with analogical, iconic representations, and a *reactive* behaviour based component (R). The role of each component is perhaps better clarified by an example: consider a person that is learning to play a tennis from a coach. Some knowledge will be taught and learnt at a symbolic level such as *"when you hit the ball with the center of the racket the trajectory can be controlled, otherwise its movement will be unpredicatable"*. However, the coach will certainly teach differently, for example, how to serve. In this case the service movement is partly described in words but mostly illustrated, focusing on key postures that have to be reached to serve correctly and negative postures that a player must keep away from. I do not claim that these postures cannot be described with a symbolic formalism but I believe diagrammatic or iconic descriptions to be more synthetic and cognitively plausible. This teaching method is also evident in ordinary tennis books in which snapshots or drawings of these key postures are presented (an example is depicted in Figure 3 [4]).

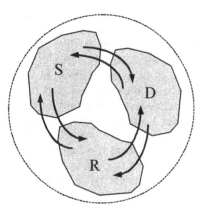

Fig. 2. HEIR cognitive architecture

Finally, when the person has learnt how to hit the ball or how to serve, he or she will probably no longer use the former representations during a tennis match but will execute a reactive behaviour in which the symbolic and diagrammatic knowledge has been compiled in order to directly couple sensing to acting. Thus the player will hit the ball with the centre of the racket because an instinctive, reflexive procedure will exhibit this behaviour without any symbolic activity.

Fig. 3. Tennis book example

The example suggests that there is no qualitative difference between the three knowledge paradigms and related components. The activity distribution between the component simply depends on the context in which the system is, and thus will vary significantly in time. When a robot has to perform a complex assembling operation most of the activity will be at the symbolic level, in which the explicit assembling plan is represented; when it is following a person the activity will focus on the diagrammatic component that reasons analogically on the different camera snapshots of the environment, in order to track the person movement correctly; when it is avoiding obstacles in its path, reactive behaviours will directly couple sensor data to the robot movement. Analogously, there is not an overall hierarchical organisation in the architecture (i.e. it is not always true that symbolic activities drive diagrammatic activities which in turn drive reactive activities), nor any component is privileged at all times, but the focus of activity, and consequently the partial control of the system, can be taken in different moments by different components. In this sense, different hierarchies in which any of the three components may occupy the top level may be dynamically interchanged depending on internal or external events. Thus, if we consider the architecture taxonomy presented in [12], HEIR does not fit into any of the categories although it has some similarities with the *layered approaches* only in the sense that it exploits hybrid reasoning formalisms and representations.

This paper will show how the proposed cognitive architecture has been implemented on a prototypical system. The properties of the architecture are discussed in detail and experimental experiences demonstrating the plausibility of the approach are also mentioned.

2. Software Architecture

The architecture is called HEIR - Hybrid Experts in Intelligent Robots. It is entirely based on a basic element called *expert*, similar to a *behaviour* [3] (but typically with a specific specialised role) or to a *skill* [2] (not only procedural but also capable of diagrammatic or symbolic reasoning). An expert is an agent that executes concurrently within the architecture, to carry out specific cognitive activity, periodically or in response to external events or activation conditions. Clearly, not all experts behave in the same way from many point of views. In fact experts can be classified as belonging to one of the three components: *symbolic*, *diagrammatic* or *reactive*. Each group corresponds to a different set of computational tasks, which differ in:

- *the type of cognitive activity carried out*. Reactive experts are mainly responsible for low-level perception and action and sensor-motor activity; diagrammatic experts are responsible for the management of the diagrammatic, iconic representations as well as for the execution of partially reactive behaviours; symbolic experts carry out tasks involving symbolic reasoning such as plan selection and adaptation, problem solving, etc..
- *timing constraints*. Reactive experts implement strict real-time behaviours, responding immediately to external stimuli such as data coming from a sensor;

diagrammatic experts, and more so symbolic experts, also need to operate in real time but their reaction times tend to be higher.

- *type of data managed*. Reactive experts deal mainly with numeric data; diagrammatic experts deal with iconic, analogical representations; symbolic experts mainly operate with symbolic information.
- *duration*. Symbolic experts can be extremely complex and temporally extensive; diagrammatic experts, and particularly reactive experts, are normally bounded both in complexity and execution time.

Clearly, this classification is only approximate. In fact, although the principal activity of an expert typically falls into one of the three classes, some activity will also be carried out into one or both of the remaining. This is the case for the many experts which contribute to the integration of the different paradigms of representation, generally represented by the arrows in Figure 2. For example, a reactive expert which interprets data from a bumper sensor placed around the body of a mobile robot will produce a symbol related to a collision situation when the robot bumps into an obstacle. This distinction is however important to clearly express and identify the different requirements to the architecture that each class of expert imposes. Moreover, in a physically distributed system, it introduces a relevant criterium for the expert distribution.

2.1 Information Management and Exchange

The support to the management and exchange of information between the experts is certainly one of the most important services the architecture provides. As mentioned above, the services required are related to the specific class the experts belong to:

- *Symbolic experts* operate on a common symbolic knowledge base, KB, to carry out all their activities: to update the stored information, to perform symbolic reasoning and to exchange information with other symbolic experts. In this context I have identified two principal requirements to the architecture: one concerning expert communication and another concerning concurrence. For the former, in order to facilitate the independent development of symbolic experts and their integration, it is important to introduce an automatic mechanism that activates and executes specific symbolic procedures of an expert depending on the content of the KB and on its modifications. This avoids a rigid coupling of different experts that would limit the reconfigurability and flexibility of the symbolic part of the architecture, without limiting the interactions. Clearly it is not plausible to rely only on this type of conditions that would inevitably explode the computational complexity of KB updates even in simple domains but other additional mechanism have to be considered. For the latter, truly concurrent behavior cannot be obtained, at least for pragmatic reasons related to the nature of symbolic inferential processes. However, considering the characteristic of such processes which cannot be constrained to strict real time responses and which typically have a long duration, it is not necessary to provide real concurrence in the system but simply a concurrent programming paradigm to facilitate expert development. In practice, the updating and querying of the KB is transparently serialized by the system, despite the concurrent execution of the single experts.

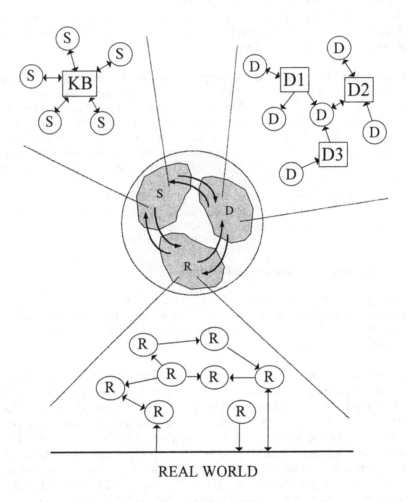

Fig. 4. Experts information management and exchange

- *Diagrammatic experts* mainly operate on diagrammatic, iconic representations. Whereas in the former cases the knowledge base is one and common to all symbolic experts, the iconic representations are many and possibly different. Moreover each icon can be managed or simply accessed by one or more experts. The architecture must then support efficient creation and sharing of generic iconic representations, specified by the creating expert, synchronising all accesses to avoid inconsistent states. In this context, since the timing requirements are more strict than in the symbolic case, real concurrence must be generally supported; instead, only atomic, non-preemptable modifications of the representations must be sequenced.

- *Reactive experts* constitute the class that mostly requires architectural support. These experts are often subject to hard real time constraints because of their interaction with the system hardware such as sensors and actuators. Moreover real time constraints characterise all reactive experts because of the necessity to handle real world environments that are both dynamic and unpredictable. Reactive experts, mostly for the same reasons, also need to communicate frequently and synchronously. This is often done throughout the use of procedure calls which constrain the structure of the reactive architecture at programming time. On the contrary, I believe that, in intelligent systems, the entire architecture must be dynamically reconfigurable to handle the sudden variations in world. Thus, the architecture must be capable of supporting timing execution constraints and synchronous communication without imposing a static expert structure.

Figure 4 illustrates the relationship between the experts and the representations accessed. Experts are depicted as lettered circles whereas representations are rectangles. Notice that in the symbolic component there is a common symbolic representation KB whereas in the diagrammatic component different diagrams can be found: D1, D2, D3. It is important to specify once more that the arrows connecting the experts to the diagrammatic representations do not signify static links but only dynamic connections. Thus an expert can operate on a particular icon at one and on a different icon at another time. Analogously the reactive experts are also interconnected only by dynamic reconfigurable links but, as their name unambiguously states, not to any representation. Therefore, in this context, the arrows simply indicate the general flow of *directed* information within the architecture. The term directed is here used to emphasise that the communication is point to point, from an expert to another expert or to a specific representation.

In the HEIR architecture directed information exchange only occurs within a single expert class. Instead, a general service (valid for both intra-class and inter-class information exchange) is provided which is in particular responsible for the integration of the different representation paradigms. This service has been named EIEP [15][16], Expert Information Exchange Protocol. It is a message passing protocol based on an efficient implementation of a blackboard [6], publish/subscribe technique for this domain of applications.

In the EIEP the exchange of information simply relies on the contents of the information regardless of the sending or receiving expert. Messages are organised in *types* depending on the information they carry. Possible types might be: *positioning, collision, sensor-data,* etc. The communication occurs based on the following principles:

- each expert selects dynamically the type of information it desires to receive. This corresponds to a *subscribe* operation to the message type.

- an expert that produces a message of a specific type informs the system. This corresponds to a *publish* operation.

The two principles allow the correct distribution of the information to the desired receiving expert without any explicit indication of the receiver by the sending expert and of the sender from the receiving expert. It is worth noting that the receiver, at the time it decides about the reception of a particular message type, has no knowledge of whether an expert that produces such a message exists. Analogously the sender does not know whether there will be any receivers. This implies that only the type of data has to be defined a priori whereas senders and receivers are defined only at runtime and can vary dynamically during the system's execution. In this way experts can be added, modified or removed dynamically allowing the entire system to adapt to different configurations depending on the real world requirements. In addition, in the EIEP, within message types, many *sub-types* giving additional hints about the data carried can be envisaged. Currently, however, though subclasses have been used even for system control messages, the relevant parameter is the first: for example, if we consider the message of type *positioning* and its subtypes *request-dynamic* and *request-static* that respectively ask for dynamic positioning of the robot during its motion and a static but more accurate localisation, the system will handle the messages in exactly the same way. It is the expert or the experts responsible for the execution of the specified behaviours that will differentiate between the two subtypes.

Thus the EIEP provides a uniform communication paradigm of representation which experts belonging to different classes can use. Again, the emphasis is put on the flexibility and reconfigurability of the architecture for which the protocol is also completely compatible with the other specific intra-class services. Moreover messages appear to be suitable for this task because they do not constrain the information contents which can be both symbolic or analogical. Note that, in this context, I have used the term analogical with respect to diagrammatic or iconic, because often the information will be in an analogical, numeric format (such as the readings from a proximity sensors) but will not, by itself, constitute an icon. The latter is instead formed by the fusion of the different analogical messages by a suitable diagrammatic expert. This protocol also offers other advantages if experts are distributed on different machines. From the opposite side, it only allows asynchronous inter-class communication. Although this would certainly be a significant limitation if it were the only method for the entire system, in the HEIR architecture it is only used to allow the different expert groups to communicate, integrate the information and maintain consistency between the different representations; in my experience these type of operations are typically based on events and thus implicitly asynchronous. An example might be a reactive expert which continuously monitors the robot batteries to verify the remaining power. When the tension level falls under a pre-defined threshold the expert produces a message indicating an emergency event or situation that requires attention. A symbolic expert might request such a message type, assert the information on the symbolic knowledge base when the message is received, and activate a set of inference procedures to handle the situation.

The directed communication services, although less general (valid only for intra-class communication), are clearly also aimed at maintaining the reconfigurability property of the components. For the diagrammatic component these services allow the creation of a diagram by an expert or the connection to existing diagrams. Again, the diagrams are characterised by their type (bitmap, APF, etc.) and role, and it is the system which provides the expert-diagram connection, eventually changing it. For example consider a system in which expert A handles a bitmap of the environment based on sensor data provided by a camera, and expert B reasons on the bitmap to recognise relevant features. If suddenly the camera stops functioning or the lighting is not sufficient, expert A may be substituted by a different expert building the bitmap based on proximity sensors. Since the bitmap has both the same type and role, the system will automatically adapt the connection without Expert B noticing the change. The same principle applies to the reactive component in which the experts do not use direct function calls to their respective interfaces but the connection is chosen by the system with an indirect call. Thus the performances remain similar but the behaviour is not constrained at programming time.

2.2 Expert Distribution

The proposed architecture is distributed at all levels, symbolic, diagrammatic or reactive, both from a cognitive and computational point of view. However, the rapid progress of communication technology offers the possibility of distributing computation not only on different processes but on a network of computers. This not only results in greater available computational power (for example, in the case of mobile robots, processing is no longer limited to the on-board unit) but it allows the robot to merge with the environment it operates in. In suitable intelligent buildings a mobile robot may open doors, turn on/off lights or even avoid obstacles based not only on its sensors and actuators but on the interaction with other robotic entities (lights, doors, etc..). In addition the range of robot interaction is now only limited by the network and thus the robot can operate remotely on the environment. Similarly users can issue commands to remote robots and receive feedback in real time [18].

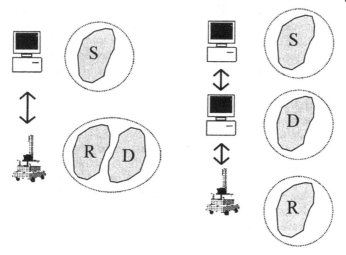

Fig. 5. Cognitive components in a network

Therefore, support for the distribution of experts on a network of different machines has been introduced among the services provided by the architecture. Although all information exchange services could be extended to function in a distributed environment, the increase in cost (in terms of efficiency in the case of a global approach) due to the current network throughput limitations would still be prohibitive. However, whereas it is more efficient to limit directed communication within a single machine, it is possible with very little overhead to extend the EIEP to a network [11]. In practice, it is then possible to distribute the symbolic, diagrammatic and reactive experts into different *components* running on different machines.

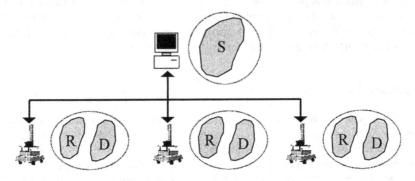

Fig. 6. Architecture in a multi-robot environment

This separation is clearly only an option that can be chosen at any time. In fact, the EIEP guarantees a protocol extension that is transparent to the user: as well as no identification of the sending or receiving expert there is also no need to identify explicitly the sending or receiving machine. Clearly there will be a significant difference due to timing and availability, dependent on the network characteristics. Figure 5 illustrates examples of how the different cognitive components can be distributed in a network of computers. Moreover other additional, non cognitive elements could be considered such as distributed interface experts, allowing the robot to be accessed remotely by different users or by a supervisor. Alternatively a multi-robot environment could be envisaged in which different autonomous robots share their knowledge of the world only one of the cognitive levels; presumably the symbolic one as shown in Figure 6.

Within the network the architecture uses a client-server model to take advantage of existing common network protocols such as TCP-IP. A component acts as a server for the lower components and it is a client of the upper ones. It is worth noting that the distinction in client and server is only necessary to correctly connect the distributed components in the network. The internal structure of the single component, whether client or server, remains identical to the user.

2.3 Application Development

Object oriented technology has been used to facilitate the development of new experts. A generic expert is in fact provided by a suitable programming interface library. This expert encapsulates all the properties and available services the system provides, allowing an implicit integration in the architecture, without any in-depth knowledge of how the services are implemented. New experts need simply to inherit this base expert class and redefine only their specific and distinguishing behaviour. Thus the derived expert will add its personal public methods that characterise the external interface of the object. Necessarily it will specify the operations that must be carried out when the expert is activated or deactivated as well as the main operation that it must execute. Other, still generic, classes are also provided for symbolic, diagrammatic and reactive experts. These classes belong to the generic base class but include the specific intra-class properties. Also in this case the user is not required to have any knowledge of the implementation of real-time services providing synchronised access to a representation or synchronous communication. Moreover, as mentioned above, communication services avoid the introduction of static programming links between the different experts. This has different advantages: it has the usual benefits of modular programming allowing the enhancement or modification of an expert or of a component of the architectures without altering the remaining experts or components and it allows the system to reconfigure itself at run time depending on the requirements of the current context.

It is also important to specify that object oriented technology is only used during the expert and system development. At run time there is no hierarchical organisation that would clearly limit real time constraint specifications.

2.4 ETHNOS

ETHNOS - Expert Tribe in a Hybrid Network Operating System, is a novel operating system that provides the services required by the proposed software architecture. It consists of:

- an object oriented application programming interface that facilitates application development by providing an easy access to the operating system's functionality. Currently the API is available for two different object oriented programming languages: C++ and Java. The latter in particular allows an ETHNOS application to communicate with Java Applets running on common www-network browsers such as *Netscape Navigator* or *Internet Explorer*.
- a run time library allowing ETHNOS applications to be executed on operating systems conforming to the Posix Real-Time specifications.

In fact, ETHNOS is not a stand-alone OS but it has been designed to extend the functionality of existing operating systems. This takes advantage of the latest commercial technology in the field while maintaining a greater compatibility for Ethnos based applications. Other implementations of the run-time library also allow the execution of these applications (using a reduced set of services) on other operating systems: Ms-Dos®, Windows® and Sun-OS Unix®.

The services ETHNOS provides are the following:

- *Expert execution*. This includes the generic real-time scheduling of the experts as well as the activation, deactivation and suspension based on EIEP messages or on knowledge updates or modifications.
- *Expert reconfigurability*. The system reorganises, transparently and dynamically, the structure of the architecture depending on the current context of execution. Synchronous communication links between reactive experts or icon access are automatically updated.
- *Expert communication*. The system takes care of all directed and non-directed, inter-class and intra-class communication, including *Symbolic knowledge base access* and *Icon management*. Moreover the system transparently identifies the sending and receiving experts, as well as the sending and receiving machines, in EIEP based communication, also limiting the use of the network channel to the essential information. In ETHNOS the EIEP has been integrated with the scheduler. Thus experts may suspend themselves on the reception of a message of a certain type or even on a combination of messages. This avoids wasting CPU time in the execution of code that cannot perform its operations because it is waiting for external data
- *Message management*. The API includes a set of functions that allow an application to create, select, read and modify ETHNOS messages.
- *Timing*. The system provides periodic and non-periodic timers. This is particularly relevant for real-time reactive experts whose behaviour often depends on the time elapsed.

3. A Practical Example

In this section an example of how the architecture may be practically used to solve the problem of obstacle avoidance is documented. The proposed solution is based on the well known evidence grids[5] and artificial potential field based approaches[11] for mobile robot navigation, which can be easily mapped into the diagrammatic component.

In Figure 7 the diagrammatic component for the above task is depicted. Two types of diagrammatic representations can be observed: the *MAP* and the *APF*. The MAP is an evidence grid, a statistical, geometric, world-centered representation of the environment in which different sensor readings can be easily fused. The APF is a robot centered representation in which obstacles correspond to high potential values and free spaces to low potential values. Three experts operate on these representations: the *Map Handler*, the *APF Handler*, and the *Navigator*. The Map Handler is responsible for the updating of the MAP on the reception of sensorial information messages (messages of type SENSOR_DATA to which the expert subscribes). The APF Handler builds the potential field on the basis of the contents of the MAP and on the robot position (received as a message of type ROBOT_POSITION to which the expert subscribes). The navigator, based on the information in the APF and on the goal position it wants to reach (received as a message of type ROBOT_GOAL to which the expert subscribes) determines periodically the speed and jog that the robot should keep. This motion information is shared, using the EIEP, as a message of type MOTION_INFO which some other expert in the system (probably a reactive expert) will receive and send to the robot actuators.

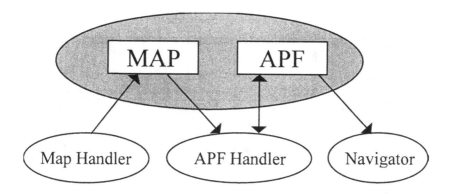

Fig. 7. An example of diagrammatic component

Thus, while sensor messages are produced by some expert in the system connected to sensor devices, the MAP is updated to reflect the changes in the environment in real time. Concurrently the APF is updated and suitable navigation parameters are chosen to avoid obstacles in the robot path towards the goal. A sample run in a simulated environment is illustrated in Figure 8 in which the robot has to move from the position indicated by the arrow to the position indicated by the dot.

In the example the remaining architectural components are not described except for their implicit role in communicating with the sensors and actuators. It is worth mentioning that two main situations may occur leading to two different hierarchical organizations.

The first situation is the most intuitive: reactive experts are connected to real sensors and actuators and are responsible for dealing with SENSOR_DATA, ROBOT_POSITION and MOTION_INFO messages, symbolic experts reason on the motivations and intentions of the robot, establishing the target positions it has to reach and producing messages of type ROBOT_GOAL. In this case a common hierarchical organization in which the symbolic component occupies the top level and the reactive component the bottom level is generated.

The second situation occurs when the robot is executing a mental simulation of a navigation action. SENSOR_DATA, ROBOT_POSITION and MOTION_INFO messages are dealt by symbolic experts which generate virtual sensor information based on their symbolic knowledge of the environment while keeping track of the virtual robot position. The goal may be determined by the reactive component: for example responding to a battery low stimulus and issuing a ROBOT_GOAL message towards the recharging position. In this context the robot must try to minimize energy consumption and therefore mentally simulates different navigations to selected a better path. Clearly this leads to a hierarchical organization in which the reactive component occupies the top most position and the symbolic component the lowest position. In a different scenario (for example if the robot is simply asked to compute a good path towards a certain position) the symbolic component itself may generate the robot goals and thus the activity will concentrate only on the symbolic and diagrammatic components.

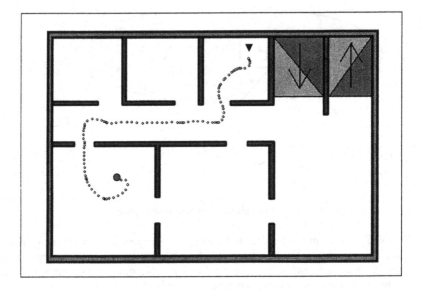

Fig. 8. Sample robot navigation in a simulated environment

4. Experimental Set-Up

The HEIR software architecture has been implemented and developed on a TRC Labmate. The mobile robot is equipped with an Intel Pentium 100 processor, a positioning system based on active beacons DLPS©, and a belt of 16 proximity sensors. The reactive and diagrammatic components were implemented on board of the mobile vehicle and written in C++ based on the ETHNOS operating system developed as an add-on to a low-level Linux RT OS. The robot was then connected throughout a 9600 baud radio link to the off-board symbolic component, running on a UNIX based version of ETHNOS on a remote Sun Spark Workstation, integrated with the prototype of a terminological system called X-Procne and written in Sicstus Prolog. For more detailed information about refer to [17].

The system has been successfully tested and used in museums or shows for public entertainment[1], meeting so far approximately more than 3,000 people. In the museum the robot had to execute different missions involving high level activities such as path planning and communication with the people it encountered, as well as low level obstacle avoidance and positioning. A photo taken during one of such public appearances is shown in Figure 9.

Fig. 9. Robot at Fair Salone Formula moving in a crowded area

With respect to other architectures presented in literature that are also capable of performing similar tasks the HEIR approach greatly differs in the way the tasks are executed. In fact, there is not a fixed hierarchical organisation (as shown in the example in the previous section) but each component takes control of the system in turn, depending on the context of execution. In the exhibitions the robot operated mostly at the diagrammatic level during navigation, using abstract potential fields to perform smooth obstacle avoidance and local path planning. It suddenly moved its focus of activity to the reactive component to deal with emergencies such as sudden obstacles or collisions. In the opposite direction, it moved the focus to the symbolic

---

[1] *Exhibition Sculture Gutenberghiane e Manifesto dell'Antilibro* , Museo della Scienza e della Tecnica, Milano, March-April 1997,
Fair Salone Formula, Magazzini del Cotone Congress Center, Genova, April 8-12 1997.

component to communicate with the people it encountered, to change its current plan or when local path planning failed. In this way, since it is not necessary to involve every component at all times, the architecture does not suffer from the typical problems concerning hybrid systems, often criticised because the overall capabilities of the system appear to be bounded to those of the symbolic high levels, which suffer from the known intrinsic limitations when coping with real words [3].

The advantages of this approach consist mainly in the flexibility of the architecture and of its single experts. In fact, different expert organisations may be dynamically used to adapt to the problem that has to be solved. Moreover different sub-hierarchies may also co-exist if more than one task has to be handled. In my opinion this property facilitates the scaling up of robot systems to solving more complex problems.

Current work is aimed at extending the functionality of the symbolic component to tasks other than navigation and simple communication. For example, a system composed of multiple HEIR based robots will be used for hospital transportation and for the Robocup® competition. It is worth mentioning that social interaction between the different robots will also be distributed among the three components, differently from other approaches [13] in which it is taken care of by a separate architectural layer.

References

[1] Proceedings of AAAI Spring Symposium on Lessons Learned from Implemented Software Architectures for Physical Agents, Stanford University, 1995.

[2] R. P. Bonasso, D. Kortenkamp, D. Miller and M. Slack, Experiences with an Architecture for Intelligent Reactive Agents, in: Intelligent Agents III - Proceedings of the Third International Workshop on Agent Theories, Architectures, and Languages (ATAL-96), edited by M. Wooldridge and J.P. Müller and M. Tambe, vol. 1037 of Lecture Notes in Artificial Intelligence, Springer-Verlag, Heidelberg, 1996.

[3] R. Brooks, "Intelligence without reason", AI Memo No. 1293, MIT Technical Report, 1991.

[4] G. Clerici, Il Tennis Facile, Mondadori, Milano, Italia, 1977.

[5] A. Elfes, Sonar-based real-world mapping and navigation, in: Autonomous Robot Vehicles, edited by Cox, I. J., Wilfong, G. T., Springer-Verlag, 233-249, 1990.

[6] R. Engelmore and T. Morgan ed., Blackboard systems, Addison-Wesley, 1988.

[7] I. Ferguson, TouringMachines: Autonomous Agents with Attitudes, Computer Laboratory, University of Cambridge, Cambridge, Technical Report 250, UK, 1992.

[8] M. Frixione, M. Piaggio, G. Vercelli and R. Zaccaria, A cognitive hybrid model for autonomous navigation, Lecture Notes in Artificial Intelligence, Vol. 992, 303-314, Springer-Verlag, 1995.

[9] M. Frixione, G. Vercelli and R. Zaccaria, Diagrammatic reasoning about actions, Technical Report DIST, 1998.

[10] B. Hayes-Roth et al., A domain-specific software architecture for adaptive intelligent systems, IEEE Transactions on Software Engineering, Vol. 21, No. 4, 1995.

[11] O. Khatib, Real time obstacle avoidance for manipulators and mobile robots, International Journal of Robotics Research, 5 (1), 90-99, 1986.

[12] J. P. Müller, in: The right agent (architecture) to do the right thing, Intelligent Agents V -- - Proceedings of the Fifth International Workshop on Agent Theories, Architectures, and

Languages (ATAL-98), edited by J.P. Muller and M.P. Singh and A.S. Rao, Lecture Notes in Artificial Intelligence, Springer-Verlag, Heidelberg , 1999.

[13] J. P. Müller, The design of autonomous agents – a layered approach, vol. 1177 of Lecture Notes in Artificial Intelligence, Springer-Verlag, Heidelberg, 1996.

[14] P. Pirjanian and H. I. Christensen, Theoretical methods for planning and control in mobile robotics, IEEE Proc. Knowledge-based Intelligent Electronic Systems, KES, Adelaide, 1995.

[15] M. Piaggio and R. Zaccaria, An Information Exchange Protocol in a Multi-Layer Distributed Architecture, IEEE Proc. Hawaii Int. Conf. on Complex Systems, 1997.

[16] M. Piaggio and R. Zaccaria, Distributing a Robotic System on a Network : the ETHNOS Approach, Advanced Robotics Journal, Vol. 12, N.8, 1998.

[17] M. Piaggio, ERASMUS - A Distributed Architecture for Intelligent Robots, Phd. Thesis, University of Genova, Italy,1998.

[18] Sheridan, T.B., "Space Teleoperation Through Time Delay: Review and Prognosis", IEEE Trans. Robotics and Automation, Vol. 9, No. 5, 1993.

A-Teams: An Agent Architecture for Optimization and Decision-Support

John Rachlin[1], Richard Goodwin[1], Sesh Murthy[1], Rama Akkiraju[1], Fred Wu[1],
Santhosh Kumaran[2], Raja Das[2]

[1] IBM T.J. Watson Research Center
Yorktown Heights, NY

[2] IBM Supply Chain Optimization Solutions
Atlanta, GA

Abstract

The effectiveness of an agent architecture is measured by its successful application to real problems. In this paper, we describe an agent architecture, A-Teams, that we have successfully used to develop real-world optimization and decision support applications. In an A-Team, an asynchronous team of agents shares a population of solutions and evolves an optimized set of solutions. Each agent embodies its own algorithm for creating, improving or eliminating a solution. Through sharing of the population of solutions, cooperative behavior between agents emerges and tends to result in better solutions than any one agent could produce. Since agents in an A-Team are autonomous and asynchronous, the architecture is both scalable and robust. In order to make the architecture easier to use and more widely available, we have developed an A-Team class library that provides a foundation for creating A-Team based decision-support systems.

1. Introduction

This paper describes an implementation of A-Teams (Talukdar et al, 1983; Talukdar et al, 1993; Talukdar et al, 1996), a multi-agent architecture which we have used to successfully deploy multi-objective decision-support systems for complex, real-world domains. Examples of these domains include manufacturing scheduling and transportation planning. Such complex optimization problems have multiple objectives and constraints. Often, there is no single dominant algorithm that can give ``the optimal'' solution to the problem because of combinatorial complexity or because multiple competing objectives make it difficult to determine which solution is optimal. The A-Team framework enables us to easily combine disparate problem solving strategies, each in the form of an agent, and enables these agents to cooperate to evolve diverse and high quality solutions. Humans, acting as agents, can use their domain expertise to guide the search and to expand the set of possible solutions by relaxing constraints. By combining the speed and accuracy of software agents with the deep knowledge of human experts, A-Team based decision-support systems improve the decision making process, which has led to significant economic advantages for our customers (Shaw 1998, Hoffman 1996).

We begin our discussion with an overview of the A-Team architecture and describe some of its advantages for creating decision-support systems. We then discuss related work and compare A-Teams to other architectures that have been used for optimization and decision support. Having introduced the A-Team architecture, we move on to describe our implementation and its key features. The implementation provides a basis for developing decision-support systems. However, creating an efficient and effective system is still more of an art than a science. To aid in the creation of A-Team systems, we present a set of principles that we have found to be useful. We conclude with an overview of A-Team based decision-support systems that have been deployed to date and discuss future research directions.

2. A-Team Overview

An asynchronous team is a collection of software agents that cooperate to solve a problem by dynamically evolving a population of solutions (Talukdar et al, 1983). In our work, we have used A-Teams to solve multi-objective optimization problems such as production and transportation scheduling for the manufacturing domain. Each element of the population created by the A-Team is a complete solution to the problem such as a production schedule for a mill or a transportation schedule for a distribution center. The representation of the problem and the solution are problem specific but uniform throughout. For example, a machine scheduling A-Team might use a representation of the problem as a list of orders and machines and the solution as a sequenced assignment of orders to machines.

Agents cooperate by sharing access to populations of candidate solutions. Each agent works to create, modify or remove solutions from a population. The quality of the solutions gradually evolves over time as improved solutions are added and poor solutions are removed. Cooperation between agents emerges as one agent works on the solutions produced by another.

Figure 1 presents an overview of the A-Team architecture. Each agent, shown as a block, encapsulates a particular algorithm. This algorithm may consist of a call to an external system. Within an A-Team, agents are autonomous and asynchronous. Each agent encapsulates a particular problem-solving method along with the methods to decide when to work, what to work on and how often to work. These decisions are evaluation driven. An agent decides when to work and what to work on by looking at the evaluations of the solutions in the population. Agents are free to use any method for deciding when to work and what to work on, but intelligent strategies look at the state of the solutions in the population and take into account the agent's ability to improve them.

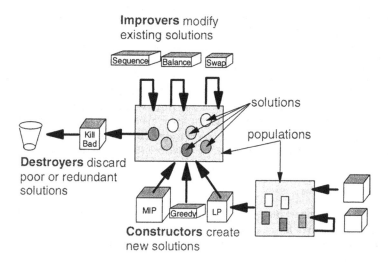

Figure 1: A-Teams consist of populations of solutions and agents that create, improve and destroy solutions.

Agents come in three flavors: constructors, improvers and destructors. *Constructors* create initial solutions and add them to the population. *Improvers* select one or more existing solutions from the population and produce new solutions that are added to the population. Technically, improvers are modifiers and may not actually make measurable improvements in the solutions they modify. They may, in fact, make random modifications that lead to worse solutions. Such modifications may be useful in that they serve to explore the solution space and, in so doing, may lead down a path to a better solution. Typically, however, improvers encapsulate domain specific methods designed specifically to effect quick directed improvement. Finally, *destroyers* keep the size of the population of solutions in check. Their main function is to delete clearly sub-optimal or redundant solutions, while keeping promising solutions. This prevents improver agents from wasting effort by working on solutions that are going nowhere.

Populations are repositories for solutions. Each population is homogenous in the sense that it holds only a single type of solution. Within a population, each solution is evaluated along a number of problem specific dimensions, resulting in an evaluation vector that determines the quality of the solution. An A-Team may contain more than one population. For example, a scheduling problem may consist of multiple sub-problems. There could be a population of solutions for each sub-problem and a population of complete solutions. The population of complete solutions can be constructed by combining solutions from the other populations. An optimization system may contain multiple A-Teams working in concert to produce complete solutions.

By sharing the set of solutions in a population, agents in an A-Team cooperate to evolve a population of good solutions. Since there is no inter-agent communication language to explicitly coordinate the behavior of sets of agents, cooperation is achieved by enabling one agent to work on the intermediate results of another. Cooperation tends to result in better solutions than could be produced by any single agent. The sequence of agent invocations that lead to the best solutions may be arbitrarily complex. (Salman *et al.*, 1997) The performance of the team, in terms of the quality and diversity of solutions and the speed with which solutions are derived, depends on the set of agents that make up the team. Later in this paper, we will have more to say about the principles that we use to create effective A-Teams.

2.1. Human as Agent

A special form of cooperation occurs between the human scheduler and the software agents (Figure 2). We have enhanced the A-Team architecture to enable humans to participate as agents so that the human scheduler can provide deep knowledge of the problem domain not captured by the software agents. Humans can also more readily adapt as circumstances of the problem change over time. By participating as agents in an A-Team, humans can generate good solutions, destroy bad ones and assist in the evaluation of solutions. Additionally, they can relax problem constraints by negotiating with concerned parties.

Complex optimization problems, such as planning and scheduling in manufacturing environments, have multiple objectives and constraints. Often, there is no single dominant algorithm that can give "the optimal" solution to the problem because of combinatorial complexity or because multiple competing objectives make it difficult to determine which solution is optimal. Heuristics for finding good solutions may be highly dependent on the specifics of the problem and may be difficult to codify. Humans can offer broad stroke guidance by seeding the population with good initial solutions. Software agents can use these solutions as a basis for further improvement. Such cooperation has been shown to be effective elsewhere (Masayuki *et al., 1991*) Conversely, the human scheduler can refine alternatives generated by software agents so as to account for special-case considerations. The human scheduler can guide improver agents by deleting alternatives that appear hopeless. When reviewing the set of non-dominated solutions and their inherent tradeoffs, the human scheduler is best able to distinguish which alternatives are worthy of more detailed consideration. Human experts understand the implications of each constraint and can negotiate to change the problem. For example, a customer may be willing to take part of an order late as long as one truckload arrives on time. Knowing when to ask for an extension is best left to the human rather than creating a complex system that tries to capture every nuance of a problem. This approach ensures that the system will be applicable to a broader range of problems. The human scheduler thus plays a highly interactive role in our system.

Within the A-Team framework, the purpose of the utility function, which evaluates solutions, is to guide search and to identify potentially good solutions for presentation to the human decision-maker. The partial utility model must capture the high level factors that contribute to a good schedule, but it does not have to compare dissimilar measures of utility that represent tradeoffs between competing interests. We use a multi-valued utility function that evaluates a schedule along a set of dimensions. For manufacturing interests, we have found that objectives can be evaluated along four broad dimensions: Time, factors that relate to on-time delivery, Quality, factors related to product quality, Money, factors related to profitability and Disruptions, factors related to the ease of manufacture. Not coincidentally, these four measures map to the interests of the customer service representatives, quality engineers, accountants and manufacturing supervisors respectively. The utility model is used to aggregate factors that contribute to each category, but comparisons between categories are left to the human scheduler who is presented with a set of schedules that represent the Pareto-optimal frontier. The scheduler can use these solutions as a basis for evaluating the tradeoffs, negotiating with other people in the company and coming to a final decision.

Presenting the human decision-maker with a set of alternatives that illustrate the tradeoffs to be made provides the information they need to make an informed decision. However, presenting too many solutions can overwhelm the decision-maker. In order to present a reasonably sized set of solutions, the system filters the population of solutions and presents only a subset. Currently, our systems present the set of non-dominated solutions. The decision maker can then choose any of these solutions, modify it and then put it back into the A-Team population in order to subject the alternative to further improvements by software-based agents.

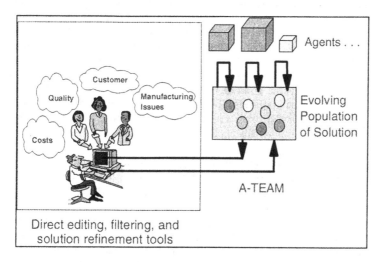

Figure 2: Decision-maker as an agent in the A-Team

2.2. A-Team Advantages

The A-Team architecture offers certain key advantages:

1. *Modular:* In an A-Team, agents are autonomous and do not depend on each other for either execution or communication. Hence, in the process of software development, agents can be built independently of each other. This enables the software solution to be developed in a modular way. Agents can be easily added or deleted from the system at any time. An analysis of the population of candidate solution alternatives often indicates what type of agent should be added to improve results. The A-Team architecture enables complex systems to be implemented incrementally and more easily maintained.

2. *Distributed:* The asynchronous nature of the A-Team makes it naturally suitable for parallelism. Since agents do not depend on each other in order to function, they can be distributed over the network and run in parallel to improve performance.

3. *Robust:* System reliability is critically important in manufacturing environments. A-Teams are robust because the failure of one agent does not lead to the failure of the entire system. If under particular circumstances an agent produces an invalid solution, or fails to produce any solution, it is unlikely that all other agents will also fail.

3. Related Architectures

The A-Team architecture was originally developed by Talukdar (Talukdar et al, 1983, Talukdar et al, 1993; Talukdar et al, 1996). A-Teams have proven to be successful in addressing hard optimization problems where no dominant algorithm exists. Application areas include: nonlinear algebraic equations (Talukdar et al, 1983), traveling salesman problems (Talukdar and de Souza, 1992), configuration of task-specific robots (Murthy, 1992), design of high-rise buildings (Quadrel, 1991), control of electric networks in real-time (Talukdar and Ramesh, 1993), diagnosis of faults in power systems (Chen and Talukdar, 1993) and constraint satisfaction problems (Gorti *et al.*, 1996). More recently, our group at IBM has applied A-Teams to planning and scheduling problems in manufacturing domains including steel (Lee et al, 1996), paper (Murthy et al, 1997) and transportation scheduling (Goodwin *et al.*, 1998). We believe that the technology is generally applicable to hard optimization problems.

According to Müller's agent architecture classification taxonomy (Müller 1998), the A-Team architecture could be classified as a software multi-agent system that is used to create software assistant agents. The multiple agents achieve an implicit cooperation by sharing a population of solutions. This is in marked contrast to the explicit cooperation that is required when agents work on a single solution, as is the case with robot soccer (Stone and Veloso 1998). The ability of agents in an A-Team to make global modifications to solutions is in contrast to some agent-based resource allocation systems where the agents are restricted to making local modifications (Dury et al. 1998).

The design of the A-Team architecture was motivated by other architectures used for optimization including blackboard systems and genetic algorithms. In fact, our A-Team infrastructure could be used to implement most aspects of these other architectures. The advantage of the A-Team architecture is that it combines a population of solutions with domain specific algorithms and limited agent interaction. In addition, rich solution evaluation metrics tends to result in a more diverse set of solutions.

Blackboard architectures enable cooperation among agents, called knowledge sources, by sharing access to a common memory and allowing agents to work on different parts of the problem (Erman, Hayes-Roth, Lesser and Reddy, 1980). The key difference is that A-Teams do not have a central scheduler responsible for sequencing agent invocations. Agents are autonomous. In addition, the A-Team population typically contains many complete solutions and uses a richer set of evaluations. This tends to produce a more diverse set of solutions rather than a single solution geared towards optimizing a specific objective function.

Genetic algorithms are based on natural selection in which a population of solutions represented as bit vectors evolves by random mutation and crossover (Holland, 1975). The solutions in an A-Team population also evolve over time, but unlike genetic algorithms, the mechanisms for creating and modifying solutions can be highly directed and take into account domain specific knowledge, rather than depending upon domain independent methods.

The ability of A-Team agents to cooperate in producing multiple candidate solutions makes it well suited for solving hard multi-objective optimization problems in a decision-support context. This is especially true in cases where the relative importance of these objectives changes constantly. (Sycara and Zeng, 1996) discuss how agent technologies can be seamlessly integrated with decision-support for information retrieval problems.

4. A-Team Implementation

Based on the A-Team architecture discussed previously, we have implemented an A-Team class library in order to make A-Team technology available to researchers, consultants, and third-party vendors. Our implementation provides the infrastructure needed to easily build complex and powerful optimization and decision-support applications. The implementation provides the basic components needed to create A-Teams, a configuration language for assembling and customizing the components and a user interface for interfacing with the resulting A-Team. To apply an A-Team to a particular problem the programmer need only write the problem specific code: an object to represent the problem, an object to represent a solution and procedures to encode problem specific algorithms. The library is designed using an object-oriented approach and is written in C++. It runs on multiple operating systems, including

AIX[1], Windows NT [2]and Linux. In this section, we describe the design of the class library.

At the conceptual level, our implementation consists of three components: *a graphical user interface, a class library and a configuration language* (Figure 3). In the rest of the section, we describe each of these components.

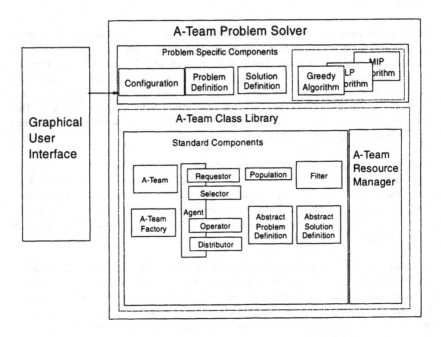

Figure 3: IBM's implementation of an A-Team framework.

4.1. User Interface

An interactive, graphical user interface allows the user to view and control the execution of a set of A-Teams. The interface displays the interactions among the agents and the evolution of the solutions within the populations. The user can use the interface to control the creation, configuration, starting, and stopping of the A-Teams. The interface also allows direct interaction with a running A-Team. The user can invoke agents and remove solutions from the population. If a problem specific editor

---

[1] Registered trademark of IBM.

[2] Registered trademark of Microsoft.

is supplied, the user can also create new solutions and add them to a population or modify existing solutions.

4.2. Class Library

The A-Team class library contains implementations of the basic components of an A-Team. These components provide the structure needed to create an A-Team as well as a rich set of standard behaviors. In most cases, these components provide all the non-problem specific functionality needed to create an A-Team. However, the library is organized in such a way as to allow a programmer to create specialized components that override the behavior of the standard components.

The components of the A-Team library are organized in a modular fashion with well-defined roles and interfaces. Individual objects represent the agents and populations in an A-Team. An A-Team object represents an instantiation of an A-Team described by a particular configuration. This object holds the agents and populations that comprise the A-Team. New instances of an A-Team are created by a factory class. Below we describe the implementation of each of these base components and their sub-components.

A-Team Factory: An A-Team factory creates new instances of A-Teams. It uses an A-Team configuration, specified using the configuration language, to create instances of A-Teams. An A-Team factory creates the populations, agents and other components that comprise an A-Team instance, it connects these components together and sets their parameters, as specified by the configuration.

1) *A-Team Object*: A-Team object encapsulates the components that comprise an instance of an A-Team. It provides a common interface for interacting with an A-Team and is used by the user interface and application programs. The interface provides mechanisms for starting and stopping the A-Team, for interacting with agents and for interacting with populations.

2) *Agents*: As well as embodying problem specific algorithms, A-Team agents must decide when to run, which solutions to work on, and what to do with any new solutions that they might generate. Correspondingly, an agent consists of four components, one component that embodies the algorithm and three decision making components, one for each decision. The decision-making components can be problem independent, while the algorithm is always problem dependent. The components of an agent are:

  - A Requestor, which requests CPU time to run the agent. A requestor is the agent's event handler. It is notified when the A-Team begins execution and can request to be notified of other events, such as a design being added to or removed from a population. Standard requestors include constructor requestors that request to run only once when an A-Team begins, improver requestors that request to run only after a population has a specified minimum number of designs and requestors with filters that request to run when the solutions in a population satisfy the filter condition. (Filters are described below.)

- A Selector, which picks solutions from a population. Constructors use null selectors, since they do not operate on existing solutions. Improvers and destroyers use their selectors to pick solutions for modification and destruction, respectively. Standard selectors include random selection and selection from the set of solutions that pass a filter.

- An Operator, which embodies the algorithm. For destroyers, the operator component is typically null. For constructors and improvers, the programmer must supply the operator, or this may consist of a call to an external system executable.

- A Distributor, which decides what to do with the results of the operator. The default strategy for constructors and improvers is to add the resulting design to the output population. The distributor for a destroyer deletes the resulting solution from the population.

3) *Populations*: A Population is a repository for solutions. It provides mechanisms for adding, deleting and copying solutions. It can also return a set of solutions that pass a given filter.

4) *Filters*: A filter embodies a test of a solution and when applied to a solution, returns either true or false. As specified above, filters are used to select solutions from a population and to gate the behavior of other components. Our implementation includes a large set of domain independent filters. We have filters that find the non-dominated set of solution, the NDFilter, filters that return the set of solutions with evaluations that exceed a given threshold, the ThresholdFilter and filters that find duplicate solutions, based on their evaluations, the DuplicateFilter. In addition, a set of composite filters allows the programmer to combine other filters in useful ways. The composite filters include the AndFilter, the OrFilter, the NotFilter, and the XorFilter. We can combine the standard filters to create new filters. For example, we could use the NDFilter, the DuplicateFilter and the AndFilter to construct a filter that returned duplicate, non-dominated solutions. In addition to the standard filters, programmers can create problem specific filters that test specific aspects of a solution.

5) *A-Team Resource Manager*: Even though A-Team agents run asynchronously, some mechanism is needed to assign resources to agents that request to run. In an implementation that uses a different thread for each agent, the operating system scheduler could perform this function. In our implementation, we use a resource manager to implement resource allocation policies and to create an abstract interface to the underlying hardware and operating system. This allows us to run an A-Team on a uni-processor, a parallel processor or on a distributed

architecture, like CORBA. Our implementation currently includes a uni-processor resource manager and a CORBA resource manager. The uni-processor manager uses a single thread of control and randomly selects an agent to run from the list of agents waiting to run. Problem specific resource allocation strategies and resource managers that learn to allocate more resources to agents that perform well have also been implemented, but are not part of the standard library yet.

6) *Abstract Definitions of Problem Specific Components*: Our implementation includes abstract placeholders for problem specific components. These abstract components can be specialized to create the components needed to represent the problem definition object and the solution definition object.

4.3. A-Team Configuration Language

The A-Team configuration language allows the user to specify the components, interconnections and parameters for an A-Team. The A-Team factory uses this specification when constructing an A-Team. Use of the configuration language reduces the amount of code that must be written and allows A-Teams to be rapidly reconfigured without recompiling. The user interface and the configuration language enable the user to dynamically re-configure A-Teams without the need to write C++ code.

The language is relatively simple, but extensible. It can be used specify all the standard components of the A-Team library and set their parameters. It can also be used to specify user-defined objects and set their parameters. Below, we give a small excerpt from a sample configuration file to give a flavor of the language.

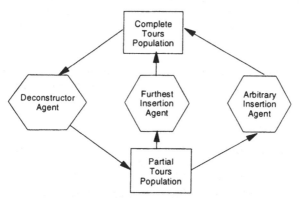

Figure 4: The connectivity between three of the agents and two of the populations in an A-Team to solve the Traveling Salesman Problem.

```
1         A tspAteam ATEAM ISA ateam
2                 WITH
3                 agents = (tspDeconstructorAgent, tspFurthestInsertionAgent,
4                                 tspArbitraryInsertionAgent, tspDestroyerAgent);
5                 populations = (tspCompleteToursPop, tspPartialToursPop);
6
7                 resource = (tspResource);
8
9                 connect = (tspDeconstructorAgent, input, tspCompleteToursPop) ;
10                connect = (tspDeconstructorAgent, output, tspPartialToursPop);
11
12                connect = (tspFurthestInsertionAgent, input, tspPartialToursPop);
13                connect = (tspFurthestInsertionAgent, output, tspCompleteToursPop);
14
15                connect = (tspArbitraryInsertionAgent, input, tspPartialToursPop);
16                connect = (tspArbitraryInsertionAgent, output, tspCompleteToursPop);
17
18                connect = (tspDestroyerAgent, input, tspCompleteToursPop);
19        END
20
21        A tspResource RESOURCE ISA UniResourceAllocator
22                WITH
23                maxInvocations = (1000);
24                trace = (TRUE);
25        END
```

This excerpt is a segment from the configuration file of a Traveling Salesman Problem (TSP) solving A-Team. Line 1 specifies that the component being described is an ATEAM that is implemented using the standard ateam object. Between the ``WITH'' and the ``END'' come the parameter settings, in this case a list of agents, populations, the connections between agents and populations, and a resource manager. In this example, there are four agents and two populations. One population contains complete solutions to the TSP problem and the other contains tour fragments. The deconstructor agent takes complete solutions and extracts efficient sub-tours and puts them into the population of tour fragments. The other two agents take zero, one or two tour fragments and create complete solutions, which are added to the tspCompleteToursPop. The definition of the tspResource begins on line 26. Here the resource manager is defined as a UniResourceAllocator. The maximum number of agent invocations is set to 1000 and tracing of agent invocations is turned on. Further details of agents and populations are defined later in the configuration file.

5. Building Effective A-Teams

The best A-teams are those that produce diverse optimal or near-optimal solutions quickly and consistently. The design of an A-Team is therefore a multi-objective optimization problem. Although diversity is only important in the context of multiple objectives, the cooperative behavior of A-Team agents is still valuable even if there is a single objective, or fitness function. (Huberman, Lukose, & Hogg 1997) offer insight into why combining multiple algorithms produces solutions that are preferable to the solutions generated by individual algorithms operating alone, and offers a measure for the degree of cooperation involved based on statistical correlation of performance. This is analogous to the way in which machine learning researchers employ ensembles of classifiers to produce higher levels of accuracy than can be achieved using any single classifier (Dietterich, 1997).

Although there is no formal theory that describes how to create an effective A-Team, our experience developing real-world applications has lead us to discover a set of guiding principles. Much of our on-going research focuses on A-Team performance measures that we use to discover good agent portfolios.

- Too great a dependence on computationally intensive agents results in fewer solutions and less agent cooperation. The result is an A-Team that takes longer to run while producing less varied results.

- Relying too heavily on simple solution-tweaking agents can result in clusters of solutions each consisting of many nearly identical solutions. In addition, simple agents may not make sufficient progress towards optimality.

- Destroyers provide selective pressure by encouraging agents to work on promising solutions and therefore critical. However, aggressive destruction can also decimate population diversity, undermining the variability of candidate alternatives available for decision-support purposes.

6. IBM Products That Use A-Teams

Using our A-Team architecture, we have built applications for paper mill scheduling, steel mill scheduling, transportation scheduling and wafer start planning for semiconductor manufacturing. These solutions have been successfully fielded at more than a dozen sites and are currently being sold worldwide. In this section, we describe some of these products.

IBM Trim[3] Optimization system (product no. 5799-A11) is a software optimization tool that gives paper companies the ability to maximize their manufacturing yield while satisfying customer requirements. The software provides multiple trim alternatives, with each alternative trim solution evaluated according to several evaluation criteria specified by the user. The optimizer combines a powerful suite of mathematical approaches and heuristics within the A-Team framework to provide to the human schedulers a diverse set of near-optimal trimming alternatives.

IBM Load Planning and Distribution optimization software application (product no. 5799-A12) provides state-of-the-art tools for distribution planners. It is designed to minimize cost and maximize vehicle utilization while maintaining on-time delivery of

---

[3] The word ``Trimming'' in paper manufacturing terminology refers to cutting paper machine reels into rolls of smaller diameter and width so as to satisfy customer demand while maximizing utilization of the reel. See (Murthy et al. 97) for further details.

products. The software considers production schedules, delivery commitments and shipment methods to produce optimized distribution schedules. We address this multi-criteria optimization problem by combining various mathematical approaches such as linear programming, integer programming and domain specific heuristics (Goodwin et al 98).

IBM Global Scheduling Optimization software (product no. 5799-A13) provides integrated enterprise-wide scheduling solutions for mills. The software produces complete production and distribution schedules for the entire enterprise which includes allocation of orders to mills and machines, grouping and sequencing orders into batches for production, trimming the for optimal manufacturing yield and producing optimal transportation schedules for the produced items. We have used the A-Team architecture in multiple layers in our global optimization software and it embodies a rich set of problem solving methods from multiple areas such as operations research and artificial intelligence.

Companies have reported substantial benefits using these technologies. One paper company customer has reported a 2 inch increase in the utilization of their reels using IBM Trim Optimization along with a 10% reduction in transportation costs using IBM Load Planning technology, recouping their investment in less than one year. These financial benefits are in addition to improvements in manufacturing yield and customer service (Shaw, 1998; Hoffman, 1996).

7. Conclusions and Future Work

We have described an agent-based architecture known as an A-Team that is now proving itself useful for addressing real-world optimization problems. An A-Team consists of a set of configurable agents and a set of populations that serve as repositories for candidate solutions. A-Teams are simple yet effective. They are simple because there is no inter-agent communication. Agents cooperate by having shared access to the solutions in a population. Nevertheless, this simple form of cooperation makes the A-Team architecture very powerful. Our A-Team implementation makes it particularly easy to incorporate unique problem-solving methods that could be custom written for the problem or even previously developed object code. A-Teams are useful for multi-objective optimization and decision-support because a set of agents can embody many different objectives and are more readily able to produce a diverse set of solution alternatives. We have discussed how our implementation further extends prior work with A-Teams by enabling the human decision-maker to act as an additional agent, able to interact with other agents by creating, refining, and destroying solution alternatives. We have also explained why A-Team-based systems are modular, robust and inherently easy to parallelize.

Building effective A-Teams depends upon the mix of agents and their individual capabilities. As part of our ongoing research, we are continuing to investigate ways of creating good combinations of agents using quantitative measures of A-Team performance. We are also investigating whether agents capable of learning and other adaptive behaviors can further improve system performance.

We are continuing to enhance our A-Team architecture, and are making the A-Team class library available to researchers, consultants and third party vendors. For information on obtaining the latest release of the A-Team library, please contact the authors.

References

Chen, C.L., Talukdar, S.N.; 1993. *Causal Nets for Fault Diagnosis.* 4th International Conference on Expert Systems Application to Power Systems, Melbourne, Australia, Jan 4-8.

Dietterich, T.; 1997. *Machine-Learning Research: Four Current Directions.* AI Magazine **18**(4): 97-136.

Dury A., Le Ber F., Chevier, V.; 1998. *A Reactive Approach for Solving Constraint-Satisfaction Problems: Assigning Land Use to Farming Territories.* In Intelligent Agents V --- Proceedings of the Fifth International Workshop on Agent Theories, Architectures, and Languages (ATAL-98); In this volume.

Erman L. D., Hayes-Roth F. Lesser V. R. and Reddy R. D; 1980. *The Hearsay-II speech-understanding system: Integrating knowledge to resolve uncertainty.* In ACM Computing Serveys 12(2).

Finin T., Labrou Y., and Mayfield J.; 1997. *KQML as an Agent Communication Language.* In Software Agents. Meno Park, AAAI Press.

Goodwin R. T., Rachlin J., Murthy S., Akkiraju R.; 1998. *Interactive Decision Support: Advantages of an Incomplete Utility Model.* AAAI Spring Symposium on Interactive and Mixed Initiative Decision-Theoretic Systems.

Gorti, S. R., Humair S., Sriram, R.D., Talukdar S., and Murthy S.; 1996. *Solving Constraint Satisfaction Problems Using A-Teams.* Artificial Intelligence for Engineering Design, **10**:1-19, Cambridge University Press.

Hoffman T; 1996. *A.I. Based Software Models Help Cut Production Costs.* Computer World September 2, 1996. http://www.computerworld.com/idx_usea.htm.

Holland J. H; 1975.*Adaptation in Natural and Artificial Systems.* University of Michigan Press, Ann Arbor MI.

Huberman, B., Lukose, R., and Hogg, T.; 1997. *An Economics Approach to Hard Computational Problems.* Science **275**:51-54.

Lee, H.S., Murthy, S., Haider, S.W., and Morse, D.; 1996. *Primary Production Scheduling at Steel-Making Industries.* IBM Journal of Research and Development.

Masayuki, N. and Morishita, S.; 1991. *Cooperative scheduling and its application to steelmaking processes.* IEEE Trans. on Industrial Electronics. **38**(2).

Müller J.; 1998. *The Right Agent (Architecture) to do the Right Thing.* In Intelligent Agents V --- Proceedings of the Fifth International Workshop on Agent Theories, Architectures, and Languages (ATAL-98); In this volume.

Murthy, S. Synergy in Cooperating Agents; 1992. *Designing Manipulators from Task Specifications.* Ph.D. Dissertation, Carnegie Mellon University.

Murthy, S., Rachlin, J., Akkiraju R., Wu F.; 1997. *Agent-Based Cooperative Scheduling.* In Constraints & Agents. Technical Report WS 1997-97-05. Menlo Park:AAAI Press.

Quadrel R.; 1991. *Asynchronous Design Environment: Architecture and Behavior.* Ph.D. Dissertation. Carnegie Mellon University.

Salman F., Kalagnanam J., Murthy S.; 1997. *Cooperative Strategies for Solving the Bicriteria Sparse Multiple Knapsack Problem.* IBM Research Report RC 21059(94164).

Shaw M.; 1998. *Madison Streamlines Business Processes with Integrated Information System.* Pulp and Paper, Volume 72, Issue 5.

Stone P., Veloso M.; 1998. *A Task Decomposition and Dynamic Role Assignment for Real-Time Strategic Teamwork.* In Intelligent Agents V --- Proceedings of the Fifth International Workshop on Agent Theories, Architectures, and Languages (ATAL-98); In this volume.

Sycara K, and Zeng D.; 1996. *Coordination of Multiple Intelligent Software Agents.* International Journal of Cooperative Information Systems.5(2 & 3)

Talukdar, S.N., Baerentzen, L., Gove, A., and Souza, P.; 1996. *Cooperation Schemes for Autonomous Agents.* Times Assincronos para Problemas Industriais, Sao Paulo.

Talukdar S.N., Pyo S.S., and Mehrotra R.; 1983. *Distributed Processors for Numerically Intense Problems.* Final Report for EPRI Project. **RP** 1983-1764-3

Talukdar S.N., and Ramesh V.C.; 1993. *Cooperative Methods for Security Planning.* 4th International Conference on Expert Systems Application to Power Systems. Melbourne, Australia, Jan 4-8.

Talukdar S.N., and Souza P.S. de.; 1992. *Scale Efficient Organizations.* In Proceedings of the 1992 IEEE International Conference on Systems, Man, and Cybernetics. Chicago, Illinois, Oct. 18-21.

Talukdar, S.N., Souza, P. de, and Murthy S.; 1993. *Organizations for Computer-Based Agents.* Engineering Intelligent Systems, 1(2).

Goal-Satisfaction in Large-Scale Agent Systems: A Transportation Example*

Onn Shehory
The Robotics Institute
Carnegie-Mellon U.
5000 Forbes Ave
Pittsburgh, PA 15213,
USA
onn@ri.cmu.edu
Tel: +1-412-268-3740
Fax: +1-412-268-5569

Sarit Kraus
Dept. of Math and CS,
Bar Ilan University,
Ramat Gan, 52900 Israel
sarit@cs.biu.ac.il
and
Inst. Adv. Comp. Studies,
Maryland U., College
Park, MD USA

Osher Yadgar
Dept. of Math and CS,
Bar Ilan University,
Ramat Gan, 52900
Israel
yadgar@cs.biu.ac.il
Tel: +972-3-5318863
Fax: +972-3-5353325

Abstract. We demonstrate the applicability of a low complexity physics-oriented approach to a large-scale transportation problem. The framework is based on modeling cooperative MAS by a physics-oriented model. According to the model, agent systems inherit physical properties, and therefore the evolution of the computational systems is similar to the evolution of physical systems. We provide a detailed algorithm to be used by a single agent and implement this algorithm in our simulations. Via these we demonstrate effective task allocation and execution in an open, dynamic MAS that consists of thousands of agents and tasks.

1 Introduction

Goal-satisfaction in MAS may require cooperation among the agents, but cooperative goal-satisfaction may be beneficial even if the agents can perform goals by themselves. Traditional task-allocation methods [15] require coordination via communication [3]. In very large agent communities there usually cannot be direct, on-line connection between all of the agents, as such a connection is too costly. Therefore, when the number of agents increases, the complexity of most of the cooperation methods becomes unbearable. To resolve the scale-up computational explosion of cooperation mechanisms in large MAS we present a different approach.

We apply a model based on methods from classical mechanics [13] to model large-scale agent systems. The physics-oriented methods are used to construct a beneficial cooperative goal-satisfaction algorithm to be used by the single agent within the system. In spite of the myriad differences between particles and computational agents, we show via simulations that, at least for the example problem that we have tested, using the physics-oriented approach enables effective cooperation and goal-satisfaction in very large agent-systems. In current research we are investigating the applicability of our model to other, non-physical domains.

---

* This material is based upon work supported in part by the NSF under grant IRI-9423967, ARPA/Rome Labs contract F30602-93-C-0241 (ARPA Order No. A716),the Army Research Lab under contract No. DAAL0197K0135 and ONR grant N00014-96-1222.

Many problems arise in large scale MAS research. In this paper we concentrate on investigating one facet—task allocation and execution within large-scale cooperative MAS.[2] More specifically, we consider cases in which cooperative autonomous agents allocate themselves to tasks. We describe and test a model that allows for the dynamic agent-task allocation and is appropriate for large-scale MAS. Testing is performed by simulating a dynamic agent system that follows our suggested mechanisms and consists of thousands of agents and tasks. To our best knowledge, this is the largest simulation of a task allocation and execution in a dynamic, open MAS. The model we present provides a solution to problems which were not addressed previously in MAS, and may be the basis for future solutions for a larger class of problem domains. We show here its applicability to one domain; in research in progress we have shown its applicability to another, less physical problem domain. Yet, more research is necessary to determine applicability to additional domains.

1.1 Assumptions, Notations and Concepts

We assume that the agents with which we deal have the ability to perceive the virtual[3] displacement in the goal-space, and can perceive the properties of other adjacent agents and goals. This may be done by sensors integrated into the agents. We also assume that each agent knows about the types of resources that other agents may have, but may be uncertain as to the particular resource-holdings of any other individual. These two assumptions are necessary since the agents are expected to propagate from state to state within the goal-space according to the properties of the surrounding agents, goals and obstacles. In order to enable such propagation, some knowledge regarding neighbors is necessary. We assume that each agent has a performance capability that can be measured using standard measurement units. The standard measurement will be used as a quantitative way of measuring the agents' success in fulfilling goals. In addition, we assume that there is a scaling method which is used to represent the displacements of the agents in the goal-space and to evaluate the mutual distances between goals and agents within this space. This assumption is necessary since virtual distances (or physical distances) are a significant factor in the model we present. We assume that goal-satisfaction can be achieved progressively. That is, a goal may be partially satisfied at one instant, and its remaining non-satisfied part may be complete at another point in time.

To present our model, we review concepts and notations from physics. The displacement vector of a particle i is denoted by r_i. v_i denotes the velocity, and a_i denotes the acceleration. The kinetic energy of a particle i is represented by k_i, and the potential is represented by V. The potential is a spatial function and therefore is sometimes called a field of potential or a potential-well. Forces can be derived from the potential. Each

---

[2] Cooperative MAS are frequently referred to as a Distributed Problem Solvers (DPS) [2] agent systems. In DPS agent systems as in cooperative MAS, agents attempt to increase the common outcome of the system.

[3] Since the goal-space is not necessarily physical, we do not assume physical distances and therefore call them virtual. In work in progress we show how such virtual distances can be modeled and computed.

particle i's mass is denoted by m_i, its displacement is denoted by the displacement vector $\mathbf{r}_i$, its momentum by $\mathbf{p}_i$ and the force that acts on it is denoted by $\mathbf{F}_i$.

1.2 Adapting Physics to MAS

MAS	Physics
identifying the environments where physics-oriented models are appropriate; matching particle properties to agents/goals	locating particle models and their properties
selecting the matter-states that can be used to model automated-agents' systems.	identifying states of matter and the particle behavior within
developing algorithms for agents' goal-satisfaction; adjusting to the physics system for validity of the algorithm	using mathematical formulation to predict and describe the properties and evolution of the selected particle model
analysis of the complexity and properties of the algorithm	theoretical and simulation-based analysis of physical particle systems behavior

Table 1. Distributed AI and physics for cooperative MAS

In the MAS that we consider, there is a large set of agents and a large set of goals they need to satisfy. Each agent has capabilities and should advance toward satisfying goals. We use a physics model that consists of particles which represent the agents and the goals to develop a distributed cooperative goal satisfaction mechanism. We first match between particles and their properties, agents and their capabilities, and goals and their properties (see table 1). Next, we identify the state of matter for modeling a community of agents and goals. The mathematical formulation that is used by physicists to describe and predict the properties and evolution of particles in these states of matter, serve as the basis for the development of algorithms for the agents. However, several modifications of the physics model are necessary to provide an efficient algorithm for automated agents.

In our model, agents and goals are modeled by dynamic particles and static particles, respectively. The match between particle properties and agent/goal properties is described in table 2. We model goal-satisfaction by a collision of dynamic particles with static particles. However, the properties of particle-collisions are different from the properties of goal-satisfaction and several adjustments are needed in order to provide the agents with efficient algorithms. These modifications are described in detail in this paper.

Automated Agents	Physics Model
community of agents satisfying goals	non-ionic liquid system
agent	dynamic particle
goal	static particle
agent's capabilities	particle's mass
(virtual) location in agent-goal space	location of particle
goal satisfaction	static-dynamic collision
algorithm for goals allocation	formal method to calculate evolution of displacement

Table 2. The match between the physics model components and the large-scale automated agents environments

2 Modeling Agents: A Physics-Oriented Approach

Classical mechanics provides a formal method for calculating the evolution of the displacement and the momentum of classical particles. For a particle i, the equations of motion are:

$$\mathbf{F}_i = m_i \ddot{\mathbf{r}}_i = m_i \mathbf{a}_i \quad \text{and} \quad \mathbf{p}_i = m_i \dot{\mathbf{r}}_i = m_i \mathbf{v}_i \tag{1}$$

The motion of a particle depends on the field of potential in which it moves and the force $\mathbf{F}_i = -m_i \nabla_{r_i} V(\mathbf{r})$. The model we present entails treating agents, goals and obstacles as particles. That is, each agent will have its equations of motion and an initial state. Note that an agent's equations of motion do not necessarily entail real physical motion. The potential field in which an agent acts represents the goals and the other agents in the environment. Subject to the potential field, agents solve the equations of motion and, according to the results, progress towards the solution of goals and either cooperate or avoid conflicts with other agents. The cooperation and conflict-avoidance are emergent properties of our physics-oriented model.

An appropriate physical system must consist of a potential that, when adapted to the agent-model, will lead the agents to successful and beneficial goal-satisfaction. The fluid model is most appropriate for our systems. As opposed to the solid state, a fluid system can evolve from its initial state into new, different states. Preferable is a model that does not require long range interactions (e.g., the non-ionic liquid model). In the model suggested in [13] the typical potential of a particle i in a non-ionic liquid was suggested (the Lennard-Jones potential). In the model developed for the specific transportation application dealt with in this paper we experimented with several different potential functions and finally concentrated on the following:

$$V(\mathbf{r})_{ij} = \gamma(\alpha \ln r_{ij} + \beta r_{ij}^{-2} + \chi r_{ij}^{-4}) \tag{2}$$

where r_{ij} corresponds to the distance of particle i from particle j. This potential diminishes after a short distance, thus implying that the interaction between the particles in the system is limited to short distances.

3   The Physics-Agent-System (PAS) Model

The cooperative MAS system with which we deal is modeled by a set of particles and a potential field. The agents in the system are modeled by dynamic particles and their potential-wells. The goals and the obstacles are modeled by static particles which are represented by fixed potential-wells. The superposition of the potential-wells of the particles, either agents or goals and obstacles, constructs a potential field. The particles move according to the field of potential and their own properties.

In the PAS model, the agent's capability of satisfying goals is represented by the mass of the particle that models it, and therefore by the potential-energy $k = mv^2/2$, which is a product of the mass, as well. Particles with a greater potential-energy model agents that can satisfy larger or more difficult goals and sub-goals. This means that a greater mass of a dynamic particle that models an agent (other properties remaining constant, and thus causing a greater potential-energy), entails a larger capability of goal-satisfaction by the agent. The mass of a fixed particle represents the size of the goal or the obstacle. This means that in order to satisfy a greater goal, which is modeled by a particle with a greater mass, more efforts are necessary on the part of the agents.

The displacement vector of a particle $\mathbf{r}_i$ models the displacement of the agent in the goal-space. Given the virtual displacement of an agent, its distances from other agents, goals and obstacles can be calculated. The potential is calculated according to these distances. The momentum vector $\mathbf{p}_i$ of particle i represents its physical velocity and is used for the calculation of the kinetic energy. In the PAS model, the velocity of a dynamic particle represents the rate of movement towards the satisfaction of a goal or a part of a goal.

3.1   Motion Towards Goal-Satisfaction

In the physical world, in general, the motion of particles is caused by the mutual attraction or repulsion between them. In the agents' system, the agents calculate the attraction (repulsion) and move according to the results of these calculations. The reaction of a particle to the field of potential will yield a change in its coordinates and energies. In our model, each agent will calculate the effect of the potential field on itself by solving a set of differential equations. According to the results of these calculations, it will move to a new state in the goal-domain (Section 3.3).

The steep decay of the potential function beyond a short distance from the center of the potential-well results in derived weak forces and negligible interaction. Physicists have shown that when the long-distance interactions are neglected, the results of simulations still agree with theoretical statistical-mechanics and thermodynamics [17, 11]. Therefore, it is common to cut off the range of interaction by cutting off the potential function after it diminishes to from 1 to 10% of its maximal value. The radius of interaction (and of the cut-off) is denoted by r_I.

Agents use numerical integration to solve the equations of motion that they must solve, with respect to time. The integration must be iterated frequently and performed with small time-steps dt. We determine the size of the time differential dt relying on the experience gathered in physics simulations [11]: we demand that a typical particle in the model will move a distance of r_0 in ~ 10 time-steps dt. This requirement implies that the average velocity $\bar{v}$ of a particle (at its initial displacement) directly affects dt by the relation $dt = r_0/\bar{v}$.

3.2   Collision and Goal-Satisfaction

The dynamics of the physical system which models the computational system leads to collisions between particles. Two types of collisions are possible: a collision between two dynamic particles, which we denote by DDC, and a collision between dynamic and static particles, denoted by SDC. In our model, the DDC represents the interaction between two agents. In order to prevent situations where agents overlap, the particles that model the agents have a mutual repulsion. The decision on which agents shall perform a specific goal will emerge from the repulsion. Dynamic particles that model agents shall have a potential that consists of a dominant repulsive component.

The SDC represents agent-goal interaction. In such interactions we would like the static particle that models the goal to attract the dynamic particle that models the agent. Adopting physical concepts, we use the notion of typical radius to specify the point from which the particle starts the collision. A typical radius σ of a particle is usually taken to be the distance from its center to the point wherein the force is zero. An SDC occurs when a dynamic particle is in the vicinity of a static particle. Vicinity here means that the distance between them is a few typical radii (r_0).

The goal-satisfaction is performed during the collision. An agent that reaches a goal may either completely or partially satisfy it. In both cases, the model requires a reduction in the magnitude of the goal. This implies that the mass of the modeling particle shall be reduced, but mass-reduction is not a physical property of such a collision. Therefore, some modifications of the model shall be done, as long as they do not affect the general evolution of the system. This will be possible if the model consists of a scheme for a temporal partition of the evolution of the system. This means that the evolution of the system will be partitioned into several time segments (different from dt, much longer), and in each temporal segment the physical evolution of the system will not depend on the other segments.

3.3   A Protocol for a Single Agent

In order to cause evolution of the system towards goal-satisfaction, each agent uses the information that it can gather by observation (e.g., via sensors) about its neighboring agents and goals and regarding its previous state. According to this information, the agent will construct the local field of potential and solve the equations of motion. The results of the equations of motion will enable the agent to decide what its next step towards goal-satisfaction will be. The exact detailed algorithm for the single agent i is as follows:

Loop and perform the goal-reaching and goal-satisfaction processes until the resources necessary for satisfying goals have been depleted or no goals within the interaction range r_I have been observed for several time-segments.

The goal-reaching process.

1. Advance the time counter t by dt.
2. Locate all of the agents and goals within the range r_I, the predefined interaction distance. Denote the distance to any neighboring entity j by r_{ij}.
3. Calculate the mutual potential (using equation 2) with respect to each of the agents and goals within the range.
4. Sum over all of the pairwise potentials $V(r_{ij})$ and calculate the gradient of the sum to derive the force F_i.
5. Using F_i and the previous state $\mathbf{r}_i(t - dt)$, $\mathbf{p}_i(t - dt)$, solve the equations of motion as described in Section 2, in equation 1.
6. The results of the equations of motion will be a new pair $\mathbf{r}_i(t)$, $\mathbf{p}_i(t)$. Move to the new state that corresponds to the displacement $\mathbf{r}_i(t)$.
7. At each time-step, after moving to a new state, calculate the new kinetic energy and potential according to the new coordinates $\mathbf{r}_i(t)$, $\mathbf{p}_i(t)$.
8. If your distance from the center of a particle that models a goal is greater than r_0, return to step 1. Otherwise, start the goal-satisfaction process.

The goal-satisfaction process.
After reaching a goal, the agent must satisfy all or at least parts of it:

- Move into the potential-well that models the goal according to the physical properties of the entities involved in the process and perform the goal.
- If m_a, the mass of the particle that models the agent, is smaller than m_g, the mass of the particle that models the goal, subtract m_a from m_g. Else, $m_g = 0$. In a case of depleting resources, m_a is reduced in a similar way. Return to step 1.

The iterative method which we propose leads to a gradual reduction in the amount and size of the goals to be satisfied, and will lead, finally, to completion of the goals.

4 Simulation

To examine our model and show its applicability to real problems we performed a set of simulations. Via these we demonstrate effective task allocation and execution in an open, dynamic MAS that consists of thousands of agents and tasks. The problem domain for which the simulations where performed is as follows. We simulate freight deliveries within a city. Such problems in real environments are commonly solved by having one or a few dispatch centers to which delivery requests are addressed and these each centrally plans and accordingly allocates delivery tasks to delivering agents. This method may face bottlenecks and inefficiency when a large number of agents and tasks is present. We demonstrate how the PAS model can overcome this limitation.

We consider the road-network of a large city. A snapshot of a part of this network is depicted in Figure 1. In this Figure squares represent messengers and circles represent tasks. The city map is represented by a lattice-like graph. The boundaries of the city are $20,000 \times 30,000$ meters. The lattice includes vertices located 200 meters apart from each other. An edge may exist between each two neighboring vertices. Each vertex represents a junction and each edge represents a road between two junctions. We designate the map a "Full Lattice" when each vertex has edges emanating to all of its neighboring vertices. A more realistic map would have some of the edges missing. To obtain such a map we use some probability to determine the existence of each edge. As a result disconnected sub-graphs "clusters" may occur. In such cases the largest cluster will be selected to represent the city. A map is termed an "X% Lattice" when lattice and cluster generation are performed taking the probability of including an edge in the lattice to X%. Note that the structure of cities and roadways regulations may prevent movement along the shortest path between two locations, as assumed by the general algorithm. Thus, in the simulation, the distance between two locations l_1 and l_2 was calculated as the shortest way that one could drive from l_1 to l_2. Furthermore, if the direction for movement[4] $\hat{v}$ calculated by the agent in the goal-reaching process algorithm does not agree with a road direction $r\hat{o}ad$, then the road with the smallest angel with $\hat{v}$ is selected for movement. This selection is not different from a physical behavior in environments with obstacles, and is therefore justified.

The simulation consists of iterations in which new freights dynamically appear at random locations on the map. The freights have an initial size which is set to $1\,kg$ in the homogeneous case and to a random value (out of a given range) in the heterogeneous cases. In addition, each freight has a random destination. Messengers (agents) follow our algorithm to perform tasks of reaching freights and delivering them to their destination.

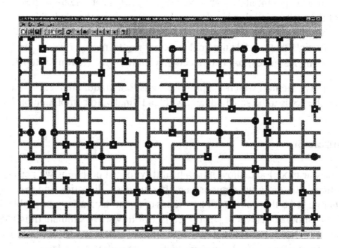

Fig. 1. A fragment of city map

We have performed several different types of simulations. These varied over the amount of tasks and agents involved, the homogeneity of agents and tasks, the reliability of communication and the intensity of the lattice map.

---

[4] The notation $\hat{v}$ refers to the direction of a vector **v**.

Our simulations were initially performed such that agents and tasks are homogeneous in that they have similar capabilities and capacities. We started with these since they are simpler to handle and predict. However, it was necessary to examine cases in which agents and tasks are not homogeneous, which are more realistic. In the homogeneous case, masses of particle were set to $1\,kg$, whereas in the heterogeneous case masses were set randomly out of a given distribution. We have also examined several lattice maps, starting from a full lattice and moving to 90% and 80% lattice maps. Since we have seen no significant difference in the performance between the different maps, we concentrated on the 90% lattice map. To learn the effect of unreliable communication on the performance we experimented with a case in which messages are passed with an arrival probability smaller than 1. Additional parameters of the simulations are as follows. During the simulation no new messengers appear. Parameter values are $\gamma = 1$ $\alpha = 4000$, $\beta = -15E5$, $\chi = 5E11$ (these are used in equation 2), R_0 is 100 meters, R_1 is 2,000 meters. Note that these values where not arbitrarily chosen. Rather, we experimented with a variety of values to fine-tune the system until we arrived at these coefficients. We sought timely task performance, and these coefficients yielded the best results.

In the homogeneous case, we considered five settings of agent and task quantities. In the 4 simulation settings in which the number of agents was 300, 400, 600 and 800 the initial number of tasks was 1200. In the case of 1200 agent the initial number of tasks was 1500. In all 5 settings additional tasks where arriving at a rate of 600 tasks per hour. The different quantities of agents in the first four settings allowed us to study the effect of the number of messengers (hence the messengers/freights ratio as well) on the system's performance. The fifth setting was aimed mainly at studying the effects of up-scaling.

The main results of the simulations are summarized in the graphs below.

- In Figure 2 the ratio between the number of messengers in the system and the number of agents that are simultaneously involved in movement towards tasks is presented. The term *Free messenger quantity* is the number of messengers which are currently moving towards freights. The other messengers are performing tasks. From the graph one can observe that as the number of messengers involved increases, so does (linearly) the number of those that simultaneously move towards tasks. This observation results in reduction in the time required for task execution (as can be seen in Figure 4).
- The term *Freight quantity* in Figure 3 is the number of freights currently waiting for a messenger to deliver them. We observe that this number drops sharply as the quantity of messengers goes up. The critical point where transition occurs is around 500 messengers. Given that 1200 tasks are present, this means that for significantly lowering the number of freights which are simultaneously waiting to be delivered it is enough to have a ratio of around 0.4 between messengers' and tasks' quantities in the system. Increasing the ratio over 0.5 does not bring about a significant increase in the performance (with respect to the numbers of freights waiting to be delivered).
- Figure 4 presents the time it takes a messenger, who successfully delivers a freight to its destination, to reach this freight. One can observe that as the number and density of messengers increases, the time which is required for a messenger to

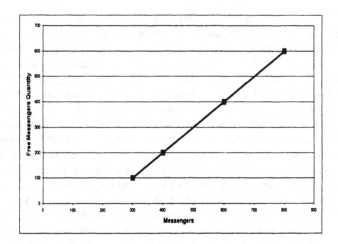

Fig. 2. The number of messengers moving towards freights (y axis) as a function of the number of messengers in the system (x axis).

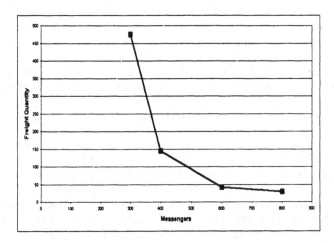

Fig. 3. The number of freights waiting for delivery (y axis) decreases as the number of agents in the system (x axis) increases.

reach a freight increases as well. This is not desirable. However, increasing the density significantly reduces the number of freights which simultaneously wait for being delivered. In addition, as shown in Figure 5, the average waiting time of the freights decreases as well.

- In Figure 5 the freight average waiting time, that is, the time that a freight that was successfully delivered to its destination has been waiting before being handled by a messenger is presented. A sharp reduction in the waiting time is observed. We observe phase transition around 500 messengers, similar to the phase transition in

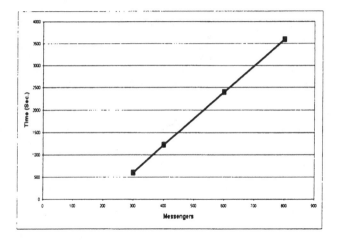

Fig. 4. The time for reaching a task (y axis) increases as the number and density of agents in the system (x axis) increases.

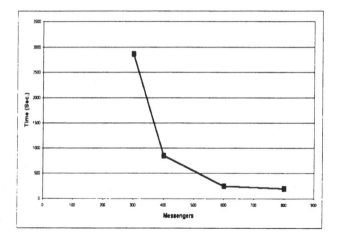

Fig. 5. The average time freights wait for delivery (y axis) decreases as a function of the number of agents in the system (x axis).

the case of *Freight quantity* (Figure 3). This further supports the observation that it is not worth while to increase the agent/task ratio to above some ratio which is, in our simulation settings, around 0.4 to 0.5.

– Figure 6 presents the average freight fulfillment time, which is the time between the freight initiation and its arrival at its destination. Less steep than in previous graphs, yet clear, is the improvement in the performance reached around 500 messengers. It is important to notice that for 600 messengers and more the task execution time is less then 1500 seconds. For a city of the size with which we deal (20 × 30 km)

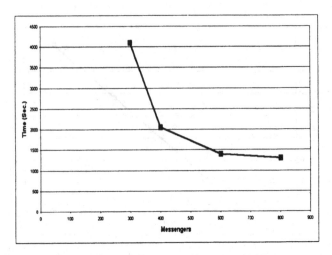

Fig. 6. The average time for task allocation and execution (y axis) decreases as the number of agents in the system (x axis) increases.

with a speed limit of 50km/hr, this is a desirable fulfillment time.

- Figure 7 presents one of the results of a set of simulations of heterogeneous ensembles of agents and tasks, where the probability of message reception varied between 50% and 100%. That is, in this simulations an agent may not receive some of the information regarding neighboring tasks and agents although this was transmitted. The initial masses of tasks was set randomly between $1kg$ and $100kg$, while the masses of the agents was set randomly between $80kg$ and $180kg$. If the capacity of an agent was smaller than the size of the task, it delivers only part of the task at a time. The number of agents in this set of simulations was 600 and the initial number of tasks was 1200. The other parameters were as in the previous simulations.

  Our results indicate that the heterogeneity of the agents does not significantly change the behavior of the system. From Figure 7 we can conclude that the freight fulfillment time increases linearly when the probability of messages arrival decreases. However, even with 50% arrival of messages, the fulfillment time is better than in the case of 400 messengers with 100% arrival of messages (see Figure 5). Similar results were obtained with respect to the other parameters.

Some additional experiments were not presented here for reasons of space. From the results presented above and these experiments we conclude the following:

- The PAS model can be applied for use in large scale agent systems to solve real problems.
- An increase in the number of agents in the system does not increase the amount of computations per agent. Thus, larger systems do not require more computation time.
- An increase in the number of agents in the system, holding the number of tasks constant, is beneficial only to some extent. Beyond some agents/tasks ratio, no

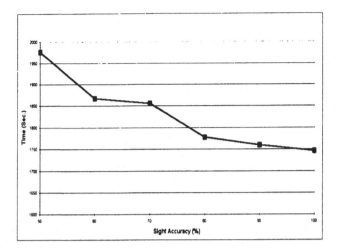

Fig. 7. The average time for task allocation and execution (y axis) decreases as the accuracy of message reception (x axis) increases.

significant improvement in performance is observed. We believe this phenomenon results from redundancy in densely populated agent systems.

- The results observed are similar for different densities of the lattice map used as well as for low probabilities of unreliable communication channels. They become better when the the distribution of tasks is not even, as typically happens in the center of large metropolitans.

5 Related Work

The issue of allocating agents to goals has widely been discussed among DAI researchers. The Contract Net Protocol (CNP) [15] uses negotiation based on task announcements, bids and contracts for task allocation. While the CNP is based on the exchange of information, the model we present minimizes the transmitted information and thus enables large-scale systems to be efficient. A study of planning in large-scale agent-systems has been presented in [19, 18]. In that research, the general-equilibrium approach from economics serves as the theoretical basis for the planning mechanism. We also discuss large-scale systems and apply an analytical model for designing the distributed planning mechanism, however we use a physics-oriented approach for cooperative MAS, not for competitive agents.

A large body of DAI research studies coordination among agents for distributed problem solving (for example, [2], PGP [5], GPGP [1], [6, 12, 20]). In [4], Durfee and Lesser study the Partial Global Planning (PGP) approach to coordination by implementing it in the Distributed Vehicle Monitoring Testbed (DVMT). The DVMT is a network of vehicle monitoring nodes. Each node has a planner that plans incrementally. Nodes do not communicate their detailed actions, but do communicate according to a meta-level organization. A PGP planner modifies local plans as required due to incoming messages. In its incremental planning and restricted communication the PGP model is similar to our model. The DVMT task domain which was used as a testbed for both PGP and GPGP includes monitoring traffic and directing it. This is performed by the agents generating tentative maps for vehicle movements in their areas. Our transportation framework is different: we require that a transportation task be attached to agents that plan for it and perform it. Therefore, our simulated transportation system is significantly different from DVMT.

The tileworld model [10] was used as a testbed for planning and task allocation and execution in multi-agent systems. The utilization of physics methods allows for a model that is significantly richer than the tileworld model. The tileworld model distinguishes (at least) two different procedures—deliberation and path planning—which are usually performed sequentially, whereas in the physics-based model an inherent property is interleaving planning and execution. And, while the tileworld proves to work successfully for systems of dozens of tasks and agents, (15 agents, 80 tasks in [6]), its computational complexity[5] will probably disable scaling up to thousands of tasks and agents. Such system size is allowed by the physics based model, as our simulations prove.

Ephrati, Pollack and Ur [6] suggest the multi-agent filtering strategy as a means for coordination among agents. They have conducted several experiments that show, that for the tile-world, this strategy improves the performance of the agents. This coordination is achieved without explicit negotiation. In our work we do not suggest a strategy, rather we suggest a method for modeling the goal-agent environment. Based upon this model we suggest a detailed algorithm for the single agent for acting efficiently in the environment.

Glance and Huberman [7] present a detailed physical formalism of the dynamics of the collective action of a system of individuals. In our work the main issue is the physical behavior of the single agent. Shoham and Tennenholtz [14] presented results of simulations that were performed in order to perceive the emergence of conventions in multi-agent systems. In our research, we discuss emergent cooperation and determine the social laws to be such—physical laws—that they will cause the emergent cooperation of the system when this cooperation is necessary. Mataric [9] proposes defining a set of basic interactions that will allow the simplification of group behavior analysis. Stone and Veloso [16] follow a similar approach for real-time coordination by introducing agent roles and formations of agents based on these roles. In our work, we concentrate on the nature of the basic interactions and adopt the physical interactions among particles to model the interactions among agents and goals. We do not pre-define formations and do not require that agent be part of such formations. Yet, our mechanism allows for evolution into such formations.

6 Conclusion

The problem of the behavior of agents in very large agent-societies imposes difficulties that are hard to solve even when the proposed solutions are of low-order polynomial

---

[5] As Kinny and Georgeff [8] state: "to reduce the complexity...we employed a simplified Tileworld with no tiles."

complexity. The approach which we present suggests a solution to some aspects of this problem. We provide a method for task allocation which is applicable to several classes of large-scale cooperative MAS. The physics-based approach we present results in complexity which is, on the side of the single agent, very low and may even be $O(1)$. Such results are possible since we use a model whose behavior is already known. Therefore, we are not required to perform the numerous explicit calculations that would have otherwise been necessary.

The model used and the algorithm that enables the single agent to act according to the model result in agents allocating themselves to goals in order for these to be satisfied. The agent-goal matching is an emergent result of the physics-oriented behavior of the agents. In cases where too many agents fit the requirements of the same goal, our model will disable some of them from reaching the goal, via mutual rejection. As we have shown, our algorithm converges to a solution within reasonable time and leads to agent-goal allocation and execution. Our method does not lead to the optimal allocation, but reaching an optimal allocation requires complete on-line information about all of the agents and goals comprising the system and, for a large class of problems, an exponential computation-time.

Our model can rely on theoretical and experimental results that are already known from physics. Nevertheless we have performed simulations which support the theoretical observations. According to results from physics, we can predict the evolution of the modeled agent-system, since it should evolve in the same manner as a corresponding physical system. The local interactions, which enable one to derive the global behavior of the system, assure a low computational complexity of the model. In very large-scale agent-systems, this approach provides a model that allows for emergent cooperative goal-satisfaction activity, as shown in our experiments.

References

1. K. Decker and V. Lesser. Designing a family of coordination algorithms. In V. Lesser, editor, *Proceedings of the First International Conference on Multi-Agent Systems*, pages 73–80, San Francisco, CA, 1995. MIT Press. Longer version available as UMass CS-TR 94–14.
2. E. Durfee. *Coordination of Distributed Problem Solvers*. Kluwer Academic Publishers, Boston, 1988.
3. E. Durfee, V. Lesser, and D. Korkill. Coherent cooperation among communicating problem solvers. *IEEE Transactions on Computers*, 36(C):1275–1291, 1987.
4. E. Durfee and V. Lesser. Predictability vs. responsiveness: Coordinating problem solvers in dynamic domains. In *Proceedings of the Seventh National Conference on Artificial Intelligence*, pages 66–71, St. Paul, MN, August 1988.
5. E. Durfee and V. Lesser. Partial global planning: A coordination framework for distributed hypothesis formation. *IEEE Transactions on Systems, Man, and Cybernetics*, 21(5), 1167–1183, September 1991. (Special Issue on Distributed Sensor Networks).
6. E. Ephrati, M. Pollack, and S. Ur. Deriving multi-agent coordination through filtering strategies. In *Proceedings of the 14th International Joint Conference on Artificial Intelligence*, pages 679–685, Montreal, Canada, August 1995.
7. N. Glance and B. Huberman. The outbreak of cooperation. *Journal of Mathematical Sociology*, 17(4):281–302, 1993.

8. D. Kinny and M. Georgeff. Commitment and effectiveness of situated agents. In *Proceedings of the Twelfth International Joint Conference on Artificial Intelligence*, pages 82–88, Sydney, Australia, August 1991.

9. M. Mataric. Kin recognition, similarity, and group behavior. In *Proceedings of the 15th Cognitive Science Society Conference*, pages 705–710, 1993.

10. M. Pollack and M. Ringuette. Introducing the tileworld: Experimentally evaluating agent architectures. In *Proceedings of the 8th National Conference on Artificial Intelligence*, pages 183–189, Boston, MA, 1990.

11. D. Rapaport. Large-scale molecular dynamics simulation using vector and parallel computers. *Computational Physics Reports*, 9(1):1–53, 1988.

12. S. Rustogi and M. Singh. The bases of effective coordination in decentralized multiagent systems. In this volume.

13. O. Shehory and S. Kraus. Cooperation and goal-satisfaction without communication in large-scale agent-systems. In *Proceedings of the 12th European Conference on Artificial Intelligence*, pages 544–548, Budapest, Hungary, 1996.

14. Y. Shoham and M. Tennenholtz. Emergent conventions in multi-agent systems: initial experimental results and observations. In *Proceedings of the 3rd Conference on Principles of Knowledge Representation and Reasoning*, Cambridge, MA, 1992.

15. R. Smith. The contract net protocol: high-level communication and control in a distributed problem solver. *IEEE Transaction on Computers*, 29(12):1104–1113, 1980.

16. P. Stone and M. Veloso. Task decomposition and dynamic role assignment for real-time strategic teamwork. In this volume.

17. C. Trozzi and G. Ciccotti. Stationary nonequilibrium states by molecular dynamics. II. Newton's law. *Physical Review A*, 29(2):916–925, 1984.

18. M. Wellman. Market-oriented programming: Some early lessons. In S. Clearwater, editor, *Market-Based Control: A Paradigm for Distributed Resource Allocation*. Chapter 4, 1995.

19. M. Wellman. A market-oriented programming environment and its application to distributed multicommodity flow problems. *Journal of Artificial Intelligence Research*, 1:1–23, 1993.

20. M. Yokoo, E. Durfee, T. Ishida, and K. Kuwabara. Distributed constraint satisfaction for formalizing distributed problem solving. In *Proceedings of the Twelfth International Conference on Distributed Computing Systems*, pages 614–621, 1992.

Task Decomposition and Dynamic Role Assignment for Real-Time Strategic Teamwork*

Peter Stone and Manuela Veloso

Computer Science Department, Carnegie Mellon University
Pittsburgh, PA 15213, USA
{pstone,veloso}@cs.cmu.edu

Abstract. Multi-agent domains consisting of teams of agents that need to collaborate in an adversarial environment offer challenging research opportunities. In this paper, we introduce *periodic team synchronization* domains, as time-critical environments in which agents act autonomously with limited communication, but they can periodically synchronize in a full-communication setting. We present a team agent structure that allows for an agent to capture and reason about team agreements. We achieve collaboration between agents through the introduction of *formations*. A formation decomposes the task space defining a set of *roles*. Homogeneous agents can flexibly switch roles within formations, and agents can change formations dynamically, according to pre-defined triggers to be evaluated at run-time. This flexibility increases the performance of the overall team. Our team structure further includes pre-planning for frequent situations. We fully implemented this approach in the domain of robotic soccer. Our simulator team made it to the semi-finals of the RoboCup-97 competition, in which 29 teams participated. It achieved a total score of 67–9 over six different games, and successfully demonstrated its flexible team structure. Using the same team structure, our small robot team won the RoboCup-97 small-robot competition, in which 4 teams participated. It achieved a total score of 13–1 over 4 games and also demonstrated its flexible team structure.

1   Introduction

A multi-agent system which involves several agents that collaborate towards the achievement of joint objectives is viewed as a *team* of agents. Most proposed teamwork structures (e.g. joint intentions, shared plans) rely on agents in a multi-agent system to negotiate and/or contract with each other in order to initiate team plans [4, 7, 8]. However, in dynamic, real-time domains with unreliable communication, complex negotiation protocols may take too much time and/or be infeasible due to communication restrictions.

Our work has been focused in time-critical environments in which agents in a team alternate between periods of limited and unlimited communication. This focus

---
* This research is sponsored in part by the DARPA/RL Knowledge Based Planning and Scheduling Initiative under grant number F30602-97-2-0250. The views and conclusions contained in this document are those of the authors and should not be interpreted as representing the official policies or endorsements, either expressed or implied, of the U. S. Government.

leads us to introduce the concept of *Periodic Team Synchronization* (PTS) domains. In PTS domains, during the limited (or no) communication periods, agents need to act autonomously, while still working towards a common team goal. Time-critical environments require real-time response and therefore eliminate the possibility of heavy communication between team agents. However, in PTS domains, agents can periodically synchronize in a safe, full-communication setting. In this paper, we introduce a flexible teamwork structure that allows for task decomposition and dynamic role assignment in PTS domains.

In PTS domains, teams are long-term entities so that it makes sense for them to have periodic, reliable, private synchronization intervals in which they can form off-line agreements for future use in unreliable, time-critical environments. This view of teams is complementary to teams that form on the fly for a specific action and keep communicating throughout the execution of that action as in [4]. Instead, in PTS domains, teams define coordination protocols during the synchronization opportunity and then disperse into the environment, acting autonomously with little or no communication possible.

It has been claimed that pre-determined team actions are not flexible or robust to failure [27]. A key contribution of our work is the demonstration that pre-determined multi-agent protocols can facilitate effective teamwork while retaining flexibility in PTS domains. We call these pre-determined protocols *locker-room agreements*. Formed during the periodic synchronization opportunities, locker-room agreements are remembered identically by all agents and allow them to coordinate efficiently. In the context of [3], locker-room agreements can be viewed as C-commitments, or commitments by team members to do the appropriate thing at the right time, as opposed to S-commitments with which agents adopt each other's goals. In the context of [5], the creation of a locker-room agreement is norm acceptance while its use is norm compliance.

In this paper, we introduce an agent architecture suited for team agents in PTS domains. The architecture allows for an agent to act appropriately based on locker-room agreements. Within the framework presented in [15], the architecture is for interactive software and hardware multi-agents.

Since the agents act autonomously and sense the world individually, they may have different views of what is best for the team. However, contrary to self-interested agents for which coordination may or may not be rational [2, 17], our agents have no individual incentives. Their performance is measured as a unit: each agent's highest goal is the success of the team.

A straightforward approach to PTS domains is to break the task at hand into multiple rigid roles, assigning one agent to each role. Thus each component of the task is accomplished and there are no conflicts among agents in terms of how they should accomplish the team goal. However such an approach is subject to several problems: inflexibility to short-term changes (e.g. one robot is non-operational), inflexibility to long-term changes (e.g. a route is blocked), and a lack of facility for reassigning roles.

We introduce instead *formations* as a team structure. A formation decomposes the task space defining a set of roles with associated behaviors. In a general scenario with heterogeneous agents, subsets of homogeneous agents can flexibly switch roles within formations, and agents can change formations dynamically. This flexibility increases the performance of the overall team. The homogeneous assumption underlying the desired flexible role-switching behavior creates a challenge in terms of determining if and when they should switch roles.

Within these PTS domains and our flexible teamwork structure, several challenges arise. For example, how to represent and follow locker-room agreements; how to determine the appropriate times for agents to change roles and/or formations; how to ensure that all agents are using the same formation; and how to ensure that all roles in a formation are filled. Since the agents are autonomous and do not share memory, they could easily become uncoordinated.

In a nutshell, the main contributions of this paper are: the introduction of the concepts of PTS domains and locker-room agreements; the definition of a general team agent architecture structure for defining a flexible teamwork structure; the facilitation of smooth transitions among roles and entire formations; and a method for using roles to define pre-compiled multi-step, multi-agent plans.

Our work is situated in an example of a PTS domain in which we conducted our research, robotic soccer [10]. In both simulated and robotic systems, teams can plan strategies before the game, at halftime, or at other breakpoints, but during the course of the game, communication is limited. There are several other examples of PTS domains, such as hospital/factory maintenance [6], multi-spacecraft missions [21], search and rescue, and battlefield combat [27].

2 Team Member Architecture

Our new teamwork structure is situated within a team member architecture suitable for PTS domains in which individual agents can capture locker-room agreements and respond to the environment, while acting autonomously. Based on a standard agent paradigm, our team member architecture allows agents to sense the environment, to reason about and select their actions, and to act in the real world. At team synchronization opportunities, the team also makes a locker-room agreement for use by all agents during periods of low communication. Figure 1 shows the functional input/output model of the architecture.

The agent keeps track of three different types of state: the *world state*, the *locker-room agreement*, and the *internal state*. The agent also has two different types of behaviors: *internal behaviors* and *external behaviors*.

The World State reflects the agent's conception of the real world, both via its sensors and via the predicted effects of its actions. It is updated as a result of processed sensory information. It may also be updated according to the predicted effects of the external behavior module's chosen actions. The world state is directly accessible to both internal and external behaviors.

The Locker-Room Agreement is set by the team when it is able to privately synchronize. It defines the flexible teamwork structure as presented below as well as inter-agent communication protocols. The locker-room agreement may change periodically when the team is able to re-synchronize; however, it generally remains unchanged. The locker-room agreement is accessible only to internal behaviors.

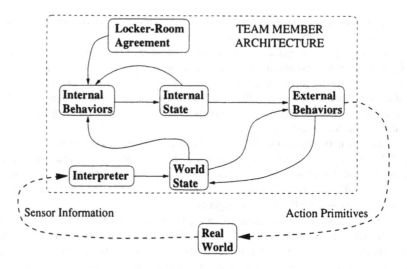

Fig. 1. The team member architecture for PTS domains.

The Internal State stores the agent's internal variables. It may reflect previous and current world states, possibly as specified by the locker-room agreement. For example, the agent's role within a team behavior could be stored as part of the internal state, as could a distribution of past world states. The agent updates its internal state via its internal behaviors.

The Internal Behaviors update the agent's internal state based on its current internal state, the world state, and the team's locker-room agreement.

The External Behaviors reference the world and internal states, sending commands to the actuators. The actions affect the real world, thus altering the agent's future percepts. External behaviors consider only the world and internal states, without direct access to the locker-room agreement.

Internal and external behaviors are similar in structure, as they are both sets of condition/action pairs where conditions are logical expressions over the inputs and actions are themselves behaviors as illustrated in Figure 2. In both cases, a behavior is a directed acyclic graph (DAG) of arbitrary depth. The leaves of the DAGs are the behavior types' respective outputs: internal state changes for internal behaviors and action primitives for external behaviors.

Our notion of behavior is consistent with that laid out in [13]. In particular, behaviors can be nested at different levels: selection among lower-level behaviors can be considered a higher-level behavior, with the overall agent behavior considered a single "do-the-task" behavior. There is one such *top-level* internal behavior and one top-level external behavior; they are called when it is time to update the internal state or act in the world, respectively. We now introduce the team structure that builds upon this team member architecture.

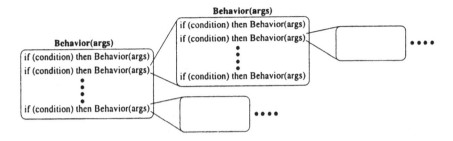

Fig. 2. Internal and external behaviors are organized in a directed acyclic graph.

3 Team Structure

Common to all players, the locker-room agreement defines the team structure while team members are acting in a time-critical environment with low bandwidth communication. In this section, we introduce a structure for capturing locker-room agreements. It defines sets of agent roles with protocols for switching among them. It can also define multi-step multi-agent plans for execution in specific situations. It indirectly affects the agent external behaviors by changing the agents' internal states via internal behaviors.

Our teamwork structure involves *flexible roles* that are organized into *formations*, which we now introduce.

3.1 Role

A *role*, r, consists of a specification of an agent's internal and external behaviors. The conditions and arguments of any behavior can depend on the agent's current role, which is a function of its internal state. At the extreme, a top-level behavior could be a switch, calling an entirely different behavior graph for each possible role. However, the role can affect the agent's overall behavior at any level of its complete behavior graph. Notice that roles need not be rigid: by specifying ranges of parameters or behavior options, the agent filling role r can be given an arbitrary amount of flexibility.

For example, a role in the robotic soccer domain, can be a position such as a midfielder. In the hospital maintenance domain, a role could specify the wing of the hospital whose floors the appropriate agent should keep clean, while in the web search domain, it could specify a server to search.

3.2 Formation

We achieve collaboration between agents through the introduction of *formations* as a team structure. A formation decomposes the task space defining a set of roles. Formations include as many roles as there are agents in the team, so that each role is filled by one agent. In addition, formations can specify sub-formations, or *units*, that do not involve the whole team. A unit consists of a subset of roles from the formation, a *captain*, and intra-unit interactions among the roles.

For a team of n agents $A = \{a_1, a_2, \ldots, a_n\}$, any formation is of the form $F = \{R, \{U_1, U_2, \ldots, U_k\}\}$ where R is a set of roles $R = \{r_1, r_2, \ldots, r_n\}$ such that $i \neq j \Rightarrow r_i \neq r_j$. Note that there are the same number of roles as there are agents. Each unit U_i is a subset of R: $U_i = \{r_{i1}, r_{i2}, \ldots, r_{ik}\}$ such that $r_{ia} \in R$, $a \neq b \Rightarrow r_{ia} \neq r_{ib}$ and r_{i1} is the captain. The map $A \mapsto R$ is not pre-specified: roles can be filled by different homogeneous agents. A single role may be a part of any number of units and formations.

Formations can affect the agent's external behaviors by specifying inter-role interactions. Since roles can be re-used among formations, their formation-specific interactions cannot be included in the role definitions. Instead these interactions are part of the formation specification.

Units are used to deal with local problem solving issues. Rather than involving the entire team in a sub-problem, the roles that address it are organized into a unit.

Roles and formations are introduced independently from the agents that are to fill them. The locker-room agreement specifies an initial formation, a map from agents to roles, and run-time triggers for dynamic changing of formations. At any given time, each agent should know what formation the team is currently using. Agents keep mappings $A \mapsto R$ from teammates to roles in the current formation. All this team structuring information is stored in the agent's internal state. It can be altered via the agent's internal behaviors. Thus, in all, the locker-room agreement is used to coordinate task decomposition among agents, to coordinate dynamic team re-alignment during time-critical stages, and for defining pre-compiled multi-agent plans. The locker-room agreement can be hard-wired or it can be the result of automatic deliberative multi-agent planning. Figure 3 illustrates a team of agents smoothly switching roles and formations over time.

Since agents are autonomous and operating in a PTS domain, during the periods of limited communication there is no guarantee that they will all think that the team is using the same formation, nor that they have accurate maps $A \mapsto R$. In fact, the only guarantee is that each agent knows its own current role. Efficient low-bandwidth communication protocols allow agents to inform each other of their roles periodically. Further details on our implemented low-bandwidth communication protocol can be found in [23].

Similarly, communication can be used as an alternative to changing formations using run-time triggers, or as a back-up should an agent not observe a run-time trigger. Although communication can be useful, we create robust behaviors for team agents which ensure that the behaviors never absolutely depend upon having correct, up-to-date knowledge of teammates' internal states: they must degrade gracefully.

4　Implementation in Robotic Soccer

Robotic soccer is a very good example of a PTS domain: teams can coordinate before the game, at half-time, and at other break points, but communication is limited during play [10, 12]. Robotic soccer systems have been recently developed both in simulation [14, 24, 25] and with real robots [1, 9, 19, 20, 28]. The research presented in this paper was first developed in simulation and it has also been successfully used on our real robot team.

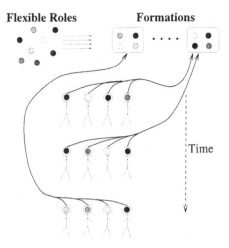

Fig. 3. Flexible roles and formations. Different roles are represented as differently shaded circles. Formations are possibly overlapping collections of roles. All roles and formations are known to all players. A player's current role is indicated by the shaded circle in its head and its current formation is indicated by an arrow to the formation. The players first switch roles while staying in the same formation; then they switch to an entirely new formation.

The soccer server [16], version 3 of which serves as the substrate simulator for the research reported in this paper, captures enough real-world complexities to be a very challenging domain. This simulator is realistic in many ways: (i) the players' vision is limited; (ii) the players can communicate by posting to a blackboard that is visible (but not necessarily intelligible) to all players; (iii) each player is controlled by a separate process; (iv) each team has 11 members; (v) players have limited stamina; (vi) actuators and sensors are noisy; (vii) dynamics and kinematics are modelled; and (viii) play occurs in *real time*: the agents must react to their sensory inputs at roughly the same speed as human or robotic soccer players. The Soccer Server was successfully used as the basis for the RoboCup-97 simulator competition in which 29 teams participated [10].

One approach to task decomposition in the Soccer Server is to assign fixed positions to agents.[2] Such an approach leads to several problems: i) short-term inflexibility in that the players cannot adapt their positions to the ball's location on the field; ii) long-term inflexibility in that the team cannot adapt to opponent strategy; and iii) local inefficiency in that players often get tired running across the field back to their positions after chasing the ball. Our formations allow for flexible teamwork and combat these problems. (As the term "position" is often used to denote the concept of "role" in the soccer domain, in this section we use the two terms interchangeably.)

---

[2] One of the teams in Pre-RoboCup-97 (IROS'96) used and depended upon these assignments: the players would pass to the fixed positions regardless of whether there was a player there.

4.1 Domain Instantiations of Roles and Formations

Figure 4 shows a sample top-level external behavior used by a team agent. The agent's top priority is to locate the ball. If the ball's location is known, it moves towards the ball or goes to its position (i.e., to assume its role), depending on its internal state. It also responds to any requested communications from teammates.

External Behavior: Play Soccer()

If (Ball Lost)	Find Ball()
If (Ball known AND Chasing)	Handle Ball(args1)
If (Ball known AND Not Chasing)	Play Position(args2)
If (Commuincate Flag Set)	Communicate()

Fig. 4. An example of a top-level external behavior for a robotic soccer player.

The referenced "Handle Ball" and "Play Position" behaviors may be affected by the agent's current role and/or formation. Such effects are realized by references to the internal state either at the level of function arguments (args1, args2), or within sub-behaviors. None of the actions in the condition-action pairs here are action primitives; rather, they are calls to lower level behaviors.

The definition of a position includes *home coordinates*, a *home range*, and a *maximum range*, as illustrated in Figure 5. The position's home coordinates are the default location to which the agent should go. However, the agent has some flexibility, being able to set its actual home position anywhere within the home range. When moving outside of the max range, the agent is no longer considered to be in the position. The home and max ranges of different positions can overlap, even if they are part of the same formations.

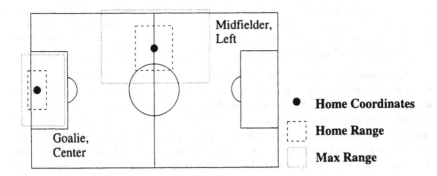

Fig. 5. Different positions with home coordinates and home and max ranges.

A formation consists of a set of positions and a set of units (as defined in Section 3.2). The formation and each of the units can also specify inter-position behavior specifications for the member positions, as illustrated in Figure 6(a). In this case, the formations specify inter-role interactions, namely the positions to which a player should consider passing the ball [26]. Figure 6(b) illustrates the units, the roles involved, and their captains. Here, the units contain defenders, midfielders, forwards, left players, center players, and right players.

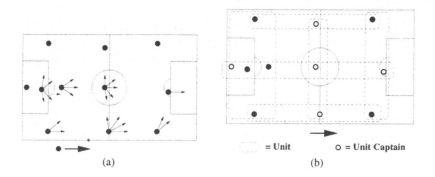

(a)   (b)

= Unit   o = Unit Captain

Fig. 6. (a) A possible formation (4-3-3) for a team of 11 players. Arrows represent passing options. (b) Positions can belong to more than one unit.

Since the players are all autonomous, in addition to knowing its own role, each one has its own belief of the team's current formation along with the time at which that formation was adopted, and a map of teammates to positions. Ideally, the players have consistent beliefs as to the team's state, but this condition cannot be guaranteed between synchronization opportunities. Another offshoot of the player's autonomy is that each is free to leave its position unilaterally, leaving the team to adjust behind it. Thus, players are not bound by their positions when presented with unexpected action opportunities.

Our team structure for PTS domains allows for several significant features in our simulated soccer team. These features are: (i) the definition of and switching among multiple formations with units; (ii) flexible position adjustment and position switching; (iii) and pre-defined special purpose plays (set plays).

4.2   Dynamic Switching of Formations

We implemented several different formations, ranging from very defensive (8-2-0) to very offensive (2-4-4).[3] The full definitions of all of the formations are a part of the

---

[3] Soccer formations are typically described as the X-Y-Z where X, Y, and Z are the number of defenders, midfielders, and forwards respectively. It is assumed that the eleventh player is the goaltender. [11]. Soccer formations are not to be confused with military-type formations in which agents must stay in precise relative positions.

locker-room agreement. Therefore, they are all known to all teammates. However during the periods of full autonomy and low communication, it is not necessarily known what formation the rest of the teammates are using. Two approaches can be taken to address this problem:

- **static formation** - the formation is set by the locker-room agreement and never changes;
- **run-time switch of formation** - during team synchronization opportunities, the team sets globally accessible run-time evaluation metrics as formation-changing indicators.
- **communication-triggered formation switch** - one team member decides that the team should switch formations and communicates the decision to teammates.

The CMUnited-97 simulator RoboCup team used run-time formation switches. Based on the amount of time left relative to the difference in score: the team switched to an offensive formation if it was losing near the end of the game and a defensive formation if it was winning. Since each agent was able to independently keep track of the score and time, the agents were always able to switch formations simultaneously.

Communication-triggered formation switches have also been implemented and tested [23].

4.3 Flexible Positions

In our multi-agent approach, the player positions itself flexibly such that it *anticipates* that it will be useful to the team, either offensively or defensively.

Two ways in which agents can use the position flexibility is to react to the ball's position and to mark opponents. When reacting to the ball's position, the agent moves to a location within its range that minimizes its distance to the ball. When marking opponents, agents move next to a given opponent rather than staying at the default position home. The opponent to mark can be chosen by the player (e.g., the closest opponent), or by the unit captain which can ensure that all opponents are marked, following a preset algorithm as part of the locker-room agreement.

As emphasized throughout, homogeneous agents can play different positions. But such a capability raises the challenging issue of when the players should change positions. In addition, with teammates switching positions, a player's internal player-position map $A \mapsto R$ could become incorrect and/or incomplete. The locker-room agreement provides procedures to the team that allow for coordinated role changing. In our case, the locker-room agreement designates an order of precedence switching among positions within each unit. When a high-priority position is left vacant, players currently filling lower-priority positions consider switching to the recently vacated position. If a player detects that another player is trying to fill the same role, it either vacates the position or informs the other player of the conflict depending on which player is closer to the position's home coordinates.

By switching positions within a formation, the overall joint performance of the team is improved. Position-switching saves player energy and allows them to respond more quickly to the ball.

4.4 Pre-Planned Set Plays

The final implemented improvement facilitated by our flexible teamwork structure is the introduction of set-plays, or pre-defined special purpose plays. As a part of the locker-room agreement, the team can define multi-step multi-agent plans to be executed at appropriate times. Particularly if there are certain situations that occur repeatedly, it makes sense for the team to devise plans for those situations.

In the robotic soccer domain, certain situations occur repeatedly. For example, after every goal, there is a kickoff from the center spot. When the ball goes out of bounds, there is a goal-kick, a corner-kick, or a kick-in. In each of these situations, the referee informs the team of the situations. Thus all the players know to execute the appropriate set-play. Associated with each set-play-role is not only a location, but also a behavior. The player in a given role might pass to the player filling another role, shoot at the goal, or kick the ball to some other location.

For example, Figure 7 illustrates a sample corner-kick set-play. The set-play designates five roles, each with a specific location, which should be filled before the ball is put back into play. Based on the home positions of the current formation, each individual agent can determine the best mapping from positions to set-play locations, i.e. the mapping that requires the least total displacement of the 5 players. If there is no player filling one of the necessary formation roles, then there must be two players filling the same role, one of which must move to the vacant role. In the event that no agent chooses to do so, the set-play can proceed with any single set-play-role unfilled. The only exception is that some player must fill the set-play-role responsible for kicking the ball back into play. A special-purpose protocol is incorporated into the set-play behaviors to guarantee such a condition.

Once the set-play-roles are filled, each player executes the action associated with its set-play-role. As illustrated by the player starting the corner-kick in Figure 7, a player could choose among possible actions, perhaps based on the opponent positions at the time of execution. No individual player is guaranteed of participating in the play. For example, the uppermost set-play position is there just in case one of the other players misses a pass or shoots wide of the goal: no player will pass directly to it. Each player leaves its set-play-role to resume its former role either after successfully kicking the ball, or after a pre-specified, role-specific amount of time.

We found that the set-plays significantly improved our team's performance. During the RoboCup-97 competitions, several goals were scored as a direct result of set-plays.

5 Results

The flexible teamwork structure improves over a rigid structure by way of three characteristics: flexible positioning within roles, set-plays, and changeable formations. We tested the benefits of the first two characteristics by playing a team with flexible, changeable positions and set-plays against a team with rigid positions and no set-plays (default team). The advantage of being able to change formations—the third characteristic—depends on the formation being used by the opponent. Therefore, we tested teams using each defined formation against each other.

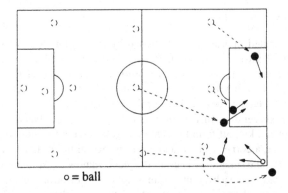

o = ball

Fig. 7. A sample corner-kick set-play. The dashed circles show the positions in the team's current formation and dashed arrows indicate the set-play-roles—black circles—that they would fill. Solid arrows indicate the direction the ball is to be kicked as part of each set-play-role.

Standard games in the soccer server system last 10 minutes. However, due to the large amount of noise, game results vary greatly. All reported results are cumulative over several games. Compiled statistics include the number of 10-minute games won, the total cumulative goals scored by each team, average goals per game, and the percentage of time that the ball was in each half of the field. The last statistic gives a rough estimate of the degree to which each team was able to control the ball.

5.1 Flexible Positions and Set-Plays

In order to test our flexible teamwork structure, we ran a team using flexible positions with set-plays against one using rigid positions and no set-plays. Both teams used a 4-4-2 formation. As shown in Figure 1, the flexible team significantly outperformed the default team over the course of 38 games.

(Game = 10 min.)	Flexible and Set-Plays	Default
Games won	34	1
Total goals	223	82
Avg. goals	5.87	2.16
Ball in own half	43.8%	56.2%

Table 1. The flexible team won 34 out of 38 games with 3 ties.

Further experimentation showed that both aspects of the flexible team contributed significantly to the team's success. Figure 2 shows the results when a team using flexible positions but no set-plays plays against the default team and when a team using set-plays but rigid positions plays against the default team, again over the course of 38 games. Both characteristics provide a significant advantage over the default team, but they perform even better in combination.

<table>
<tr><td colspan="3" align="center">Only Flexible Positions</td></tr>
<tr><td>(Game = 10 min.)</td><td>Flexible</td><td>Default</td></tr>
<tr><td>Games won</td><td>26</td><td>6</td></tr>
<tr><td>Total goals</td><td>157</td><td>87</td></tr>
<tr><td>Avg. goals</td><td>4.13</td><td>2.29</td></tr>
<tr><td>Ball in own half</td><td>44.1%</td><td>55.9%</td></tr>
</table>

Only Flexible Positions				Only Set-Plays		
(Game = 10 min.)	Flexible	Default		(Game = 10 min.)	Set-Plays	Default
Games won	26	6		Games won	28	5
Total goals	157	87		Total goals	187	108
Avg. goals	4.13	2.29		Avg. goals	4.92	2.84
Ball in own half	44.1%	55.9%		Ball in own half	47.6%	52.4%

Table 2. Only using flexible positions and only using set-plays works better than using neither.

5.2 Formations

In addition to the above tests, we tested the various formations against each other, as reported in Table 3. Each entry shows the goals scored for and against when a team using one formation played against a team using another formation over the course of 24 10-minute games. The right-most column collects the total goals scored for and against the team using that formation when playing against all the other teams. In all cases, the teams used flexible positions, but no set-plays.

formations	4-3-3	4-4-2	3-5-2	8-2-0	3-3-4	2-4-4	totals
4-3-3		68-60	68-54	24-28	59-64	70-65	289-271 (51.6%)
4-4-2	60-68		68-46	22-24	51-57	81-50	282-245 (53.5%)
3-5-2	54-68	46-68		13-32	61-72	75-73	249-313 (44.3%)
8-2-0	28-24	24-22	32-13		27-28	45-36	156-96 (61.9%)
3-3-4	64-59	57-51	72-61	28-27		87-69	308-267 (53.6%)
2-4-4	65-70	50-81	73-75	36-45	69-87		293-385 (43.2%)

Table 3. Comparison of our different formations. Entries in the table show the number of goals scored. Total (and percentage) cumulative goals scored against all formations appear in the right-most column.

The results show that the defensive formation (8-2-0) does the best. However the total goals scored when using the defensive formation is quite low. On the other hand, the 3-3-4 formation performs well with a high goal total.

This detailed study allowed us to devise an effective formation-switching strategy for RoboCup-97. Our team [22] used a 4-4-2 formation in general, switching to a 8-2-0 formation if winning near the end of the game, or a 3-3-4 formation if losing. This strategy, along with the flexible teamwork structure as a whole, and the novel communication paradigm, helped us to perform well in the tournament, making it to the semi-finals in a field of 29 teams and out-scoring opponents by a total score of 67-9 [18].

We also used this flexible teamwork structure on our CMUnited-97 small robot team which won the RoboCup-97 small-size robot competition, out-scoring opponents by a total score of 13–1 [18]. Although developed in simulation, all of the teamwork concepts apply directly to real robot teams as well. We were able to reuse the code textually from our simulator clients on the robots and immediately achieve variable formations, flexible positions, and position switching.

Unlike the simulated agents, the robots have a global view, seeing the entire field via an overhead camera. Nonetheless, the agent control modules are distributed, enabling the use of the same team member architecture, including locker-room agreement and formation structure, as was originally developed in simulation. Our robotic system is described in detail in [28].

6   Conclusion

In this paper, we introduced a flexible team structure for periodic team synchronization (PTS) domains. The structure allows for multi-agent tasks using homogeneous agents to be decomposed into flexible roles. Roles are organized into formations, and agents can fill any role in any formation. Agents dynamically change roles and formations in response to changing environments. The team structure includes pre-planning for frequent situations, and agents act individually, but keep the team's goals in mind. This flexible team structure builds upon our team agent architecture, which maintains both an internal and world state, and a set of internal and external behaviors. Coordination is achieved through limited communication and pre-determined procedures as part of a locker-room agreement.

Our teamwork structure will apply in PTS domains such as hospital/factory maintenance, multi-spacecraft missions, search and rescue, and battlefield combat. We presented the implementation of our approach in the robotic soccer domain, which we have used as a substrate to our research. We participated in the RoboCup-97 simulator and small-size real robot competitions. Our flexible team structure approach was developed in the simulator team and subsequently also successfully used in the real robot team.

References

1. Minoru Asada, Eiji Uchibe, Shoichi Noda, Sukoya Tawaratsumida, and Koh Hosoda. Coordination of multiple behaviors acquired by vision-based reinforcement learning. In *Proc. of IEEE/RSJ/GI International Conference on Intelligent Robots and Systems 1994 (IROS '94)*, pages 917–924, 1994.
2. A. L. C. Bazzan, R. H. Bordini, and J. A. Campbell. Moral sentiments in multi-agent systems. In J. P. Müller, M. P. Singh, and A. S. Rao, editors, *Intelligent Agents V — Proceedings of the Fifth International Workshop on Agent Theories, Architectures, and Languages (ATAL-98)*, Lecture Notes in Artificial Intelligence. Springer-Verlag, Heidelberg, 1999. In this volume.

3. Cristiano Castelfranchi. Commitments: From individual intentions to groups and organizations. In *Proceedings of the First International Conference on Multi-Agent Systems (ICMAS-95)*, pages 41–48, Menlo Park, California, June 1995. AAAI Press.

4. Philip R. Cohen, Hector J. Levesque, and Ira Smith. On team formation, 1997.

5. R. Conte, C. Castelfranchi, and F. Dignum. Autonomous norm-acceptance. In J. P. Müller, M. P. Singh, and A. S. Rao, editors, *Intelligent Agents V — Proceedings of the Fifth International Workshop on Agent Theories, Architectures, and Languages (ATAL-98)*, Lecture Notes in Artificial Intelligence. Springer-Verlag, Heidelberg, 1999. In this volume.

6. Keith S. Decker. Task environment centered simulation. In M. Prietula, K. Carley, and L. Gasser, editors, *Simulating Organizations: Computational Models of Institutions and Groups*. AAAI Press/MIT Press, 1996.

7. Barbara J. Grosz. Collaborative systems. *AI Magazine*, 17(2):67–85, Summer 1996.

8. L. Hunsberger. Making SharedPlans more concise and easier to reason about. In J. P. Müller, M. P. Singh, and A. S. Rao, editors, *Intelligent Agents V — Proceedings of the Fifth International Workshop on Agent Theories, Architectures, and Languages (ATAL-98)*, Lecture Notes in Artificial Intelligence. Springer-Verlag, Heidelberg, 1999. In this volume.

9. Jong-Hwan Kim, editor. *Proceedings of the Micro-Robot World Cup Soccer Tournament*, Taejon, Korea, November 1996.

10. Hiroaki Kitano, Yasuo Kuniyoshi, Itsuki Noda, Minoru Asada, Hitoshi Matsubara, and Eiichi Osawa. RoboCup: A challenge problem for AI. *AI Magazine*, 18(1):73–85, Spring 1997.

11. Michael L. LaBlanc and Richard Henshaw. *The World Encyclopedia of Soccer*. Visible Ink Press, 1994.

12. A. K. Mackworth. On seeing robots. In A. Basu and X. Li, editors, *Computer Vision: Systems, Theory, and Applications*, pages 1–13. World Scientific Press, Singapore, 1993.

13. Maja J. Mataric. Interaction and intelligent behavior. MIT EECS PhD Thesis AITR-1495, MIT AI Lab, August 1994.

14. Hitoshi Matsubara, Itsuki Noda, and Kazuo Hiraki. Learning of cooperative actions in multi-agent systems: a case study of pass play in soccer. In *Adaptation, Coevolution and Learning in Multiagent Systems: Papers from the 1996 AAAI Spring Symposium*, pages 63–67, Menlo Park, CA, March 1996. AAAI Press. AAAI Technical Report SS-96-01.

15. J. P. Müller. The right agent (architecture) to do the right thing. In J. P. Müller, M. P. Singh, and A. S. Rao, editors, *Intelligent Agents V — Proceedings of the Fifth International Workshop on Agent Theories, Architectures, and Languages (ATAL-98)*, Lecture Notes in Artificial Intelligence. Springer-Verlag, Heidelberg, 1999. In this volume.

16. Itsuki Noda and Hitoshi Matsubara. Soccer server and researches on multi-agent systems. In *Proceedings of the IROS-96 Workshop on RoboCup*, November 1996. Soccer server is available at http://ci.etl.go.jp/ noda/soccer/server/index.html.

17. S. Ossowski and A. García-Serrano. Social structure in artificial agent societies: Implications for autonomous problem-solving agents. In J. P. Müller, M. P. Singh, and A. S. Rao, editors, *Intelligent Agents V — Proceedings of the Fifth International Workshop on Agent Theories, Architectures, and Languages (ATAL-98)*, Lecture Notes in Artificial Intelligence. Springer-Verlag, Heidelberg, 1999. In this volume.

18. Results of RoboCup-97. Accessible from http://www.RoboCup.org.

19. Michael K. Sahota, Alan K. Mackworth, Rod A. Barman, and Stewart J. Kingdon. Real-time control of soccer-playing robots using off-board vision: the dynamite testbed. In *IEEE International Conference on Systems, Man, and Cybernetics*, pages 3690–3663, 1995.

20. Randy Sargent, Bill Bailey, Carl Witty, and Anne Wright. Dynamic object capture using fast vision tracking. *AI Magazine*, 18(1):65–72, Spring 1997.

21. Peter Stone. Multiagent learning for autonomous spacecraft constellations. In *Proceedings of the NASA Workshop on Planning and Scheduling for Space*, 1997.

22. Peter Stone and Manuela Veloso. The CMUnited-97 simulator team. In Hiroaki Kitano, editor, *RoboCup-97: Robot Soccer World Cup I*, pages 387–397. Springer Verlag, Berlin, 1998.

23. Peter Stone and Manuela Veloso. Communication in domains with unreliable, single-channel, low-bandwidth communication. In Alexis Drogoul, Milind Tambe, and Toshio Fukuda, editors, *Collective Robotics*, pages 85–97. Springer Verlag, Berlin, July 1998.

24. Peter Stone and Manuela Veloso. A layered approach to learning client behaviors in the RoboCup soccer server. *Applied Artificial Intelligence*, 12:165–188, 1998.

25. Peter Stone and Manuela Veloso. Towards collaborative and adversarial learning: A case study in robotic soccer. *International Journal of Human-Computer Studies*, 48(1):83–104, January 1998.

26. Peter Stone and Manuela Veloso. Using decision tree confidence factors for multiagent control. In Hiroaki Kitano, editor, *RoboCup-97: Robot Soccer World Cup I*, pages 99–111. Springer Verlag, Berlin, 1998.

27. Milind Tambe. Towards flexible teamwork. *Journal of Artificial Intelligence Research*, 7:81–124, 1997.

28. Manuela Veloso, Peter Stone, Kwun Han, and Sorin Achim. The CMUnited-97 small-robot team. In Hiroaki Kitano, editor, *RoboCup-97: Robot Soccer World Cup I*, pages 242–256. Springer Verlag, Berlin, 1998.

Agent Languages and Their Relationship to Other Programming Paradigms

John-Jules Ch. Meyer

Utrecht University

1 Introduction

One of the two panels held this year at ATAL was to address the topic of agent-oriented languages, and particularly their relationship with other (i.e. traditional) programming paradigms. What triggered this panel is the observation that while there have been several proposals for agent-oriented languages the professional programmer has not really picked these up, and continues to employ familiar and more traditional paradigms and languages such as Java, C++, relational and object-oriented databases, and CORBA. So it seemed a good idea to reflect a bit on the position of agent-oriented programming as opposed to well-established paradigms such as object-oriented programming, distributed programming and logic programming.

To this end a number of well-known experts having experiences with these familiar paradigms as well as having an interest in intelligent agents were asked to discuss various questions related to the above theme. The panelists were Jean-Pierre Briot (Laboratoire d'Informatique de Paris 6 & CNRS), Keith Clark (Imperial College, London), Jacques Ferber (Université Montpellier II) and Carl Hewitt (MIT AI Lab). I myself served on the panel as a moderator. The questions I put to the panelists were the following:

- Is there a need for special agent-oriented languages anyway? (Or can every 'agent-oriented' thing be done as easily with familiar paradigms: OO, LP, ...)
- What is the current state of agent-oriented languages: Agent0, PLACA, AgentSpeak, ...; is there a need for new agent-oriented languages?
- What makes a language agent-oriented? Should there be an explicit mention (by means of language primities or so) of BDI-like features in the language?
- Is there a need for formal semantics and formal methods for specification & verification of agent programs?
- What are the expectations for the future of agent languages? (Are they as popular as OO languages nowadays in 10 years time?)

We had a lively discussion on these issues on stage at ATAL'98. In order to record some of it for 'posterity', so to speak, the organisers asked me to compile something for the proceedings. The way I've implemented this request is by asking the panelists to reflect once again on the questions and related issues they think is important as to the panel's topic. Here they are in full, after which I'll conclude with some reflections on these statements. The panelists are gratefully thanked for their contribution. (Unfortunately, Jacques was not able to provide me with a statement, so that his is lacking.)

2   Statement by Jean-Pierre Briot:

Regarding the whole set of questions asked, I would like to discuss the four following points.

- First, I think that when one speaks about agent languages, there are different kinds of language concerns, at least:
  - Programming languages for expressing the algorithmic part of the agent.
  - Knowledge representation languages for expressing the knowledge part (acquaintances, mental state, . . .) - in case of cognitive agents.
  - Communication/coordination language between agents - message passing (objects, actors) is too unconstrained to be called a communication language, but proposals like KQML or FIPA ACL get closer.

  I do not think we need (and could find) one agent language for all of these different language concerns. I think we should rather build upon existing high level programming languages (specially object/actor-oriented as they provide a good basic structuring model - see for instance the study by Les Gasser and myself published in the book "DAI: Theory and Praxis", Kluwer, 1992). Also please refer to current special series on Actors and Agents in IEEE Concurrency Journal.

  We may then use different components for different concerns: knowledge base, perception, reasoning (different kinds, e.g. planning, constraints, case-based reasoning, . . .), communication, coordination, . . . I think agent languages like Agent0 or BDI are somehow both too general (for a given application) and too specific (for various applications). I do not mean rejecting works like Agent0. Its idea of a control loop tackles well what I believe is one of the fundamental machinery of an agent, i.e., the balance between reaction (to communication and perception) and pro-action (based on mental states for cognitive agents) - in other words selection and adaptation of actions. But I do not want to necessarily express everything in terms of Agent0 or BDI.

  Then, having different components within a single agent means being able to compose, schedule and coordinate them. For some architectural proposal in that direction, see for instance work by Zahia Guessoum on the DIMA modular agent architecture and its meta-control through a state/transition model (published in the proceedings of MAAMAW'96).

- Second, I think that probably the most fundamental difference between cooperative agents (multi-agent) and conventional programming (distributed objects) is more at the level of design than at the level of programming language. Compared to conventional (object-oriented) design methodologies, identification of agents ("finding the agents") depends heavily on the explicit identification of relational and organizational behaviors, in complement to basic domain behaviors. See for instance the Cassiopee methodology proposed by Anne Collinot and Alexis Drogoul (published in the first issue of the new Journal on Autonomous Agents and Multi-Agent Systems, Kluwer).

  Needless to say, such methodologies should complement conventional object-oriented methodologies (with an organizational dimension).

– Third, one thing agent-oriented programming may learn from the object-oriented community is the notion of "design pattern". - Actually, Robert Tolksdorf gave a presentation at AgentsWorld'98 where he also advocated the use of design patterns for agents. It is interesting to note that we both reached, although completely independently, similar conclusions. -

The idea is in capitalizing on design expertise of the community, that is the mapping of design solutions to patterns of problems. The key aspect is to be able to well document for various classes of problems what patterns may apply, or do not apply, and may collaborate with other known patterns. For instance it would be valuable to well document known usages of well identified coordination protocols (e.g., variations of contract net protocol). And also bring to the surface redundant patterns of interaction which are buried deep into applications code.

Catalogs of patterns should be linked to the methodology and its environment. That is, from a given analysis (see my second point) identifying requirements for coordination between some agents, help at finding known patterns and protocols of coordination for actual implementation.

– Last, for me one of the main motivations of multi-agent systems is when control must be distributed. I mean, because of logical, physical, or/and temporal distribution. On large scale distributed architectures, fault tolerance becomes crucial as one cannot exclude the possibility of failures (processor or/and network).

I believe that in order to be able to run multi-agent systems on a large scale and not just on single (or only a few) machine(s), we need to use distributed protocols for ensuring maximal reliability (e.g., by replicating critical agents and communications). Note that, in the case of reactive agents, some degree of redundancy is often built-in within organizations and interaction protocols, e.g. in the case of ant nests. But cognitive agents usually completely lack such properties. One example of application field where fault tolerance is critical is crisis management and decision systems.

What I see as a promising direction is the possibility for the agents themselves to dynamically adapt the protocols to the ongoing situation (perception by agents of the environment and the possibly changing requirements/priorities from the users, as well as representation by agents of the problem solving process). The reason is that distributed protocols for fault tolerance may be costly to support and adapting them dynamically may improve the reliability and the use of resources in a large scale agent system.

3 Statement by Keith Clark

My answers to the questions posed above are as follows:

3.1 Is there a need for special agent-oriented languages anyway?

The short answer is no, we do not need special agent oriented programming languages at this stage. The main reason is that we are still experimenting with different agent architectures, agent comunication languages and coordination mechanisms and it is too early to freeze any of these into an agent programming language. Instead, it is better to use something like a concurrent OO language, with knowledge representation and symbolic message capabilities to prototype agent applications and concepts. Such a language could be extensible, in the way that Prolog is, so that the programming syntax can be tailored to fit particular application areas or agent design concepts. In this way, different agent programming languages will emerge, out of the applications and the conceptual experiments. This is the pragmatic, bottom up approach to agent language design.

3.2 Is there a need for new agent-oriented languages?

As I remarked above, what we need to do now is to experiment with different multi-agent architectures using a more low level language rather than propose an alternative to the above proposed agent languages. They have, however served a useful purpose in highlighting certain styles of agent programming.

3.3 What makes a language agent-oriented? Should there be an explicit mention of BDI-like features in the language?

No, that will depend on the application. The beliefs can be implicitly represented in the state of an agent implemented as a concurrent object, its desires can be implicit in its proactive and reactive behaviour, as can its intentions. An intensional description or specification of what a program does may usefully employ BDI concepts, and they are probably also useful design concepts for many applications, but they do not need to be explicitly supported by separate syntactic categories in the programming language.

3.4 Is there a need for formal semantics and formal methods for specification & verification of agent programs?

Down stream, this will become important, when we know what different agent pro-gramminmg languages we need to use for our agent applications.

3.5 What are the expectations for the future of agent languages? (In 10 years as popular as OO languages nowadays?

No, I see any particular agent language being a bespoke language for a niche set of applications. What may be in more widespead use are the concurrent OO languages I mentoned in answer to the first question, which are general purpose agent 'imple-mentation' languages. Such languages will support the programming of mobile agents and support standardised interfaces to non-agent software, such as Corba's IIOP or the internet's TCP/IP, or their successors.

4 Carl Hewitt, Negotiation Science and Technology: A Call to Action

The thesis here is that we greatly need to increase our understanding of scientific and technical issues for developing negotiation science and technology.

4.1 Opportunities

Negotiation has always been of immense importance to humans. Now the Internet is rapidly becoming an indispensable media infrastructure. This is part of a larger trend in which digital technologies are becoming ubiquitous. These digital technologies are increasingly being used to make all kinds of arrangements in commerce, education, government, etc. There is a pressing need for negotiation technology for making these arrangements by facilitating coordination, collaboration, intermediation, etc. In commerce, negotiation technology impacts how products are designed, marketed, manufactured, and distributed. For example, electronic mail has already had significant impact - both beneficial and harmful - on social interaction. Interactive applications have grown tremendously with the growth of the Internet. Traditional uses of telecomputing are being reevaluated and modified. New developments in wireless communications will accelerate the adoption and use of digital interactive communication among computer systems that will in turn drive the need for new negotiation science and technology.

The need is to identify critical research issues that are central to the development and use of negotiation science and technology. Characterizing negotiation is currently a topic of considerable controversy. As a starting point one characterization of negotiation is the following:

Negotiation is interactive communication for arranging (joint) activities. As used here, negotiation is inherently reflexive and self-referential because negotiation specifically includes the interactive communication for arranging the communication that is itself the negotiation.

Other characterizations include goals, interdependence, intentions, desires, consensus, agreement, commitment, strategies, tactics, turn taking, bargaining, compromise etc. as important aspects of negotiation. All of these and more will need to be developed.

The need is to develop, analyze, and compare multiple characterizations and applications of negotiation science and technology.

4.2 Impact

Negotiation science and technology impact a wide range of applications and processes, indicating the need for cross-disciplinary research. The pressing is to assess current negotiation research and to identify areas of critical and pressing need. Some of these scientific and technical characteristics include issue management, negotiation moves, turn taking, closure, etc.

The Web provides enabling technology to use negotiation in many important applications. For example in electronic commerce, vendors are typically loath to compete on price alone. They would like to be able to offer services and amenities in order to differentiate themselves. Negotiation technology affords the potential to increase market differentiation and efficiency by engaging potential customers in electronic negotiations. Vendors can entertain, educate, and customize their offerings. Currently online transaction technology can be quite rigid, e.g., using forms, structured workflow, etc.

Negotiation has the potential to make online transactions more flexible in the following aspects:

- applicable to more circumstances
- more robust in the face of contention, conflict, and misunderstanding
- better able to handle uncertainty

These characteristics are critical for the development of future organizational information systems.

4.3 The Charge

The charge is:

- To assess and identify research areas that are strategic, timely, and most pressing for the successful development and application of negotiation science and technology.
- To develop research priorities aimed at defining high-impact areas for sponsors, research institutions, and other members of the community.
- To build understanding of how cross-discipline and cross-institution collaborations can be developed.

Meeting this charge will provide resources for defining, clarifying, and rationalizing research on negotiation science and technology. Negotiation science and technology is a pressing, fertile, high-impact area. It is critical to research in Multi-Agent Systems, organizational and management science, political science, and engineering science and management. Research in this area is in its critical initial stages with active research groups forming in North America, Europe/Middle East, and the Pacific Rim.

The need is to increase the breadth and depth of community participation to galvanize scientific activity in this research area. Activities must be developed to promote a critical airing and discussion of scientific issues, approaches, and technologies that will provide foundations and directions for the development of a much stronger, more productive, and long-lasting research capability.

Multiple aspects of negotiation science and technology must be addressed including the following:

1. *Teaching and Learning.* E.g., learning to negotiate and negotiating to learn.
2. *Negotiation Breakdowns:* Detection, causes, and cures.
3. *Negotiation Moves:* Digital and/or physical
4. *Exploration and Search.* E.g., negotiation in exploration and exploration in negotiation.
5. *Market Mechanisms.* E.g., negotiation in the marketplace and using market mechanisms for negotiation.
6. *Foundations and Semantics of Negotiation.*
7. *Applications of Negotiation Science and Technology.*
8. *Frameworks, Languages, and Systems for Negotiation.*

4.4 Summary

The charge is to define, clarify, and focus research on negotiation science and technology. As discussed above, negotiation science and technology is a pressing, fertile, high-impact area. It is critical to research in Multi-Agent Systems, organizational and management science, political science, and engineering science and management. Research in this area is in its critical initial stages with active research groups forming in North America, Europe/Middle East, and the Pacific Rim.

5 Reflection and conclusion

After having seen the above thought-provoking statements by the various panelists I cannot resist to put forward some of my own thoughts concerning them. For instance, I agree with Jean-Pierre that agent-orientedness is probably indeed in the first instance more a thing at the conceptual level than at the implementational level: it is a way of 'thinking about programs'. However, I believe that it also very important that such a way of thinking is supported by the right kind of programming languages. So for me agent-oriented languages should really be able to express the very concepts that are employed to design / devise the agents (contrary to Keith's opinion). In my opinion this implies that we need languages in which the mental attitudes of agents (viz. knowledge, beliefs, desires and intentions) are expressible explicitly, e.g. by language primitives (but, of course, we should not strive for one all-encompassing language, and I totally agree with Jean-Pierre here). To my mind stopping at the conceptual level would be the same as letting the programmer think in (terms of) objects but not use a truly object-oriented programming language. Even stronger, I claim that unless there is some match between conceptual level and implementational level, agent-oriented programming will not really catch on. It is much harder to match the specification and implementation of a program (e.g. prove its correctness) if the specification and the implementation are put in completely different conceptual terms (i.e. use different concepts, such as intentions in the specification while these are hidden somehow in the program). This holds in my opinion both for the formal and informal specification of agent programs. (By the way, in view of my background it will come as no surprise that I maintain that (eventually) having formal semantics and verification means available renders an enormous support to really understand the behaviour of agent programs and prove their correctness with mathematical rigour, the latter being of crucial importance in e.g. life-critical applications.) A fortiori all this holds with respect to multi-agent systems, where–as Carl states–social attitudes such as negotiation and related ones should be analyzed and developed further, and here, too, I believe that some of the primitive social attitudes should be expressed adequately in the programming language that will be used to program such systems. This is particularly important to accommodate for agents reasoning about each other's mental state. I believe that in this sense the agent languages to date are not nearly yet sufficiently expressible for this purpose. So there remains a lot to be done.

Finally, as opposed to Keith's opinion, I really think it is worth-while already to look at a 'top-down' approach to agent language design as well (besides the 'bottom-up' one as advocated by Keith and Jean-Pierre), if only it were for a scientific objective to bridge the 'gap' between agent theories (such as those employing those modal logics) and agent programming. Playing around with several kinds of primitives at this level may also provide useful insight in how to go about with the agent-oriented way of thinking.

A Survey of Agent-Oriented Methodologies*

Carlos A. Iglesias[1]**, Mercedes Garijo[2] and
José C. González[2]

[1] Dep. TSC e Ing. Telemática, E.T.S.I. Telecomunicación
Universidad de Valladolid, E–47011 Valladolid, Spain
cif@tel.uva.es
[2] Dep. de Ingeniería de Sistemas Telemáticos, E.T.S.I. Telecomunicación
Universidad Politécnica de Madrid, E–28040 Madrid, Spain
{mga,jcg}@gsi.dit.upm.es

Abstract. This article introduces the current agent-oriented methodologies. It discusses what approaches have been followed (mainly extending existing object-oriented and knowledge engineering methodologies), the suitability of these approaches for agent modelling, and some conclusions drawn from the survey.

1 Introduction

Agent technology has received a great deal of attention in the last few years and, as a result, the industry is beginning to get interested in using this technology to develop its own products. In spite of the different developed agent theories, languages, architectures and the successful agent-based applications, very little work for specifying (and applying) techniques to develop applications using agent technology has been done. The role of agent-oriented methodologies is to assist in all the phases of the life cycle of an agent-based application, including its management.

This article reviews the current approaches to the development of an agent-oriented (AO) methodology. To avoid building a methodology from scratch, the researchers on agent-oriented methodologies have followed the approach of extending existing methodologies to include the relevant aspects of the agents. These extensions have been carried out mainly in two areas: object oriented (OO) methodologies (Section 2) and knowledge engineering (KE) methodologies (Section 3). We will review (1) why each area can be relevant for developing an AO methodology, (2) what problems were found in applying directly the existing methodologies without extending them and (3) what solutions have been proposed. We will also review some particular approaches (Section 4), formal approaches (Section 5) and software-engineering techniques proposed by agent researchers (Section 6). Finally, some conclusions are drawn (Section 7).

* This research is funded in part by the Commission of the European Community under the ESPRIT Basic Research Project *MIX: Modular Integration of Connectionist and Symbolic Processing in Knowledge Based Systems*, ESPRIT-9119, and by the Spanish Government under the CICYT projects TIC91-0107 and TIC94-0139

** This research was partly carried out while the first author was visiting the Dep. Ingeniería de Sistemas Telemáticos (Universidad Politécnica de Madrid).

2 Extensions of Object-Oriented Methodologies

2.1 Advantages of the approach

Several reasons can be cited that justify the approach of extending object-oriented methodologies.

Firstly, there are similarities between the object-oriented paradigm and the agent-oriented paradigm [5, 27]. Since the early times of distributed artificial intelligence (DAI), the close relationship between DAI and Object-Based Concurrent Programming (OBCP) [2, 15] was established. As stated by Shoham [43], the agents can be considered as *active objects*, objects with a mental state. Both paradigms use message passing for communicating and can use inheritance and aggregation for defining its architecture. The main difference [43] is the constrained type of messages in the AO paradigm and the definition of a state in the agent based on its beliefs, desires, intentions, commitments, etc.

Another possible advantage comes from the *commonly usage* of object-oriented languages to implement agent-based systems because they have been considered a natural framework [2, p. 34].

The *popularity* of object-oriented methodologies is another potential advantage. Many object-oriented methodologies are being used in the industry with success such as Object Modelling Technique (OMT) [41], Object Oriented Software Engineering (OOSE) [21], Object-Oriented Design [3], RDD (Responsibility Driving Design) [48] and Unified Modelling Language (UML) [8]. This experience can be a key to facilitate the integration of agent technology because on the one hand, the software engineers can be reluctant to use and learn a complete new methodology, and on the other hand, the managers would prefer to follow methodologies which have been successfully tested. So we could take advantage of their experience for learning quicker.

The three common views of the system in object-oriented methodologies are also interesting for describing agents: *static* for the object structure objects and their structural relationships; *dynamic* for describing the object interactions; and *functional* for describing the data flow of the methods of the objects.

Finally, some of the techniques for object identification can also be used for identifying agents: use cases [21] and classes responsibilities collaborations (CRC) cards [48].

2.2 Aspects not addressed

In spite of the similarities between objects and agents, obviously, agents are not simply objects. Thus, object-oriented methodologies do not address these different aspects [43, 5, 24].

Firstly, though both objects and agents use message-passing to communicate with each other, while message-passing for objects is just method invocation, agents distinguish different types of messages and model these messages frequently as speech-acts and use complex protocols to negotiate. In addition, agents analyse these messages and can decide whether to *execute* the requested action.

Another difference consists in that agents can be characterised by their mental state, and object-oriented methodologies do not define techniques for modelling how the agents carry out their inferences, their planning process, etc.

Finally, agents are characterised by their social dimension. Procedures for modelling these social relationships between agents have to be defined.

2.3 Existing solutions

In this section the following agent-oriented methodologies are reviewed: *Agent-Oriented Analysis and Design* [5], *Agent Modelling Technique for Systems of BDI agents* [27], *MASB* [31, 32] and *Agent Oriented Methodology for Enterprise Modelling* [24].

Agent-Oriented Analysis and Design by Burmeister

Burmeister [5] defines three models for analysing an agent system: the *agent model*. that contains the agents and their internal structure (beliefs, plans, goals,...); the *organisational model*, that describes the relationships between agents (inheritance and roles in the organisation); and the *cooperation model*, that describes the interactions between agents.

The process steps for the development of each model are:

– *Agent Model:* agents and their environment are identified using an extension of CRC cards for including beliefs, motivations, plans and cooperation attributes.
– *Organisational Model:* proposes the identification of the roles of each agent and the elaboration of diagrams using OMT notation for the inheritance hierarchy and the relationships between the agents.
– *Cooperation Model:* cooperations and cooperation partners are identified, and the types of interchanged messages and used protocols are analysed.

Agent Modelling Technique for Systems of BDI agents

This method [27] defines two main levels (external and internal) for modelling BDI (Belief, Desire and Intention) agents.

The *external viewpoint* consists of the decomposition of the system into agents and the definition of their interactions. This is carried out through two models: the *agent model*, for describing the hierarchical relationship between agents and relationships between concrete agents; and the *interaction Model* [26], for describing the responsibilities, services and interactions between agents and external systems.

The *internal viewpoint* carries out the modelling of each BDI agent class through three models: the *belief model*, which describes the beliefs about the environment; the *goal model*, which describes the goals and events an agent can adopt or respond to; and the *plan model*, which describes the plans an agent can use to achieve its goals.

The development process of the *external viewpoint* starts with the identification of the roles (functional, organisational, etc.) of the application domain in order to identify the agents and arrange them in an agent class hierarchy described using OMT like notation. Then the responsibilities associated to each role are identified, together with the services provided and used to fulfill the responsibilities. The next step is the identification of the necessary interactions for each service and both the speech-act and information content of every interaction. Finally, the information is collected in an *agent instance model*.

The development of the *internal viewpoint* starts with the analysis of the different means (plans) of achieving a goal. The plans for responding to an event or achieving a goal are represented using a graphical notation similar to Harel statecharts [18], but adding the notion of failure of the plan. Finally, the beliefs of the agent about the objects of the environment are modelled and represented using OMT notation.

Multi-Agent Scenario-Based Method (*MASB* method)

This method [31, 32] is intended to be applied for MAS in the field of cooperative work (CSCW). The analysis phase consists of the following activities:

- *Scenario description:* identification using natural language of the main roles played by both the human and the software agents, objects of the environment and the typical scenarios.
- *Role functional description:* description of the agent roles using *behaviour diagrams*, which describe the processes, the relevant information and the interactions between the agents.
- *Data and world conceptual modelling:* modelling of the data and knowledge used by the agent using entity-relationship diagrams (or object-oriented diagrams) and entity life-cycle diagrams.
- *System-user interaction modelling:* simulation and definition of different suitable interfaces for human-machine interaction in every scenario.

The design phase consists of the following activities:

- *MAS architecture and scenario description:* selection of the scenarios to be implemented and the roles played by the agents in these scenarios.
- *Object modelling:* refines the world modelling of the analysis, defining hierarchies, attributes and procedures.
- *Agent modelling:* specification of the elements defined in the data conceptual modelling step of the analysis as belief structures. A graphical notation is proposed for describing the decision process of a agent, taking into account beliefs, plans, goals and interactions.
- Finally, two steps are stated though not developed: *conversation modelling* and *system design overall validation*.

Agent oriented methodology for Enterprise modelling

This methodology [24] proposes the combination of object-oriented methodologies (OOSE) and enterprise modelling methodologies IDEF (Integration DEfinition for Function modelling) [12] and CIMOSA (Computer Integrated Manufacturing Open System Architecture) [28]). The identified models are:

- *Function Model:* describes the functions (inputs, outputs, mechanisms and control) using $IDEF_0$ diagrams that include the selection of the possible methods depending on the input and the control.

- *Use Case Model:* describes the actors involved in each function, using OOSE use case notation.
- *Dynamic Model:* this model is intended for analysing object interactions. The use cases are represented in event trace diagrams.
- *The Agent Oriented System:* is a compound of:
  - *Agent Identification:* the actors of the use cases are identified as agents. The main functions of an agent are its goals and the possibilities described in the $IDEF_0$ diagrams.
  - *Coordination protocols or scripts:* they are described in state diagrams.
  - *Plan invocation: sequence diagrams* extend event trace diagrams to include conditions for indicating when a plan is invoked.
  - *Beliefs, Sensors and Effectors:* inputs of the functions should be modelled as beliefs or obtained from objects via sensors, and achieved goals should be modelled as changes to beliefs or modifications via effectors.

3 Extensions of Knowledge Engineering Methodologies

3.1 Advantages of the approach

Knowledge engineering methodologies can provide a good basis for MAS modelling since they deal with the development of knowledge based systems. Since the agents have cognitive characteristics, these methodologies can provide the techniques for modelling this agent knowledge.

The definition of the knowledge of an agent can be considered as a *knowledge acquisition process*, and only this process is addressed in these methodologies.

The extension of current knowledge engineering methodologies can take advantage of the acquired experience in these methodologies. In addition, both the existing tools and the developed ontology libraries and problem solving method libraries can be reused.

Although these methodologies are not as extendable as the object-oriented ones, they have been applied to several projects with success.

3.2 Aspects not addressed

Most of the problems subject to knowledge engineering methodologies are present in designing MAS: knowledge acquisition, modelling and reuse. Nevertheless, these methodologies conceive a knowledge based system as a centralised one. Thus, they do not address the distributed or social aspects of the agents, or their reflective and goal-oriented attitudes.

3.3 Existing solutions

Several solutions have been proposed for multi-agent systems modelling extending *CommonKADS* [42]. The main reason of the selection of this methodology among the knowledge engineering methodologies is that it can be seen as a European standard for knowledge modelling. *CommonKADS* defines the modelling activity as the building of a number of separate models that capture salient features of the system and its environment.

We will review the extensions *CoMoMAS* [16] and *MAS-CommonKADS* [19], though there have been other preliminary works [9, 25, 37, 47].

The *CoMoMAS* methodology

Glaser [16] proposes an extension to the methodology *CommonKADS* [42] for MAS modelling. The following models are defined:

- *Agent Model:* this is the main model of the methodology and define the agent architecture and the agent knowledge, that is classified as social, cooperative, control, cognitive and reactive knowledge.
- *Expertise Model:* describes the cognitive and reactive competences of the agent. It distinguishes between task, problem solving (PSM) and reactive knowledge. The *task knowledge* contains the task decomposition knowledge described in the task model. The *problem-solving knowledge* describes the problem solving methods and the strategies to select them. The *reactive knowledge* describes the procedures for responding to stimuli.
- *Task Model:* describes the task decomposition, and details if the task are solved by a user or an agent.
- *Cooperation Model:* describes the cooperation between the agents. using conflict resolution methods and cooperation knowledge (communication primitives, protocols ad interaction terminology).
- *System Model:* defines the organisational aspects of the agent society together with the architectural aspects of the agents.
- *Design Model:* collects the previous models in order to operationalisate them, together with the non-functional requirements.

The *MAS-CommonKADS* methodology

This methodology [19] extends the models defined in *CommonKADS*, adding techniques from object-oriented methodologies (OOSE, OMT) and from protocol engineering for describing the agent protocols (SDL [20] and MSC96 [40]).

The methodology starts with a *conceptualisation phase* that is an informal phase for collecting the user requirements and obtaining a first description of the system from the user point of view. For this purpose, the use cases technique from OOSE [40] is used, and the interactions of these use cases are formalised with MSC (*Message Sequence Charts*) [39]. The methodology defines the models described below for the analysis and the design of the system, that are developed following a risk-driven life cycle. For each model, the methodology defines the constituents (entities to be modelled) and the relationships between the constituents. The methodology defines a textual template for describing every constituent and a set of activities for building every model, based on the development state of every constituent (empty, identified, described or validated). These activities facilitate the management of the project.

This extension defines the following models:

- *Agent Model:* describes the main characteristics of the agents, including reasoning capabilities, skills (sensors/effectors), services, goals, etc. Several techniques are proposed for agent identification, such as analysis of the actors of the conceptualisation phase, syntactic analysis of the problem statement, application of heuristics for agent identification, reuse of components (agents) developed previously or usage of CRC cards, which have been adapted for agent oriented development.

- *Task Model:* describes the tasks (goals) carried out by agents, and task decomposition, using textual templates and diagrams.

- *Expertise Model:* describes the knowledge needed by the agents to carry out the tasks. The knowledge structure follows the KADS approach, and distinguishes domain, task, inference and problem solving knowledge. Several instances of this model are developed for modelling the inferences on the domain, on the agent itself and on the rest of agents. The authors propose the distinction between *autonomous problem solving methods*, that decompose a goal into subgoals that can be directly carried out by the agent itself and *cooperative problem solving methods*, that decompose a goal into subgoals that are carried out by the agent in cooperation with other agents.

- *Coordination Model:* describes the conversations between agents, that is, their interactions, protocols and required capabilities. The development of the model defines two milestones. The first milestone is intended to identify the conversations and the interactions. The second milestone is intended to improve these conversation with more flexible protocols such as negotiation and identification of groups and coalitions. The interactions are modelled using the formal description techniques MSC (Message Sequence Charts) and SDL (Specification and Description Language).

- *Organisation Model:* describes the organisation in which the MAS is going to be introduced and the organisation of the agent society. The description of the multiagent society uses an extension of the object model of OMT, and describes the agent hierarchy, the relationship between the agents and their environment, and the agent society structure.

- *Communication Model:* details the human-software agent interactions, and the human factors for developing these user interfaces.

- *Design model:* collects the previous models and is subdivided into three submodels: *application design:* composition or decomposition of the agents of the analysis, according to pragmatic criteria and selection of the most suitable agent architecture for each agent; *architecture design:* designing of the relevant aspects of the agent network: required network, knowledge and telematic facilities and *platform design:* selection of the agent development platform for each agent architecture.

This methodology has been successfully applied in several research projects in different fields, as intelligent network management (project CICYT TIC94-9139 *PROTEGER: Multi-Agent System for Network and Service Management*) and development of hybrid systems with multiagent systems (project ESPRIT-9119 MIX, Modular Integration of Symbolic and Connectionist Knowledge Based Systems).

4 Other approaches

The methodology *Cassiopeia*

The methodological approach called *Cassiopeia* [7], distinguishes three main steps for designing a MAS, applied to the robot soccer teams domain. Firstly, the elemental agent behaviours are listed using functional or object oriented techniques. Then the relational behaviours are analysed, that is, the dependencies between the agents are studied using a coupling graph. Finally, the dynamics of the organisation are described, that is, who can start or end a coalition, by analysing the coupling graph.

Cooperative Information Agents design

Verharen [46] proposes a methodology from a business process perspective. The methodology proposes the following models:

- *Authorisation model:* describes the authorised communication and obligations between the organisation and the environment and the internal communications using authorisation diagrams. After identifying the current situation, it is redesigned for improving the efficiency of the business processes.
- *Communication model:* refines the previous model describing in detail the contracts between the agents, using petri nets. The transactions between the agents are modelled using transaction diagrams that describe the relationship between speech-acts and goals.
- *Task model:* specifies the task decomposition using task diagrams.
- *Universe of Discourse model:* concerns the modelling of the content of the messages exchanged between the agents, using object-oriented techniques.

5 Formal Approaches

Several formal approaches have tried to bridge the gap between formal theories and implementations [10]. Formal agent theories are [10] *agent specifications* that allow the complete specification of the system. Though formal methods are not easily scalable in practice [13], there are specially useful for verifying and analysing critical applications, prototypes and complex cooperating systems.

Traditional formal languages such as Z have been used [30], providing an elegant framework for describing a system at different levels of abstractions. Since there is no notion of time in Z [30, 10, 13], it is less well suited to specifying agent interactions.

Another approach has been the use of temporal modal logics [49] that allows the representation of dynamic aspects of the agents and a basis for specifying, implementing and verifying agent based systems. The implementation of the specification can be done [49] by directly executing the agent specification with a language such as *Concurrent Metatem* [14] or by compiling the agent specification.

The usage of formal languages for multi-agent specification such as *DESIRE* [4] are a very interesting alternative to be used as detailed design language in any methodology. *DESIRE* (framework for DEsign and Specification of Interacting REasoning components) proposes a component-based perspective based on a task decomposition.

6 Techniques based on the experience of agent developers

The definition of methodologies for developing multiagent systems is a recent development. Nevertheless, multiagent systems have been successfully applied to different fields using different multiagent platforms. During this application, some agent developers have taken a software engineering perspective. Although they have not "formally" defined an AO methodology, they have given general guidance for MAS development. In this section, some of these recommendations are reviewed. Another important contribution is a collection of common mistakes of agent system developers [50].

The *ARCHON* experience

ARCHON [6, 45] is a complete development environment for MAS, which proposes a methodology for analysing and designing MAS.

The *analysis* combines a *top-down* approach, that identifies the system goals, the main tasks and their decomposition and a *bottom-up* approach, that allows the reuse of preexisting systems, constraining the top-down approach.

The *design* is subdivided into agent community design and agent design. The *agent community* design defines the agent granularity and the role of each agent. Then the authors propose the design of the user interfaces. Finally, the skills and interchanged messages are listed. The *agent design* encodes the skills for each agent (plans, rules, etc.).

The *MADE* experience

MADE [51, 36] is a development environment for rapid prototyping of MAS. It proposes a development methodology for designing MAS, extending the five stages for knowledge acquisition proposed by Buchanan *et al* [11]: Identification, Conceptualisation, Decomposition (added for agent identification), Formalisation, Implementation and Testing (here the integration of the MAS is added).

Coordination languages

There are several coordination languages that can be an alternative to interaction modelling and included in an AO methodology: (1) using *finite state representation* for conversations such as COOL [1] and *AgentTalk* [29]; (2) using a *formal language* which takes advantage of formal description techniques of protocol engineering such as *Yubarta* [38].

The *AWIC* Method

The *AWIC* method [34] proposes an iterative design approach. In every cycle, five models are developed, an agent is added to the system, and the overall system is tested. The proposed models are:

- *A: The agent model*. The developing of this model consists of the identification of the active agents of the problem, the specification of their tasks, sensors, actuators, world knowledge and planning abilities. Then a suitable agent architecture should be specified for each agent.
- *W: The world model*. This model represents the environment the agents operate in, detailing the world laws that minimise the coordination between agents and testing if the agent tasks are feasible in the world.
- *I: The interoperability model*. This model defines how the world reflects the actions of the agents and how the agents perceive the world.
- *C: The coordination model*. This models specify the protocols and interchanged messages among agents and study the suitability of joint planning or social structuring.

The decentralising refinement method

An interesting approach to bridge the gap among theory and practice is the decentralising refinement method [44]. This method proposes to start with a centralised solution to the problem. Then a general problem-solving method is abstracted out. The next step is the identification of the assumptions made on the agents' knowledge and capabilities, and the relaxation of these assumptions in order to obtain more realistic versions of the distributed system. Finally, the system is specified with a formal language. The method takes into account the reuse of the problem-solving methods, by identifying connections among parts of the problems and the agents that solve them.

7   Conclusions

This article has shown that there are several emerging agent-oriented methodologies. The reviewed methodologies are mainly extensions to known object-oriented or knowledge engineering methodologies. Which relevant aspects of object-oriented and knowledge engineering can be reused and which aspects are not covered have been discussed. In addition, the models and modelling process of these agent-oriented methodologies have been shown.

Several open issues not included in the reviewed methodologies can be cited, such as mobile agents design and user interface design [17] that is mentioned but not particularly developed in any methodology.

After the reviewing of these agent-oriented methodologies, several questions can arise:

- *Why are AO methodologies necessary?* The question of the need of AO methodologies have been mentioned previously in [22, 23, 33, 13]. Obviously, the engineering approach [13] to agent-based systems development is a key factor for their introduction in industry. This principled development will be specially needed as the number of agents in a system increases. The standard advantages of an engineering approach, such as management, testing and reuse should be applied in the development of agent-based systems.

– *Is agent technology mature enough for defining agent-oriented methodologies?* As long as there are no standard definitions of an agent, an agent architecture, or an agent language, we could think that the methodologies presented here will only be used by individual researchers to program their agent based application using their own agent language, architectures and theories. The methodologies reviewed here have shown that there is a conceptual level for analysing the agent-based systems, no matter the agent theory, agent architecture or agent language they are supported by. This conceptual level should describe:

- *Agent Models:* the characteristics of each agent should be described, including skills (sensors and effectors), reasoning capabilities and tasks.
- *Group/Society Models:* the relationships and interactions between the agents.

The lack of standard agent architectures and agent programming languages is actually the main problem for operationalising the models, or providing useful "standard" code generation. Since there is no standard agent architecture, the design of the agents needs to be customised to each agent architecture. Nevertheless, the analysis models are independent of the agent architectures, they describe what the agent-based system has to do, but not how this is done.

– *What is the relationship between AO methodologies and agent architectures*

Agent architectures are taken into account in different ways in two of the reviewed methodologies. *CoMoMAS* selects the agent architecture during the analysis, while *MAS-CommonKADS* considers that it is a design issue, and the agent architecture should be selected depending on the requirements of the analysis. In addition, *MAS-CommonKADS* proposes an expertise model of a generic agent architecture that guides the knowledge acquisition process.

A first solution to the problem of the selection of an agent architecture is addressed by Müller [35], that presents some guidelines about which type of architecture is best suited for which type of application.

– *Are the reviewed AO methodologies just individual efforts, or are they converging efforts?*

As we have stated previously, the reviewed AO methodologies can be compared since they use the same key concepts: mental state, tasks, interactions and group modelling. They propose complementary modelling techniques, though the degree of elaboration of these methodologies is quite different.

References

1. Mihai Barbuceanu and Mark S. Fox. Capturing and modeling coordination knowledge for multi-agent systems. *Journal on Intelligent and Cooperative Information Systems*, July 1996.
2. Alan H. Bond and Les Gasser. An analysis of problems and research in DAI. In Alan H. Bond and Les Gasser, editors, *Readings in Distributed Artificial Intelligence*, pages 3–36. Morgan Kaufmann Publishers: San Mateo, CA, 1988.
3. Grady Booch. *Object-Oriented Design with Applications.* Benjamin/Cummings, Redwood City, CA, 1991.

4. F. M. T. Brazier, B. M. Dunin-Keplicz, N. R. Jennings, and Treur J. DESIRE: Modelling multi-agent systems in a compositional formal framework. *Int Journal of Cooperative Information Systems*, 1(6):67–94, January 1997.

5. Birgit Burmeister. Models and methodology for agent-oriented analysis and design. In K Fischer, editor, *Working Notes of the KI'96 Workshop on Agent-Oriented Programming and Distributed Systems*, 1996. DFKI Document D-96-06.

6. David Cockburn and Nick R. Jennings. ARCHON: A distributed artificial intelligence system for industrial applications. In G. M. P. O'Hare and N. R Jennings, editors, *Foundations of Distributed Artificial Intelligence*, pages 319–344. John Wiley & Sons, 1996.

7. Anne Collinot, Alexis Drogoul, and Philippe Benhamou. Agent oriented design of a soccer robot team. In *Proceedings of the Second International Conference on Multi-Agent Systems (ICMAS-96)*, pages 41–47, Kyoto, Japan, December 1996.

8. Rational Software Corporation. *Unified Modelling Languaje (UML) version 1.0*. Rational Software Corporation, 1997.

9. Rose Dieng. Specifying a cooperative system through agent-based knowledge acquisition. In *Proceedings of the International Workshop on Cooperative Systems (COOP'95)*, pages 141–160, Juen-les-Pis, January 1995. Also published in *Proc. of the 9th International Workshop on Acquisition Knowledge for Knowledge-Based Systems*, Banff, Canada, February - March 1995, pages 20-1 – 20-20.

10. M. d'Inverno, M. Fisher, A. Lomuscio, M. Luck, M. de Rijke, M. Ryan, and M. Wooldridge. Formalisms for multi-agent systems. *The Knowledge Engineering Review*, 3(12), 1997.

11. B. G. Buchanan et al. Constructing an expert system. In F. Hayes-Roth, D. A. Waterman, and D. Lenat, editors, *Building Expert Systems*. Addison-Wesley, 1983.

12. FIPS Pub 183. Integration definition for function modeling (IDEF0). Software Standard. Modelling techniques. FIPS Pub 183, Computer Systems Laboratory National Institute of Standards and Technology, Gaithersburg, Md. 20899, 1993.

13. M. Fisher, J. Müller, M. Schroeder, G. Staniford, and G. Wagner. Methodological foundations for agent-based systems. In *Proceedings of the UK Special Interest Group on Foundations of Multi-Agent Systems (FOMAS). Published in Knowledge Engineering Review (12) 3, 1997*, 1997. http://www.dcs.warwick.ac.uk/ fomas/fomas96/abstracts/ker3.ps.

14. M. Fisher and M. Wooldridge. On the formal specification and verification of multi-agent systems. *International Journal of Cooperative Information Systems*, 1(6):37–65, 1997.

15. Les Gasser and Jean-Pierre Briot. Object-based concurrent processing and distributed artificial intelligence. In Nicholas M. Avouris and Les Gasser, editors, *Distributed Artificial Intelligence: Theory and Praxis*, pages 81–108. Kluwer Academic Publishers: Boston, MA, 1992.

16. Norbert Glaser. *Contribution to Knowledge Modelling in a Multi-Agent Framework (the Co-MoMAS Approach)*. PhD thesis, L'Universtité Henri Poincaré, Nancy I, France, November 1996.

17. Lynne E. Hall. User design issues for distributed artificial intelligence. In G. M. P. O'Hare and N. R Jennings, editors, *Foundations of Distributed Artificial Intelligence*, pages 543–556. John Wiley & Sons, 1996.

18. D. Harel. Statecharts: A visual formalism for complex systems. *Sci. Computer Program*, 8:231–247, 1987.

19. Carlos A. Iglesias, Mercedes Garijo, José C. González, and Juan R. Velasco. Analysis and design of multiagent systems using MAS-CommonKADS. In AAAI'97 Workshop on Agent Theories, Architectures and Languages, Providence, RI, July 1997. ATAL. (An extended version of this paper has been published in *INTELLIGENT AGENTS IV: Agent Theories, Architectures, and Languages*, Springer Verlag, 1998.

20. ITU-T. Z100 (1993). CCITT specification and description language (SDL). Technical report, ITU-T, June 1994.

21. I. Jacobson, M. Christerson, P. Jonsson, and G. Övergaard. *Object-Oriented Software Engineering. A Use Case Driven Approach.* ACM Press, 1992.

22. N. R. Jennings and A. J. Jackson. Agent-based meeting scheduling: A design and implementation. *Electronic Letters, The Institution of Electrical Engineering,* 31(5):350–352, March 1995.

23. N. R. Jennings and M. Wooldridge. Applying agent technology. *Applied Artificial Intelligence,* 9(6):357–370, 1995.

24. Elisabeth A. Kendall, Margaret T. Malkoun, and Chong Jiang. A methodology for developing agent based systems for enterprise integration. In D. Luckose and Zhang C., editors, *Proceedings of the First Australian Workshop on DAI,* Lecture Notes on Artificial Intelligence. Springer-Verlag: Heidelberg, Germany, 1996.

25. J. Kingston. Modelling interaction between a KBS and its users. *Newsletter of BCS SGES Methodologies Interest Group,* 1, August 1992. Also available from AIAI as AIAI-TR-141.

26. D. Kinny. The AGENTIS agent interaction model. In J. P. Müller, M. P. Singh, and A. S. Rao, editors, *Intelligent Agents V — Proceedings of the Fifth International Workshop on Agent Theories, Architectures, and Languages (ATAL-98),* Lecture Notes in Artificial Intelligence. Springer-Verlag, Heidelberg, 1999. In this volume.

27. David Kinny, Michael Georgeff, and Anand Rao. A methodology and modelling technique for systems of BDI agents. In W. van der Velde and J. Perram, editors, *Agents Breaking Away: Proceedings of the Seventh European Workshop on Modelling Autonomous Agents in a Multi-Agent World MAAMAW'96, (LNAI Volume 1038).* Springer-Verlag: Heidelberg, Germany, 1996.

28. K. Kosanke. *CIMOSA - A European Development for Enterprise Integration.* IOS Press, 1993.

29. Kazushiro Kuwabara, Toru Ishida, and Nobuyasu Osato. AgenTalk: Coordination protocol description for multiagent systems. In *Proceedings of the First International Conference on Multi-Agent Systems (ICMAS-95),* page 455, San Francisco, CA, June 1995.

30. Michael Luck, Nathan Griffiths, and Mark d'Inverno. From agent theory to agent construction: A case study. In J. P. Müller, M. Wooldridge, and N. R. Jennings, editors, *Intelligent Agents III (LNAI 1193),* Lecture Notes in Artificial Intelligence. Springer-Verlag: Heidelberg, Germany, 1997.

31. B. Moulin and L. Cloutier. Collaborative work based on multiagent architectures: A methodological perspective. In Fred Aminzadeh and Mohammad Jamshidi, editors, *Soft Computing: Fuzzy Logic, Neural Networks and Distributed Artificial Intelligence,* pages 261–296. Prentice-Hall, 1994.

32. Bernard Moulin and Mario Brassard. A scenario-based design method and an environment for the development of multiagent systems. In D. Lukose and C. Zhang, editors, *First Australian Workshop on Distributed Artificial Intelligentce, (LNAI volumen 1087),* pages 216–231. Springer-Verlag: Heidelberg, Germany, 1996.

33. H. Jürgen Müller. (Multi)-agent systems engineering. In *Second Knowledge Engineering Forum,* Karlsruhe, February 1996.

34. H. Jürgen Müller. Towards agent systems engineering. *International Journal on Data and Knowledge Engineering. Special Issue on Distributed Expertise,* (23):217–245, 1996.

35. J. P. Müller. The right agent (architecture) to do the right thing. In J. P. Müller, M. P. Singh, and A. S. Rao, editors, *Intelligent Agents V — Proceedings of the Fifth International Workshop on Agent Theories, Architectures, and Languages (ATAL-98),* Lecture Notes in Artificial Intelligence. Springer-Verlag, Heidelberg, 1999. In this volume.

36. G.M.P O'Hare and M.J. Wooldridge. A software engineering perspective on multi-agent system design: Experience in the development of MADE. In Nicholas M. Avouris and Les Gasser, editors, *Distributed Artificial Intelligence: Theory and Praxis*, pages 109–127. Kluwer Academic Publishers: Boston, MA, 1992.

37. Arturo Ovalle and Catherine Garbay. Towards a method for multi-agent system design. In M. A. Bramer and R. W. Milne, editors, *Proceedings of Expert Systems 92, the 12th Annual Technical Conference of the British Computer Society Specialist group on Expert Systems, Research and Development in Expert Systems IX*, British Computer Society Conference Series, pages 93–106, Cambridge, U.K., December 1992. Cambridge University Press.

38. Alejandro Quintero, María Eugenia Ucrós, and Silvia Takhashi. Multi-agent systems protocol language specification. In *Proccedings of the CIKM Workshop on Intelligent Information Agents*, December 1995.

39. Björn Regnell, Michael Andersson, and Johan Bergstrand. A hierarchical use case model with graphical representation. In *Proceedings of ECBS'96, IEEE International Symposium and Workshop on Engineering of Computer-Based Systems*, March 1996.

40. Ekkart Rudolph, Jens Grabowski, and Peter Graubmann. Tutorial on message sequence charts (MSC). In *Proceedings of FORTE/PSTV'96 Conference*, October 1996.

41. J. Rumbaugh, M.Blaha, W. Premerlani, F. Eddy, and V. Lorensen. *Object-Oriented Modeling and Design*. Prentice-Hall, 1991.

42. A. Th. Schreiber, B. J. Wielinga, J. M. Akkermans, and W. Van de Velde. CommonKADS: A comprehensive methodology for KBS development. Deliverable DM1.2a KADS-II/M1/RR/UvA/70/1.1, University of Amsterdam, Netherlands Energy Research Foundation ECN and Free University of Brussels, 1994.

43. Yoav Shoham. Agent-oriented programming. *Artificial Intelligence*, 60(1):51–92, March 1993.

44. Munindar P. Singh, Michael N. Huhns, and Larry M. Stephens. Declarative representations of multiagent systems. *IEEE Transactions on Knowledge and Data Engineering*, 5(5):721–739, October 1993.

45. L. Z. Varga, N. R. Jennings, and D. Cockburn. Integrating intelligent systems into a cooperating community for electricity distribution management. *International Journal of Expert Systems with Applications*, 7(4):563–579, 1994.

46. Egon M. Verharen. *A Language-Action Perspective on the Design of Cooperative Information Agents*. PhD thesis, Katholieke Universieit Brabant, the Netherlands, March 1997.

47. Hans-Peter Weih, Joachim Schue, and Jacques Calmet. CommonKADS and cooperating knowledge based systems. In *Proceedings of the 4th KADS User meeting*, GMD, Bonn, 1994.

48. R. Wirfs-Brock, B. Wilkerson, and L. Wiener. *Designing Object-Oriented Software*. Prentice-Hall, 1990.

49. M. Wooldridge. Agents and software engineering. *AI*IA Notizie XI*, 3, September 1998.

50. M. Wooldridge and N. R. Jennings. Pitfalls of agent-oriented development. In P. Sycara and M. Wooldridge, editors, *Agents '98: Proceedings of the Second International Conference on Autonomous Agents*. ACM Press, May 1998.

51. Michael Wooldridge, Greg O'Hare, and Rebecca Elks. FELINE: A Case Study in the Design and Implementation of a Co-operating Expert System. In *Proceedings of the International Conference on Expert Systems and their Applications (Avignon-91*. Avignon-91, May 1991.

The Agentis Agent Interaction Model

David Kinny

Intelligent Agent Laboratory
Department of Computer Science
University of Melbourne
Parkville 3052, Australia
dnk@cs.mu.oz.au

Abstract. Agentis is a framework for the implementation of commercial, interactive, process-driven application systems, and is based upon an underlying agent
technology (presently dMARS) that provides core agent functionality. These systems are intended to be programmed *by the business process owner* – application
functionality is defined by a set of procedure and data definitions in an abstract
process description language called GEM, and the framework is designed to allow
these specifications to be easily modified and extended by their owner after the
system has been implemented and commissioned. The tool set that supports the
specification process has an industry-standard look-and-feel and is designed to be
intuitive to non-technical users such as business analysts. Its use is supported by a
methodology that guides specification refinement, helping to take agent-oriented
programming out of the research lab and into the world of commerce and industry.
The Agentis framework provides structure and functionality not provided by the
underlying dMARS system. Key conceptual components are an *agent model* that
defines standard agent types, and an agent *interaction model* based on explicit notions of services and tasks, a strictly typed agent communication language, a set
of protocols that provide reliable, concurrent provision of services and tasks, and
conventions for structuring agents into a hierarchy and controlling their activity.
Concrete components are built-in agents that provide services for system management and monitoring, and standard interfaces that facilitate the integration of
the Agentis system with other system components such as middleware, databases,
user interfaces, web browsers and servers, and legacy systems. In a companion paper to this one, we have described and formally specified the interaction protocols
that are a key element of the interaction model [3]. In this paper we motivate and
present the design of the Agentis interaction model and describe its functionality.

1 Introduction

Agent technologies such as dMARS [2, 10] are now sufficiently robust and mature to
serve as the basis for commercial application systems, however they do not constrain
to any great extent the structure of the Multi-Agent System (MAS) which is developed.
While this lack of constraint is an advantage for research purposes and in some complex
engineering applications, the large design space that results and the lack of predefined,
higher-level component abstractions tend to complicate the design process and and in-
hibit software reuse. This is a barrier to the use of such technologies in the world of commerce and industry, as are other limitations which are perhaps more specific to dMARS.

dMARS is a generic BDI [1,6] agent technology, based upon compilation of agent specifications directly into C++ code. As a result of this approach, it is fast, efficient, and portable to a wide range of platforms. However, it lacks standard interfaces and provides only basic functionality in the all important area of communication, with I/O primitives that allow agents to send and reply to messages, and a C++ library that permits applications to be built that can communicate with agents. The intention is that system developers build upon these primitives a communications subsystem that fulfils application specific requirements, and build appropriate interfaces to non-dMARS system components. dMARS agents are programmed in a powerful graphical plan language which has a long pedigree [7], but which also has a long learning curve and operates at a level of abstraction that is too low for business application development.

The approach taken to addressing these issues in the development of the Agentis system has been to define a standard *multiagent architecture* that is sufficiently constrained to effectively guide system design, but sufficiently configurable to allow the creation of systems that cover a range of scales from small applications running on a single host, to those with thousands of customers and agents, running on many distributed hosts. The framework provides much functionality that is absent from dMARS, and support for integration with industry-standard system components such as middleware, databases, user interfaces, web browsers and servers, and also with non-standard components such as legacy systems.

Application development is supported by a business-friendly programming environment and toolset that allow the specification of process and data models in a graphical language (GEM) which is more conventional than the dMARS language, operates at a higher level of abstraction, and is guided by a comprehensive methodology. GEM primitives are the usual operations for manipulation of local data, subgoals which are achieved in a context-sensitive manner, and *service* and *task* requests to other agents or *interface processes*, such as user and database interfaces. GEM specifications are compiled directly into dMARS code, which is then embedded in particular agents within the framework.

A key objective of this approach is to decouple the specification of business processes and data from the framework and infrastructure which supports them. As a consequence, it is possible to change and extend the application behaviour entirely at the GEM level without the need to make any changes to the standard software components of the Agentis system, or to the custom interface processes that may have been developed as part of the application system. The effect is to provide the process owners with an application system in whose development they are key players, and which they can rapidly change and extend without having to depend upon the system supplier or their IT department to make the necessary modifications. The GEM development methodology plays a central role in making this flexibility accessible to business analysts.

The commercial focus of Agentis is upon interactive application systems such as call centers and web sites which customers use directly via the internet, touchtone phones, or voice recognition systems, or indirectly via a customer service representative (CSR). Alternatively, the customers may be internal to a business with interaction occurring via conventional user interfaces running on their desktop computers. Key business drivers are to facilitate rapid process change and to provide highly personalized services to each individual customer, which can be done quite naturally using the context-sensitivity of GEM process specifications. Agentis is a commercially available software product. It has been used to implement a web-based application system that matches job seekers with employment agencies, and is being used to develop applications in the healthcare industry and other business areas.

Agentis has its origins in several threads of research and development that have been performed at the Australian AI Institute in the last few years, including research into an agent system design methodology [12] and modelling technique [11], which has guided the design of the development environment and the GEM programming language and methodology[1], and the lessons learned from the development (in dMARS) of a large-scale call centre application system. The major conceptual advance has been the development and refinement of a standard multi-agent architecture and a model of interaction between agents which together comprise the Agentis *Agent Interaction Model* which is the subject of this paper.

We commence by introducing the elements of this model and relating it to previous work. In subsequent sections we focus upon the interaction component of the model. In a companion paper, we provide a description and formal specification of the interaction protocols that are key elements of the interaction model [3].

2 Modelling Agents and their Interactions

In previous work on agent system modelling [11], we have presented two models that together describe the structure of a multi-agent system, viewing agents from an external perspective:

1. An *Agent Model* describes the hierarchical relationships among different abstract and concrete agent classes, and identifies the agent instances which may exist within the system, their multiplicity, and when they may come into existence.

2. An *Interaction Model* describes the responsibilities of an agent class, the services it provides, their associated interactions, and the control relationships between agent classes, such as responsibilities for agent creation and deletion, and delegation. It includes the syntax and semantics of inter-agent communication, and communication between agents and other system components, such as user interfaces.

In this section we briefly review the essential elements of the Agentis agent model. In the next section we will focus upon the Agentis interaction model and the major functionality it provides.

Overview of the Agentis Agent Model

The key elements of the Agentis agent model are:

– an inheritance hierarchy of abstract and concrete (instantiable) agent classes,

---

[1] A survey of the state of the art in agent-oriented methodologies may be found elsewhere within this volume [9].

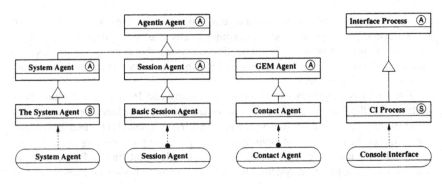

Fig. 1. Agentis Agent Class and Instance Model

- a specification of constraints upon class instantiation, i.e., of what agents may exist,
- an initial agent configuration and a specification of which agents may be created and deleted at runtime, i.e., the statics and dynamics of the elements of the MAS, and
- a specification of how agents are mapped to operating system processes.

The first element is of lesser importance within the Agentis system, since all agent classes are predefined within the framework, and it is only the behaviour of one particular class that can be modified by user specifications.

Figure 1 depicts the basic Agentis agent class and instance model, which captures all but the last of these elements. Classes are denoted by rectangular icons and instances by oval icons. Details of the individual classes, such as their attributes, are omitted here for clarity. Inheritance relations are represented by edges bearing a triangle with a vertex pointing towards the superclass, and instantiation relationships by a dotted vector from instance to class. Abstract classes are distinguished by the adornment Ⓐ and statically instantiated classes by Ⓢ. The filled circles ● adjacent to the Session and Contact agent instance icons indicate that they may be instantiated multiple times. By contrast, only one Console Interface process is permitted (per host system).

Agent Classes An Agentis system is a hierarchy[2] of agents and other processes, called *interface processes*, with which they interact. The agents are instances of one of three classes.

System agents are created at system startup and provide process control and other services to suitably privileged requestors. There is at least one such agent (**The** System Agent) on every host, which provides services that allow for the creation and deletion of other agents, system monitoring, event and error logging, etc. System agents provide predefined sets of services, and are part of the Agentis infrastructure.

---

[2] There are in fact two quite distinct hierarchies; the inheritance hierarchy among agent classes in the agent model, and the control hierarchy that exists among agents at runtime. The latter is captured in the interaction model.

Contact agents are created for each customer contact. This may be an incoming or out-going call, another form of contact such as a request via a web-server, or activation of a *commitment* resulting from an earlier contact. Contact agents cache data related to the contact, and provide personalized services to the customer. They provide a set of application-specific services and tasks defined by GEM specifications.

Session agents are created when a customer service representative logs on. Their services enable the CSR to manipulate contacts, and include login, contact transfer, future commitments and logout. A session agent may have a number of contact agents associated with it at any time. Session agents are part of the infrastructure.

An application system may contain more than one different type of each of these classes of agents, and may contain multiple instances of a given agent type. Related agents may be grouped into processes in various ways, as permitted by the dMARS system.

Note that only contact agents are generated by the Agentis GEM compiler. System and session agents are programmed directly in the dMARS language and provide functionality that is not application specific. In a sense, the system and session agents and interface processes provide a virtual environment in which the contact agents operate.

Interface Processes As well as instances of these agent classes, different types of interface processes exist.

User interface (UI) processes typically request services from Agentis agents, and perform tasks upon request by the agent, which are usually requests for information relevant to the service being provided. Each session and contact agent has an associated user interface process.

DataServer interface (DSI) processes provide various information storage and retrieval services, linking to components such as databases and digital libraries.

Console interface (CI) processes allow the system manager to request services from the system agent.

System interface (SI) processes allow external systems or processes to control and monitor the execution of an Agentis system.

Various standard interfaces are available as part of the Agentis infrastructure, providing, for example, services for accessing industry-standard components such as ODBC-compliant databases. Custom interfaces, such as GUI's, will usually be developed as part of the application framework using a C++ or JAVA API that implements the interaction model. Interface processes are permitted to be multi-functional, combining more than one of these interface types in a single process.

Agent Instances An agent instance model specifies how and when these agent classes may be instantiated. The standard initial configuration consists of a single system agent and console interface process, and possibly other interface processes[3]. The agent system

---

[3] In order to provide as much flexibility as possible in the design and configuration of the application-specific components of the system, the creation and deletion of interface processes is not directly managed by Agentis.

is extended dynamically as CSR's log in and/or customers make contact. Any appropriately privileged interface process may request the system agent to create a new session agent, and in doing so, must specify the interface processes with which that agent will interact. Similarly, the user interface associated with a session agent may request it to create a new contact agent, which has its own associated interface processes. Contact agent creation may also be done indirectly by a request to the system agent.

Agent to Process Mapping Agentis inherits the scalability and flexibility of the underlying dMARS system. Agents may be mapped to individual operating system processes, or combined, with multiple agents in a single process. Agent processes communicate transparently via TCP/IP sockets and may be distributed across multiple host systems. The usual mapping combines a session agent and all its subsidiary contact agents within a single process. Communications between these agents is optimized – messages are passed internally within the process rather than via socket connections.

The way in which agents are mapped to processes determines, amongst other things, the number of TCP socket connections required to support inter-agent communications. Each process requires, at minimum, a TCP port on which it can establish connections to other processes, and in addition may require a second port on which it can accept connections from other agent or interface processes.

3 The Agentis Interaction Model

Having introduced the essential elements of the agent model, we can proceed to describe the interaction model. For ease of exposition, in what follows we will refer to Agentis agents and interface processes collectively as agents, distinguishing them only where necessary. The key elements of the model are:

- a conceptual model of agent interaction based upon notions of services and tasks and associated concepts such as registration and notification,
- a communication language and its associated set of communication protocols, and
- a set of associations and control relationships between agents that further constrain their communication and behaviour.

We consider each of these elements in detail in the sections that follow.

3.1 The Conceptual Model

Agents in the Agentis framework exist to perform *services*, which are complex activities executed by a provider agent for a requestor, and *tasks*, which are simpler activities that are performed by the requestor or provider as an element of the provision of a service. Agents may also perform activities in response to both external and internal events. The requestor may be any agent but most commonly is a UI process, i.e., the services are initiated (directly or via a CSR) by the customers. Tasks provide the mechanism for interaction with the customer during the provision of a service. DSI processes, by contrast, provide services to Agentis agents rather than requesting them, but may notify agents of

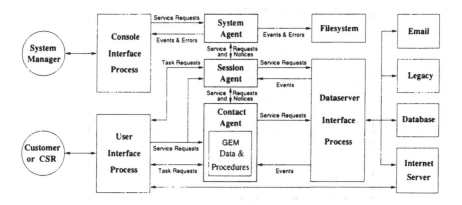

Fig. 2. Agentis Agent Interactions

significant events that have occurred. This model is depicted in Figure 2. The dotted box delineates the extent of the Agentis system.

Execution of a service is initiated by a request message being sent; this must be accepted or declined within a certain time. If accepted, a service agreement comes into force and both provider and requestor have certain obligations to fulfill. The basic obligation of the provider is to inform the requestor of progress towards completion and of the final outcome. Both may also need to perform certain tasks, upon request, to facilitate the execution of the service. The requestor has the right at any time after acceptance to cancel the service, and may also suspend and resume its execution. Execution of a task always occurs in the context of an existing service provision and proceeds in a similar manner, except that a valid task request may not be declined, and suspend/resume is not supported.

The services provided by an agent have unique names and are grouped into named *service classes*. In order to request an agent's services, a requestor must first *register* with the provider for a particular service class. If the registration request is accepted, the provider then supplies information to the requestor about services of that class, including their parameter type signatures, their current availability, and whether multiple instances of a service may be requested concurrently. Thus a provider may offer different groups of services to different clients, and the services' availability may depend on the identity and privileges of the requestor.

The primary purpose of registration is to provide detailed information about services *at runtime*, so that the knowledge that must be built in to client applications is minimized, and service definitions may be modified and extended without the need to recompile interface processes. Registration also serves three other purposes: to provide access control, to make available information about dynamic changes in service availability, and to establish control relationships between agents in the runtime hierarchy. We discuss this latter aspect in Section 3.3.

3.2 Communication Language and Protocols

The interaction protocols, described in detail elsewhere [3], operate at four levels: registration, service, task, and notification. The latter level permits agents to notify each other of relevant conditions or events, and to perform simple queries.

Each level has a corresponding language consisting of a set of message types which are specified by schemas. For example, at the registration level, these are:

(R) $\Longrightarrow$ (P) Register-Request (Request-id, Service-Class)
(R) $\Longleftarrow$ (P) Register-Accept (Request-id, Regn-id, Service-Descriptor-Set)
(R) $\Longleftarrow$ (P) Register-Decline (Request-id, RD-Reason)
(R) $\Longleftarrow$ (P) Register-Update (Regn-id, Service-Descriptor-Set)
(R) $\Longleftrightarrow$ (P) Register-Cancel (Regn-id, RC-Reason)

In general, messages carry typed attributes which may be simple, e.g., identifiers, reasons, and names of services, or complex, e.g., service descriptors and I/O parameter lists. Both static and dynamic checking techniques can be applied to verify the type-correctness of messages. The encoding of the messages is an implementation decision. In the current Agentis system they are encoded using the native dMARS encoding, however they could straightforwardly be encoded using the primitives of an agent communication language such as KQML [4] or that proposed by the Foundation for Intelligent Physical Agents (FIPA) [5].

The protocols were originally specified by means of finite state machines with associated textual description. One shortcoming of this approach is that it does not adequately capture constraints that cross different protocol levels, for example, that a task request message must carry a valid current service instance identifier, and dependencies that arise between different protocol instances at the same level. Accordingly, we have been developing complete formal specifications of the protocols [3] in the Z specification language.

The design objectives that the protocols fulfil or support are to provide:

– authentication and control of access to agent services,
– reliable request and provision of multiple concurrent services and tasks,
– strongly typed message parameters and runtime parameter type checking,
– flexible, efficient communication of information between agents,
– immunity to message collisions that may occur as a result of the asynchronous nature of the underlying message transport mechanism,
– reliable termination and detection of protocol errors, and
– automatic protocol shutdown on error or termination.

We consider briefly how these objectives are achieved in the following sections.

Authentication and access control Authentication and access control occur in two ways. Firstly, agents will only accept registration requests from certain others who must be identified when the agent is created. With the exception of the system agent, which uses a more complex access control technique, they will only accept service, task, and notification requests from registered agents. Secondly, agents are organized at runtime in a hierarchy that restricts and localizes communication, preventing them from sending messages to inappropriate recipients. We describe this hierarchy in Section 3.3.

Concurrent services and tasks Upon registration, requestors are sent information about the services available to them in the form of *service descriptors* – data structures whose attributes are the service's name, class, I/O parameter signature, arity, and current availability. When a service's availability changes, the provider notifies registered agents of the change via Update messages.

For example, consider a graphical user interface presented to a customer. It might display several icons for different services that may be requested, but initially all except the customer authentication service would be greyed-out to indicate unavailability. Once the customer had successfully completed authentication, other services would become available, and the provider agent would notify the GUI process of the change in availability. Note that the logic that determines availability is located in the GEM procedures, not the GUI.

Requestors may issue multiple concurrent requests to different providers, to the same provider for different services, or even for different instances of the same service. The arity attribute specifies how many concurrent instances of a service are permitted. Continuing the example, when a service of unit arity is initiated, the GUI process could automatically grey-out its icon until the service is completed, based on its knowledge of the service properties, without action by the agent.

The protocol supports concurrent requests in the following way. Each request must contain a unique[4] *request identifier*, which the provider includes in its response to the requestor, allowing the latter to match requests to responses no matter what their sequence of arrival. When a request is accepted, the provider supplies an identifier that is used for the duration of the interaction. The protocol implementation also detects and rejects requests that violate the declared service arity.

Strongly typed message parameters Services and tasks have declared I/O type signatures which specify their mandatory input, optional input, and output parameters. Parameters are named and typed, and parameter passing is by keyword. This makes possible complete type checking of all message attributes at runtime, and partial static checking at compile time. Note that partial correctness is guaranteed for contact agents and interface processes, since the GEM language elements that cause communication and the interface API's operate at a level of abstraction which conceals the message structures. Runtime type errors are detected and logged to the system error log, as are other errors such as duplicated or omitted parameters. Again, this is invaluable for debugging and may be disabled for efficiency in a production system.

There is one important extension to this typing system: certain services and tasks are *generic*; the number and type of their I/O parameters may vary at runtime, but only in accordance with the value of a mandatory parameter that carries type signature information, somewhat like the *varargs* mechanism in C++. Effectively, the runtime type signature extends the declared type signature, permitting, for example, the construction of a database interface process whose services can interpret arbitrary SQL queries.

---

[4] More precisely, the combination of requestor, request identifier, and protocol level must be unique from the perspective of the provider, so different requestors may safely use the same request identifiers, avoiding the need for global coordination of request identifier allocation.

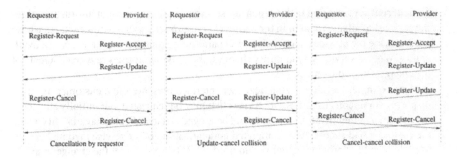

Fig. 3. Registration Interaction Scenarios

Flexible, efficient communication of information As previously mentioned, the service and task protocols allow the provider to send information about execution status and partial results prior to completion. This feature is often not required, hence is not mandated by the protocols. For simple services that can be quickly completed, even the minimal ⟨Request, Accept, Complete, Acknowledge⟩ sequence is unnecessarily inefficient. Accordingly, it is permitted to abbreviate the protocol by returning a final status and output parameters in the accept message (provided this is done within the applicable timeout period), at which point the protocol execution is complete.

Immunity to message collisions The protocols assume that the underlying transport layer provides sequenced, accurate, asynchronous, point-to-point message delivery, subject to unpredictable finite delay, or notification of delivery failure; a set of assumptions supported under the FIPA model [5]. Due to the asynchronicity, the observed sequence of transmission and reception may differ for the two agents. Figure 3 depicts three scenarios for a registration level interaction. The left diagram depicts a normal situation, where the requestor eventually terminates the interaction by sending a Cancel message, to which the provider responds with an acknowledgement. In the middle diagram, the same occurs, but note that an Update sent by the provider is received by the requestor after it has sent the Cancel. In the right diagram, both requestor and provider "simultaneously" cancel the interaction.

The protocols are designed to ensure that all collisions that may legally occur (i.e., excluding those caused by protocol violations) are benign and that, where possible and useful, the parties to the interaction can detect such situations. For example, the acknowledgement of a registration Cancel is another Cancel, which will usually carry the reason acknowledge, but in the event of a cancel collision will carry some other reason. Similarly, the protocol explicitly permits that the requestor may receive an update after it has sent a cancel, but not after it has received its acknowledgement. Other examples occur in the service protocol, where a Cancel or Suspend message from the requestor may collide with a Complete message from the provider.

Our claims about the behaviour of the protocols in collision situations are based on careful engineering and have not been formally validated. We are investigating the use of CSP [8] and other approaches to prove these and other protocol properties.

Reliable termination and detection of protocol errors The protocols are designed to ensure that all protocol violations are straightforwardly detectable. They are detected by the implementation both on transmission and receipt of messages. This may seem somewhat redundant, but is invaluable for the validation of a protocol implementation[5], and may be partially disabled in a production system for efficiency. Detectable errors include sending a message of a type not legal in a particular protocol state, sending a legal message type with incorrect attributes such as an invalid identifier or an inappropriate reason code, or failing to send a message within a specified timeout period. The action taken on such errors is to terminate the protocol execution immediately[6].

It is also important, for efficiency, that both agents know precisely when a protocol execution has terminated and no further messages relating to it can legally be received. At that point, resources associated with the protocol instance may be released. This is why the protocols incorporate a handshake on termination in all cases where a message collision is possible, since otherwise the agent might have to wait long enough for any delayed but legal message to arrive, or risk generating a spurious protocol error. Note that in order to detect reliably an invalid reuse of a request identifier, the provider must retain a record of all identifiers previously used by a requestor[7]. This is impractical in practice, and instead a minimal history is kept which effectively detects the most likely error cases.

In general, it is not possible to offer a proof of termination of the protocols since there is no *a priori* restriction on the duration of a registration, nor on the time taken to perform a service. Timeouts apply only to the generation of a response to a request, a control such as suspend/resume, or a termination sequence. We believe, however, that it is possible to do so under some stronger set of assumptions, such as where service execution is not infinitely delayed.

Automatic protocol shutdown on error or termination When a protocol execution completes, either normally or due to error or cancellation, associated protocol instances must be shutdown in a coordinated manner. These may be service interactions in the context of a registration, task interactions in the context of a service, or secondary service requests to other agents that arose during service execution. The protocol implementations implement controlled shutdown automatically; outstanding services and tasks that have been requested are cancelled, and those being provided are completed immediately with a failed status.

---

[5] There are actually three separate implementations of the protocols: in dMARS agents, and in the C++ and JAVA API's used by interface processes.

[6] There are other ways in which messages may be incorrect, e.g., a request whose I/O parameters violate the service type signature, however these and other errors such as requesting an unknown or unavailable service are not protocol errors as they are handled within the protocol, e.g., by declining the request.

[7] Alternatively, if identifiers are taken from a totally ordered domain, the constraint can be imposed that they be used in a monotonic sequence.

3.3 Associations and Control Relationships

Agentis agents are organized into a communications hierarchy which is established at runtime by a sequence of creation and registration steps. The hierarchy may span multiple host machines, and changes over time as agents are created and deleted as people log in and out, and customers make contact. The hierarchy serves two purposes: to localize and minimize the latency of inter-agent communications, and to establish control relationships between agents. On each host, the root of the local hierarchy is the system agent running on that host. One such system agent, the *primary* (usually the first created), is the designated root of the entire Agentis system. *Secondary* system agents on other hosts register as children of this agent.

When a system agent creates a child session agent, the latter immediately registers with its parent, which notifies it of the identity of the UI and DSI processes with which it will be associated. The session agent will accept registrations only from these agents, and from children it creates. Similarly, a contact agent becomes a child of the session agent that creates it, and a parent to its interface processes. Agents can communicate only with their ancestors and immediate children. Thus all agents can communicate with the system agent on their local system, which provides them with event and error logging services. System agents can also, via session agents, interrogate any Agentis agent for system monitoring purposes.

Agentis agents are thus associated in a strict tree structure, with a system agent and all of its session and contact children residing on a single host. More flexibility is permitted in the way interface processes are associated with Agentis agents. Each session and contact agent must have at least one associated UI process, and zero or more DSI processes, but these may be located on a different host, such as a desktop. A single UI or DSI interface process may be associated with a session agent and all of its child contact agents. It is even possible to have a single UI or DSI process associated with all of the session and contact agents on a host or in an entire system, though performance considerations limit the applicability of this option to smaller systems.

As mentioned before, registration establishes control relationships between agents. Agents control their children in the following manner. A newly created Agentis agent, other than the primary system agent, must successfully register with its parent before it will accept registration requests from its nominated interfaces. If at any time the parent cancels the registration, this is an imperative which forces the agent to shutdown. Before acknowledging the cancellation, it must cancel the registrations of all its children, wait for acknowledgments from them, and terminate any current services or task interactions with its parent.

By contrast, an agent that intends to shutdown may not cancel its registration with its parent until it has already shutdown its children and completed all service and task interactions with its parent. This asymmetry is required to avoid a premature termination of communication between parent and child that might otherwise occur in the event of a registration cancel collision. Interface processes, which are always leaf nodes in the hierarchy, are not required to shutdown when a parent cancels their registration, since they may have multiple parents, but must obey the same constraint on when they may initiate registration cancellation.

4 Comparison and Conclusions

An approach commonly taken in the design of agent communication frameworks, such as that proposed by FIPA [5], is to provide a comprehensive set of generic primitives for communication with which it is possible to perform queries about mental states, request arbitrarily complex actions, enquire about the existence of agents with particular capabilities, employ multiple languages and ontologies, broadcast, etc. Often no particular communication protocols are mandated, and no structural constraints are placed upon communication between agents other than those that relate to standard elements such as directory, router, and broker agents.

By contrast, the Agentis interaction model employs a small set of specialized communicative acts, a single common language and ontology, and a fixed set of communication protocols that support multiple concurrent interactions between agents which are elements of a structured hierarchy, within which communication is localized for security and efficiency. These interactions primarily concern not the performance of actions but the provision of services; more complex, abstract activities which occur within a contractual framework which mandates certain behaviour, including how the contract may be terminated. A similar model of service provision as a contract was used by Flores in the Action Workflow framework [13]. Information about services and their availability is provided at runtime by a local rather than global registration mechanism. Negotiation is reduced to a ⟨Request, {Accept, Decline}⟩ sequence, though clearly more complex negotiation protocols may be built upon this.

The model of interaction adopted in the Agentis System is thus highly constrained, and its communication language is much less flexible and expressive than others that have been developed. Its protocols, however, are efficient, flexible, and deal effectively with concurrency and problems that may arise when communication is both full-duplex and asynchronous – problems which are usually left to the agent designer to manage or ignore. Message content is strictly typed and type checked, including at the level of application-specific content. The overall focus is upon providing an industrial strength implementation of useful high-level functionality which simplifies the task of the agent and interface process designer, and supports the decoupling of the specification of agent behaviour from the infrastructure which supports it.

Acknowledgements

This paper was researched and written while the author was at the Australian Artificial Intelligence Institute. The author wishes to thank the Institute for the support which made possible its preparation and presentation.

References

1. Michael E. Bratman. *Intentions, Plans, and Practical Reason.* Harvard University Press, Cambridge, MA, 1987.
2. M. d'Inverno, D. Kinny, M. Luck, and M. Wooldridge. A formal specification of dMARS. In *Intelligent Agents IV: Proceedings of the Fourth International Workshop on Agent Theories, Architectures, and Languages (ATAL-97). LNAI 1365*, Providence, RI, 1997. Springer.

3. Mark d'Inverno, David Kinny, and Michael Luck. Interaction protocols in Agentis. In *Proceedings of the Third International Conference on Multi-Agent Systems (ICMAS-98)*, Paris, 1998.

4. T. Finin and R. Fritzson. KQML — a language and protocol for knowledge and information exchange. In *Proceedings of the Thirteenth International Workshop on Distributed Artificial Intelligence*, pages 126–136, Lake Quinalt, WA, July 1994.

5. Foundation for Intelligent Physical Agents. *FIPA 97 Specification Part 2: Agent Communication Language*, November 1997. Version 1.0.

6. Michael P. Georgeff and Felix Ingrand. Decision-making in an embedded reasoning system. In *Proceedings of the Eleventh International Joint Conference on Artificial Intelligence, IJCAI-89*, pages 972–978, Detroit, MI, 1989.

7. Michael P. Georgeff and Amy L. Lansky. Procedural knowledge. In *Proceedings of the IEEE Special Issue on Knowledge Representation*, volume 74, pages 1383–1398, 1986.

8. C. A. R. Hoare. *Communicating Sequential Processes*. Prentice Hall, Englewood Cliffs, NJ, 1985.

9. C. A. Iglesias, M. Garijo, and J. C. Gonzalez. A survey of agent-oriented methodologies. In J. P. Müller, M. P. Singh, and A. S. Rao, editors, *Intelligent Agents V — Proceedings of the Fifth International Workshop on Agent Theories, Architectures, and Languages (ATAL-98)*, Lecture Notes in Artificial Intelligence. Springer-Verlag, Heidelberg, 1999. In this volume.

10. David Kinny. *The Distributed Multi-Agent Reasoning System Architecture and Language Specification*. Australian Artificial Intelligence Institute, Melbourne, Australia, 1993.

11. David Kinny and Michael Georgeff. Modelling and design of multi-agent systems. In *Intelligent Agents III: Proceedings of the Third International Workshop on Agent Theories, Architectures, and Languages (ATAL-96). LNAI 1193*, Budapest, 1996. Springer.

12. David Kinny, Michael Georgeff, and Anand Rao. A methodology and modelling technique for systems of BDI agents. In *Agents Breaking Away: Proceedings of the Seventh European Workshop on Modelling Autonomous Agents in a Multi-Agent World, MAAMAW '96. LNAI 1038*, Eindhoven, The Netherlands, 1996. Springer.

13. R. Marshak. Action technology's workflow products – coordinating activities of people as they work together. *Workgroup Computing Report*, 16(5):4–11, 1993.

Content Based Routing as the Basis for Intra-agent Communication

Nikolaos Skarmeas and Keith L. Clark

Department of Computing
Imperial College
London
{ns4,klc}@doc.ic.ac.uk

Abstract. In this paper, an agent architecture is proposed that can be used to integrate pre-existing components that provide the domain dependent agent functionality. The key integrating feature of the agent is an active message board that is used for inter-component, hence intra-agent communication. The board is active because it automatically forwards messages to components, they do not have to poll the message board. It does this on the basis of message pattern functions that components place on the board using advertisement messages. These functions can contain component provided semantic tests on the content of the message, they can also communicate with any other component whilst they are being applied. In addition an agent management toolkit, called ALFA, is described which offers a set of agent management services. This toolkit consists of a number of servers for storing the code of the components and symbolic descriptions of what agents regarding their component makeup. A third server uses all this information to facilitate launching new agents.

1 Introduction

With the advances in Object Oriented technology, the construction of off-the shelf components that can be used and re-used for the construction of large software systems has become fashionable. The re-use can be employed either at the design level which involves abstract patterns ([2]), or at the more concrete level that involves components implemented in some specific language. This leads to a new style of software construction called *component oriented* ([15]).

In parallel, especially for distributed applications, another style of programming is often used, called *agent oriented*. In this style of programming the entities of the application are viewed as agents which are capable of accomplishing complex tasks.

A number of software architectures have been proposed for building agents. A common approach, for the internal architecture of an agent, is the separation of the agent functionalities into two main categories: the domain independent and the domain dependent one. The *domain dependent* part of the agent deals with the (possibly local) problem solving activities of the agent. The *domain independent* part deals with the communication oriented activities of the agent and other features such as knowledge base management.

The domain dependent part of the agent usually consists of a number of quasi-independent modules, different agents comprising different collections of modules. One way of designing and implementing the domain dependent part is to hardwire into the components the inter-component, hence the intra-agent communication. However, this has the disadvantage of creating inflexible architectures. Deletions and additions of components affect the overall agent functioning and usually result in the need to re-engineer some of the other components. Therefore, what is needed is a way of allowing the components to communicate with each other which allows dynamic deletion, addition and modification of components. A standard approach is the use of a message board, a shared repository of messages which components can use as their communication bus. The advantage of a message board is that the components can be heterogeneous -implemented in different programming languages - and can be written independently. When we code one component C all that we need to assume is a standard language for inter-component communication. When C needs a service S from another component all we need do is program C to place a message requesting S on the message board. We do not need to know the identity of the other component that provides service S. Indeed there may be several, and it may be useful to have them all respond to the service request. Moreover, between requests for the service S some or all of the components offering S may be replaced, allowing dynamic upgrading and reconfiguration of the agent.

A Corba ORB offers a limited message board facility for components for it offers message routing and implementation independence for object components. But its message routing requires a destination address. The destination address can be found by use of an ORB trader or yellow pages directory object, but a more high level message board would automatically route the message to the appropriate component, based on the content of the message.

The rest of this paper explains in detail a proposal for an active message board architecture that can be used to integrate components based on content's routing of messages to appropriate destination components. The message board acts as an intelligent router because it actively forwards messages to one or more of the other agent components based on the content of the message. It does not wait to be polled by the components. As with a KQML match maker, the message board finds out which component or components to send the message to using message pattern advertisements sent to the message board by the components. However, a crucial difference between our proposed message board and a KQML match maker is that the advertised patterns are not themselves KQML messages, they are not even symbolic expressions. Instead they are active patterns - test functions to be applied to each message sent to the message board. If the function succeeds, the message board knows that the component that advertised the active pattern is interested in receiving the message.

The major advantage of sending message patterns as functions is that we can incorporate semantic tests on the content of the message. The semantic tests are supplied by the advertiser, either as additional code included with the message test, or on demand. It can be provided on demand because in our implementation, using the April programming language ([14]), the active message pattern can communicate with the advertiser to get extra information regarding the acceptability of the message when the test is applied. In effect, each advertiser supplies the semantic information to the message board, but without the need for the message board to be able to understand this information. The message board simply executes the test function. The inability of a KQML style matchmaker to support application specific semantic tests on behalf of advertisers is a recognised shortcoming ([10]).

Each message pattern advertised by each component, C, is applied by the message board to each new message placed on the board. Whether or not the message is forwarded to C now depends on qualifications, concerning the destinations, specified by the sender. For example, the sender can specify one or all destinations (KQML broker-one or broker-all). In addition, it can attach an optional filter function to be applied to the list of identities of all the potential destinations to prune the set. This destination filter function can embed client semantics regarding appropriate destinations. For example, the filter function can directly query each potential destination, to ask them meta queries about quality of service, current task load etc. Only destinations offering the right quality of service will be left in the pruned destination set. All of these get sent the message.

This bilateral control of the message routing, by both senders and receivers, provides a powerful mechanism for processing and routing messages, more powerful than the contents routing of a KQML match maker and much more powerful than Linda style tuple spaces, or blackboards, which are passive message repositories that must be continually polled by processes for messages of interest.

The message board does not need to be used for every communication between components, but it is good policy to use it for each communication that opens a transaction. Subsequent communications for that transaction can be direct inter-component communications.

As we mentioned above, our message board is implemented using the April language but its functionality could be realised in any language offering code mobility and communication or call back facilities, for example, Java. The message board is part of an April based agent toolkit that we have used to build two agent based applications [17],[1]. This toolkit, contains also an agent management layer. This layer consists of a collection of servers that offer a set of management services for configuring a network of agents based on our component architecture.

Section 2 gives more detail of our component based agent architecture. Section 3 describes an example agent. Section 4 gives details of the implementation in the April language. Section 5 describes the management layer.

2   The agent architecture

Agent architectures range from quite abstract proposals of what agents should comprise ([5]) to more concrete artifacts designed for specific kinds of applications (viz. [6], [11]). A common approach (nicely summarised in [12] p115 and [7] p86), is an agent comprising a set of interrelated components whose functionality contributes to the overall agent behaviour. Each component can have its own private knowledge base but it is often useful to have an agent wide knowledge base that the components share. The *knowledge base* component is a domain independent component, although its contents will be domain dependent. It is also useful to have two other domain independent components. An agent *head*, or *communicator*, which communicates with other external agents or non-agent applications, and a *meta-component* that allows for dynamic reconfiguration of the domain dependent components. This architecture, which is more fully described in [16] is depicted in Figure 1 and explained below. All the components are concurrently executing components.

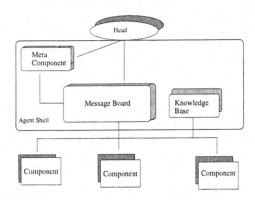

Fig. 1. The agent architecture

2.1   The knowledge base

The knowledge base component keeps information shared by all the other components. It is the global memory for all the components of the agent (each of which may also have private memory) and can be used to store information such as the beliefs, intentions and plans of the agent as well as meta-level information about other agents and the capabilities of the behavioural (the domain dependent) components. This knowledge base can be accessed and updated by all the other agent components. For the current implementation of the knowledge base, a deductive extension to April, called AprilQ ([4]), is used that provides a high level syntax for retrieving and updating information.

2.2 Behavioural components

The specific behaviour that the agent exhibits is implemented by a number of behavioural (domain dependent) components. The behavioural components will generally differ from agent to agent. A behavioural component can be composite, indeed it can itself be another agent. So agents can have a recursive structure. These behavioural components are changeable over the lifetime of the agent. This allows the agent to be reconfigured and gives it the ability to adapt to new requirements that its environment imposes. The manipulation of the behavioural components is the purpose and role of the *meta-component*.

2.3 Message board

The agent components interact with each other in two ways. They store and retrieve information from the shared knowledge base. They also interact via messages. The message interaction is supported by the active message board. Any agent component can place messages intended for one or more other components on the message board. It never explicitly reads from the message board. Components can join and withdraw without disrupting the functionality of the rest of the agent. When a new component is added to the agent it registers itself with the message board using a symbolic name and then sends advertisement messages to the board giving it a set of active message patterns. The message board stores the symbolic name together with the low level process identity of the component (needed for message forwarding) in its 'white pages' directory. It stores the advertisements, linked with the symbolic name of the component, in its 'yellow pages' directory. Because of the advertisements the component will be sent messages in the future. If the new component is pro-active, it may also place messages on the message board requesting services. It just needs to know the required format of the request, not the identities of the other components capable of servicing these requests.

An active message pattern is of the form

```
filter_pattern :: auxiliary_test_code
```

It is applied by the message board to each new message M placed on it. If the filter pattern matches the message, the auxiliary test code is executed. This usually further processes and tests parts of the message extracted as a result of the successful match with the filter pattern to make sure the message really is of interest to the component C that lodged it. However, it can also do arbitrary processing on behalf of C. As part of this processing it can communicate with other agent components. It can even communicate with C, or the component that sent the message, to determine whether or not M is really of interest to C *at this time*. If this test code succeeds, C is a *potential destination* for the message.

If the message M was communicated as a broker-all message, all the potential component destinations are found by applying each of the message board's active message patterns to the message. Then, the destination filter function which the sender may have attached to the message is applied to prune this set of potential destinations. The message M is then forwarded to each destination in the pruned set, if there are any. Finally, the message is retained on the message board until its sender specified expiry time. This is in case a component C' subsequently advertises an active pattern that successfully applies to the message, between the time of its receipt and its expiry time. If so, providing this component also satisfies the destination filter function, the message is forwarded to C'. The default expiry time for a broker message is immediate, in which case the message is not usually retained by the message board. It will only be retained if no suitable destination was found at the time of receipt.

There is a similar scenario for a message M' communicated to the message board as a broker-one single destination message. The main difference is that M' will be forwarded to at most one component destination and, after forwarding, is not retained by the message board even if its expiry time has not lapsed. It will only be retained if its expiry time has not been reached *and* no suitable destination component has yet been found.

Once the message has been forwarded, the receiver can reply directly to the component that placed the message on the board. We assume that the sender field of the message contains either the sender's symbolic name, as registered with the message board, or its low level process identity. If the former, the reply can be sent via the message board as a forward message which only requires white pages lookup by the message board. If the latter, the message is communicated directly, bypassing the message board, using the direct process to process communication.

2.4 Agent head

Agents also have a process that deals with incoming messages from other agents. This is the purpose of the head communicator which is the external communication interface of the agent. The head communicator is also a security wall to the outside world. Incoming messages arrive first at it, and are then put on the the the message board in order to be forwarded to the appropriate agent components, based on their content. Therefore, outside agents do not have direct access to the message board which is the internal agent backbone. The head may discard messages that are from unknown agents, or which are not syntactically well formed.

3 An example agent

In order to illustrate the above concepts, consider an agent that implements a travel agency which can be contacted for a ticket reservation. This agent can offer tickets for European and Asian flights. The agent has a broker component that deals with customer requests and two airline interface components dealing with the interaction with the airlines for price information and reservations. Each airline interface component deals with a particular geographical area (Figure 2). The agent also maintains a database with information regarding frequent customers, containing their address details and other personal information.

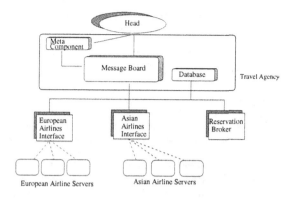

Fig. 2. A travel agent scenario

Assume that a message for a price quote for a fare between London and Tokyo arrives with date constraints and a constraint on the fare (fare < 700). This message is forwarded to the Broker because it is the only component to advertise an interest in requests for price quotes. The broker then consults the data base to see if there is information about the sender, perhaps the software agent for some customer, such as the airline preferences of the customer. Let us assume that either the customer is unknown, or it is known that they do not insist on non-stop flights. Because of this, and because of the low fare constraint, the Broker places a broker-all message on the message board for a flight reservation and fare quote without the constraint 'non-stop-direct'. This way, it will perhaps get replies from the European Airlines Interface component as well as the Asian Airlines Interface component, with the former offering cheaper quotes involving a change of flight.

4 The implementation platform

As an implementation platform for the above framework, we use the April language ([14],[13]). April offers a number of significant features such as: concurrency, symbolic list based computation, pattern matching, TCP/IP based communication between processes on different hosts, higher order features, advanced macro processing. These features can be extremely useful for the implementation of agent based applications. Our agent platform is implemented as a macro extension of April augmented with a set of predefined functions and processes.

A KQML message of the form:

```
"(request
   :language April
   :ontology ticket_reservation
   :reply_with id1
   :sender ''klc_agent@zeus.ic.ac.uk''
```

```
    :content "[(destination, Tokyo), ((From, London),
             (departure_date,"7/2/97"), (return_date,"14/2/97")]"
)"
```

can be represented as the April data value:

```
(request, [(language,April), (ontology,ticket_reservation),
          (reply_with ,id1), (sender, ''klc_agent@zeus.ic.ac.uk'')
          (content, [(destination, Tokyo), (From, London),
                    (departure_date,"7/2/97"),(return_date,"14/2/97")])])
```

The active patterns that components advertise via the message board are
represented as boolean function closures that take as argument a data value
which is the April representation of a KQML message. The Broker component
might send the message board something like:

```
(advertise, [(pattern_name,asian_tickets),
            (sender, Broker),
            (content, {(request,?LabelValuePairs) ::
               (content, any?Content) in LabelValuePairs  and
               (destination, any?Destination) in Content and
               is_true{ asian_city(Destination) or
                        european_city(Destination) } ! kb }) ])
```

which is macroed into a message of the form:

```
(advertise,
    [(pattern_name,asian_tickets),
     (sender, Broker),
     (content,{lambda(?M) ->
        M={(request, ?LabelValuePairs) ::
           (content, any?Content) in  LabelValuePairs and
           (destination, any?Destination) in Content and
           valof{
               (ask_if, {lambda(?DB)-> {
                   Destination in lookup(asian_city,DB) or
                   Destination in lookup(european_city,DB)}}
               ) >> kb;

               (reply, yes) :: sender == kb -> valis true
               | (reply, no) :: sender == kb -> valis false}
       }}) ])
```

in which the content is a function closure (the lambda) to be applied to a message
M. We will not explain the macro expanded code here. A detailed discussion of
the use of April macros and the code generated is given in [16].

The above message, when received by the message board, will cause it to
store the symbolic name of the component, Broker, the pattern name and the
code. It stores this triple in its table of current active patterns. Notice the test
condition

```
is_true { asian_city(Destination) or european_city(Destination) } ! kb
```

of the active pattern.

This is a direct query to the knowledge base component of the agent whose identity is held in the variable kb (it does not go via the message board). This is expanded into an explicit communication of a query function to the knowledge base (>> is April's message send operator). The query function will be applied to the data DB in the knowledge base. If the query function returns true, a (reply,yes) message will be returned as response. This is also an example of the power of the active patterns, which not only do local processing but can include calls to arbitrary test functions and communication to other components. This communication can be back to the component that sent the active pattern. The test functions could have been defined in and be private to the sender of the active pattern. Their code is automatically packaged up in the function closure that is the active pattern.

4.1 The message board

We adopt the KQML approach of having messages sent to the message board wrapped in an outer message with a performative indicating the senders intent. The message board takes appropriate action according to the performative of the wrapper message.

As well as broker messages the message board also accepts forward messages that give symbolic names for the destination. When a component is added to an agent, the first thing it does is register with the message board giving a symbolic name. The table of symbolic names paired with the process identity of the component that registered the name is the white pages directory of the message board. (The process identity is something like a CORBA inter-orb object reference. The process identity of the sender of any message is provided by the April communications system, on request, when a message is received). The table of registered active patterns is its yellow pages directory. Neither can be directly consulted. They are implicitly consulted by sending either a forward or broker message to the message board. On receipt of a:

```
(forward, [(content,M), (to,R)])
```

message, the board will forward M to the component that registered with the name R. For a

```
(forward_to_all,[(content,M), (to, [List of Component Names])])
```

it will send M to the list of the named components. If the destination name is not known, then a broker message:

```
(broker, [(content,M)])
```

can be sent to the message board. The message board will apply all the current active patterns to the message M and will forward M to the component that lodged the first pattern function it finds that successfully applies to M.

There is also a broker_all message and in both broker messages there can be a filter field giving a filter function which expresses the senders preferences with respect to the destinations. A destination filter of the form:

```
lambda(?D) -> is_true { has_capability(....)!kb
                and current_no_of_tasks(N)!D and N<4}
```

can be used to filter out any destination D which the knowledge base does not record as having a particular capability, or which has a current number of task in excess of 3. This information is obtained by querying D (current_no_of_tasks(N)!D). The assumes that D is itself multi-threaded and is able to answer the query whilst concurrently executing these tasks. The query will be answered using D's private knowledge base.

A component's message patterns are sent to the message board as a

```
(advertise, [(pattern_name,N),(sender,S),(content,<function defn>)])
```

message. Here, S is the symbolic name that the component has registered with the message board.

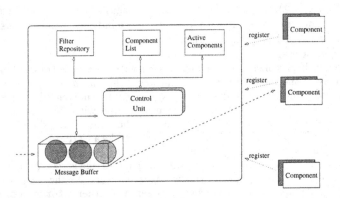

Fig. 3. The message board internal structure

The internal architecture of the message board is depicted in Figure 3. The Component List is a list of records that contain the symbolic name of each registered component and its low level process identity (needed for forwarding messages). This name indirection allows a component with a particular symbolic name N to be replaced by another process offering the same message interface. All that is needed is a protocol which first deregisters the old process with that name and then registers the new process using the same name N. Since all forward messages and advertisements (held in the Filter repository) use the symbolic name and not the process identity, the new process will transparently replace the old as far as the other components and message board is concerned. This possibility of component upgrade is the reason why the message board should always be used for the opening communication of a conversation or transaction between components, using either a broker or forward message.

The `Active components` list is a sublist of all the registered components. After registration a component must send an explicit `activate` message to be put on the active list. It can also send a `deactivate` message to get itself removed. Only active components get sent messages. This mechanism allows a component to temporarily suspend its availability.

When a message is placed in the message buffer it is processed by the control unit which accesses the three lists: `component list, active list, filter repository`.

4.2 Behaviour components

Components are implemented as April processes, which when they start executing immediately try to attach to the agent. The attachment involves sending a "registration" message to the agent head and consequently to the message board, and (optionally) the registration of active patterns on the message board. The implementation of the `reservation_broker` of the previous example is sketched below.

```
reservation_broker()
{
  (init_input, (string?agent_name,
                  string?plug_in_name, input_type[]?Input) -> {
    /* Get information about the agent and
       specific inputs for the component. */

    /* Attaching to the Agent.  Get message board (mboard)
       and database (DB) handles form the agent.*/
    (handle?mboard,
     handle?DB) = attach_to_agent(plug_in_name, MyHandle, agent_name);

    (advertise, ...) >> mboard;   /* Register active patterns */

    ... /* Rest of code */
}
```

All the components are implemented as no argument procedures in order to maintain a uniform view of them. This has proven useful for their persistent storage (see also Section 5.1). When the component is forked as a process it is sent a message containing the name of the agent that it will attached to (`agent_name`), the name under which it will get attached (`plug_in_name`) and other initial data that needs to be given to the component (`Input`). The `plug_in_name` will be the symbolic name which will be used by the message board to identify the component. The Input is a list of attribute/value pairs. The component picks up this information using the message receive statement:

```
(init_input, (string?agent_name,
                string?component_name, input_type[]?Input) -> ...
```

which is the first statement executed by the component. For the specific example, the creation of the `reservation_broker` component would be achieved using:

```
handle?H = fork reservation_broker;

(init_input, ("travel_agent", "reservation_broker",
            [(destinations, ["asia", "europe"])])]) >> H;
```

This will fork the "reservation broker" process and will send all the "bootstrapping" information via the `init_input` message to the process, identified by the handle H, i.e. the `reservation_broker`. After this information is received by the reservation broker, the call `attach_to_agent` will perform the appropriate steps for attaching the component to the agent. Essentially, this means asking the agent for the handle identifier of its message board and database process components storing these in local variables `mboard` and `DB` of the broker, and registering its `plug_in_name` with the message board. After getting hold of the message board address, it then registers its patterns before executing the rest of the component code.

5   The agent management toolkit

The agent architecture described above is supported by an agent management toolkit[1]. This consists of a set of server that offer agent management services. A server for persistently storing components is supplied. Components implemented as closures can be stored in this server. They can be dynamically fetched from this server and attached to agents. Descriptions of agents can be provided and stored in a separate *agent library*. These descriptions specify the components an agent consists of. The descriptions can be retrieved, and based on them, the appropriate components can be fetched from the code server and attached to the agent. An integrated mechanism for creating agents is provided by a management unit (illustrated in Figure 4) which provides the glue between these servers.

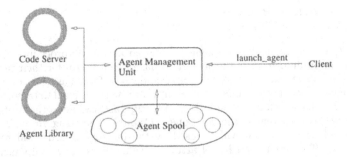

Fig. 4. The Agent Management component

---

[1] The agent architecture and this layer are called ALFA (Agent Layer For April).

It controls a spool of agents and can be requested to create a new agent and add it into the spool.

5.1 Code server

The component-oriented approach, allows agents to be easily customised. Components can be added or deleted from an agent description, so that it has different set of capabilities when launched. Alternatively, after being launched new components can be added and old ones replaced.

The code for agent components can be stored in a special process, called the *code server*. Other processes can contact the code server in order to retrieve the code they need. When the agent is started up, for example, the code for each component is retrieved from the code server, before being launched as described in Section 4.2. The following program sketches the implementation of this code server:

```
code_server()
{
    /* Table for storing component closures */
    definition CodeTable schema (string?code_name, (){}?code);
    ... /* Load any pre-registered closures */

    repeat {
      ({add_code}, (string?code_name, (){}?CodeAbstraction)) -> {
          ... /* Adding a new closure */ }
      | (retrieve_code, string?code_name) -> {
          ... /* Retrieving a code abstraction */ }
      | (delete_code, string?code_name) -> {
          ... /* Deleting a registered closure */ }
    } until quit;
};
```

The code server maintains a database table (CodeTable) where the closures are stored. They are stored as pairs with type (string, {}()), which contain a symbolic name for the code abstraction and the abstraction[2]. The symbolic name is used for retrieving and deleting the code. This code table is persistently backed-up to the file system.

When a process wants to register a new piece of code that can be used later either by itself or by other processes, it sends a **add_code** message to the code server. In this message it includes the name of the closure and the closure as a procedure abstraction that takes no input arguments. For example, in order to register the code for the **reservation_broker** process the following message needs to be sent to the code server:

```
(add_code, ("reservation_broker",
            reservation_broker)) >> handle??"CodeServer"
```

For deleting code the **delete_code** message is provided. The name of the closure has to be specified. For retrieving a specific closure now, the message:

---

[2] {}() is the April type for a no argument procedure.

```
(retrieve_code, string?code_name) -> ...
```

is provided. When it is received the code is fetched from the CodeTable and it is sent back in the form of a message like the following:

```
(retrieved_code, (code_name, CodeAbstraction)) >> replyto;
```

If for some reason the code is not found, either because it does not exist or a wrong name was specified, an error message is generated.

In order, for example, to retrieve the code for the "reservation_broker" process the following statements should be used:

```
(retrieve_code, "reservation_broker") >> handle??"CodeServer";
(retrieved_code, ("reservation_broker", (){}?componentCode)) -> {
    spawn_component(componentCode, "travel_agent", "reservation_broker",
                                    [(destinations, ["asia", "europe"]);
};
```

And after the retrieved_code message is received the componentCode can be executed. A special procedure, spawn_component is provided that will fork the component process and send the input arguments as a message, in the manner described in Section 4.2.

```
spawn_component((){}?componentCode, string?agent_name,
                string?plug_in_name, input_type[]?Input) {
    /* fork component */
    handle?H = fork componentCode;

    /* supply component with initial input information.
       It is the first message received by the component. */
    (init_input, (agent_name, plug_in_name, Input)) >> H;
}
```

The spawn_component procedure is passed the identity of the agent to which the component is being attached (agent_name), the name under which it will be known (plug_in_name) and input information (Input). Now as soon as the component is forked, it will attach itself to the agent.

The code retrieval and component launch have been wrapped up under a single routine called launch_component, the implementation of which is:

```
launch_component(string?agent_name, string?component_name,
                 string?plug_in_name, input_type[]?Input)
{
    (retrieve_code, component_name) >> handle??"CodeServer";
    /* Retrieving component code */
    (retrieved_code, (component_name, (){}?componentCode)) -> {
        /* Forking component */
        spawn_component(componentCode, agent_name, plug_in_name, Input);
    };
};
```

5.2 The agent library

The agent is constructed by attaching a set of pre-defined components to its message board. These components are implemented as April processes and are stored in the code server. If we had to describe the agent in some symbolic form, that form would basically include the list of the agent components. An agent description in general has the format:

```
(agent_name,
    [ (component_name, plug_in_name, [ ... /* Input information */])
      ... /* Other components */ ]
)
```

The description contains the agent name, and the list of names of the components. For the travel agent example, the description would be similar to:

```
("travel_agent", [ /* Component descriptions */
  ("reservation_broker", "reservation_broker",
                          [(destinations, ["asia","europe"])]),
  ( "airline_interface", "european_airline_interface", [
                (destination, "europe"),
                (european_airlines, ["lufthansa", "ba"]) ]),
  ( "airline_interface", "asian_airline_interface", [
                (destination, "asia"),
                (asian_airlines, ["jal", "ana", "korean_airlines"]) ])
])
```

This is the description of the agent with name "travel_agent" which consists of three components described above, namely a central "reservation_broker" and two components that handle the interface with airline servers ("european_airline_interface", "asian_airline_interface"). For the airline interface components the same component code is used, customised with different information regarding the destination of the flights and the airlines that it deals with.

Ideally, what we would like, is to have a library of such agent descriptions which can be re-used. Other entities can retrieve symbolic agent descriptions and use them to launch (possibly customised) instances of them. We have developed such a server and we call it the *agent library*. It is an April server which maintains a table of agent descriptions. This server is publically forked under the name "AgentLibrary". It can be sent description, asked to delete old ones, and asked to provide description based on its symbolic name. For example, a client process can send the message

```
(new_instance_description, "travel_agent",
     ... /* The travel agent description */) >> handle??"AgentLibrary";
```

which includes the description of the travel agent given above. Later we can retrieve this description by name and launch the agent using the procedure:

```
launch_agent(string?agent_name) {
    /* Fork generic agent components, i.e. meta-component,
```

```
    message board, head, database. */
fork mu(){agent_proc(agent_name)};

/* Retrieve the description of the agent */
(supply_agent_description, agent_name) >> handle??"AgentLibrary"
(description_is, agent_name, ?agentDescription) -> {

    /* Retrieve the list of components from the agent description */
    comp_type[]?componentDescription = agentDescription.components;

    /* Launch the individual components */
    for (string?component, string?plug_in_name,
                        input_type?Input) in componentDescription do {
        launch_component(agent_name, component, plug_in_name, Input);
    };
}
};
```

The result of a `launch_agent` call is to create a new instance of the `agent_proc` process which will automatically launch the domain independent components of the agent (meta-component, message board, database, head). As soon as the generic components are launched, it will get hold of the agent description from the agent library (`supply_agent_description` message); then extract the list of component descriptions (`componentDescription`) and launch them one at a time (`for ... do ...` loop).

5.3 The management platform

The above servers and procedures offer a collection of tools that provide quite a powerful and open platform for building agents. The agent management platform provides the top level interface. It provides a high level, easy to use interface to external clients for creating and managing agents. An external client, can launch an agent simply by sending a message such as:

```
(launch_agent, "travel_agent") >> handle??"ManagementPlatform"
```

to the "ManagementPlatform". The management platform also provides the capability of suspending and killing agents. There is also a graphical interface for visualising the current state of the multi-agent system and for invoking the services offered by the platform.

6 Discussion and Conclusions

Software construction increasingly follows a component oriented style, where components are constructed and used off the shelf for the construction of complex software systems. The construction of agent systems could also follow this philosophy ([8], [15]).

In this paper, an agent architecture is proposed that can be used to integrate pre-existing components. Even components written in a conventional language such as C can be integrated by providing a wrapper that accepts our KQML style messages, mapping them into internal procedure calls, and which sends the required advertisements. April has a C and Java API, which allows Unix processes written in these languages to read and write April messages. Using it, we can implement components whose main functionality is not programmed in April.

The integrating component of the agent is the message board. Attached components provide a symbolic name which is used when messages need to be forwarded to a specific component. This is used to identify the component in all other communications with the message board. It allows for dynamic component replacement. Furthermore, a content based approach to message routing has been also adopted. Components can specify active patterns in the form of code abstractions that the message board uses in order to route messages between components, when the name of a suitable destination component is not known.

Other agents do not have direct access to the message board. Messages from the outside reach the message board via a communication module, the agent head, that acts as a communication mediator between the agent components and the external entities. A network of agents can be integrated using an inter-agent message board of the functionality as the internal message board. This allows for a recursive agent structure, in which components themselves are agents.

In addition to the infrastructure for constructing a single agent, a set of additional servers are supplied which comprise a complete agent management toolkit. For persistently storing components a special persistency server called *code server* is provided. Also, the description of the components that comprise a single agent can be stored in another server, called the *agent library*. A central agent management server is used as the glue. It receives requests for launching agents and by interacting with the other two servers takes all the appropriate steps to launch the agents.

This infrastructure has been used to develop two concrete agent based applications. One is an agent layer for managing telecommunication networks ([17]). The other ([1]), communicates with a Java-based control software to control the environmental conditions in an office in accordance with the location and preferences of the occupants.

A similar approach, starting from an underlying agent architecture on which layers are built that can be used for the development of domain specific agent based applications is presented in [9]. The architecture assumed there is a BDI based architecture. Also, in [3] the issue of semantics of inter-agent communication based on speech acts is addressed, something that is not explicitly dealt in the work presented in this paper.

References

1. M Boman, P. Davidsson, N. Skarmeas, K. L Clark, and R. Gustavvson. Energy Saving and Added Customer Value in Intelligent Buildings. *PAAM'98*, 1998.

2. F. Buschmann and et al. *A System of Patterns: Pattern Oriented Software Architecture*. Wiley and Sons, 1996.

3. B. Chaib-draa and D. Vanderveken. Agent communication language: Toward semantics based on success and satisfaction. In J. P. Müller, M. P. Singh, and A. S. Rao, editors, *Intelligent Agents V — Proceedings of the Fifth International Workshop on Agent Theories, Architectures, and Languages (ATAL-98)*, Lecture Notes in Artificial Intelligence. Springer-Verlag, Heidelberg, 1999. In this volume.

4. K. L. Clark and N. Skarmeas. A Harness Language for Cooperative Information Systems. In M. Papazoglou and G. Schlageter, editors, *Cooperative Information Systems: Trends and Directions*. Academic Press, 1998.

5. Y. Demazeau and Jean Pierre Müller. Decentralised Artificial Intelligence. In Y. Demazeau and Jean Pierre Müller, editors, *Decentralised Artificial Intelligence*, pages 3–13. Elsevier Science Publisher, 1990.

6. H. Heugeneden, editor. *IMAGINE final report*. Siemens, Munich, Germany, 1994.

7. L.P. Kaelbling. A situated automata approach to the design of embedded systems. *SIGART Bulletin*, 1991.

8. E. A. Kendall and M. T. Malkoum. Design Patterns for the Development of Multiagent Systems. In C. Zhang and D. Lukose, editors, *Multi-Agent Systems: Methodologies and Applications*. Springer Verlag, 1997.

9. D. Kinny. The AGENTIS agent interaction model. In J. P. Müller, M. P. Singh, and A. S. Rao, editors, *Intelligent Agents V — Proceedings of the Fifth International Workshop on Agent Theories, Architectures, and Languages (ATAL-98)*, Lecture Notes in Artificial Intelligence. Springer-Verlag, Heidelberg, 1999. In this volume.

10. D. Kuokka and L. Harada. On using KQML for Matchmaking. *Proceedings of the First International Conference on Multi-Agent Systems*, pages 239–245, 1995.

11. V. R. Lesser and Daniel D. Corkill. The Distributed Vehicle Monitoring Testbed: A Tool for Investigating Distributed Problem Solving Networks. *The AI Magazine*, pages 15–33, Fall 1994.

12. P Maes. The agent network architecture (ANA). *SIGART Bulletin*, 1991.

13. F. McCabe. April reference manual. Technical report, Fujitsu Laboratories Ltd., Japan, 1996.

14. F. McCabe and K. L. Clark. April – Agent PRocess Interaction Language. *Intelligent Agents*, 1994.

15. T. D. Meijler and O. Nierstrasz. Beyond Objects: Components. In M. Papazoglou and G. Schlageter, editors, *Cooperative Information Systems: Trends and Directions*. Academinc Press, 1998.

16. Nikolaos Skarmeas. *Agents as Objects with Knowledge Based State*. Imperial College Press, December 1998.

17. N. Skarmeas and K. L. Clark. Intelligent Agents for Telecoms Applications (IATA'96). *IATA'96 Workshop of the European Conference on Artificial Intelligence*, August 1996.

Agent Communication Language: Towards a Semantics Based on Success, Satisfaction, and Recursion

Brahim Chaib-draa[12] and Daniel Vanderveken[3]

[1] Laval University, Computer Science Department
Pavillon Pouliot, Ste-Foy, PQ, Canada, G1K 7P4
chaib@ift.ulaval.ca
[2] DFKI GmbH Stuhlsatzenhausweg 3, D-66123 Saarbrücken, Germany
[3] Département de Philosophie, Pavillon Ringuet, CP 500
UQTR, Trois-Rivières, PQ, Canada G9A 5H7
Daniel_Vanderveken@uqtr.uquebec.ca

Abstract. Searle and Vanderveken's model of speech acts is undoubtedly an adequate model for the design of communicating agents because it offers a rich theory which can give important properties of protocols that we can formalize properly. We examine this theory by focusing on the two fundamentals notions, *success* and *satisfaction*, which represent a systematic, unified account of both the truth and the success conditional aspects. Then, we propose an adequate formalism--the situation calculus-for representing these two notions (in a recursive way) in the context of agent communication language. The resulting framework is finally used for (1) the analysis and interpretation of speech acts; (2) the semantics and descriptions of agent communication languages.

1 Introduction

Speech act theory deals with natural language utterances. In fact, it was developed to deal with utterances like "I declare open the conference", that are not easy classified as being true or false, but rather are actions. Later it was extended to deal with all utterances, with the primary vision that all utterances are *actions* of some sort or the other [2,3,17]. In distributed AI and more specifically in multiagent systems, one of the most natural ways in which intelligent interaction may occur is through communication, especially communication about action. Agents may command, request, advise, report, or permit each other to do certain actions. They may also promise actions of their own, or prohibit those of others. Therefore, speech act theory can be considered as a foundation for communication among agents. In this paper, we present a new semantics for this kind of communication based on success and satisfaction; two notions which represent a systematic, unified account of both the truth and the success conditional aspects.

2 Theory of Speech Acts: An Unified Account of both the Truth and the Success Conditional Aspects

Linguists have long acknowledged the illocutionary aspects of sentence meaning in their analysis of the different syntactic types of sentences in natural language. Using speech act theory, one can reformulate as follows their analysis of the meaning of most current types of sentences [18,20,21]: *representatives* or *assertives* which represents a state of affairs, e.g. statements; *directives* which ask the hearer to do something, e.g. orders; *commissives* which lead the speaker to commit herself to doing something, e.g. promises; *expressives* which express a certain psychological state, e.g. congratulations; *declaratives* which bring something about in the world, e.g. an excommunication.

Most elementary illocutionary acts that are the meaning of sentences in a context of utterance consist of an illocutionary force f together with a propositional content p (an elementary act will be therefore represented by $\langle f, p \rangle$) [18]. For example, the two utterances "You will leave the party" and "Leave the party!" have the same propositional content, namely that you will leave the party; but the first of these has the illocutionary force of an assertion about the future and the second has the illocutionary force of an order.

In order to analyze the logical form of illocutionary acts, one must define recursively their conditions of success and of satisfaction, as well as the truth conditions of their propositional content. The *conditions of success* of an illocutionary act are the conditions that must be obtained in a possible context of utterance in order that the speaker succeed in performing that act in that context. For example, a condition of success of a promise is that the speaker commit himself in carrying out a future course of action. The *conditions of satisfaction* of an illocutionary act are the conditions that must be obtained in a possible context. For instance, a condition of satisfaction of a promise is that the speaker carries out in the world the future course of action represented by the propositional content.

In fact, in speech act theory the notion of satisfaction is a generalization of the notion of *truth* that is needed to cover all possible illocutionary forces. Just as an assertion is satisfied if and only if (iff) it is true, a promise is satisfied iff it is kept, a request is satisfied iff it is granted, a question is satisfied iff it is answered, etc. In case of satisfaction of an illocutionary act, there is a success of fit between language and the world. The propositional content is true in the sense that it represents an actual state of affairs in the world of utterance.

According to Searle and Vanderveken [18], each illocutionary force can be divided into: (1) an illocutionary point, (2) a mode of achievement of that point, (3) propositional content, (4) preparatory and (5) sincerity conditions and finally, (6) degree of strength. We will now explain the nature of these components.

1. The Illocutionary Point. Illocutionary point is the principal component of an illocutionary force f because it determines the direction of fit of utterances with that force. More precisely, it determines how the propositional content is related in the speaker's mind to the world of utterance and in particular,

through which direction the success of fit must be achieved in order that the speech act can be satisfied. As pointed out elsewhere [18], there are four directions of fit and five and only five illocutionary points of utterances in language: the *assertive, commissive, directive declarative,* and the *expressive points.* The four direction of fit are as follows

(i) *The words-to-world direction of fit.* Here, when the illocutionary act $\langle f, p \rangle$ is satisfied, its propositional content fits a state of affairs existing in the world. Speech acts with the assertive point such as, for example, predictions, conjectures and objections have the words-to-world direction of fit. Their point is to represent how the things are in the world.

(ii) *The world-to-words direction of fit.* When the illocutionary act $\langle f, p \rangle$ is satisfied, the world is transformed to fit the propositional content. Speech acts with the commissive or directive point such as, promises, recommendations, supplications and demands have the world-to-words direction of fit. Their point is to get the world to be transformed by the future course of action of the speaker (commissives) or the hearer (directives) in order to match the propositional content of the utterance.

(iii) *The double direction of fit.* Here, when the illocutionary act $\langle f, p \rangle$ is satisfied, the world is transformed by an action of the speaker to fit the propositional content by the fact that the speaker represents it as being so transformed. Speech acts with the declarative illocutionary point such as for example, acts of appointing, nominating and endorsing, have the double direction of fit. Their point is to get the world to match the propositional content by saying that the propositional content matches the world.

(iv) *The empty direction of fit.* For some illocutionary acts, there is no question of success or failure of fit, and their propositional content is in general presupposed to be true. Speech acts with the expressive point such as for example, apologies, thanks, congratulations, etc., have the empty direction of fit. Their point is to express a propositional attitude of the speaker about the state of affairs represented by the propositional content. The point here is not to represent that state of affairs as actual or to try to get it to be actual in the world.

2. Mode of Achievement. Most purposes of our actions, and particularly illocutionary points, can be achieved in various ways or by different means. The mode of achievement of an illocutionary force determines how its point must be achieved on the propositional content in case of successful performance of an act with that force. For example, in a command the speaker must invoke a position of *authority* over the hearer and in a request he must give *option of refusal* to the addressee. The modes of achievement of illocutionary forces precisely state the conditions of achievement of their point. In English, they are expressed by adverbs such as for example "surely" and "whether you like it it or not" which modify the verb in sentences such as (a) "Surely, he is here" and (b) "Whether you like it or not, do it!". Special other modes of achievement include "humbly" and "politely" which modify the performative verbs.

3. **Propositional Content Conditions.** Many illocutionary forces impose conditions on the set of propositions that can be taken as propositional contents of acts with that force in a context of utterance. For example, the propositional content of a promise must represent a speaker's future course of action. The propositional content of a report must represent a state of affairs which is either past or present with respect to the moment of utterance, etc.

4. **Preparatory Conditions.** Whenever a speaker attempts to perform an illocutionary act, he *believes* that certain propositions hold in the context of his utterance. For example, a speaker who promises to do something presupposes that his future action promotes the hearer's utility. The preparatory conditions of an illocutionary force f determine which propositions the speaker believes if he were performing an act with that force and a propositional content p in a possible context of utterance.

5. **Sincerity Conditions.** Of course, by performing an illocutionary act, the speaker also *expresses* mental states of certain psychological modes about the state of affairs represented by the propositional content. For example, a speaker who promises something expresses an *intention* to do what he promises, and a speaker who requests a hearer to do something expresses a desire that he do it. As in the case of propositional content and preparatory conditions, some sincerity conditions are determined by the illocutionary point. For example, all assertive illocutionary forces have the sincerity condition that the speaker believes the propositional content.

6. **Degree of Strength.** Evidently, the mental states which enter into the sincerity conditions of speech acts are expressed with different degrees of strength depending on the illocutionary force. For example, the degree of strength of the sincerity conditions of a supplication is greater than that of request, because a speaker, who supplicates, expresses a stronger desire than a speaker who requests. Degree of strength is in general orally expressed by the intonation contour in English. Precisely, an increase in the degree of strength of the intonation contour serves in general to increase the degree of the sincerity conditions. Adverbs like "sincerely" also serves to strengthen the degree of strength of the sincerity condition in sentences such as "I sincerely advise you to do it".

3   The Situation Calculus: A Logical Formalism for Reasoning About Knowledge and Action

The situation calculus [10] seems to be an adequate formalism for reasoning about actions and their effects on the world. Axioms are used to specify the prerequisites of actions as well as their effects. Recently, Reiter [14] has given a set of conditions under which the explicit specification of frame axioms can be avoided. This solution is extended to the frame problem to cover *knowledge-producing actions*, that is, actions whose effects are to change a state of knowledge [15]. Notice that Reiter's approach does not, address the ramification problem, his approach fails in the presence of state constraints. To remedy this, Lin [9] proposed a two step procedure for determining an axiomatization (using situation calculus) which monotonically solves some versions of the ramification and qualification problems.

With situation calculus, we can also encode messages which depend on the words and the *situation* in which the words are uttered. In this perspective, just as in situation calculus, the encoding and decoding functions take an extra argument representing the current situation.

For these reasons, we pursue the perspective of situation calculus for reasoning about actions in multiagent systems, and specially the reasoning about speech acts for the communication between agents. To achieve this, we incorporate semantics of intensional logic and illocutionary logic in the situation calculus. We will now present briefly the situation calculus, then we will show how we will use such calculus for reasoning about knowledge and action.

In situation calculus, terms are used to represent states of the world -i.e. *situations*. If α is an action and s a situation, the result of performing a situation α in s is represented by $do(\alpha, s)$. $Poss(\alpha, s)$ means that it is possible to perform the action α in the situation s. The constant S_0 is used to denote the initial situation; and there is also an ordering relation on situations $\succ$, where $s' \succ s$ stands for "s' can be reached from s by a sequence of one or more actions". A *fluent* F is a function defined on situations. For instance, in the blocks world, the location of a given block x is a fluent whose value are the possible locations of blocks. In the language of the situation calculus, the value of this fluent at s for a block x is denoted by $location(x, s)$. More generally, $F(do(\alpha, s))$ means that F becomes true in the successor situation $do(\alpha, s)$; and $\neg F(do(\alpha, s))$ means that F becomes false in the same successor situation.

Before we treat epistemic fluents, let us introduce an alternative formulation in order to facilitate the logical formalism for reasoning about knowledge and action. Rather than introduce a situational argument to all of the predicates in our domain, we can instead reify predicates like loc, making objects out of sentences such as $loc(b, l)$. More precisely, instead of writing $loc(b, l, s)$ to indicate that the location of b is l in situation s, we can write $loc(b, l)[s]$, where $loc(b, l)$ is now an object of our domain instead of a sentence. What $loc(b, l)[s]$ says is that the object $loc(b, l)$ holds in the situation s. One advantage of reification is that it allows us to quantify over sentences (now objects) being reified. For instance, if we want to say that *nothing* holds in some situation s_1, we could write this as:

$$\forall p \; \neg p[s_1]$$

If we have not adopted sentence reification in our domain, this axiom would involve quantification over predicates and would therefore not be a legitimate sentence of first-order logic.

However, some atomic formula like $Poss$ and do are binary functions, whose arguments are an action and a situation and in this case it is important to use the reification appropriately. For instance, if we express by $move(x, y)$ the action of placing x on top of y, we can describe the effect of this action by the following axiom: $Poss(move(x, y), s) \supset on(x, y)[do(move(x, y), s)]$

Now, we introduce some binary accessibility relations over situations, where a situation s' is understood as being accessible for an agent i from a situation s if as far as i believes (for example) in situation s, he might be in situation s'. Thus, something is believed in s if it is true in every s' accessible from s, and conversely something is not believed if it is false in some accessible situation. Therefore, the usual belief operator can be treated as an operator which reflects a mental state and which can hold or not in some situation s. To this end, we introduce a binary relation $B_i(s', s)$, read as "s' is accessible for i from s". Thus relation $B_i(s', s)$ holds in s iff s' is compatible with what i believes in s. We can now introduce the object $bel(i, p)$ read as "agent i believes p" and define it as:

$$bel(i, p)[s] \stackrel{\text{def}}{=} \forall s' \; B_i(s', s) \supset p[s'] \tag{1}$$

This is the usual "knowledge" operator and is considered here as primitive modal operator. Concerning this operator, we assume the usual axiom schemata corresponding to a "weak S5" modal logic.

We assume here that *goal* is not a primitive atomic predicate, as in Cohen and Levesque [5], because this predicate is based on the relation G_i, which is constrained by B_i. In fact, the relation G_i can be defined as the intersection of B_i and an accessibility relation expressing the fundamental notion of "interest", i.e., the set of situations that an agent *would wish were true*. We call such a relation I_i, and the corresponding predicate *wish*. In these conditions, $wish(i, p)$ means "agent i has an interest that p is true". This predicate is defined by the following:

$$wish(i, p)[s] \stackrel{\text{def}}{=} \forall s' \; I_i(s', s) \supset p[s'] \tag{2}$$

As $G_i = B_i \bigcap I_i$, this allows to us to introduce the "goal" predicate which is defined by:

$$goal(i, p)[s] \stackrel{\text{def}}{=} \forall s' \; G_i(s', s) \supset p[s'] \tag{3}$$

Now it is time to give our formalization of ability. In fact, we base this formalization on that of Moore [11], which in spite of its relative simplicity, does get at the essential connection between the ability of agents to achieve goals and the knowledge they have about relevant actions. To formalize this ability, we introduce firstly two operators for which situations will not be referred to explicitly: $res(a, p)$ and $agt(i, a)$. The first operator $res(a, p)$ will mean that it is possible for the event denoted by a to occur and that, it it did, the formula p would then be true. The semantics of this operator is similar to the operator RES of Moore [11]. The second operator $agt(i, a)$ says here that agent i is the only agent for the action a.

In these conditions, the operator $can(i, a, p)$ read as "agent i can achieve p by performing action a" satisfies the following:

$$\forall i \, \exists x \; bel(i, (x = a) \wedge agt(i, x) \wedge res(a, p))[s] \supset can(i, a, p)[s] \tag{4}$$

This captures the fact that an agent i can achieve p by performing act a if he knows what action a is, and he knows that p would be true as result of his performing a. Notice that 4 is not bidirectional because it is impossible for an agent to know from the very beginning of this action, particularly if it is complex, "what" she is going to do every step.

We also need a formal definition of "commitment". For this purpose, we augment our formal system with a new accessibility relation C_i which is Euclidean, transitive, serial and such as $C_i \subseteq I_i \cap B_i$. According to our intuition, C_i accesses situations which the agent i regards as both desirable and possible. The situations in C_i are consequently those in which the agent does the action(s) that she has decided to do. Now we can define a predicate $cmt(i, p)$ read as "agent i is committed to achieving p" and define it as:

$$cmt(i,p)[s] \overset{\text{def}}{=} \forall s' \; C_i(s', s) \supset p[s'] \tag{5}$$

Another mental state is the "intention" for which we need a weak notion of an agent *having* a plan [13]. We note this version of plan

$$has.plan(i, \pi, p)$$

This means that i has the plan π to achieve p. Notice that our weak notion of having a plan states: (1) i believes that he can execute each act in π; (2) i believes that executing the acts in π will entail the performance of p and, (3) i believes that each act in π plays a role.

Now, we can define a new predicate $int(i, p)$ read as "the agent i intends to achieve p" as:

$$int(i,p)[s] \overset{\text{def}}{=} \exists \pi \; cmt(i,p)[s] \land has.plan(i, \pi, p)[s] \tag{6}$$

How should various feature of intentions follow from previous definitions?

1. *Intentions must be consistent.* This means that an agent cannot be committed to two simultaneous conflicting actions. This is the case since situations are internally consistent and according to the definition of cmt, the two actions must occur in all the situations in relation by C_i.
2. *Intentions are not closed under expected consequence.* This follows from the fact that we do not want cmt to be closed under (expected) implication. Particularly, $cmt(i, p) \land bel(i, p \supset q)$ does not imply $cmt(i, q)$.
3. *Intentions must be realistic.* An agent might believe that she will do some action without having a plan, that is, without having an idea on how to do it. Therefore, she can have a commitment, but not an intention.

Finally, we need to formalize "Obligations" as they are used, for instance, in the promises to reflect the mode of achievement. Obligations represent what an agent *should* do, according to some set of norms; its formal aspects are generally examined using Deontic Logic (e.g., [22]).

Obligations are generally different from and cannot be reduced to intentions and goals, Thus, although knowing that p is not compatible with her goals, an agent may be obliged to make p true for respecting norms or social laws. We assume here that agents plan their actions to violate as few rules as possible. In the case of obligations, an agent chooses to violate her obligations or not depending on the price to pay. As a first approximation, we can expressed "i is obliged to j to make p true" by $oblig(i, j, p)$ which is defined by the following:

$$oblig(i, j, p)[s] \stackrel{\text{def}}{=} (\exists s_l \succ s) \land (\forall s'.s \succ s' \succ s_l)$$

$$\neg p[s_l] \land whish(i, p)[s'] \supset violating(i, j, p)[s_l] \tag{7}$$

Thus, if p is not achieved by i in some limit situation s_l, i violates her agreement between i and j on p. Such a violation is represented by the predicate $violating(i, j, p)$. Evidently, between situations s and s_l, agent i has an interest that p would be true. We state that by $whish(i, p)[s']$.

To sum up, the knowledge and action approach developped here is in fact a contribution to the belief, desire, intention (BDI) model. Nowadays, it is widely accepted that the bahavior of any agent is mainly governed by the specific way it handles the rational balance between its beliefs, desires, and intentions. Other papers in this book refer to the BDI model [7], [12], [16], [24].

4 Semantics of Speech Acts based on Success, Satisfaction and Recursion

The condition of success of an illocutionary act are the conditions that must be obtained in a possible situation (i.e. context) in order that the speaker succeed in performing that act in that situation. For instance, a condition of success of a request is that the speaker attempts to get the hearer to carry out the future course of action represented by p.

Moreover, communication between agents can fail even illocutionary acts are successfully performed. In this case, the illocutionary act(s) of this communication are not satisfied. For example, a request which is successfully performed by a speaker is satisfied, only if the hearer makes its propositional content true by carrying out in the multiagent environment the course of action that it represents. More generally, the conditions of satisfaction of a speech act corresponds to the conditions under which we would affirm that the given speech act has been satisfied.

In fact, conditions of success and of satisfaction are a part of semantics of speech acts. A formal semantics is important for MAS because we need a rigorous understanding of communication in order to design and analyze a multiagent systems. To this end, we propose in this section to capture conditions of success and satisfaction in the situation calculus, by using the different operators introduced in the previous section. To do this, we adopt the following Singh's notations [19]: (1) a message m is a pair $\langle f, p \rangle$, where f identifies the illocutionary force, and p the proposition. In this notation, f is an atomic symbol from the set {assertive, directive, commissive, declarative and expressive}; and p is a logical formula; (2) a communication from i to j is represented by $comm(i, j, m)$. If we consider $says.to(i, j, m)$ as the only action that agent i can perform to make $comm(i, j, m)$ true, then

$$Poss(says.to(i,j,m),s) \supset comm(i,j,m)[do(says.to(i,j,m),s)]$$

We need also to express the psychological states that enter into sincerity conditions which different degrees of strength depending on the illocutionary force (see Section 2). For this purpose, we use integers which serve to measure the degrees of strength of illocutionary forces. By convention we select zero (0) to represent the *neutral degree of strength* that is characteristic of the primitive illocutionary forces of utterances (such as assertion); +1 represents the next stronger degree of strength (e.g. testimony); +2 the next stronger degree of strength (e.g. solemn acts of swearing that something is the case). Similarly, -1 represents the greatest degree of strength smaller than 0 (e.g. conjecture), and so on. If $degree(\tau)$ represents the degree of strength of an act of type τ, then $degree(\tau) = k$ means that if the act τ is performed in situation s, the speaker S expresses psychological states with degree k. With such a degree of strength, we can order the speech acts for each illocutionary force. Thus, the following illustrates "some" degrees in the case of $\langle directive, p \rangle$:

$$degree(order) = degree(command) = degree(require) = +1$$
$$degree(ask) = degree(tell.to) = degree(request) = 0$$
$$degree(suggest) = degree(advise) = degree(recommend) = -1$$

We have similar orders for the assertives, commissives, declaratives and expressives (details are in [21]). A such order between speech acts has in fact many implications in cooperative systems communication. For instance, an act of *request* or *ask* type lets the Hearer H know that the Speaker S is either of the same rank or a lower rank. Thus, H can grant or refuse the request by returning messages with either an assert or answer type. Roles have as function to reflect the position of each agent in the hierarchy of the multiagent system and to determine what reasoning strategies to use. To compare the ranking differences of agents, we can assign a number to every role as in COSMO [23]. For example, for two agents i of $role_i$ and j of $role_j$, agent i ranks higher than j iff $v(role_i) > v(role_j)$ where $v(role_x)$ denotes the role value of an agent x.

4.1 The Conditions of Success

As Searle and Vanderveken [18] pointed out, the conditions of success of elementary acts are uniquely determined by the components of their illocutionary force and by their propositional content.

Proposition 1: An illocutionary act of the form $\langle f, p \rangle$ is *successfully performed* in the context of an utterance (s) iff the conditions of success of $\langle f, p \rangle$ hold in s. Formally, we state this by the following:

$$success(comm(S, H, \langle f, p \rangle), s) \equiv cond.success(\langle f, p \rangle)[s] \qquad (8)$$

In this formulation, $success(comm(S, H, \langle f, p \rangle), s)$ states if the act $\langle f, p \rangle$ between S and H is successfully performed, in situation

$s = do(says.to(S, H, \langle f, p \rangle), s_u)$, or not. Moreover, $cond.success(\langle f, p \rangle)$ expresses if the conditions of success of $\langle f, p \rangle$ hold or not in s. Finally, s_u stands for the situation of utterance.

As specified in Section 2, the conditions of success (*cond.success*) for an illocutionary act of the form $\langle f, p \rangle$ with respect to s are:

1. the speaker achieves the *illocutionary point* of the force f on the proposition p;
2. the speaker achieves this illocutionary point with the *mode of achievement* of f;
3. p satisfies the *propositional content conditions* of f with respect to s;
4. the speaker presupposes the propositions determined by the *preparatory conditions* of f;
5. the speaker expresses, with the *degree of strength* of f, the psychological states of the modes determined by the *sincerity conditions* of f about the state of affairs represented by p.

These conditions can be formulated for any speech acts using the situation calculus and the different operators introduced in the previous section. For example, a speaker S makes a **promise** for the hearer H in a context of utterance (s) if and only if the following conditions (i.e. *cond.success*) hold in $s = do(says.to(S, H, \langle commissive, p \rangle), s_u)$:

1. S commits herself to make p true (illocutionary act). $cmt(S, p)[s]$
2. S is obligated to H to make p true (mode of achievement). $oblig(S, H, p)[s]$
3. The propositional context of the utterance is that the speaker *will do* "something" to make p true (propositional content conditions).
   $\exists a \, \exists s' \, (s' \succ s) \, bel(S, p)[do(a, s')]$
4. S presupposes that he is capable of doing some action a to make p true and that p is in the interest of H (preparatory conditions);
   $\exists a \, can(S, a, p)[s] \wedge bel(S, goal(H, p))[s]$
5. S expresses with the degree of strength of a promise, an intention to make p true (Sincerity conditions with a degree of strength).
   $int(S, p)[s] \wedge degree(promise)[s]$

We can state similar conditions of success for $\langle assertive, p \rangle$, $\langle directive, p \rangle$, $\langle declarative, p \rangle$, and $\langle expressive, p \rangle$. For example, S requests H about p, in some context iff, in this context: (1) S expresses a wish to get H to carry out the future course of action represented by p (illocutionary point); (2) in this whish, S gives a (more or less total) option of refusal to H (mode of achievement); (3) p has the general propositional content condition that its content represents a future course of action of H (condition on p); (4) S presupposes that the hearer is capable of doing some action a to achieve p (preparatory condition); (5) and finally, S expresses with a normal degree of strength a wish that H do that act (sincerity condition).

Similar conditions of success can be formulated for the other illocutionary forces. Details about this formulation are given in [4].

Finally, it is important to note that a speech act can be *successful* though *defective*. Thus, a speaker S might actually succeed in asserting or promising something even though he has not enough evidence for her assertion or her promise might be insincere. In fact, an ideal speech act is one which is both successful and nondefective. Evidently, nondefectiveness implies success, but not conversely. We generally assume that there are only two ways that an act can be successfully performed though still be defective. First, *some* of the preparatory conditions might not be the case in the real world and yet the act might still be performed. The sincerity conditions might not obtain, in other words, the act can be successfully performed even though it be insincere.

4.2 The Conditions of Satisfaction

The conditions of satisfaction of elementary illocutionary acts of the form $\langle f, p \rangle$ are a function of the truth-conditions of their propositional content and of the direction of fit of their illocutionary force [18,20,21]. Generally, the speaker expresses the proposition p with the aim of achieving a success of fit between language and the world from a certain direction. On the basis of the previous considerations on direction of fit (see Section 2), we adopt the following proposition about the conditions of satisfaction of illocutionary acts in general semantics.

Proposition 2: An illocutionary act $\langle assertive, p \rangle$ with the words-to-world direction of fit is satisfied in a situation s of utterance iff p holds in s. Formally, if we express the satisfaction with the words-to-world direction of fit by $satis_{wd}^{wl}$, then this proposition becomes:

$$satis_{wd}^{wl}(comm(S, H, \langle assertive, p \rangle), s) \equiv p[s] \wedge p[s_u] \qquad (9)$$

with $s = do(says.to(S, H, \langle assertive, p \rangle), s_u)$ and s_u is the situation of utterance. •

Thus, the success of fit between words and things is achieved by the fact that the expressed propositional content matches a state of affairs existing in general, independently in the world.

In the case of the world-to-words or the double direction of fit, the conditions of success of commissives and directives are part of their conditions of satisfaction. Indeed, unlike assertive utterances, commissive and directive utterances have conditions of satisfactions that are not independent of these utterances. An assertion is "true" iff its propositional content corresponds to an existing state of affairs no matter how it got into existence. On the other hand, a promise is kept or an order is obeyed only if the speaker or hearer carries out in the world a future course of action because of the promise or the order. Similarly, a declaration is satisfied only if the speaker makes its propositional content true by saying that it is true in the performance of that declaration. Now, we can state the following proposition about the satisfaction.

An illocutionary act $\langle f, p \rangle$ with the world-to-words direction $\langle world, words \rangle$ of fit is satisfied ($satis$) in some situation s iff p holds in s *because of* the performance of this illocutionary act.

As sincerity conditions of $\langle commissive, p \rangle$ and $\langle directive, p \rangle$ are $int(S, p)$ and $int(H, p)$ respectively, and that "intention" has been defined as a "commitment + having-plan" (see Definition 6) we can relate the performance of commissives and directives to the execution of plans by the speaker S and hearer H. To do this, we assume that π in $has.plan(i, \pi, p)$ represents the set of acts $[\pi_1, \ldots, \pi_n]$. In these conditions, $do(\pi_n, do(\pi_{n-1}, \ldots, do(\pi_1, s))) \ldots)$ is a situation denoting the world history consisting of the sequence of actions $[\pi_1, \ldots, \pi_n]$. In light of these considerations, we consider firstly the satisfaction of $\langle commissive, p \rangle)$ and $\langle directive, p \rangle)$ by stating the two following propositions:

Proposition 3: An illocutionary act $\langle commissive, p \rangle$ with the world-to-words direction of fit is satisfied in some situation s iff p holds in s *because of* the performance of this illocutionary act. Formally, if we express the satisfaction with the world-to-words direction of fit by $satis_{wl}^{wd}$, then this proposition is:

$$satis_{wl}^{wd}(comm(S, H, \langle commissive, p \rangle), s) \equiv$$
$$\exists s', s'' \ (s \succeq s' \succeq s'') \ Poss(\pi_i, s') \ldots Poss(\pi_n, s') \wedge$$
$$success(comm(S, H, \langle commissive, p \rangle), s'') \supset$$
$$p[do(\pi_n, do(\pi_{n-1}, \ldots, do(\pi_1, s'))) \ldots)$$

$$(10)$$

Proposition 4: An illocutionary act $\langle directive, p \rangle$ with the world-to-words direction of fit is satisfied in some situation s iff p holds in s *because of* the performance of this illocutionary act. As the satisfaction with the world-to-words direction is expressed by $satis_{wl}^{wd}$, we can state:

$$satis_{wl}^{wd}(comm(S, H, \langle directive, p \rangle), s) \equiv$$
$$\exists s', s'' \ (s \succeq s' \succeq s'') \ Poss(\pi_i, s') \ldots Poss(\pi_n, s') \wedge$$
$$success(comm(S, H, \langle directive, p \rangle), s'') \supset$$
$$p[do(\pi_n, do(\pi_{n-1}, \ldots, do(\pi_1, s'))) \ldots)$$

$$(11)$$

Notice that in the case of $\langle commissive, p \rangle$ the agent which is in charge of the execution of the set of acts $[\pi_1, \ldots, \pi_n]$ is the speaker S, whereas in the case of $\langle directive, p \rangle$ it is the hearer H. Finally, the situation s represents $do(\pi_n, do(\pi_{n-1}, \ldots, do(\pi_1, s'))) \ldots)$ and s' is the situation in which all preconditions of $[\pi_1, \ldots, \pi_n]$ hold, finally, s'' is the situation where $comm(S, H, \langle directive, p \rangle)$ is successfully performed.

As stated previously, a $\langle declarative, p \rangle$ is satisfied only if the speaker S makes its propositional content true by saying that it is true in the performance of that declaration. This statement leads to the following proposition:

Proposition 5: An illocutionary act $\langle declarative, p \rangle$ with the double direction of fit is satisfied in some situation s iff p holds in s *because of* the performance of this illocutionary act. If the satisfaction with the double direction of fit is expressed by $satis_{dble}$, then this proposition becomes:

$satis_{dble}(comm(S, H, \langle declarative, p \rangle), s) \equiv$

$success(comm(S, H, \langle declarative, p \rangle), s) \supset$
$$p[do(says.to(S, H, \langle declarative, p \rangle), s_u)]$$

$$(12)$$

Finally, in the case of the empty or null direction of fit, there is no question of success or failure of fit, and the propositional content is in general presupposed to be true. Such are the expressives that have null or empty direction of fit. Their point is to express a mental attitude of the speaker S about the state of affairs represented by p. Formally, we represent this by $m(S, p)$ where m is a psychological mode which determines a particular direction of fit between mind and the world, and p is the propositional content which represents the state of affairs to which they are directed. As we see, in the case of the empty direction of fit, it is not to represent that state of affairs as actual or to try to get it to be actual in the world.

Proposition 6: An illocutionary act $\langle expressive, p \rangle$ with the empty direction of fit is satisfied in some situation s iff $m(S, p)$ holds in s *because of* the performance of this illocutionary act. If the satisfaction with the empty direction of fit is expressed by $satis_\emptyset$, then this proposition becomes:

$satis_\emptyset(comm(S, H, \langle expressive, p \rangle), s) \equiv$

$success(comm(S, H, \langle expressive, p \rangle), s) \supset$
$$m(S, p)[do(says.to(S, H, \langle expressive, p \rangle), s_u)]$$

$$(13)$$

Finally, it is important to note that *the set of illocutionary forces of possible utterances is recursive.* Consequently, there are five primitive illocutionary acts with an illocutionary act, no special mode of achievement of that point, a neutral degree of strength and only the propositional content, and the preparatory and sincerity conditions which are determined by their point. These primitive forces are : $\|assert\|$ for the assertives, $\|commit\|$ for the commissives, $\|direct\|$ for the directives, $\|declare\|$ for the declaratives and finally, the primitive expressive illocutionary force which is realized syntactically in the type of exclamatory sentences (there is no illocutionary verb or performative in English that names the primitive expressive). $\| \|$ is the function that assigns to each illocutionary verb the force or type of speech act that it names. Such a function can be associated to a propositional content as for instance $\|assert\|(p)$.

Proposition 7: Other illocutionary forces (than primitives) are obtained from the primitive illocutionary forces by a finite number of application of the following operations: i) adding propositional content conditions, ii) adding preparatory conditions, iii) adding sincerity conditions, iv) restricting the mode of achievement and finally, v) increasing the degree of strength.

These operations are Boolean operations (see [21] for details). Here are some examples of derived illocutionary forces. The illocutionary force $\|promise\|$ is obtained from the primitive commissive force $\|commit\|$ by imposing a special mode of achievement of the commissive point involving the undertaking of an obligation. $\|pledge\|$ is obtained from $\|commit\|$ by increasing the degree of strength of the sincerity conditions, etc.

5 Applications of our Approach

5.1 Contributions to the Analysis and Interpretation of Speech Acts

Our semantics, expressed into a tractable language (the situation calculus), is useful for several reasons. First, it enables us to analyze *illocutionary force markers* and to interpret a great number of speech acts. Second, it also enables us to make a reasoned dictionary of *illocutionary verbs* of actual natural language by way of a systematic breakdown of lexicalized forces into their components. Third, our theory is also useful to describe the various sorts of entailment and relative inconsistency that can exist between actual sentences expressed in the same contexts with related conditions of success and satisfaction. Such entailments and inconsistencies might be important in the context of Agent Communication Language (ACL). For example, a sentence S_1 such as "I ask you if you are busy" *illocutionarily entails* the sentence S_2 "Are you busy?". Thus a speaker could not perform S_1 without also performing S_2 in the same context. Similarly, the two sentences "How nice of you to finish the job j_1" and "I regret that you have done j_1" are *illocutionary incompatible* because they express in the same contexts speech acts that are not simultaneously performable. The formal model presented here can also generalize the traditional truth conditional notions of entailment and consistency and apply them to non-declarative sentences. For example, the imperative sentence S_3 "Please, touch me by email tomorrow morning!" can be said to entail *truth-conditionally* the sentence S_4 "you are able to touch me by email tomorrow morning". Thus, S_3 expresses in a given context a request which cannot be satisfied unless the assertion expressed by S_4 in the same context is true. Similarly, the imperative sentence S_5 "email piece of information P_1 ... and do not email P_1!" is truth-conditionally inconsistent since it expresses in all contexts a directive which is not satisfiable.

Thus, the approach presented here can be used to formally analyze illocutionary forces. Such an analysis is useful to formalize human interactions as well as the communications among software agents.

5.2 Agent Communication Language: Towards a Semantics of KQML performatives

The semantics developed by authors of KQML turns around the well known approach: speakers and hearers have *only* to recognize each other's intentions. This approach, which was initiated by [1] considers in fact that the only kinds of things that are *intrinsically*, as opposed to derivatively, meaningful are not linguistic acts like the act of asserting that something is the case, the act of requesting someone to make something the case, or the act of promising to make something the case, but rather *mental states* like the state of believing, desiring or intending. With a such approach, some aspects of the success are not considered (as for instance the "degree of strength" and some facets of the preparatory conditions) and cannot derive from the mental states of the intervening parties. In our point of view, the degree of strength and the preparatory conditions are very important for the interactions among agents as explained in Section 2. To remedy to this, we give here our semantics for some performatives used in KQML [8]: achieve(S, H, p), and tell(S, H, p).

Firstly, achieve(S, H, p) performative should be analyzed in our framework as a $\|request\|$ addressed by S to H in order to achieve p. Notice that request is a directive illocutionary act that allows for the possibility of refusal and consequently, it can be granted or refused by H. In these conditions, $\|request\|$ differs from the primitive directive $\|direct\|$ (see previous section) only by the fact that the mode of achievement allows H the possibility of refusing to carry out the future course of action represented by p. In our framework, this can be expressed by:

$$success(comm(S, H, \|request\|(p)), s) \equiv$$
$$success(comm(S, H, \|direct\|(p)), s) \land \forall s'(s' \succ s') \ \neg oblig(H, S, p)[s']$$

The condition of satisfaction of $comm(S, H, \|request\|(p))$ is determined by **Proposition 5**.

Secondly, tell(S, H, p) performative should be analyzed here as an $\|assert\|$ that p. With our semantics, all other assertives of KQML (untell, sorry and error) should be analyzed in our framework according to the **Proposition 7**. Precisely, these assertives are obtained from the primitive illocutionary force $\|assert\|$ by a finite number of application of the following operations: i) adding propositional content conditions, ii) adding preparatory conditions, iii) adding sincerity conditions, iv) restricting the mode of achievement and finally, v) increasing the degree of strength. In fact, all KQML performatives should be expressed in our framework using recurrence. In this way, KQML "performatives" can be extended since developers have some guidance on how to formulate new performatives. Thus in the case of assertives for instance, developers have only to develop performatives which may differ from one another in respects such as their mode of achievement (the difference, for example, between arguing and testifying that p); their degree of strength (the difference, for example, between insisting that p and conjecturing that p), their propositional content conditions (the difference, for example, between a prediction and a report), their preparatory conditions (the difference, for example, between reminding and informing that p), or their sincerity conditions (the difference, for example, between asserting and complaining).

6 Conclusion

The model of speech acts presented in this paper represents a systematic, unified account of both the truth and the success-conditional aspects. In this model, meaning and use are logically related and linguistic competence is not dissociated from performance. On the contrary, linguistic competence is constructed as the speaker's ability to understand which illocutionary acts can be performed by literal utterances in the various possible contexts of use of this language.

We have proposed an adequate formalism (the situation calculus) for representing this model in the context of agent communication language. Finally, we have explained how the resulting model allows us to (1) contribute to the analysis and interpretation of speech acts; (2) contribute to the semantics of agent communication language as KQML.

This work is only the beginning and we plan to extend it, in particulier to conversations taking into account social interactions of autonomous agents, and specially the private and global views on communication as developed by Dignum [6].

Acknowledgments:

This research was supported by the Natural Sciences and Engineering Research Council of Canada (NSERC), by the Social Sciences and Humanities Research Council (SSHRC) of Canada, by the Fonds pour la Formation des Chercheurs et l'aide à la Recherche (FCAR) du Québec and in part, by the German Research Centre for AI (DFKI).

References

1. J. F. Allen and C. R. Perrault. Analysing intention in utterances. *Artificial Intelligence*, 15(3):143–178, 1980.
2. J. L. Austin. *How to Do Things With Words*. Oxford University Press: Oxford, England, 1962.
3. K. Bach and R. M. Harnich. *Linguistic Communication and Speech Acts*. MIT Press: Cambridge, MA, 1979.
4. B. Chaib-draa. On the success and satisfaction of speech acts for computational agents. Rapport DIUL–RR–9409, Département d'Informatique, Université Laval, 1994.
5. P. R. Cohen and H. J. Levesque. Intention is choice with commitment. *Artificial Intelligence*, 42:213–261, 1990.
6. F. Dignum. Social interactions of autonomous agents; private and global views on communications. In *ModelAge'97 Workshop*. 1997.

7. C. G. Jung. Emergent mental attitudes in layered agents. In J. P. Müller, M. P. Singh, and A. S. Rao, editors, *Intelligent Agents V — Proceedings of the Fifth International Workshop on Agent Theories, Architectures, and Languages (ATAL-98)*, LNAI. Springer-Verlag, Heidelberg, 1999. In this volume.

8. Y. Labrou and T. Finin. semantics and conversations for an agent communication language. In *Proceedings of the 15th International Joint Conference on Artificial Intelligence (IJCAI-97)*. Nagao, Japan, 1997.

9. F. Lin and R. Reiter. State constraints revised. *Journal of Logic and computation. Special Issue on Actions and Process*, 1994.

10. J. McCarty and P. Hayes. Some philosophical problems from the standpoint of artificial intelligence. In B. Meltzer and D. Mitchie, editors, *Machine Intelligence, Vol. 4*, pages 463–502. Edinburgh University Press, 1969.

11. R. C. Moore. A formal theory of knowledge and action. Report no. CSLI-85-31, Center for the Study of Language and Information, Menlo Park, CA, 1985.

12. M. Móra, J. G. Lopes, R. Viccari, and H. Coelho. BDI models and systems: reducing the gap. In J. P. Müller, M. P. Singh, and A. S. Rao, editors, *Intelligent Agents V — Proceedings of the Fifth International Workshop on Agent Theories, Architectures, and Languages (ATAL-98)*, LNAI. Springer-Verlag, Heidelberg, 1999. In this volume.

13. M. E. Pollack. Plan as complex mental attitudes. In Morgan J. Cohen, P. R. and M. E. Pollack, editors, *Intentions in Communication*, pages 77–103. MIT Press, 1990.

14. R. Reiter. *Knowledge in Action: Logical Foundation for Describing and Implementing Dynamical Systems*. Unpub. Draft, CS Departement Toronto University, 1996.

15. R. Scherl. The frame problem and knowledge-producing actions. In *Proceedings of the Eleventh National Conference on Artificial Intelligence (AAAI-93)*, pages 689–695, Washington DC, 1993.

16. K. Schild. On the relationship between BDI logics and standard logics of concurrency. In J. P. Müller, M. P. Singh, and A. S. Rao, editors, *Intelligent Agents V — Proceedings of the Fifth International Workshop on Agent Theories, Architectures, and Languages (ATAL-98)*, LNAI. Springer-Verlag, Heidelberg, 1999. In this volume.

17. J. R. Searle. *Speech Acts: An Essay in the Philosophy of Language*. Cambridge University Press: Cambridge, England, 1969.

18. J. R. Searle and D. Vanderveken. *Foundations of Illocutionary Logic*. Cambridge University Press: Cambridge, England, 1985.

19. M. P. Singh. On the semantics of protocols among distributed intelligent agents. Report DFKI-TMI-91-09, DFKI The German Research Center for AI, 1991.

20. D. Vanderveken. *Meaning and Speech Acts: Formal Semantics of Success and Satisfaction*. Cambridge University Press: Cambridge, England, 1990.

21. D. Vanderveken. *Meaning and Speech Acts: Principles of Language Use*. Cambridge University Press: Cambridge, England, 1990.

22. G. H. von Wright. Deontic logic. *Mind*, 60:1–15, 1951.

23. S. T. C. Wong. COSMO: a communication scheme for cooperative knowledge-based systems. *IEEE Transactions on Systems, Man and Cybernitics*, 23(3):809–824, 1993.

24. M. J. Wooldridge and S. D. Parsons. Intention reconsideration reconsidered. In J. P. Müller, M. P. Singh, and A. S. Rao, editors, *Intelligent Agents V — Proceedings of the Fifth International Workshop on Agent Theories, Architectures, and Languages (ATAL-98)*, LNAI. Springer-Verlag, Heidelberg, 1999. In this volume.

Control Structures
of Rule-Based Agent Languages

Koen V. Hindriks, Frank S. de Boer,
Wiebe van der Hoek and John-Jules Ch. Meyer

University Utrecht, Department of Computer Science
{koenh,frankb,wiebe,jj}@cs.ruu.nl

Abstract. An important issue when defining a rule-based agent programming language is the design of interpreters for these programming languages. Since these languages are all based on some notion of *rule*, an interpreter must provide some means of selection from a set of such rules. We provide a concrete and intuitive ordering on rules on which this selection can be based. This ordering is inspired by the common sense metaphor of intelligent agents in Artificial Intelligence. Furthermore, we provide a language with a formal semantics for programming agent interpreters. The main idea is not to integrate this language into the agent language itself, but to provide the constructs for building interpreters at another (meta) level of specification. The operational semantics is accordingly specified at the meta level, by means of a (meta) transition system. Using this language we make a comparison between several interpreters for agent languages in the literature.

1 Introduction

In a previous paper we discussed a number of features of agents, defined a programming language incorporating these features, and gave an operational semantics of this language by means of a transition system ([3]). Among these features are those of beliefs, goals, and rules to modify the goals. One of the major aims of the design of agent languages is to incorporate to some level the intuitive meanings associated with these common sense notions into the programming language. In this paper we continue the pursuit for such languages by incorporating a common sense based selection mechanism, and make a comparison with some of the other rule-based agent languages in the literature.

In [3] we noted that the basic difference between a number of agent languages resides in their *control structure*, from which we then abstracted. The main purpose of a control structure for agent languages is to specify which goals to deal with first and which rules to apply during the execution of an agent program. We think that the mechanisms of selection in agent languages are relevant for the design and correctness of agent programs, and therefore should be made explicit in the semantics of the agent language.

One of the main ideas of this paper is to separate the semantic specification of the basic constructs of an agent language from its control structure. The reason to separate them into an object and meta level is that the specification of the selection mechanisms at a meta level gives us two independent systems. We can leave the semantics of the agent language as it is, and also obtain the advantages associated with the modularity of two different systems. By separating these two systems *any* suitable agent language specified at the object level can be plugged into *any* interpreter specified at the meta level. Moreover, we provide for a general framework to specify the main features of control structures of agent languages and to compare the control mechanisms of these languages. In this paper we compare the languages AGENT-0 ([10]), AgentSpeak(L) ([9]), and our own proposal for an agent language, 3APL ([3]).

The formalisation of this two-level approach is achieved by defining two transition systems (which are a means to specify the operational semantics of programming languages. Cf. [8]). The first defines the semantics of the agent language, whereas the second, the *meta transition system*, defines the semantics of the meta language for programming interpreters. In the meta language a number of expressive operators for programming an interpreter for the object language are available, allowing the programmer to specify a selection mechanism for the programming language. The semantics of the meta language specifies the mechanisms for selection of goals and rules in rule-based languages.

2 A Rule-Based Agent Programming Language

In this section we define a *minimal* agent programming language that includes *goals* and *rules*. It is a simplified agent language that we mainly introduce for illustrative purposes. The main simplification is that it does not contain any programming variables. We have left variables out of the language since it would only complicate matters and is irrelevant for the purposes of the paper. Details of incorporating variables in a rule-based agent language can be found in our [3]. We start by defining the syntax.

Definition 1. *(Syntax)*
Let A be a set of *basic action symbols*, and $\mathcal{L}$ be a *propositional language*.
The set of *goals* $\mathcal{L}^g$ is defined by:

(i) $A \subseteq \mathcal{L}^g$,
(ii) if $\phi \in \mathcal{L}$, then $\phi? \in \mathcal{L}^g$, and
(iii) if $\pi_1, \pi_2 \in \mathcal{L}^g$, then $\pi_1; \pi_2, \pi_1 + \pi_2 \in \mathcal{L}^g$.

The set of *rules* $\mathcal{L}^p$ is defined by:

(i) if $\pi, \pi' \in \mathcal{L}^g \cup \{\Box\}$ and $\phi \in \mathcal{L}$, then $\pi \leftarrow \phi \mid \pi' \in \mathcal{L}^p$.

π is called the *head* of the rule, ϕ is called the *guard* of the rule, and π' is called the *body* of the rule. $\Box$ is used to denote an *empty* head or body.

An agent program consists of a set of initial goals, a set of initial beliefs, and a set of rules to modify goals. Basic actions are updates on beliefs. An agent program specifies how a basic action transforms beliefs.

Definition 2. An *agent program* is a tuple $\langle \mathcal{T}. \Pi_0, \sigma_0, \Gamma \rangle$ where

- $\mathcal{T} : A \times \wp(\mathcal{L}) \rightarrow \wp(\mathcal{L})$ is a (partial) function which yields the update on beliefs that is denoted by the basic action symbol,
- $\Pi_0 \subseteq \mathcal{L}^g$ is a set of *initial goals*,
- $\sigma_0 \subseteq \mathcal{L}$ is a set of propositional formulae, also called *initial beliefs*,
- $\Gamma \subseteq \mathcal{L}^p$ is a set of *rules*, also called the *rule base* of the agent.

A *configuration* is a pair $\langle \Pi, \sigma \rangle$, with $\Pi \subseteq \mathcal{L}^g$ and $\sigma \subseteq \mathcal{L}$, consisting of the goals and beliefs at a particular moment during execution. Π is called the *goal base*, σ is called the *belief base*. The goal and rule base are the only components of an agent that change during execution of the agent program. We identify a goal base Π with the goal base including the empty goal $\Pi \cup \{\Box\}$.

The *operational semantics* of the agent language is defined by a Plotkin-style transition system ([8]). Formally, a transition system is a deductive system which allows to *derive* the transitions of a program. A transition system consists of a set of *transition rules* that specify the meaning of each programming construct in the language. Such a rule consists of some premises and a conclusion. A transition system defines a transition relation $\longrightarrow$ on configurations. The transition rules transform these configurations.

The top level of our agent language consists of a goal base and a belief base. A goal base or set of goals is executed by executing one of the goals from this set. Thus, we may pick any goal in a goal base of a given configuration and try to execute it and transform the goal base accordingly.

Definition 3. *(execution rule for goal execution)*

$$\frac{\langle \pi_i, \sigma \rangle \longrightarrow \langle \pi_i', \sigma' \rangle}{\langle \{\pi_0, \ldots, \pi_{i-1}, \pi_i, \pi_{i+1}, \ldots, \pi_n\}, \sigma \rangle \longrightarrow \langle \{\pi_0, \ldots \pi_{i-1}, \pi_i', \pi_{i+1}, \ldots, \pi_n\}, \sigma' \rangle}$$

The premise of this rule transforms a single goal from the goal base together with the given belief base. The other rules in the transition system deal with transformations of such goal-belief base pairs.

A basic action is a basic update operator on the belief base. Given a set of beliefs a basic action may transform this set into another set of beliefs, as specified in the execution rule for basic actions. A test checks if a certain proposition follows from the belief base. It does not modify the belief base. The symbol E is used to denote termination in the transition system.

Definition 4. *(execution rules for basic actions and tests)*

$$\frac{\mathcal{T}(a, \sigma) = \sigma'}{\langle a, \sigma \rangle \longrightarrow \langle E, \sigma' \rangle} \qquad \frac{\sigma \models \phi}{\langle \phi?, \sigma \rangle \longrightarrow \langle E, \sigma \rangle}$$

Definition 5. *(execution rule for sequential composition)*

$$\frac{\langle \pi_1, \sigma \rangle \longrightarrow \langle \pi_1', \sigma' \rangle}{\langle \pi_1; \pi_2, \sigma \rangle \longrightarrow \langle \pi_1'; \pi_2, \sigma' \rangle}$$

Definition 6. *(execution rule for nondeterministic choice)*

$$\frac{\langle \pi_1, \sigma \rangle \longrightarrow \langle \pi_1', \sigma' \rangle}{\langle \pi_1 + \pi_2, \sigma \rangle \longrightarrow \langle \pi_1', \sigma' \rangle} \qquad \frac{\langle \pi_2, \sigma \rangle \longrightarrow \langle \pi_2', \sigma' \rangle}{\langle \pi_1 + \pi_2, \sigma \rangle \longrightarrow \langle \pi_2', \sigma' \rangle}$$

The rules of definitions 5 and 6 are standard (cf. [8]). All the transition rules presented thus far deal with the execution of a goal. By using these rules, a goal is transformed by goal *execution* of either a basic action or test. Another goal transformation method is goal *revision* by means of applying a rule from the agent program to a goal. In that case, the goal is deleted and the body of the rule is substituted for the old goal. Note that since we identified a goal base Π with $\Pi \cup \{\Box\}$ an empty head $\Box$ of a rule trivially unifies with a goal in the goal base.

Definition 7. *(application of rules)*

$$\frac{\pi \leftarrow \phi \mid \pi' \in \Gamma \text{ and } \sigma \models \phi}{\langle \pi, \sigma \rangle \longrightarrow \langle \pi', \sigma \rangle}$$

Notation 8. Let $\Pi = \{\pi_0, \ldots, \pi_{i-1}, \pi_i, \pi_{i+1}, \ldots, \pi_n\}$, and $\Pi' = \{\pi_0, \ldots, \pi_{i-1}, \pi_i', \pi_{i+1}, \ldots, \pi_n\}$. We use the following expressions as shorthands:

- $\langle \Pi, \sigma \rangle \overset{\pi_i, \pi_i'}{\longrightarrow} \langle \Pi', \sigma' \rangle$ for a transition $\langle \Pi, \sigma \rangle \longrightarrow \langle \Pi', \sigma' \rangle$ that is provable without using rule application,
- $\langle \Pi, \sigma \rangle \overset{\pi, \pi'}{\longrightarrow}$ for the fact that there are Π', σ' such that $\langle \Pi, \sigma \rangle \overset{\pi, \pi'}{\longrightarrow} \langle \Pi', \sigma' \rangle$,
- $\langle \Pi, \sigma \rangle \overset{\pi_i, \gamma, \pi_i'}{\longrightarrow} \langle \Pi', \sigma \rangle$ for a transition $\langle \Pi, \sigma \rangle \longrightarrow \langle \Pi', \sigma' \rangle$ that is provable by using rule application with $\gamma = \pi \leftarrow \phi \mid \pi'$,
- $\langle \Pi, \sigma \rangle \overset{\pi, \gamma, \pi'}{\longrightarrow}$ for the fact that there is a Π' such that $\langle \Pi, \sigma \rangle \overset{\pi, \gamma, \pi'}{\longrightarrow} \langle \Pi', \sigma \rangle$.

If $C \overset{\pi, \pi'}{\longrightarrow}$, we say that goal π is *executable in C*; if $C \overset{\pi, \gamma, \pi'}{\longrightarrow}$, we say that the rule-goal pair $\langle \gamma, \pi \rangle$ is *applicable in C*.

3   Control in Agent Languages

An important issue in rule-based languages is the selection of which rules to use at a particular time during execution. This problem is addressed by constructing a particular *control structure* for the language. There are two basic assumptions that can be made about such a control structure. On the one hand one could argue that the control structure should not matter for program design and therefore should be hidden from the programmer. We will call this the *black-box assumption*. On the other hand, one could argue that the control structure is relevant for program design, and the particular choices of implementation should be available to the programmer. This assumption could be called the *glass-box assumption* (cf. discussions of a similar issue in constraint programming languages, [5]). We will argue for the *glass-box assumption* in this paper; it offers a viable option only if this approach is based on a number of principles. In a glass-box approach, for example, the control structure should have an intuitive and logical structure. This is necessary since it must be possible to use the logic of the control structure to design agent programs.

In any rule-based language, like for example Prolog, one has to deal with one important issue: how to select a rule from a set of applicable rules during execution. In this section we will focus on this problem. A control structure basically is a solution to this problem (and a number of others, as will become clear below). There are, however, a number of important differences between logic programming and rule-based agent programming. Theoretically, the selection of logic clauses in logic programming does not matter as long as the selection mechanism is *fair* (cf. [6], where the selection mechanism is called a *search rule*). Since the aim of logic programming is declarative programming where the order of logic clauses does not matter, theoretically at least, the particular selection mechanism could be hidden from the programmer. In practice, of course, Prolog differs a great deal from this ideal. The aim of declarativity, however, is to *hide the selection mechanism* from the programmer.

This should be different for agent programming, we think. The aim of agent programming is, in our view, to design practical tools and develop a formal theory for programming agents based on the common sense metaphor. The agent paradigm in Artificial Intelligence, therefore, is an attempt to design programming constructs which can usefully be viewed as the counterparts of the common sense notions of goal, plan, belief, etc. It is important in implementing this philosophy to retain as many as possible of the intuitive meanings of these notions in the formal counterparts. This is one of the reasons for a *glass-box approach* to the selection of (planning) rules.

Another reason, more in the line of traditional software design, for making the particular details of the control structure available to the programmer is that these details matter for the design of programs. The issue is well-known in the context of rule-based languages. For example, for the rule-based language OPS5 a number of selection mechanisms have been proposed (cf. [1]). One of these mechanisms, *rule clustering*, seems also particularly useful for our purposes. Our proposal for a selection mechanism, however, is derived from the philosophy of intelligent agents as outlined in the previous paragraph.

We will use the simple agent language of the previous section to discuss the selection of rules. This language includes a variety of rules which is representative for agent languages. Among others, it includes the well-known type of rule $a \leftarrow \phi \mid \pi$ where a is a simple head. A second type of rule supported by the language are rules with empty head. We call such rules *condition-action rules*. Still more general rules are allowed, where the head may be any goal. The latter type allows the modification of complex goals.

These rules may have several purposes. Based on their purpose, we can classify rules into *reactive rules*, *means-end rules*, and *revision rules*. Reactive rules commonly are triggered in situations in which a certain type of behaviour is needed urgently. The type of situation is specified by the guard of the rule, and the type of behaviour by the body of the rule. Typically, these rules have an empty head. Means-end rules specify in the body of the rule the means to achieve a goal as specified in the head. Revision rules are useful for modifying, or dropping (rules with empty body) of complex, goals.

We want to propose one further distinction in the class of revision rules. In general, there are two types of situations an agent might want to revise his goals. In the first type, something goes wrong and at least the means to achieve a goal of the agent have to be revised, whereas, in the second type, it is possible to select a more optimal strategy to replace the current means an agent uses to achieve one of its goals. If something goes wrong, there basically exist two strategies to deal with the failure. The agent may drop his current goal because of the failure, since it is no longer feasible or the costs to achieve it in some other way are too high. Or, alternatively, the agent may substitute some alternative means to deal with the failure situation and try to achieve the goal in some other way. In the second type of situation a different issue is at stake. In this case the *means* to achieve a goal are found to be suboptimal and a more optimal way of achieving the same goal is possible. According to these distinctions we introduce four classes of rules: the class $\mathcal{R}$ of *reactive rules*, $\mathcal{M}$ of *means-end rules*, $\mathcal{F}$ of *failure rules*, and, finally, the class $\mathcal{O}$ of *optimisation rules*.

We argue that one can assign a total order to these classes, in an intuitive way, as follows: $\mathcal{R} > \mathcal{F} > \mathcal{M} > \mathcal{O}$. The order on the rules reflects the priorities assigned to them. The class of reactive rules has the highest priority, which reflects the purpose these rules are generally used for. These rules are not related to the current goals of an agent at all, but reflect a low-level goal of the agent (cf. [4]). A reactive rule specifies a behaviour encoded by the body of the rule which is needed urgently in a situation specified by the guard of the rule. A good example is a behaviour to avoid collision with something which suddenly crosses the path of a robot. Note that it is also vital to immediately *execute* the behaviour after *firing* the reactive rule. The order imposed on the different types of rules implements a particular *revision strategy* an agent uses to reconsider its goals or plans (cf. also [12]).

The second-highest priority is assigned to the class of failure rules, which should at least revise the means to achieve a goal of an agent. The reason for this revision typically is that the means to achieve a current goal of the agent are not suitable in the current situation the agent is in. Therefore, if the agent would pursue his goal by using the current means as specified the agent would almost certainly fail. The purpose of the failure rules is to avoid this type of failure and to revise the means to achieve and possibly the goal the agent is after. The means in need of revision are specified by the head of a failure rule, the situation that gives rise to the failure by the guard of the rule, and the strategy to avoid the failure by the body of the rule. The high priority assigned to this rule is justified because of the pressing need to avoid behaviour which could potentially lead to catastrophic consequences.

After reacting to urgent situations and avoiding failure, the agent should use its time to find the means to achieve its goals. The lower priority assigned to means-end rules reflects our assumption that it is very important to avoid failure, and that only after this has been accomplished the agent should worry about how to achieve a goal the agent currently pursues. Nevertheless in the normal case this is the natural mode of functioning for an agent, since otherwise it would never achieve any of its goals.

The lowest priority is assigned to optimisation rules which have the purpose to achieve better performance of an agent or a higher success rate. Without these types of rules nothing would go wrong, things would only be achieved less optimal. Thus, although an agent could do without them, to build optimal agents these rules serve their purpose.

The control structure we propose is a specialised version of the well-known sense-update-act cycle which is used in a number of rule-based agent languages:

```
1. Get sense data S
2. Update belief base with S
3. Select which rule R to fire
4. Update goal base by firing R
5. Select goal G to execute
6. Execute (part of) G
7. Goto 1
```

The control structure can be divided into three main sections. To make this division we assume the goal base of an agent is divided into sense, reactive, and other goals: $\Pi = \Pi_{sense} \cup \Pi_{reactive} \cup \Pi_{rest}$. Steps (1) and (2) together constitute the *sensing phase*. In this paper, however, we do not deal with sensing or communication and we will therefore not discuss steps (1) and (2) but leave this for future research. Steps (3) and (4) constitute the *rule application phase*. In the previous section we have discussed a selection mechanism for firing rules. The priorities assigned to the rules can be used in step (3) to select which rules to fire. Steps (5) and (6) constitute the *execution phase*. Keeping the purpose of reactive rules in mind, if a reactive rule has been fired at step (4), at step (5) a reactive goal from $\Pi_{reactive}$ should be selected for execution. This selection strategy establishes a link between the application and execution phase. A question concerning step (6) is how much of a goal is executed during step (6). Several reasons suggest that only a part of the selected goal(s) should be executed. First of all, an interpreter implementing the control structure cannot decide whether a goal is completely executable. Secondly, failure rules operate on goals in the goal base; if a complex goal would be executed completely there is no purpose anymore in having failure rules preventing failure while executing the goal. Other interesting features of the execution phase, for example, goal selection based on goal prioritisation, are left for future research.

4 A Language for Programming Control Structures

As noted above, in most agent languages a distinction is made between an *execution phase* and a *rule application phase* in the interpreter for the language (this is so, for example, in AgentSpeak(L) [9], AGENT-0 [10], [4]). In the execution phase some of the goals are (partly) executed, while in the rule application phase some kind of planning by second principles, i.e. by rules, is done.

We now present our meta language for programming an interpreter for agent languages. Its design is guided by the needs of a programmer of an interpreter for agent languages. First of all, we need the regular imperative constructs (or some other means for programming in general) to program control flow. Imperative constructs seem most suitable for the purpose of building an interpreter since interpreters usually specify some sequential order of execution (cf. the control structure of the previous section). Secondly, we need a number of *basic actions* or constructs, roughly corresponding to the transition rules of the agent language and the application and execution phases. Here, we have chosen four actions corresponding to the steps (3) to (4) of the control structure in the previous section. And thirdly, we need constructs to express a preference order over goals and rules. Also, the interpreter should have the means to access all the features of an agent program, like its set of rules, and the current configuration the agent program is in.

Starting with the syntax, the goal and rule terms of the meta language are used to access the goal base and rule base of the agent program of the object language in the meta language. The terms range over sets of goals or sets of rules. Therefore, the operators of the meta language for building complex terms are the usual set operators.

Definition 9. Let $\mathsf{Var}_\Pi, \mathsf{Var}_\Gamma$ be given sets of variables.
The set of *goal terms* $\mathfrak{T}_\Pi$ is defined by: (i) $\mathsf{Var}_\Pi \subseteq \mathfrak{T}_\Pi$, (ii) $\emptyset, \Pi \in \mathfrak{T}_\Pi$, (iii) if $g_0, g_1 \in \mathfrak{T}_\Pi$, then $g_0 \cap g_1, g_0 \cup g_1, g_0 - g_1 \in \mathfrak{T}_\Pi$, and (iv) if $g \in \mathfrak{T}_\Pi$, then $max_\Pi(g) \in \mathfrak{T}_\Pi$.
The set of *rule terms* $\mathfrak{T}_\Gamma$ is defined by: (i) $\mathsf{Var}_\Gamma \subseteq \mathfrak{T}_\Gamma$, (ii) $\emptyset, \Gamma \in \mathfrak{T}_\Gamma$, (iii) if $r_0, r_1 \in \mathfrak{T}_\Gamma$, then $r_0 \cap r_1, r_0 \cup r_1, r_0 - r_1 \in \mathfrak{T}_\Gamma$, (iv) if $r \in \mathfrak{T}_\Gamma$, then $max_\Gamma(r) \in \mathfrak{T}_\Gamma$.

The goal and rule terms are the usual set terms, constructed from the set operators $\cap$, etc. $\emptyset$ is a constant denoting the empty set. Furthermore, Γ is a rule term constant denoting the set of rules of an agent program. The goal term Π, however, is a variable which denotes the goal base of the current object configuration during execution. The set operators are extended with one more operator, the *max* function. The goal and rule term functions *max* return the maximal goals respectively rules in a given set under the goal and rule orderings.

Definition 10. The set of *meta statements* $\mathfrak{S}$ is defined by:

- if $G \in \mathsf{Var}_\Pi, g \in \mathfrak{T}_\Pi$, then $G := g \in \mathfrak{S}$,
- if $R \in \mathsf{Var}_\Gamma, r \in \mathfrak{T}_\Gamma$, then $R := r \in \mathfrak{S}$,
- if $g, g' \in \mathfrak{T}_\Pi$, then $g = g', g \neq g' \in \mathfrak{S}$,
- if $r, r' \in \mathfrak{T}_\Gamma$, then $r = r', r \neq r' \in \mathfrak{S}$,
- if $g \in \mathfrak{T}_\Pi, G \in \mathsf{Var}_\Pi$, then $selex(g, G) \in \mathfrak{S}$,
- if $G, G' \in \mathsf{Var}_\Pi$, then $ex(G, G') \in \mathfrak{S}$,
- if $r \in \mathfrak{T}_\Gamma, g \in \mathfrak{T}_\Pi, R \in \mathsf{Var}_\Gamma$, then $selap(r, g, R) \in \mathfrak{S}$,

- if $R \in \mathsf{Var}_\Gamma$ and $G, G' \in \mathsf{Var}_\Pi$, then $ap(R, G. G') \in \mathfrak{S}$,
- if $\beta, \beta' \in \mathfrak{S}$, then $\beta; \beta', \beta + \beta', \beta^* \in \mathfrak{S}$.

The meta language includes assignment of sets of goals or rules to goal or rule variables, tests for equality on the goal and rule terms, and the regular programming constructs for sequential composition, nondeterministic choice, and iteration. The meta language includes two actions *selex* and *selap* for selection and two actions *ex* and *ap* for respectively execution of goals and application of rules to goals. These four actions are calls to the object agent system to test and select, or to perform object transition steps corresponding to execution of goals or application of rules. The first argument position of the actions *selex* and *ex* should be filled with an input term denoting the set of goals from which to select or execute. The second argument position should be substituted with an output variable. The first two argument positions of *selap* and *ap* should be substituted with input terms denoting the set of goals respectively rules from which to select or respectively apply a rule to a goal. The third argument position should be substituted with an output variable.

Let us remark that, if in some context a *planning system* is defined, then we could also introduce an action $plan(g, r, G', R')$ for adding new rules to the rule base of the program. (g, r are input terms; in G' the set of goals for which a plan has been found could be stored, and in R' the set of plans found.) The suggestion of incorporating a planning system in the language *PLACA* (cf. [11]) possibly can be viewed as such an action. Note that in this case, the rule term Γ no longer is a constant.

Now we define the operational semantics of the meta language. The transition relation of the meta transition system is denoted by $\Longrightarrow$ denoting a relation on meta configurations, which are pairs consisting of a program statement and a meta state. Meta level states should include the information about object level features an agent interpreter should be able to access, like the object configuration and the rule base of an agent program. Furthermore, a meta state should keep track of the values of variables used in the meta program.

Definition 11. A *meta state*, or *m-state* τ is a tuple $\langle \langle \Pi, \sigma \rangle, \Gamma, <_\Pi, <_\Gamma, V \rangle$, where $\langle \Pi, \sigma \rangle$ is an *object configuration*, $\Gamma \subseteq \mathcal{L}^p$ is a set of *object rules*, $<_\Pi$ is an ordering on the set of goals $\mathcal{L}^g$ of the object language, $<_\Gamma$ is an ordering on the set of rules $\mathcal{L}^p$ of the object language, and V is a *variable valuation* of type : $(\mathsf{Var}_\Pi \to \wp(\mathcal{L}^g)) \cup (\mathsf{Var}_\Gamma \to \wp(\mathcal{L}^p))$.

The orderings on goals and rules in an m-state are used to define the selection mechanisms for them. Here, we assume these orderings do not change. Since they actually are features of the agent program, we could formally incorporate them into the definition of agent programs.

An *m-configuration* is a pair $\langle \beta, \tau \rangle$ where β is a program statement and τ an m-state. We also write an m-configuration as a six-tuple, listing all the elements of an m-state as elements of an m-configuration. We leave out the rule base and orderings of the configuration, since they are constants.

Definition 12. *(semantics of terms)*
Given an order $<_o$ on a set X, let $max_o(X) = \{x \in X \mid$ there is *no* $x' \in X$ such that $x <_o x'\}$. Furthermore, let $\tau = \langle\langle \Pi, \sigma\rangle, \Gamma, <_\Pi, <_\Gamma, V\rangle$ be an m-state, and T range over goal and rule terms. Then the interpretation function $[\![\cdot]\!]_\tau : (\mathfrak{T}_\Pi \to \wp(\mathcal{L}^g)) \cup (\mathfrak{T}_\Gamma \to \wp(\mathcal{L}^p))$ is defined by:

- $[\![T]\!]_\tau = V(T) \cap \Pi$, for $T \in Var_\Pi \cup Var_\Gamma$,
- $[\![\Pi]\!]_\tau = \Pi$, $[\![\Gamma]\!]_\tau = \Gamma$,
- $[\![\emptyset]\!]_\tau = \emptyset$,
- $[\![T_0 \oplus T_1]\!]_\tau = [\![T_0]\!]_\tau \oplus [\![T_1]\!]_\tau$, for $\oplus \in \{\cap, \cup, -\}$,
- $[\![max(T)]\!]_\tau = max([\![T]\!]_\tau)$.

We will drop the subscript referring to the state in the rest of this paper, as the context will make clear which state is referred to.

The selection action $selex(g, G)$ selects a goal which is executable in the current object configuration from a given set of goals $[\![g]\!]$. The goal selected must be maximal with respect to the ordering on the set of all goals, i.e. a goal is not chosen if there is a goal in $[\![g]\!]$ which is executable and greater with respect to the ordering on goals. The selection action returns a singleton set with the selected goal in the output variable G.

Definition 13. *(execution rule for selex)*

$$\frac{\langle \Pi, \sigma\rangle \xrightarrow{\pi, \pi'}}{\langle selex(g, G), \langle \Pi, \sigma\rangle, V\rangle \Longrightarrow \langle E, \langle \Pi, \sigma\rangle, V\{\{\pi\}/G\}\rangle}$$

such that $\pi \in [\![g]\!]$, and there is *no* $\delta \in [\![g]\!]$ such that $\delta >_\Pi \pi$ and $\langle \Pi, \sigma\rangle \xrightarrow{\delta, \delta'}$.

If there is no executable goal in the set of goals denoted by g, then the selection action returns the empty set in G.

$$\frac{\langle \Pi, \sigma\rangle \xrightarrow{\pi, \pi'} \text{ for all } \pi \in [\![g]\!], \pi' \in \mathcal{L}^g}{\langle selex(g, G), \langle \Pi, \sigma\rangle, V\rangle \Longrightarrow \langle E, \langle \Pi, \sigma\rangle, V\{\emptyset/G\}\rangle}$$

The selection action $selap(r, g, R)$ selects a rule from $[\![r]\!]$ that is applicable to a goal from $[\![g]\!]$ in the current object configuration. The action first selects a maximal goal from $[\![g]\!]$ to which a rule from $[\![r]\!]$ can be applied, and then selects a maximal rule from $[\![r]\!]$ which is applicable to that goal. This order of maximisation is explained by the fact that an agent program is *goal-driven*, not *rule-driven*. I.e, an agent tries to achieve its goals, not to apply its most preferred rules. The selected rule is returned as a singleton set in the output variable R.

Definition 14. *(execution rule for selap)*

$$\frac{\langle \Pi, \sigma\rangle \xrightarrow{\pi, \gamma, \pi'}}{\langle selap(r, g, R), \langle \Pi, \sigma\rangle, V\rangle \Longrightarrow \langle E, \langle \Pi, \sigma\rangle, V\{\{\gamma\}/R\}\rangle}$$

such that

1. $\gamma \in [\![r]\!]$, $\pi \in [\![g]\!]$,
2. there is *no* $\delta >_\Pi \pi$, $\delta \in [\![g]\!]$ such that:

   there is a $\theta \in [\![r]\!]$ such that: $\langle \Pi, \sigma \rangle \xrightarrow{\delta, \theta, \delta'}$,
3. there is *no* $\theta >_\Gamma \gamma$ such that $\theta \in [\![r]\!]$ and $\langle \Pi, \sigma \rangle \xrightarrow{\pi, \theta, \pi'}$.

If there is no rule applicable to a goal in the denotation of r and g, then the empty set is returned in R.

$$\frac{\langle \Pi, \sigma \rangle \xcancel{\xrightarrow{\pi, \gamma, \pi'}} \text{ for all } \pi \in [\![g]\!], \gamma \in [\![r]\!], \pi' \in \mathcal{L}^g}{\langle selap(r, g, R), \langle \Pi, \sigma \rangle, V \rangle \implies \langle E, \langle \Pi, \sigma \rangle, V\{\emptyset/R\} \rangle}$$

Informally, the meaning of the action $ex(G, G')$ is to (partly) execute as many goals from $[\![G]\!]$ from the current state as possible. The choice to execute *all* executable goals from $[\![G]\!]$ introduces a duality with the selection of *some* goal by the action *selex*. A maximal subset of $[\![G]\!]$ is chosen in such a way that each goal can be (partly) executed in sequence when the goals of the subset are ordered appropriately. Each of these goals is only partly executed, i.e. only one transition step according to the object agent transition system is made. The reason for partly executing a goal is that in general it is undecidable to check whether or not a program will halt, while it is possible to decide whether a basic action or test can be performed. Furthermore, the goals are transformed by using basic action or test transition rules, and no rules are applied to a goal in the subset.

The semantics of the action $ex(G, G')$ is defined by iteration. $ex(G, G')$ is executed by arbitrarily choosing an executable goal from $[\![G]\!]$, deleting this goal from $[\![G]\!]$, executing the goal at object level, and returning the new goal in output variable G', until no goals from $[\![G]\!]$ can be executed including the case $[\![G]\!] = \emptyset$.

In the sequel, let us write $X := +x$ for the substitution $([\![X]\!] \cup \{x\})/X$ and, similarly, $X := -x$ for $([\![X]\!] \setminus \{x\})/X$

Definition 15. *(execution rule for ex)*

$$\frac{\langle \Pi, \sigma \rangle \xrightarrow{\pi, \pi'} \langle \Pi', \sigma' \rangle, \pi \in [\![G]\!]}{\langle ex(G, G'), \langle \Pi, \sigma \rangle, V \rangle \implies \langle ex(G, G'), \langle \Pi', \sigma' \rangle, V\{G := -\pi, G' := +\pi'\} \rangle}$$

$$\frac{\langle \Pi, \sigma \rangle \xcancel{\xrightarrow{\pi, \pi'}} \text{ for all } \pi \in [\![G]\!], \pi' \in \mathcal{L}^g}{\langle ex(G, G'), \langle \Pi, \sigma \rangle, V \rangle \implies \langle E, \langle \Pi, \sigma \rangle, V \rangle}$$

The meta basic action $ex(G, G')$ is a call to the object agent language system to execute a maximal subset of goals from the set $[\![G]\!]$ and recording the result of executing those goals in G' (resulting in a change to the variable valuation V). The variable G is also changed and contains the remaining goals which are not executable in the current object state. The second transition rule specifies the termination condition of the iteration.

The iterative definition of ex implicitly defines an executable sequence of goals from $[\![G]\!]$ that is maximal, i.e. which cannot be extended with other executable goals from $[\![G]\!]$. The execution rules for ex do not demand that a sequence from $[\![G]\!]$ is chosen that is the longest sequence relative to all other executable sequences, i.e. it is a local maximum. To find a global maximum would require a lookahead facility that checks whether or not a sequence of goals from $[\![G]\!]$ can be extended or not. In case a longest sequence is asked for such a facility is needed to be able to compare sequences with different prefixes.

As before, an iterative definition of the semantics of ap is given. Informally, the action $ap(R, G, G')$ applies as many rules from $[\![R]\!]$ to as many goals from $[\![G]\!]$ as possible, recording the change to the goal base as a result of this action in G'. We have to distinguish two cases. The first case concerns the application of a condition-action rule. In this case, a condition-action rule from $[\![R]\!]$ is applied, the rule is removed from $[\![R]\!]$, and the result is stored in the variable G'. The rule has to be removed from $[\![R]\!]$ to guarantee termination of ap. The second case concerns the case that a rule modifies a goal from G. In this case an arbitrary goal from G is chosen and an arbitrary rule from R is chosen that is applicable to the chosen goal; the goal is deleted from $[\![G]\!]$, and the result of applying the rule to the goal is stored in the output variable G'. We require that for all variables $G, \square \notin [\![G]\!]$.

Definition 16. *(execution rule for ap)*

$$\frac{\langle \Pi, \sigma \rangle \xrightarrow{\pi, \gamma, \pi'} \langle \Pi', \sigma \rangle, \pi = \square}{\langle ap(R, G, G'), \langle \Pi, \sigma \rangle, V \rangle \Longrightarrow \langle ap(R, G, G'), \langle \Pi', \sigma \rangle, V\{R := -\gamma, G' := +\pi'\} \rangle}$$

$$\frac{\langle \Pi, \sigma \rangle \xrightarrow{\pi, \gamma, \pi'} \langle \Pi', \sigma \rangle, \pi \in [\![G]\!]}{\langle ap(R, G, G'), \langle \Pi, \sigma \rangle, V \rangle \Longrightarrow \langle ap(R, G, G'), \langle \Pi', \sigma \rangle, V\{G := -\pi, G' := +\pi'\} \rangle}$$

$$\frac{\langle \Pi, \sigma \rangle \xrightarrow{\pi, \gamma, \pi'}\!\!\!\!/\;\; \text{for all } \pi \in [\![G]\!], \gamma \in [\![R]\!], \pi' \in \mathcal{L}^g}{\langle ap(R, G, G'), \langle \Pi, \sigma \rangle, V \rangle \Longrightarrow \langle E, \langle \Pi, \sigma \rangle, V \rangle}$$

The third rule specifies the termination condition of the iteration. Similar remarks regarding local maxima as made for the action ex can be made for ap.

The transition rules for the regular programming constructs define the usual semantics assigned to them. Here, we omit the rules for sequential composition and nondeterministic choice; they are the counterparts in the meta-language of the rules of definitions 5 and 6.

Definition 17. *(assignment for program variables)*
Let $T \in \text{Var}_\Pi$ and $T' \in \mathfrak{T}_\Pi$, or $T \in \text{Var}_\Gamma$ and $T' \in \mathfrak{T}_\Gamma$.

$$\langle T := T', \langle \Pi, \sigma \rangle, V \rangle \Longrightarrow \langle E, \langle \Pi, \sigma \rangle, V\{[\![T']\!]/T\} \rangle$$

Definition 18. *(test on terms)* Let $T, T' \in \mathfrak{T}_\Pi$, or $T, T' \in \mathfrak{T}_\Gamma$.

$$\frac{[\![T]\!]_\tau = [\![T']\!]_\tau}{\langle T = T', \tau \rangle \Longrightarrow \langle E, \tau \rangle} \qquad \frac{[\![T]\!]_\tau \neq [\![T']\!]_\tau}{\langle T \neq T', \tau \rangle \Longrightarrow \langle E, \tau \rangle}$$

Definition 19. *(nondeterministic repetition)*

$$\frac{\langle \beta_1, \sigma_m \rangle \Longrightarrow \langle \beta_1', \sigma_m' \rangle}{\langle \beta_1^*, \sigma_m \rangle \Longrightarrow \langle E, \sigma_m \rangle \qquad \langle \beta_1^*, \sigma_m \rangle \Longrightarrow \langle \beta_1'; \beta_1^*, \sigma_m' \rangle}$$

5 Three interpreters

We now can use the formal tools and the meta programming language to design and compare interpreters for three agent programming languages in the literature: AGENT-0, AgentSpeak(L), and 3APL. Doing so, we had to deal with the fact that the main features of the AGENT-0 interpreter are outlined in [10], but this discussion of the interpreter is informal. Also, we abstracted from multi-agent features and time in AGENT-0. It seems, however, that the essentials of the AGENT-0 interpreter are not affected by this.

Concerning AgentSpeak(L), the differences with our agent language seem bigger than they really are. It is possible to formally show that a number of notions like event and intention which are not available in the simple agent language of this paper are redundant (cf. [2]). Therefore, one can define an interpreter for the regimented version of AgentSpeak(L) without these notions. Of course, 3APL is equivalent to the agent language defined in section 2 except for the lack of variables. The interpreters for the three languages are defined below.

	AGENT-0	AgentSpeak(L)	3APL
	REPEAT	WHILE $(\Pi \neq \emptyset)$ DO	WHILE $(\Pi \neq \emptyset)$ DO
		BEGIN	BEGIN
Step 3		selap(Γ, Π, R);	selap(Γ, Π, R);
Step 4	$G := \Pi$; $R := \Gamma$;	$G := \Pi$;	$G := \Pi$; $G' := \emptyset$;
	ap$(R, G, \_)$;	ap$(R, G, \_)$;	ap(R, G, G');
Step 5	$G := \Pi$;	selex(Π, G);	IF $R \subseteq$ max(Γ)
	ap$(\Delta, G, \_)$;		THEN $G := G'$
			ELSE selex(Π, G);
Step 6	ex$(\Pi, \_)$	ex$(G, \_)$	ex$(G, \_)$
	UNTIL TRUE;	END;	END;

In the table, we use '$\_$' at argument positions for output variables in the actions ex and ap if the results returned by these actions need not be recorded in any variable. For example, $ex(G, \_)$ does not record the resulting goals of execution in a variable.

The strategy for executing goals and applying rules in AGENT-0, is to execute all executable goals and apply all applicable rules in every cycle of the interpreter. This strategy can be directly programmed by the actions *ex* and *ap*. By simply supplying these actions with the current goal base and all the rules of the agent program, these actions execute and apply as many as possible in the current configuration. In AGENT-0 step 3 and 5 of the control structure in section 3 therefore are empty: no selection is made. One extra feature of AGENT-0 is that it leaves to the interpreter to decide, at each cycle, whether a goal in the goal base is still considered feasible. If not, the interpreter removes the goal from the goal base. We can mimic this feature by introducing a set of failure rules Δ with empty bodies to drop a goal under certain circumstances in which the goal is considered infeasible. These conditions should be stated as the guard of the rule. Step 5 in the interpreter for AGENT-0 performs this function (see table).

At the other extreme of the spectrum, AgentSpeak(L) executes and applies each cycle of the interpreter at most one goal and one rule. The selection mechanisms used in AgentSpeak(L) are not made explicit in [9], so we can not comment on the orderings used. The interpreter implements each of the steps (3) to (6) of the control structure of section 3. Neither in AgentSpeak(L) nor in AGENT-0 there exists any link between the execution and application phase of the interpreters. We mean by this that no information that results from the execution phase is used in the application phase or vice versa. This can be concluded from the interpreters by noticing that no output variables of one of these phases is used as input in the other phase (cf. step 5 in the table).

The main difference between AgentSpeak(L) and 3APL is that 3APL does have a link between the application and the execution phase. If a reactive rule is fired in the application phase, the body of this rule is inserted in the goal base, and should be executed in the next execution phase. This body is returned in the output variable of the action *ap*. The link between the phases can be read from the program text: the output variable G' of $ap(R, G, G')$ is used as an input variable in the first branch of the IF-THEN-ELSE in the execution phase. In the execution phase it is tested whether or not a reactive rule was fired. If so, the corresponding reactive goal is executed. It is assumed that there always are reactive rules in agent programs. However, this assumption can be removed by a few changes to the interpreter. Thus, in 3APL the ordering as defined in section 3 is explicitly used to guide the execution of the agent program. The rule with highest priority is selected to apply to the selected goal, and depending on the result of this choice the goal for execution is determined.

6 Conclusion

We developed formal tools to compare a number of rule-based agent programming languages. The main results of this comparison can be summarised as follows. When the features of communication and time are dropped from AGENT-0, a simple programming language remains. In particular, AGENT-0 lacks (imperative programming) constructs to program control flow. AgentSpeak(L) mainly is an imperative programming language with belief bases as its domain of computation. A notable feature of 3APL is the general goal revision it allows by means of generalised rules. In a nutshell, the interpreters highlight the following differences between the languages. AGENT-0's interpreter is a-selective: it tries to execute as many goals and apply as many rules as possible. This contrasts with the selective execution of goals and application of rules of AgentSpeak(L) and 3APL. However, the selection mechanism of AgentSpeak(L) is not made explicit, while that of 3APL is outlined in this paper.

We argued for a glass-box approach when building interpreters for rule-based agent languages. A glass-box approach argues for making the selection of goals and rules during execution of the agent program explicit. This is particularly important for the design of agent programs. The extreme ends of the spectrum of selection mechanisms illustrated by AGENT-0 on the one hand and AgentSpeak(L) and 3APL on the other hand provide evidence for our claim that a glass-box approach should be taken. We then developed a selection mechanism for rules, which was based on the common sensical view of agents as complex mental entities consisting of beliefs, goals, plans, etc. The selection mechanism proposed is incorporated into a more general control structure known as the sense-update-act cycle.

The importance of these issues makes it imperative to define programming constructs with a clear and formal semantics in which these control structures can be formally stated. We achieved this goal by designing a meta programming language including a number of expressive constructs for programming agent interpreters. The total agent system then becomes a two level system. The object level corresponds to the agent language, while the meta level corresponds to the meta language for programming interpreters. This approach allows a great flexibility concerning the choice of agent language and type of interpreter.

In the future we want to extend our framework with priorities on goals, and a selection mechanism based on priorities assigned to goals. By experimenting with the rule-ordering argued for in this paper in a mobile robot setting we hope to substantiate our claims with empirical results. The particular features of rule and goal selection built into our language 3APL constitute the basic architecture of 3APL agents. A question which remains for future research is in what ways the architectural constraints imposed are related to the design of particular types of agents (cf. [7]). We also want to look at a formal proof system based on the operational semantics in this paper.

References

1. Thomas Cooper and Nancy Wogrin. *Rule-based Programming with OPS5*. Morgan Kaufmann, 1988.
2. Koen V. Hindriks, Frank S. de Boer, Wiebe van der Hoek, and John-Jules Ch. Meyer. A Formal Embedding of AgentSpeak(L) in 3APL. Technical Report UU-CS-1998-07, University Utrecht, Department of Computer Science, 1998.
3. Koen V. Hindriks, Frank S. de Boer, Wiebe van der Hoek, and John-Jules Ch. Meyer. Formal Semantics for an Abstract Agent Programming Language. In

Munindar P. Singh, Anand Rao, and Michael J. Wooldridge, editors, *Intelligent Agents IV (LNAI 1365)*, pages 215 229, 1998.

4. Robert Kowalski and Fariba Sadri. Towards a unified agent architecture that combines rationality with reactivity. *Proc. International Workshop on Logic in Databases (LNCS 1154)*, 1996.

5. Robert Kowalski, F. Toni, and G. Wetzel. Towards a declarative and efficient glass-box clp language. In N.E. Fuchs and G. Gottlob, editors, *Proc. of the 10th Logic Programming Workshop*. University of Zurich (ifi-Report Nr. 94.10), 1994.

6. J.W. Lloyd. *Foundations of Logic Programming*. Springer, 1987.

7. J. P. Müller. The right agent (architecture) to do the right thing. In J. P. Müller, M. P. Singh, and A. S. Rao, editors, *Intelligent Agents V -- Proceedings of the Fifth International Workshop on Agent Theories, Architectures, and Languages (ATAL-98)*, Lecture Notes in Artificial Intelligence. Springer-Verlag, Heidelberg, 1999. In this volume.

8. G. Plotkin. A structural approach to operational semantics. Technical report, Aarhus University, Computer Science Department, 1981.

9. Anand S. Rao. AgentSpeak(L): BDI Agents Speak Out in a Logical Computable Language. In W. van der Velde and J.W. Perram, editors, *Agents Breaking Away*, pages 42 55. Springer, 1996.

10. Yoav Shoham. Agent-oriented programming. *Artificial Intelligence*, 60:51 92, 1993.

11. Sarah Rebecca Thomas. *PLACA, An Agent Oriented Programming Language*. PhD thesis, Department of Computer Science, Stanford University, 1993.

12. M. J. Wooldridge and S. D. Parsons. Intention reconsideration reconsidered. In J. P. Müller, M. P. Singh, and A. S. Rao, editors, *Intelligent Agents V Proceedings of the Fifth International Workshop on Agent Theories, Architectures, and Languages (ATAL-98)*, Lecture Notes in Artificial Intelligence. Springer-Verlag, Heidelberg, 1999. In this volume.

A Reactive Approach for Solving Constraint Satisfaction Problems

Arnaud Dury[1], Florence Le Ber[2,1], and Vincent Chevrier[1]

[1] LORIA, B.P. 239, 54506 Vandœuvre-lès-Nancy cedex, France
[2] INRA LIAB, 54280 Champenoux, France

Abstract. We propose in this paper a multi-agent model for solving a class of Constraint Satisfaction Problems: the assignment problem. Our work is based on a real-world problem, the assignment of land-use categories in a farming territory, in the north-east of France. This problem exhibits a function to optimize, while respecting a set of constraints, both local (compatibility of grounds and land-use categories) and global (ratio of production between land-use categories). We developed a model using a purely reactive multi-agent system that builds its solution upon conflicts that arise during the resolution process. In this paper, we present the reactive modelling of the problem solving and experimental results from two points of view: the efficiency of the problem being solved and the properties of the problem solving process.

1 Introduction

In Europe today, farm enterprises are disappearing or modifying their farming systems with a resulting increase in land available for rent or sale. In addition, land use is changing and these changes cause many problems, such as pollution, erosion and landscape changes. We need to understand and simulate the organization of farming territories and their dynamics in order to predict these problems and to develop techniques or new farm management methods to solve them.

We developed a model to simulate the organization of farming territories [7]. We took the example of mixed crop-livestock farming systems in the north-east of France. They are grouped in different categories and their main features are described. For instance, the LMI type is described as follow: hay, corn and cereals are used to feed dairy and beefs cattle; dairy cattle is grazed about 6 months a year. The required production or area of each land-use category depends on the number of animals, the stocking rate of pastures and the expected yield of crops and hay meadows.

The relief of the north-east of France is a succession of gently sloping plateaus (calcareous soils) interspersed with valleys (clay and alluvial soils). The settlements are grouped. The location of land-use categories depends on their constraints and preferences: dairy cow pastures must be located very near the village (max 1 km), crops grow better on limestone, the slope must be less than 10%, corn must be near the village (max 2 km), the other crops can be located further away, and so on.

Our model is simple: a farming system occupies the territory of the village where the farm buildings are located. Each village territory is divided into zones according to the local values of the following characteristics: distance to village, soil and slope. The farming systems are described as sets of land-use categories (crops and meadows) which have to achieve a goal (production or area) and to respect constraints. The problem is to assign the land-use categories to the territory respecting the priorities of the farming systems, the constraints of the land-use categories and the characteristics of the territory. We suggest a reactive multi-agent system to solve this problem [8].

2 Related Works

Related research can be divided into two main categories: constraint satisfaction problem solving with cognitive multi-agent and reactive agents approaches.

The first category uses communicative, cooperative agents. Yokoo [13] defined agents that work separately on differents aspects of the problem, but communicate with each other in order to prevent conflict when several agents try to gain access to the same variable of the problem. Conry, Ghedira [2,6] used communication to allow agents to exchange local information that helps them achieve a more global view of the impact of their own decisions. Finally, agents exchange information to detect particular situations (like an overconstrained one) and react accordingly [2].

Being cognitive, such agents also implement complex strategies to optimize their problem solving process. In [6], agents use a taboo mechanism to avoid endless loops. In [13], agents are able to detect a "quasi-local-minimum" and escape from it. In [2] a negotiation protocol is introduced in order to provide backtracking capacity to the system.

Reactive approaches have been applied to similar problems, as Mueller has shown in [9]. Drogoul, Ohira [4,10] based these approaches on situated agents trying to achieve satisfaction in an environment that represents the problem domain. They try to achieve satisfaction by acting on their environment; such actions generally being "moving". An acting agent may attack another: Ferber based Eco-Resolution on such behaviors [5]. Agents perceive and react to force-fields defined in their environement; these force-fields are, in return, built upon the previous actions of the agents [10,1].

The reactive approaches use neither a complex strategy, nor an advanced communication protocol. Their simplicity allows the solving of oversized problems, previously unreachable by "classical" methods (see [4], for an application to the N-Puzzle problem). These systems can easily be adapted to new constraints at run-time [10,1].

3 A Multi-Agent Model to Assign Land Use

Our system is composed of reactive agents whose goal is to conquer spatial zones in the environment. The agents are clustered in groups that represent the land-use categories while the environment represents the territory which is to be occupied.

The problem solving process is based on the following principles: an agent can conquer a zone in the environment and then contribute to the satisfaction of its group; the zones are more or less attractive for an agent; when searching for a zone, an agent chooses the most attractive one. If the zone is free the agent occupies it; if it is already occupied, the two agents have to fight, and the outcome is determined by the respective strengths of their groups. Finally, the strength of a group decreases while its satisfaction increases, in order to ensure that groups farther from their objectives gain an advantage over those closer.

This model is not based on the agronomist's or the farmer's reasoning. For instance, ranking the groups by their respective strength has nothing to do with the agronomist's way of ranking land-use categories [7]. The purpose of this model is to make fast simulations of land-use organizations at a regional scale in order to test hypotheses. It is not to reproduce the real organization of a farming system.

3.1 The Environment

The environment is a set of zones, each of these is fully described by a set of data which are: *distance* to the village, *slope*, *soil* and *surface*. There is no modelling of the two-dimensionnal topology of the real ground. The set of zones in the environment is denoted Z.

3.2 The Society

A land-use category (denoted l with $l \in \{corn, cereals, cow\text{-}pasture, etc.\}$) corresponds to an agent group g_l. Each group is characterized by three main parameters:

- the number (n_l) of agents of the group, an agent of g_l is denoted a_{lj} with $j \in [1, n_l]$;
- a goal (denoted $Goal_l$) that is a quantity to produce or an area to cover;
- a production function (denoted $Prod_l(soil, slope, distance, surface)$), which computes the production or the area covered by the land-use category as a function of the features of the environment; its value is null when these features are not convenient for the land-use category;

Four values are used for problem solving:

- The current achievement of the goal at a resolution cycle t is:

$$A_l^t = \sum_{j \in [1, n_l]} Prod_{lj}^t$$

where $Prod_{lj}^t$ is the contribution of the agent a_{lj} at cycle t (see paragraph 3.3);
- the distance to the goal at cycle t: $D_l^t = |1 - A_l^t/Goal_l|$;
- the satisfaction of the group at cycle t: $S_l^t = A_l^t/Goal_l$ which increases since the group is achieving its goal;
- the strength of the group at cycle t: $Str_l^t = (Goal_l/A_l^t)^d$, d is a positive and non zero integer; the strength decreases when the group approaches its goal.

3.3 The agents

An agent belongs to a group and shares some information with the other agents of its group (the goal, the production function). The agent's behavior is guided by the search for a zone in order to be able to produce and thereby to contribute to the achievement of its group goal.

An agent can be free (it will be supposed to occupy the null zone denoted by z_0) or placed (that is occupying a zone).

An agent a_{lj} contributes to the achievement of its group goal at cycle t according to the following definitions:

- the agent is free, its contribution is null: $Prod_{lj}^t = Prod_l(z_0) = 0$
- the agent is placed on a zone z of the environment, its contribution is:

$$Prod_{lj}^t = Prod_l(z) = Prod_l(soil_z, slope_z, distance_z, surface_z)$$

The strength of an agent at a cycle t corresponds to the strength of its group at cycle $t+1$ for which we suppose the agent will change state or zone. Thus, an agent is going to win a fight if and only if it does not lose at $t+1$ a fight with the previously defeated. This local heuristic is designed to lead the system towards stability. The general expression of the strength is:

$$Str_{lj}^t(z', z) = Str_l^{t+1} = \left(\frac{Goal_l}{A_l^t - Prod_l(z') + Prod_l(z)} \right)^d, d \in N^*$$

for an agent occupying the zone $z' \in Z \cup \{z_0\}$ and trying to conquer the zone $z \in Z \cup \{z_0\}$.

According to this general formula, the strength of an attacked placed agent is:

$$Str_{lj}^t(z', z_0) = (Goal_l/(A_l^t - Prod_l(z')))^d$$

Finally, agents are provided with a function to enable them to rank the zones and to choose which zone to try to conquer. This aspect will be detailed in the next section.

4 The Problem Solving Process and its Dynamic

The problem solving process is iterative. It starts with every agent being free and the environment being complete. One after another, each group chooses an agent to activate. It chooses either a free agent or a placed agent, depending on its own current satisfaction and the state of the environment.

The agent determines a zone to be conquered: its strategy is to maximize its contribution to its group, while minimizing the loss inflicted on the other groups. If the chosen zone is free, the agent occupies it. A fight arises if the zone is already occupied, and the stronger agent wins the fight. The other has to flee. The process stops when all the groups are unable to occupy the zones they would like to occupy. These steps are described next.

In our work, as in [11], the social structure biases autonomous agent behaviour. In contrary to [11], our system is not based on co-ordination, but rather on conflicts. Agents in our model are guided by a field of potential (that is the attractiveness of the zones for the agents) over the problem domain. A similar use of a potential field can be found in [12].

4.1 The Behaviour of the Groups

Each group can adopt two behaviors, one of expansion and another of optimization.

- **expansion**: this behavior leads the group to occupy the maximum number of zones. It therefore chooses free agents. Thus, the number of free zones will decrease if this agent is successful.
- **optimization**: the group leaves a zone to occupy another that reduces the distance to the goal. This behavior is achieved by placed agents. Thus, the number of free zones will not change.

The choice between these two behaviors is tied to group satisfaction: the greater the group satisfaction, the more the optimization behavior is used. The group randomly chooses the agent to be activated amongst those under consideration (that is, free or placed ones).

4.2 The Behavior of the Agents

An agent's behavior is not directly related to its group's behavior. The activated agent (either placed or free) looks for an attractive zone to occupy. In order to avoid a fight, it will first look for free attractive zones. If there are any such zones, it will occupy one of them. If there are not, the activated agent will have to drive another agent away from its zone.

Choosing a Zone. An agent a_{lj} has to contribute to the achievement of its group goal. Leaving the zone z' ($z' \in Z \cup \{z_0\}$) to occupy a zone z, it will try to decrease its group's distance to the goal. The profit is:

$$Profit_{lj}(z', z) = D_l^t - D_l^{t+1} = |1 - \frac{A_l^t}{Goal_l}| - |1 - \frac{A_l^t - Prod_l(z') + Prod_l(z)}{Goal_l}|$$

If this value is positive, then the zone z is attractive for the agent a_{lj}. This heuristic was implemented to help the convergence of our system.

The agent a_{lj} first examines the free attractive zones. It rates them as follow:

$$M_{lj}^t(z) = Prod_l(z)/Goal_l$$

and occupies the zone with the highest grade. In this case, the zone occupied by the agent is simply that with maximal production.

If there are no free attractive zones, the agent examines zones what are occupied. Let the zone z be occupied by an agent a_{km} ($k \neq l$), the mark is:

$$M_{lj}^t(z) = \frac{Profit_{lj}(z', z)}{-Profit_{km}(z, z_0)} \cdot \frac{Str_l^t}{Str_k^t}$$

The agent a_{lj} chooses to "attack" the zone with the higher grade.

The latter case is more complex than the former: the grade formula was chosen to embody two heuristics. The first is an heuristic of "mutual respect": each agent tries to maximize its expected gain, while minimizing the loss potentially inflicted to another agent, currently placed on the zone being rated. Thus, the groups both approach their goals. The second heuristic is one of "prudence": it prevents the agent from choosing a zone whose occupant is too strong.

Fighting for a zone. The outcome of the fight between an agent a_{lj} (active, placed on z') and an agent a_{mk} (placed on z and attacked) depends on the ratio of $Str_{lj}^t(z', z)$ and $Str_{mk}^t(z, z_0)$. If $Str_{lj}^t(z', z) > Str_{mk}^t(z, z_0)$, the agent a_{lj} wins and it will then occupy the zone. The agent a_{mk} becomes free. If this does not occur, both agents remain in their previous states.

5 Experiments

We conducted experiments to assess this model according to two points of view:

1. its efficiency with respect to the problem being solved. In this case we were interested in the quality of the results;
2. the problem solving process and its properties. In this case, we were interested in the dynamics of the problem-solving process.

Our experimental data set consisted of two territory data (228 and 210 zones) from a Geographic Information System of the Vittel plateau in the east of France [3] and three sets of constraints: one weak, one average, one strong, representing the goals of the land-use categories of LMI farming systems (five land-use categories, as shown in Table 1). Each constraint set is defined according to the needs of a certain number of dairy cows. For instance the average set of constraints is defined for 430 dairy cows.

	corn (ton)	cereals (quintal)	hay (quintal)	cow pasture (hectare)	heifer pasture (hectare)
weak c-set	2106	8073	7020	300	362
average c-set	3024	11592	10080	430	520
strong c-set	4212	16146	14040	600	724

Table 1. Goals of the 5 land-use categories for each constraint set (c-set).

Crossing constraint sets and territories provided us with 6 problem configurations to test our system. First, we ran the system on each of the 6 configurations 1000 times.

Then we conducted experiments on the dynamics of the process, varying data at runtime. Results were produced by our system, coded in C, running on a Pentium Pro 200 MHz, under Solaris.

5.1 Evaluating the results

The agronomic expert requires the following criteria which define the quality of a result:

- final goal achievements of the groups (i.e., land-use categories) should be high: their mean value should be close to the optimum defined by the expert (see Table 2);
- final goal achievements should be close to each other: their standard deviation should be low.

The optimum is defined according to the expert's results [7] when allocating the same land-use categories with the same objectives on the same territory. The second requirement should be linked to the viability of the farming systems: crops and meadows are used to feed cattle; they cannot replace each other as animal feed.

	210 zones	228 zones
weak c-set	100%	100%
average c-set	71%	79%
strong c-set	51%	56%

Table 2. Value of the expert's optimum (average goal achievement) for each constraint set (percentage).

We computed the mean value and the standard deviation of the final goal achievements for the 1000 runs of our system on each configuration (see Figures 1, 2, 3, 4, 5, and 6).

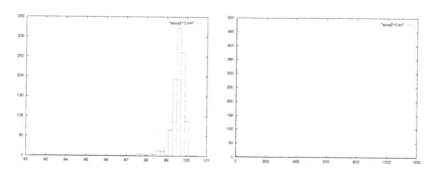

Fig. 1. Mean-values and standard-deviations of the goal achievements (percentage) of the 5 groups (weak constraint set, 210 zones).

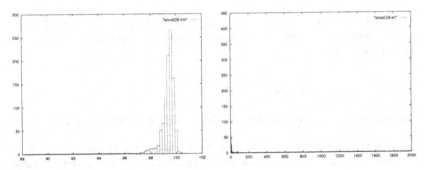

Fig. 2. Mean-values and standard-deviations of the goal achievements (percentage) of the 5 groups (weak constraint set, 228 zones).

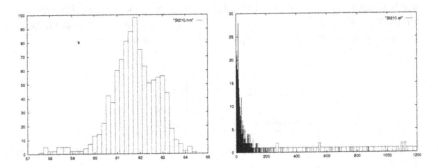

Fig. 3. Mean-values and standard-deviations of the goal achievements (percentage) of the 5 groups (average constraint set, 210 zones).

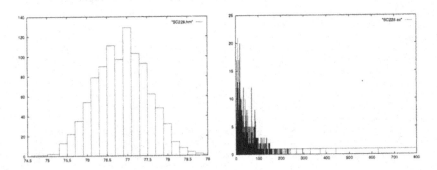

Fig. 4. Mean-values and standard-deviations of the goal achievements (percentage) of the 5 groups (average constraint set, 228 zones).

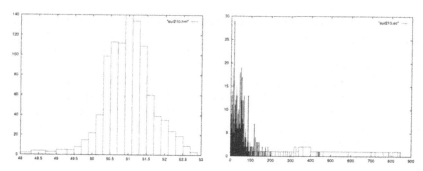

Fig. 5. Mean-values and standard-deviations of the goal achievements (percentage) of the 5 groups (strong constraint set, 210 zones).

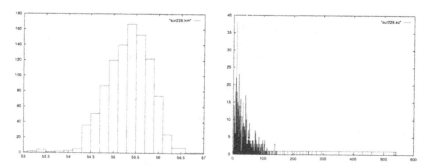

Fig. 6. Mean-values and standard-deviations of the goal achievements (percentage) of the 5 groups (strong constraint set, 228 zones).

In the weak constraint set (see Figures 1 and 2), most results are near 100% goal achievement. The standard deviation is very small and is reduced to a vertical narrow line at $x = 0$ coordinate. In this case our model produced satisfactory results according to the expert's requirements.

In the average constraint set (see Figures 3 and 4) mean values are a little below the expert's optimum on most tries. The standard deviation is also debased. In the strong constraint set (see Figures 5 and 6), the mean value is mostly better than the expert's optimum (there are a high number of values better than expert's ones : 51% and 56%), but the standard deviation is generally not good.

5.2 The Properties of the Problem-Solving Process

We were interested in two categories of properties:

1. those linked to a standard problem-solving process (at the beginning, every agents is free and the environment is complete): convergence, stability;
2. those related to the ability of our model to adapt itself to varying problem data: modification of the number of zones or of the number of groups at run-time.

Standard resolution. A **stable** state of the problem-solving process is characterized by the stability of the land-use categories over time: no further zone will undergo a change in assignment. **Convergence** is concerned with the ability of the system to gradually near the expert's optimum for each land-use category.

Figure 7 shows the goal achievements of each group at run time and is representative of a typical run of the system. It shows that our system exhibits the two previous properties. Stability is achieved at step 40. Convergence is not strict (the expert's optimum is 79% in this case).

Moreover, due to the design of our model, the problem-solving process respects all constraints at each step. Thus, stopping the system at any step will provide a solution. This aspect, together with convergence, defines an **anytime** property [14]: the system can be stopped at any step and provide a solution whose quality increases over time.

Modifying the number of zones. In the first set of experiments, the system started with an empty environment (no zone available) and the zones became available step-by-step during the resolution process. This experiment restricted the search space of the problem in the initials steps of the resolution. Figure 8 (left) shows the evolution of goal achievements for an average constraint data set (compare with Figure 7 for a standard run).

These experiments were also conducted with the weak and strong constraint sets. Results can be summarized as follow:

– when the constraints are weak, the results of the step-by-step runs are close to each other, and closer to the expert's optimum than in a standard run;
– when the constraints are strong, the results are of a lower quality than in a standard run.

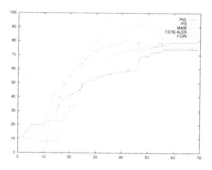

Fig. 7. Evolution of the goal achievements (percentage) during a run (228 zones, 5 groups, average constraint set): this run shows a convergent evolution toward a stable state of overall good quality.

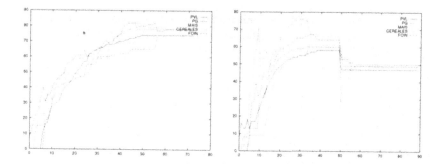

Fig. 8. Left: Evolution of the goal achievements (percentage) during a run with step-by-step available zones (228 zones, 5 groups, average constraint set). Right: Standard run and suppression of 60 zones at step 50 (210 zones, 5 groups, average constraint set).

In the second set of experiments, we withdrew zones (potentially previously allocated) at run-time. We first ran the system as usual, waited for a stable state, then withdrew randomly 20% of the zones, and again waited for a stable state to be reached. As shown in Figure 8 (right), our model can recover from the disturbance, and converge to a new stable state. Final results were of good quality, according to the expert's requirements.

Modifying the number of land-use categories. We studied the insertion of a new land-use category at run-time. Figure 9 (left) shows a standard run with six land-use categories (insertion was done at step 0); results are of good overall quality. Figure 9 (right) shows the system evolution when introducing a new land-use category at step 70: the system is able to recover from the introduction and converges to a stable state.

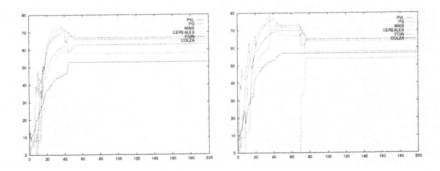

Fig. 9. Adding a new land-use category during a standard run (5 groups). Left: coleseed at step 0 (i.e., standard run with 6 groups). Right: coleseed at step 70.

We also studied the deletion of a land-use category at run time: the system was able to recover (i.e., the average goal achievement increases) but the final states were of poor quality (see Figure 10 for run example).

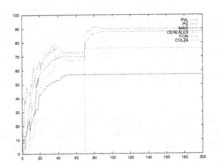

Fig. 10. Withdrawing a land-use category during a standard run (6 groups): coleseed at step 70.

6   Discussion

We have proposed a model to simulate the organization of farming territories. This model used a reactive approach in which interaction was mainly based on conflicts.

The results we obtained on real data sets were promising. First, the system produced results that were on par with the expert's requirements, although we did not introduce any explicit expert knowledge in our model. Instead, we designed heuristics embodied in the behaviors of the groups and of the agents: equilibrium between strength and satisfaction, expansion, optimization, self-satisfaction, "mutual respect", "prudence".

In all the experiments the system was able to converge to a stable state that respected the problem constraints and thus represented a solution to the problem. Moreover, the underlying process is anytime and is able to adapt itself to run-time changes in the problem data. Self-adaptation was experimentally stated when changing the number of zones (changes in the search space) and when adding or removing a land-use category (changes in the search constraints).

However, we still have to validate such properties with further experiments based on other real data sets and to complete the assessment of the results by comparing them with classical methods of constraint-satisfaction problem-solving.

Our system differs from the other multi-agent systems for constraint-solving: in contrast to cognitive designs we did not introduce any explicit backtracking behavior, nor any explicit behaviour for escaping from local optima. Our approach is rather similar to Eco-Resolution, but differs in the chaining process of agression, which our model lacks. In our system, each agression is settled immediately and the losing agent has to flee to the z_0 zone.

The zone-choice mechanism can be seen as defining a field of values over the territory, these values then being used to guide the agents in their choices. These choices, in return, modify the field. In this respect, our work shares features with the systems of [10] and [1]. From the agronomic point of view, some questions remain unanswered. For instance, the territories used in our experiments are highly heterogeneous: the size of the zones they are made of varies greatly from one zone to another. This has caused some problems when trying to obtain a low standard-deviation between the goal achievements of the different land-uses. Another question concerns the lack of topological information: our system is not able to locate the same land-use category in neighbouring zones. Finally, we considered a single farming system in one particular territory. We did not model several farming systems in competition over the same territory.

From the algorithmic point of view we have still to compare our approach to more classical ones in the field of CSP. Currently, we are building a resolution system based on simulated annealing. We intend to compare the quality of the results and the dynamic properties of the solving process in each system.

7 Conclusion

We have built a multi-agent model to solve a CSP, which is to assign land use on farming territories. Our model provides us with an incremental approach to the solution. The problem-solving process exhibits interesting properties: the system produces results that fit the expert's requirements; the dynamic of the problem-solving process is convergent to a stable state and is an anytime process, emerging from conflict-based local interactions. Furthermore, the model exhibits self-adaptation properties that enable it to maintain features that define "good" states through external disturbance.

This model could be applied without difficulty to similar problems in the assignment field, such as room assignment.

Future work will focus on the comparison of these results with classical methods of constraint-satisfaction problem-solving and with new data sets. Thanks to its high speed resolution[1], the model can be used to simulate land-use organization in a large space. Some extensions are under consideration. Firstly, we could design a dynamic sub-division of zones at run time: this would enable the system to homogenize the territory, by subdividing the biggest zones. Secondly, we need to take the topology into account to model neighboring constraints. Finally, we could introduce agents of various levels, such as farming system agents, to solve problems of competitive farming systems on the same territory.

References

1. C. Baeijs, Y. Demazeau, and L. Alvares. Sigma application of multi-agent system to cartographic generalization. In *Agents Breaking Away, Proceedings of Modeling Autonomous Agents in Multi-Agent World 96*, pages 163–176, 1996.
2. S. Conry, K. Kuwabara, V. Lesser, and R. A. Meyer. Multistage negotiation for distributed constraint satisfaction. *IEEE Transactions on Systems, Man and Cybernetics*, 21(6):1463–1477.
3. J.-P. Deffontaines, M. Benoît, J. Brossier, E. Chia, F. Gras, and M. Roux. Agriculture et qualité des eaux, diagnostic et propositions pour un périmètre de protection. Technical report, INRA, 1993. 334 pages.
4. A. Drogoul. *De la Simulation Multi-Agents à la résolution collective de problèmes*. PhD thesis, Université Paris VI, 1993.
5. J. Ferber and E. Jacopin. The framework of eco-problem solving. In *Proceedings Modeling Autonomous Agents in Multi-Agent World 90*, 1990.
6. K. Ghedira. Co-optimisation combinatoire : fondement et exemples.
7. F. Le Ber and M. Benoît. Modelling the spatial organisation of land use in a farming territory. Example of a village in the plateau lorrain. *Agronomie: Agriculture and Environment*, (18):101–113, 1998.
8. F. Le Ber, V. Chevrier, and A. Dury. A multi-agent system for the simulation of land use organization. In *Proceedings 3rd workshop on Artificial Intelligence in Agriculture*, Makuhari, Japan, April 1998. IFAC.
9. J. P. Müller. The right agent (architecture) to do the right thing. In J. P. Müller, M. P. Singh, and A. S. Rao, editors, *Intelligent Agents V — Proceedings of the Fifth International Workshop on Agent Theories, Architectures, and Languages (ATAL-98)*, Lecture Notes in Artificial Intelligence. Springer-Verlag, Heidelberg, 1999. In this volume.
10. T. Ohira, R. Sawatari, and M. Tokoro. Distributed interactions with computon. In *Agents breaking away, proc. of Modeling Autonomous Agents in Multi-Agent World 96*, 1996.
11. S. Ossowski and A. García-Serrano. Social structure in artificial agent societies: Implications for autonomous problem-solving agents. In J. P. Müller, M. P. Singh, and A. S. Rao, editors, *Intelligent Agents V — Proceedings of the Fifth International Workshop on Agent Theories, Architectures, and Languages (ATAL-98)*, Lecture Notes in Artificial Intelligence. Springer-Verlag, Heidelberg, 1999. In this volume.
12. O. Shehory, S. Kraus, and O. Yadgar. Goal satisfaction in large scale agent-systems: A transportation example. In J. P. Müller, M. P. Singh, and A. S. Rao, editors, *Intelligent Agents V — Proceedings of the Fifth International Workshop on Agent Theories, Architectures, and Languages (ATAL-98)*, Lecture Notes in Artificial Intelligence. Springer-Verlag, Heidelberg, 1999. In this volume.

---

[1] The experimentally assessed complexity is O(number of zones).

13. M. Yokoo and K. Hirayama. Distributed breakout algorithm for solving distributed constraint satisfaction problems. In *Proceedings International Conference on Multi-Agent Systems 96*, pages 401–408, 1996.

14. S. Zilberstein. Using anytime algorithms in intelligent systems. *AI Magazine*, 17(3):73–83.

Increasing Resource Utilization and Task Performance by Agent Cloning *

Onn Shehory, Katia Sycara, Prasad Chalasani, and Somesh Jha

The Robotics Institute
Carnegie Mellon University
Pittsburgh, PA 15213, U.S.A.
Tel: +412-268-8818
{onn,katia,chal,sjha}@cs.cmu.edu

Abstract. Agents in a multi-agent system may face situations where tasks overload their computational capacities. Usually, this problem is solved by passing tasks to others or agent migration to remote hosts. We propose agent cloning as a more comprehensive approach to balancing local agent overloads. According to our paradigm, agents may clone, pass tasks to others, die or merge. We discuss the requirements of implementing a cloning mechanism and its benefits in a Multi-Agent System (MAS), and support our claims with simulation results.

1 Introduction

Assume a multi-agent system (MAS) that receives a stream of tasks. The agents have *capabilities* which indicate the types of tasks they can perform and *capacities* which indicate the amounts of resources that the agents can access and use for task execution. Tasks are categorized by types that can be handled by agents with appropriate capabilities. The problem discussed in this paper is the situation where the task flow to an agent overloads it. Such overloads are of two different general categories:

1. An agent in a MAS is overloaded, but the MAS as a whole has the required capabilities and capacities.
2. The MAS as a whole is overloaded, i.e., the agents that comprise the MAS do not have the necessary capacities (however there may be idle resources in the computational system where the agents are situated).

As a result of such overloads, the MAS will not perform all of the tasks in time, although the required resources may be available to it. The following solutions suggest themselves:

1. Overloaded agents should pass tasks to others agents which have the capabilities and capacities to perform them.
2. Overloaded agents create new agents or migrate to other hosts, to perform excess tasks and utilize unused resources .

* This material is based upon work supported in part by ARPA Grant #F33615-93-1-1330, by ONR Grant #N00014-96-1222, and by NSF Grant #IRI-9612131.

In this paper we present *agent cloning* as a means for implementing these solutions and discuss the required reasoning, decision making and actions that are necessary for an agent within the system to perform cloning.

In particular, we consider cloning in an open environment, such as the Internet, where agents might dynamically and unpredictably appear or disappear. To study MAS issues in such an environment, we use the RETSINA domain-independent infrastructure [18]. In RETSINA, there are three types of agents: *providers*, who possess certain capabilities and perform tasks that require these capabilities; *requesters*, who have tasks to be performed and who locate agents with the required capabilities to whom they delegate the tasks; *middle agents* such as matchmakers [5], by whom requester agents locate provider agents. Provider agents advertise their capabilities to middle agents and requesters ask the latter to find providers with required capabilities. Our cloning mechanism is applied to this RETSINA infrastructure as follows. When an agent perceives an overload it can find, through middle agents, provider agents with appropriate capabilities (similar to its own) to whom it can consider transferring tasks. When no such providers are found, a clone may be created. Once created, a clone should advertise itself with a middle agent (as any agent in the system does), thus it becomes known to the multi-agent society.

In this paper we provide an analysis of the circumstances under which agents should consider cloning, and present experimental results on how cloning affects the performance of a MAS. Our simulation results show that using our cloning protocols to address local overloading problems improves agent and system performance.

2   The Cloning Approach

Cloning is a possible response of an agent to overloads. Agent overloads are due, in general, either to the agent's limited capacity to process current tasks or to machine overloads. Other approaches to overloads include task transfer and agent migration. Task transfer, where overloaded agents locate other agents which are lightly loaded and transfer tasks to them, is very similar to processor load balancing. Agent migration, which requires that overloaded agents, or agents that run on an overloaded machine,[2] migrate to less loaded machines, is closely related to process migration and to the recently emerging field of mobile agents [1]. Agent migration can be implemented by an agent creating its clone on a remote machine, transferring its tasks[3] to the clone, and dying. Thus, agent mobility is an instance of agent cloning (although mechanisms which are specifically designed for mobility may be more efficient in some cases). A main difference between load balancing and agent cloning is that, while the first explicitly discusses machine loads and process migration, the latter, in addition, considers a different type of load—the agent load. Agent load is unique in its reference to agent capabilities (i.e., its expertise), and not only to resources and capacities. It may also

---

[2] We assume some correlation between machine load and agents' loads, however these are different overloads.

[3] When tasks are already partially executed, it may be possible to transfer to the clone the remaining sub-tasks. If this is not possible (and a state is not passed), the clone may need to re-start executing the tasks.

happen that an agent capacity is overloaded, however the machine on which it is running is not overloaded.

Therefore, cloning is a superset of task transfer and process migration: it includes them and adds to them as well. Cloning does not necessarily require migration to other machines. Rather, a new agent is created either on the local or a remote machine. Note that there may be several agents running on the same machine, and having one of them overloaded does not necessarily imply that the others are overloaded (although we expect some correlation between overloads). Agent overload does not imply machine overload, and therefore local cloning (that is, on the same machine) may be possible. As shown in the load balancing literature [10], within a distributed system there is a high probability of having some of the processors idle, while others are highly loaded. Cloning takes advantage of these idle processing capacities.

To perform cloning, an agent must reason about its own load (current and future), its host load as well as capabilities and loads of other machines and agents. Accordingly, it may decide to: create a clone; pass tasks to a clone; merge with other agents; or die. Merging of two agents, or self-extinction of underutilized agents is an important mechanism to control agent proliferation with resulting overload of network resources. Detailed consideration of this problem, however, is outside of the scope of this paper.

Reasoning with regards to cloning starts by considering local cloning. This will prevent the communication overhead of trying to access and reason about remote hosts. Once local cloning is found infeasible or non-beneficial, the agent proceeds to reason about remote cloning. If remote cloning is decided upon, an agent should be created and activated on a remote machine. Assuming that the agent has access and a permit to work on this machine, there may be two main methods to perform this cloning: (1) creating the agent locally and letting it migrate to the remote machine (similar to a mobile agent) or, (2) creating and activating the agent on the remote machine. While the first method requires very little on the part of the remote machine, it requires mobilization properties as well as additional resource consumption on local host. The second method, while avoiding mobilization and local resource consumption, requires that a copy of the agents' code be located on the remote machine. Similar requirements also hold for mobile agent applications [7, 19], since an agent server or an agent dock is required.

Since the agent's own load and the loads of other agents vary over time in a non-deterministic way, the decision of *whether and when* to clone is non-trivial. Prior work [4] has presented a model of cloning based on prediction of missed task deadlines and idle times on the agent's schedule in the RETSINA multi-agent infrastructure [18]. In this paper (Section 4), we present a stochastic model of decision making based on dynamic programming to determine the optimal timing for cloning.

Suppose a clone has been created and activated. Several questions yet remain with respect to this clone. These regard its autonomy, its tasks, its lifetime, and its access to resources. *Autonomy* refers to independent clone vs. a subordinate one. Having been created and activated, an independent clone is not controlled by its creator. Therefore, such a clone will continue to exist after completion of the tasks provided by its initiator agent. Hence, a mechanism for deciding what it should do afterwards is necessary. Such a mechanism must allow the clone to reason about the agent- and task-environment, and accordingly decide whether it should continue to work on other tasks (if necessary and if the computational resources allow), merge with others, or perform self extinction.

A *subordinate* clone will remain under the control of its initiator. This will prevent the complications arising in the independent clone case - i.e., it is not necessary to decide what to do after the tasks that were delegated to the clone are accomplished. However, in order to manage a subordinate agent, the initiating agent must be provided with a control mechanism for remote agents. Regardless of the details of such a mechanism, it will require additional communication between the two agents, thus increasing the communication overhead of such a cloning method and the MAS vulnerability to communication flaws. In addition, control of other agents is a partially centralized solution, which might violate the reason for using a multi-agent system in the first place.

3 Cloning Initiation

An agent should consider cloning:

1. If it cannot perform all of its tasks on time by itself nor can it decompose them so that they can be delegated to others.
2. If (1) is false, but there is no lightly-loaded agent that can receive and perform its excess tasks (or sub-tasks when tasks are decomposable).
3. If there are sufficient resources for creating and activating a clone agent (either on the same machine or on a remote one).
4. If the efficiency of the clone agent and the original agent is expected to be greater than that of the original agent alone.

The above requirements may be difficult for an agent to determine. Later in this paper we discuss the methods according to which agents reason about themselves and their environment to make this determination.

The necessary information used by an agent to decide whether and when to initiate cloning comprises parameters that describe both local and remote resources. In particular, the necessary parameters are as follows:

- The CPU and memory loads, both internal to the agent (which result from planning, scheduling and task-execution activities of the agent) and external (on the agent host and possibly on remote hosts).
- The CPU performance[4], both locally and remotely.
- The load on the communication channels and their transfer rate, both locally and remotely.
- The current queue of tasks, the resources required for their execution and their deadlines.
- The future expected flow of tasks.

To acquire the above information an agent must be able to read the operating system variables. In addition, the agent must have self awareness on two levels—an agent internal level and a MAS level. The internal self awareness should allow the agent to

---

[4] We utilize standard methods (e.g., MIPS) to estimate it.

realize what part of the operating system retrieved values are its own properties (that is, agent internal parameters). The system-wise self awareness should allow the agent to find, possibly via middle agents [5], information regarding available resources on remote machines. Without middle agents, servers that are located on the remote hosts can supply such information upon request.[5] When such information is not available, an agent may compute the expected values of the attributes of remote machines relying on probability distributions either specifically by machine id (e.g., IP address) or groupwise, by machine type.

4   Optimizing When to Clone

Each agent A_i has a load tuple $l_i = \langle p_i, m_i, c_i \rangle$ (processing load p_i, memory load m_i and communication load c_i). This load results from the agent's tasks' makeup. In general, an agent's load is time dependent and is denoted by $l_i(t)$. The time t is measured in discrete units. The distance d_{ij} between agents A_i and A_j is the network latency based on the communication route between the machines on which the agents are running. To assess the time a remote clone should consume for performing its given tasks, the computational resources of the remote machine must be considered. These are the CPU performance (e.g., given in MIPS), the size of memory (MB) and the communication capabilities (transmission rate and number of ports).

An agent should decide on cloning at the optimal time. Each decision regarding cloning has a value, calculated with respect to loads and distances as a function of time. A_i has a valuation function $Val_i(l_i, \overline{L_i}, d, t)$, where $\overline{L_i}$ is a set of loads of agents $A_j, j \neq i$, and $d = \{d_{ij}\}, j \neq i$ a set of distances to other agents.[6] We describe the possible decisions of A_i by a decision tree $T_i = \langle V_i, E_i, t, R_i, r_i \rangle$, where V_i is a set of decision points (the nodes of the tree), $E_i \subseteq V_i \times V_i$ the tree edges, $\tau : V_i \to \mathbf{N}$ function that attaches time (in natural numbers) to nodes (equivalent to the level of the node in T), $R_i \in V_i$ the root of T_i, and r_i a discount rate which the agent uses in cases where it assumes that the value of a decision is discounted over time (otherwise $r_i = 0$).

Decision points have two types of valuation functions: (i) valuation of a decision which is made independently of other nodes in the tree, denoted by $V_I^i(v_j)$, where v_j is the evaluated node; (ii) valuation of a decision which is made dependent on other decisions in the tree denoted by $Value_i(v_j)$. In case (i), if no independent decision can be made at node v_j, the independent value assigned to it is $V_I^i(v_j) = 0$. Otherwise, node v_j is assigned an independent value $V_I^i(v_j) = Val_i(l_i, \overline{L_i}, d, \tau(v_j))$. In case (ii), the value of a node v_j is defined by the following recursive valuation function:

$$Value_i(v_j) = \begin{cases} Val_i(l_i, \overline{L_i}, d, \tau(v_j)) & \text{if } V_I^i(v_j) \neq 0 \\ \frac{1}{1+r_i} \sum_{k=1}^m p_k \cdot Value_i(v_k) & \text{otherwise} \end{cases}$$

where the sum is over all of the edges (v_j, v_k) emanating from v_j and p_k is the probability of (v_j, v_k) being chosen. Given this representation, we can use standard

---

[5] In our simulation we have examined both of these methods as well as matchmaking for acquiring information with regards to remote hosts and found no significant difference in performance.

[6] Although Val_i may depend on other agents' loads, such dependency is not required.

dynamic programing methods to compute the optimal decision with respect to a given decision tree. For the cloning mechanisms this implies a cloning timing which is optimal with respect to the available information with regards to future loads. Although this optimization is local to an agent and not global to the system, simulation results (Section 6) show a significant increase in the overall system performance.

5   The Cloning Algorithm

One may find two main approaches to load balancing [16]: (1) overloaded processors that seek other, idle (or just random other) processors to let them perform part of the processes; (2) idle (or lightly-loaded) processors that look for processes to increase their load. These approaches are sometimes merged or combined with additional heuristics. Both approaches, (1) and (2), may be utilized when designing a cloning algorithm for agents. However, in the case of cloning in open, dynamic systems, considerable difficulties arise. Both (1) and (2) require that an agent locate other agents for task delegation. When matchmaking agents are used, a cloning mechanism that follows approach (1) only requires that underloaded agents advertise their capabilities. Thus, overloaded agents may contact the underloaded ones via matchmaking. Similarly, approach (2) requires that overloaded agents advertise their overloads and required capabilities and resources. Though, in addition, (2) requires that underloaded *machines* will be known to the overloaded agents as well, so that they can serve as potential targets for overload transfer. This information is not given in an open, dynamic system. It could be provided if each machine in the system runs an agent whose sole task would be supplying such information. This would lead to an undesirable overhead of communication and computation. To avoid this overhead we utilize the first approach. That is, we provide a cloning mechanism to be used by agents who perceive or estimate self-overloads.

5.1   Overview of Cloning Procedure

The cloning procedure consists of the following components:

- Reasoning before cloning: includes the reasoning about the (possibly dynamic) task list with respect to time restrictions and capability and resource requirements. The consideration of the task list as well as agent capabilities, capacities, loads and machine loads results in a decision to clone or transfer tasks to already existing agents.
- Task splitting: includes reasoning that considers the time intervals in which overloads are expected and accordingly selects tasks to be transferred, which results in task splitting.
- Cloning: includes the creation and activation of the clone, the transfer of tasks, and the resulting inevitable updates of connections between agents via matchmaking. The following are the basic actions to be taken:
    - Create a copy of its code. This copy, however, may have to undergo some modification.

- When cloning while performing a specific task, an agent should pass to its clone only the relevant sub-tasks and information which are necessary for the tasks passed to the clone. Otherwise, the clone may face the same overload problem as its creator. Note that in contrast to the typical approach to agent migration [2], the cloning paradigm does not require the transfer of an agent state. The only transfer necessary is of the set of tasks to be performed by the clone.[7]
- Reasoning after cloning: collects information regarding the benefits of the cloning and environmental properties (such as task stream distribution), and statistically analyzes them, as a means of learning for future cloning.

While the reasoning of whether to initiate cloning is performed continually (i.e., when there are changes in the task schedule or if previous attempts to clone have failed), the cloning itself is a one-shot procedure.

5.2 The Cloning Protocol

Details of the protocol are given below. We denote arrays by [ ] and procedures by ( ).

- The type resources is a tuple $\langle p, m, c \rangle$ where p is the processing load, m is the memory load and c is the communication load.
- Arrays:
  task TaskList[], TaskSplit[], ProspectiveTasks[] tasks that have already arrived, tasks to send to others, candidate tasks for split, respectively.
  boolean OverloadAt[] indicates agent or machine being overloaded.
  boolean CanPassTasks[] indicates an agent's ability to pass tasks.
  resources RequiredAt[] quantifies the resources required by agent or task.
- Procedures:
  TransferTasks(agent) transfer the tasks in TaskSplit to agent.
  boolean CanCloneLocally() checks if the resources available on local host are sufficient for running a clone with the tasks in TaskSplit.
  boolean CanCloneRemotely() checks if the resources available on remote hosts are sufficient for running a clone with the tasks in TaskSplit.
  CloneLocally() create and activate a clone on local host.
  CloneRemotely() create and activate a clone on remote host.
  ReasonAfterCloning() collect information about time and resources used by clones on various machines, compute their averages, variances and predictors.
  GetCurrentTaskList() get the tasks in TaskList.
  GetExpectedTaskFlow() lookup given distribution or rely on predictors.
  resources CalculateRequiredResourcesAt(t) compute resources necessary for the tasks to be performed at time interval t by summing resources necessary for tasks at t with respect to resource types.
  resources GetSelfCapacity(agent) get the predefined maximal ability

---

[7] One may distinguish two components of an agent state: machine and operating system state vs. planning and task execution state. Agent cloning does not require the transfer of the first, however may require transfer of some parameters related to the latter. Nevertheless such parameters are passed as part of the transferred tasks, and not as a distinguished state.

of agent to utilize resources.

`agent[] LocateAgentsWithAppropriateCapabilities()` query a matchmaker for such agents.

`resources AcquireAgentLoads(agent)` query agent for its loads (an agent will look up its OS variables to find acquire this information).

- Main reasoning and cloning protocol:

```
for each time interval t:
   OverloadAt[t] = ReasonAboutOverloads(t) // current and future
   if (OverloadAt[t]) CanPassTasks[t] = FindUnderloadedAgents(t)
   if (CanPassTasks[t]) ReasonForTaskSplit(), TransferTasks()
   else if (CanCloneLocally()) CloneLocally(),
    ReasonForTaskSplit(), TransferTasks()
   else if (CanCloneRemotely()) CloneRemotely(),
    ReasonForTaskSplit(), TransferTasks()
   else Sorry(can't split or clone)
ReasonAfterCloning()
```

- The reasoning methods:

- `ReasonAboutOverloads(t)`
   `GetCurrentTaskList()`
   `GetExpectedTaskFlow(t)` // a distribution may either be given, or computed by
      // `ReasonAfterCloning()` after previous cloning incidents
   `RequiredAt[t] = CalculateRequiredResourcesAt(t)` // for current and
      // future tasks
   `SelfCapacity = GetSelfCapacity(t)` // find l_i, subtract from max capacity,
      // get machine $\langle p, m, c \rangle$, find the agent's part of it
   `if (SelfCapacity >= RequiredAt[t]) return FALSE`
      `else return TRUE`

- `FindUnderloadedAgents()`
   `LocateAgentsWithAppropriateCapabilities()` // contact a matchmaker
   `for each agent found:`
      `AgentLoads = AcquireAgentLoads()` // query the agent for this info.
      `If (AgentLoads at t > RequiredAt[t] - SelfCapacity -`
       `ResourcesForCloning) add agent to UnderloadedList`
   `return UnderloadedList`

- `ReasonForTaskSplit()`
   // Note: tasks are either one-shot or periodic (performed more than once). A periodic
   // task can be described as a set of one-shot tasks. Each one-shot task has a time interval
   // t in which it should be performed.
   `for each t where OverloadAt[t] = TRUE:`
      `for each Task in TaskList, if (TimeInterval(Task) = t)`
      `add Task to ProspectiveTasks`
   `Periods = periods of periodic tasks in ProspectiveTasks`

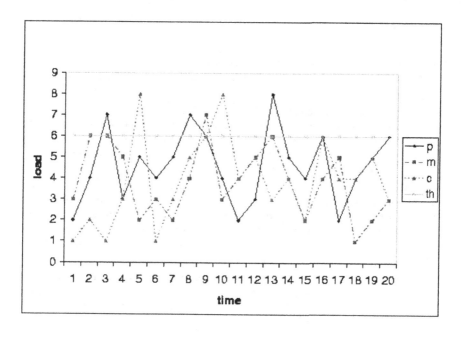

Fig. 1. CPU, memory and communication loads

```
if (Periods ≠ ∅), for each period p in Periods:
  if (OverloadAt[·] has a period p) move one corresponding
  Task at a time from TaskList to TaskSplit.
  for each t, Recompute OverloadAt[t] // some will become false
else
  for each t where (OverloadAt[t] = TRUE): // until none are true
  move one Task with TimeInterval = t to TaskSplit
  Recompute OverloadAt[t]
```

The above algorithms sketch the guidelines of the reasoning about cloning. We illustrate the task-split mechanism by the following example. Suppose the current and future tasks have been scheduled. At each point in time, the required resources are the sum of the resources required for all of the tasks that were scheduled to be executed at this point. Figure 1 brings an example of the sums of three resources: cpu(p); memory(m); communication(m), with respect to time. The maximal capacity of the agent is depicted by the threshold horizontal line (th) leveled at 6. One can observe overloads whenever any type of resource crosses this threshold. A periodic overload can be observed at times 3,8,13 with a period of 5 time units. Other overloads do not seem periodic. When attempting to prevent overloads, the agent first looks for tasks with a period that fits the period of the overloads and puts them in the `TaskSplit`. After recomputing the loads, it transfers one-shot tasks, if still necessary.

6 Simulation

To examine the properties of the cloning mechanism and its advantages, a simulation was performed. The simulation results show that (on average), the additional performance as a result of cloning (if any) outweighs the efforts put into cloning.

The method of simulation was as follows. Each agent was represented by an agent-thread that simulated the resource-consumption and the task-queue of a real agent. The simulated agent has a reasoning-for-cloning method which, according to the resource-consumption parameters and the task-queue, reasons about cloning. As a result of this reasoning, it may create a clone by activating another agent-thread (either locally or remotely). During the simulation, information is collected about the usage of CPU and the memory and communication consumption of the agents. Each agent-thread receives a stream of tasks according to a given distribution. For each task it creates a task-object that consumes time and memory and requires communication. Some of these task-objects are passed to the clone agent-thread. The simulation was performed with and without cloning, to allow comparison.

An agent-thread in the simulation must be subject to CPU, communication and memory consumption similar to those consumed by the agent it models in the MAS. Such information was collected from the real agent-system (RETSINA [6]) prior to the simulation as described below.

Agent type	Mem. size	CPU(1)	CPU(3)	Comm.(1)	Comm.(3)
Matchmaker	7.5 MB	43%	18-20%	94%	42%
Information	9.5-12 MB	45%	18-22%	94%	42%
Task	7 MB	44%	18-20%	94%	12%
Interface	9.6 MB	41%	18-20%	94%	15%

Fig. 2. Resource consumption

To properly simulate the RETSINA agents, we measured the resource consumption of the various types of its agents, when running 1 or 3 agents on each machine (in Figure 2, when relevant, referred to by parentheses). The platforms on which these agents were examined are Sun Ultra-1s with 64MB, running Solaris. The resource consumption is summarized in the Figure 2. As one can observe, when running alone all types of agents consume 40% to 45% of the CPU, whereas when running 3 agents on the same machine each consumes around 20% of the CPU. Not surprisingly, this results in a slower task performance. The same effect holds for usage of the available bandwidth.

We simulated the agent system with and without cloning, with the following settings:

- Number of agents: 10 to 20.
- Number of clones allowed: 10.
- Number of tasks dynamically arriving at the system: up to 1000.

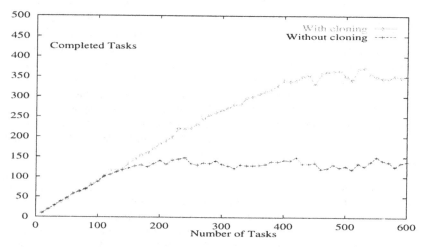

Fig. 3. Task execution with and without cloning

- Task distribution with respect to the required capabilities and resources for execution: normal distribution, where 10% of the tasks are beyond the ability of the
agents to perform them within their particular deadlines.
- Agent capacity: an agent can perform 20 average[8] tasks simultaneously.

The results of the simulation are depicted in Figure 3. The graph shows that for small
numbers of tasks (0 to 100) a system which practices cloning performs (almost) as well
as a system with no cloning (although difficult to see in the graph, the performance is
slightly lower due to the reasoning costs). However, when the number of tasks increases,
the cloning system performs much better. Nonetheless, beyond some threshold, (around
350 tasks) even the cloning cannot help. Note that in the range 150 to 350 tasks cloning
results in task performance which is close to the optimal (85% as compared to 90%
which, in our setting, is the optimal), where optimality refers to the case in which all
of the available resources are efficiently used for task performance (which does not
necessarily imply that all of the tasks are performed).

---

[8] An average task is one that the requires average resources (the center value of a normal
distribution).

7 Related Work

The idea of agent composition and decomposition was previously introduced in [9]. Although the ideas presented there by Ishida *et al* have some similarities to agent cloning and merging, there are several important differences. In [9], the issue of distributed problem solving was addressed. Our MAS is not a DPS system in the sense that it is not provided with a global goal which it must solve[9] nor is it designed for such a specific goal. Instead, we have an open system of autonomous agents, where each receives its own tasks, possibly from different sources, and they each try to satisfy its tasks, occasionally via cooperation. Our agents are heterogeneous, i.e., they have different capabilities and capacities, whereas the agent described in [9] seem to all be of a single type—rule firing agents. Therefore the only type of load discussed there is the rule firing load. This load may inaccurately represent the actual use of resources in the system. We measure operating systems' resource use directly and upon such loads carry out decisions for cloning and merging, thus balancing their use. Another limitation introduced in Ishida's work is the requirement to establish synchronization between agents. In contrast, our agents work asynchronously.

Methods for procedure cloning [3] and object cloning [12] were presented in the software engineering literature. The first serves as means for inter-procedural optimization, and the latter is used for eliminating parametric polymorphism and minimizing code duplication to overcome some typical inferior performance of object-oriented programs. Agent cloning is performed differently and has a different aim. Although it attempts to improve the system's performance (as other cloning paradigms do), it concentrates on balancing the work loads of agents, not on the other computational issues. In addition, it allows for agent mobility.

The issue of agent load balancing was previously studied in [14], where the authors concentrate on multi-agent reinforcement learning in the context of adaptive load balancing. The MAS dealt with in that research was dynamic in the sense that resources and tasks were given probabilistically, and the agents had to efficiently allocate resources to tasks in order to optimize the global resource usage, while ensuring fairness. The underlying load balancing of the cloning paradigm has some similarities, however is conceptually different. Cloning intends to optimize the resource usage of the whole system, and our simulation results show that to some extent this was achieved. However we do not address the issue of fairness. More significantly, we deal with a system in which, in addition to resource and task dynamics, agents may dynamically appear and disappear, thus increasing the complexity of the load balancing. Finally, while the agents in [14] attempt to adapt their resource selection to the behavior of other agents (using reinforcement learning), our agents attempt to either delegate tasks to other existing agents or create other agents that will perform the overloading tasks.

In [11] different approaches to agent mobility are discussed, concentrating on messengers, which are mobile threads of execution who coordinate without central control. The salient features of messengers are their mobility, the creation of new messengers at run-time and collaboration and dynamic formation of sets of messengers for this collaboration. These properties seem quite similar to our requirements for MAS with cloning.

---

[9] Yet, one may view the goal of increasing overall system performance as such a goal.

However there is a major difference—messengers rely on a shared memory for their functioning. This implies a strong restriction on their autonomy, which is unacceptable in MAS. Nevertheless, the π-calculi presented for messengers may be used to describe cloning MAS as well.

Mobile agents are an approach to remote computing which, in contrast to remote procedure calls, allows for sending the procedures to be performed on the remote host [19]. The procedure as well as its state are transported, and processing on the remote host is performed under previously-given authentication constraints. Cloning supports remote computing as well (however does not require it), but does not require the transmission of a procedure (or agent) state. This property significantly simplifies the performance of remote computing (especially due to the complexity encapsulated in state transmission).

In this volume, several issues with relevancy to agent cloning are addressed. Cloning is aimed at increasing agent and system performance. In the context of MAS, achieving this requires coordination and cooperation among the agents, both the pre-existing and the newly-cloned. For small groups of agents, using formations for real-time synchronization and agreements among the agents, as suggested in [17], may be applicable. However, the major limitation of that approach is the implicit assumption of a close environment. Significant modifications of that model are necessary to adjust it to an open environment (to which the cloning approach refers). Coordination in large-scale agent systems is addressed in [15]. There, the major role of coordination is to allow for effective, low complexity task-agent allocation. Combining agent cloning and the physics-based model may further improve efficiency in large-scale agent systems. This combination awaits advances on the physics-based approach research, where it is necessary to show applicability to non-physical domains. Regardless of the size of the systems and the specific mechanism, cloning can benefit from coordination. When developing coordination for systems where cloning is implemented, it may also be beneficial to consider the concepts that affect coordination. These concepts are described and experimented with in [13].

8 Conclusion

Agent cloning is the action of creating and activating a clone agent (locally or remotely) to perform some or all of an agent's tasks. Cloning is performed when an agent perceives or predicts an overload, thus increasing the ability of a MAS to perform tasks. We presented agent cloning as a means for balancing the loads and improving the task performance of a MAS running on several remote machines. We provided explicit methods of implementation and tested these methods by simulation. We found that for large numbers of tasks, cloning significantly increases the portion of tasks performed by a MAS. In a MAS where tasks require information gathering on the web (e.g., RETSINA), the additional reasoning needed for cloning is small compared to task execution requirements. Currently we are in the process of embedding the cloning protocol into each autonomous agent in the RETSINA MAS. In future work we intend to use the cloning mechanisms to achieve agent mobility. In addition, we are developing protocols for agent merging or self-extinction. These should increase the efficiency of garbage-collection and monitoring of the cloning activity.

References

1. D. Chess, B. Grosof, C. Harrison, D. Levine, C. Parris, and G. Tsudik. Itinerant agents for mobile computing. In *[8]*, pages 267–282. 1997. (Reprinted from *IEEE Personal Communications, 1995*).

2. R. Clark, C. Grossner, and T. Radhakrishnan. CONSENSUS and COMPROMISE: Planning in cooperating expert systems. *Int. Journal of Intelligent and Cooperative Information Systems (submitted)*.

3. K. Cooper, M. Hall, and K. Kennedy. Procedure cloning. In *Proceedings of the International Conference on Computer Languages*, pages 96–105. IEEE Computer Society, April 1992.

4. K. Decker, K. Sycara, and M. Williamson. Intelligent adaptive information agents. In *Proceedings of the AAAI-96 workshop on Intelligent Adaptive Agents*, Portland, Oregon, 1996.

5. K. Decker, K. Sycara, and M. Williamson. Middle-agents for the internet. In *Proceeding of IJCAI-97*, pages 578–583, Nagoya, Japan, 1997.

6. K. Decker, A. Pannu, K. Sycara, and M. Williamson. Designing behaviors for information agents. In W. Lewis Johnson, editor, *Proceedings of the First International Conference on Autonomous Agents*, New York, 1997. ACM Press.

7. R. Gray, D. Kotz, G. Cybenko, and D. Rus. D'agents: Security in a multiple-language, mobile-agent system. In Giovanni Vigna, editor, *Mobile Agent Security*, Lecture Notes in Computer Science. Springer-Verlag, 1998.

8. M. Huhns and M. Singh, editors. *Readings in Agents*. Morgan Kaufmann, San Francisco, 1998.

9. T. Ishida, M. Yokoo, and L. Gasser. An organizational approach to adaptive production systems. In *Proceedings of the National Conference on Artificial Intelligence*, pages 52–58, July 1990.

10. M. Livny and M. Melman. Load balancing in homogeneous broadcast distributed systems. In *Proceedings of the ACM Computer Network Performance Symposium*, April 1982.

11. G. Di Marzo, M. Muhugusa, and C. Tschudin. Survey of theories for mobile agents. Working paper, The Computing Science Center, University of Geneva, Switzerland, November 1995.

12. J. Plevyak and A. Chien. Type directed cloning for object-oriented programs. In *Proceedings of the Workshop for Languages and Compilers for Parallel Computers*, pages 37–51, Columbus, Ohio, August 1995.

13. S. Rustogi and M. Singh. The bases of effective coordination in decentralized multiagent systems. In this volume.

14. A. Schaerf, Y. Shoham, and M. Tennenholtz. Adaptive load balancing: a study in multi-agent learning. *Journal of Artificial Intelligence Research*, 2:475–500, 1995.

15. O. Shehory, S. Kraus, and O. Yadgar. Goal satisfaction in large-scale agent systems: a transportation example. In this volume.

16. B. A. Shirazi, A. R. Hurson, and K. M. Kavi, editors. *Scheduling and Load Balancing in Parallel and Distributed Systems*. IEEE Computer Society Press, New York, 1995.

17. P. Stone and M. Veloso. Task decomposition and dynamic role assignment for real-time strategic teamwork. In this volume.

18. K. Sycara, K. Decker, A. Pannu, M. Williamson, and D. Zeng. Distributed intelligent agents. *IEEE Expert*, pages 36–45, December 1996.

19. J. White. Mobile agents. In J. Bradshaw, editor, *Software agents*, chapter 19, pages 437–472. AAAI Press and the MIT Press, 1996.

An Index to Volumes 1–5 of the *Intelligent Agents* Series

Michael Wooldridge* and Jörg P. Müller[†]

* Department of Electronic Engineering, Queen Mary & Westfield College
London E1 4NS, United Kingdom
M.J.Wooldridge@elec.qmw.ac.uk

[†] John Wiley & Sons Ltd., International House
London W5 5DB, United Kingdom
jpm@wis-dev.wiley.co.uk

Abstract. We present a subject classified index to all articles that have appeared in the first five volumes of the *Intelligent Agents* series. Papers are classified using the classification scheme for agent-related research activities developed by the AGENTLINK project (see http://www.AgentLink.org/). These research activities are summarised in Table 1.

1.1: Agent Control Architectures

ATAL-94: [34, 49, 69, 73]. ATAL-95: [46, 12, 37]. ATAL-96: [41]. ATAL-97: [98, 16, 119]. ATAL-98: [40, 80].

1.1.1: Deliberative/Cognitive Control Architectures

ATAL-94: [1, 34, 69]. ATAL-96: [13]. ATAL-97: [28]. ATAL-98: [128].

1.1.2: Reactive/Behavioural Control Architectures

ATAL-95: [46, 42]. ATAL-97: [98, 24].

1.1.3: Hybrid Architectures

ATAL-94: [36, 81]. ATAL-95: [12]. ATAL-96: [83, 78, 26]. ATAL-98: [54].

1.1.4: Layered Architectures

ATAL-94: [36, 81]. ATAL-95: [12]. ATAL-96: [83, 78, 26]. ATAL-98: [54].

1.2: Foundations of Agency

ATAL-94: [18]. ATAL-96: [19].

1.2.1: Practical Reasoning/Planning & Acting

ATAL-94: [7, 29, 1, 85]. ATAL-95: [118, 112, 86, 2]. ATAL-97: [48]. ATAL-98: [50, 90, 128].

1.2.2: Rational Action & Agency

ATAL-94: [18, 29, 49, 85]. ATAL-95: [86, 2]. ATAL-96: [75, 114, 15, 13]. ATAL-97: [28, 60, 31]. ATAL-98: [54, 128].

1.2.3: Decision Making, Decision Theory & Agency

ATAL-94: [85]. ATAL-95: [86]. ATAL-96: [129]. ATAL-98: [93].

1.2.4: Agent Representation & Specification Formalisms

ATAL-94: [7]. ATAL-95: [118, 94, 105, 115, 127, 43, 120, 65]. ATAL-96: [58, 39, 67, 75, 30, 8, 96, 13, 99, 26, 4, 126, 66]. ATAL-98: [20, 40, 47, 54, 74, 97, 117].

1.2.5: Semantics of Agency & Logics of Agency

ATAL-94: [7, 22, 29, 32, 109, 38, 113, 123]. ATAL-95: [62, 118, 94, 105, 115, 127, 65]. ATAL-96: [41, 125, 121, 67, 75, 30, 8, 96, 27, 26, 126, 66]. ATAL-97: [48, 60, 31]. ATAL-98: [23, 40, 47, 74, 97].

1.2.6: Computational/Complexity Issues of Agency

ATAL-95: [94]. ATAL-96: [126]. ATAL-98: [97].

1.2.7: Adaptation, Learning, & Agency

ATAL-95: [46]. ATAL-96: [129].

2.1: Cooperation

ATAL-94: [18, 44]. ATAL-97: [100]. ATAL-98: [57, 87].

2.1.1: Cooperation Protocols

ATAL-94: [44]. ATAL-95: [5, 79].

2.1.2: Models and Formalisms for Cooperation

ATAL-95: [11, 79]. ATAL-96: [14, 15, 61, 78]. ATAL-98: [50, 101, 111].

Research Areas

RA1: Micro/agent-level issues in agent technology

   1.1: Agent control architectures

      1.1.1: deliberative/cognitive agent control architectures & planning

      1.1.2: reactive/behavioural agent control architectures

      1.1.3: hybrid agent control architectures

      1.1.4: layered agent control architectures

   1.2: Foundations of agency

      1.2.1: practical reasoning/planning and acting

      1.2.2: rational action & agency

      1.2.3: decision making, decision theory, & agency

      1.2.4: agent representation & specification formalisms

      1.2.5: semantics of agency & logics of agency

      1.2.6: computational/complexity issues of agency

      1.2.7: adaptation, learning, & agency

RA2: Macro/society level issues in agent technology

   2.1: cooperation

      2.1.1: cooperation protocols

      2.1.2: models and formalisms for cooperation

      2.1.3: game/economic theoretic models of cooperation

      2.1.4: conflict detection & resolution in multi-agent systems

      2.1.5: coalitions & coalition formation

      2.1.6: planning by/for multiple agents

   2.2: coordination

      2.2.1: coordination techniques and protocols

      2.2.2: coordination languages & systems

   2.3: computational market systems

      2.3.1: market-based control

      2.3.3: market-oriented programming

   2.4: communication

      2.4.1: agent communication languages

      2.4.2: speech acts

   2.5: negotiation, bidding, and argumentation

   2.6: foundations of multi-agent systems

      2.6.1: emergence of cooperation and social action

      2.6.2: sociology, ethology, and their relationship to multi-agent systems

      2.6.3: emergent functionality and swarm behaviour in multi-agent systems

      2.6.4: semantics of multi-agent systems & logics of multi-agent systems

      2.6.5: computational/complexity issues of multi-agent systems

      2.6.6: multi-agent and cooperative learning

RA3: Agent system implementation issues

   3.1: environments & testbeds for agent system development

   3.2: programming languages, tools, & libraries for agent system development

   3.3: relationship of agents to objects and other paradigms (e.g., logic programming)

   3.4: standardised scenarios for evaluating agent systems

   3.5: benchmarks for agent systems

   3.5: evaluating agent systems

RA4: Best-practice in agent system development

   4.1: standards for (multi-) agent systems

      4.1.1: agent communication standards

      4.1.2: agent management standards

      4.1.3: agent interaction standards

      4.1.4: libraries, tools, testbeds for implementing agent standards

      4.1.5: relationship of agent standards to other standards (e.g., CORBA MAF)

   4.2: agent-based software engineering

      4.2.1: analysis & design techniques for agent systems

      4.2.2: specification techniques for agent systems

      4.2.3: verification techniques for agent systems

      4.2.4: relationship of agent-based software engineering to other disciplines (e.g., OO)

   4.3: pragmatics of agent-based software development

   4.4: experience with agent development projects

   4.5: commercialising agent technology

Table 1. Research areas.

2.1.3: Game/Economic Theoretic Models for Cooperation

ATAL-95: [11].

2.1.4: Conflict Detection & Resolution for Agent Systems

ATAL-95: [21]. ATAL-98: [33].

2.1.5: Coalitions & Coalition Formation

ATAL-97: [103]. ATAL-98: [111].

2.1.6: Planning by/for Multiple Agents

ATAL-95: [21]. ATAL-96: [78]. ATAL-97: [64]. ATAL-98: [50].

2.2: Coordination

ATAL-94: [44]. ATAL-95: [11]. ATAL-96: [4]. ATAL-97: [106, 24, 64, 103]. ATAL-98: [95, 111].

2.2.1: Coordination Techniques & Protocols

ATAL-97: [106, 24, 64, 103].

2.3.1: Market-Based Control

ATAL-95: [77].

2.3.2: Market-Oriented Programming

ATAL-95: [77]. ATAL-97: [100].

2.4: Communication

ATAL-96: [89, 114, 83, 15, 27, 84, 4]. ATAL-97: [119, 104, 63].

2.4.1: Agent Communication Languages

ATAL-95: [71]. ATAL-97: [63]. ATAL-98: [20, 117].

2.4.2: Speech Acts

ATAL-98: [20].

2.5: Negotiation, Bidding, and Argumentation

ATAL-96: [83, 129, 78, 84]. ATAL-97: [100, 104].

2.6.1: Emergence of Cooperation and Social Action

ATAL-95: [112]. ATAL-96: [19, 61]. ATAL-98: [6, 23, 87, 101].

2.6.2: Sociology, Ethology, and Their Relationship to Agents

ATAL-94: [110, 122]. ATAL-96: [19]. ATAL-98: [6, 23, 87].

2.6.3: Emergent Functionality and Swarm Behaviour

ATAL-94: [122].

2.6.4: Semantics & Logics of Multi-Agent Systems

ATAL-94: [22, 32, 110, 124]. ATAL-95: [43, 120, 10]. ATAL-96: [39, 67, 30, 8, 96, 14, 27, 61]. ATAL-97: [3, 106, 104, 55]. ATAL-98: [6, 9, 35, 102, 117].

2.6.6: Multi-Agent and Cooperative Learning

ATAL-96: [61].

3.1: Environments and Testbeds for Agent System Development

ATAL-94: [124, 36, 81]. ATAL-95: [37, 5, 53, 42, 70, 79, 108]. ATAL-96: [14, 92]. ATAL-97: [82, 116]. ATAL-98: [51].

3.2: Programming Languages & Tools for Agent Development

ATAL-94: [17, 38, 72, 91, 113, 123]. ATAL-95: [10, 65]. ATAL-96: [68, 92, 66]. ATAL-97: [3, 64, 76, 48, 55, 25]. ATAL-98: [57, 47, 51, 90, 93, 102, 107].

3.3: Relationship of Agents to Other Paradigms (e.g., OO)

ATAL-94: [17, 72, 91]. ATAL-95: [53]. ATAL-96: [41, 58, 89, 125, 99]. ATAL-97: [3, 76, 25]. ATAL-98: [33, 107].

3.5: Benchmarks for Agent Systems

ATAL-94: [36]. ATAL-95: [71]. ATAL-97: [76]. ATAL-98: [33, 95].

4.1.1: Agent Communication Standards

ATAL-95: [71]. ATAL-96: [89]. ATAL-97: [63].

4.2: Agent-based Software Engineering

ATAL-94: [17, 38, 91, 113, 123]. ATAL-96: [68, 121]. ATAL-97: [59, 98, 16, 88, 56, 82, 116, 52, 45]. ATAL-98: [51, 80].

4.2.1: Analysis & Design Techniques for Agent Systems

ATAL-96: [58]. ATAL-97: [59, 88, 52, 45].

4.2.2: Specification Techniques for Agent Systems

ATAL-94: [32, 124]. ATAL-96: [39]. ATAL-98: [9, 35].

4.2.3: Verification Techniques for Agent Systems

ATAL-98: [9, 35].

4.2.4: Relationship of Agents to Software Engineering

ATAL-94: [73]. ATAL-96: [125, 92]. ATAL-97: [16, 52, 45].

4.3: Pragmatics of Agent-based Development

ATAL-95: [62]. ATAL-96: [68, 121]. ATAL-97: [59, 56].

4.4: Experience with Agent Development Projects

ATAL-94: [122]. ATAL-96: [84]. ATAL-97: [88, 82, 116, 25]. ATAL-98: [80].

4.5: Commercialising Agent Technology

ATAL-98: [57, 93].

References

1. J. S. Aitken, F. Schmalhofer, and N. Shadbolt. A knowledge-level characterisation of multi-agent systems. In M. J. Wooldridge and N. R. Jennings, eds., *Intelligent Agents: Theories, Architectures, and Languages (LNAI Volume 890)*, pages 179–190. Springer-Verlag: Berlin, Germany, 1995.

2. J.-F. Arcand and S.-J. Pelletier. Cognition based multi-agent architecture. In M. J. Wooldridge, J. P. Müller, and M. Tambe, eds., *Intelligent Agents II (LNAI Volume 1037)*, pages 267–282. Springer-Verlag: Berlin, Germany, 1996.

3. A. K. Bansal, K. Ramohanarao, and A. Rao. Distributed storage of replicated beliefs to facilitate recovery of distributed intelligent agents. In M. P. Singh, A. Rao, and M. J. Wooldridge, eds., *Intelligent Agents IV (LNAI Volume 1365)*, pages 77–92. Springer-Verlag: Berlin, Germany, 1998.

4. M. Barbuceanu and M. Fox. The design of a coordination language for multi-agent systems. In J. P. Müller, M. J. Wooldridge, and N. R. Jennings, eds., *Intelligent Agents III (LNAI Volume 1193)*, pages 341–356. Springer-Verlag: Berlin, Germany, 1997.

5. M. Barbuceanu and M. S. Fox. The architecture of an agent building shell. In M. J. Wooldridge, J. P. Müller, and M. Tambe, eds., *Intelligent Agents II (LNAI Volume 1037)*, pages 235–251. Springer-Verlag: Berlin, Germany, 1996.

6. A. L. C. Bazzan, R. H. Bordini, and J. A. Campbell. Moral sentiments in multi-agent systems. In J. P. Müller, M. P. Singh, and A. S. Rao, eds., *Intelligent Agents V*, pages 113–131. Springer-Verlag: Berlin, Germany, 1999. In this volume.

7. J. Bell. Changing attitudes. In M. J. Wooldridge and N. R. Jennings, eds., *Intelligent Agents: Theories, Architectures, and Languages (LNAI Volume 890)*, pages 40–55. Springer-Verlag: Berlin, Germany, 1995.

8. M. Benerecetti, A. Cimmatti, E. Giunchiglia, F. Giunchiglia, and L. Serafini. Formal specification of beliefs in multi-agent systems. In J. P. Müller, M. J. Wooldridge, and N. R. Jennings, eds., *Intelligent Agents III (LNAI Volume 1193)*, pages 117–130. Springer-Verlag: Berlin, Germany, 1997.

9. M. Benerecetti, F. Giunchiglia, and L. Serafini. A model checking algorithm for multiagent systems. In J. P. Müller, M. P. Singh, and A. S. Rao, eds., *Intelligent Agents V*, pages 163–176. Springer-Verlag: Berlin, Germany, 1999. In this volume.

10. C. Beyssade, P. Enjalbert, and C. Lefèvre. Cooperating logical agents: Model, applications. In M. J. Wooldridge, J. P. Müller, and M. Tambe, eds., *Intelligent Agents II (LNAI Volume 1037)*, pages 299–314. Springer-Verlag: Berlin, Germany, 1996.

11. C. Bicchieri, E. Ephrati, and A. Antonelli. Games servers play: A procedural approach. In M. J. Wooldridge, J. P. Müller, and M. Tambe, eds., *Intelligent Agents II (LNAI Volume 1037)*, pages 127–142. Springer-Verlag: Berlin, Germany, 1996.

12. R. P. Bonasso, D. Kortenkamp, D. P. Miller, and M. Slack. Experiences with an architecture for intelligent, reactive agents. In M. J. Wooldridge, J. P. Müller, and M. Tambe, eds., *Intelligent Agents II (LNAI Volume 1037)*, pages 187–202. Springer-Verlag: Berlin, Germany, 1996.

13. L. M. Botelho and H. Coelho. Emotion-based attention shift in autonomous agents. In J. P. Müller, M. J. Wooldridge, and N. R. Jennings, eds., *Intelligent Agents III (LNAI Volume 1193)*, pages 277–292. Springer-Verlag: Berlin, Germany, 1997.

14. F. Brazier, C. Jonker, and J. Treur. Formalisation of a cooperation model based on joint intentions. In J. P. Müller, M. J. Wooldridge, and N. R. Jennings, eds., *Intelligent Agents III (LNAI Volume 1193)*, pages 141–156. Springer-Verlag: Berlin, Germany, 1997.

15. P. Bretier and D. Sadek. A rational agent as the kernel of a cooperative spoken dialogue system: Implementing a logical theory of interaction. In J. P. Müller, M. J. Wooldridge,

and N. R. Jennings, eds., *Intelligent Agents III (LNAI Volume 1193)*, pages 189–204. Springer-Verlag: Berlin, Germany, 1997.

16. J. Bryson and B. McGonigle. Agent architecture as object oriented design. In M. P. Singh, A. S. Rao, and M. J. Wooldridge, eds., *Intelligent Agents IV (LNAI Volume 1365)*, pages 15–30. Springer-Verlag: Berlin, Germany, 1998.

17. H.-D. Burkhard. Agent-oriented programming for open systems. In M. J. Wooldridge and N. R. Jennings, eds., *Intelligent Agents: Theories, Architectures, and Languages (LNAI Volume 890)*, pages 291–306. Springer-Verlag: Berlin, Germany, 1995.

18. C. Castelfranchi. Guarantees for autonomy in cognitive agent architecture. In M. J. Wooldridge and N. R. Jennings, eds., *Intelligent Agents: Theories, Architectures, and Languages (LNAI Volume 890)*, pages 56–70. Springer-Verlag: Berlin, Germany, 1995.

19. C. Castelfranchi. To be or not to be an agent. In J. P. Müller, M. J. Wooldridge, and N. R. Jennings, eds., *Intelligent Agents III (LNAI Volume 1193)*, pages 37–40. Springer-Verlag: Berlin, Germany, 1997.

20. B. Chaib-draa and D. Vanderveken. Agent communication language: Toward semantics based on success and satisfaction. In J. P. Müller, M. P. Singh, and A. S. Rao, eds., *Intelligent Agents V*, pages 363–379. Springer-Verlag: Berlin, Germany, 1999. In this volume.

21. J. Chu-Carroll and S. Carberry. Conflict Detection and Resolution in Collaborative Planning. In M. J. Wooldridge, J. P. Müller, and M. Tambe, eds., *Intelligent Agents II (LNAI Volume 1037)*, pages 111–126. Springer-Verlag: Berlin, Germany, 1996.

22. A. Cimatti and L. Serafini. Multi-agent reasoning with belief contexts: the approach and a case study. In M. J. Wooldridge and N. R. Jennings, eds., *Intelligent Agents: Theories, Architectures, and Languages (LNAI Volume 890)*, pages 71–85. Springer-Verlag: Berlin, Germany, 1995.

23. R. Conte, C. Castelfranchi, and F. Dignum. Autonomous norm-acceptance. In J. P. Müller, M. P. Singh, and A. S. Rao, eds., *Intelligent Agents V*, pages 99–112. Springer-Verlag: Berlin, Germany, 1999. In this volume.

24. S. Coradeschi and L. Karlsson. A behavior-based approach to reactivity and coordination: A preliminary report. In M. P. Singh, A. S. Rao, and M. J. Wooldridge, eds., *Intelligent Agents IV (LNAI Volume 1365)*, pages 107–112. Springer-Verlag: Berlin, Germany, 1998.

25. R. S. Cost, I. Soboroff, J. Lakhani, T. Finin, E. Miller, and C. Nicholas. TKQML: A scripting tool for building agents. In M. P. Singh, A. S. Rao, and M. J. Wooldridge, eds., *Intelligent Agents IV (LNAI Volume 1365)*, pages 336–340. Springer-Verlag: Berlin, Germany, 1998.

26. D. David. Reactive and motivational agents: Towards a collective minder. In J. P. Müller, M. J. Wooldridge, and N. R. Jennings, eds., *Intelligent Agents III (LNAI Volume 1193)*, pages 309–324. Springer-Verlag: Berlin, Germany, 1997.

27. F. Dignum and B. van Linder. Modelling social agents: Communication as action. In J. P. Müller, M. J. Wooldridge, and N. R. Jennings, eds., *Intelligent Agents III (LNAI Volume 1193)*, pages 205–218. Springer-Verlag: Berlin, Germany, 1997.

28. F. Dignum and R. Conte. Intentional agents and goal formation. In M. P. Singh, A. S. Rao, and M. J. Wooldridge, eds., *Intelligent Agents IV (LNAI Volume 1365)*, pages 231–244. Springer-Verlag: Berlin, Germany, 1998.

29. P. Dongha. Toward a formal model of commitment for resource-bounded agents. In M. J. Wooldridge and N. R. Jennings, eds., *Intelligent Agents: Theories, Architectures, and Languages (LNAI Volume 890)*, pages 86–101. Springer-Verlag: Berlin, Germany, 1995.

30. A. F. Dragoni and P. Giorgini. Belief revision through the belief-function formalism in a multi-agent environment. In J. P. Müller, M. J. Wooldridge, and N. R. Jennings, eds., *Intelligent Agents III (LNAI Volume 1193)*, pages 103–116. Springer-Verlag: Berlin, Germany, 1997.

31. H. Duc. Approximate reasoning about combined knowledge. In M. P. Singh, A. S. Rao, and M. J. Wooldridge, eds., *Intelligent Agents IV (LNAI Volume 1365)*, pages 275–280. Springer-Verlag: Berlin, Germany, 1998.

32. B. Dunin-Keplicz and J. Treur. Compositional formal specification of multi-agent systems. In M. J. Wooldridge and N. R. Jennings, eds., *Intelligent Agents: Theories, Architectures, and Languages (LNAI Volume 890)*, pages 102–117. Springer-Verlag: Berlin, Germany, 1995.

33. A. Dury, F. Le Ber, and V. Chevrier. A reactive approach for solving constraint satisfaction: Assigning land use to farming territories. In J. P. Müller, M. P. Singh, and A. S. Rao, eds., *Intelligent Agents V*, pages 397–411. Springer-Verlag: Berlin, Germany, 1999. In this volume.

34. B. Ekdahl, E. Astor, and P. Davidsson. Towards anticipatory agents. In M. J. Wooldridge and N. R. Jennings, eds., *Intelligent Agents: Theories, Architectures, and Languages (LNAI Volume 890)*, pages 191–202. Springer-Verlag: Berlin, Germany, 1995.

35. J. Engelfriet, C. M. Jonker, and J. Treur. Compositional verification of multi-agent systems in temporal multi-epistemic logic. In J. P. Müller, M. P. Singh, and A. S. Rao, eds., *Intelligent Agents*, pages 177–193. Springer-Verlag: Berlin, Germany, 1999. In this volume.

36. I. A. Ferguson. Integrated control and coordinated behaviour: A case for agent models. In M. J. Wooldridge and N. R. Jennings, eds., *Intelligent Agents: Theories, Architectures, and Languages (LNAI Volume 890)*, pages 203–218. Springer-Verlag: Berlin, Germany, 1995.

37. K. Fischer, J. P. Müller, and M. Pischel. A pragmatic BDI architecture. In M. J. Wooldridge, J. P. Müller, and M. Tambe, eds., *Intelligent Agents II (LNAI Volume 1037)*, pages 203–218. Springer-Verlag: Berlin, Germany, 1996.

38. M. Fisher. Representing and executing agent-based systems. In M. J. Wooldridge and N. R. Jennings, eds., *Intelligent Agents: Theories, Architectures, and Languages (LNAI Volume 890)*, pages 307–323. Springer-Verlag: Berlin, Germany, 1995.

39. M. Fisher. If Z is the answer, what could the question possibly be? In J. P. Müller, M. J. Wooldridge, and N. R. Jennings, eds., *Intelligent Agents III (LNAI Volume 1193)*, pages 65–66. Springer-Verlag: Berlin, Germany, 1997.

40. M. Fisher. Representing abstract agent architectures. In J. P. Müller, M. P. Singh, and A. S. Rao, eds., *Intelligent Agents V*, pages 227–241. Springer-Verlag: Berlin, Germany, 1999. In this volume.

41. S. Franklin and A. Graesser. Is it an agent, or just a program? In J. P. Müller, M. J. Wooldridge, and N. R. Jennings, eds., *Intelligent Agents III (LNAI Volume 1193)*, pages 21–36. Springer-Verlag: Berlin, Germany, 1997.

42. S. Giroux. Open reflective agents. In M. J. Wooldridge, J. P. Müller, and M. Tambe, eds., *Intelligent Agents II (LNAI Volume 1037)*, pages 315–330. Springer-Verlag: Berlin, Germany, 1996.

43. P. J. Gmytrasiewicz. On Reasoning About Other Agents. In M. J. Wooldridge, J. P. Müller, and M. Tambe, eds., *Intelligent Agents II (LNAI Volume 1037)*, pages 143–155. Springer-Verlag: Berlin, Germany, 1996.

44. F. Guichard and J. Ayel. Logical reorganization of DAI systems. In M. J. Wooldridge and N. R. Jennings, eds., *Intelligent Agents: Theories, Architectures, and Languages (LNAI Volume 890)*, pages 118–128. Springer-Verlag: Berlin, Germany, 1995.

45. R. E. Gustavsson. Multi-agent systems as open societies — a design framework. In M. P. Singh, A. S. Rao, and M. J. Wooldridge, eds., *Intelligent Agents IV (LNAI Volume 1365)*, pages 327–336. Springer-Verlag: Berlin, Germany, 1998.

46. H. H. Hexmoor. Learning from routines. In M. J. Wooldridge, J. P. Müller, and M. Tambe, eds., *Intelligent Agents II (LNAI Volume 1037)*, pages 97–110. Springer-Verlag: Berlin, Germany, 1996.

47. K. V. Hindriks, F. S. de Boer, W. van der Hoek, and J.-J. Ch. Meyer. Control structures of rule-based agent languages. In J. P. Müller, M. P. Singh, and A. S. Rao, eds., *Intelligent Agents V*, pages 381–396. Springer-Verlag: Berlin, Germany, 1999. In this volume.

48. K. V. Hindriks, F. S. de Boer, W. van der Hoek and John-Jules Ch. Meyer. Formal semantics for an abstract agent programming language. In M. P. Singh, A. S. Rao, and M. J. Wooldridge, eds., *Intelligent Agents IV (LNAI Volume 1365)*, pages 215–230. Springer-Verlag: Berlin, Germany, 1998.

49. J. Huang, N. R. Jennings, and J. Fox. An agent architecture for distributed medical care. In M. J. Wooldridge and N. R. Jennings, eds., *Intelligent Agents: Theories, Architectures, and Languages (LNAI Volume 890)*, pages 219–232. Springer-Verlag: Berlin, Germany, 1995.

50. L. Hunsberger. Making SharedPlans more concise and easier to reason about. In J. P. Müller, M. P. Singh, and A. S. Rao, eds., *Intelligent Agents V*, pages 81–98. Springer-Verlag: Berlin, Germany, 1999. In this volume.

51. C. A. Iglesias, M. Garijo, and J. C. Gonzalez. A survey of agent-oriented methodologies. In J. P. Müller, M. P. Singh, and A. S. Rao, eds., *Intelligent Agents V*, pages 317–330. Springer-Verlag: Berlin, Germany, 1999. In this volume.

52. C. Iglesias, M. Garijo, J. C. González, and J. R. Velasco. Analysis and design of multiagent systems using MAS-CommonKADS. In M. P. Singh, A. S. Rao, and M. J. Wooldridge, eds., *Intelligent Agents IV (LNAI Volume 1365)*, pages 313–326. Springer-Verlag: Berlin, Germany, 1998.

53. C. A. Iglesias, J. C. González, and J. R. Velasco. MIX: A general purpose multiagent architecture. In M. J. Wooldridge, J. P. Müller, and M. Tambe, eds., *Intelligent Agents II (LNAI Volume 1037)*, pages 251–266. Springer-Verlag: Berlin, Germany, 1996.

54. C. G. Jung. Emergent mental attitudes in layered agents. In J. P. Müller, M. P. Singh, and A. S. Rao, eds., *Intelligent Agents*, pages 195–209. Springer-Verlag: Berlin, Germany, 1999. In this volume.

55. C. G. Jung and K. Fischer. A layered agent calculus with concurrent, continuous processes. In M. P. Singh, A. S. Rao, and M. J. Wooldridge, eds., *Intelligent Agents IV (LNAI Volume 1365)*, pages 245–258. Springer-Verlag: Berlin, Germany, 1998.

56. G. A. Kaminka and M. Tambe. Social comparison for failure detection and recovery. In M. P. Singh, A. S. Rao, and M. J. Wooldridge, eds., *Intelligent Agents IV (LNAI Volume 1365)*, pages 127–142. Springer-Verlag: Berlin, Germany, 1998.

57. D. Kinny. The AGENTIS agent interaction model. In J. P. Müller, M. P. Singh, and A. S. Rao, eds., *Intelligent Agents V*, pages 331–344. Springer-Verlag: Berlin, Germany, 1999. In this volume.

58. D. Kinny and M. Georgeff. Modelling and design of multi-agent systems. In J. P. Müller, M. J. Wooldridge, and N. R. Jennings, eds., *Intelligent Agents III (LNAI Volume 1193)*, pages 1–20. Springer-Verlag: Berlin, Germany, 1997.

59. D. Kinny, J. Treur, L. Gasser, S. Clark, and J. P. Müller. Panel: Methodologies for multi-agent systems. In M. P. Singh, A. S. Rao, and M. J. Wooldridge, eds., *Intelligent Agents IV (LNAI Volume 1365)*, pages 1–2. Springer-Verlag: Berlin, Germany, 1998.

60. F. Koriche. Approximate reasoning about combined knowledge. In M. P. Singh, A. S. Rao, and M. J. Wooldridge, eds., *Intelligent Agents IV (LNAI Volume 1365)*, pages 259–274. Springer-Verlag: Berlin, Germany, 1998.

61. D. Kraines and V. Kraines. The threshold of cooperation among adaptive agents: Pavlov and the Stag Hunt. In J. P. Müller, M. J. Wooldridge, and N. R. Jennings, eds., *Intelligent Agents III (LNAI Volume 1193)*, pages 219–232. Springer-Verlag: Berlin, Germany, 1997.

62. C. Krogh. The rights of agents. In M. J. Wooldridge, J. P. Müller, and M. Tambe, eds., *Intelligent Agents II (LNAI Volume 1037)*, pages 1–16. Springer-Verlag: Berlin, Germany, 1996.

63. Y. Labrou and T. Finin. Semantics for an agent communication language. In M. P. Singh, A. S. Rao, and M. J. Wooldridge, eds., *Intelligent Agents IV (LNAI Volume 1365)*, pages 209–215. Springer-Verlag: Berlin, Germany, 1998.

64. J. Lee and E. H. Durfee. On explicit plan languages for coordinating multiagent plan execution. In M. P. Singh, A. S. Rao, and M. J. Wooldridge, eds., *Intelligent Agents IV (LNAI Volume 1365)*, pages 113–126. Springer-Verlag: Berlin, Germany, 1998.

65. Y. Lésperance, H. J. Levesque, F. Lin, D. Marcu, R. Reiter, and R. B. Scherl. Foundations of a logical approach to agent programming. In M. J. Wooldridge, J. P. Müller, and M. Tambe, eds., *Intelligent Agents II (LNAI Volume 1037)*, pages 331–346. Springer-Verlag: Berlin, Germany, 1996.

66. R. Li and L. M. Pereira. Knowledge-based situated agents among us. In J. P. Müller, M. J. Wooldridge, and N. R. Jennings, eds., *Intelligent Agents III (LNAI Volume 1193)*, pages 375–390. Springer-Verlag: Berlin, Germany, 1997.

67. A. Lomuscio and M. Colombetti. QLB: A quantified logic for belief. In J. P. Müller, M. J. Wooldridge, and N. R. Jennings, eds., *Intelligent Agents III (LNAI Volume 1193)*, pages 71–86. Springer-Verlag: Berlin, Germany, 1997.

68. M. Luck, N. Griffiths, and M. d'Inverno. From agent theory to agent construction: A case study. In J. P. Müller, M. J. Wooldridge, and N. R. Jennings, eds., *Intelligent Agents III (LNAI Volume 1193)*, pages 49–64. Springer-Verlag: Berlin, Germany, 1997.

69. J. Malec. A unified approach to intelligent agency. In M. J. Wooldridge and N. R. Jennings, eds., *Intelligent Agents: Theories, Architectures, and Languages (LNAI Volume 890)*, pages 233–244. Springer-Verlag: Berlin, Germany, 1995.

70. B. Malheiro and E. Oliveira. Consistency and context management in a multi-agent belief revision testbed. In M. J. Wooldridge, J. P. Müller, and M. Tambe, eds., *Intelligent Agents II (LNAI Volume 1037)*, pages 361–375. Springer-Verlag: Berlin, Germany, 1996.

71. J. Mayfield, Y. Labrou, and T. Finin. Evaluating KQML as an agent communication language. In M. J. Wooldridge, J. P. Müller, and M. Tambe, eds., *Intelligent Agents II (LNAI Volume 1037)*, pages 347–360. Springer-Verlag: Berlin, Germany, 1996.

72. F. G. McCabe and K. L. Clark. April — agent process interaction language. In M. J. Wooldridge and N. R. Jennings, eds., *Intelligent Agents: Theories, Architectures, and Languages (LNAI Volume 890)*, pages 324–340. Springer-Verlag: Berlin, Germany, 1995.

73. D. Moffat and N. Frijda. Where there's a Will there's an agent. In M. J. Wooldridge and N. R. Jennings, eds., *Intelligent Agents: Theories, Architectures, and Languages (LNAI Volume 890)*, pages 245–260. Springer-Verlag: Berlin, Germany, 1995.

74. M. Móra, J. G. Lopes, R. Viccari, and H. Coelho. BDI models and systems: reducing the gap. In J. P. Müller, M. P. Singh, and A. S. Rao, eds., *Intelligent Agents V*, pages 11–27. Springer-Verlag: Berlin, Germany, 1999. In this volume.

75. A. Moreno and T. Sales. Dynamic belief analysis. In J. P. Müller, M. J. Wooldridge, and N. R. Jennings, eds., *Intelligent Agents III (LNAI Volume 1193)*, pages 87–102. Springer-Verlag: Berlin, Germany, 1997.

76. M. Mulder, J. Treur, and M. Fisher. Agent modelling in METATEM and DESIRE. In M. P. Singh, A. S. Rao, and M. J. Wooldridge, eds., *Intelligent Agents IV (LNAI Volume 1365)*, pages 193–208. Springer-Verlag: Berlin, Germany, 1998.

77. T. Mullen and M. P. Wellman. Some issues in the design of market-oriented agents. In M. J. Wooldridge, J. P. Müller, and M. Tambe, eds., *Intelligent Agents II (LNAI Volume 1037)*, pages 283–298. Springer-Verlag: Berlin, Germany, 1996.

78. J. Müller. A cooperation model for autonomous agents. In J. P. Müller, M. J. Wooldridge, and N. R. Jennings, eds., *Intelligent Agents III (LNAI Volume 1193)*, pages 245–260. Springer-Verlag: Berlin, Germany, 1997.

79. J. P. Müller. A markovian model for interaction among behavior-based agents. In M. J. Wooldridge, J. P. Müller, and M. Tambe, eds., *Intelligent Agents II (LNAI Volume 1037)*, pages 376–391. Springer-Verlag: Berlin, Germany, 1996.

80. J. P. Müller. The right agent (architecture) to do the right thing. In J. P. Müller, M. P. Singh, and A. S. Rao, eds., *Intelligent Agents V*, pages 211–225. Springer-Verlag: Berlin, Germany, 1999. In this volume.

81. J. P. Müller, M. Pischel, and M. Thiel. Modelling reactive behaviour in vertically layered agent architectures. In M. J. Wooldridge and N. R. Jennings, eds., *Intelligent Agents: Theories, Architectures, and Languages (LNAI Volume 890)*, pages 261–276. Springer-Verlag: Berlin, Germany, 1995.

82. M. Nodine and A. Unruh. Facilitating open communication in agent systems: The InfoSleuth infrastructure. In M. P. Singh, A. S. Rao, and M. J. Wooldridge, eds., *Intelligent Agents IV (LNAI Volume 1365)*, pages 281–296. Springer-Verlag: Berlin, Germany, 1998.

83. P. Noriega and C. Sierra. Towards layered dialogical agents. In J. P. Müller, M. J. Wooldridge, and N. R. Jennings, eds., *Intelligent Agents III (LNAI Volume 1193)*, pages 173–188. Springer-Verlag: Berlin, Germany, 1997.

84. T. Norman, N. Jennings, P. Faratin, and A. Mamdani. Designing and implementing a multi-agent architecture for business process management. In J. P. Müller, M. J. Wooldridge, and N. R. Jennings, eds., *Intelligent Agents III (LNAI Volume 1193)*, pages 261–276. Springer-Verlag: Berlin, Germany, 1997.

85. T. J. Norman and D. Long. Goal creation in motivated agents. In M. J. Wooldridge and N. R. Jennings, eds., *Intelligent Agents: Theories, Architectures, and Languages (LNAI Volume 890)*, pages 277–290. Springer-Verlag: Berlin, Germany, 1995.

86. T. J. Norman and D. Long. Alarms: An implementation of motivated agency. In M. J. Wooldridge, J. P. Müller, and M. Tambe, eds., *Intelligent Agents II (LNAI Volume 1037)*, pages 219–234. Springer-Verlag: Berlin, Germany, 1996.

87. S. Ossowski and A. García-Serrano. Social structure in artificial agent societies: Implications for autonomous problem-solving agents. In J. P. Müller, M. P. Singh, and A. S. Rao, eds., *Intelligent Agents V*, pages 133–148. Springer-Verlag: Berlin, Germany, 1999. In this volume.

88. V. Parunak, J. Sauter, and S. Clark. Toward the specification and design of industrial synthetic ecosystems. In M. P. Singh, A. S. Rao, and M. J. Wooldridge, eds., *Intelligent Agents IV (LNAI Volume 1365)*, pages 45–61. Springer-Verlag: Berlin, Germany, 1998.

89. C. Petrie. What is an agent? In J. P. Müller, M. J. Wooldridge, and N. R. Jennings, eds., *Intelligent Agents III (LNAI Volume 1193)*, pages 41–44. Springer-Verlag: Berlin, Germany, 1997.

90. M. Piaggio. HEIR — a non-hierarchical hybrid architecture for intelligent robots. In J. P. Müller, M. P. Singh, and A. S. Rao, eds., *Intelligent Agents V*, pages 243–259. Springer-Verlag: Berlin, Germany, 1999. In this volume.

91. A. Poggi. DAISY: An object-oriented system for distributed artificial intelligence. In M. J. Wooldridge and N. R. Jennings, eds., *Intelligent Agents: Theories, Architectures, and Languages (LNAI Volume 890)*, pages 341–354. Springer-Verlag: Berlin, Germany, 1995.

92. A. Poggia and G. Adorni. A multi language environment to develop multi agent applications. In J. P. Müller, M. J. Wooldridge, and N. R. Jennings, eds., *Intelligent Agents III (LNAI Volume 1193)*, pages 325–340. Springer-Verlag: Berlin, Germany, 1997.

93. J. Rachlin, R. Goodwin, S. Murthy, R. Akkiraju, F. Wu, S. Kumaran, and R. Das. A-Teams: An agent architecture for optimization and decision-support. In J. P. Müller, M. P. Singh, and A. S. Rao, eds., *Intelligent Agents V*, pages 261–276. Springer-Verlag: Berlin, Germany, 1999. In this volume.

94. A. S. Rao. Decision procedures for propositional linear-time Belief-Desire-Intention logics. In M. J. Wooldridge, J. P. Müller, and M. Tambe, eds., *Intelligent Agents II (LNAI Volume 1037)*, pages 33–48. Springer-Verlag: Berlin, Germany, 1996.

95. S. K. Rustogi and M. P. Singh. The bases of effective coordination in decentralized multiagent systems. In J. P. Müller, M. P. Singh, and A. S. Rao, eds., *Intelligent Agents V*, pages 149–161. Springer-Verlag: Berlin, Germany, 1999. In this volume.

96. G. Sandu. Reasoning about collective goals. In J. P. Müller, M. J. Wooldridge, and N. R. Jennings, eds., *Intelligent Agents III (LNAI Volume 1193)*, pages 131–140. Springer-Verlag: Berlin, Germany, 1997.

97. K. Schild. On the relationship between BDI logics and standard logics of concurrency. In J. P. Müller, M. P. Singh, and A. S. Rao, eds., *Intelligent Agents V*, pages 47–61. Springer-Verlag: Berlin, Germany, 1999. In this volume.

98. M. Schoppers and D. Shapiro. Designing embedded agents to optimize end-user objectives. In M. P. Singh, A. S. Rao, and M. J. Wooldridge, eds., *Intelligent Agents IV (LNAI Volume 1365)*, pages 3–14. Springer-Verlag: Berlin, Germany, 1998.

99. M. Schroeder, I de Almeida Móra, and L. Moniz Pereira. A deliberative and reactive diagnosis agent based on logic programming. In J. P. Müller, M. J. Wooldridge, and N. R. Jennings, eds., *Intelligent Agents III (LNAI Volume 1193)*, pages 293–308. Springer-Verlag: Berlin, Germany, 1997.

100. R. Schwartz and S. Kraus. Bidding mechanisms for data allocation in multi-agent environments. In M. P. Singh, A. S. Rao, and M. J. Wooldridge, eds., *Intelligent Agents IV (LNAI Volume 1365)*, pages 61–76. Springer-Verlag: Berlin, Germany, 1998.

101. O. Shehory, S. Kraus, and O. Yadgar. Goal satisfaction in large scale agent-systems: A transportation example. In J. P. Müller, M. P. Singh, and A. S. Rao, eds., *Intelligent Agents V*, pages 277–292. Springer-Verlag: Berlin, Germany, 1999. In this volume.

102. O. Shehory, K. Sycara, P. Chalasani, and S. Jha. Increasing resource utilization and task performance by agent cloning. In J. P. Müller, M. P. Singh, and A. S. Rao, eds., *Intelligent Agents V*, pages 413–426. Springer-Verlag: Berlin, Germany, 1999. In this volume.

103. O. Shehory, K. Sycara, and S. Jha. Multi-agent coordination through coalition formation. In M. P. Singh, A. S. Rao, and M. J. Wooldridge, eds., *Intelligent Agents IV (LNAI Volume 1365)*, pages 143–155. Springer-Verlag: Berlin, Germany, 1998.

104. C. Sierra, N. R. Jennings, P. Noriega, and S. Parsons. A framework for argumentation-based negotiation. In M. P. Singh, A. S. Rao, and M. J. Wooldridge, eds., *Intelligent Agents IV (LNAI Volume 1365)*, pages 177–192. Springer-Verlag: Berlin, Germany, 1998.

105. M. P. Singh. Semantical considerations on some primitives for agent specification. In M. J. Wooldridge, J. P. Müller, and M. Tambe, eds., *Intelligent Agents II (LNAI Volume 1037)*, pages 49–64. Springer-Verlag: Berlin, Germany, 1996.

106. M. P. Singh. A customizable coordination service for autonomous agents. In M. P. Singh, A. S. Rao, and M. J. Wooldridge, eds., *Intelligent Agents IV (LNAI Volume 1365)*, pages 93–106. Springer-Verlag: Berlin, Germany, 1998.

107. N. Skarmeas and K. L. Clark. Content based routing as the basis for intra-agent communication. In J. P. Müller, M. P. Singh, and A. S. Rao, eds., *Intelligent Agents V*, pages 345–362. Springer-Verlag: Berlin, Germany, 1999. In this volume.

108. A. Sloman and R. Poli. SIM_AGENT: A toolkit for exploring agent designs. In M. J. Wooldridge, J. P. Müller, and M. Tambe, eds., *Intelligent Agents II (LNAI Volume 1037)*, pages 392–407. Springer-Verlag: Berlin, Germany, 1996.

109. M. Soutchanski and E. Ternovskaia. Logical formalization of concurrent actions for multiagent systems. In M. J. Wooldridge and N. R. Jennings, eds., *Intelligent Agents: Theories, Architectures, and Languages (LNAI Volume 890)*, pages 129–144. Springer-Verlag: Berlin, Germany, 1995.

110. G. Staniford and R. Paton. Simulating animal societies with adaptive communicating agents. In M. J. Wooldridge and N. R. Jennings, eds., *Intelligent Agents: Theories, Architectures, and Languages (LNAI Volume 890)*, pages 145–159. Springer-Verlag: Berlin, Germany, 1995.

111. P. Stone and M. Veloso. Task decomposition and dynamic role assignment for real-time strategic teamwork. In J. P. Müller, M. P. Singh, and A. S. Rao, eds., *Intelligent Agents V*, pages 293–308. Springer-Verlag: Berlin, Germany, 1999. In this volume.

112. M. Tambe and P. S. Rosenbloom. Agent tracking in real-time dynamic environments. In M. J. Wooldridge, J. P. Müller, and M. Tambe, eds., *Intelligent Agents II (LNAI Volume 1037)*, pages 156–170. Springer-Verlag: Berlin, Germany, 1996.

113. S. R. Thomas. The PLACA agent programming language. In M. J. Wooldridge and N. R. Jennings, eds., *Intelligent Agents: Theories, Architectures, and Languages (LNAI Volume 890)*, pages 355–369. Springer-Verlag: Berlin, Germany, 1995.

114. D. Traum. A reactive-deliberative model of dialogue agency. In J. P. Müller, M. J. Wooldridge, and N. R. Jennings, eds., *Intelligent Agents III (LNAI Volume 1193)*, pages 157–172. Springer-Verlag: Berlin, Germany, 1997.

115. P. Traverso, L. Spalazzi, and F. Giunchiglia. Reasoning about acting, sensing, and failure handling: A logic for agents embedded in the real world. In M. J. Wooldridge, J. P. Müller, and M. Tambe, eds., *Intelligent Agents II (LNAI Volume 1037)*, pages 65–78. Springer-Verlag: Berlin, Germany, 1996.

116. W. Van de Velde, S. Geldof, and R. Schrooten. Competition for attention. In M. P. Singh, A. S. Rao, and M. J. Wooldridge, eds., *Intelligent Agents IV (LNAI Volume 1365)*, pages 297–312. Springer-Verlag: Berlin, Germany, 1998.

117. R. M. van Eijk, F. S. de Boer, W. van der Hoek, and J.-J. Ch. Meyer. Information-passing and belief revision in multi-agent systems. In J. P. Müller, M. P. Singh, and A. S. Rao, eds., *Intelligent Agents V*, pages 29–45. Springer-Verlag: Berlin, Germany, 1999. In this volume.

118. B. van Linder, W. van der Hoek, and J. J. Ch. Meyer. How to motivate your agents. In M. J. Wooldridge, J. P. Müller, and M. Tambe, eds., *Intelligent Agents II (LNAI Volume 1037)*, pages 17–32. Springer-Verlag: Berlin, Germany, 1996.

119. E. M. Verharen, F. Dignum, and S. Bos. Implementation of a cooperative agent architecture based on the language-action perspective. In M. P. Singh, A. S. Rao, and M. J. Wooldridge, eds., *Intelligent Agents IV (LNAI Volume 1365)*, pages 31–44. Springer-Verlag: Berlin, Germany, 1998.

120. J. M. Vidal and E. H. Durfee. Recursive agent modeling using limited rationality. In M. J. Wooldridge, J. P. Müller, and M. Tambe, eds., *Intelligent Agents II (LNAI Volume 1037)*, pages 171–186. Springer-Verlag: Berlin, Germany, 1996.

121. G. Wagner. Practical theory and theory-based practice. In J. P. Müller, M. J. Wooldridge, and N. R. Jennings, eds., *Intelligent Agents III (LNAI Volume 1193)*, pages 67–70. Springer-Verlag: Berlin, Germany, 1997.

122. P. Wavish and M. Graham. Roles, skills, and behaviour: a situated action approach to organising systems of interacting agents. In M. J. Wooldridge and N. R. Jennings, eds., *Intelligent Agents: Theories, Architectures, and Languages (LNAI Volume 890)*, pages 371–385. Springer-Verlag: Berlin, Germany, 1995.

123. D. Weerasooriya, A. S. Rao, and K. Ramamohanarao. Design of a concurrent agent-oriented language. In M. J. Wooldridge and N. R. Jennings, eds., *Intelligent Agents: Theories, Architectures, and Languages (LNAI Volume 890)*, pages 386–402. Springer-Verlag: Berlin, Germany, 1995.

124. M. J. Wooldridge. This is MYWORLD: The logic of an agent-oriented testbed for DAI. In M. J. Wooldridge and N. R. Jennings, eds., *Intelligent Agents: Theories, Architectures, and Languages (LNAI Volume 890)*, pages 160–178. Springer-Verlag: Berlin, Germany, 1995.

125. M. J. Wooldridge. Agents as a Rorschach test: A response to Franklin and Graesser. In J. P. Müller, M. J. Wooldridge, and N. R. Jennings, eds., *Intelligent Agents III (LNAI Volume 1193)*, pages 47–48. Springer-Verlag: Berlin, Germany, 1997.

126. M. J. Wooldridge. A knowledge-theoretic semantics for Concurrent METATEM. In J. P. Müller, M. J. Wooldridge, and N. R. Jennings, eds., *Intelligent Agents III (LNAI Volume 1193)*, pages 357–374. Springer-Verlag: Berlin, Germany, 1997.

127. M. J. Wooldridge. Time, knowledge, and choice. In M. J. Wooldridge, J. P. Müller, and M. Tambe, eds., *Intelligent Agents II (LNAI Volume 1037)*, pages 79–96. Springer-Verlag: Berlin, Germany, 1996.

128. M. J. Wooldridge and S. D. Parsons. Intention reconsideration reconsidered. In J. P. Müller, M. P. Singh, and A. S. Rao, eds., *Intelligent Agents V*, pages 63–79. Springer-Verlag: Berlin, Germany, 1999. In this volume.

129. D. Zeng and K. Sycara. How can an agent learn to negotiate? In J. P. Müller, M. J. Wooldridge, and N. R. Jennings, eds., *Intelligent Agents III (LNAI Volume 1193)*, pages 233–244. Springer-Verlag: Berlin, Germany, 1997.

Index

operative Work
CTL 50, 164, 166
CTL* 50, 59, 197
cumulative language composition 183
Cypress planner 213, 225

DAI, see *Distributed Artificial Intelligence*
Das, R. 261
databases
    object-oriented 309
    relational 309
DCOM *xviii*
de Boer, F. *xi*, 29, 381
decentralizing refinement 326
decentralized multiagent system 149
decision *xiv*, 99, 116
    support 261, 265
    theory 428
declarative past 188
declaratives 364, 375
default persistence 187
defeasible reasoning 14
delegation 101
deliberation 63, 66
    function 66
deliberative
    agents 212
    component *xvi*
    rule 231
deontic logic 369
dependence
    relation 137
        types 137
    structure *xiv*, 136, 138
design
    methodologies 310, 317
    pattern 311
desire 4, 8, 17, 65
    candidate 20
    preference graph 20
    preference relation 20
    triggers 24
DESIRE (methodology) 43, 178, 324
destroyer 263
deterministic environments 67

development tools 431
diagrammatic
    component *xvi*, 244, 255
    expert 248
    knowledge xvi
    reasoning 244
Dignum, F. 99
DIMA 310
directives 364, 374
disagreement point 141
    monotonicity 142
Distributed Artificial Intelligence 128, 318
distributed problem-solving *xiv*, 133
distributed resource allocation 215
Distributed Vehicle Monitoring Testbed 289
dMARS 8, 213, 225, 332
Dury, A. 397
DVMT, see Distributed Vehicle Monitoring Testbed
dynamic action selection 213
dynamic logics 53

ECO problem solving 213, 225
egoism, effects of 124
EIEP, see *Expert Information Exchange Protocol*
eligible intentions 19
ELP, see *Extended Logic Programming*
emergent
    behavior 100
    functionality 431
emotion 100, 108, 113
empowerment 101
Engelfriet, J. 177
enterprise modeling 320
environment 30, 64, 399
error 341
error tolerance 154
ETHNOS 253
ethology 431
event calculus 15
evolution
    of benevolence 126
    of goal achievement 407

Springer
and the
environment

At Springer we firmly believe that an international science publisher has a special obligation to the environment, and our corporate policies consistently reflect this conviction.

We also expect our business partners – paper mills, printers, packaging manufacturers, etc. – to commit themselves to using materials and production processes that do not harm the environment. The paper in this book is made from low- or no-chlorine pulp and is acid free, in conformance with international standards for paper permanency.

Springer

Lecture Notes in Artificial Intelligence (LNAI)

Lecture Notes in Computer Science